"This edited volume provides a much-needed complement to similar, recent volumes exploring topical issues in public sector accounting, auditing and governance. It has a broad scope in terms of the topics covered, theories applied and geographical representation. The chapters are all written by established public sector accounting scholars and cover a range of burning issues that require attention from practitioners, policymakers and researchers".

Sven Modell, *Alliance Manchester Business School,*
University of Manchester

"This book provides an up-to-date, in-depth reflection on the most important and recent evolutions in public sector accounting scholarship and practices, offering international, plural perspectives on the challenges facing accountants and accounting systems in the public sphere. This is a fundamental reading to appreciate the scale and variety of such challenges, ranging, among others, from the widening of the scope of accounting to encompass public value and sustainability, to the strengthening of the roles of control systems to support change as well as risk management, to the rethinking of auditing, or the search for stronger community engagement".

Ileana Steccolini, *University of Essex and*
University of Bologna

"Routledge Handbooks are marvelous assemblies of scholarship in a specialised field. I welcome this *Handbook of Public Sector Accounting*. The Handbook contains a smorgasbord of coverage by well-known scholars on public sector accounting. Also, the coverage is global, with contributions covering various regions, nation states and sectors. The Handbook highlights contemporary issues in public sector accounting, auditing and accountability".

James Guthrie, *Member of the Order (AM),*
Macquarie Business School, Australia

THE ROUTLEDGE HANDBOOK OF PUBLIC SECTOR ACCOUNTING

The Routledge Handbook of Public Sector Accounting explores new developments and transformations in auditing, management control, performance measurement, risk management and sustainability work in the contemporary world of the public sector and the functioning of accounting and management in that realm. It focuses on critical analysis and reflection with respect to changing risk and crisis management patterns in the public sector in the current Covid-19 and post-Covid-19 era, across diverse social, political and institutional settings globally.

This research-based edited book, targeted at scholars, professionals, teachers and consultants in the fields of public sector accounting, auditing, accountability and management, offers high-level insights into the new architecture and execution of such activities in the emerging post-pandemic world. The chapters are written by leading scholars in the accounting and public administration disciplines internationally and provide important assessments, frameworks and recommendations concerning a wide variety of institutions, practices and policies with a view to addressing the many emerging societal, governmental and professional issues. Spanning theoretical, empirical and policy discussion contributions, the book's chapters will be readily accessible to accounting, auditing and management audiences alike.

Tarek Rana is an associate professor of accounting in the School of Accounting, Information Systems and Supply Chain at RMIT University, Melbourne, Australia. He teaches management accounting, forensic business investigation and data analytics. His research interests are in the areas of strategic management, management control systems, performance measurement, risk management and sustainability, with a focus on not-for-profit and public sector organizations.

Lee Parker is a research professor in accounting at the University of Glasgow. His previous academic posts include the Universities of Glasgow, Dundee, Monash, Griffith, Flinders, Adelaide, South Australia, the Royal Holloway University of London, RMIT University Melbourne, an honorary professorship at the University of St Andrews, and visiting professorships in the USA, UK, Australasia, Asia and the Middle East.

ROUTLEDGE INTERNATIONAL HANDBOOKS

THE ROUTLEDGE HANDBOOK OF PUBLIC SECTOR ACCOUNTING

Edited by Tarek Rana and Lee Parker

NEW YORK AND LONDON

Cover image: ALotOfPeople

First published 2024
by Routledge
605 Third Avenue, New York, NY 10158

and by Routledge
4 Park Square, Milton Park, Abingdon, Oxon, OX14 4RN

Routledge is an imprint of the Taylor & Francis Group, an informa business

Library of Congress Cataloging-in-Publication Data
Names: Rana, Tarek, editor. | Parker, Lee D. (Lee David), editor.
Title: The Routledge handbook of public sector accounting /
edited by Tarek Rana and Lee Parker.
Description: New York, NY : Routledge, 2024. |
Includes bibliographical references and index.
Identifiers: LCCN 2023018695 | ISBN 9781032282510 (hardback) |
ISBN 9781032282589 (paperback) | ISBN 9781003295945 (ebook)
Subjects: LCSH: Accounting.
Classification: LCC HJ9733 .R68 2024 | DDC 657/.458–dc23/eng/20230727
LC record available at https://lccn.loc.gov/2023018695

ISBN: 978-1-032-28251-0 (hbk)
ISBN: 978-1-032-28258-9 (pbk)
ISBN: 978-1-003-29594-5 (ebk)

DOI: 10.4324/9781003295945

Typeset in Times New Roman
by Newgen Publishing UK

Tarek Rana *dedicates this book to his wife, Afsana Siddique; sons, Sabir Ahmed and Jabir Ahmed; and parents, Kabir Ahmed and Ranuara Begum, in recognition of their unconditional love, boundless inspiration and continuous support throughout his career.*

Lee Parker *dedicates this book to the memories of long-time mentors and friends, the late Professors John Eldridge and Don Bowes (University of Glasgow) and his close colleagues the late Professors Rob Gray (University of St Andrews) and Jeffrey Unerman (University of Lancaster).*

CONTENTS

REVIEW PROCESS

Routledge stands unrivalled as the foremost commercial publisher in the realms of social sciences and humanities, catering to a discerning academic audience by offering multidisciplinary research books. Our mission is to continually elevate scholarly discourse and foster intellectual growth through the dissemination of cutting-edge, thought-provoking research.

At the heart of Routledge's publication process lies the indispensable element of peer review, ensuring that every research-based book we release meets our exacting standards. We employ esteemed independent scholarly referees who, working anonymously, provide unbiased, critical evaluations of each work. Authors receive these invaluable review reports, augmented by the expert insights of our dedicated editors, Tarek Rana and Lee Parker, who collaborate closely to refine and polish the book's content.

Moreover, each book we publish is assigned an International Standard Book Number (ISBN), underscoring our commitment to maintaining a cohesive and responsible publishing process. Both the editors and authors share the responsibility of ensuring the highest quality for each volume, further solidifying Routledge's reputation as the pre-eminent publisher in the fields of social sciences and humanities.

FIGURES

TABLES

CONTRIBUTORS

Daniela Argento is an associate professor in management control and accounting at the Faculty of Business, Kristianstad University (Sweden), where she coordinates the research environment Governance, Regulation, Internationalization and Performance (GRIP). Dr Argento conducts research on various topics including governance, control and performance of public service organizations; implementation of smart city strategies; challenges of collaborative innovation projects; sustainability and integrated reporting; organizational and accounting change; relationships between internal and external auditors; and the influence of performance metrics on academics' identity. She has extensive experience in applying qualitative research methodologies and various theoretical lenses. Dr Arto is part of a wide network of scholars as she regularly collaborates with both Swedish and international colleagues in various research projects. Her diverse research has resulted in the publication of articles in journals such as *Accounting, Auditing & Accountability Journal*; *Meditari Accountancy Research*; *Journal of Management Control*; *Journal of Accounting and Organizational Change*; *Organization & Environment*; *Public Administration & Development*; *Public Money & Management*; *Utilities Policy*; *International Journal of Public Sector Management*; *Public Organization Review*; *International Review of Administrative Sciences*; and *International Journal of Public Policy*.

Michela Arnaboldi is Full Professor of accounting finance and control at Politecnico di Milano. She is the director of Institution and Public Administration at Polimi Graduate School of Management. She is member of the board of the Department of Management Economics and Industrial Engineering, where she is part of the PhD board. She is coordinator of Urbanscope, the interdepartmental Lab of Politecnico di Milano on the use of analytics for decision-making. She is author of over 70 papers published on national and international journals and conference proceedings

Enrico Bracci is a full professor of accounting at the University of Ferrara, Italy. He has published numerous research articles and books in the field of accounting and public administration. His research interests include management accounting, public management, public value and risk management. He has also served as an editorial board member and reviewer for several journals and conferences in accounting.

Manuel Castelo Branco is an assistant professor at the Faculty of Economics, University of Porto, Portugal, and is interested in Corporate Social Responsibility (CSR) and the reporting thereof,

CSR education, and accounting and the public interest. He is also a researcher at CEF.UP and Fraud Economy and Management Observatory (OBEGEF). His teaching focus is in the areas of accounting and CSR. His academic work has been published in journals such as *Accounting, Auditing & Accountability Journal*; *Journal of Business Ethics*; *Journal of Cleaner Production*; and *British Accounting Review*.

Sara Brorström holds a position as an associate professor in Management and Organization at the Department for Business Administration, School of Business Economics and Law, Gothenburg University. Her research is on public sector strategic management, collaborative organizations, city planning and sustainability.

Usman W. Chohan is the director for Economics & National Affairs at the Center for Aerospace & Security Studies (CASS). He is also founder of the International Association of Hyperpolyglots (HYPIA), director of the Critical Blockchain Research Initiative (CBRI), and is on the top 20 Business Authors on the Social Science Research Network (SSRN). He has a PhD from University of New South Wales (UNSW) and an MBA from McGill University. He is fluent in seven Indo-European languages (English, Spanish, French, Portuguese, Hindi, Urdu, Punjabi), and conversant in various languages from other linguistic families. He has global four-sector leadership experience that involves the public sector (the World Bank), the private sector (the National Bank of Canada), academia (UNSW Australia), and NGOs (CBRI, HYPIA). His global orientation has led him to call ten different countries on five continents "home".

Mark Christensen is Full Professor, Accounting and Management Control Department, École Supérieure des Sciences Economiques et Commerciales (ESSEC) Business School. After completing his BA (Hons) at Macquarie University, Mark embarked on what turned out to be a three-part career involving the public sector, consulting and academia. He holds a PhD from the University of Adelaide and his research interests are broadly themed along considerations of accounting as a socio-technical construction. His research of public sector accrual accounting is highly cited. His publications cover matters such as public sector accrual accounting, performance reporting, comparative international studies, consultants in accounting change, accounting history, environmental sustainability and budgeting, audit as an instrument of blame, and related topics. He has published in journals that include *Accounting, Auditing & Accountability Journal*; *Accounting, Organizations & Society*; *Accounting Education*; *Accounting History*; *Australian Accounting Review*; *Contemporary Accounting Research*; *Critical Perspectives on Accounting*; *European Accounting Review*; *International Review of Administrative Sciences*; *International Journal of Public Sector Management*; and *Financial Accountability & Management*. His academic appointments have included associate dean, international; director, postgraduate research and studies; director, master of professional accounting; associate professor and professor. Prior to joining ESSEC, he was employed by the University of New South Wales, the University of New England, Southern Cross University and Copenhagen Business School, whilst invitations to visit have been issued to him by Hokkaido University, Cardiff Business School, Copenhagen Business School, the University of Nordland, the University of Siena and Nanzan University.

Carolyn Cordery is an adjunct professor of accounting in the School of Accounting and Commercial Law, Victoria University of Wellington, New Zealand. Carolyn is chair of the New Zealand Accounting Standards Board (NZASB) and a member of the Australian Accounting Standards Board (AASB) and of the Practitioner Advisory Group of the International Financial Reporting for Non-Profit Organisations (IFR4NPO) project. Carolyn's research focuses on not-for-profit organisations' accounting and accountability. She is particularly interested in how these organisations are regulated as well as the impact of their resourcing (by donors/philanthropists, grants, contracts, volunteers etc.) and the resource constraints that cause many of these organisations to be financially vulnerable. Much of her work is based on international comparisons. Carolyn also researches public sector audit as a means of accountability. Her Routledge book (with Professor David Hay) on the structures, opportunities and challenges of Supreme Audit Institutions was published in late 2020. She has undertaken a number of commissioned research projects, and published work in relevant international journals such as: *Accounting, Auditing & Accountability Journal*; *Accounting History*; *Financial Accountability and Management*; *Accounting & Finance*; *Journal of Accounting and Public Policy*; *Public Management Review*; and *Public Money and Management*. Her paper titled "Accounting History and Religion: A Review of Studies and a Research Agenda" (*Accounting History*, 20(4) pp 430–463), won the 2015 Robert W. Gibson Manuscript Award. Her teaching areas include accounting information systems and financial reporting research methods. Professionally, Carolyn is a Fellow of Chartered Accountants Australia and New Zealand. She is also a Fellow of CPA Australia.

Suresh Cuganesan is Deputy Dean (Students & External Partnerships) and Professor in the Discipline of Strategy, Innovation and Entrepreneurship at the University of Sydney Business School. Suresh is passionate about education that is fit-for-purpose and impactful given our changing society and work environments. He provides strategic oversight across the University of Sydney Business School's portfolio of education programmes and work-integrated learning offerings, working closely with industry and government; liaises with the university on strategic recruitment approaches for the Business School; and works to enhance the student experience and graduate employability. He has delivered executive education and post-graduate learning programmes across countries in Europe as well in Asia, with a particular focus on Singapore, Hong Kong and India. Education innovations that Suresh has led have been recognised internationally for their industry engagement and student impact, including the Global Education Award from QS ReImagine Education. A key initiative that Suresh is currently focused on involves harnessing the incredible multicultural diversity in Australia's higher education student communities to create stronger person-to-person ties to support and enhance closer connections across the Indo-Pacific region. On the research front, Suresh specialises in the areas of strategy, organisational design and strategic financial management. His current research areas investigate: how technology and data innovations impact work and organisations, and how organisations can achieve better outcomes through being more open, collaborative and transparent. Suresh has published numerous academic research articles in leading international and national journals and has won multiple Australian Research Council Grants for his research.

Hans de Bruijn is Professor of public administration in the Faculty of Technology, Policy and Management at Delft University of Technology. His research focuses on governance issues at the intersection of politics, management and technology, such as decision-making about large-scale infrastructure projects; the privatization and deregulation of utilities; safety and security; river management, regulation and inspection; the managing of professionals; and various types of government policy relating to technology. Such issues are usually characterised by a high degree of complexity. Governance involves a network of interdependent actors who behave strategically and know how to play the game. The types of problems that arise in this context are often ambiguous in nature, and the relevant information is often contested. Unforeseen dynamics are also very common. Hans de Bruijn has written several books on these issues, including *Management in Networks: On Multi-Actor Decision Making"* (Routledge, 2008, with Ernst ten Heuvelhof) and *Process Management: Why Project Management Fails in Complex Decision-Making Processes"* (Springer, 2010, with Ernst ten Heuvelhof and Roel in 't Veld). He has also published on the management of professional organisations, including: *Managing Professionals* (Routledge, 2010) and *Managing Performance in the Public Sector* (Routledge, 2007, 2nd ed.).

Enrico Deidda Gagliardo is Vice Chancellor, Full Professor of Planning and Control of Public Administrations, director of the Master PERF.ET, member of the Technical Commission for Performance at the Department of Public Administration, established by Decree of the Minister for Simplification and Public Administration pursuant to Article 4 of Presidential Decree 105/2016, and participant in the Technical Table at the National Anti-Corruption Authority for the preparation of the National Anti-Corruption Plan 2016, with particular reference to small municipalities and metropolitan cities.

Adina Dudau is a senior lecturer in the Adam Smith Business School, University of Glasgow. After quite a series of career shifts (including civil service, as well as private and voluntary sector roles in Romania, Greece and the UK), Adina entered academia in 2005, when she started her PhD in inter-organisational management, followed by a postdoc in the Engineering and Physical Sciences Research Council (EPSRC) project "Under Dark Skies: Port Cities, Extreme Events, Multi-Scale Processes and the Vulnerability of Controls around Counter Terrorism". She became was appointed lecturer in 2012, and is currently senior lecturer in management, associate research director and PGR director in Adam Smith Business School. On 1 August 2022, Adina joined SGSSS as associate director and Lead of the Economies, Minds and Technologies Hub. Adina's research is highly interdisciplinary and anchored in public management. She draws on several theoretical lenses, including risk and crisis management, complexity theory, positive organisational behaviour and management control. She has published in general management, public management, business education and accounting journals, such as *European Management Journal*; *Public Management Review*; *Academy of Management Learning & Education*; and *Financial Accountability & Management*. She is on the board of International Research Society for Public Management (IRSPM) and of the Public and Nonprofit Division of Academy of Management (AOM), as well as on the editorial boards of *Public Management Review*; *Public Administration*; *Public Money & Management*; *Journal of Public Budgeting*; *Accounting & Financial Management*; and *Asia-Pacific Journal of Public Administration*. Adina led on a number of special issues in some of these journals and is associate editor for *Public Management Review* and *Journal of Management Inquiry*.

Kim Eriksson is a senior lecturer at the School of Business and Economics at Linnaeus University. Kim teaches courses in management accounting at bachelor and master levels. In his research, Kim studies management accounting and control in public sector organisations. His research interest is, broadly stated, the construction of and conditions for management accounting and control as well as management accounting and control in everyday organisational life.

Alvise Favotto is a senior lecturer in the Adam Smith Business School, University of Glasgow. He joined the Adam Smith Business School in 2015 as a lecturer in management accounting. Previously, he worked in political science at the University of Glasgow, and at Ca' Foscari, University of Venice. In his research, Alvise focuses on management control and governance systems, with a particular interest in corporate social responsibility and labour relations.

Laurence Ferry is an award-winning professor in accounting for democracy at Durham University Business School (UK), an established author, founding director of the International Centre of Public Accountability (ICOPA), and head of Department for Accounting. Laurence is a senior leader on the Dean's Faculty Executive Team, a senator on the University Senate, and a member of the Senior Common Room at Castle, University College. He earned his PhD from the Warwick Business School, and is a qualified chartered accountant, a prestigious elected Fellow of the Chartered Institute of Public Finance and Accountancy (CIPFA), and holds a first-class accounting degree. His research, impact, teaching and consulting cover accounting, auditing and accountability with a specific focus on the public sector where he is a very well recognized world-leading expert in public financial management. Internationally, he is a Senior Distinguished Visiting Fellow in Accounting at Rutgers University (USA), co-director of the Durham Rutgers Accounting Analytics Network (DRAAN), and a member of the CIPFA International Advisory Board undertaking thought leadership for how accounting, auditing and accountability can improve social, economic and environmental well-being for citizens of the world. This includes an Economic and Social Research Council (ESRC)-funded comparative project on "Voice(s) of Accountability at Supreme Audit Institutions" that involves CIPFA and the International Organisation of Supreme Audit Institutions (INTOSAI) for INCOSAI Congress 2022, which internationally covers seven geographic regions and around 200 countries.

Giorgia Gobbo has a PhD in accounting and finance. She is a research fellow at the University of Ferrara in the Department of Economics and Management.

Delfina Gomes is Assistant Professor at the School of Economics and Management. She has been a visiting professor at RMIT University, Australia and Edinburgh Business School, Scotland. Her main research field of research is accounting history. The main research projects at the moment are: accounting and religion; accounting and war; accounting and the state; accounting profession. She has published in academic journals such as *Accounting, Auditing & Accountability Journal*; *European Accounting Review*; *Accounting History*; and *Accounting Education*. She is on the editorial board of *Accounting, Auditing & Accountability Journal* and *Accounting History*, among other international journals. She is active in refereeing articles for a number of leading accounting journals. She was awarded a prize from the Academy of Accounting Historians, the 2009 Margit F. Schoenfeld and Hanns Martin W. Schoenfeld Scholarship in Accounting History, and has also been Trustee of the Academy since 2016.

Giuseppe Grossi is Research Professor in accounting at Nord University (Norway), Kristianstad University (Sweden), and Kozminski University (Poland). He holds a PhD in business administration from the University of Pisa (Italy). He was visiting scholar in several universities Europe, Asia, Australia, New Zealand and South America. Giuseppe's diverse research focuses on governmental accounting, hybrid forms of governance and performance of knowledge-intensive public organizations, state-owned enterprises and smart cities. He has extensive experience in conducting country and comparative studies with senior and emerging scholars from different disciplines around the world. He collaborates as expert with national and local governments, Supreme Audit Institutions, and the European Court of Auditors. Giuseppe's publications appear in leading accounting and public management journals. He is co-chair of the Special Interest Group on Hybrid Governance of the International Research Society on Public Management (IRSPM) and sits in the board as vice-chair of the Comparative International Government Accounting Research (CIGAR) Network. He is on the editorial board of several accounting and public management journals, is editor-in-chief of the *Journal of Public Budgeting, Accounting & Financial Management*, and associate editor of *Qualitative Research in Accounting & Management* (Emerald).

Suzana Grubnic is reader in accounting, director of Programme Quality at Loughborough University. Suzana joined Loughborough University's School of Business and Economics in October 2011 and is a reader in Accounting. Suzana's research interests are in the areas of: sustainability accounting and accountability in public services; management control for sustainability strategy; and, partnership working in local government. Her research has been funded by the Chartered Institute of Management Accountants (CIMA), the British Academy, and the British Accounting & Finance Association Special Interest Group on Public Services Accounting. In general, Suzana's research seeks to understand the outworking and transformative potential of sustainability accounting in the public and private sectors. She has conducted her research in the National Health Service, local authorities, large multinational companies, and small and medium-sized enterprises.

Alison Hart is a research analyst at the University of Sydney. She has a masters of arts by research and her research interests are in the areas of business and management and policy.

Geoffrey Heath has been a fellow in public sector accounting at Keele University since August 2010, having previously been a lecturer in accounting. he came to Keele in September 2002 from Staffordshire University, where he was an academic for many years. Before that he worked in National Health Service finance, where he qualified as a chartered management accountant. He has a degree in politics and sociology from the University of Kent, a PGCE from Liverpool University and a Lic. Phil (Soc. Sc.) by publication from Luleå University, Sweden.

Linda Höglund is an associate professor in business administration at the School of Business, Society and Engineering (EST). She is also part of the Academy of Management Accounting and Control in Central Government (AES), Stockholm Business School, Stockholm University. She teaches within accounting and management control with a special focus on strategy work. She conducts research in mainly strategic management, management control and strategic entrepreneurship within a context of the public sector using qualitative methods. Currently she mainly works with two large projects following strategic work at Swedish Public Employment Service and Region Stockholm.

Noel Hyndman is Honorary Professor and Professor Emeritus at Queen's University Belfast (where he was Professor of accounting and director of the Centre for Not-for-Profit and Public-Sector Research), and Honorary Professor at Durham University Business School. Noel has been a member of the UK Charity SORP Committee since 2006. He is associate editor of *Financial Accountability & Management* and *Abacus*, and was a non-executive director of the Northern Ireland Audit Office until 2022. His publications focus on public-sector/charity accounting and reporting.

Georgios Kominis is a senior lecturer in the Adam Smith Business School, University of Glasgow. George graduated from the Technological Educational Institution of Piraeus in Athens with a BSc in business administration. He was employed in the accounting department of Greenpeace Greece for two years (1994–1996) as chief accountant. During the period from 1996 to 2002, he attended and successfully completed postgraduate studies at the University of Glasgow (MAcc, PhD) that resulted in his appointment as lecturer in 2002. George undertakes research in the area of management control. His main interests include the impact of management control systems on human behaviour in contemporary organisations, the design of incentive schemes and reward packages for middle managers, and the determinants of dysfunctional behaviour in the managerial setting. In the last four years, and partly with the financial support of the Chartered Institute of Management Accountants Research Foundation, his research programme has mainly concentrated on systems of performance measurement, evaluation and reward, and the way these influence the process of motivation at the middle management level. George is a member of the editorial board of *Scientific Touristic Journal*, and he frequently reviews papers for a number of leading international accounting journals, including *Management Accounting Research*, *Accounting and Business Research*, and the *British Accounting Review*.

John Kommunuri is a senior lecturer in accounting at the Auckland University of Technology (AUT), New Zealand. John's doctoral research is on the price informativeness of management earnings forecasts (MEFs) of S&P 500 firms and the moderating effect of earnings quality on the stock price informativeness of MEFs. Before joining AUT in 2005, John served as an academic at Unitec Institute of Technology. Recently, he also served as an academic at RMIT. Having worked as an accountant in Auckland and taught various subjects both in undergraduate and postgraduate programmes, John brings his accounting and finance practical knowledge and teaching experience.

Mariannunziata Liguori is Professor of accounting and co-director of the International Centre of Public Accountability at Durham University Business School, where she moved after having worked at Queen's University Belfast. She was awarded a PhD by Bocconi University, where she previously worked. Mariannunziata is chair of the British Accounting & Finance Association (BAFA)'s Public Services and Charities SIG and an editorial board member of *Financial Accountability & Management* and *Journal of Public Budgeting, Accounting & Financial Management*. She publishes in a number of leading journals in the field.

Chu Yeong Lim has worked for 15 years in the financial control, management reporting, risk management and treasury functions of international banks and multinational companies such as Credit Suisse, Citibank, Standard Chartered Bank, GIC, DBS Bank and Shell Eastern Petroleum (Pte) Ltd. He has taught introductory, intermediate and advanced financial accounting courses, and valuation courses in Singapore Management University and Singapore Institute of Technology. He has taught executive and postgraduate courses on financial accounting and valuation. He is active in the accounting profession, being a member of the Institute of Internal Auditors Education Committee, an external reviewer of the professional qualification examinations, a technical accounting adviser to PKF LLP and a former member of the Institute of Singapore Chartered Accountants Financial Reporting Committee. He has publications in the *Journal of Accounting and Public Policy*; *Journal of Banking and Finance*; *Issues in Accounting Education*; *British Accounting Review*; and *Information & Management*, among other journals. Chu Yeong holds a PhD in accounting from the University of Manchester, an MBA from the University of Warwick, and a bachelor of accountancy (First Class Honors) from Nanyang Technological University (NTU). His professional qualifications include Chartered Accountant Singapore and CPA Australia.

Jamus Lim is an associate professor of economics at ESSEC Business School, one of the top business schools in Europe, and a member of the Fourteenth Parliament of Singapore, representing Sengkang. Previously, he was chief economist of the ThirdRock Group, an investment management and wealth advisory, a lead economist at the Abu Dhabi Investment Authority – where he oversaw economic inputs underlying tactical and strategic asset allocation for the sovereign fund's multi-hundred-billion dollar portfolio – and before that, a senior economist with the World Bank, where he led a number of initiatives on macroeconomic forecasts, along with analysis of trade, finance and governance issues in East Asia, the Middle East,and Africa. His research expertise and interests lie at the intersection of international macro-finance, political economy and development economics, and his work has appeared in leading academic journals such as the *Journal of Monetary Economics* and *Journal of Money, Credit, and Banking*, along with policy flagships such as the World Bank's Global Economic Prospects and the joint IMF–World Bank Global Monitoring Report. A seasoned communicator, his ideas have been featured in print media such as the *Financial Times* and *Straits Times*, and he also regularly shares his views on radio and television outlets such as CNA. An old Rafflesian, he graduated with first-class honours in economics from the University of Southern Queensland, and went on to graduate work at the London School of Economics, the University of California and Harvard University. In his wild, impetuous youth, Jamus was variously a drummer, a rugby player and a solitaire junkie; today, his more mundane pursuits have led him to the trails, gym, kitchen and cellar (typically in reverse order).

Eva Lövstål is director of the Master's in Industrial Economics and Management Programme. She presently teaches management control, strategy, innovation and entrepreneurship. Her current research deals with management control practices in innovation contexts. Eva has long experience of higher education teaching.

Melina Manochin is an associate professor in accounting at the Birmingham Business School of the University of Birmingham. Melina's research views accounting as a control and accountability practice of situated agents within various contexts. Her research interests include management accounting and control, accounting pedagogy, sustainability and accountability, interdisciplinary perspectives on accounting and research methodology. Melina's work includes a number of studies in empirical fields such as public services, housing associations, health care services, local authorities, NGOs and sell-side analysts. Melina is the module leader in the Public Sector Accounting and Governance (BSc final year), Management Accounting (MSc), and Dissertation (MSc) modules.

Maria Mårtensson is a professor in the Department of Management School of Business and Economics at Linnaeus University, Sweden and Stockholm Centre for Organizational Research (SCORE), Stockholm University, Stockholm, Sweden.

Adelaide Martins is an assistant professor at the School of Economics and Management in the University of Porto (FEP.UP). She holds a PhD in business administration and a MSc in industrial and firm economics in the University of Minho. She has developed a career in research and teaching in the area of accounting, and is the supervisor of PhD theses and MSc dissertations. Her academic work has been published in journals such *Critical Perspectives on Accounting*; *Qualitative Research in Accounting and Management*; *Journal of International Accounting*; and *Auditing & Taxation*, among other international journals, and she is a regular reviewer in international journals.

Sara Giovanna Mauro graduated in management and governance, English-language curriculum in accounting and governance at the University of Siena in 2012 (December), and earned a PhD in management at Scuola Superiore Sant'Anna in 2016 (November). She studied abroad at the University College Cork (UCC) (Ireland) and the New Jersey Institute of Technology (USA), and has research experience abroad at the University of Tampere (Finland) and Kristianstad University (Sweden). She is currently a postdoctoral research fellow. Her main research interests are in performance measurement and management, public sector budgeting and co-production of public services.

Henry Midgley is an assistant professor in the Department of Accounting at Durham University. He arrived at Durham after spending 13 years at the National Audit Office, the UK's Supreme Audit Institution, where he qualified as an accountant. He was an author of several value-for-money inquiries, including work focused on equity returns to Public Finance Initiatives (PFI) contracts, the regulation of charities, the troubled families payment-by-results scheme, contract management in the Ministry of Justice and Home Office and more general papers on principles to manage Provider Failure and Payment-by-Results delivery models. Whilst at the National Audit Office (NAO), from 2015 to 2018, he went on secondment to the House of Commons. He worked for the Public Administration and Constitutional Affairs Committee as the committee's main adviser on several different inquiries. These included inquiries into the collapse of the outsourcer Carillion, fundraising in the charity sector, the process of public appointments and the role of government accounts in promoting democracy within the UK. Dr Midgley earned his PhD from Cambridge University in 2008, with a thesis which focused on notions of Parliamentary accountability and democracy in the seventeenth century. He has an undergraduate degree in history from Oxford University. He has published on diverse topics including quantification in education policy in the nineteenth century, the role of accountability in the seventeenth century, the history of the UK's select committee system and the constitutional role of financial scrutiny in the UK's political system. He is a member of the Executive of the Study of Parliament Group, where he edits the Group's newsletter.

Jodie Moll is an associate professor of accounting at the Queensland University of Technology, Australia. She has been working in academia for more than 20 years. The focus of her work is on real-world problems. Her research aims to provide new theoretical ideas about the rapidly changing business landscape and the critical role and impact of the accounting systems and practices created for organizing and managing it. In more recent times, her research interests include understanding how the role of management accounting is changing to address disruptive technology innovations such as cloud, big data and artificial intelligence. She is also interested in revenue management. She holds an Honorary Reader position at the University of Manchester. Research that she has undertaken has been published in journals such *Management Accounting Research* and *Accounting, Organizations and Society*.

Anil K. Narayan is a professor in accounting and head of the Department of Accounting at the Auckland University of Technology (AUT), New Zealand. He has extensive teaching and post-graduate research supervision experience. Anil is a Chartered Accountant, Australia and New Zealand (CA ANZ), a Fellow of the Certified Practising Accountant (FCPA) Australia, and a Fellow Certified Management Accountant (FCMA) Australia and New Zealand. He served on the NZ National Council of CPA Australia for 12 years. Prior to joining AUT, he held various senior management and senior accounting positions in public and private sector organisations. Anil's primary research focus is on accounting and accountability issues in the public tertiary education sector. He has a special research interest in accounting education for Pacifica students and also researches in management accounting and sustainability accounting issues. Anil has published widely in highly ranked international refereed journals such as *Accounting, Auditing & Accountability Journal* (*AAAJ*); *Financial Accountability & Management*; *Accounting History*; *Meditari Accountancy Research*; *Public Money & Management*; *Accounting* Research; and *Pacific Accounting Review*. He regularly presents papers at international conferences, referees papers for a range of accounting journals and serves on the editorial boards of the *AAAJ*; *Accounting History*; *Accounting Forum*; and *Meditari Accountancy Research*.

Lee Parker is a research professor in accounting at the University of Glasgow. His previous academic posts include the Universities of Glasgow, Dundee, Monash, Griffith, Flinders, Adelaide, South Australia, Royal Holloway University of London and RMIT University Melbourne, an honorary professorship at the University of St Andrews, and visiting professorships in the USA, UK, Australasia, Asia and the Middle East. As a research professor in the Adam Smith School of Business, Professor Parker is focused on supporting the research programme in the accounting group, including advisory services to staff researchers, PhD students and supervisory teams, research projects mentoring and international networking. He is a 2020 member of the Australian Accounting Hall of Fame and a 2016 Hall of Fame Member of the Australian Centre for Social and Environmental Accounting Research. His research has been published in over 250 articles and books on management and accounting, with a Google Scholar H score of 73 and cited in over 22,000 publications. Scopus SciVal lists him as one of the highest published scholars in the accounting discipline globally. He is joint founding editor of the globally leading interdisciplinary research journal *Accounting, Auditing & Accountability Journal* and serves on over 20 journal editorial boards internationally.

Tarek Rana is an associate professor of accounting in the School of Accounting, Information Systems and Supply Chain at RMIT University, Melbourne, Australia. He teaches management accounting, forensic business investigation and data analytics. His research interests are in the areas of strategic management, management control systems, performance measurement, risk management and sustainability, with focus on not-for-profit and public sector organisations. His publications span journal articles, book chapters, books, research monographs and editorials. His publications appeared in reputable accounting, management and interdisciplinary journals such as *Accounting Auditing & Accountability*; *British Accounting Review*; *Financial Accountability & Management*; *Qualitative Research in Accounting and Management*; *Meditari Accountancy Research*; *Intelligent Systems in Accounting*; *Finance & Management*; *Business Strategy and the Environment*; *Public Money & Management*; *Journal of Accounting & Organisational Change*; *Journal of Cleaner Production*; *and Journal of Intellectual Capital.* Further to his academic record, Dr Rana is Chartered Accountant and Chartered Management Accountant, and brings a professional record of accomplishment including partnership in accounting firms, board membership and governance experience as both executive and non-executive director.

Andre Rodrigues is a doctoral (PhD) student at the University of Glasgow, UK.

Alexander Styhre is Chair of Organization Theory and Management, Department of Business Administration, School of Business, Economics and Law, University of Gothenburg. Styhre earned his PhD from the School of Economics and Management, Lund University, in 1998. In 1999, Styhre was recruited to the Industrial Economics Department, Chalmers University of Technology. In 2002, Styhre became docent (associate professor) in business administration at Chalmers, and in 2006 he was assigned the title professor at the same university. Between 2008 and 2010, Styhre was chair of operations management at University of Technology. In January 2010, Styhre was appointed chair of organization and management at the School of Business, Economics and Law, University of Gothenburg. Styhre has published widely in the field of organization and his work has appeared in, for example, *Journal of Management Studies*; *Organization Studies*; and *Academy of Management Review*. His most recent books published are *Institutionalizing Assisted Reproductive Technologies: The Role of Science, Professionalism, and Regulatory Control* (co-authored with Rebecka Arman, Routledge, 2016) and *The Financialization of the Firm* (Edward Elgar, 2015). Styhre is the former editor-in-chief of *Scandinavian Journal of Management* and has served on the board of several journals and reviewed extensively for, for example, *Organization Studies* and *Journal of Management Studies*. Styhre is currently part of the committee for Handelsbankens Forskningsstiftelser and supervises three doctoral students.

Mouhcine Tallaki is a research fellow in the Department of Economics and Management on the topic of the models of governance and control of the public–private partnership for the non-core management of healthcare facilities. He obtained the title of PhD in economics, curriculum in business economics and financial intermediaries (XXIV cycle), at the Faculty of Economics of the University of Ferrara. Thesis title "Management Control Systems and National Culture in Multinationals: Case of Companies in the Mediterranean Area".

Floris van Kimpren is a dual PhD candidate in the Organisation & Governance section of the faculty of Technology, Policy and Management and at the Department of Management Engineering at Politecnico di Milano. He earned his bachelor's degree in systems engineering, policy analysis and management and his master's degree in engineering and policy analysis from Delft University of Technology (TU Delft). During his master's programme, he spent an exchange semester at Politecnico di Milano. Before starting a PhD, he followed the L.E.A.D. Programme, a one-year traineeship from X!Delft, a part of the TU Delft valorisation centre. In his research, Floris is focused on the use of machine learning techniques for supporting decision-making on wicked problems. Specifically, he researches the implicit or explicit institutions or "rules of the game" that govern the behaviour of stakeholders along the entire development and use cycle of machine learning when applied for supporting decision-making on wicked issues. He studies this in the setting of public organizations such as inspectorates or similar executive agencies. With his research he wants to contribute to a more conscious development and use of machine learning in public organizations.

PREFACE

Accounting, auditing, management control, performance measurement and risk management are undeniably critical components of governance and accountability in the public sector. These essential elements have long been recognized as fundamental to the efficient functioning of public sector organisations (PSOs), ensuring public value and maintaining trust between these PSOs and their various stakeholders.

In recent years, our knowledge of public sector management has advanced considerably, thanks to numerous insightful studies in accounting, management and public administration. However, the emergence of the latest global crisis, the Covid-19 pandemic, has given rise to previously unanticipated risks, challenges and pressures on PSOs across the globe. As we strive to adapt to the new normal, it is increasingly clear that there is a pressing need for innovative approaches to accounting, management control, performance measurement and risk management in the public sector. Moreover, understanding how these practices can be integrated with sustainability measures is crucial for PSOs to successfully navigate and survive in this crisis-ridden environment.

Now, more than ever, the demand for impactful solutions and innovative processes in public sector accounting, management control and risk management is on the rise. This book highlights the growing need for such innovations, emphasizing their potential to improve public sector performance and enhance accountability in a world where uncertainty is the new norm.

Accounting plays a pivotal role in ensuring the accuracy and transparency of financial and non-financial information, enabling public sector stakeholders, such as government entities, citizens, investors, and regulators, to make informed decisions. By providing reliable data, accounting helps maintain the integrity and credibility of PSOs, fostering trust among stakeholders.

Through the 19 chapters in this book, we make a compelling case for the integration of management control, performance measurement, risk management and sustainability in PSOs. These crucial elements can act as catalysts for innovation and the development of novel processes, leading to improved outcomes and accountability. For instance, effective management control systems provide PSOs with the necessary tools to monitor, evaluate their performance and provide feedback to identify areas for improvement and allocate resources more efficiently. Risk management practices, on the other hand, equip PSOs with the knowledge and strategies required to anticipate, assess and mitigate potential risks, thereby ensuring their resilience in the face of adversity. Finally, integrating sustainability practices into the public sector's financial management and accountability framework can lead to long-term benefits, promoting responsible decision-making and contributing to the overall well-being of society.

So the new Covid-19 pandemic-normal world has accentuated the importance of accounting, management control, performance measurement risk management and sustainability in the public sector. As PSOs grapple with the challenges of the post-pandemic era, embracing new approaches and processes in these areas will be instrumental in delivering impactful outcomes, enhancing performance, ensuring accountability, and ultimately, fostering public value, trust and innovation.

PART I

Public management, governance and accountability

1

PUBLIC SECTOR ACCOUNTING, MANAGEMENT CONTROL AND RISK MANAGEMENT

An overview

Tarek Rana and Lee Parker

Accounting, management control and risk management in times of crisis

Public sector organizations (PSOs) are integral to any country's economy and welfare. PSOs deliver many essential services in a country, including health, education, employment, industry, social services, immigration and defence (Alford & O'Flynn, 2012). Over the past three years, the global pandemic Covid-19 has introduced unprecedented risks, challenges and pressures on PSOs worldwide. The pandemic has disrupted public services during this unprecedented global crisis (Leoni et al., 2021, 2022). Tackling public sector challenges during a crisis requires organizational, institutional, political, societal and technological actions (Leoni et al., 2021, 2022). Leoni et al. (2021) identify how uncertainty and crisis can induce changes that impact the PSO's design, use and understanding of accounting, management control and accountability practices.

Recent geopolitical events, particularly during the Covid-19 pandemic, have intensified the demand for more public services and a growing interest in understanding public sector management during and after the event (Andrew et al., 2020). For example, during the Covid-19 pandemic, Australia, like other countries around the world, experienced severe shortages and high demand for services in many essential areas, including food, agriculture, education, health and medical products. The global nature of this pandemic has exacerbated the problem since today's public services are more dynamic, complex and sometimes more international than in the past. This makes them more susceptible to failure in many locations worldwide when confronted with significant disruptions such as Covid-19. Uncertainties and risks associated with a global pandemic highlight the importance of securing a robust understanding of and new knowledge concerning the implications of pandemics for PSOs and the services they provide.

In this new "pandemic-normal" world, evidence exists of an increasing demand for accounting, management control and risk management innovations and new processes. While prior studies have improved our understanding of public sector management, these global circumstances raise new issues. Thus, our understanding of how public sector accounting, management control, risk management and sustainability practices can assist public organizations in navigating and surviving such a challenging global environment is minimal (Chabrak & Gendron, 2015; Leoni et al., 2021, 2022). Remedying this knowledge gap warrants global research to bring out the multifaceted nature of the challenges and impacts in various contexts and address research questions concerning the roles and

DOI: 10.4324/9781003295945-2

implications of accounting, management control and risk management tools in addressing these challenges.

This chapter critically reflects on this book's examination of accounting, management control, risk management and sustainability processes and practices. It explores new developments and transformations in accounting, auditing, management control, performance measurement and risk management work in contemporary society. In doing so, it highlights the importance of developing new understandings of how public organizations can effectively deliver essential public services to the broader community, particularly during significant disruptions such as a pandemic. As mentioned earlier, public services in a pandemic are inevitably more susceptible to the risk of failure, so PSOs need to become more resilient, dynamic, complex and agile to navigate current and future pandemics and other major crises.

Public sector accounting and management in Covid-19 crisis: Australian experience

We offer an introductory reflection by setting the scene concerning the Australian Covid-19 pandemic experience as a national case with which we editors are familiar. This is intended to provide a brief impression of one country's significant experiences to illustrate the macro-conditions to which PSOs are challenged to respond. Like many other countries, Australia has been influenced by neoliberalism, an economic ideology that advocates for free markets, privatization, deregulation and limited government intervention in the economy. This ideology has dominated Australia and other Western countries for decades, shaping economic policies and government responses to crises like the Covid-19 pandemic. Since the onset of this pandemic, there has been a growing emphasis on neoliberal ideology through government approaches to budget repairs. Andrew et al. (2020) examined the immediate budgetary responses to the Covid-19 pandemic by the Australian government and argued that neoliberalism had constrained the ability of the Australian government to respond to crises through budgetary action. One of the main ways neoliberalism has limited government responses to crises is through prioritising fiscal austerity and balanced budgets. This has reduced public spending on essential services and social welfare programmes, making it more difficult for governments to provide support during a crisis like the Covid-19 pandemic. Another way neoliberalism has constrained government responses is in privatizing public services and infrastructure. This has resulted in a lack of public capacity to respond to crises, as essential services like healthcare and emergency response have been outsourced to private providers primarily motivated by profit.

In another study, in the Covid-19 context, Parker et al. (2023) explore the impact of neoliberalism on Australia's public higher education system, focusing on the flaws in the university system that were revealed by the Covid-19 pandemic. They argue that the conditions created by neoliberal policies have limited universities' capacity to respond to a crisis like Covid-19. This study analyses neoliberal policies and New Public Management (NPM) practices to provide an overview of the Australian public sector university system up to 2021 and its transformation by stealth. One of the critical impacts of this transformation has been that Covid-19-related public health measures have caused a significant short-term downturn in the number of international students studying in Australia, which has created a financial crisis for universities, resulting in many tens of thousands of university staff losing their jobs and courses being cut. The chapter also highlights the accountingization of individual academic and university performance due to neoliberal policies. The quantified performance metrics associated with accountingization have become universities' new language, and revenue generation and expenditure have been privileged over contributing to the nation and society. Overall, the chapter calls for a radical rethinking of the public sector university mission for the ultimate benefit of the Australian community. This includes moving away from the neoliberal model that prioritizes revenue generation over social and community benefits, and towards a model that prioritizes public good and community impact. Additionally, the chapter argues for increased public funding for universities and the restoration of academic freedom, which the current neoliberal model has eroded. We highlight this recent study as providing just one example of the risk management failures and potential management control and accountability implications of neoliberal policy impacts on many different types of organizations across the public sector

In examining Australia as just one developed economy case of response to the Covid-19 crisis, the Australian public sector accounting response can be summarized as follows:

- Rapid deployment of fiscal stimulus measures: The Australian government quickly introduced several fiscal stimulus measures to support businesses, households and the economy at large. These measures included wage subsidies, cash payments and tax relief measures. However, these were targeted at select parts of the economy and were not extensive or inclusive.
- Flexibility in accounting standards and reporting requirements: The Australian Accounting Standards Board and the Australian Securities and Investments Commission provided flexibility in accounting standards and reporting requirements to help entities respond to the Covid-19 crisis. This included allowing the deferral of lease payments and the recognition of government grants on an accrual basis.
- Increased focus on financial management: The Covid-19 crisis highlighted the importance of effective financial management in the public sector. The Australian government emphasized the need for financial discipline and transparency in the management of public funds.
- Increased collaboration between government agencies: The Covid-19 crisis necessitated increased collaboration between agencies at all levels. The Australian federal government worked closely with state and territory governments and other key stakeholders to coordinate the response to the crisis.

Overall, the Australian public sector accounting response to the Covid-19 crisis focused on providing financial support to those affected by the crisis while maintaining financial discipline and transparency in the management of public funds. The response was characterized by flexibility, increased financial and risk management focus, and increased collaboration between government agencies.

The Australian government's response to the Covid-19 crisis involved a range of risk management strategies to protect public health, the economy and social well-being. These strategies were implemented across federal, state and territory government levels, as well as across various agencies and departments.

- Enhanced enterprise risk management (ERM): The crisis highlighted the importance of effective ERM in the public sector. The Australian government implemented enhanced risk management processes and practices to address the uncertainties posed by the Covid-19 crisis.
- Preparing for the Pandemic: The Australian government began preparing for pandemic impacts early on by establishing a National Incident Room and developing a pandemic plan based on the World Health Organization's guidelines. This plan was updated and refined as the situation evolved.
- Coordinated National Response: The federal government worked with state and territory governments to establish a coordinated national response. This involved establishing a national cabinet to provide a forum for collaboration and decision-making. The national cabinet included the prime minister, state and territory premiers and chief ministers, and relevant federal government ministers.

- Border Protection Measures: The government introduced border protection measures to prevent the spread of the virus. This included travel bans, mandatory quarantine for all international arrivals, and the closure of state borders.
- Public Health Measures: The government implemented a range of public health measures to slow the spread of the virus, including social distancing, hand hygiene and mask-wearing. These measures were communicated to the public through various channels, including television advertisements and social media.
- Economic Support: The government introduced a range of economic support measures to help some groups of individuals and businesses affected by the pandemic. This included income support payments, tax relief and business grants and loans to selected target groups.
- Vaccine Roll-Out: The government also implemented a nationwide vaccine roll-out plan, prioritizing vulnerable populations and essential workers. The roll-out has continued to be managed by state and territory governments in partnership with the federal government.

Overall, the Australian government's response to the Covid-19 crisis involved a range of risk management strategies, including border protection measures, public health measures, economic support and vaccine roll-out. These strategies were developed and implemented coordinated across federal, state, and territory government levels, aiming to protect public health, the economy and social well-being.

The Covid-19 crisis in Australia required the implementation of various management control tasks by the public sector to ensure effective governance, accountability, performance management and risk management. Some of these tasks included:

- Strategic Planning: The public sector must develop and implement strategic plans to effectively manage the crisis. This involved developing policies, procedures and guidelines to guide decision-making and ensure consistency across all levels of government.
- Resource Management: The public sector had to manage and allocate resources effectively, including personnel, financial resources and equipment, to ensure a coordinated response to the crisis. This involved identifying and procuring necessary equipment and supplies, deploying staff to areas of need and ensuring adequate funding for response efforts.
- Risk Management: The public sector had to manage risks associated with the crisis, including identifying and mitigating potential risks, developing contingency plans and monitoring and reporting on risk management activities.
- Communication: The public sector had to communicate effectively with the public, stakeholders and other agencies to ensure transparency and clarity of information. This involved developing communication strategies and materials, regularly updating the public on the status of the crisis and addressing public concerns and questions.
- Performance Monitoring: The public sector had to monitor and evaluate the performance of response efforts to ensure that objectives were being met and resources were being used effectively. This involved developing key performance indicators, collecting and analysing data and reporting on performance to relevant stakeholders.
- Coordination and Collaboration: The public sector had to coordinate and collaborate effectively across agencies and levels of government to ensure a cohesive and effective response to the crisis. This involved establishing partnerships, sharing information and resources and coordinating response efforts to maximize efficiency and effectiveness.

Overall, Australia's public sector faced a range of management control tasks in responding to the Covid-19 crisis. These tasks aimed at contributing to effective governance, accountability and performance, and required coordination and collaboration across all government and stakeholders. This one particular national case is offered simply as an illustrative overview of the many PSO challenges and organizing strategies triggered by the onset of this particular global pandemic. Of course, different national locations, with their differing contexts and government/public sector structures and processes, have produced different approaches and outcomes. Some of these unique national and international contexts and experiences will become evident across the chapters in this book that cover a range of international circumstances.

Themes and scope of the book and contributions

The new global circumstances occasioned by this particular global crisis, its durability and ongoing impacts raise a raft of new issues as depicted by the chapters in this book. Thus, our understanding of how public sector accounting and management control practices can assist public organizations in navigating and surviving in this challenging environment offers major insights that emerge from the contributions of these chapters. The book addresses the need for new understandings of how public organizations can effectively deliver essential public services to the broader community, particularly during a pandemic. Several chapters analyse the Covid-19 crisis responses of different governments and PSOs, drawing on ideas from neoliberalism, resilience and governmentality, among other perspectives. Considering the unique settings and examples from many parts of the world, this book explores the dynamics between accounting, management control and risk management as lessons and innovations for future pandemics. In so doing, it highlights contemporary issues such as reforms, technological advancement, increased social and community involvement and expectations, increased demand for public value, the developing of risk management ideas and practices, sustainability reporting and management, and the proliferation of enabling government policies and regulations for agile and resilient public management. The chapters in this book show that public services in a pandemic are inevitably more susceptible to the risk of failure, so PSOs need to become more agile and resilient to navigate future pandemics. Set in this context, this book has reimagined the dynamics between accounting, management control and risk management for future pandemics. It also addresses technological advancement, increased social/community movements/expectations, and the proliferation of government policies and regulations for agile public management, as discussed in the following section.

This research-based edited book, targeted at scholars, professionals, teachers and consultants in public sector accounting, auditing, accountability and risk management, offers high-level insights into the new architecture and execution of such activities in the emerging post-Covid-19 world. Several important themes emerged from the chapters that follow, namely "public management, governance and accountability", "public sector accounting and auditing issues", "management control, innovation and change", "performance management and public value", "risk management and disclosure" and "sustainability accounting and management". The chapters within these themes critically analyse relevant topics in the context of past and current pandemics. They focus on issues crucial to understanding the contemporary world of public management and the functioning of accounting and sustainability reporting in that realm. For example, the sustainability theme shows that sustainability reporting is a crucial tool for promoting sustainability practices in the public sector. Such reporting helps public sector entities consider the impacts of their operations and decision-making on society, the environment and the global economy. By disclosing information about their sustainability practices, PSOs and Supreme Audit Institutions (SAIs) can provide stakeholders with insights into how they address sustainability issues and progress towards achieving Sustainable Development Goals (SDGs). Sustainability reporting, therefore, potentially plays an essential role in promoting transparency and accountability in the public sector, enabling stakeholders to make better-informed decisions and hold public entities accountable for their actions.

Their discussions of management control incorporate the processes and systems PSOs use to achieve efficient and effective objectives delivery. They also address related issues of establishing performance metrics, monitoring progress and taking corrective action to improve PSO accountability, transparency and performance. The chapters in this book also reveal how risk management in the public sector involves identifying, assessing and managing risks that may impact achieving public sector objectives. It involves formulating and executing risk strategies related to risk management, aimed at controlling the effects of potential threats, while concurrently identifying and capitalizing on new strategic opportunities. Effective risk management is therefore tailored towards assisting PSOs to make informed decisions, improve resilience and enhance public trust.

This book offers a major resource that addresses a wide range of public sector issues, drawing on the latest research from the international public sector accounting research community. Its key contributions can be summarized as follows:

- Documenting the implications of a crisis, such as the Covid-19 pandemic, for public sector management, governance and accountability.
- Highlighting the role of accounting and auditing in improving public sector management in a new world.
- Examining the role of public sector accounting and management in managing risks, including using risk management frameworks.
- Providing insights into how management control systems can enhance performance management and assist with risk management.
- Challenging previous frameworks for understanding public sector accounting and management and reconceptualizing these frameworks in a post-Covid-19 era.
- Recognizing that the boundaries between management control systems, performance management and risk management are often blurred or temporary and that these boundaries may disappear during a crisis.
- Illustrating how organizational and institutional models that previously sustained public sector management are transforming in response to the Covid-19 pandemic and other emerging societal and environmental issues.

Overall, the contributions of this book carry implications not only for public sector accounting and management, but also for policymakers, practitioners and scholars in these fields. It provides a timely and valuable resource for understanding the challenges and opportunities facing PSO organizations in a rapidly changing world, and for developing strategies and practices to enhance their resilience, effectiveness, and accountability.

Overview of the chapters

In the present chapter (Chapter 1), Rana and Parker (2023) provide an overview of the book by highlighting the importance of practical public sector accounting, management control, risk management and sustainability reporting in managing essential public services during the COVID-19 pandemic. The chapter argues that the Covid-19 pandemic has highlighted the need for PSOs to become more resilient, dynamic, complex and agile in responding to crises. Effective public sector accounting and management control are crucial in ensuring that public resources are used efficiently and effectively to provide essential services to the broader community. This chapter shows that these functions are critical in contributing to the integrity of management and accountability of PSOs by providing accurate and transparent financial and non-financial information to stakeholders, including citizens, investors, governments and regulators. Rana and Parker argue that risk management is essential in identifying and managing risks associated with delivering public services during a pandemic. This includes identifying potential risks and developing contingency plans to mitigate those risks. In addition, Rana and Parker contend that sustainability reporting ensures that PSOs consider the social, environmental and economic impacts of their operations and decision-making. Sustainability reporting provides stakeholders with information on how PSOs address sustainability issues and their progress towards achieving SDGs.

In Chapter 2, Christensen et al. (2023) analyse Singapore's response to the Covid-19 crisis, arguing that crisis management should not be confined to analysis "in time" but also be considered how it "makes time". Drawing on the Singaporean case, the chapter shows that PSOs were able to mobilize crisis time to formulate government responses to citizens through public policy developments and budgetary practices. The corpus of documentary coverage of Covid-19 from the first half of 2020 to the first quarter of 2022 is examined in terms of government budgeting and health policy decisions to draw insights into neoliberalism and temporalization of a citizenry in the social and political context of Singapore. The frames of neoliberalism and temporalization provide focus to this chapter, revealing that Singapore has adopted a variant of neoliberalism over the last four decades. Singapore PSOs have meshed the country's policies and concepts of shared responsibility with budgeting principles based on intergenerational views of the citizenry. This is founded on arguments regarding the prevalence of a Singaporean-style neoliberalism in which big government and market forces coexist and which can be differentiated from those anchored-on Margaret Thatcher's and Ronald Reagan's tenets of neoliberalization (Lapsley & Miller, 2019). Singapore's substantial response involved using past financial reserves rather than government debt without adopting a balance sheet view of the strategy – Singaporean neoliberalism privileges individual decision-making within caveats formed by generational relationships and societal structures. A Singaporean city-state model of neoliberalism reveals possible future mutations of an eco-political philosophy dominant in other parts of the world. This chapter extends temporalization studies as a foundation to implement a unique variant of neoliberalism.

In their study, Chapter 3, Brorström and Styhre (2023) present an analysis of how the city of Gothenburg in Sweden manages a grand challenge associated with vulnerable public services in the context of the Covid-19 crisis. The city had to act quickly to respond, prompting bottom-up responses at the local city level. Brorström and Styhre discuss a strategic process within the city of Gothenburg with the ambition to tackle criminality and segregation in vulnerable city districts. The process involved establishing new routines and managing the performance of these initiatives in a setting where organizational boundaries and accountability were blurred and not well defined. The city's leadership initiated the strategic process, recognizing the need to address the root causes of criminality and segregation in vulnerable city districts. The process involved engaging local stakeholders and establishing a network of actors from various organizations, including public and private sectors, civil society and academia. The new routines that were established included creating an interdisciplinary team that developed a comprehensive action plan based on evidence-based practices, establishing a task force to coordinate the plan's implementation, and allocating resources to support the initiatives. Given the blurred organizational boundaries and accountability, performance management was critical to the strategic process. The city established a monitoring and evaluation system to track the initiatives' progress and assess their impact. The system involved setting performance targets, collecting and analysing data and reporting results to stakeholders. The chapter highlights the challenges of managing a grand challenge in a complex setting where organizational boundaries and accountability are blurred. Brorström and Styhre emphasize the importance of engaging local stakeholders, establishing clear routines and processes, and adopting a performance management approach to track progress and assess impact. The chapter also provides insights into how the city of Gothenburg managed a grand challenge associated with vulnerable public service in the context of the Covid-19 crisis. The chapter demonstrates the importance of adopting a strategic process that involves engaging local stakeholders, establishing clear routines and processes, and adopting a performance management approach to manage performance in a complex setting.

Ferry and Midgley (2023), in Chapter 4, explore the experience of the National Audit Office (NAO) in the UK in its efforts to digitalize and develop a data analytics capacity. The chapter explores the embeddedness of entrepreneurship towards technological change in public sector audit by utilizing two frames – professional logic and democratic logic. The professional logic arises from the accounting specialism and the need to improve audit quality, efficiency and effectiveness through data analytics. Ferry and Midgley argue that the NAO recognized the potential benefits of data analytics, such as identifying anomalies and patterns in large data sets and reducing the risk of fraud and error. The professional logic permitted and justified the adoption of data analytics techniques within the NAO, as it aligned with the NAO's mission to improve the quality of public sector auditing. The democratic logic arises from the NAO's constitutional purpose, and mandate set out by Parliament to ensure transparency, accountability and value for money in public funds. The NAO recognized that data analytics could enhance its ability to carry out its constitutional mandate by providing more insightful and evidence-based audit findings. The democratic logic also legitimized the adoption of data analytics techniques within the NAO as it aligned with the NAO's role in promoting public accountability and transparency. Ferry and Midgley demonstrate how the NAO's adoption of data analytics was legitimized through the utilization of professional and democratic logic frames, which permitted and justified the adoption of data analytics techniques while limiting the extent to which change could immediately happen. The NAO's experience provides insights into the challenges and opportunities in digitalizing the public sector and highlights the importance of aligning technological change with the public sector's constitutional mandate and purpose.

Chapter 5 by Hyndman and Liguori (2023) highlights the relationship between accounting change and crises in the public sector. While the existing literature tends to view change as a reaction to external crises and shocks, such as the Covid-19 pandemic or the 2008 global financial crisis, Hyndman and Liguori argue crises can provide reforms and opportunities for the development of new systems and processes. The chapter proposes new lenses for interpreting accounting change in the public sector, including the role of power and politics, organizational culture's influence and technology's impact. Hyndman and Liguori reiterate that public sector accounting and accountability systems play a critical role in ensuring the effective management of public resources and promoting transparency and accountability in government operations. However, the chapter argues that as public sector challenges evolve, these systems must adapt and adjust accordingly to ensure they remain relevant and practical.

In Chapter 6, Argento and Lövstål (2023) explore the challenges of collaborative innovation projects in the public sector and how they can be managed using different control forms. Specifically, the study draws on public management and management control literature and empirical observations from the Digital Innovation for Dementia Care (DIDEC) project in Perstorp Municipality, Sweden. The DIDEC was a collaborative innovation project to develop innovative products and services for dementia care. The authors found that tensions in collaborative innovation projects can be effectively managed by balancing formal and informal management control forms throughout the project's different stages and in different parts of the project organization. This progressive balance can help ensure that the project achieves its goals while maintaining the flexibility and creativity required for successful innovation. However, Argento and Lövstål found that this balance can be destabilized by unexpected crises such as the outbreak of Covid-19. During this crisis, the dominance of formal controls focused on achieving predetermined targets, resulted in neglecting the unexpected added value of the DIDEC project. This chapter highlights the importance of carefully managing the tensions in collaborative innovation projects in the public sector. By balancing formal and informal control forms, project leaders can help ensure that innovation projects achieve their goals while maintaining flexibility and creativity.

Cuganesan and Hart (2023), in Chapter 7, explore the challenges of generating positive outcomes from major infrastructure development projects that often face opposition from local communities and social movements. The chapter uses a social capital lens to analyse a cancelled infrastructure project and the strategies used by the government authority and social movement to engage public support. Cuganesan and Hart highlight the importance of building public support for infrastructure projects through strategies such as openness and civic engagement. It argues that relying on bureaucratic authority and technical expertise cannot overcome opposition from social movements and local communities. Instead, project authorities must use social capital-building strategies to build public legitimacy and support for their proposals. The authors find that government authorities' failure to engage in similar social capital-building strategies can lead to the contested process of proposing infrastructure developments to the public. The chapter's contribution to public management and accounting literature identifies specific strategies project authorities must consider when engaging with the public and responding to social movements. The chapter emphasizes the importance of openness and civic engagement in shaping and managing infrastructure projects, which can help generate positive outcomes while minimizing opposition and negative impacts on local communities and the environment. This failure can reduce public support and legitimacy, creating barriers to successfully implementing infrastructure development projects.

Focusing on issues surrounding Strategic Management Accounting (SMA), in Chapter 8, Eriksson, Höglund and Mårtensson (2023) present a case study of the Swedish Public Employment Service's (SPES) use of a balance scorecard (BSC) as a tool for SMA. The study aims to enhance our understanding of how PSOs use SMA to balance long-term objectives with short-term evaluations. Eriksson, Höglund and Mårtensson suggest that SPES's operational managers and controllers use the BSC to create active management and control while remaining reactive with a short-term focus. This approach reflects the agency's desire to become a flexible organization that can quickly adapt to changes in its environment. The chapter provides insights into how PSOs can use SMA to balance strategic and operational objectives in a rapidly changing environment. The chapter argues that using SMA in the public sector is characterized by the desire for flexibility and the ability to adapt to short-term changes. The case study of the SPES illustrates how operational managers and controllers use the balanced scorecard as an SMA tool to create active management and control while being reactive with a short-term focus. The chapter suggests that SMA creates flexibility, enabling flexibilization and reproducing a neoliberal discourse. This differs from the traditional understanding of SMA as providing long-term direction and stability. Instead, SMA becomes a responsive and fluid practice concerning changes and the desire for flexibility in contemporary public management discourse. This chapter shows how operational managers and controllers use the BSC as an SMA tool to create active management and control while being reactive with a short-term focus. The chapter highlights the importance of understanding the context and attributes of an SMA tool in managing and internalizing changes and capturing several issues. The notion of flexibilization is proposed to understand how SMA is used in this context, as the desire to become a flexible agency characterizes the studied managers and controllers and their use of SMA.

In Chapter 9, Krimpen, de Bruijn and Arnaboldi (2023) provide a conceptual overview of the literature on machine learning (ML) algorithms, focusing on the specific characteristics of public decision-making and their implications for the use of ML algorithms. The chapter shows that using ML algorithms in public decision-making has been a topic of interest in academia and in practice. While the potential benefits of these algorithms in improving services and outcomes for citizens are often highlighted, there are also numerous challenges and risks associated with their use. These challenges include a lack of transparency, accountability and ethics. However, Krimpen, de Bruijn and Arnaboldi argue that there is a need to explore further the specific characteristics of public decision-making and how they interact with ML algorithms. The chapter outlines the unique characteristics of public decision-making, such as the presence of multiple stakeholders, the need to balance competing interests and the importance of public trust and legitimacy. The chapter further discusses the implications of these unique characteristics of public decision-making for using ML algorithms. These implications include the potential amplification of existing challenges, such as a lack of transparency and accountability, the potential for unintended consequences and the need for ongoing monitoring and evaluation. The chapter shows that using ML algorithms in public decision-making is complex and raises significant challenges. Specifically, the wickedness of public decisions, such as the high level of uncertainty, the involvement of multiple stakeholders with conflicting interests, and the high degree of interdependence between decisions, can exacerbate issues associated with ML algorithms, such as opacity, accountability and the risk of discrimination. The authors argue that existing approaches to address these challenges, such as transparency and explainability techniques, are limited in their effectiveness in the public sector. This is due to the complex nature of public decision-making and the lack of consensus on what constitutes a fair and ethical decision.

Chapter 10, by Grossi and Mauro (2023), presents a study on how the European Union (EU) sets its performance budget and how performance is conceptualized and measured to guide the delivery of public value and contributes to the literature on performance budgeting at the EU level and public value budgeting, which are underdeveloped research streams. The chapter shows that the EU budget results from a complex negotiation process between different actors and perspectives, and it plays a crucial role in managing relationships across different levels of government. In light of the current extraordinary times and the size of the current EU budget, it is essential to understand how performance is defined and measured to allocate resources effectively. The concept of public value and the pursuit of performance budgeting is increasingly relevant, but defining and measuring them remains a challenge. The study analysed available documents and interviews with European Commission experts in the EU budget process and reforms. The chapter also highlights that the EU's performance budgeting approach is suitable for enhancing the delivery of public value, as it aligns budget allocation and resource allocation decisions with the achievement of public goals. The use of performance-based budgeting also contributes to transparency and accountability, as it allows for tracking how resources are used and the impact they have on achieving public goals. However, the chapter noted that there is still room for improvement in impact measurement and in developing indicators to capture the full range of impacts produced from multiple perspectives. Overall, the chapter provides insights into the EU's performance budgeting approach and its potential to enhance the delivery of public value.

In an alternate context, Chohan (2023), in Chapter 11, highlights how the Covid-19 pandemic has presented significant challenges to public management and public value theory. This chapter reflects on these challenges and presents several lessons for the PSOs. One lesson is the importance of considering a "global" public in public value creation, as the pandemic has highlighted the interconnectedness of the world and the need for coordinated global responses. Another lesson is the crucial role of civil society in responding to the pandemic, as individuals and organizations have mobilized to provide support and services where governments have been unable to. The predominance of private interest has been highlighted, as private businesses have been granted significant influence over public policy decisions and resource allocation during the pandemic. The chapter also discusses the politics of accounting, as the pandemic has exposed the limitations of traditional measures of public value and the need for new ways of measuring impact. The surprising successes and failures of public value creation during the pandemic are also examined, as are the underlying public value problems that the crisis has exacerbated. This chapter argues that PSO managers should continue to monitor the Covid-19 pandemic and be prepared for ongoing and future disruptions to public value. This requires a shift in mindset from simply reacting to crises to proactively building resilience and adaptability in public systems and services. It also requires a recognition of the importance of collaboration and cooperation across different levels of government, civil society and private actors. The lessons learned from the Covid-19 pandemic can provide valuable insights for PSO managers to understand better the complexities and challenges of creating, preserving and protecting public value in a rapidly changing and uncertain world. Overall, the chapter concludes that the pandemic has prompted a re-examination of what is valuable and what is valued and that this will have implications for public value theory and public management going forward.

Grubnic and Heath (2022), in Chapter 12, explore the use of performance measures concerning public health during the UK's Covid-19 crisis. It begins by providing a background to the UK experience and then examines the potential theoretical lenses of deliberative democracy, agonistic pluralism and "agonistic deliberation". The chapter considers the role of performance information in helping to make sense of the crisis and contributing to public debates, focusing on politicians, professional experts and members of the public. Grubnic and Heath discuss the innovative presentation and use of public health information in the UK during the pandemic. They highlight the importance of instrumental rationality between the government and the public, and some degree of communicative rationality between the government and non-affiliated scientists in the context of "agonistic deliberation". The chapter identifies various stakeholder groups interested in how the government performed in discharging responsibilities concerning the Covid-19 pandemic. It focuses on three groups of stakeholders: the government, independent experts and the general public. The interrelationships between these groups and performance management are an important topic, yet under-researched, and have considerable societal implications. The chapter adopts theoretical framings that provide new insights into performance measurement. These framings, which combine the concepts of deliberative democracy and agnostic pluralism, have been relatively little used in the academic accounting literature but have great potential for providing perceptive insights. The resulting notion, which the chapter calls "agonistic deliberation", helps illuminate the issues and emergent performance measurement in the UK during the Covid-19 crisis. The chapter argues that during a crisis, it is particularly desirable to allow many voices to be heard to recognize a common citizenship and access vital information that would not be available otherwise. For example, the care home scandal could have been avoided if care home managers, residents and their families had been consulted. This highlights the importance of a multi-stakeholder approach to democratic debate and decision-making during a crisis.

In Chapter 13, Rodrigues, Dudau, Kominis and Favotto (2023) argue that effective management control systems (MCS) are crucial for addressing strategic risks and uncertainties organizations face, including PSOs. While research suggests that PSOs are exposed to as much risk as private enterprises, there is insufficient examination and theorization on how MCS can account for risk in PSOs. The chapter proposes a theoretical framework for examining the interplay between risk and control in PSOs to address this gap. The proposed framework highlights the importance of integrating risk management into the design and implementation of MCS and the need for a dynamic approach to managing risk at times of crisis and uncertainty. Consistent with Mahama et al. (2022) and Rana et al. (2022, 2019), the chapter argues that PSOs face unique challenges in managing risk, including balancing multiple stakeholder interests and potential political interference. The proposed framework seeks to address these challenges by emphasizing the importance of developing a risk-aware organizational culture and promoting collaboration and communication across different levels of the organization. The framework draws upon the levers of control framework, which posits that the essence of control lies in successfully managing tensions between various factors, including innovation and predictability, enablement and coercion, and current and future strategy. These factors are associated with different types of risks and uncertainties, and the key consideration for designing MCS in (PSOs) is to strike an acceptable balance between risks associated with opportunity-seeking behaviours and those associated with "check box" compliance (Rana et al., 2022).

Chapter 14, by Moll (2023), explores how Australian higher education institutions have been affected by the Covid-19 pandemic and how they have communicated these risks to their stakeholders through their annual reports. To examine the financial position and risk disclosures of Australian public universities, the authors analysed the annual reports of 37 institutions for 2019 and 2020. This builds upon the work of Carnegie et al. (2021a, 2021b), who previously analysed university annual reports. The chapter seeks to deepen our understanding of the institutions' risk management practices by examining changes in universities' risk profiles and how these are communicated. The study's findings suggest that Australian universities have experienced significant financial risks due to the pandemic. These risks include declines in international student enrolment, reductions in government funding and increased expenses associated with transitioning to online learning. The authors also found that while universities disclose information about these risks in their annual reports, there is significant variation in the quality and usefulness of these disclosures. Moll argues that effective risk management requires transparent and applicable risk disclosures to stakeholders, similar to those of corporations. The chapter highlights the importance of risk disclosure in effective risk management and the potential consequences of inadequate risk reporting for stakeholder trust and organizational resilience. As such, it calls for a greater emphasis on transparent reporting practices in the Australian higher education sector, particularly in times of crisis.

Chapter 15, by Bracci, Deidda-Gagliardo, Gobbo and Tallaki (2023), highlights the importance of integrating performance management, risk management and public value management for PSOs. Italy introduced an integrated plan for PSOs and public administrations except for schools (The Italian acronym for this plan is PIAO). The basic idea is to effectively address the excessive array of planning tools currently in use and remedy the resulting fragmentation. The case study on implementing PIAO in Italian public administration provides insights into the tools, processes and actors contributing to making public value an integrating mechanism between performance management and risk management). The study found that integrating performance management, risk management, and public value management requires the involvement of multiple actors, such as top management, middle managers and front-line staff, and various tools, such as risk assessment matrices and performance scorecards. The case study results suggest that integrating performance, risk, and public value management through the PIAO reform can reduce cultural and ideological barriers and align PSOs' objectives towards a public value management perspective. Including public value at the centre of the planning process can motivate public managers and employees towards public value, leading to more effective performance and risk management. This represents a shift from previous NPM reforms focusing mainly on short-term financial performance and efficiency. The chapter concludes that integrating performance management, risk management, and public value can lead to better decision-making, increased accountability and improved public service delivery. However, further studies are needed to evaluate the effectiveness of the PIAO reform and its ability to achieve its objectives.

In Chapter 16, Narayan and Kommunuri (2023) argue that one of the emerging challenges in the public sector includes the Covid-19 pandemic. They argue that this crisis has brought new risks and uncertainties that traditional risk management systems may not adequately address. Implementing an ERM system can help PSOs manage risks and uncertainties in a more integrated, proactive and comprehensive manner. ERM systems can help identify, assess, prioritize and manage risks across the entire PSO, including strategic, operational, financial and compliance risks. The chapter also highlights the importance of governance and MCS in supporting the implementation and effectiveness of ERM systems. Effective governance structures and processes can help provide oversight, accountability and strategic direction for ERM implementation.

Conversely, MCS can provide the necessary tools, processes and techniques for risk identification, assessment and monitoring (Mahama et al., 2022; Rana et al., 2022). The chapter also discusses the role of digital technologies in enabling ERM implementation and enhancing its effectiveness. The chapter argues that using digital technologies can also help increase transparency and accountability in risk management practices by providing real-time reporting and data analysis. This can help public entities identify emerging risks and take timely actions to mitigate them. The chapter also argues that digital platforms can facilitate stakeholder engagement and communication, allowing risk managers to engage with stakeholders and communicate risk management strategies more effectively. Furthermore, adopting digital technologies enables public entities to achieve greater cost efficiencies in risk management, reducing the costs associated with traditional paper-based systems and manual data processing. Incorporating digital technologies into ERM systems can significantly enhance the effectiveness and efficiency of risk management practices in the public sector.

Cordery and Manochin's (2023) discussion of the Indian case, in Chapter 17, focuses on the challenges of achieving the SDGs by 2030 and the need for polycentric approaches to governance to address complex multilevel problems. It highlights that progress towards achieving the SDGs has been slow, and reports from the SAIs of member states indicate that states are yet to define goals, relevant data are missing, and citizens lack a voice in stakeholder processes. The chapter emphasizes that achieving the SDGs requires cooperation and action from diverse actors beyond traditional bureaucratic or market-based regulatory approaches. It discusses the features of the UN's polycentric SDG governance and monitoring structures, including high-level political debates and attendant reports, and how nations are called to account for their commitments to achieve the SDGs. Polycentric governance offers a way to address complex problems that traditional bureaucratic or market-based regulatory approaches cannot handle alone. The SDGs provide an example of polycentric governance in action, as their achievement requires cooperation and action from a diverse range of actors, including governments, civil society and the private sector. The SDGs also emphasize the importance of leaving no one behind, addressing social and economic inequalities and climate change. This allows for greater flexibility and adaptability in responding to complex problems and opportunities for learning and innovation. The chapter also highlights the challenges of interdependency, opportunities for learning, and sufficient resources to achieve the SDGs. However, achieving the SDGs is complex and challenging, and progress has been slow. Challenges include the lack of defined goals, missing or irrelevant data, and a lack of citizens' voices in stakeholder processes. A polycentric approach that involves a range of actors and promotes vertical independence is essential to overcome these challenges. The chapter notes that these issues will continue to drive public sector responses towards SDG success in networks, especially in challenging times.

Gomes, Martins and Branco (2023), in Chapter 18, argue that PSOs face a complex and uncertain institutional environment in a crisis when addressing sustainability challenges. As such, they often rely on impression management strategies to communicate their actions and achievements to their stakeholders. The chapter proposes a framework for sustainability-related impression management and accountability, considering the social and political contexts in which PSOs operate. This framework moves away from an individualistic approach to ethics and emphasizes the importance of considering the public good when evaluating the accountability of PSOs. By highlighting the role of impression management in public sector sustainability, this chapter contributes to the ongoing debates on accountability and sustainability in the public sector.

Chapter 19 by Rana and Parker (2023) proposes several directions for future research at the intersection of MCS and risk management in public sector accounting and management contexts based on the themes and topics that emerged from the book chapters. One important consideration is that accounting and control are not neutral activities but a social practice that reflects and reinforces societal values and norms. Accounting systems can enable and constrain efforts to address emerging challenges such as the Covid-19 crisis, climate change, supply chain management and cybersecurity. For instance, traditional accounting systems may not adequately capture the impacts of the crisis on government activities, leading to underinvestment in initiatives that promote sustainable development. Similarly, accountability systems prioritizing financial performance over social outcomes may incentivize short-term decision-making and hinder long-term planning. Therefore, the chapter argues that policymakers and stakeholders should critically reflect and dialogue on the role of public sector accounting and accountability systems in addressing emerging challenges. This should involve considering a range of perspectives and incorporating diverse stakeholder input into the design and implementation of these systems. Among suggested directions, the chapter contends that the public sector is inherently uncertain and that future research should focus on how PSOs can manage risk and uncertainty effectively. The chapter also argues that innovation is an aspect of public sector service delivery and that future research should explore how PSOs can effectively adopt and use digital technologies to innovate to improve their operations and services.

Conclusion

In summary, this chapter offers an analytical overview and reflection on the contributions made by the authors in this book concerning the changing risk and crisis management patterns in the public sector, particularly in the context of the Covid-19 pandemic. It highlights the diverse social, political and institutional settings in which the chapters provide new knowledge and developments in public sector accounting and management, management control, performance measurement, risk management and sustainability perspectives. Overall, the chapter emphasizes the relevance and importance of the book's contributions to enhancing PSOs' resilience, accountability and sustainability in the face of the challenges posed by the Covid-19 pandemic and other emerging societal and environmental issues.

The contributing researchers provide critical assessments, frameworks and recommendations for addressing emerging societal, governmental and professional issues in PSOs, practices and policies. Their contributions span theoretical, empirical and policy discussions and will be helpful for both scholars and practitioners in public sector accounting, auditing and management. Prior studies have improved our understanding of accounting and management in the public sector, and the new global circumstances due to Covid-19 have raised a raft of new issues, some of which are captured in this book. Thus, new understandings of how public sector accounting and management control can assist government organizations in navigating and surviving in this challenging environment have been very limited, but the chapters in this book provide essential new contributions. Those contributions span various issues, including digitization, stakeholder engagement and collaboration, governance and reporting practices, performance and risk management relationships, public value and decision-making, and strategic and change processes. Hence we offer a crucially important contribution to understanding how PSOs can assess, manage and govern during and post a pandemic crisis era.

To this end, in Chapter 19, we identify further research required to expand these themes and consolidate the knowledge developed in this book. We invite the readers to explore the following chapters and consider our recommendations for future research.

References

Alford, J., & O'Flynn, J. (2012), *Rethinking public service delivery: Managing with external providers.* Bloomsbury.

Andrew, J., Baker, M., Guthrie, J. & Martin-Sardesai, A. (2020). Australia's COVID-19 public budgeting response: The straitjacket of neoliberalism. *Journal of Public Budgeting, Accounting & Financial Management, 32*(5), 759–770.

Carnegie, G. D., Guthrie, J. & Martin-Sardesai, A. (2021a). Public universities and impacts of COVID-19 in Australia: risk disclosures and organisational change. *Accounting, Auditing, and Accountability, 35*(1), 61–73.

Carnegie, G. D., Martin-Sardesai, A., Marini, L., & Guthrie, J. (2021b). Taming the black elephant: assessing and managing the impacts of COVID-19 on public universities in Australia. *Meditari Accountancy Research, 30*(6), 1783–1808.

Chabrak, N., & Gendron, Y. (2015). Promoting research from the "periphery": Engaging critically with the global financial crisis. *Critical Perspectives on Accounting, 30*, 1–8.

Lapsley, I., & Miller, P. (2019). Transforming the public sector: 1998–2018. *Accounting, Auditing & Accountability Journal, 32*(8), 2211–2252.

Leoni, G., Lai, A., Stacchezzini, R., Steccolini, I., Brammer, S., Linnenluecke, M., & Demirag, I. (2021). Accounting, management and accountability in times of crisis: Lessons from the COVID-19 pandemic. *Accounting, Auditing & Accountability Journal, 34*(6), 1305–1319.

Leoni, G., Lai, A., Stacchezzini, R., Steccolini, I., Brammer, S., Linneluecke, M., & Demirag, I. (2022). The pervasive role of accounting and accountability during the COVID-19 emergency, *Accounting Auditing and Accountability Journal, 35*(1), 1–19.

Mahama, H., Rana, T., Marjoribanks, T., & Elbashir, M.Z. (2023). Principles-based risk regulatory reforms and management control practices: a field study. *Accounting, Auditing & Accountability Journal, 36*(3), 773–800. https://doi.org/10.1108/AAAJ-10-2020-4983

Parker, L., Martin-Sardesai, A., & Guthrie, J. (2023). The commercialised Australian public university: An accountingized transition. *Financial Accountability & Management, 39*(1), 125–150.

Rana, T., Wickramasinghe, D., & Bracci, E. (2019). New development: Integrating risk management in management control systems – lessons for public sector managers. *Public Money & Management, 39*(2), 148–151.

Rana, T., Wickramasinghe, D., & Bracci, E. (2022). Management accounting and risk management – research and reflections. *Public Money & Management, 42*(6), 361–364.

2

PUBLIC MANAGEMENT AND CRISIS

Lessons for neoliberalism drawn from a city-state

Mark Christensen, Chu Yeong Lim and Jamus Lim

Public management and crisis

Political incantations of neoliberalism may have a familial lineage with US president Ronald Reagan as the father and UK prime minister Margaret Thatcher as the mother. Amongst other (in)famous sayings these two are remembered for, two separate but interconnected claims stand out:

> There is no such thing as society.
>
> *(Thatcher, 1987)*

and

> Government is not the solution to our problem; government is the problem [...] our present troubles parallel and are proportionate to the intervention and intrusion in our lives that result from unnecessary and excessive growth of government.
>
> *(Reagan, 1981)*

This chapter aims to draw lessons for neoliberalism from Singapore"s Covid-19 response via public sector management and accounting settings. At its core, it is a story that refutes the above claims of Thatcher and Reagan. It demonstrates a clear and important need to leverage societal behaviour, while mounting a governmental effort, in response to an external crisis. Nevertheless, the Singaporean response demonstrates how neoliberalism has been invoked in preparation for, and implementation of, budgeting settings and ancillary healthcare policies that have contributed to Singapore"s Covid-19 successes. Thus, it demonstrates a successful implementation of neoliberalism, which has contributed to a Covid-19 experience envied by many other countries.

Singapore was early to respond, had preparations ready for a pandemic,[1] devoted significant resources to the health and economic responses, and kept the death rates at a seven-day moving average of 1.9 for unvaccinated elderly aged more than 70 years old and 0.1 for vaccinated elderly aged more than 70 years old on 12 April 2022, despite a very high case load (MOH, 2022a). An extended period of lockdown – in Singaporean parlance, a "Circuit Breaker" – was implemented in 2020, and economic activity was adversely affected. Gross domestic product (GDP) fell by 12.6 per cent in the second quarter of 2020, following a 0.3 per cent contraction in the first. Employment saw its largest ever decline; the seasonally adjusted unemployment rate rose to 2.9 per cent and

DOI: 10.4324/9781003295945-3

was expected to reach an all-time high (Heng, 2020b). However, in the July 2020 national election, the government's parliamentary representation remained robust (88 per cent of seats), and its crisis management has been praised both in Singapore and internationally (RMIT, 2020; Gordon, 2020). In 2021, Singapore applied a dual-pronged strategy of national vaccination free to all residents and calibrated safe management measures. The economy recovered to a high positive 15.3 per cent in the second quarter of 2021, tapering to 3.4 per cent in the first quarter of 2022 (CNA, 2022).

Singapore's Covid-19 response has been a dexterous combination of ingredients that are sometimes viewed as incompatible. Whilst it has been highly interventionist, it has been couched within a neoliberal context that has relied upon, and further deepened, a temporalization of the Singaporean population. Singapore had positioned itself for a pandemic and, following that preparation, it mobilized government-controlled resources and public policy settings to proactively respond to the crisis. The overarching finding of this project is that the synergy between societal coherency, neoliberalism and a temporalized population has been mobilized to positive effect in Singapore's Covid-19 response. Singapore also presents a neoliberal model with lessons for other jurisdictions.

A substantial corpus of data on Singapore's Covid-19 situation has arisen. This study reviews the early part of that corpus and qualitatively analyses the sources related to public policy settings and budgeting decisions made largely in the absence of "lessons" from other countries due to the early nature of the pandemic. This chapter adopts the following structure in presenting that analysis. First, the concepts of neoliberalism and temporalization are outlined, and this is followed by an overview of Singapore's early overall response together with its historical context. In the next section, public policy healthcare settings are described as a shared responsibility, built upon a citizenry that sees itself within the context of time. In the subsequent section, the analysis of Singapore's Covid-19 health settings and budgetary response is provided, including how citizens were persuaded that the budgetary settings were expressions of generation-based action. The final section concludes with an analysis of Singapore's deft combination of neoliberalism and temporalization to combat Covid-19.

Concepts for interpreting the public policy settings in Singapore's Covid-19 response

Two underlying concepts are discernible in Singapore's Covid-19 response: neoliberalism and the temporalizing of Singapore's citizens. This section clarifies the meanings of these concepts.

Neoliberalism asserts that "well-being can best be advanced by liberating individual entrepreneurial freedoms and skills within an institutional framework characterized by strong private property rights, free markets and free trade" (Harvey, 2005, p. 2). The neoliberalism framework collects "certain logics, practices and techniques of government" (Morales et al., 2014, p. 424) which in Singapore have developed over almost four decades (Naruse & Gui, 2016) around policy settings built on shared responsibility, but premised on self-help and limited government assistance (albeit not minimal governmental *presence*), executed via continuous policy feedback and modification (typically couched as "pragmatism"; Tan, 2012).

Within Singapore's reliance on shared responsibility is a strong pattern of temporalization. Temporalization refers to

> the creation of time, which finds meaning in one's interpretation of foundational moments and elements of disjuncture and continuity [...] (where) the act of temporalizing for one individual or group does not occur in isolation from the existence of other individuals or groups, the emphasis must be put on co-presence, co-relationality and co-adaptations ... (since) temporalization is a technology of orchestration.
>
> *(Montsion, 2014, p. 1489)*

Temporality is evidenced in (a) time-related policy change, where certain age groups' characteristics become incorporated into policy developments; and (b) frequency of policy changes that recognize, and invoke, implications of the past for the future as a significant element of public policy. Temporality becomes an enabler of a neoliberal approach of "governing through freedom" that differentiates over time and across age groups. In Singapore, this is recognized as a theme that "requires people to be free and self-managing in different spheres of everyday life – health, education, bureaucracy, the professions, etc." (Ong, 2007, p. 4). However, that freedom is exercised within the goalposts and rules set by Singaporean public policy.

The thesis that Singapore's style of neoliberalism relies on temporalizing citizens is supported by studies across a wide range of public policies. In the non-health-related fields, studies have covered pension schemes (Hardin, 2014), ethnic change (Montsion, 2014), migratory strategies of governing (Ong, 2007), anti-suicide programmes (Chua, 2011), foodscapes (Bishop, 2011), service performance reporting in universities (Rana et al., 2022), social work (Chow & Bracci, 2020), and neoliberal disabled "workfare" regimes (Soldatic, 2013). Outside temporalism as a frame of reference, Parker et al. (2021) and Parker (2020) examined the impact of neoliberalism on Australia public universities during Covid-19 measures. Hopper (2020) also observed the different emphases by governments on financial policies, information and control systems, discourse with experts, degree of accountability and leadership that led to multiple problems during Covid-19. However, neoliberalism is not always supported by the people. Broadbent (2020) found the English government response to Covid-19 based on an New Public Management approach undermined public trust, while Lapsley (2020) observed there were challenges that the UK National Health System faced during the pandemic. Nyland et al. (2020) found a group of politicians resisted New Public Management in healthcare. In contrast to the above studies, the present study of Singapore's Covid-19 response aims to contribute to the literature showing temporalization as an important part of neoliberal implementations in the context of Singapore's healthcare.

Brief overview of Singapore's early Covid-19 response and its context

Singapore's 55 years of sovereignty are built on struggles to survive with only 5.7 million residents and few natural resources other than its location as a trade and travel hub (SDS, 2020). After separation from the Malaysian Federation, vulnerability was high and sacrifice through hard work was extolled as essential to surviving. This ethos continued to the current day, with Singapore having a per capita income within the middle-to-upper range internationally and stable economic growth. It maintains a competent civil service by international standards, and enjoys stable political leadership (Painter, 2004). The crucially important element of this background is the ethos of self-sacrifice for the nation's survival (Tan, 2012) which builds up reserves for use in the current crisis.

Turning to the Covid-19 response, it began as early as 2 January 2020 when the Ministry of Health (MOH) advised of a virus in Wuhan. It urged the public to "adopt precautions such as: […] Practise frequent hand washing with soap […] wear a mask if you have respiratory symptoms" (MOH, 2020). By 20 January, the MOH had established a strategy which included some exceptional elements (for the time): (1) very detailed contact tracing, separated into known clusters and transmission pathway; (2) clear and publicly released documentation of cases; and, (3) some relevant case history of pertinent cases. An illustration of the detailed nature of the contact tracing is available at CNA (2020). The first Covid-19 case was detected and immediately isolated on 23 January 2020 and a whole-of-government response was also announced on the same day as the beginning of a concerted campaign to lift public awareness of the virus and precautions that each resident was asked to observe.

The identification of a Covid-19 cluster of foreign worker dormitories on 30 March 2020 led to the government imposing a circuit breaker on 7 April 2020. The circuit breaker was a softer mode of lockdown, with social gatherings, dining out and physical presence in workplaces prohibited.

However, people were allowed to leave their homes to carry out essential activities such as purchase of food/groceries and visits to doctors. The circuit breaker reduced the number of infected cases. With the reduction in infected cases, the government gradually lifted the restrictions in phases – Phase 1 on 2 June 2020, Phase 2 on 19 June 2020 and Phase 3 on 31 December 2020. In 2021, the appearance of the new Delta variant of the Covid-19 virus led to tightened rules, disallowing indoor mask-off activities completely during Phase 2 Heightened Alert on 16 May 2021; limiting social gathering group sizes to two and disallowing dining-in at food and beverage establishments on 22 July 2021 (MOH, 2021); and limiting social gathering group sizes and dining-in at food and beverage establishments to two during Phase 3 Heightened Alert on 14 June 2021. (Tambyah & Lum, 2022)

That Singapore was quick to enact a pre-existing strategy to respond to Covid-19, was in no small part due to lessons it learnt during the 2003 SARS epidemic (Anon. 2020). SARS killed 33 people and cost the Singaporean economy S$1 billion (Khalik, 2020). By 4 January 2020, the popular press was observing developments in Wuhan and drawing comparisons with SARS (Khalik, 2020). Singaporeans were quick to recognise the risk, as did the government. Physical resources were already in place (personal protective equipment stockpiles; a specialized hospital and research facility for communicable disease; and personnel and systems for tracing contacts). A series of measures were put in place ranging from keeping physical distances to more than one metre, requiring mask-wearing, doing contact tracing and limiting the number of people in physical gatherings to five. The early targeted containment measures helped suppress the number of infections (Ansah et al., 2021). In addition, Singapore had the social capital built by a strong awareness of epidemics and communicable diseases. Indeed, Singaporeans have a high awareness of health matters and their roles in protecting themselves against adverse health outcomes. Still, Covid-19 posed new challenges compared to SARS. Firstly, the scale and spread of Covid-19 is far greater than that of SARS. As of 13 April 2022, there were 499 million Covid-19-infected cases and six million deaths worldwide (WHO, 2022). Singapore's government had to learn and adapt with varying measures, taking a balanced and measured approach towards protecting public health and the economy. To understand Singapore's response to Covid-19, it is important to understand Singaporeans' attitudes towards healthcare, as discussed in the next section.

Healthcare settings in Singapore: citizenry responsibility

In many countries, citizens look to the government to take care of their health. Such is also the case in Singapore; however, that expectation is accompanied by an acceptance by the citizens of a mutual obligation to effectively co-fund the availability of health services in a quasi-market mix of private and public sector provision. That provision is grounded upon the narrative that market forces drive healthcare providers to provide efficient, quality healthcare at affordable prices. However, as healthcare is a societal responsibility, the government is accountable to ensure that basic affordable healthcare is available to citizens. Yet it has been apparent since nationhood (1965) that variations to public policy settings have been crafted for the state to acquit that responsibility. Between 1983 and 2015, 35 significant changes were made: national savings schemes; subsidies; means-testing calibrations; hospital organization; and performance matters such as licensing, quality assurance, performance indicators, infrastructure, and health service financing (Loh, Lim, & Christensen, 2021), some of which (such as subsidies) have been applied to manage the Covid-19 situation.

The healthcare reforms, seen as a whole, reveal a governmental willingness to interfere, and a gradual devolution of additional responsibility to the individual. It is not a "set and forget" approach in which the market is allowed to dominate; the reforms also reflect the changes facing Singapore's healthcare where communicable tropical diseases, tuberculosis and pneumonia have been replaced in importance by non-communicable or chronic diseases such as diabetes and cancer (Basu, 2016). Coupled with an ageing population, the profile of changing healthcare demand dictates that younger citizens in good health need to be motivated to prepare for the future. In that light, the discussion below illuminates that the reforms deal with, and utilize, the matter of temporality, as has been observed of other neoliberal reforms elsewhere (Chua, 2011) and in Singapore (Montsion, 2014).

Behind the successes of Singapore's health system (see Loh et al., 2021 for a brief review), the overall picture is one of dedicated effort to implement a neoliberal programme of self-governance by citizens who accept a shared responsibility for healthcare as a natural consequence of state–citizen relations (Soldatic, 2013). Importantly, that acceptance is within an environment that protects citizens if they are unable to pay the expense of a co-contribution, while offering the achievement of an efficient, quality-focused healthcare sector as the quid pro quo for societal acceptance of co-contribution payments. As a result, Singapore has achieved expenditure control and high-quality outcomes that outperform many countries (Heng, 2020e). Under pandemic conditions, the protection of all, regardless of income, is a substantial weapon for achieving societal acceptance of government policy.

Whilst Singapore's policy instrument structure has achieved remarkable success, both relatively and absolutely, that success is frequently expressed in terms of present-day achievement. However, the thesis of this chapter is that a feature deserving of attention in understanding Singapore's neoliberal success is the consistent way that the policy suite has succeeded in temporalizing Singaporeans in terms of their views of themselves through "practices of temporalization as constitutive and vital components of everyday projects of self-care" (Chua, 2011, p.16). With that understanding of Singapore's healthcare system, the next section turns to Singapore's Covid-19 responses in terms of public policy settings and budgeting.

Analysis of Singapore's Covid-19 health settings and budgetary response

Covid-19 health settings

Around the world, sovereign nations have embarked on a mixture of health-related policy actions and economy-related fiscal reactions to the downturn caused by Covid-19. These measures seek to curtail human interaction and manage the consequential economic damage. Singapore has been no different. On a scale of 0 to 100, Singapore's "Response Stringency Index" changed 11 times between 22 January and 1 August 2020, ranging from a low of 14 to a high of 85 (OxCGRT, 2020). Those index changes reflect varying degrees of intrusion in daily life and commerce: school and workplace closures; public events cancellations and gathering size restrictions; public transport closures; stay-at-home requirements; internal movement restrictions and electronic recording; and international travel restrictions.

The 11 changes in response stringency were indicative of the Singaporean government's tendency to be early – and frequent – in its responses to external events. Its usage of outright closure (of schools, businesses and public gatherings) was later than a number of other countries, whereas its public awareness campaigns preceded most other countries', and the frequency of changes was higher than most (OxCGRT, 2020). Also notable in the response was a focus on mobilizing the citizenry: three separate free face mask distributions to all households; active testing and safe management measures at senior residential care homes; charging late travellers for health services and isolation fees; and marshalling unused buildings (for example, convention centres, hotels) for isolation of infected people and development of temporary hospital facilities.

As the Covid-19 pandemic evolved with new variants in 2021, the government started sourcing for Covid-19 vaccines from pharmaceutical companies across the world. The government approved the Pfizer BioNTech vaccine for residents above 16 years old in December 2020, and the Moderna vaccine in February 2021 (Tambyah & Lum, 2022). In 2021, the government strategy in the fight against Covid-19 turned towards the vaccination of its people. This was a major switch in strategy from the initial phase when vaccines were not available and safe management measures were the only way to minimize infection cases. The government secured supplies of the Pfizer BioNTech, Moderna and Sinovac Covid-19 vaccines and provided the vaccines for free to all residents (securing purchases of vaccines in advance and delivery for free is also part of budgetary action discussed in the next section). The fight against Covid-19 applied a mix of vaccination and safe management measures in 2021 and 2022. The government imposed differentiated treatment for the vaccinated and unvaccinated in social gathering restrictions, workplace access and even access to healthcare treatment for infections. The differentiated measures incentivized residents to take up the vaccination. The string of measures led to 93 per cent of the population having received at least one vaccine dose as of 10 April 2022 (MOH, 2022a).

With high vaccination rates, the government gradually reverted to Phase 2 Heightened Alert (dubbed the "stabilization phase") on 27 September 2021. Six months later, the measures were further eased, with the limit on group sizes and dining-in increased to ten, masks made optional outdoors, and the full reopening of borders for fully vaccinated travellers, as well as the lifting of restrictions on live performances. The rules for infected residents were streamlined to three protocols. Individuals who were unwell followed Protocol 1 where they visit doctors and depending on severity of their symptoms and age/risk level (elderly, immunocompromised), and were referred to hospital or self-isolated at home. Individuals who were well, though tested positive, followed Protocol 2 where they self-isolate at home, except for high-risk individuals who visited doctors. Individuals who were close contacts of infected cases followed Protocol 3 where they self-monitor for five days. (MOH, 2022b) The streamlined protocols were part of the "living with Covid strategy" and aimed at mitigating the hospital case load during the Omicron variant wave when infected cases rose to a high of 25,731 infections on 22 February 2022 before dropping to 4,420 infections on 12 April 2022 (MOH, 2022c).

Singapore's policy responses adapted to the evolving pandemic situation by securing supplies of vaccine for the population coupled with the gradual relaxation of safe measurement measures and the opening of the borders. This dual-pronged approach of pushing for high vaccination rates in the population and varying degrees of safe management measures, depending on the infection rates, balanced protection of public health with economic growth and livelihoods. The strategy gradually shifted towards a longer term strategy of living with Covid-19 (MOH, 2022b). The gradual relaxation of safe management measures and the opening of borders allowed economic growth of Singapore to turn from a trough of negative 13.3 per cent in second quarter 2020, negative 5.8 per cent in third quarter, and negative 2.4 per cent in fourth quarter 2020, to positive 1.6 per cent in first quarter 2021 and high positive 15.3 per cent in second quarter 2021, slowing down to 7.1 per cent in third quarter 2021 and 5.9 per cent in fourth quarter 2021 (Hirschmann, 2022). The negative economic consequences of Covid-19 and the subsequent economic recovery have a precedent in the Spanish flu epidemic 1918–1920. Salterio (2020) summarized the historical economic evidence of Spanish flu and used simulations under various scenarios of infection rates to predict economic effects early on during the Covid-19 pandemic.

The trajectory of health policy settings described above can be characterized as being highly responsive to the incidence of infection, location of sources of infection, identification of means by which infection was being transmitted, vaccination as a primary tool to combat infection and to living with Covid-19 by practicing social responsibility (MOH, 2022b). By late 2021, Singapore's response was perhaps emerging internationally as a more or less standard approach. However, a distinguishing aspect was the extremely high rates of vaccination achieved in very short periods in Singapore. A strong theme in public communications about Covid-19 was the need to behave as a society to overcome "the challenge of a generation" (Lee, 2020), and thus to be willing to forego personal predilections and freedoms to achieve the betterment of all. The media campaign also touted the act of vaccination as part of the responsibility for every individual (NCID, 2022). The underlying thinking behind the streamlined protocols, such as Protocol 2 where infected individuals could self-isolate at home, is that all individuals are encouraged to practise social responsibility (MOH, 2022d). Resonance with that sense of individual contribution is found by Yates and Difrancesco (2022) in a

Spanish NGO, whilst in a study of the early Covid-19 response in Italy, Lazzini et al. (2022) underline the importance of emotions and moods at a personal level. Increasingly, that theme of personal sacrifice and social responsibility invoked previous and future generations of Singaporeans. That theme was also pronounced in the budgetary actions, as described in the next section.

Singapore's budgetary responses

Singapore's budgetary actions in the first half of 2020 were unprecedented in its short national history. Less than one month after detecting the first Covid-19 infection in Singapore, the government announced a sizeable budgetary response; it subsequently produced three additional extraordinary budgets (see Table 2.1), with S$92.9 billion total budgeted COVID-19-related expenditure (close to 20 per cent of GDP, among the highest in the world).

Importantly, the expenditures also evoked significant temporality. The prime minister specifically noted that the amount was "the largest fiscal intervention in [Singapore's] history" (Lee, 2020), befitting of the largest crisis the nation was facing since independence. The structure of those budgeted expenditures (and foregone tax collections) comprised three heads: a "Solidarity Payment", a "Care and Support Package" and a "Stabilization and Support Package". However, that macro-structure hides a complexity of detailed programmes, each with its unique eligibility requirements. For example, the "Care and Support Package" constituted 16 separate payments, rebates or vouchers.

The armoury of programmes aimed to spread budgetary support across societal groupings and over time. Societal groupings have used proxies for indicators of need, including the number of bedrooms in social housing; value of home; age of citizen; income level; income loss; employment; and Covid-19-related isolation as well as combinations of indicators. The complexity of programmes is beyond the scope of this chapter; however, while almost all Singaporean residents qualified for government support, their eligibility, typical of the neoliberal ethos, had to be "proven".

Industry support programmes were also unveiled in the four Covid-19 budgets in 2020. Beyond the interesting names of these budgets focusing on societal and personal characteristics, these budgets presented sector-calibrated programmes whereby some sectors, such as tourism, received higher levels of support. The amount of S$20 billion had also been set aside for loan schemes at low interest rates and generous repayment terms (IMF, 2020). In the year 2020, S$115 billion needed to be financed.

In Budget 2021, the government further set aside S$11 billion for a Covid-19 Resilience Package. This package consisted of three prongs. The first prong provided S$4.8 billion towards public health and safe reopening measures including vaccination. The second S$700 million towards extension of a job support scheme to cover wages of workers in sectors hard-hit by the pandemic such as aviation and tourism. The third prong provided S$870 million targeted support and relief for the aviation sector as well as S$133 million for the transport sector and S$45 million for the arts, culture and sports sector. The package also consisted of skills training schemes for workers and temporary bridging loans for businesses (MOF, 2021). Budget 2022 continued to provide a S$500 million jobs and business support package for workers and businesses in sectors that have not fully recovered,

Table 2.1 Four budgets in three months 2020

2020 Budget names	Date	COVID-19-related expenditure (S$ billion)
Unity	18 February 2020	6.4
Resilience	26 March 2020	48.4
Solidarity	6 April 2020	5.1
Fortitude	26 May 2020	33.0 (Total: S$92.9 bil.)

Source: Heng, 2020e.

such as the food and beverage, retail, and tourism and hospitality sectors (MOF, 2022). These budgets contained elements of shared responsibility and cohesion in the midst of a pandemic crisis.

Somewhat obscured by the support programmes' ubiquity and quantum, a clear significance throughout the complexity has been an attention to age. The discourse explaining the distribution of programmes' personal expenditures (mostly the "Care and Support Package") and their financing have both invoked the age of citizens and the government-defined "generation" to which they belong. These generations are frequently recognized across many spheres of Singaporean life, and so generation per se is a meaningful means of calibrating public policy settings. Given the short and threatened history of Singapore, each generation is conceptualized in terms of what it has contributed to Singapore, and what Singapore owes to each generation.

The Covid-19 public awareness campaign has been built on a societal view, embedded in generations. Two generations in particular are important: the "Pioneer Generation", who made sacrifices in Singapore's nascency, and the "Merdeka Generation", born in the 1950s and associated with Singapore's independence. Much Covid-19 policy explanation was founded on these generations having provided sacrifices, and the need to respect future generations so they will not be burdened by Covid-19-related expenditure. A good illustration of that rationale was in the prime minister's 7 June 2020 national broadcast:

> Our nation was born in crisis. When we were granted independence, it was expected that we would fail and come crawling back [...] We proved otherwise [...]. The Pioneer Generation fought to master their destiny [...] the Merdeka Generation put heart and soul into making Singapore succeed. Together, they weathered many storms, always looking ahead, never flinching at hard choices and challenges [...]
>
> Now, at another hinge in our history, it is our turn to face the crisis of a generation. The choices that we make now will define who we are as a people, and what values and ideals we pass on to future generations. Confronting adversity, do we yield to anger, fear and bitterness? Or will we be true to ourselves, [...] and continue to trust and depend on one another?
>
> *(Lee, 2020)*

The deputy PM (and finance minister) also relied on the generation-based argument in his Fortitude Budget speech. He noted the four budgets' unprecedented expenditures reflect that: "The battle against COVID-19 will (have) [...] more ups and downs. Our generation must have the fortitude to persevere, to adapt and to emerge stronger, just like our founding generation" (Heng, 2020b). Further, the speech directly linked expenditures to the savings of prior generations: "Our Past Reserves are our strategic asset, built up through prudence and hard work of our people, across generations (on) the principle that our Past Reserves are to be used only in exceptional circumstances". A total of S$52 billion has been drawn from Past Reserves, and the surpluses generated in 2015–2019 budgets have been expended in the four Covid-19 budgets.[2] Thus, additional debt was avoided, but this entailed depletion of past generations' "reserves":[3]

> As a young nation, we have been fortunate over the years, our people and our Government have been prudent and disciplined in saving and growing our reserves. We are now able to tap into this to respond decisively, without burdening our children [from younger generations].
>
> *(Heng, 2020c)*

The concept of "reserve" fundamentally embeds temporality (it is a stock of financing from the past), and complements a generational view of society (Hardin, 2014). In a prescient pre-Covid-19 speech (January 2020), Deputy PM Heng spelt out the generational logic behind reserves:

the reservoir of trust between Singaporeans and the Government, [provides] confidence to make sacrifices for the greater good, and for future generations. This is the formula behind our success, and this has kept Singapore exceptional. This approach must remain core to the Government's mission, especially as we grapple with longer-term issues facing us.

(Heng, 2020a)

Singapore's public sector finance is supported, in part, by a constitution-mandated system of "Past Reserves" and "Surpluses". Both are effectively results of past surplus budgetary outcomes, where government funds inflow exceeded its use of funds within each budgetary period. "Surpluses" are generated in the current government's budgets, whereas "Past Reserves" are past government surpluses plus investment earnings less annual Net Investment Returns Contributions (NIRC). Whilst the quantum and the constituent parts of the Past Reserves are secret, the NIRC is known to be significant (for 2019, it accounted for almost 18 per cent of the recurrent budget, or S$17 billion; MOF, 2020). Importantly, the constitution also mandates that governments do not carry a deficit at the end of their term, that the ceiling for the NIRC contribution is set at 50 per cent, and that draws on reserves require presidential approval. Taken together, these clauses virtually guarantee a growing reserve under normal circumstances, which even more underscores the significance of the Covid-19 budgets.

These principles were in full display in the rhetoric of the Covid-19 budgets. The Past Reserves are the total assets minus liabilities of specific governmental entities in the constitution's Fifth Schedule,[4] and these physical or financial stores of future worth are conferred a reified, privileged status, rather than being simply a useful fiscal management tool. In the 2020 Budget Round-Up Debate, the reserves were variously referred to as a "Golden Goose", "our rainy-day fund" and "the exceptional feature of our Budgets this Financial Year" (Heng, 2020d). Budget 2021 also made the same point: "We were able to mount a whole-of-government response to Covid-19, without incurring a huge debt for future generations, because successive generations have built up strong reserves ahead of this crisis" (MOF, 2021). The drawdown of Past Reserves and the full depletion of the 2015–2019 government surplus was seen to be the "strategic asset" that protected another, new, generation: the "Lockdown Generation", the children of millennials. This differs from

most countries [where] borrowing is the only way to fund their large stimulus packages. [...] [Their] future generations will be required to shoulder this debt, in the form of higher taxes, higher inflation, or lower returns on their retirement assets [and they] will also be affected in other ways. [...] The "Lockdown Generation" in these countries will end up paying for this crisis a long way down the road.

(Heng, 2020d)

The apparent purity of Singapore's balanced budgetary rule was also emphasized: "We also spend equitably, with the principle that each generation bears the cost of the benefits that they enjoy. That is why we do not borrow to fund our recurrent spending" (Heng, 2020d).

Whilst the outcome, to date, has been successful by averting an even worse economic contraction of at least 12.4 per cent in 2020 and saving 155,000 jobs on average over 2020 and 2021 (MOF, 2021), Singapore also presents paradoxical phenomena resulting from the temporalization of its citizens. Given the high level of education in Singapore, it seems surprising that the much-touted decision to reduce government assets (Past Reserves) was not challenged as being essentially a financing decision, but rather a grateful use of prior generations' sacrifices "without burdening our children" (Heng, 2020c). Scant discourse – even during a general election campaign – has reached into the reality that Past Reserves are merely governmental assets, and their depletion is financially akin to increasing debt when considering the Singapore government's financial position. The relative desirability of increasing debt during a low interest regime was not subject to public discussion nor was attention turned towards asset shedding in a period of declining asset values.[5] Thus, consistent with other crises (Morales et al., 2014), the limiting neoliberal mantra ("debt bad, surplus good") remains unchallenged rather than being reset by the Covid-19 once-in-a-century event. This mantra of low debt being a good thing could be due to the Asian mentality of saving being good and borrowing bad, shown in a survey that Asians are averse to borrowing (Reuters, 2011).

Amid the pandemic crisis, a common theme has been calls for social cohesion and consideration of the greater good to create a vibrant economy. The use of fiscal reserves to support specific sector businesses and workers hardest hit by the pandemic has been made along this theme (MOF, 2021). The move to strengthen the social compact included new pillars of support to help people get training for new jobs (ComCare) and to uplift lower-wage workers (Workfare) (MOF, 2022). These new pillars add on the existing schemes of the Central Provident Fund (CPF; retirement funds for Singapore citizens) and the 3Ms healthcare schemes (MediSave, MediShield and MediFund: for details, refer to Loh et al. (2021)). The various schemes provide safety nets for citizens in areas of healthcare, (un)employment and retirement.

The Budgets reflect the government's aim to create a more equitable society, such as higher property taxes for properties of higher values, particularly investment properties typically held by more wealthy individuals (MOF, 2022). At the same time, Budget 2022 also contained investments in new capabilities: S$200 million to build digital capabilities in businesses; S$25 billion (equivalent to 1 per cent of GDP, similar to other small, advanced economies) in research and development under the RIE2025 (RIE: Research, Innovation and Enterprise) strategy; S$600 million to implement digital and automation solutions for the small to medium-sized enterprises (MOF, 2022). These investments to boost productivities and new capabilities are consistent with neoliberal policies to encourage entrepreneurship and innovation, and to build future reserves. The pursuit of neoliberalism is carried out under an overarching umbrella of shared social responsibility and temporalization where past reserves are tapped to help the citizens during the crisis and budgets are made to invest in the future and create future reserves for contingencies (Heng, 2020f). The "living with Covid" strategy allows the economy to recover, investments to be made and reserves to be built for future generations. Temporalization here is not just a case of reaping past fruits but also planting the seeds for the future, connecting the past, present and future generations.

Conclusion

As Bourdieu (2000) observed, practice should not be confined to analysis *in time*, but practice should also be considered as to how it *makes time*. The Singaporean response to Covid-19, in its public policy settings and its budgetary actions, demonstrates how the government has been able to mobilize time as a means of couching responses to its citizens. To date, this has been successful in protecting the health of Singaporeans and mediating the collateral economic damage. The economy rebounded in 2021 and 2022 from the contractions in 2020. The temporalized citizenry has had high levels of trust in government based on the belief that past generations' sacrifices (in the tangible form of "Past Reserves") can be used to provide the resources required to ensure health and economic recovery, and the reserves continue to be built for future generations through investments in new capabilities. This extends beyond financial resources and goes into social capital being "the intangible bonds that unite our multi-racial society" (Heng, 2020d). Thus, in Singapore, there is powerful evidence that the political "parents" of neoliberalism were wrong on two counts: "society" *does* exist and government *can* be the solution to problems.

Singapore's lessons on Covid-19 and neoliberalism go beyond disproving Thatcher's and Reagan's tenets. The lessons extend into proof that neoliberalism depends on a citizenry accepting its temporalization, and politicians masterfully using opportunities, even during major crises, to present consistent and coherent arguments that serve the interests of neoliberal policy settings. As found by Ahn and Wickramasinghe (2021) in Korea's reactions to Covid-19, citizens and government were both driven by desires around issues of health, safety and legitimacy. Instead of taking a balance sheet perspective where net assets are the focus unaffected by choices between borrowing or selling assets, a generational view disciplines the citizenry. The consequence is increased respect from living citizens towards future citizens and those passed. Perhaps, that is the true sense of what a society or a community can deliver, and it is not contrary to a Singaporean style of neoliberalism where "big government" and market forces coexist whilst the former dominates.

Singapore's Covid-19 early response provides lessons regarding neoliberalism. Singapore's model of neoliberalism has contrarian features: state-owned assets dominate the free market in preference to privatization; frequent and pervasive government interventions occur in a structured market – not just during crises; and the government maximizes rhetorical claims of society (or community). However, stronger underpinnings of neoliberalism survive. Notably, we observe discourse invoking personal responsibilities and a fiscal stranglehold of surplus budgets over each electoral cycle. The strength of neoliberalism's philosophical underpinning of fiscal management is noteworthy since, even in a crisis, it is apparently so important that it must be preserved in the Singaporean model. This form of neoliberalism thereby rationalizes the use of reserves during the crisis with an increased reliance on a pattern of temporalization through shared responsibility in society.

Based on Singaporean experience to date, neoliberalism appears to be surviving the deadly Covid-19 pandemic, but it can do so in large part because of the Singaporean sense of society. The effectiveness of this type of neoliberalism as a response to Covid-19 in the longer term and beyond Singapore are areas of future research.

Notes

1 The 2019 Global Health Security Index (cited by RMIT 2020) ranked Singapore the world's 11th most prepared for an epidemic.
2 This is all the more remarkable given how, historically, the government had always been reticent to draw down on reserves, even in the midst of the Asian financial crisis (Chua, 1999), which had hitherto been the most severe economic challenge the nation faced.
3 "Reserves" are artefacts of Singapore's contested beginning since it decided to fully back its new currency in 1967 with foreign currency reserves. Since then, reserves have been crucial to the compulsory savings scheme (CPF), which in 2015 had net investments of S$ 300 billion – 75% of that year's GDP.
4 Fifth Schedule entities are investment vehicles; the main ones are CPF Board, MAS, HDB, GIC and Temasek. See: www.mof.gov.sg/policies/our-nation's-reserves/Section-I-What-comprises-the-reserves-and-who-manages-them
5 During the Budget Round-Up Debate, one ruling party Member suggested raising debt in the historic low interest rate regime, but deputy PM Heng repeated the argument that surplus drawdown protected future generations.

References

Ahn, P., & Wickramasinghe, D. (2021). Pushing the limits of accountability: Big data analytics containing and controlling COVID-19 in South Korea. *Accounting, Auditing & Accountability Journal, 34*(6), 1320–1331. https://doi.org/10.1108/AAAJ-08-2020-4829

Anonymous (2020). Disease surveillance: Pandemic-proofing the planet. *The Economist*, 27 June.

Ansah, J.P., Matchar, D.B., Shao Wei, S.L., Low, J.G., Pourghaderi, A.R., Siddiqui, F.J. et al. (2021). The effectiveness of public health interventions against COVID-19: Lessons from the Singapore experience. *PLOS ONE, 16*(3): e0248742. https://doi.org/10.1371/journal.pone.0248742

Basu, R. (2016). *Safe but soulless: Nursing homes need a new narrative*. Lien Foundation.

Bishop, P. (2011). Eating in the contact zone: Singapore foodscape and cosmopolitan timespace. *Continuum: Journal of Media & Cultural Studies, 25*(5), 637–652. https://doi.org/10.1080/10304 312.2011.597846

Bourdieu, P. (2000). *Pascalian meditations* (Richard Nice, Trans.). Stanford University Press (Original work *Méditations pascaliennes*, published 1997, Seuil).

Broadbent, J. (2020). The response to Covid-19 in England: Political accountability and loss of trust. *Journal of Accounting & Organizational Change, 16*(4), 527–632.

Chow, D., Bracci, E. (2020). Neoliberalism, accounting, and the transformation of subjectivities in social work: A study on the implementation of personal budgets. *Financial Accountability & Management, 36*, 151–170.

Chua, J. (2011). Making time for the children: self-temporalization and the cultivation of the anti-suicidal subject in South India. *Cultural Anthropology, 26*(1), 112–137.

Chua, M.H. (1999, 10 March). $6bn surplus government can use. *Straits Times*. https://eresources.nlb.gov.sg/newspapers/Digitised/Article/straitstimes19990310-1.2.2

Channel New Asia (CNA) (2020, 30 March). Singapore reports 35 more COVID-19 cases, 3 new clusters identified. www.channelnewsasia.com/news/singapore/covid-19-coronavirus-singapore-cases-moh-mar-30-12589390

Channel New Asia (CNA) (2022, 14 April). Singapore economy grows 3.4% in Q1, slower than previous quarter. www.channelnewsasia.com/singapore/economy-singapore-gdp-grows-q1-2022-mti-advance-estimates-2623476

Gordon, E. (2020, 2 March). COVID-19: Lessons from Singapore and how it handled SARS. *The World*. www.pri.org/stories/2020-03-02/covid-19-lessons-singapore-and-how-it-handled-sars

Hardin, C. (2014). Neoliberal temporality: Time-sense and the shift from pensions to 401(k)s. *American Quarterly, 66*(1), 95–118.

Harvey, D. (2005). *A brief history of neoliberalism.* Oxford University Press.

Heng, S.K. (2020a). Singapore Perspectives Conference 2020 Opening Address. 20 January. www.pmo.gov.sg/Newsroom/DPM-Heng-Swee-Keat-at-the-Singapore-Perspectives-Conference-2020

Heng, S.K. (2020b). Ministerial Statement on Singapore's Fortitude Budget. 26 May. www.mof.gov.sg/newsroom/speeches/ministerial-statement-on-singapore's-fortitude-budget

Heng, S.K. (2020c). *Budget 2020 Booklet*. 15 April. www.singaporebudget.gov.sg/docs/default-source/budget_2020/download/pdf/fy2020_supplementary_budget_booklet_eng.pdf

Heng, S.K. (2020d). Fortitude Budget Debate Round-Up Speech. 9 June. www.singaporebudget.gov.sg/budget_2020/fortitude-budget/fortitude-budget-debate-round-up-speech

Heng, S.K. (2020e). Fortitude Budget Debate Round-Up Speech. 22 June. www.singaporebudget.gov.sg/budget_2020/budget-debate-round-up-speech

Heng, S.K. (2020f). Reserves needed to prepare for contingencies. 3 September. www.mof.gov.sg/news-publications/media-articles/reserves-needed-to-prepare-for-contingencies-dpm-heng-swee-keat

Hirschmann, R. (2022). Impact of COVID-19 outbreak on YoY growth rate quarterly GDP Singapore 2020–2021. 3 January. www.statista.com/statistics/1103400/singapore-covid-19-impact-yoy-growth-rate-quarterly-gdp/

Hopper, T. (2020). Swimming in a sea of uncertainty – business, governance and the coronavirus (COVID-19) pandemic. *Journal of Accounting & Organizational Change, 16*(4), 533–539.

International Monetary Fund (IMF). (2020). Policy responses to COVID-19. www.imf.org/en/Topics/imf-and-covid19/Policy-Responses-to-COVID-19#S

Khalik, S. (2020, 4 January). Lessons from SARS will help Singapore tackle virus from China. *Straits Times*. www.ncid.sg/News-Events/News/Documents/ST%204%20Jan%202020.pdf

Lapsley, I. (2020). An uncertain, erratic story: The pandemic in the UK. *Journal of Accounting & Organizational Change, 16*(4), 549–555.

Lazzini, A., Lazzini, S., Balluchi, F., & Mazza, M. (2022). Emotions, moods and hyperreality: Social media and the stock market during the first phase of COVID-19 pandemic. *Accounting, Auditing & Accountability Journal, 35*(1), 199–215. https://doi-org.ezp.essec.fr/10.1108/AAAJ-08-2020-4786.

Lee, H.L. (2020). Overcoming the crisis of a generation. *Prime Minister National Broadcast*. www.pmo.gov.sg/Newsroom/National-Broadcast-PM-Lee-Hsien-Loong-COVID-19

Loh, C.M., Lim, C.Y., & Christensen, M. (2021). Temporalizing the healthy self-governing citizen: Singapore's successful healthcare neoliberal project. In Z. Hoque (Ed.), *Public sector reform and performance management in emerging economies: Outcomes-based approaches in practice* (pp. 136–154). Routledge.

Ministry of Finance (MOF) (2020). *How do Singaporeans benefit from our Reserves?* www.mof.gov.sg/Policies/our-nation's-reserves/Section-III-How-do-Singaporeans-benefit-from-our-Reserves

Ministry of Finance (MOF) (2021). *Budget 2021. Emerging Stronger Together.* www.mof.gov.sg/docs/librariespr
ovider3/budget2021/download/pdf/fy2021_budget_statement.pdf

Ministry of Finance (MOF) (2022). *Budget 2022. Charting Our New Way Forward Together.*
www.mof.gov.sg/singaporebudget/budget-2022/budget-statement

Ministry of Health (MOH). (2020, 2 January). Precautionary measures in response to severe pneumonia cases in
Wuhan, China. MOH News Highlights. www.moh.gov.sg/news-highlights/details/precautionary-measures-
in-response-to-severe-pneumonia-cases-in-wuhan-china

Ministry of Health (MOH). (2021, 20 July). *Going Back to Phase 2 Heightened Alert.*
www.moh.gov.sg/news-highlights/details/going-back-to-phase-2-heightened-alert

Ministry of Health (MOH). (2022a, 15 April). *Vaccination Statistics.* www.moh.gov.sg/covid-19/vaccination/
statistics

Ministry of Health (MOH). (2022b, 15 April). *Living with COVID-19.*
www.covid.gov.sg/

Ministry of Health (MOH). (2022c, 15 April). *COVID-19 Situation Report.*
www.moh.gov.sg/covid-19/testing/situation-report-pdf

Ministry of Health (MOH). (2022d, 15 April). *Social Responsibility Key to Living with COVID.*
www.moh.gov.sg/news-highlights/details/social-responsibility-key-to-living-with-covid-19#:~:text=We%20en
courage%20all%20individuals%20to,for%20at%20least%2072%20hours

Montsion, J. (2014). Chinese ethnicities in neoliberal Singapore? State designs and dialect(ical) struggles of
community associations. *Ethnic and Racial Studies, 37*(9), 1486–1504.

Morales, J., Gendron, Y., & Guénin-Paracini, H. (2014). State privatization and the unrelenting expansion of
neoliberalism: The case of the Greek financial crisis. *Critical Perspectives on Accounting, 25*(6), 423–445.

Naruse, C., & Gui, W. (2016). Singapore and the intersections of neoliberal globalization and postcoloniality.
Interventions, 18(4), 473–482.

National Centre for Infectious Diseases (NCID). (2022). *Singapore's COVID-19 Vaccination Programme.
Protect Yourself and Your Loved Ones.* www.ncid.sg/Documents/EN_Vaccine%20Brochure.pdf

Nyland, K., Ahlgren, P.C., & Lapsley, I. (2020). NPM resistence: A political intervention. *Financial Accountability
& Management, 36*(4), 376–400.

Ong, A. (2007). Neoliberalism as a mobile technology. *Transactions of the Institute of British Geographers,
32*, 3–8.

OxCGRT (2020). *Oxford COVID-19 Government Response Tracker.* www.bsg.ox.ac.uk/research/research-proje
cts/coronavirus-government-response-tracker

Painter, M. (2004). The politics of administrative reform in East and Southeast Asia: From gridlock to continuous
self-improvement? *Governance, 17*(3), 361–386.

Parker, L. (2020). Australian universities in a pandemic world: Transforming a broken business model? *Journal
of Accounting & Organizational Change, 16*(4), 541–548.

Parker, L., Martin-Sardesai, A., & Guthrie, J. (2021). The commercialized Australian public university: An
accountingized transition. *Financial Accountability & Management, 36*, 151–170.

Rana, T., Ahmed, Z. U., Narayan, A., & Zheng, M. (2022). An institutional theory perspective on public
sector reform and service performance reporting by New Zealand universities. *Journal of Accounting &
Organizational Change, 18*(3), 461–484.

Reagan, R. (1981). Inauguration Speech. Ronald Reagan Presidential Foundation and Institute. www.reaganfou
ndation.org/media/128614/inaguration.pdf

Reuters. (2011, 29 June). Asians more averse to borrowing, prefer local banks – survey. www.reuters.com/article/
asia-borrowingsurvey-idUSL3E7HT09N20110629

RMIT Fact Check (2020, 9 April). Singapore is often praised for its coronavirus response. *ABC News.* www.abc.
net.au/news/2020-04-07/comparing-australia-with-singapore-coronavirus/12107106?nw=0

Salterio, S.E. (2020). Accounting for the unaccountable – coping with COVID. *Journal of Accounting &
Organizational Change, 16*(4), 557–578.

Singapore Department of Statistics (SDS). (2020). Singapore population. www.singstat.gov.sg/modules/infog
raphics/population

Soldatic, J. (2013). Appointment time: Disability and neoliberal workfare temporalities. *Critical Sociology,
39*(3), 405–419.

Tan, K. (2012). The ideology of pragmatism: Neo-liberal globalisation and political authoritarianism in Singapore.
Journal of Contemporary Asia, 42(1), 67–92. https://doi.org/10.1080/00472336.2012.634644

Tambyah, P., & Lum, L. (2022, 10 February). Looking to 2022: What lies ahead in the Covid-19 pandemic. National
University of Singapore. news.nus.edu.sg/looking-to-2022-what-lies-ahead-in-the-covid-19-pandemic/

Thatcher, M. (1987). Interview for Woman's Own ("no such thing as society"). Margaret Thatcher Foundation. 23 September. www.margaretthatcher.org/document/106689

World Health Organization (WHO). (2022). WHO Coronavirus (COVID-19) Dashboard. https://covid19.who.int/

Yates, D., & Difrancesco, R. (2022). The view from the front line: Shifting beneficiary accountability and inter-relatedness in the time of a global pandemic. *Accounting, Auditing & Accountability Journal, 35*(1), 85–96. https://doi.org/10.1108/AAAJ-08-2020-4811

3

MANAGING A GRAND CHALLENGE AT THE LOCAL LEVEL

The case of especially vulnerable neighbourhoods in a Swedish city

Sara Brorström and Alexander Styhre

Introduction

Grand challenges cut across organizational boundaries, responsibilities and interests (e.g. Bryson et al., 2017; Brorström & Diedrich, 2022) and examples are climate change, poverty, and segregation (George et al., 2016). Tackling grand challenges require organizational and political action, as well as new technical solutions (Pimentel, Cho, & Bothello, 2022; Ferraro, Etzion, & Gehman, 2015). Grand challenges are often described as "wicked", meaning that they are complex, where the solutions of today might turn out to be the problems of tomorrow (Farrell, 2011; Termeer & De Wulf, 2019). Bours, Wanzenböck and Frenken (2021) argued that when attempting to tackle grand challenges, there is no time to wait for large structural initiatives; instead, action from the bottom up and at the local level is needed. However, making progress in grand challenges depends on "a concerted effort among diverse participants who bring different skills to the problem" (Grodal & O'Mahoney, 2017, p. 1801), but that collaboration between actors is needed has proven to be a challenge of its own (Crosby & Bryson, 2005; Coutore et al., 2022). Grodal and O'Mahoney (2017) further argued that many initiatives to tackle grand challenges falls short because of their initial goals, which are difficult to translate into practice. Others have claimed that there is a need for pragmatic approach, to accept that these challenges are inherently uncertain (Ansell & Boin, 2019). This implies accepting that crisis and failures will always occur, as was already argued by Perrow and Guillen (1990, p. 78): "organizations are always failing to some degree, for they are imperfect and refractory tools".

Over the past recent years there has been an intense debate in Sweden, and neighbouring Nordic countries, about what the police authority refers to as "vulnerable neighbourhoods" and "especially vulnerable neighbourhoods". The label "especially vulnerable neighbourhoods" is used by the police to indicate neighbourhoods where criminals have a considerable impact on the local community and where residents experience a higher level of lack of safety and fear compared to other neighbourhoods. The national police authority present, every second year, a list of neighbourhoods that are "vulnerable", "risk areas" or "especially vulnerable". The majority of these neighbourhoods are located within or near larger cities (Gerell, Puur, & Guldåker, 2022). This list is based on a combination of measurable indicators and a more qualitative assessment. Municipalities are naturally working towards removing neighbourhoods from this list, and as a result of this development, cities are adopting policies and strategies to tackle the challenges encountered there (c.f. Grander, Roelofs,

DOI: 10.4324/9781003295945-4

& Salonen, 2022). One such attempt is reported in this chapter, and the aim of the chapter is to analyse the practices of managing a grand challenge locally in public organizations. The grand challenge in focus here is thus to improve the neighbourhoods that are on the police list, to ultimately get them removed from the list. The challenge is complex and composed of different aspects as expressed by interviewees, exemplified by poverty, criminality, segregation, unemployment and so on. In this chapter we analyse actions taken at the local level, and we further want to understand what role is played by measuring and assessments of the work in this process. This interest responds to calls for research that focuses on wicked problems or grand challenges, and their implications for accounting (Jacobs & Cuganesan, 2014; Steccolini, 2019). Chenhall, Hall and Smith (2013, p. 269) argued that accounts of performance are "critical because it is in discussions over the different metrics, images and words that can be used to represent performance that the actual worth of things is frequently debated and contested". How to measure actions taken in response to the development in especially vulnerable neighbourhoods was of great importance in the empirical case reported here. There was a need to show that actions taken were leading to improvements. Nevertheless, how and what to measure was a challenge due to the existence of conflicting values and interests. The empirical data comes from the Swedish city of Gothenburg. Here, the city council entrusted the task of tackling challenges encountered in especially vulnerable neighbourhoods to the Framtiden group in 2020. Framtiden is a municipal housing group consisting of a parent corporation, one development corporation that is planning and building new housing units; five municipal housing corporations (MHCs) that are to provide rental housing; one corporation managing public space such as neighbourhood squares and shopping malls; and one corporation providing emergency security services in various neighbourhoods. In particular, the role of the MHCs is crucial in these neighbourhoods as they own a large share of the building stock. When the politicians in Gothenburg in their annual budget for the year 2020 selected the Framtiden housing group to work towards removing the current six neighbourhoods in the city labelled "especially vulnerable" on the police authority's list , a strategy was quickly drafted with the aim of removing the target neighbourhoods from the list before the year 2025. This strategic document entailed investments in new housing and renovation of the existing stock as well as projects targeting local schools, unemployment, activities for youths and zero tolerance against criminality. The character of this document implies that collaborations with other organizations is crucial, for instance, if to work towards the local schools, the school department needed to be part of it. This moreover meant that if the housing group is to reach its targets, this is not something they could manage by themselves.

Literature review: tackling grand challenges at the local level

According to Ferraro et al. (2015) grand challenges have three overarching features. Firstly, they are *complex*, which means that they entail many interactions and associations, emergent understandings and nonlinear dynamics. Secondly, grand challenges confront organizations with *radical uncertainty*, which implies that actors cannot define possible future states of the world, and therefore not predict the consequences of actions. Thirdly, grand challenges are *evaluative*, which means that they cut across jurisdictional boundaries, and values and new concerns that need to be tackled are revealed along the way. This further implies that, the tackling of grand challenges often results in various collaborations (Thomasson et al., 2020; Laegreid & Rykkja, 2021; Carstensen et al., 2022).

Scholars have attempted to find the best way of tackling grand challenges and Ferraro et al. (2015) claimed that grand challenges are best addressed by what they call "robust action", which are actions that include: *participatory architecture*, or a way of allowing diverse actors to interact in a constructive way and over time; *multivocal inscription*, which is a discursive and material activity that sustains various interpretations, and that create coordination of actions; and *distributed experimentation*, which are actions that generate small wins and learning over time which will increase engagement and as a result also lead to abandoning ineffective measures. Small wins will over time add up to a big win, and the trick is to "not to go for it all at once, but to go for it small step by small step" (Bryson, 1988, p. 13; c.f. Weick, 1984). This also builds on the idea that even though changes are described as small, this does that not mean that they are trivial in the long term (Vermaak, 2013). Termeer and DeWulf (2019) explored the literature on small wins and came up with a list of five mechanisms that drive small wins: energizing, learning by doing, logic of attraction, the bandwagon effect and coupling. The *energizing mechanism* is based on motivational drivers. *Learning by doing* is based on the idea that each step will result in outcomes that will present and expand ideas of what is possible and worth trying. The *logic of attraction mechanism* means that resources tend to flow towards winners, which indicates that it is important to tell the story of success, and finally the *bandwagon effect* which is described as psychological phenomenon where people do something because other people do it. However, even though it might be beneficial to aim for small wins, Bours, Wanzenböck and Frenken (2021) argue that the "institutional barriers" are hardest to overcome. These could be organizational barriers or knowledge barriers, and barriers in the form of rules and regulations.

The role of calculative practices in relation to grand challenges

In situations of conflicting interests and logics, such as the tackling of grand challenges, the role of accounting practices has previously been emphasized (Ahrens & Chapman, 2002; Chenhall, Hall, & Smith, 2013). Accounting practices in general have an impact on what is being valued by organizations and individuals (Kornberger et al., 2015) as accounting practices and numbers are important in decision-making. Accounting has therefore been argued to be a major force in shaping societies, markets and how organizations are being managed (Tregidga & Laine, 2022). This has, however, been discussed as an issue, for example when tackling environmental challenges, as the focus of accounting practices is on an entity, an organization or a project, and ignores the systemic features of grand challenges (Gray, 2010). This entails that tensions could arise between an organization's narrow focus and broader societal values (Burns & Jollands, 2020; Killian & O'Regan, 2020). However, accounting practices can also give voice to various concerns and priorities when there are conflicting values (Chenhall, Hall, & Smith, 2013). This is because actors from different organizations can hold various views of how the organization is performing and different information might coexist and become layered (Cooper et al., 1996). In their study of a non-governmental organization, Chenhall, Hall and Smith (2013) found three processes where different accounts provided a fertile arena for debate: firstly, the authors found that accounts that manage tensions between different evaluative principles are always imperfect, which implies a "give and take" between different values. Secondly, they argue that accounts can facilitate friction through making attributes visible that are of importance to actors with different evaluative practices. Thirdly, the authors show how debates about the mechanics of accounting practices can lead to a "stuckness" where debate is needed about the underlying principles of the evaluative practices. Moreover, Cuganesan et al. (2012) observed that accounting practices are important when it comes to shaping organizational boundaries. They moreover showed how accounting practices have reshaped strategy and given rise to new forms of management accounting. From the perspective of a grand challenge, this is an interesting conclusion as it might imply that accounting practices could reshape the initial ambitions. On the same note, Jacobs and Cuganesan (2014) asked the question of how to account for outcomes in the long run when there is a short-term focus on yearly budget processes and efficiency (c.f. Brorström, 2023). They further posed the question of how to measure what actions are working, given their wicked nature. The question of measurability becomes even tricker as the tackling of grand challenges requires a bottom-up perspective and a collection of actors (Sachs, 2012). Another interesting link to explore is that to the accountability of the collaborating organizations since, as argued by Pesci et al. (2020, p. 5), they have a "double bottom line of accountability". This implies that they are to provide information on "their mission without losing the link to their financial result". Costa and Pesci (2016) claimed that stakeholders' need for information is a driver for accountability, making it important to identify who the stakeholders are and what they want. In practice, this is often linked to metrics and measurements, and naturally what to measure and how to measure becomes important. Glasser (2019, p. 63) stated: "what we choose to measure is ultimately a manifestation of what we care about". Regarding the specificity of vulnerable neighbourhoods, Hincks (2017) argued that there have been several attempts to measure deprivation, but the problem is that these measures become only "snapshots" and fail to show change over time. Grander, Roelofs and Salonen (2022) argued, for instance, that people might move from the neighbourhood when they have opportunity, and that improvement in the neighbourhood at large is thus not captured. In line with this reasoning, this chapter explores the tension between the long-term goals of creating change in vulnerable neighbourhoods and organizational accounting practices within the Swedish housing sector in the city of Gothenburg.

Method, case and context

The city of Gothenburg in western Sweden has been claimed to be one of the most segregated cities in Europe, something that has been discussed and dealt with by politicians and civil servants in the city for years (e.g. Brorström, 2015). As mentioned above, the politicians on the city council, through their annual budget in 2020, selected Framtiden housing group to come up with ways of tackling this challenge, with the specific aim of removing the six neighbourhoods in the city currently on the police authority's list of "especially vulnerable neighbourhoods". As mentioned, this list identifies neighbourhoods in Sweden that are geographically limited, characterized by low socio-economic status and where criminals have a certain degree of impact on the local community. In response, the Framtiden group adopted a new strategic document with the overall aim of removing all neighbourhoods in the city from the list before the year 2025. This is to be done through large investments in the neighbourhoods in the form of new housing and by renovating existing facilities. There is also a large focus on social projects, aiming at improving the neighbourhoods by investing in the people living there. These social investments can be summed up in three overarching categories: investments in employment projects, investments in local schools, and a social investment fund that is to support projects in the two other categories. The large ambition entails an increased need to collaborate with other actors, since the MHCs alone cannot solve the issue of being placed on the police list. The mere type of problems facing these neighbourhoods shows there is a good reason for working together, yet this creates challenges of its own.

The Swedish public housing system is built up by MHCs with the task and responsibility to provide rental apartments that are generally directed to all citizens (Holmquist & Turner, 2014). These MHCs became an important instrument for implementing the Swedish government's housing policy, which builds on the principles that the MHCs are almost entirely owned by municipalities and are open to all citizens, meaning that they are not only directed towards specific target groups (Hedman, 2008; Emilsson & Öberg, 2022). This makes Sweden, together with Denmark, the only countries in Europe without a social housing system (Grander, 2019). Swedish MHCs have also been argued to be an important tool for creating inclusiveness in cities, and their social responsibility is regulated (Grander, 2017). However, in 2011 there was a change in legislation in Sweden that implied that MHCs need to meet profit margins decided by the politicians and to be "business-like" (Westerdahl, 2021). This means that they are to compete on the same market terms as private rental companies, while at the same time they have the responsibility to provide housing for the general public. In other words, actions carried out by the MHCs must be economically justified (Grander, 2017). The ability to combine these two responsibilities has been questioned: is it possible to maintain social responsibility while meeting profit margins? We can study this potential dilemma facing the city of Gothenburg, which aimed to remove all the highly vulnerable neighbourhoods from the police list before the year 2025, yet at the same time doing that based on business-like principles.

Data collection

The data were collected from three sources. First, interviews were conducted with employees at the municipal housing group Framtiden involved in managing and overseeing the strategy and its implementation, and with employees at housing corporations (municipal and private) as well as other organizations, in the neighbourhoods of Hjällbo, Bergsjön Biskopsgården and Tynnered. These three neighbourhoods have been listed as "especially vulnerable neighbourhoods", and the fourth, Tynnered, was in 2021 listed as "only" vulnerable. The interviews were structured on the basis of an interview guide, were recorded, and lasted for about 1.5 hours. In total, 28 interviews were conducted, and the sample included district managers, project leaders, business development directors in private and municipal housing corporations, CEOs of municipal housing corporations, and employees at city departments. Second, the researchers also participated during project meetings within the Hjällbo urban development project as well as within the Bergsjön BID organization. These meetings included discussions of contractual conditions and agreements and involved information sharing between actors working in these neighbourhoods. During such participative observations, field notes were written to account for the issues being addressed and the topics being debated in the project team. Third, and finally, internal documents and reports issued by the participant organizations were retrieved and used as input material for understanding how the new strategy was to be managed within the parent company and the MHCs.

Data analysis

The interviews were first transcribed verbatim by a professional writing bureau. These interview transcripts were then coded, with all the interviews read through and then coded into themes in accordance with the first-order coding described by Gioia, Corley and Hamilton (2013). These themes where then coded in a second-order coding, and through this process the number of codes reduced. In this process, we were looking for accounts of what problems the new strategic intentions were to tackle and how. We were further looking for claims about the role of the MHCs, and the other collaboration partners and possible challenges to these collaborations. In relation to these challenges and the roles, we analysed the role and conflicting accounts of performance assessment to get closer to the overall goal of being removed from the police list before the end of 2025. Finally, we also added the insights from the empirical data and literature on tackling grand challenges and accounting practices.

Findings: managing a grand challenge at the local level

An interviewee stated the reason why the city council had chosen the housing group Framtiden to tackle the issues in the vulnerable neighbourhoods was due to their ability to act:

> Well, I think it has to do with our ability to act. We have an ambition that goes a long way back about not evaluating things to death, but to make sure to act. And that is what makes a difference to people.
>
> *(Manager, housing group Framtiden)*

Another reason had to do with a lack of action on the part of other actors:

> They [the housing corporation] needed to step up as the society had slipped away, that is my opinion. They had to, "hello, we need this if it is going to be alright here". And there is something not right in that.
>
> *(Employee, school department, City of Gothenburg)*

Other interviewees described the process of actors leaving the vulnerable neighbourhoods but the MHCs remaining. One reason for why this is the case, is due to several reorganizations of the city organization. One of these interviewees implied that the city districts which acted locally, were removed in 2021. As a consequence, services that were managed by the city district, such as civic offices, were withdrawn from the neighbourhoods and left service gaps. Beyond removing the city districts, the management of the school sector, as well as social services had been reorganized in recent years. Together, these organizational changes suggested that residents in the vulnerable neighbourhoods increasingly turned to the MHCs operating there for all kinds of issues. Interviewees argued that this development had changed their role and implied that they needed competences not required previously; they are still traditional facility managers but also inhabit several other roles. These new roles are also captured in the strategic document that Framtiden adopted in 2020, with its large investments in employment, in improving school results and with a zero tolerance towards criminality. The expectation is that this large investment will encourage other actors to follow. In interviews, this role of Framtiden housing group was often referred to as them being the ones to "take the lead". One of the interviewees said:

> We need to do what we can and take the lead. But I would like to see a similar investment from the police. [...] Let's match up, allocate resources and, because that is what we do within the corporation, we take resources elsewhere and put them within these six neighbourhoods. What if the school would do the same? And the social services?
>
> *(District manager, MHC)*

This suggests that actions by the MHCs put pressure on others also to act. However, interviewees mentioned that there is a risk as well that when the housing corporations "take the lead", other actors might step back instead of taking on the much-needed common responsibility. Some interviewees, as an example, expressed frustration over private housing corporations operating in the neighbourhoods, which were said not to invest as much in their properties as the public ones. The extent of renovation and investment undertaken was said to differ across neighbourhoods, as one interviewee noted: "They [private housing corporation] take part in some forums, but we think they should do as much as we do. They do not invest in their properties" (Employee, MHC). Even so, there is an opinion held by the interviewees that the strategy gives them a momentum "never seen before". This means that even though they would like others to follow suit, the MHCs now have a reason to pressure others. They hope this will yield results over time. There is a pragmatic view of the ongoing work, as there are no answers, no right or wrong; there is a need to try different solutions and see what works. One interviewee from one of the MHCs described this in the following way:

> You are on your toes and extra aware. You should be amenable for all kinds of ideas and not just say no, but "yes, let's try". [...] to succeed you need to try, everything should be tried if you ask me.
>
> *(Employee, MHC)*

This statement illustrates the often-illustrated pragmatic approach towards action in the neighbourhoods.

The content and implication of the strategic intention

The strategy document drafted by the Framtiden Group, which was to be implemented within the MCHs, had a focus on new urban development as well as on renovating the existing stock in the neighbourhoods. There was also, as mentioned above, a strong focus on social aspects, aiming for better school results, increased employment and meaningful after-school activities for youths. The content and ambition of this strategy document made sense for most of the persons interviewed, even though most thought that the goal would not be met by 2025. One of the district managers for one of the neighbourhoods said:

> The strategy is very ambitious, but it is about time that we invest in these neighbourhoods. I can only agree about that. I can only agree that there should be no vulnerable neighbourhoods.
>
> *(District manager, municipal housing corporation)*

An interviewee from a private housing corporation argued that from their perspective, the strategy was welcome, as they work together with other housing corporations with the aim of improving the neighbourhoods. To work together made sense even though the organizations are of various sizes and have different shares of the apartments. "We have 200 apartments here and [other corporations] have 5,000, but we still face the same problems", one interviewee from a private housing corporation said. Helping each other out could be through communication about solutions that worked out well and about deciding on similar investments. To have similar solutions across organizations was described as a good thing as there should be no obvious differences between how, for instance, the garbage is taken care of depending on what housing corporation you rent from. Another upside of working together is that the contact net gets larger, and it becomes easier to approach other actors together, for example, city departments. Nevertheless, the city council gave the task to the Framtiden group and not to any other organization, something that implies that what the employees can do is to talk and try to mobilize action. As the challenges encountered were associated with issues that were the responsibility of other actors, this was described as a potential problem and regarded by some as a sign of these other actors not being able to act or to step up when needed. One example given was how there is no prioritization of projects in these neighbourhoods within the city planning office. According to one of the interviewees, this suggests that the plan to add more housing through urban development will take more time than anticipated. One of the interviewed expressed this at a policy level:

> If we have a task to produce 3,000 new housing units within these neighbourhoods, in the coming ten years, that is not going to happen. It is impossible if we do not have any plans. There is just one department that can produce plans. Then they also need to say that they should produce 3,000 housing units in the coming years.
>
> *(Manager, Framtiden group parent company)*

Different priorities across organizations were also regarded as a challenge at a more practical level: "I think that as a targeted area, we should have some priority. When we call someone, they should just ask when and where and fix it" (Employee MHC). Wanting to do something quickly but having to wait for others was described as frustrating. One recurrent criticism, and a potential reason for why there was not similar prioritization at other organizations, was that the process of drafting the strategy had been too much top down and too fast. Interviewees in hindsight said that at least the top management at the subsidiaries should have been more involved as this could have saved time in the later stages.

In relation to this, some interviewees pointed out that the strategy did not include key learnings from employees working locally in the neighbourhoods and, as a result, the employees felt excluded. Early in the process, how to measure and illustrate the meaning of the work done, was being discussed.

Creating measurability

As there are such large investments by the Framtiden Group, there is also a need to assess and measure how well the MHCs perform over time, and whether the neighbourhoods are getting closer to the goal of being removed from the police list. This entails several challenges, as how the list is being developed is not totally transparent and there are conflicting values at play. However, the Framtiden parent company does a qualitative assessment three times each year, which is a conversation between the CEO at Framtiden and the CEOs at the various MHCs where different parameters are talked about. As the overarching goal of removing the neighbourhoods from the police list is based on an assessment by the police, however, the interviewees are not sure that it is good help for the work in MHCs. One of the employees at the head office explains:

> The goal is clear, no especially vulnerable neighbourhoods in 2025. And the ones that can judge that are the police. I was first trying to figure out how they do that and had a lot of discussions with them. But I should have realized that the measurements are built on the work of the police. If they look at [one neighbourhood], about 150 individuals are the key. But we care for all people within the neighbourhood.
>
> *(Employee, Head Office)*

The interviewees argue that employees at the MHCs have a better knowledge of the people living in the neighbourhoods compared to any other actor. Every year a survey is sent out to all tenants that measures a lot of different aspects. It could, however, be difficult to be sure exactly what these measures show. One interviewee who worked in one of the neighbourhoods as a development leader mentioned that the "feeling of safety" had increased over the years. It is, however, difficult to deduce why this was the case. The interviewee said that this "feeling" is something that could easily change if a negative event occurred in the neighbourhood, such as a shooting. Another interviewee explained: "if there has been a shooting, then the evaluations [from the tenants] get worse". A bad "feeling" within a neighbourhood could also easily spill over into the results of other measurements, not only those having to do with safety. Another interviewee from one of the MHCs said that the easiest way of measuring how well they are performing, is to see how much damage there is within the neighbourhoods.

> As far as I know, there has not been a single break-in to the cellars this year. That is a good result. We do not have a lot of glass shards either. The costs for this can be seen in our budget.

The interviewee explained further:

> Five, seven, ten years ago, when the police were not as active [here], we had the glassworker here every day […] a great sum was spent on that, and on damages and break-ins. But when the police started to work actively, that gave results.

The interviewees argued that they had the survey and the ongoing work with the tenants and the everyday work with the facilities under control, as these are tools that have been used for a long time. To measure all the extra projects that have been started as a consequence of the new strategy is more difficult:

Is it connected to any change in socio-economic status if we employ 100 youths over summer? Does it change the governmental income support in the future? Quite hard to say actually.

(Employee, Framtiden parent company)

Another challenge is that different parts of the strategy are more or less difficult to assess. One interviewee from one of the MHCs said:

The efforts in the strategy are totally different. To make buildings safer [technically through better locks etc.], we know when that is done, it is a check in the margin. But, when we have reached the maximal effect with how we work with no tolerance towards criminality, what does that mean?

At the same time; existing statistics can be interpreted in different ways. If more crimes are reported, it looks worse, but compared to another neighbourhood, where the tenants do not dare to report incidents, the feeling of unsafeness is probably more widespread. This is also one reason why the results of the surveys carried out by the MHCs might differ from the overall statistics, and is one reason why the communication between the local police and the MHCs is of great importance. Another example of the challenge is difficulty in measuring socio-economic statistics. One of the employees at the head office at Framtiden said:

The statistic on the numbers of the unhealthy is going down. Is that because people are feeling better? Or is it due to a change in the way of measuring the unhealth at the Swedish Social Insurance Agency?

(Employee, Framtiden parent company)

Despite its difficulties, there was a need to measure the effects of ongoing work, as many new projects were started.

Measuring the results of various projects

As the goal of being removed from the police list lay far into the future at the same time as investments were made in various projects, it became important to measure the impact of these. One interviewee described how previously many projects were supported by the MHCs but not carried out through collaboration or partnering, and there had subsequently been no assessment. One interviewee argued that this had led to a problem of "sparkler projects": short-term projects where it had been difficult to see whether they led to any changes in the long run. The interviewees indicated that all the money that was made available because of the new strategy came with great responsibility. The intent now is to do projects together with others and not only to support projects. For actors working in the targeted neighbourhoods, this means that they need to connect all projects with the larger ambition. This is a difficult endeavour, as one interviewee said about the lack of evaluation on how well the projects are performing:

No one has had any clue; they have scattered money around. But no one has known, what is it that we gain from all this? Do they even practice? [the example of basketball practices for youths] […] it is difficult if you have a lot of organizations involved, you cannot keep track of all of them.

(District Manager, private housing corporation)

Another interviewee, a CEO for one MHC, agreed about the lack of control:

> We do not have any systematic model [about some help with school home-work projects]. [...] we have put in money and support but ... we cannot see how it is connected to the development of this neighbourhood.

The challenge goes both ways. It is important to connect projects with the overall strategy and the socio-economic development in the neighbourhoods. Interviewees, however, explained that it is difficult to see any improvement in the socio-economic statistics, as this is something that changes slowly, and that when individuals are better off, they might move to another neighbourhood. This means, then, that the statistics on neighbourhoods are unchanged, yet people are better off. It is also important to keep in mind that the projects, even small ones, can be important for the people taking part in them. One of the interviewed, as an example, talked about how basketball was the way out of criminality for one of the youths taking part. This is not visible in the overall neighbourhood statistics, but obviously important for that person.

As a final point, when assessing the impact of the strategy, there is the fact that the goal of the strategy is something that requires collaboration across a lot of organizational boundaries, yet the strategy is developed and decided on by the parent company Framtiden AB. Even so, one reason for it not to succeed could be that other actors do not follow, as discussed previously. The employees at Framtiden could, however, not blame others, as one of the employed at the parent company said: "we cannot say that this went to hell because [another actor] did not do what they were supposed to. That is an analysis some other will have to do". This portrays the difficulty of aiming at a shared, grand challenge at the local level. It signals the importance of targeting other actors and helping them see the importance of being part of the solutions. In this process, it is also important to be able to illustrate small wins along the way.

Discussion – tackling grand challenges at the local level

The case reported opinions on how the challenge in the neighbourhoods under study were being managed too much top down, yet from a global perspective the MHC is tackling the challenge at a local level (c.f. Bours, Wanzenböck, & Frenken, 2021). This way of dealing with development in the neighbourhoods studied was a response to ongoing development and there was no time to wait for others to act first. This presents difficulties as, at the same time, when it comes to grand challenges, there is a need for concerted efforts between several actors (Grodal & O'Mahoney, 2017).

The empirical data shows a pragmatic view of how the strategic goal is to be realized. There is a need to act that comes with an attitude that it is better to try something out, see how it works, and then act again. This approach is in line with how previous literature has suggested that grand challenges are to be tackled pragmatically in this manner, and aim for small wins (Bryson, 1988). There is an attitude that the challenge is grand, so the least they can do is to try. That the MHCs have this role can be explained by their being in a "freer" role compared to the city departments or other actors, and they are, at least initially, experiencing fewer institutional barriers (Bours, Wanzenböck, & Frenken, 2021). This focus on action also resembles an *energizing mechanism* – a strong motivation to act, and in similar ways a *bandwagon effect*, as there is an expectation that other actors will follow (Teremeer & DeWulf, 2019). However, there is also a need to uphold what Teemer and DeWulf (2019) called the *logic of attraction mechanism*, suggesting the need to uphold communication about the need to act, and to communicate that the challenge is shared, to not lose momentum. There is otherwise a risk that potential collaborators, instead of stepping up, will back off. There is a need to communicate that tackling the challenges in the especially vulnerable neighbourhoods requires what Ferraro et al. (2015) called a *participatory architecture,* allowing various actors to interact in a constructive way and over time. To communicate that the ongoing actions are leading to something valuable, becomes important. There is a potential catch-22 here: it is important to communicate and illustrate the importance of the ongoing work at the same time as there is a need to be responsive and reflexive on how the work is proceeding, and if necessary, to change direction (c.f. Ferraro et al., 2015). Moreover, as there are potential tensions between long-term development and short-term activities (Brorström, 2021), and between the narrow objective of the organization and the overall societal values (Burns & Jollands, 2020; Killian & O'Regan, 2020), this means that there is a risk of the new strategic intentions leading to more projects, but without knowing how they contribute to the overarching aim. The ongoing work of finding the right ways of measuring the work becomes crucial to being able to illustrate how actions taken lead in the right direction – to improve the living conditions in the targeted neighbourhoods and, as a result, to be removed from the police list before 2025. However, as this goal is seen as difficult, if not impossible to meet, there is instead a focus on short-term measures that can illustrate that the actions are important, even though the goal might not be met. Grodal and Mahoney (2017) argued that many efforts to tackle grand challenges fall short because of their initial goal. In the case here, it thus became important to keep discussing this goal, and by doing that to uphold a debate about the underlying principles for assessing the development (Chenhall, Hall, & Smith, 2013). To illustrate the small wins becomes crucial to making the employees at the MHCs as well as the collaborating partners keep going and to illustrate the small steps on the road to the big win (Bryson, 1988). Perhaps these ongoing discussions are the most valuable outcome of the assessment work, and the ambitious goal thus has another important role: to show the importance and the urge to act, to do something.

The role of measuring performance

Even though the work of measuring how well the organizations perform might be most important to keep alive discussions on the underlying principles of the work, there are also practical implications. In the case reported here, there was the magnitude of the investment by the Framtiden Group, something that made measuring of the outcomes important from a societal perspective, as it was imperative that spending this large sum would end up showing positive results. Similarly, as there had been criticism towards the process of being too top down, the assessment could prove to be a way of making actors follow. as they see the importance and to include them, if not earlier, in this process. Yet, how and what to measure is not easy to decide, and the empirical material may reveal tensions and conflicting values when this is discussed. There is, for one, an existing gap between the overall statistics of the neighbourhood – that signal large socio-economic issues – and the microlevel "solutions" that focus on individuals. Whether these activities lead the development closer to the goal is unclear and difficult to measure. Similarly, the empirical material shows that existing measurements are valued differently depending on who you ask. For example, there seems to be a gap between how employees at the management level regard the existing assessment compared to employees working "at the ground level". At the management level, there is an interest in overall statistics on the neighbourhoods, yet the people working on the ground, close to the tenants, seem to be more reluctant to accept that information and would rather discuss the underlying causes of the data and more detailed accounts of how they perform, such as the cost for shattered glass over time. There is a need to showcase good results. The issue is thus that a project might be a success, even if it is helping only one person. This is, however, not visible in the overall statistics. When the MHCs, as an example, provide children in local schools with breakfast, the result of this might not be traceable in socio-economic statistics, yet the children do not need to be hungry until lunch, and all can agree that it is a good result, no matter the measurability of it. This dilemma illustrates the complexity of measuring long-term ambitions in a short-time perspective, and if all projects needed to be traceable in an overall perspective, the neighbourhoods might lose important activities. Again, to trace the small wins and communicate them might therefore be a way forward towards managing the grand challenge at a local level. However, it is also important to discuss the development in the vulnerable neighbourhoods from a larger perspective, as people might move from the neighbourhoods when possible (c.f. Grander, Roelofs, & Salonen, 2022). Measuring the work towards the goal in this specific case is also a challenge since how the actual goal, to be removed from the police list, is measured is not totally transparent and is for the police authority to decide on. This, again, shows the need for ongoing discussion of the goal, how it can be understood, and the underlying principles for measuring it (Chenhall, Hall, & Smith, 2013).

To conclude, the MHCs play an interesting role as they invest in social projects based on business principles (Westerdahl, 2021). For the people interviewed in the study underlying this chapter, this does not seem to be an issue but is rather a circumstance that allows for all kinds of actions. However, over time this might create tension between what is good in the short run and what is good in the long run (Jacobs & Cuganesan (2014), and it is difficult to know whether the actions today will lead to being closer to the large ambitions. This chapter thus illustrates both the need to measure and capture development when managing grand challenges, and the complexities when doing it. This poses the question, if we are to find new, innovative ways of managing grand challenges locally, do we not also need to find other means of measuring and evaluating the progress? This link between measurements and the overall development in grand challenges is worth further discussion and research.

References

Ahrens, T., & Chapman, C. (2002). The structuration of legitimate performance measures and management: day-to-day contests of accountability in a UK restaurant chain. *Management Accounting Research, 13*(2), 151–171.

Ansell, C., & Boin, A. (2019). Taming deep uncertainty: The potential of pragmatist principles for understanding and improving strategic crisis management. *Administration & Society, 51*(7), 1079–1112.

Bours, S. A., Wanzenböck, I., & Frenken, K. (2021). Small wins for grand challenges. A bottom-up governance approach to regional innovation policy. *European Planning Studies, 30*(11), 1–28.

Brorström, S. (2015). Strategizing sustainability – the case of River City Gothenburg'. *Cities, 42*(Part A), 25–30.

Brorström, S. (2023). The sustainability shift: The role of calculative practices in strategy implementation. *Financial Accountability & Management, 39*(1), 3–17.

Brorström, S., & Diedrich, A. (2022). Boundaries of collaboration – the case of a temporary housing complex for refugees in Sweden. *Public Management Review, 24*(4), 536–557.

Bryson, J. (1988). Strategic planning: Big wins and small wins. *Public Money & Management, 8*(3), 11–15.

Bryson, J., Sancino, A., Benington, J., & Sørensen, E. (2017). Towards a multi-actor theory of public value co-creation. *Public Management Review, 19*(5), 640–654.

Burns J., & Jollands S. (2020) Acting in the public interest: accounting for the vulnerable. *Accounting and Business Research, 50*(5), 507–534.

Carstensen, M. B., Sørensen, E., & Torfing, J. (2022). Why we need bricoleurs to foster robust governance solutions in turbulent times. *Public Administration, 101*(1), 36–52.

Chenhall, R. H., Hall, M., & Smith, D. (2013). Performance measurement, modes of evaluation and the development of compromising accounts. *Accounting, Organizations and Society, 38*(4), 268–287.

Cooper, D. J., Hinings, B., Greenwood, R., & Brown, J. L. (1996). Sedimentation and transformation in organizational change: The case of Canadian law firms. *Organization Studies, 17*(4), 623–647.

Costa, E., & Pesci, C. (2016). Social impact measurement: Why do stakeholders matter? *Sustainability Accounting, Management and Policy Journal, 7*(1), 99–124.

Couture, F., Jarzabkowski, P., & Lê, J. K. (2022). Triggers, traps, and disconnect: How governance obstacles hinder progress on grand challenges. *Academy of Management Journal* (in press).

Crosby, B. C., & Bryson, J. M. (2005). *Leadership for the common good: Tackling public problems in a shared-power world* (Vol. 264). John Wiley & Sons.

Cuganesan, S., Dunford, R., & Palmer, I. (2012), Strategic management accounting and strategy practices within a public sector agency, *Management Accounting Research, 23*(4), 245–260.

Emilsson, H., & Öberg, K. (2022). Housing for refugees in Sweden: Top-down governance and its local reactions. *Journal of International Migration and Integration, 23*(2), 613–631.

Farrell, K. N. (2011). Snow White and the wicked problems of the West: A look at the lines between empirical description and normative prescription. *Science, Technology, & Human Values, 36*(3), 334–361. https://doi.org/10.1177/0162243910385796

Ferraro, F., Etzion, D., & Gehman, J. (2015). Tackling grand challenges pragmatically: Robust action revisited. *Organization Studies, 36*(3), 363–390.

George, G., Howard-Grenville, J., Joshi, A., & Tihanyi, L. (2016). Understanding and tackling societal grand challenges through management research. *Academy of Management Journal, 59*(6), 1880–1895.

Gerell, M., Puur, M., & Guldåker, N. (2022). Swedish conditions? Characteristics of locations the Swedish Police label as vulnerable. *Nordic Journal of Urban Studies, 1*, 40–62.

Gioia, D. A., Corley, K. G., & Hamilton, A. L. (2013). Seeking qualitative rigor in inductive research: Notes on the Gioia methodology. *Organizational Research Methods, 16*(1), 15–31.

Glasser, H. (2019). Toward robust foundations for sustainable well-being societies: learning to change by changing how we learn. In J. W. Cook (Ed.), *Sustainability, human well-being, and the future of education* (pp. 31–89). Palgrave Macmillan.

Grander, M. (2017). New public housing: A selective model disguised as universal? Implications of the market adaptation of Swedish public housing. *International Journal of Housing Policy, 17*(3), 335–352.

Grander, M. (2019). Off the beaten track? Selectivity, discretion and path-shaping in Swedish public housing. *Housing, Theory and Society, 36*(4), 385–400.

Grander, M., Roelofs, K., & Salonen, T. (2022). Area-based development initiatives: A means to an end or an end in itself? – a literature overview on the case of Sweden. *Nordic Social Work Research, 12*(2), 243–255.

Gray, R. (2010). Is accounting for sustainability actually accounting for sustainability … and how would we know? An exploration of narratives of organisations and the planet. *Accounting, Organizations and Society, 35*(1), 47–62.

Grodal, S., & O'Mahony, S. (2017). How does a grand challenge become displaced? Explaining the duality of field mobilization. *Academy of Management Journal, 60*, 1801–1827.

Hedman, E. (2008). *A history of the Swedish system of non-profit municipal housing.* Boverket.

Hincks, S. (2017). Vulnerable neighbourhoods in transition: Divergent pathways of change in the Greater Manchester city-region. *Urban Studies, 54*(4), 1038–1061.

Holmqvist, E., & Turner, L. M. (2014). Swedish welfare state and housing markets: Under economic and political pressure. *Journal of Housing and the Built Environment, 29*, 237–254. https://doi-org.ezproxy.ub.gu.se/10.1007/s10901-013-9391-0

Jacobs, K., & Cuganesan, S. (2014). Interdisciplinary accounting research in the public sector: Dissolving boundaries to tackle wicked problems. *Accounting, Auditing & Accountability Journal, 27*(8), 1250–1256.

Killian, S., & O'Regan, P. (2020). Accounting, the public interest and the common good. *Critical Perspectives on Accounting, 67–68*(6), 102144. https://doi.org/10.1016/j.cpa.2019.102144

Kornberger, M., Justesen, L., Madsen, A. K., & Mouritsen, J. (Eds.). (2015). *Making things valuable.* Oxford University Press.

Lægreid, P., & Rykkja, L. H. (2022). Accountability and inter-organizational collaboration within the state. *Public Management Review, 24*(5), 683–703.

Perrow, C., & Guillen, M. F. (1990). *AIDS disaster: Failure of organizations in New York and the nation.* Yale University Press.

Pesci, C., Costa, E., & Andreaus, M. (2020). Using accountability to shape the common good. *Critical Perspectives on Accounting, 67*, 102079.

Pimentel, E., Cho, C. H., & Bothello, J. (2022). The blind spots of interdisciplinarity in addressing grand challenges. *Critical Perspectives on Accounting, 93*, June 2023.

Sachs, J. (2012). From millennium development goals to sustainable development goals. *The Lancet, 379*(9832), 2206–2211.

Steccolini, I. (2019). Accounting and the post-new public management: Re-considering publicness in accounting research. *Accounting, Auditing & Accountability Journal, 32*(1), 255–279.

Termeer, C., & Dewulf, A. (2019). A small wins framework to overcome the evaluation paradox of governing wicked problems. *Policy and Society, 38*(2), 298–314. https://doi.org/10.1080/14494035.2018.1497933

Thomasson, A., Lapsley, I., & Steccolini, I. (2020). "Managing" wicked problems: Uncovering the roles of budgets, financial systems, and collaboration. *Financial Accountability & Management, 36*, 113–116.

Tregidga, H., & Laine, M. (2022). On crisis and emergency: Is it time to rethink long-term environmental accounting? *Critical Perspectives on Accounting, 82*, 2022.

Vermaak, H. (2013). Planning deep change through a series of small wins. *Academy of Management Proceedings, 1*, 1–25.

Weick, K. E. (1984). Small wins: Redefining the scale of social problems. *American Psychologist, 39*(1), 40–49.

Westerdahl, S. (2021). Yield and the city: Swedish public housing and the political significance of changed accounting practices. *Critical Perspectives on Accounting, 80*, 102161.

PART II

Public sector accounting and auditing issues

4

INSTITUTIONAL ENTREPRENEURSHIP IN A SUPREME AUDIT INSTITUTION

The National Audit Office and the use of data in financial audit

Laurence Ferry and Henry Midgley

Introduction

Currently, public sector audit faces a changing context, including altering roles for the auditor and relationships with parliaments and other bodies (Liston-Heyes & Juillet, 2022a). This changing context does not just relate to accounting and audit's objectives, but it also relates to what accountants and auditors do to achieve those objectives. Accounting is one of a series of professions that is likely to be transformed in the twenty-first century by technology (Suskind & Suskind, 2015). Digitalization promises to have radical effects on the ways in which numbers can be used to hold people to account (Leoni & Parker, 2019; She & Michelon, 2019). In the private sector, audit has become increasingly technological – with technologies such as blockchain and big data offering auditors different routes to offer assurance to their stakeholders (Vasarhelyi et al., 2015; Manita et al., 2020; Atayah & Alashatar, 2021; Lombardi et al., 2021). As governments increasingly use digital technology to conduct their activities, those who hold them to account are required to adjust their methodologies (Torres & Cabeza, 2022). In audit specifically, some of the same arguments that apply for the private sector work within the public sector, with auditors increasingly using technology to reframe their own activities (Aquino et al., 2022).

However, despite this set of changes to the way that audit will function in the future, one recent literature review of accountability in the public sector identified "a dearth of accounting scholarship investigating public service digitalization's relevance to and potential implications for public sector accounting, accountability and accountants" (Agostino, Saliterer, & Steccolini, 2022, p. 153). This finding has been repeated for audit itself (Otia & Bracci, 2022; Ferry et al., 2022b). There is some evidence that public sector audit has been slow so far to adapt to change. Otia and Bracci (2022) suggested that despite the existence of a few pioneers, Supreme Audit Institutions (SAIs) had been conservative in the way that they approached new data.[1] They suggested that one element SAIs should focus on in order to improve their adoption of the new technology was leadership. In this chapter, we assess the role of leadership, particularly at junior levels, within the UK's SAI in adapting the practice of audit to new technology and how it is channelled by the dominant logics that inform public sector audit's development in the UK.

There are many studies in the accounting literature that focus on leadership as a mechanism to cope with change (Funnell, 2003; Opara et al., 2021; Orlandi, 2021; Ferry & Midgley, 2022).

DOI: 10.4324/9781003295945-6

Institutional entrepreneurship is described by its advocates as the "activities of actors who have an interest in particular institutional arrangements and who leverage resources to create new institutions or to transform existing ones" (Maguire et al., 2004, p. 657). Institutional entrepreneurship is a useful lens, therefore, to look at the way that an institution – public sector audit – is being transformed by technology in a particular country. Much of the scholarship on institutional entrepreneurship stresses how far the entrepreneur is embedded within the institutional framework in which they operate, importing the justifications for change from the contradictions or rationalities given to them by that framework. This results in what Garud et al. (2007, pp. 958, 961) describe as "embedded agency".

In this chapter, we examine the experience of the National Audit Office (NAO) [2] in the UK in its efforts to digitalize. We focus on their development of a data analytics capacity – called the Data Analytics Research Team (DART), which was set up in 2017 to increase the NAO's use of data analytics in its audits. The research question underpinning the chapter is to seek to understand how this change took place and how it was legitimated. The chapter examines the embeddedness of the entrepreneurship towards technological change in public sector audit, through the utilization of two frames: a professional logic arising out of accounting specialism and a democratic logic arising out of the NAO's constitutional purpose and mandate set out by Parliament. We then show how these two frames permitted and justified the adoption of data analytics techniques within the NAO, as well as limited the extent to which change could immediately happen.[3]

Institutional entrepreneurship

In this section of the chapter, we establish three things. The first part of this section describes the current state of scholarship concerning the digitalization of audit and specifically the use of data analytics. The second part describes the literature on institutional entrepreneurship and justifies the argument that entrepreneurs are able to secure change when they use their embedded agency to do so. The third part develops two institutional logics, which underpin public sector audit and are therefore available to institutional entrepreneurs in this space.

Change in digitalization in audit

Audit is one profession that observers expect to be revolutionized by the development of technology over the next century (Suskind & Suskind, 2015). Whilst not all auditors or audit firms within the private sector may, at present, have sufficient skills to prosper in this new world, there is an expectation that in order to survive, auditors will need to develop their skills (Appelbaum et al., 2021). The possibilities for this technology in both the public and the private sector are immense: Power (2022, p. 3) suggested that digitalization at its most basic was "eliminating cumbersome paper-based processes" yet suggested that these technologies may be part of a "a radical epistemic shift in the way we know persons, organizations and economies".

There are different ways in which technology may affect the practice of audit. The current literature identifies, among other things, big data, blockchain and artificial intelligence as potential drivers of change in auditing. Lombardi et al. (2021) and Wang and Kogan (2018) suggested blockchain could have similar effects, enabling the use of smart contracting and through better interrogation of business information systems.[4] Issa et al. (2016, p. 1) suggested that audit was "prime for partial automation" through artificial intelligence due to its labour intensiveness and range of decision structures.[5] Kokina and Davenport (2017, p. 116) identify the fact that audit tasks are often "structured and repetitive and therefore can be automated" using artificial intelligence.

There has been considerable scholarship around big data in particular. Cao et al. (2015) saw the transformational potential of big data. This assertion was also supported by the survey of the literature conducted by Applebaum et al. (2018), who identified numerous specific improvements big data could make to audit. This is supported by many within the industry: a survey of 216 senior audit managers in Scandinavia found that they recognized that data analytics was useful but that use was limited (Eilifson et al., 2020). In the audits sampled by Elifson et al. (2020, p. 93), data analytics was often used for journal entry testing, the calculating of sample sizes, selection of samples, the summarizing of ledgers, simple judgemental methods, identification of outliers or groups, performance of two- or three-way matching, reconciliations, recalculations and the making of statistical calculations from data for predictive analysis. Sallijeni et al. (2019) and Kend and Nguyen (2022) analysed the implications of data analytics for auditors in the private sector and described the potential opportunities and limitations of this technology for private sector audit.

Whilst in the private sector there have been several studies of the effects of technology on audit, in the public sector there have been fewer. Agostino, Bracci, and Steccolini (2022) argued that whilst a lot of attention had been paid to the ways in which digital technology might change public services, "far less attention has been devoted to the accounting and accountability implications connected with the adoption and use of digital technologies". This issue is particularly relevant for accounting journals, which "appear to have mostly ignored the digitalized public sector" (Agostino, Saliterer, & Steccolini, 2022). This gap prompted Mattei et al. (2021) to suggest that scholars of public sector audit needed to explore the adoption of digital technology given its potential for enhancing transparency and accountability. Ferry et al. (2022b) echoed this call, suggesting that digitalization was a challenge that public sector auditors faced. Rana et al. (2022, p. 358) identified "relatively few" studies of digitalization in performance audit. Agostino, Saliterer, and Steccolini (2022) draw attention to the fact that a lack of scholarship may encourage a utopian sense of the possibility of the digitalization of audit. Aquino, Lino, de Azevaldo, and da Silva (2022) reinforced this research by suggesting that digital technology in Brazil shaped the nature of the questions that auditors asked.

The adoption of these new technologies has been driven by a number of factors. Alles (2015) suggested that as audit clients in the private sector became increasingly focused on big data, then audit firms would be forced to follow. Krieger et al. (2021) suggested that the technological capacity of individual firms was a key limiting factor on change in the private sector. However, Elifson et al. (2020), Kend and Nguyen (2022), and Cao et al. (2022) suggest that regulation and inspection may be a factor in reducing the take-up of data analytics.

In the public sector, compulsion has been used to force the adoption of digital technology in accounting (Lino et al., 2022). Otia and Bracci (2022) found that SAIs defined digital transformation according to their own level of maturity and suggested that digital transformation in SAIs had to take place alongside transformations in culture and people. They suggested that SAIs were less interested in leadership and culture than in technology and process. In this sense, this bears out the observation of Agostino, Saliterer, and Steccolini (2022) that realism is required about the potential of this new technological revolution and how far it will change public sector accountability. In this study, we examine the factors which facilitated institutional entrepreneurship within the NAO and in particular the arguments that members of particular teams were able to draw on to advocate for change. This requires us to analyse both institutional entrepreneurship itself in the following section of the literature review, and the institutional logics underpinning the UK SAIs in the final section.

Institutional entrepreneurship

Institutional entrepreneurship explains agency within and outside of institutions. Institutions are patterns of activity by which individuals and organizations are structured and organized (Greenwood et al., 2017). Entrepreneurs, on the other hand, are individuals who take responsibility for taking decisions – the key to that being, there is an individual who can take "decisions that run counter to conventional wisdom" (Hébert & Link, 1989). That individual may be an individual person (Hébert

& Link, 1989), though scholars have also drawn attention to the role that teams or even organizations can play as entrepreneurs (Aldrich, 2011; Ahrens & Ferry, 2018). Institutional entrepreneurship therefore represents an attempt to add back agency into the study of institutions (Battilana et al., 2009). It enables scholars to study how agency disrupts structures, without deciding the priority of either agency or structure in shaping the world: both rely upon each other intrinsically (Tiberius et al., 2020).

Within public sector accounting, accountants have frequently drawn on ideas about institutional entrepreneurship to explain change or resistance to change. Institutional entrepreneurship cannot just rely upon "personal professional autonomy, legitimacy and expertise" but has to be built upon through strategies that legitimate the change itself (Major et al., 2018). Successful entrepreneurs employ strategies, which rely upon rewards, rhetorical and even pedagogical techniques to achieve change (Sutheewasinnon et al., 2016). Hyvönen et al. (2012) emphasized that institutional entrepreneurs required both tools of communication and also a receptive audience to succeed in their objectives. Ahrens and Ferry (2018) stressed the role that practice memory played in enabling Newcastle City Council (and the field of local government more broadly) to resist central government cuts in England during the 2010s. Ahrens and Ferry (2018, p. 15) define practice memory as the way in which past practices are remembered socially and form a context for current practices within an organization. Institutional entrepreneurs will see more opportunities and exploit them more effectively, the more that they are invested in those cultural narratives about the institutions they inhabit (Löhlein & Müßig, 2020).

SAIs and their logics

This analysis of institutional entrepreneurship makes the rhetoric with which institutions justify themselves incredibly important. Liston-Heyes and Juillet (2022b) found that the behaviour of auditors is determined by the context in which they are embedded. Radcliffe (1998) argued that understanding what he described as the rationalities underpinning public sector audit was crucial to understanding its development. Within this chapter, we seek to explore the institutional logics in which the auditors who developed data analytics within the NAO were embedded. The concept of institutional logics is well known within accounting. An institutional logic refers to the way a social world works – it is a "contingent set of rules, premiums and sanctions" that agents "create and recreate in such a way that their behaviour and accompanying perspective are to some extent regularized and predictable" (Jackall, 1988, p. 112). They therefore are practices and symbolic constructions that underpin the identities and interactions of their members and thereby guide human action within institutions (Greenwood & Suddaby, 2006). As a result, they define what counts as a problem and a solution, and constitute agendas of economic and political control as well as organizational reward (Freidland & Alford, 1987).

In the context of public sector audit, there are two main institutional logics at work. The first logic is a democratic logic that ties the value of public sector audit back to democracy (Pallot, 2003; Funnell, 2007; Ferry et al., 2019; Ferry et al., 2022, Ferry et al., 2023). The NAO's predecessor organization, the Exchequer and Audit Department, was initially founded in the 1860s to support Parliamentary financial control of the executive (Dewar & Funnell, 2017). The NAO was created in 1983 out of the Exchequer and Audit Department and was granted more freedoms and more funding to further support parliamentary scrutiny of the executive (Dewar & Funnell, 2017; Midgley, 2019; Ferry & Midgley, 2022). Developments in audit thus have implications for citizens and their ability to use audited information or audit reports to hold the government to account (Ferry & Ahrens, 2022). The second major logic lying behind public sector audit is a professional logic that seeks legitimacy in professional external expertise and an implicit link between that expertise and the development of better management within the public sector (Stewart & Connolly, 2022). The adoption of standards for accounts and audit is described by influential global actors as necessary for "strong" financial management (Bakre et al., 2021, p. 5). Hazgui et al. (2022) show that auditors have embraced this professionalization as a way of defending their position as commentators on the public sector.

The argument that these two logics coexist in public sector audit is not new. Bowerman et al. (2003, p. 5) pointed to a risk that the NAO would justify itself on "managerialist" grounds rather than on parliamentary grounds. Skærbæk (2009) pointed out that in Denmark the audit office saw itself both as a modernizer of the public sector and as an independent auditor. Morin and Hazgui (2016) suggested that in the NAO, auditors internalized a double mission – to hold government to account before Parliament and to act as enablers of best practice in public sector administration. Free et al. (2020) suggested that the professionalization of audit was the product of international comparison and learning. Dewar and Funnell (2017, p. 218) argued that in financial audit, the NAO perceived a requirement to keep up with the "latest professional standards". In this chapter, we will show that these two institutional logics were relied upon by senior managers and entrepreneurs within the NAO to justify and establish the increased use of data analytics within NAO audit.

Methodology

The NAO is the SAI of the UK. It was established in 1983 (although a predecessor organization was founded in the nineteenth century) as a body responsible to Parliament. The NAO produces two main forms of output. It audits the financial accounts of the UK government and provides certificates for those accounts, which confirm that the accounts are true and fair and regular. The NAO also publishes reports on the economy, efficiency and effectiveness with which public money is spent by the Westminster government in the UK (within the NAO, this is commonly described as value-for-money audit). Bodies responsible to the devolved parliaments in Scotland, Wales and Northern Ireland have their own audit arrangements which audit the devolved administration's responsibilities (Foster & Knox, 2022). The NAO audits both the entire UK government and, where powers have been devolved to Scotland, Wales and Northern Ireland, it audits the English policy response. The Comptroller and Auditor General (C&AG), the NAO's head, has complete discretion over the ways in which their function is performed, although they are accountable to Parliament for the use of their resources. Therefore, the NAO has a great deal of autonomy in how it organizes itself and how it deploys its resources to meet its objectives.

The NAO has several unique features as an organization that flow out of its set-up. Firstly, it is an organization whose fundamental activities are prescribed by law – and they cannot easily change without either legislative change or a negotiated settlement with government. Major changes to the NAO's remit during the period covered by this chapter included acquiring extra responsibilities for the audit of value for money across the whole of local government in the UK (Ferry et al., 2022a). (The NAO does not audit either the accounts or the value for money of spending in individual local authorities). Whereas the C&AG has complete discretion in how they carry out their work, they have followed the accounting profession in how they conduct their financial audits, with special considerations for issues which are unique to the public sector such as regularity. Secondly, the NAO is headed by a C&AG who is appointed for a non-renewable term of ten years. This chapter covers a period in which there was a change in C&AG: Lord Morse's term finished in 2019 and he was replaced by the current C&AG, Gareth Davies. Thirdly, the organization is quite small, with an average total of 939 staff employed in 2020–2021 (NAO, 2022).

In order to understand how the data analytics team developed at the NAO and what the motivations behind the data analytics development in the NAO were, we carried out 30 interviews. The interviewees occupied different positions within the NAO and were spread across central teams engaged in digitalization work, value for money-focused teams, financial audit-focused teams, and senior leaders within the organization. We also interviewed several members of staff who had left the organization and some outside stakeholders from the UK Parliament, the NAO's main client.

Table 4.1 Employment status of interviewees

Employment Status	Number of interviewees
Current NAO employees	18
Former NAO employees	10
Members of Parliamentary staff	2

Table 4.2 Role of interviewees

Role within digitalization in the NAO	Number of interviewees
Member of central digital delivery team	12
Line member of staff with expertise in financial audit	9
Line member of staff with expertise in value-for-money audit	10
Senior leaders within the NAO (Director and above)	6
Members of Parliamentary staff	2

Interviewees were told that their input would remain anonymous, and they were also given opportunities to question the research team on the design of the study. A breakdown of the 30 interviewees by different categories is provided in Table 4.1, which gives the current employment status of interviewees, and in Table 4.2, which sets out their roles within digitalization at the NAO.

Within the NAO, interviewees performed different roles – these are summarized in Table 4.2 – though the total does not sum to 30 as some members of staff performed multiple roles.

One of the authors worked at the NAO between 2008 and 2021 and was familiar with the changes described in the chapter. The other researcher has worked externally with the NAO closely and has a long experience of the organization. Interviewees were selected based on the authors' experience of the NAO and also on the feedback of previous interview subjects who suggested further contacts. Care was taken to ensure that interviews were held with people who were involved in the development of data analytics or the DART, and those who were not, as well as those who were customers of the services of the programme, in order that perceptions were balanced. As the programme was publicized widely within the NAO, views of people such as staff on the VFM service line who did not use the outputs of the programme were relevant to understanding its impact.

Findings

Initially we set out what the NAO had achieved with regard to big data and data analytics in the first section of our findings. The second section explains senior management's accommodating attitude to change and innovation within the organization, and sets out their motivation for supporting and sponsoring change, without personally directing it. In the third section, we explain how the DART and others within the NAO exploited this opportunity to further their own projects and contribute therefore to the development of the NAO's digital audit.

Digitalization and DART

The NAO relied upon computers and digital technology to manage its audits, collect audit evidence and store audit findings from the early 2000s onwards. It had invested in standardized audit software in which tests were set out and findings and evidence were produced against those tests. In the early 2010s, the NAO transitioned to cloud-based computer software and remote internet access from the client site (Participant 23). This and a new set of audit software enabled the NAO to use its digital infrastructure more collaboratively, with individual team members now able to work on the audit file simultaneously. There were attempts to interrogate the data coming out of financial audit, but these were often "ad hoc data analytics" (Participant 1). Individual members of staff across the office were doing their own work on data analytics within their own audits, which went beyond what was centrally available, but this was bespoke work to individual clients and often relied upon the skills of individual audit teams. There was some capacity that was available to teams but not a huge amount.

Whilst in 2014, senior managers in the NAO could see the need for the development of further data analytics, they had not created a separate team for doing this within financial audit. Initial developments were made by the team responsible for using data on value-for-money audit and then the DART was set up as a "separate function created specifically to cater for the needs of analytics in financial audit" (Participant 5). The team grew out of both the Financial Audit central team who had expertise in the use of data on financial audit and also the value-for-money team, which focused on the use of statistics elsewhere (Participant 17, Participant 5).

The DART was set up in 2017, though some preparatory work was done in 2016. Implementation was spread out across 2018, 2019 and 2020 but was an ongoing process (Participant 25). Initially, the team was small and was a group of young staff with an interest in the issues. One of the main members of staff at that point described their role as "the main brief we had at the very beginning was very much to try and find problems to solve" (Participant 1). The purpose behind the team was to "try and be a bit more strategic in what was happening to try and set up the capability within the office because before it's just individuals, and to try and grow more capabilities" (Participant 1). The team was made up of newly qualified accountants, trainee accountants, a senior data scientist, interns who later obtained full-time jobs as data scientists in the NAO, and a long-term financial auditor who had previously been working on data analytics by himself on audits. The team was built out of networks within the NAO: one member described his recruitment as "very informal" with a focus on getting "some people into the room who have the skills" (Participant 25).

The DART worked in coalition with others in the NAO. These included members of the Financial Audit central team, who were responsible for the overall quality of the NAO's audit and were therefore able to influence financial auditors working on individual departments. However, they also worked closely with others, including those advancing the development of modelling within the organization and the development of analysis within value-for-money audit, and there was a considerable degree of "cross-fertilization" of ideas between these teams (Participant 20). These other NAO staff described themselves in similar ways to the DART: for example, speaking about their "natural affinity with technology" and how their "own passions and my own agendas and desire to press forward with technologies" drove forward a programme of technological development (Participant 16).

Initially, the DART took on specific projects such as examining journals testing for the audit team who examined the BBC's accounts within the NAO and doing data analysis for the NAO on the prison system. The team then moved into developing more tools for solving "general problems" across all audits (Participant 25). These tools focused on bringing together data to support the financial audit opinion. Key developments included:

- The Audit Information Management System, a cloud-based system, which enabled teams to input, store and use data centrally.
- A journals risk assessment tool which enabled the identification of journals that were anomalies or inherently risky (for example, identifying all journals which had been posted at unusual times such as over the weekend).
- An analysis tool that reconciled the Trial Balance and the General Ledger. The Trial Balance should summarize the General Ledger and the new tool allowed an NAO auditor to swiftly identify any discrepancies between the two documents.

As one experienced financial auditor put it to us, "the main pillar or focus is around improving data and how that data itself is stored and accessed" (Participant 25). This improvement was supposed to be introduced across all financial audits within the organization. However, the DART also did specific work for some teams: assisting, for example, in providing an automated solution to the consolidation of some school accounts into the Department for Education's accounts. The process that is described here is not finished. Despite the considerable achievements that the DART has made, some within the office described to us some cultural resistance to the change that was begun (Participants 17, 23, 27).

The top-down logic of change

For the DART to be able to perform this role, it required permission from senior management. The DART had good links with senior management and was able to influence them (Participant 1). Both C&AGs during the time period covered by this work were digitally aware (Participant 9). Partly this was due to a convergence of views about the problems facing the NAO. Senior management saw digitalization and increased manipulation of data as important for both contextual and regulatory reasons. During our interviews, senior leaders pushed back on the notion that the NAO could opt out of digitalization. They saw that change was inevitable and argued that "digitalization [is]. kind of like being modern" (Participant 9). Senior managers believed that Parliament would expect and require the NAO to be led by data in the future (Participant 9).

Senior managers in the NAO saw data as embodying a challenge to public sector audit. The profusion of data raised expectations about what audit could do and how granular audit might be. There was a sense that financial audit in the public sector had to keep pace with financial audit in the private sector. As a senior member of staff told us, adoption in the public sector "mirrors relatively speaking the one which is happening in the private sector", with the acknowledgement that the NAO did not have the size or financial muscle of some of the large accounting firms (Participant 9). Another senior manager pointed out that "the organizations we audit, if they weren't audited by the NAO would be audited by a big four [audit firm] [...] so we are always trying to track what they do" (Participant 17). This was the sense outside the organization as well, as summed up by another of our participants, who said that

> the NAO tries to do what the firms do, they see the firms do it and you know its all the talk [...] firms were moving to use this technology and therefore the NAO felt that in order to demonstrate their value and keeping up with the firms [...] they need to demonstrate quality, efficiency, etc.
>
> *(Participant 21)*

A further important driver was that the NAO acquired new clients like the BBC where "we had to do it [use data analytics] because otherwise we could not physically deliver that service" (Participant 25). This was important as these audits were similar to company audits and the NAO had to demonstrate "we can do this audit, just as well as a firm can" (Participant 21). Senior managers where driven by regulatory changes to the structure of audit itself. In contrast to the DART members themselves (discussed below), for example, senior managers argued that the "regulator expects us to use analytics on journals" (Participant 17). They suggested that a more technological approach to audit was also an expectation of the regulator (Participant 17).

Senior managers were therefore aware that the NAO had to digitalize but sometimes they lacked the expertise to understand how this might happen. The NAO was in a position where its legal status was guaranteed – any threat to the organization was a long-term one. Consequently, staff believed the organization opted to change over a period of time using an incremental approach. One member of staff summed up DART's impact as being part of a story. In his view, the team "wasn't a great success", but viewed in another context, it took the NAO "forward again [...] it identified the need for a day to day function to support data analytics in the financial audit function" (Participant 16). This embodied a model of change within the organization in which individuals with a passion could make incremental changes and then, once change had to get established, it had to achieve senior and organizational sponsorship (Participant 16). DART was described by one senior participant in our study as "a development function without all the support" (Participant 17). There was a sense amongst some staff that the NAO was about "18 months or so behind wherever the cutting edge happens to be at any given time", but that "I think in a public sector context, particularly when we're spending taxpayers' money, that, that feels entirely pragmatic and sensible" (Participant 19).

The bottom-up logic of change

These logics for change within senior management were mirrored by team members in DART. Staff came to the team from different backgrounds and with different experiences, but they all recognized a problem involving government and data. For example, one key individual described her experience in Parliament as the source for her work in the team:

> There were a number of issues with the quality of data and, you know, there was a skills gap and the ability of organizations, particularly within the public sector, to kind of make use of this data in a meaningful way. And so when I was part of that inquiry, and learned quite a lot about kind of what was going on in the public sector, it also really encouraged me to develop those skills because it was very clear to me like the kinds of analysis you could do if you learned to code essentially or use advance analytics tools.
>
> *(Participant 22)*

This experience made her go away and learn how to do statistics and use digital technology to improve her own knowledge of how they worked. Specifically, financial auditors saw the profusion of data both as a threat and an opportunity. Another member of the team told us that financial audit was:

> fundamentally a nineteenth- to early twentieth-century process that it assumes that data volumes will be reasonably low and therefore manageable, and approaches like sampling for example will be a reasonable response to that, when actually the reality these days in the public as well as the private sector is that there is vast quantitative data.
>
> *(Participant 11)*

She was not alone. Another participant told us that "the main focus of our attention has been to develop tools which allow us to look across the whole population rather than previously our financial audit has been very sample driven" (Participant 13). The case for change rested upon the assertion that "genuinely, I don't believe you can perform an audit on a 60 million transaction organization without the use of data analytics" (Participant 11). Given that financial audit was taking place "in a more digital age", public sector audit could be "left behind" by the profusion of data out there (Participant 25).

The second main inspiration for the team itself was their view of the experience they had as trainees. As one senior member of the team put it to us, her interest in DART developed out of her frustrations when she was working as a junior auditor a couple of years earlier. She told us, "I remember distinctly being a first-year trainee and thinking, Why am I doing this? A computer can do this better" (Participant 11). She explained it as a contradiction within the profession as a whole:

> We have these extraordinarily bright, extraordinarily thoughtful, creative people and we put them through a three-year training programme to sort of knock that out of them, so that they can do a general ledger to trial balance reconciliation accurately to the nth degree when the reason we have accountancy as a chartered profession and the reason we spent so much time and effort and money training people to this expertise is so that they can apply subtle judgement.
>
> *(Participant 11)*

This sense that accountants at the NAO should be liberated by technology was part of the appeal of the team's efforts. This experience also motivated the kinds of problems that DART attempted to change: for example, the journals testing related to a particular issue at the NAO with the audit of government departments, which have large numbers of journals and where it is a challenge for the auditor to identify anomalies (Participant 21).

DART team members' enthusiasm for change was driven by their experience of working on financial audits in the NAO. Consequently, they were naturally predisposed to align their ideas about the development of audit within the NAO with the ideas of the senior leadership team. In some places, their ideas went further. For example, with respect to the role of trainees, DART members saw technology as having a revolutionary impact that would change the nature of audit work (Participant 17). The team was also motivated by the democratic purpose of audit: they identified that "Parliament will not be able to fulfil its scrutiny function effectively unless the NAO digitizes, unless it does that properly" (Participant 11).

Conclusion

This chapter explains the ability of institutional entrepreneurs within an SAI to further change – in this case the increased use of data analytics within public sector audit. The chapter does not comment on the successful implementation of this change. However, many interviewees told us that based on their subsequent experience (often after leaving the NAO), the NAO in this area was ahead of other Supreme Audit Institutions and at least in line with medium-sized private sector audit firms, and at times in line with the big four (Participant 11, Participant 17). The study does suggest that there were limitations to the success of the NAO's approach to change in this area (Participants 17, 23 and 27), but this has to be put in the context of the comparison with other organizations. There is a gap in the literature surrounding the implementation of digitalization in the public sector, including in audit (Ferry et al., 2022b). SAIs in general have proved resistant to digitalization (Otia & Bracci, 2022) and this chapter offers a contribution to the literature through examining how the NAO managed to introduce data analytics into its financial audit.

Scholars of institutional entrepreneurship have argued that entrepreneurs have success in trying to reshape institutions if they use arguments that are embedded in the institutions they seek to change. This is borne out by our study. The arguments offered by the institutional entrepreneurs in the NAO for improving the NAO's data analytics were based on practical audit experience and a rhetoric of modernization that they shared with senior management. Alongside Aldrich (2011), this chapter suggests that this was achieved neither by a single individual (though there were key people involved) nor by a single team, but by several individuals working across several teams within an organization. The NAO adopted a model effectively which relied upon its members of staff generating ideas in line with the cultural expectations of senior management and working together to achieve their goals across team boundaries. Agency and structure therefore were not alternatives, but actually worked together to generate change. Senior management may not have had the detailed understanding that team members on DART had, nor shared all of DART members' aspirations, but it is clear that they created space for DART to innovate within. This chapter therefore reinforces the insights of Tiberius et al. (2020) that structure and agency work together rather than separately. The limits to this approach also became visible during our interviews – as suggested above, DART was a stage within, rather than the culmination of, a process.

In the context of a conservative organization like an SAI, what the chapter suggests is that a mixed model of organizational support for change and institutional entrepreneurship can work to create an iterative process that leads to incremental change. Given that SAIs have struggled to digitalize in the main, the example of the UK NAO's approach to digitalization may be attractive to other practitioners. Taking advantage of a small organization where close links between the teams and senior management can be built and a common understanding of a problem can be sustained, the NAO has been able to allow staff the freedom to explore their own passions and then eventually back that exploration with organizational muscle. The process is unfinished and its results remain to be seen and require continued effort by the organization to sustain, but in contrast to Otia and Bracci's (2022) research, it is clear that many of the participants in our study viewed DART's work positively and saw it as a basis for further improvement.

In terms of the scholarship of SAIs, this chapter also contributes to the debate about the purpose of these bodies. Whereas scholars have argued that democratic motivations have or should be important to the continuing existence of SAIs (Dewar & Funnell, 2017; Ferry & Midgley, 2022), this chapter suggests that SAIs themselves are as exercised about their role as auditors as they are about their role as constitutional guardians. The literature which discusses the different logics embedded within public sector audit often approaches it by studying performance auditors, but this study examines the role of a team of technical experts largely supporting financial audit. As Bakre et al. (2021) suggest, financial auditors in the public sector are worthy objects of study themselves. The interesting questions for researchers that arise from this chapter relate to how this discussion of audit technology can relate to the democratic purposes of audit and what impact its links to the professional world will eventually have on its function in public sector audit in the long term.

Notes

1 Supreme Audit Institutions audit central government.
2 Since 1922, the UK has included England, Scotland, Wales and Northern Ireland. The National Audit Office is the Supreme Audit Institution of the UK and audits central government and has some involvement in the audit of English local government. There are separate audit institutions for the devolved governments in Northern Ireland, Wales and Scotland.
3 The term "big data" refers to extremely large data sets that may be analysed computationally to reveal patterns, trends and associations.
4 Blockchain is a system in which a record of transactions made in bitcoin or another cryptocurrency is maintained across several computers that are linked in a peer-to-peer network.
5 Artificial intelligence is a system by which a computer mimics cognitive functions that humans associate with other human minds.

References

Agostino, D., Bracci, E., & Steccolini, I. (2022). Accounting and accountability for the digital transformation of public services. *Financial Accountability & Management, 38*(2), 145–151.

Agostino, D., Saliterer, I., & Steccolini, I. (2022). Digitalization, accounting and accountability: a literature review and reflections on future research in public services. *Financial Accountability & Management, 38*(2), 152–176.

Ahrens, T., & Ferry, L. (2018). Institutional entrepreneurship, practice memory and cultural memory: choice and creativity in the pursuit of endogenous change of local authority budgeting. *Management Accounting Research, 38*, 12–21.

Aldrich, H. E. (2011). Heroes, villains and fools: institutional entrepreneurship NOT institutional entrepreneurs. *Entrepreneurship Research Journal, 1*(2), 1–4.

Alles, M. G. (2015). Drivers of the use and facilitators and obstacles of the evolution of big data by the audit profession. *Accounting Horizons, 29*(2), 439–449.

Appelbaum, D., Showalter, D. S, Sun, T., & Vasarhelyi, M. A. (2021). A framework for auditor data literacy: A normative position. *Accounting Horizons, 35*(2), 5–25.

Appelbaum, D. A., Kogan, A., & Vasarhelyi, M. A. (2018). Analytical procedures in external auditing: A comprehensive literature survey and framework for external audit analytics. *Journal of Accounting Literature, 40*, 83–101.

Aquino, A. C. B., Lino, A. F., & de Azevedo, R. R. (2022). The embeddedness of digital infrastructures for data collection by the courts of accounts. *Revista Contabilidade & Finanças, 33*(88), 46–62.

Aquino, A. C. B., Lino, A. F., de Azevedo, R. R., & da Silva, P. B. (2022). Digital affordances and remote public audit practice. *Financial Accountability & Management, 38*(3), 447–467.

Atayah, O. F., & Alshatar, M. M. (2021). Audit and tax in the context of emerging technologies: A retrospective analysis, current trends and future opportunities, *International Journal of Digital Accounting Research, 21*, 95–128.

Bakre, O. M., McCartney, S., & Fayemi, S. O. (2021). Accounting as a technology of neo-liberalism: The accountability role of IPSAS in Nigeria. *Critical Perspectives on Accounting.* https://doi.org/10.1016/j.cpa.2020.102282

Battilana, J., Leca, B., & Boxbaum, E. (2009). How actors change institutions: Towards a theory of institutional entrepreneurship. *Academy of Management Annals, 3*, 65–107.

Bowerman, M., Humphrey, C., & Owen, D. (2003). Struggling for supremacy: The case of UK public audit institutions. *Critical Perspectives on Accounting, 14*, 1–22.

Cao, M., Chychyla, R., & Stewart, T. (2015). Big data analytics in financial statement audits. *Accounting Horizons, 29*(2), 423–429.

Cao, T., Duh, R. R., Tan, H. T., & Tu, X. (2022). Enhancing auditors' reliance on data analytics under inspection risk using fixed and growth mindsets. *Accounting Review, 97*(3), 131–153.

Dewar, D., & Funnell, W. (2017). *A history of British National Audit: The pursuit of accountability.* Oxford University Press.

Eilifson, A., Kinserdal, F., Messier, W. F., & McKee, T. E. (2020). An exploratory study into the use of data analytics on audit engagements. *Accounting Horizons, 34*(4), 75–103.

Ferry, L., & Ahrens, T. (2022). The future of regulatory space in local government audit: A comparative study of the four nations of the United Kingdom. *Financial Accountability & Management, 38*(3), 376–393.

Ferry, L., Ahrens, T., & Khalifa, R. (2019). Public value, institutional logics and practice variation during austerity localism at Newcastle City Council. *Public Management Review, 21*(1), 96–115.

Ferry, L., Ruggiero, P., & Midgley, H. (2022). Where is public sector auditing: A comparative analysis. In L. Ferry & P. Ruggiero (Eds.), *Auditing practices in local government: An international comparison* (pp. 149–160). Emerald.

Ferry, L., & Midgley H. (2022). Democracy, accountability and the creation of the UK NAO as a defence of liberty. *Accounting, Auditing & Accountability Journal, 35*(2), 413–438.

Ferry, L., Midgley, H., Murphie, A., & Sandford, M. (2022a). Auditing governable space – a study of place based accountability in England. *Financial Accountability & Management.* https://doi.org/10.1111/faam.12321

Ferry, L., Midgley, H., & Ruggiero, P. (2023). Regulatory space in local government audit: An international comparative study of 20 countries. *Public Money & Management, 43*(3), 233–241. https://doi.org/10.1080/09540962.2022.2129559

Ferry, L., Radcliffe, V.S., & Steccolini, I. (2022b). The future of public audit. *Financial Accountability and Management, 38*(3), 325–336.

Foster, H., & Knox, C. (2022). The "eyes and ears of Parliament": Devolved public accounts committees in the UK. *Journal of Legislative Studies.* https://doi.org/10.1080/13572334.2022.2079860

Free, C., Radcliffe, V. S., Spence, C., & Stein, M. J. (2020). Auditing and the development of the modern state. *Contemporary Accounting Research, 37*(1), 485–513.

Friedland, R., & Alford, R. (1987). Bringing society back in: Symbols, practices and institutional contradictions. In S. Lash & S. Whimster (Eds.), *Max Weber, rationality and modernity* (pp. 232–263). Allen and Unwin.

Funnell, W. (2003). Enduring fundamentals: constitutional accountability and auditors-general in the reluctant state. *Critical Perspectives on Accounting, 14*, 107–132.

Funnell, W. (2007). The reason why: The English constitution and the latent promise of liberty in the history of accounting. *Accounting, Business and Financial History, 17*(2), 265–283.

Garud, R., Hardy, C., & Maguire, S. (2007). Institutional entrepreneurship as embedded agency: An introduction to the special issue. *Organisation Studies, 28*(7), 957–969.

Greenwood, R., Oliver, C., Lawrence, T. B., & Meyer, R. E. (2017). Introduction: Into the fourth decade. In *The SAGE handbook of organizational institutionalism* (pp. 1–23). SAGE.

Greenwood, R., & Suddaby, R. (2006). Institutional entrepreneurship in mature fields: The big five accounting firms. *Academy of Management Journal, 49*(1), 27–48.

Hazgui, M. Triantafillou, P., & Christensen, S. E. (2022). On the legitimacy and apoliticality of public sector performance audit: Exploratory evidence from Canada and Denmark. *Accounting, Auditing & Accountability Journal*, 35(6), 1375–1401. https://doi.org/10.1108/AAAJ-04-2020-4508

Hébert, R. F., & Link, A. N. (1989). In search of the meaning of entrepreneurship. *Small Business Economics, 1*, 39–49.

Hyvönen, Järvinen, J., Oulasvirta, L., & Pellinen, J. (2012). Contracting out municipal accounting: The role of institutional entrepreneurship. *Accounting, Auditing & Accountability Journal, 25*(6), 944–963.

Issa, H., Sun, T., & Vasarhelyi, M. A. (2016). Research ideas for artificial intelligence in auditing: The formalization of audit and workforce supplementation. *Journal of Emerging Technologies in Accounting, 13*(2), 1–20.

Jackall, R. (1988). *Moral mazes: The world of corporate managers*. Oxford University Press.

Kend, M., & Nguyen L. A. (2022). The emergence of audit data analytics in existing audit spaces: Findings from three technologically advanced audit and assurance service markets. *Qualitative Research in Accounting & Management, 19*(5), 540–563.

Kokina, J., & Davenport, T. H. (2017). The emergence of artificial intelligence: How automation is changing audit. *Journal of Emerging Technologies in Accounting, 14*(1), 115–122.

Krieger, F., Drews, P., & Velte, P. (2021). Explaining the (non-)adoption of advanced data analytics in auditing: A process theory. *International Journal of Accounting Information Systems, 41*, 1–24.

Leoni, G., & Parker, L. (2019). Governance and control of sharing economy platforms: Hosting on Airbnb. *British Accounting Review, 51*(6), 1–22.

Lino, A. F., Aquino, A. C. B., & Neves, F. R. (2022). Accountants postures under compulsory digital transformation imposed by oversight bodies. *Financial Accountability & Management, 38*(2), 202–222.

Liston-Heyes, C., & Juillet, L. (2022a). What has become of the audit explosion? Analyzing trends in oversight in the Canadian government. *Public Administration, 100*(4), 1073–1090. https://doi.org/10.1111/padm.12793

Liston-Heyes, C., & Juillet, L. (2022b). Institutional embeddedness and the language of accountability: Evidence from 20 years of Canadian public audit reports. *Financial Accountability & Management, 38*(4), 608–632. https://doi.org/10.1111/faam.12336

Löhlein, L., & Müßig, A. (2020). At the boundaries of institutional theorizing: individual entrepreneurship in episodes of regulatory change. *Accounting, Organizations and Society, 83*, 1–21.

Lombardi, R., De Villiers, C., Moscariello, N., & Pizzo, M. (2021). The disruption of blockchain in auditing – a systematic literature review and an agenda for future research. *Accounting, Auditing and Accountability Journal, 35*(7), 1534–1565. https://doi.org/10.1108/AAAJ-10-2020-4992

Maguire, S., Hardy, C., & Lawrence, T.B. (2004). Institutional entrepreneurship in emerging fields: HIV/Aids treatment advocacy in Canada. *Academy of Management Journal, 47*, 657–679.

Major, M., Conceição, A., & Clegg, S. (2018). When institutional entrepreneurship failed: The case of a responsibility centre in a Portuguese hospital. *Accounting, Auditing & Accountability Journal, 31*(4), 1199–1229.

Manita, R., Elommal, N., Baudier, P., & Hikkerova, L. (2020). The digital transformation of external audit and its impact on corporate governance. *Technological Forecasting and Social Change, 150*, 1–10.

Mattei, G., Grossi, G., & Guthrie, J. (2021). Exploring past, present and future trends in public sector auditing research: A literature review. *Meditari Accountancy Research, 29*(7), 94–134.

Midgley, H. (2019). The National Audit Office and the select committee system 1979–2019. *Parliamentary Affairs, 72*(4), 779–798.

Morin, D., & Hazgui, M. (2016). We are much more than watchdogs: the dual identity of auditors at the National Audit Office. *Journal of Accounting & Organizational Change, 12*(4), 568–589.

National Audit Office (NAO). (2022). *Annual Report and Accounts 2021–22*. National Audit Office (NAO) corporate information.

Opara, M., Okafor, O. N., Ufodike, A., & Kalu, K. (2021). Institutional entrepreneurship: Collaborative change in a complex Canadian organization. *Accounting, Auditing & Accountability Journal, 34*(9), 284–314.

Orlandi, A. (2021). The emergence of double entry bookkeeping in Tuscan firms of the thirteenth and fourteenth centuries. *Accounting History, 26*(4), 534–551.

Otia, J. E., & Bracci, E. (2022). Digital transformation and the public sector auditing: The SAI's perspective. *Financial Accountability & Management, 38*(2), 252–280.

Pallot, J. (2003). A wider accountability? The audit office and New Zealand's bureaucratic revolution. *Critical Perspectives on Accounting, 13*(1–2), 133–155.

Power, M. (2022). Afterword: Audit Society 2.0? *Qualitative Research in Accounting & Management.* http://dx.doi.org/10.1108/QRAM-03-2022-0040

Radcliffe, V. (1998). Efficiency audit: An assembly of rationalities and programmes. *Accounting, Organizations and Society, 23*(4), 377–410.

Rana, T., Steccolini, I., Bracci, E., & Dessalegn, G. M. (2022). Performance auditing in the public sector: A systematic literature review and future research avenues. *Financial Accountability & Management, 38*(3), 337–359.

Salijeni, G., Samasanova-Taddei, A., & Turley, S. (2019). Big data and changes in audit technology: Contemplating a research agenda. *Accounting and Business Research, 49*(1), 95–119.

She, C., & Michelon, G. (2019). Managing stakeholder perceptions: Organised hypocrisy in CSR disclosures on Facebook. *Critical Perspectives on Accounting, 61*, 54–76.

Skærbæk, P. (2009). Public sector auditor identities in making efficiency auditable: The National Audit Office of Denmark as independent auditor and moderniser. *Accounting, Organisations and Society, 34*(8), 971–987.

Stewart, E., & Connolly, C. (2022). UK public sector fiscal reporting: Clear and contradictory. *Accounting Forum.* https://doi.org/10.1080/01559982.2022.2133339

Suskind, R., & Suskind, D. (2015). *The future of the professions: How technology will transform the work of human experts.* Oxford University Press.

Sutheewasinnon, P., Hoque, Z., & Nyamori, R.O. (2016). Development of a performance management system in the Thailand public sector: Isomorphism and the role and strategies of institutional entrepreneurs. *Critical Perspectives on Accounting, 40*, 26–44.

Tiberius, V., Rietz, M., & Bouncken, R.B. (2020). Performance analysis and science mapping of institutional entrepreneurship research. *Administrative Sciences, 10*(3), 69.

Torres, L., & Cabeza, I. (2022). Local government auditing in Spain. In L. Ferry & P. Ruggiero (Eds.), *Auditing practices in local government: An international comparison* (pp. 121–130). Emerald.

Vasarhelyi, M., Kogan, A., & Tuttle, B.M. (2015). Big data in accounting: An overview. *Accounting Horizons, 29*(2), 381–396.

Wang, Y., & Kogan, A. (2018). Designing confidentiality preserving Blockchain-based transaction processing systems. *International Journal of Accounting Information Systems, 30*, 1–18.

5

ACCOUNTING CHANGE IN THE PUBLIC SECTOR

Rearranging deck chairs on the *Titanic*?

Noel Hyndman and Mariannunziata Liguori

Introduction

Change and crisis are concepts often intertwined (Liguori & Steccolini, 2012; Al Mahameed et al., 2021). In the public sector, change in accounting systems has frequently been seen largely as a reaction to external influences (Liguori & Steccolini, 2012; Hodges & Lapsley, 2016), this view having been particularly strengthened in recent years as a reaction to emergencies such as the Covid-19 pandemic, the 2008 Great Recession and ongoing climate-change challenges. However, accounting in the public sector is not new to such challenges. Ideas related to New Public Management (NPM)[1] (and associated accounting changes) were themselves introduced, from the 1970s onwards, largely in response to ballooning public sector expenditure and perceived widespread inefficiencies (seen as crises themselves). Crises provide the conditions for great reforms, and the opportunity to develop new systems and roles. In light of the long history and research on public sector accounting change and the more recent developments and crises, this contribution sets out to provide some possible lenses to reinterpret processes of accounting change and crises, finally suggesting possible ways forward.

Now, perhaps more than ever before, there is the need to reflect on the roles public sector accounting and accountability systems (however broadly these terms are defined) have played so far, and consider possible beneficial future adjustments to systems as they seek to underpin emerging (and new) challenges. In doing this, it must always be remembered that accounting is not a socially neutral activity and it contains the potential both to support and, at times, to hamper processes of change (Catchpowle & Smyth, 2016).

The chapter is structured as follows: firstly, it explores the meaning of accounting change, particularly focusing on the process of change and how it might lead merely to changes in the tools and systems of accounting (incremental change), or, alternatively, how it might result in radical change, whereby actors' thoughts and actions (interpretive schemes) are also affected. This is presented to offer an overview of some of the ideas and concepts that are used in the subsequent sections of the chapter. This is followed by a more articulated discussion of the links between crisis (a time of intense difficulty or danger) and accounting change, illustrating how a crisis provides a fertile ground for the implementation of change and the possible disruption of existing systems. This is augmented in the subsequent section by reflecting on NPM, which (we posit) represented a discourse largely emerging from a perceived crisis (or sequence of crises), and a number of related key accounting changes . Finally, the chapter concludes with thoughts on what we can learn, and the proposal of future research

DOI: 10.4324/9781003295945-7

questions and themes that may further our understanding of the role of public sector accounting in responding to crises. Are new tools and systems merely cosmetic (the deckchairs on the *Titanic* only having been rearranged) or, more positively, have they been developed and used to enhance the effectiveness, efficiency and efficacy of public sector policies, as a basis for improving public-service delivery (thus, preventing the ship from sinking)?

Accounting change and change processes

In both accounting and organizational theory, the definition of what constitutes change, and its relationship with the external environment, has always been at the centre of a lively debate (Quattrone & Hopper, 2001, Christensen et al., 2019). Accounting change has been examined across different geographical and temporal spaces to try to explain variations (Hyndman & Liguori, 2018). Resistance to accounting change (Christiaens & Rommel, 2008; Jayasinghe et al., 2021), as a factor in slowing down processes of change or even turning suggested possible adjustments into "unresolved" (or "unresolvable") contestable notions, has been identified as an issue, alongside debates regarding "the appropriate model" to support a particular change implementation (Vaivio, 1999; Liguori & Steccolini, 2012). According to Quattrone and Hopper (2001), how and why accounting information is produced and changed, and its effects on the organization, are the result of the dynamic interaction between the context and the fabrications of knowledge within the organization itself. It is argued that accounting has the ability to connect multiple organizational worlds, times and spaces, rather than representing a static and centred measurement activity for predetermined ends.

Change is usually defined as the process of making something different (possibly by a far-reaching replacement, or by a significant alteration or modification). It identifies differences in form, quality or state of a certain entity or practice over time (van de Ven & Poole, 1995). An important body of literature has focused on the antecedents and consequences of accounting change (Jones & Mellett, 2007; Liguori & Steccolini, 2012; Hyndman & Liguori, 2018). Understanding accounting change is important in order to be able to predict both likely future individual behaviours, and possible organizational reactions to crises and subsequent structural adjustments. This is an ongoing concern in relation to both external reporting (for instance, in deciding whether or not to embrace international accounting standards) and within organizations (for example, in relation to designing new control systems that highlight non-financial performance measures). The extant literature has typically examined the dichotomy between exogenous and endogenous factors affecting change, and the extent to which adopting organizations are successful (in terms of both implementation and in relation to desired outcome).

In order to explain the final outcome/success of change, public sector accounting studies have largely focused on exogenous factors, such as technology, market and institutional pressures (Modell et al., 2007; Liguori & Steccolini, 2012), and endogenous factors, such as leadership, capabilities, culture and power (Gigli & Mariani, 2018; Odia & Oke, 2018). The most-utilized theoretical lens in public sector accounting studies on change has overwhelmingly been institutional theory (Powell & DiMaggio, 1991; Scott, 2001). Here, a number of authors (Modell et al., 2007; Liguori & Steccolini, 2012; Hyndman & Liguori, 2018 and 2019) have focused on the institutionalization of change as a result of external social and technical influences (albeit emphasizing different aspects of the same broad theory). In doing so, they explored the ability of an organization to change by investigating how institutionalized norms, values and practices affect an organization's available choice set, as well as individual behaviours and decisions. While institutional theory remains one of the main theoretical lenses utilized in public sector accounting research, more recently, studies have also looked at accounting change, broadly defined, through the lenses of epistemic communities (Irvine et al., 2011), governmentality (Christensen et al., 2019), and actor-network theory (Christensen & Skærbæk, 2010). Recent literature has also highlighted the important role of agency during change, using, for instance, ideas from institutional entrepreneurship (Argento et al., 2018) and considerations of the role of accountants and the accounting profession (Christensen et al., 2019).

Other studies have examined the process of accounting change itself (Burns & Scapens, 2000; Liguori, 2012a and 2012b; ter Bogt & Scapens, 2019). Processes of change have generally been classified through four main models that highlight change in terms of: (i) natural evolution (as continuous competitive selection of the fittest); (ii) life cycle and stages of pre-ordered regulated change; (iii) dialectic conflict (between thesis, antithesis and synthesis), and (iv) teleology (as purposeful change and action towards a predetermined aim) (van de Ven & Poole, 1995; van de Ven & Sun, 2011). Change can, therefore, be seen as either continuous or punctuated. In this respect, punctuated equilibrium theory (Miller & Friesen, 1984) suggests that organizations go through relatively long periods of evolutionary convergence that are interspersed with (or punctuated by) relatively short periods of dramatic revolutionary change often triggered by changes in the external environment (Brown & Eisenhardt, 1997). According to this view, organizations might address change through ad-hoc, punctuated responses (Fox-Wolfgramm et al., 1998). However, many authors, especially in organization theory, have argued that indiscriminate rapid/revolutionary change across many different organizational elements rarely accurately describes how change actually takes place. Indeed, change can happen at different paces, both evolutionary (when change occurs slowly and gradually) and revolutionary (when change happens swiftly and affects most parts of an organization simultaneously) (Liguori, 2012a). Moreover, despite the strength of external influences, pressures to implement and accept changed practices may vary among organizations, and these are influenced by both structures and the potential role of agency. Attempts to address these aspects in accounting studies have employed institutional approaches to investigate relationships between the socially constructed institutional realm (structure) and the realm of action (agency) (Burns & Scapens, 2000; Hyndman & Liguori, 2018).

A competing interpretation of a punctuated process of change has been offered by archetype theory (Liguori & Steccolini, 2012; Hyndman & Liguori, 2018). An archetype is defined as a set of structures and systems that reflects a certain interpretive scheme, made up of ideas, beliefs and values (Greenwood & Hinings, 1993). Accounting structures and systems can, therefore, be seen as embodiments of ideas and values (such as NPM ones) that are associated with an overarching and prevailing interpretive scheme. According to this approach, change is not indiscriminate, but happens differently on the basis of the levels involved (i.e. systems and structures and/or interpretive schemes). The consistency of change with an existing archetype defines the distinction between incremental and radical change. The former takes place when organizations modify their structures and systems in a way that is consistent with the existing archetype. Radical change, instead, involves a shift in both structures and systems and values/interpretive schemes from an existing archetype to a new one (Greenwood & Hinings, 1996). The concept of incremental change similarly recalls the idea of "first order" change used in some accounting studies (Laughlin, 1991; Broadbent, 1992), which involves shifts in managerial arrangements and organizational systems, but where the interpretive schemes remain largely untouched and undisturbed. Conversely, radical change implies the idea of "second order" change, where major shifts also occur in the core value systems (interpretive schemes) of an organization.

Accounting change and recent crises: an overview

For many years, accounting has been at the centre of attention for its role in shaping and being shaped by crises (Tregidga & Laine, 2022). While most studies still tend to replicate the internal versus external dichotomy of change, they also show an increasing awareness of the role that accounting can play in affecting major societal issues, often going far beyond traditional organizational boundaries. Moreover, accounting research has recently started to investigate, more systematically, natural disasters and humanitarian crises (Sargiacomo et al., 2014; Sargiacomo, 2015), trying to explore the role of accounting and the way in which accountability may enhance trust in such circumstances from a critical and interpretive perspective (Sciulli, 2018). While for some changes introduced as a result of recent crises (such as environmental disasters and the Covid-19 pandemic) it may be a tad early to express a definite judgement, most of the related accounting and reporting changes were initially presented as radical improvements for accountability and transparency (especially towards citizens). However, in reality, the so-far quite limited and scattered implementation of these would seem to suggest a less disruptive, more incremental, process of change.

For instance, Hopwood (2009), reflecting on the 2008 financial crisis and how it highlighted problems and inadequacies in existing accounting systems, claimed that accounting studies often examined current practices, but only seldom challenged and questioned them. It was argued, under this perspective, crises have the potential to generate managerial innovations, and accounting should be studied within its community rather than at a distance. Perhaps unsurprisingly, both externally and internally orientated accounting practices have been found to have changed as a result of the 2008 financial crisis, with this underpinning even greater momentum towards harmonization and isomorphism (Bhimani, 2008). Although not specifically looking at the public sector, van Der Stede (2011) highlighted an increased demand for disclosure as a consequence of this crisis. For example, calls were made for greater scrutiny and external disclosure of a range of organizational arrangements that were previously considered internal matters only. Commenting on this, van Der Stede argued that these calls could be viewed as opportunities to explore change by revisiting previously researched topics in new ways. This could result in a greater appreciation of their wider roles in society, particularly when used in different cultures and countries. Similar reflections came to the fore in public sector literature, in relation to both the 2008 "Great Recession" (Hodges & Lapsley, 2016) and, in general, when reflecting on austerity policies that brought about a number of adjustments in the tools and technologies of accounting (Bracci et al., 2015; Barbera et al., 2020). Some of these adjustments (such as those related to budget flexibility and NPM) have been found to be associated with processes of both radical and incremental change (for a more in-depth discussion, see the following section).

The connection between crises and the role of accounting in the public sector has been identified also in relation to environmental challenges. For example, suggesting the achievement of marginal incremental changes, it is contended that environmental accounting (despite the challenge of agreeing how such a concept might be operationalized and constructed) has failed to provide a long-term approach and create a sense of urgency in the collective response, with this failure being even more pronounced during the Covid-19 pandemic (Tregidga & Laine, 2022). Notwithstanding this, calculative practices (accounting numbers) have been shown to have considerable power as they can be captured, monitored and used (at times, almost as ammunition) to develop and reinforce policy and steer individual behaviour (Tregidga & Laine, 2022; Polzer & Goncharenko, 2022). Crises can, therefore, represent the trigger, excuse or learning space for accounting change. Cho et al. (2022), for instance, while recognizing the difficulties and limitations of traditional environmental accounting, saw great potential in its multidisciplinarity and ability to bring different management and decision-making areas together. They suggested that adopting a system approach, rather than a single-organization focus, can bolster strategy formulation and generate more effective outcomes.

A significant body of literature on the crisis generated by the Covid-19 pandemic has recently relatively quickly developed. Many of these studies point out changes implemented with the aim of reducing uncertainty and ambiguities connected to the crisis (Grossi et al., 2020; Bastida et al., 2022). An observation of responses across countries, moreover, suggests that the most "successful" (potentially radical) reactions to the health emergency have occurred where social, ecological and financial considerations (reinforced by novel accountability tools) have come together (Leoni et al., 2022). Throughout Europe, in particular, accounting and performance measurement have been increasingly found to support governments in their decisions and monitoring activities (Mitchell et al., 2021;

Polzer & Goncharenko, 2022). Also, in countries with different administrative traditions (such as South Korea), the pandemic has provided the context for increased government surveillance based on control measures that hold citizens increasingly accountable (Ahn & Wickremasinghe, 2021).

NPM (and related changes) as a response to crisis

Since the 1970s, many Western governments have engaged in reform processes aimed at improving public sector practices, frequently embracing so-called NPM ideas, seen as a necessary replacement for Traditional Public Administration (TPA). A main area of change has involved far-reaching adjustments in accounting systems (ter Bogt, 2008; Vivian & Maroun, 2018). Justifications are often framed in terms that good (better) information is needed to ensure good (better) decisions (making government more effective and efficient), and to underpin accountability processes (reinforcing good governance). The origins of NPM, however, can be traced to the post–World War II crisis in Western economies. After the war, almost all developed Western economies expanded the role of government rapidly, with spending of social programmes being a particular feature. For example, in the USA, public social spending as a per cent of GDP rose from 0.56 per cent in 1930 to 8.86 per cent in 1980 (Ortiz-Ospina & Roser, 2016). Comparable figures for France and the UK are 1.05 per cent and 2.24 per cent respectively (1930), and 20.23 per cent and 15.59 per cent (1980). The increased role of the state was largely due to the rise in expectations and a demand for greater equality following the conflict. A recurring theme at this time was that for citizens to participate appropriately in society, they had to have at least minimum access to services such as health, education and housing (Sanderson, 1996). By the 1970s, major concerns about the impact of this began to be expressed, with particular focus on limited private incentives for innovation, and the tendency towards inefficiency (and lack of competition) in public-service provision (Flynn & Strehl, 1996; Lane, 2000; Bovaird & Loffler, 2003; Pollitt & Bouckaert, 2017).

This "crisis" forced governments to examine, among other things, the role of the state, the way public services were delivered to citizens, and the accountability of the public sector. Such reflections (frequently framed as an impending public sector crisis by right-of-centre political leaders) provided the foundation for the articulation and crafting of NPM reforms, and momentum to push related NPM accounting changes into the public sector. Indeed, without such changes, it has been argued that the potential beneficial impact of many of the NPM-inspired policies would be weakened (Chan, 2003; Likierman, 2003). As a consequence, and as a response to the then newly identified "crisis" (or crises), there was a significant and progressive movement away from bureaucratic, TPA-related accounting routines and towards more "modern" and business-like tools in many governments, both at a central and a local level. This could be interpreted, following previous theoretical considerations, as an example of a planned and intended, disruptive and punctuated process of change, where a sequence of external jolts and reforms contributed to reshape a whole range of both intra- and inter-organizational accounting structures and systems (Liguori, 2012b).

With respect to financial accounting, budgetary control and performance management systems (key components of all accounting systems), reactions to this crisis (or crises) resulted in: cash accounting being replaced with accrual accounting; much greater flexibility in budgeting, with significant devolution of budgets and strict annuality relaxed to permit less-centralized control; and a much stronger emphasis on performance management both at the individual and the organizational level. The information from these systems often fed into, and supported, other more-specific accounting-related decision-making, reporting and accountability processes.[2] But has such a disruptive, sometimes revolutionary, process of change actually improved decision-making and accountability? Or, is this current architecture of accounting incapable of addressing crises and unduly complex, possibly even undermining public sector values? In the last 20 years, several systematic literature reviews have been carried out on public sector accounting research and accounting change (including Broadbent &

Guthrie, 2008; De Vries & Nemec, 2013). While the contribution in this chapter does not aim to repli-cate such significant and valuable efforts of systematization of the topic, it offers a critical perspective on public sector accounting change, building on this existing literature.

With respect to financial accounting, moves from cash-based to accrual-based private sector-style accounting systems have been common in many countries, at both the national and the local level. Accrual accounting, in particular, often claimed as superior to cash accounting, has represented a real groundbreaking, disruptive change. It was argued that, among other things, traditional cash systems have inherent biases against capital investment, while accrual accounting encourages better-informed decisions on the balance between current and capital expenditure, and provides a more meaningful basis for deter-mining cost (Cavanagh et al., 2016). Such views suggest that accrual accounting can provide accurate, objective information to support rational decision-making. However, a key criticism of the application of such systems to the public sector is that proponents have deliberately oversold and under costed them (Lapsley et al., 2009). Moreover, potential problems regarding the development, implementation and use of such systems have been highlighted by a range of researchers. Among these concerns are: the unnecessary complexity of the systems themselves (Connolly & Hyndman, 2006); the fact that key users (including politicians and senior managers) have great difficulty in understanding (and engaging with) the information produced (Brusca Alijarde, 1997; Guthrie, 1998; Ezzamael et al., 2005); and the claim that accrual accounting fails to focus on key public sector issues (Ezzamel et al., 2007; Newberry & Pont-Newby, 2009). It has also been opined that if accrual accounting systems are to be used, reporting schedules employed (and financial reporting standards adopted) should be kept as simple as possible, and the needs (and abilities) of politicians and managers ought to be central in system design decisions (Hyndman, 2016). However, there is little evidence to suggest such an approach has generally been followed. Indeed, based on a review of governmental accounting experiences, Christiaens and Rommel (2008) argued that, because of the complexity of systems (expert talk) and the limitations of many users to engage with the information, if accrual accounting is applied in public sector settings at all, its use should be restricted to business-like (parts of) government.

Budgets are representations of planned spending (and possibly performance) of an organization over a particular period of time (often a year). Budget rules can vary by country and by level of government. However, typically, under TPA, budgets: specify (by types/heads of expenditure) what (usually) cash amounts can be spent in the future period; allow no (or limited) virement (thereby restricting the ability to move money from one part of a budget to another); require the principle of annuality to be followed (compelling budget holders to spend their budget by the period end, or, if unspent, to surrender it to the centre); and oblige the budget holder, ex-post, to report on the budget available and actual spending against it. Overall, this aims to ensure centralized control of finance. Aspects of such an approach jar with proponents of NPM, and relaxation of these tendencies has been observed in contemporary budgeting and control systems in a variety of settings. For instance, in the UK, Hyndman et al. (2007) examined the impact of the apparent abolition of annuality and its replacement with end-year flexibility (EYF). This was viewed as an aspect of NPM thinking related to less centralized control and greater local freedoms in budgeting. Among the research findings were the following: annuality continued to impact on the vast majority of budget holders despite its apparent abolition; and, any significant additional freedoms were restricted to very high organiza-tional levels. Interestingly, in the UK, in 2011, in response to the government revenue impacts of the 2008 global financial crisis, EYF was abolished and replaced with a much more restrictive, and centrally controlled, system of "Budget Exchange", a reversion to TPA principles as a response to the crisis. In terms of the choice regarding the use of cash or accrual budgeting, Reichard and van Helden (2016) explored the use of both accrual-based and cash-based systems of external reporting and budgeting. While recognizing the influence of NPM, and that, via such a lens, having accrual-based systems for both budgeting and reporting seemed consistent and preferable, they opined that there are good reasons for not doing this. They argued that, even if accrual-based systems are used for external reporting purposes (with it remaining a moot point whether or not this is desirable), there is a strong case, based on logic, understandability and ease of use, for retaining cash as the focus for the budgeting system. Similar conclusions were drawn by Christiaens and Rommel (2008). Moreover, the challenges of using performance information in the construction of public sector budgets (especially where output/outcome information is difficult/impossible to standardize) have been shown to generate significant dysfunctional effects, often resulting in the abandonment, or major revisions, of initially introduced, performance aspects of such systems (Edwards et al., 1996; Galarraga et al., 2020; Poulsen et al., 2022).

A key theme of many of the NPM structural reforms in the public sector is that strategy should come about by highly systematized forms of planning. Such an approach encourages the development of detailed architectures of performance replete with specific and quantified goals, objectives, targets and performance measures. As a consequence, a myriad of performance management systems have been developed across many aspects of the public sector (departments, agencies, hospitals, schools, universities etc.) and in many counties. These seek to steer individuals and organizations towards desired outcomes and provide the basis for a discharge of performance accountability (Birrell & Gray, 2018; Berri et al., 2019; Dal Mas et al., 2019). Yet, such an approach is not problem free. Often these systems are based on simple production (or logic) models of performance (using the terms input, output and impact; W.K. Kellogg Foundation, 2004) with an emphasis on efficiency and effectiveness. While this may work well when an organization has easily identifiable (and relatively few) standardized outputs, and clearly specified (and easily quantified) objectives, this is frequently not the case with public sector organizations. Many of these, on the contrary: have multiple (and competing) goals and objectives that are difficult to quantify; lack a direct and knowable link between intentions and outcomes; and, if required, can be manipulated (or gamed) to accord with evaluation processes being used at higher organizational levels (Grossi et al., 2019). Moreover, such systems encourage a concentration on "quantification" and a lack of regard for "judgement" in evaluative processes. This is particularly problematical when dealing with multiple higher-level outputs/impacts where "softer" judgement by qualified evaluators is often critical. Additional difficulties arise when systems are developed by those far removed from the point of delivery, offering an abundance of different numbers related to (continually changing) specific aspects of the organization's activity, and where overall "scores" are framed into "objective" league table formats for external reporting (Wiggins & Tymms, 2002; Muller, 2018). In both healthcare and education, for example, this has been a particular issue, with inappropriate systems frequently encouraging significant mission drift; with highly questionable ethical, organizational and individual behaviour; and with an undermining of the social ethos (and contribution) of the organization (Broadbent & Guthrie, 2008; Lilford & Pronovost, 2010; Parker, 2012; ter Bogt & Scapens, 2012; Poulsen et al., 2022). In many of these settings, the realization of the effect of inappropriate performance frameworks led to discontinuance (or extreme modification) of the original systems, but often not before significant damage was already done (Murphy et al., 2019). Moreover, even in systems where "success" is claimed, it has been shown that there is still a tendency for financial imperatives to dominate and for short-run issues to take precedence over longer-term strategic thrusts (Ferry & Murphy, 2018; Kloot & Martin, 2000).

Accounting change: rearranged deck chairs or a buoyancy aid to reduce the likelihood (and impact) of crises? – Discussion and concluding remarks

How has the process of accounting change played out, and to what extent can such changes support the avoidance of crisis and/or facilitate appropriate responses to crisis? Given the size, range and variety of changes to public sector accounting, and the various countries in which change has occurred, such questions have no simple, universally applicable, answers, but are largely rhetorical devices to reflect on what has occurred and suggest what has been learnt. What we know is that, under the widespread influence of NPM ideas (developing from a crisis itself), disruptive and radical accounting changes occurred in a number of Western democracies. As discussed, these still affect behaviours and shape responses to new crises to this day. So what have we learnt?

In terms of financial accounting, perhaps what needs to be acknowledged most is that accrual accounting is complex expert talk. In its most technical version, it is very difficult for non-specialists to appreciate its particular nuances. At present, most users do not (and cannot) understand its complexities, be they public sector managers, politicians or the electorate generally. New accrual accounting systems (for example, those supporting environmental reporting) are in place, often facilitated by external providers who may benefit significantly from the system development support they have provided. However, a lack of knowledge of the concept of accrual accounting weakens its potential use in the political sphere (undermining democratic accountability), in relation to many day-to-day public sector management decisions (weakening its decision-making potential), and in terms of the general populace (diminishing its ability to provide wider financial accountability). New tools are often set in place, but with limited enhancement of understanding and limited use, consequently resulting in incremental change rather than the radical change often espoused by the proponents of the instrument. In such a context, the extent of the effectiveness of the new financial accounting systems in highlighting, combating or pre-empting a crisis (i.e. a time of intense difficulty or danger) is inevitably quite limited. If change is to be more than cosmetic/incremental, users of the information (especially managers and politicians) need to be educated in terms of what the numbers mean. In the language of O'Neill (2006), the information has to be both "accessible to" and "assessable by" key stakeholders if it is to be useful and lead to substantial, meaningful (radical) change. There is limited evidence to date that this has been achieved.

As far as budgeting is concerned, it is interesting to note that many of the accounting modifications initially introduced were developed with the aim of providing managers (be it in local or central government) with freedom and flexibility to improve spending decisions. Greater budget responsibility was provided to those close to the delivery interface, with the expectation that this would facilitate more effective management, and, ultimately, reduce public sector expenditure. New reporting systems were developed to facilitate this. Again, this was initially seen as a reaction to the public sector spending crisis that provided the foundation for the emergence of NPM. However, difficulties with regard to this aspect have become evident in terms of managing the budget (with many new budget holders often having limited previous experience of detailed financial management) and the related problems of having to generate and use accrual information (see the comments on understandability above). Interestingly, as a reaction to another crisis (the 2008 financial crisis), a number of countries rowed back on some previous NPM budget changes to ensure greater central control. Such a trajectory has been supported and advised by the International Monetary Fund itself during the Covid-19 pandemic (Curristine et al., 2020). While periods of crisis can, indeed, trigger substantial reforms, this particular aspect marked a reversion to the TPA principles of public management. Therefore, it can be suggested that, during crises, processes of change and reform do not necessarily take on a linear trajectory. Rather, oscillations of accounting change can occur, with the direction (and type) of change being affected by the type of crisis. During the 2008 financial crisis, for instance, short-term financial control ideas seemed to trump the desire to get both better long-term spending effectiveness and lower baselines for budgets.

Finally, the widespread development of performance frameworks is perhaps the accounting change most frequently viewed as having the greatest potential in terms of improving management and accountability processes in the public sector (Hyndman & Liguori, 2018; Muller, 2018). However, it is also the area with the most striking examples of problems relating to the design and operation of systems, and where, frequently, major dysfunctional consequences emerge very visibly and starkly. These relate, among other things, to: the privileging of unsuitable metrics; chaos and misunderstanding facilitated by too many (and poorly aligned) measures; extensive gaming of systems; and simplistic evaluation processes focusing on numbers to the exclusion of much-needed judgement and context considerations. Yet, arguably, performance measurement is also the accounting area where most "new stuff" (tools and systems) has emerged and which most individuals (well beyond finance specialists) have taken note of. Metrics and indicators, for instance, have proved essential in the management of the recent Covid-19 pandemic. It is clear that individuals and organizations have changed their focus as a consequence of the use of such systems, but not necessarily always for "good" (in terms of both the organization and society at large). Indeed, given widespread problems in their use, these systems appear to go through a continual process of adjustment and reinvention (develop, review, abandon/ revise), and have an almost constant major influence on the direction of organizations and reactions of individuals. Is this incremental, radical or just chaotic change? Or is it a necessary iterative and heuristic process to support a journey towards a desired teleological aim? In this respect, significant problems seem to arise more often when: frameworks are developed away from those responsible for service delivery; "league tables" (often using a variety of measures, some of which have dubious validity) are generated that have widespread external visibility; and funding is heavily associated with the achievement of "good" numbers. Conversely, in cases where performance measures are used in a "softer", less transactional, manner, primarily directed at internal consumption, and have a learning and development focus, system problems seem to be less severe (Eden & Hyndman, 2001). Performance management frameworks probably represent the area which is most amenable to supporting how governments and society grapple with crises that are not largely financial (see, for example, health or climate change). Well-developed non-financial performance frameworks can give visibility to problems in advance, facilitating (in the language of Snow & Benford, 1988) a "call to arms" that can motivate discussion, reflection and action (Ferry & Murphy, 2018; Murphy et al., 2019).

If this is what we have learnt, how can we now tackle new challenges/crises and move forward? The literature and ideas discussed throughout this chapter suggest three main areas of reflection that could be addressed by both academics and practitioners in the not-too-distant future. These are outlined below in the form of broad research questions.

How do we (governments, practitioners in the sector, academics, society at large) define and construct a crisis and its meaning?

While we have witnessed an increasing number of studies dealing with accounting and crises/external shocks, it is important to remember that individual constructions of a crisis (and the subsequent solutions to it) are likely to affect behaviours and coping mechanisms. Is a major change or crisis (such as financial recessions, environmental disasters etc.) identified only when this is perceived to be radical/disruptive (or second order, involving both systems and ideas/values)? And how does the individual and collective construction of a crisis happen? Shedding more light on these aspects may help predict reactions and suggest more appropriate strategies of actions, not only from a theoretical point of view but also at a policy level.

How are accounting systems and technologies understood by different actors and levels of government, and how can these be made (realistically and practically) useful to anticipate and manage periods of crisis?

As discussed earlier in the chapter, the role of agency (and skills) is important during processes of change, something that has also been rediscovered in more recent accounting research. More studies are needed to unpack key actors' cognitive black boxes and their understanding of the purpose and use of accounting tools. It is argued that both research and practice should respectively strive to explore and implement changes that actually matter and, especially, can be understood and used widely inside an organization.

How does the role and shape of accounting tools and practices (including accrual accounts, budgets and performance measures) transform in light of different processes of change and crises?

Previous literature and theory suggest that processes of change can be characterized by a different pace, and that crises and disruptive changes can, in reality, take place with both evolutionary and revolutionary paces. We could, however, expect different processes of change and crisis to be associated with a greater introduction and use of certain accounting tools rather than others. This aspect has been, so far, less investigated, although it has clear implications on the effectiveness of the choices made, as well as the meaningfulness of the accounting information generated and communicated during crises.

These research themes are, of course, only indicative and three of many possible others that could be posed about the relationship between accounting and crisis. How we shall answer these (and similar) questions in the future will help us gauge and understand whether accounting tools (and the way they are implemented and used) are merely a means to rearrange the deck chairs on the *Titanic* at a time of crisis, or they can actually be used as devices that have the potential to stop ships (and governments) from sinking.

Notes

1 Hood (1991) suggested that NPM is a convenient (though loose) term that is shorthand for a set of broadly similar administrative doctrines. He identifies the main theme of NPM as including: a shift in emphasis from policymaking to management skills; the stressing of output rather than process; and the introduction of much greater competition through restructuring and the development of contract relationships. In contrast, he opines that Traditional Public Administration (TPA) ideas dominated public service delivery regimes since the late nineteenth century to the early 1980s, these having at their centre the rule of law, where politics and administration are clearly separated and the hegemony of professionals is dominant. More recently, an assertion that the NPM emphasis has itself been superseded by New Public Governance (NPG) (a wide and more inclusive system of ideas, based on partnerships among government, business and citizens) has been debated (Rhodes, 1997; Osborne, 2006 and 2010), although Hyndman et al. (2014) suggest that the three approaches (TPA, NPM and NPG) are not mutually exclusive and, in many countries, result in progressive sedimentation (or layering) of ideas over time, with NPM ideas still dominating.

2 For example, this is the case in the use of accounting information in decisions relating to the outsourcing and financing of capital projects (Lapsley & Pallot, 2000; Demirag et al., 2012; Jansson et al., 2021; Tallaki & Bracci, 2021; Verweij & van Meerkerk., 2021). Given the length constraints of this chapter, detail regarding these more specific decision situations, albeit worthy of examination and reflection, is not discussed.

References

Ahn, P., & Wickramasinghe, D. (2021). Pushing the limits of accountability: Big-data analytics containing and controlling COVID-19 in South Korea. *Accounting, Auditing and Accountability Journal, 34*(6), 1320–1331.

Al Mahameed, M., Belal, A., Gebreiter, F., & Lowe, A. (2021). Social accounting in the context of pro-found political, social and economic crisis: The case of the Arab Spring. *Accounting, Auditing &Accountability Journal, 34*(5), 1080–1108.

Argento, D., Peda, P., & Grossi, G. (2018). The enabling role of institutional entrepreneurs in the adoption of IPSAS within a transitional economy: the case of Estonia. *Public Administration and Development, 38*, 39–49.

Barbera, C., Jones, M., Korac, S., Saliterer, I., & Steccolini, I. (2021). Local government strategies in the face of shocks and crises: The role of anticipatory capacities and financial vulnerability. *International Review of Administrative Sciences, 87*(1), 154–170.

Bastida, F., Bracci, E., & Hoque, Z. (2022). Accounting for unstable environments in the public sector: managing post-COVID-19 times. *Journal of Public Budgeting, Accounting & Financial Management, 34*(1), 1–26.

Beeri, I., Uster, A., & Vigoda-Gadot, E. (2019). Does performance management relate to good governance? A study of its relationship with citizens' satisfaction with and trust in Israeli local government. *Public Performance & Management Review, 42*(2), 241–279.

Bhimani, A. (2008). The role of a crisis in reshaping the role of accounting. *Journal of Accounting and Public Policy, 27*(6), 444–454.

Birrell, D., & Gray, A. M. (2018). Outcomes-based approaches and the devolved administrations. C. Needham, E. Heins, & J. Rees (Eds.), *Social Policy Review, 30*, 67–86.

Bovaird, T., & Loffler, E. (2003). *Public management and governance*. Routledge.

Bracci, E., Humphrey, C., Moll, J., & Steccolini, I. (2015). Public sector accounting, accountability and austerity: More than balancing the books? *Accounting, Auditing & Accountability Journal, 28*(6), 878–908.

Broadbent, J. (1992). Change in organisations: A case study of the use of accounting information in the NHS. *British Accounting Review, 24*(4), 343–367.

Broadbent, J., & Guthrie, J. (2008). Public sector to public services: 20 years of contextual accounting research. *Accounting, Auditing & Accountability Journal, 21*(2), 129–169.

Brown, S. L., & Eisenhardt, K. M. (1997). The art of continuous change: Linking complexity theory and time-paced evolution in relentlessly shifting organizations. *Administrative Science Quarterly, 42*(1), 1–34.

Brusca Alijarde, M. (1997). The usefulness of financial reporting in Spanish local governments. *Financial Accountability & Management, 13*(1), 17–34.

Burns, J., & Scapens, R. W. (2000). Conceptualizing management accounting change: An institutional framework. *Management Accounting Research, 11*(3), 3–25.

Catchpowle, L., & Smyth, S. (2016). Accounting and social movements: An exploration of critical accounting praxis. *Accounting Forum, 40*(3), 220–234.

Cavanagh, J., Flynn, S., & Moretti, D. (2016). *Implementing accrual accounting in the public sector*. International Monetary Fund.
www.imf.org/external/pubs/ft/tnm/2016/tnm1606.pdf

Chan, J. (2003). Government accounting: An assessment of theory, purposes and standards, *Public Money & Management, 23*(1), 13–20.

Cho, C. H., Senn, J., & Sobkowiak, M. (2022). Sustainability at stake during COVID-19: Exploring the role of accounting in addressing environmental crises. *Critical Perspectives on Accounting, 82*. https://doi.org/10.1016/j.cpa.2021.102327

Christensen, M., Newberry, S., & Potter, B. N. N. (2019). Enabling global accounting change: Epistemic communities and the creation of a more business-like public sector. *Critical Perspectives on Accounting, 58*, 53–76.

Christensen, M., & Skærbæk, P. (2010). Consultancy outputs and the purification of accounting technologies. *Accounting, Organizations and Society, 35*(5), 524–545.

Christiaens, J., & Rommel, J. (2008). Accrual accounting reforms: Only for business-like (parts of) governments. *Financial Accountability & Management, 24*(1), 59–75.

Connolly, C., & Hyndman, N. (2006). The actual implementation of accruals accounting: Caveats from a case within the UK public sector. *Accounting, Auditing & Accountability Journal, 19*(2), 272–290.

Curristine, T., Doherty, L., Imbert, B., Sheik Rahim, F., Tang, V., & Wendling, C. (2020). *Budgeting in a crisis: Guidance for preparing the 2021 budget*. International Monetary Fund. www.imf.org/-/media/Files/Publications/covid19-special-notes/en-special-series-on-covid-19-budgeting-in-a-crisis-guidance-on-preparing-the-2021-budget.ashx

Dal Mas, F., Massaro, M., Lombardi, R., & Garlatti, A. (2019). From output to outcome measures in the public sector: A structured literature review. *International Journal of Organizational Analysis, 27*(5), 1631–1656.

De Vries, M., & Nemec, J. (2013). Public sector reform: An overview of recent literature and research on NPM and alternative paths. *International Journal of Public Sector Management, 26*(1), 4–16.

Demirag, I., Khadaroo, I., Stapleton, P., & Stevenson, C. (2012). The diffusion of risks in public private partnership contracts. *Accounting, Auditing & Accountability Journal, 25*(8), 1317–1339.

Eden, R., & Hyndman, N. (2001). Rational management, performance targets and executive agencies: Views from agency chief executives in Northern Ireland. *Public Administration, 79*(3), 579–598.

Edwards, P., Ezzamel, M., Robson, K., & Taylor, M. (1996). Comprehensive and incremental budgeting in education: The construction and management of formula funding in three English local education authorities. *Accounting, Auditing & Accountability Journal, 9*(4), 4–37.

Ezzamel, M., Hyndman, N., Johnsen, A., Lapsley, I., & Pallot, J. (2005). Conflict and rationality: Accounting in Northern Ireland's devolved assembly. *Financial Accountability & Management, 21*(1), 33–55.

Ezzamel, M., Hyndman, N., Johnsen, A., Lapsley, I., & Pallot, J. (2007). Experiencing institutionalization: The development of new budgets in the UK devolved bodies. *Accounting, Auditing & Accountability Journal, 20*(4), 11–40.

Ferry, L., & Murphy, P. (2018). What about financial sustainability of local government! A critical review of accountability, transparency, and public assurance arrangements in England during austerity. *International Journal of Public Administration, 41*(8), 619–629.

Flynn, N., & Strehl, F. (1996). *Public sector management in Europe*. Prentice Hall.

Fox-Wolfgramm, S. J., Boal, K. B., & Hunt, J. (1998). Organizational adaptation to institutional change: A comparative study of first-order change in prospector and defender banks, *Administrative Science Quarterly, 43*(1), 87–126.

Galarraga, J., Black, B., Pimentel, L., Venkat, A., Sverha, J., Frohna, W., Lemkin, D., & Pines, J. (2020). The effects of global budgeting on emergency department admission rates in Maryland. *Annals of Emergency Medicine, 75*(3), 370–381.

Gigli, S., & Mariani, L. (2018). Lost in the transition from cash to accrual accounting. *International Journal of Public Sector Management, 31*(7), 811–826.

Greenwood, R., & Hinings, C. (1996). Understanding radical organisational change: Bringing together the old and the new institutionalism. *Academy of Management Review, 21*(4), 1022–1054.

Greenwood, R., & Hinings, C. R. (1993). Understanding strategic change: The contribution of archetypes. *Academy of Management Journal, 36*(5), 1052–1081.

Grossi, G., Ho, A. T., & Joyce, P. G. (2020). Budgetary responses to a global pandemic: International experiences and lessons for a sustainable future. *Journal of Public Budgeting, Accounting & Financial Management, 32*(5), 737–744.

Grossi, G., Kallio, K., Sargiacomo, M., & Skoog, M. (2019). Accounting, performance management systems and accountability changes in knowledge-intensive public organizations: A literature review and research agenda. *Accounting, Auditing & Accountability Journal, 33*(1), 256–280.

Guthrie, J. (1998). Application of accrual accounting in the Australian public sector – rhetoric or reality. *Financial Accountability & Management, 14*(1), 1–19.

Hodges, R., & Lapsley, I (2016). A private sector failure, a public sector crisis – reflections on the great recession. *Financial Accountability & Management, 32*, 265–280.

Hood, C. (1991). A public management for all seasons? *Public Administration, 69*(1), 3–19.

Hopwood, A. (2009). The economic crisis and accounting: Implications for the research community. *Accounting, Organizations and Society, 34*(6/7), 797–802.

Hyndman, N. (2016). Accrual accounting, politicians and the UK – with the benefit of hindsight. *Public Money & Management, 36*(7), 477–479.

Hyndman, N., Jones, R., & Pendlebury, M. (2007). An exploratory study of annuality in the UK public sector: Plus ça change, plus c'est la même chose? *Financial Accountability & Management, 23*(2), 215–237.

Hyndman, N., & Liguori, M. (2018). Achieving radical change: A comparative study of public-sector accounting in Westminster and Scotland. *Accounting, Auditing & Accountability Journal, 31*(2), 428–455.

Hyndman, N., & Liguori, M. (2019). Accounting change in the Scottish and Westminster central governments: A study of voice and legitimation. *Financial Accountability & Management, 35*(4), 390–412.

Hyndman, N., Liguori, M., Meyer, R., Polzer, T, Rota, S., & Seiwald, J. (2014). The translation and sedimentation of accounting reforms: A comparison of the UK, Austrian and Italian experiences. *Critical Perspective on Accounting, 25*(4–5), 388–408.

Irvine, H., Cooper, C., & Moerman, L. (2011). An epistemic community as influencer and implementer in local government accounting in Australia. *Financial Accountability & Management, 27*, 249–271.

Jansson, M., Carlström, E., Karlsson, D., & Berlin, J. (2021). Drivers of outsourcing and backsourcing in the public sector – from idealism to pragmatism. *Financial Accountability & Management, 37*(3), 262–278.

Jayasinghe, K., Adhikari, P., Soobaroyen, T., Wynne, A., Malagila, J., & Abdurafiu, N. (2021). Government accounting reforms in Sub-Saharan African countries and the selective ignorance of the epistemic community: A competing logics perspective. *Critical Perspectives on Accounting, 78*,(2), 102246. https://doi.org/10.1016/j.cpa.2020.102246

Jones, M., & Mellett, H. (2007). Determinants of changes in accounting practices: accounting and the UK Health Service. *Critical Perspectives on Accounting, 18*(1), 91–121.

Kloot, L., & Martin, J. (2000). Strategic performance management: A balanced approach to performance management issues in local government. *Management Accounting Research, 11*(2), 231–251.

Lane, J. E. (2000). *New public management*. Routledge.

Lapsley, I., Mussari, R., & Paulsson, G. (2009). On the adoption of accrual accounting in the public sector: A self-evident and problematic reform. *European Accounting Review, 18*(4), 719–723.

Lapsley I., & Pallot J. (2000). Public sector capital: Policy reforms and accounting mutations. In E. Caperchione & R. Mussari (Eds.), *Comparative issues in local government accounting* (pp. 35–52). Springer.

Laughlin, R. (1991). Environmental disturbances and organisational transitions and transformations: Some alternative models. *Organization Studies, 12*(2), 209–232.

Leoni, G., Lai, A., Stacchezzini, R., Steccolini, I., Brammer, S., Linnenluecke, M., & Demirag, I. (2022). The pervasive role of accounting and accountability during the COVID-19 emergency. *Accounting, Auditing & Accountability Journal, 35*(1), 1–19.

Liguori, M. (2012a). The supremacy of the sequence: Key elements and dimensions in the process of change. *Organization Studies, 33*(4), 507–539.

Liguori, M. (2012b). Accounting and public sector reforms: A comparison of Italian and Canadian municipalities. *Financial Accountability & Management, 28*, 437–463.

Liguori, M., & Steccolini, I. (2012). Accounting change: Explaining the outcomes, interpreting the process. *Accounting, Auditing & Accountability Journal, 25*, 27–70.

Likierman, A. (2003). Planning and controlling UK public expenditure on a resource basis. *Public Money & Management, 23*(1), 45–50.

Lilford, R., & Pronovost, P. (2010). Using hospital mortality rates to judge hospital performance: A bad idea that just won't go away. *British Medical Journal, 340*, 955–957.

Miller, D., & Friesen, P. (1984). *Organizations: A quantum view.* Prentice-Hall.

Mitchell, F., Nørreklit, H., Nørreklit, L., Cinquini, L., Koeppe, F., Magnacca, F., Mauro, S. G., Jakobsen, M., Korhonen, T., Laine, T., & Liboriussen, J. M. (2021). Evaluating performance management of COVID-19 reality in three European countries: A pragmatic constructivist study. *Accounting, Auditing & Accountability Journal, 34*(6), 1345–1361.

Modell, S., Jacobs, K., & Wiesel, F. (2007). A process (re)turn? Path dependencies, institutions and performance management in Swedish central government. *Management Accounting Research, 18*, 453–475.

Muller, J. (2018). *The tyranny of metrics.* Princeton University Press.

Murphy, P., Ferry, L., Glennon, R., & Greenhalgh, K. (2019). *Public service accountability: Rekindling a debate.* Palgrave Macmillan.

Newberry, S., & Pont-Newby, S. (2009). Whole of government accounting in New Zealand: The ownership form of control. *Public Money & Management, 29*(4), 235–242.

O'Neill, O. (2006). Transparency and the ethics of communication. In C. Hood & D. Heald (Eds.), *Transparency: The key to better governance?* Proceedings of the British Academy (pp. 74–90). Oxford University Press.

Odia, J. O., & Oke, S. (2018). Change in management accountant roles: A comparative study of two public-sector organizations in Nigeria. *Journal of Accounting, Finance and Auditing Studies, 4*(3), 198–222.

Ortiz-Ospina, E., & M. Roser (2016). *Government spending.* Our world in data. https://ourworldindata.org/government-spending

Osborne, S. P. (2006). The new public governance? *Public Management Review, 8*(3), 377–387.

Osborne, S. P. (2010). *The new public governance? Emerging perspectives on the theory and practice of public governance.* Routledge.

Parker, L. (2012). From privatised to hybrid corporatised higher education: A global financial management discourse. *Financial Accountability & Management, 28*(3), 247–268.

Pollitt, C., & Bouckaert, G. (2017). *Public management reform: A comparative analysis – into the age of austerity.* Oxford University Press.

Polzer, T., & Goncharenko, G. (2022). The UK COVID-19 app: The failed co-production of a digital public service. *Financial Accountability & Management, 38*, 281–298.

Poulsen, M. L., Bukh, P. N., & Christensen, K. S. (2022). (Dys)functionality of intentions or outcomes? Performance funding of Danish schools. *Accounting, Auditing & Accountability Journal, 36*(1), 267–294. https://doi.org/10.1108/AAAJ-12-2020-5034.

Powell, W., & DiMaggio, P. J. (1991). *The new institutionalism in organizational analysis.* University of Chicago Press.

Quattrone P., & Hopper, T. (2001). What does organizational change mean? Speculations on a taken for granted category. *Management Accounting Research, 12*, 403–435.

Reichard, C., & van Helden, J. (2016). Why cash-based budgeting still prevails in an era of accrual-based reporting in the public sector. *Accounting, Finance & Governance Review, 23*(1), 43–65.

Rhodes, R. (1997). *Understanding governance: Policy networks, governance, reflexivity and accountability.* Open University Press.

Sargiacomo, M. (2015). Earthquakes, exceptional government and extraordinary accounting. *Accounting, Organizations and Society, 42*, 67–89.

Sargiacomo, M., Ianni, L., & Everett, J. (2014). Accounting for suffering: Calculative practices in the field of disaster relief. *Critical Perspectives on Accounting, 25*(7), 652–669.

Sciulli, N. (2018). Weathering the storm: Accountability implications for flood relief and recovery from a local government perspective. *Financial Accountability & Management, 34*, 30–44.

Scott, W. R. (2001). *Institutions and organizations*. SAGE.

Snow, D., & Benford, R. (1988). Ideology, frame resonance, and participant mobilization. In B. Klandermans, H. Kriesi, & S. Tarrow (Eds.), *From structure to action: Social movement participation across cultures* (pp. 197–217). JAI Press.

Tallaki, M., & Bracci, E. (2021). Risk allocation, transfer and management in public–private partnership and private finance initiatives: A systematic literature review. *International Journal of Public Sector Management, 34*(7), 709–731.

ter Bogt, H. (2008). Management accounting change and new public management in local government: A reassessment of ambitions and results – an institutionalist approach to accounting change in the Dutch public sector. *Financial Accountability & Management, 24*(3), 209–241.

ter Bogt, H., & Scapens, R. (2012). Performance management in universities: effects of the transition to more quantitative measurement systems. *European Accounting Review, 21*(3), 451–497.

ter Bogt, H., & Scapens, R. (2019). Institutions, situated rationality and agency in management accounting: A research note extending the Burns and Scapens framework. *Accounting, Auditing & Accountability Journal, 32*(6), 1801–1825.

Tregidga, H., & Laine, M. (2022). On crisis and emergency: Is it time to rethink long-term environmental accounting? *Critical Perspectives on Accounting, 82*(2), 102311. https://doi.org/10.1016/j.cpa.2021.102311

Vaivio, J. (1999). Exploring a "non-financial" management accounting change. *Management Accounting Research, 10*(4), 409–437.

van de Ven, A. H., & Poole, M. S. (1995). Explaining development and change in organizations. *Academy of Management Review, 20*(3), 510–540.

van de Ven, A. H., & Sun, K. (2011). Breakdowns in implementing models of organization change. *Academy of Management Perspectives, 25*(3), 58–74.

van der Stede, W. A. (2011). Management accounting research in the wake of the crisis: Some reflections. *European Accounting Review, 20*(4), 605–623.

Verweij, S., & van Meerkerk, I. (2021). Do public–private partnerships achieve better time and cost performance than regular contracts? *Public Money & Management, 41*(4), 286–295.

Vivian, B., & Maroun, W. (2018). Progressive public administration and new public management in public sector accountancy: An international review. *Meditari Accountancy Research, 26*(1), 44–69.

Wiggins, A. , & Tymms, P. (2002). Dysfunctional effects of league tables: A comparison between English and Scottish primary schools. *Public Money & Management, 21*(1), 43–48.

PART III

Management control, innovation and change

6

COLLABORATIVE INNOVATION AND MANAGEMENT CONTROL IN TIMES OF CRISIS

Tensions of a disrupted project in public healthcare

Daniela Argento and Eva Lövstål

Introduction

The public sector is increasingly relying on projects to innovate public service delivery (Godenhjelm & Johanson, 2018). Organizing work in projects is appealing because ad-hoc, temporary projects are argued to be an organizational solution that enables both flexibility and control (Fred, 2020; Godenhjelm & Johanson, 2018). Projects usually involve different internal and external stakeholders whose collaboration is viewed as a source for innovation. As proposed by Agger and Sørensen (2018, p. 56),

> collaboration between public employees from different public agencies and levels of governance as well as between public actors and private firms, civil society actors and citizens with different mindsets, experiences, ideas, knowledge and skills can reveal the deficiencies of existing policies, services and governance practices and inspire the development, realization and diffusion of new ones.

However, collaborative innovation projects within the public sector entail management challenges due to their inherent complexities. Firstly, multi-stakeholder projects are intricate because the involved stakeholders can bear different and potentially competing interests, goals and demands. Secondly, these kinds of projects display a multitude of management principles and practices that compete for attention (Agger & Sørensen, 2018; Fred, 2020). For example, the manager of a public innovation project needs to deal with the formalities of public sector organizations and funding agencies, at the same time as being flexible and responsive to unforeseeable reactions and events. In addition, the temporary nature of projects requires the manager to create and control a transitory organization while having to consider, and maybe being constrained by, the permanent public sector organization and its ordinary duties (Fred, 2020). Furthermore, given that such projects rely on collaboration, the project manager must foster and steer horizontal relationships among stakeholders. Simultaneously, vertical relationships need to be sustained to cope with the traditional hierarchies of the public sector. Accordingly, collaborative innovation projects in the public sector are filled with tensions derived from coexisting and often competing management principles and practices as well as different stakeholder demands.

DOI: 10.4324/9781003295945-9

The literature has discussed organizational tensions in the context of innovations (e.g. Potočnik et al., 2022; Smith et al., 2017), management control (e.g. Lövstål & Jontoft, 2017; van der Kolk et al., 2020) as well as interorganizational collaborations (e.g. Lewis et al., 2010). Some studies have focused on public organizations specifically (e.g. Agger & Sørensen, 2018; Lee, 2022). Research has also discussed and studied how tensions can be managed by practitioners, for example through the use of communication (Lewis et al., 2010) and a balanced use of controls (e.g. Mundy, 2010). However, more knowledge about where the tensions arise within collaborative innovation projects and how they are dealt with is needed. This chapter aims to explore tensions and how they evolve and influence the control practices in a collaborative innovation project within the public sector. It adds to previous research by studying project tensions over time, thereby increasing the understanding of the dynamics of collaborative innovation projects and the role of controls in dealing with tensions (see also Stevens & Agger, 2017). The chapter also complements previous research by particularly addressing how the balancing of controls is affected by an unexpected crisis (Covid-19) and the accountability constraints of funding agencies which impose strict deadlines and target achievement expectations. In a period of crisis, such as the Covid-19 pandemic, tensions might be even more evident because strategic and long-term issues need to be considered along with immediate solutions to overcoming the crisis (Kober & Thambar, 2022; Pradies et al., 2021). Since crises imply threats to organizations, and consequently increase safeguarding behaviour, tensions between project stakeholders' interests and goals might also be intensified.

The empirical focus is on Digital Innovation in Dementia Care (DIDEC), a collaborative innovation project in the field of dementia care implemented in the Municipality of Perstorp in the south of Sweden. Dementia is a healthcare field that has been neglected from an innovation perspective, while the number of people with dementia illness is increasing quite dramatically (Brankaert & den Ouden, 2013; OECD, 2015; Seabrooke & Alisoun, 2014). The complexity and character of the disease require innovation methods built on collaboration among many stakeholders (Brankaert & den Ouden, 2013) with complementary expertise and resources, such as care centres, health professionals, entrepreneurs and funders (Lee et al., 2010; Ramirez, 1999). The project was financed by one of the European Union's (EU's) funding programmes.

The findings show how the tensions emerging in the DIDEC project were well managed through balancing the use of both formal and informal controls. Unfortunately, the project had to be stopped due to the Covid-19 pandemic. Even if good results were produced and a long-term positive impact was expected, the project was interrupted by the need to comply with formal targets and expected results set in the funding agreement. The case illustrates how tensions, first being approached as dualities in which competing demands are dealt with simultaneously, turn into real dilemmas which cannot be solved. Contrary to Kober and Thambar (2022), who claimed that controls can be helpful to navigate a crisis, we argue that formal controls easily override informal ones in times of crisis because of external pressures and the temporary nature of the project.

The remainder of the chapter is structured as follows. The next section reviews the public management/administration and management control literature that is relevant in the context of collaborative innovation projects in the public sector. The following section presents the research method, while the next two sections illustrate the findings. The chapter ends by discussing findings and advancing final reflections.

Tensions within collaborative innovation projects in the public sector

Tensions, intended as competing demands, are an inevitable feature of organizational life which managers must respond to (Gaim & Wåhlin, 2016; Smith & Lewis, 2011). Tensions can occur on different organizational levels as well as in project organizations (Lövstål & Jontoft, 2017; Smith & Lewis, 2011). They can also take various forms and be approached differently. Several researchers suggest a paradoxical approach to tensions, acknowledging that competing demands are contradictory yet interdependent and need to be dealt with simultaneously (Gaim & Wåhlin, 2016; Lewis et al., 2017; Sharma & Bansal, 2017). Thus, paradoxes – like dualities – reflect a both-and perspective. On the contrary, trade-offs and dilemmas suggest an either-or situation in which one contradictory demand is selected or prioritized (Gaim et al., 2018).

Different types of tensions can exist in collaborative innovation projects in the public sector and for various reasons (see e.g. Agger & Sørensen, 2018; Lewis et al., 2010; Lövstål & Jontoft, 2017). Due to complex multi-stakeholder settings characterized by different agendas, goals and expectations, one type of tension emerges from the availability of resources and different interpretations of the desired results (cf. Smith & Lewis, 2011). In principle, a project organization is a means of integrating the competencies and skills of different stakeholders with the aim of achieving the goal and targets of the project (Lee et al., 2010; Laya et al., 2018). However, while some stakeholders might focus on quality aspects (i.e. long-term impact of the results of the project), others are more concerned with the achievement of the maximal return (i.e. efficient use of resources within the time frame of the project) or aim for maximal uniqueness (i.e. the innovativeness of the project) (Blomberg, 2013). Thus, to continuously align interests and goals, and create a common win-win feeling, these different and sometimes competing demands have to be managed.

A second type of tension emerges due to stakeholders' potentially diverging opinions on how the project should be managed and good results achieved (cf. Agger & Sørensen, 2018; Marrewijk et al., 2008). Projects aimed at innovating public service delivery lead to the establishment of temporary organizations and require the appointment of project managers who work at the interface of different organizational boundaries (see Turner & Müller, 2003). Process-related tensions can occur because project managers in a public setting need to respect the predefined procedures and criteria typical of public sector bureaucracy (Agger & Sørensen, 2018). Similarly, funding agencies, such as the EU, often promote a traditional approach to project management, characterized by standardized procedures, timelines and deadlines, as well as well-defined budgets and targets (Büttner & Leopold, 2016). Other stakeholders, such as entrepreneurs and public employees, expect more flexible work methods which allow for experimentation and mutual learning.

A third type of tension relates to project organization structures and relationships. Acting at the border of several organizations can create tensions between external stakeholders and the internal dynamics of the permanent organization as well as inside the temporary project organization (Lewis et al., 2010). Accordingly, in collaborative innovation projects, contacts with external stakeholders must be handled at the same time as fostering close relationships with internal members. Drawing on the concepts of Godenhjelm and Johanson (2018), both strong and weak ties have to be managed. A project manager also needs to consider the permanent organization and its structure and tasks on the one hand, and the temporary project organization on the other. In addition, and considering the public context, there may be a tension between different forms of authority (Agger & Sørensen, 2018). The public organization is characterized by a hierarchical authority structure, whereas a collaborative innovation project requires a structure of horizontal decision-making and network communication (see also Godenhjelm et al., 2015).

Combination of control forms

Steering, coordination and control are crucial to dealing with the tensions that arise in collaborative innovation projects in the public sector. The temporary and complex nature of projects which focus on innovation, and are carried out in collaboration, impact the choice and combination of controls. Effective controls are needed to support collaboration and ensure that stakeholders constantly agree upon the core content and value of innovations, as well as support processes and working methods over time (Hakanen & Jaakkola, 2012). The term "management control" refers to the use of techniques and procedures that encourage and ensure employees act consistently with organizational goals (Bürkland et al., 2019; Merchant & Van der Stede, 2017). The term is no longer associated with a command-and-control approach based on top-down management, formal agreements and quantitative performance measures (Davila et al., 2009). It is approached from a more holistic and softer perspective, including a variety of controls forms (Artto et al., 2011; Chenhall, 2003). In the context of collaborative innovation projects, conventional control ideas emphasize elements such as regulation, goal congruence and standardization, whereas innovation asks for creativity, flexibility and long-term returns (Adler & Chen, 2011; Davila et al., 2009; Lövstål & Jontoft, 2017). Holistic approaches to control, incorporating also enabling, interactive and informal control forms, suggest that a well-balanced use of different control forms can be a way of dealing with tensions (Mundy, 2010).

The management control literature has delved into classifying control forms. A common classification distinguishes between formal and informal controls (Collier, 2005; Grafton & Mundy, 2011; Pan Fagerlin & Lövstål, 2020). Formal controls include plans, written contracts and other organizational mechanisms for ensuring cooperation leads to goal achievement (Collier, 2005; Dekker, 2004). They are implemented to ensure that the involved parties accomplish their duties (Klein Woolthuis et al., 2005; Van Dooren et al., 2010). Informal control is instead related to mechanisms such as group norms, socialization and culture inducing self-regulation (Collier, 2005; Dekker, 2004). Informal controls include trust, open communication and dialogue (Almqvist, 2001; Van der Meer-Kooistra & Vosselman, 2000). Trust is intended as the willingness to believe the other party might not act opportunistically (Dekker, 2004; Edelenbos & Klijn, 2007; Van der Meer-Kooistra & Vosselman, 2000). It facilitates cooperation among parties (Näslund, 2018; Högberg et al., 2018) and can enhance the capacity to solve problems and foster innovation (Edelenbos & Klijn, 2007; Klijn et al., 2010). Good communication and dialogue among the stakeholders are means of keeping interests constantly aligned and ensuring that the potentially different agendas do not collide (Argento & Peda, 2015). In sum, informal controls, such as shared beliefs and values between organizations, can be an effective and efficient means of monitoring the behaviour of partners (Grafton & Mundy, 2011).

Research on the combination between formal and informal controls has produced mixed findings (Klein Woolthuis et al., 2005; Six, 2013; Seal & Vincent-Jones, 1997; Ditillo et al., 2015). It has been argued that if there is trust between parties, then there is no need for detailed contracts (Van der Meer-Kooistra & Vosselman, 2000). If low or no trust exists, the use of tight contracts is advocated as it can be expected that the interactions between parties are of a more conflicting nature (Seal & Vincent-Jones, 1997). In this sense, the use of tight contracts can be beneficial in the early stages of a collaborative innovation project when trust has not yet been developed. Formal controls based on accounting figures can interact with trust-building behaviours (Vosselman & van der Meer-Koistra, 2009). Informal controls can reinforce formal controls in public sector settings characterized by intense vertical and horizontal relationships (Nyland et al., 2017). In addition, if controls are too rigid and repressive, partners' knowledge generation will suffer having a negative effect on innovation and project performance. Informal controls can enable parties to explore alternative options to solve problems and develop new suggestions (Edelenbos & Klijn, 2007; Klijn et al., 2010). However, excessive freedom may lead the project team towards dispersive, unfocused and ineffectual efforts which might not promote project performance (Ylinen & Gullkvist, 2014). A complementary use of formal and informal forms of control can therefore enhance the performance of a collaborative innovation project as each form compensates for the weakness and potential side effects of the other one.

The balancing act that managers perform when implementing project control systems becomes more challenging when a sudden crisis threatens the fate of a collaborative innovation project.

A worldwide pandemic, like the one caused by Covid-19, is likely to affect the public sector, and innovation attempts can be hampered due to the sudden need to redirect resources and attention elsewhere (Argento et al., 2020). The abrupt scarcity of resources and the need to solve unplanned problems, in addition to emerging and not necessarily aligned views on the problem to be solved, challenges the ability of project managers, and the project organization, to meet the original goals, thus escalating the tensions between the project's competing demands and expectations. The focus tends to be oriented towards short-term, internal operational matters, while long-term strategic issues might be neglected. The use of adequate control forms can prevent this short-term focus from happening (Kober & Thambar, 2022).

Empirical setting and method

This chapter builds upon the results of our engagement in the collaborative innovation project named Digital Innovation for Dementia Care (DIDEC) from September 2017 to March 2021. The project was funded by the European Union Regional Development Fund with the aim of improving the quality of life of individuals with dementia by developing new technological solutions and innovative products for dementia care. To fulfil this aim, DIDEC relied on the creation of a *living lab* in the real-life setting of the Österbo dementia care centre (from now on Österbo), which is located in Perstorp (region Skåne, in the south of Sweden) and owned by the Municipality of Perstorp. A living lab is a set-up that can foster collaborative creation of innovations (Gascó, 2017) allowing entrepreneurs and health professionals to test various solutions in the daily life of people living in dementia care centres. A living lab is characterized by the continuous interaction of various stakeholders that wish to jointly innovate the products and services for people with dementia (Brankaert & den Ouden, 2013).

The living lab was meant to allow companies to co-create innovative solutions in collaboration with the personnel and management of Österbo. Key stakeholders of the living lab were the Municipality of Perstorp (the formal project owner), three project managers, the managers and employees of Österbo, companies willing to test new solutions and products, two science incubators (co-funders), and the EU (main funder). The project organization consisted of a steering group including project managers, representatives of the Municipality and the science incubators, and researchers (without voting rights). While the project was up and running, the crisis caused by the Covid-19 pandemic brought the entire project to a halt, and after an initial six-month suspension, due to the prohibition against accessing elderly care centres, the project was forced to stop.

The research presented in this chapter is based on an interventionist research approach (Suomala et al., 2014; Lukka & Wouters, 2022). The possibility of acting as interventionist researchers and closely following the various stages of the DIDEC project, enabled us to collect rich data by studying collaborative innovation processes over three and a half years, which suggests that the study can be classified as a longitudinal field study. The empirical research involved both moments of active participation in living lab activities and steering group meetings, where we could advise project managers and owners on how to proceed in, for example, the contacts with entrepreneurs and interactions with employees, and moments of autonomous reflections. This is in line with an interventionist approach where the researchers intervene within the studied real-life setting, but also take a step back in order to produce trustworthy and valid scientific findings (Suomala et al., 2014; Lukka & Wouters, 2022). A descriptive summary of the project learnings is available in Argento and Lövstål (2021).

To reach a broad and deep understanding of the development of DIDEC, mixed methods of empirical data collection were used. The data collection methods were primarily of a qualitative character, but some minor quantitative analysis of questionnaires occurred as well. Methodological triangulation, or the use of multiple methods of data collection, enhances the validity of this research project

(Thomas, 2004) and allows for a deeper comprehension of the tensions that emerged throughout the project and how these tensions were dealt with through the project managers' use of controls. The following data collection methods were used:

- *Observations* in approximately 25 meetings, workshops and training sessions took place. The observations can be defined as "open participant observations" (Thomas, 2004) because we had an explicit role within the DIDEC project and were known by the participants. During such observations, systematic diaries were written to keep track of the themes that were discussed, the decisions that were made, the challenges/problems encountered, and the different perspectives/feedback of various actors. We constantly compared our impressions and made joint reflections about the data that was being collected.
- Ten semi-structured *interviews* were conducted with project managers, one representative of the Municipality of Perstorp, the managers of the two departments of Österbo in which testing took place, one entrepreneur representing the company that tested their product in the living lab, and three innovation advisers of the science incubators. In addition, informal conversations with health professionals took place during workshops and training sessions that we observed.
- Formal *documents*, such as descriptions of DIDEC's project goals and work processes, communications plans, illustrative presentations of innovation models, and reports of the steering group meetings, as well as email conversations, are additional data that we collected. We systematized those documents and materials in our archive. The analysis of these documents is appropriate for the longitudinal character of this field study and allowed us to corroborate the findings stemming from the interviews and observations.
- Short *questionnaires* were administered on two occasions. The activities of the DIDEC living lab included workshop sessions with about 30 participants. Participants were asked to answer questionnaires with the aim of understanding how they evaluated the usefulness and effectiveness of workshops.

Taking an active role as interventionist researchers meant that project managers and owners regularly shared their plans and working documents with us. In addition, we constantly shared our observations and results stemming from collected data, as well as discussed practical implications with project managers and owners. Therefore, we also suggested to implement some control forms that could be beneficial to solve the tensions emerging during various stages of the project implementation and in different parts of the project organization.

The data analysis consisted of three steps. The first step entailed the identification of the project's main stakeholders and their specific interests, expressed as agendas and actions (see Table 6.1).

The second step aimed at depicting stakeholders' interactions during the implementation of the project and how interests reflected in their agenda and actions that were undertaken caused various tensions. We identified episodes that were perceived as unexpected or problematic by the project management, the steering group or by us, and that caused discussion or consultation. These episodes have been carefully documented in our observation notes and in email conversations. In many cases, tensions between conflicting project demands explained the episodes. In the third step, we focused on project managers' introduction and use of different control forms during the project implementation process.

The DIDEC project and its tensions

The project consisted of five stages. In the *preparation stage* (Fall 2017), the Municipality of Perstorp took the initiative to write an application for the DIDEC project whose purpose was to (1) increase

Table 6.1 Stakeholder interests

Stakeholders	Agenda	Actions
Ambassadors	Facilitation of project implementation	Acting as intermediaries between project management and employees
Employees of Österbo dementia care centre	Improvement of health are services for people with dementia at Österbo and their own working conditions	Making their voices heard
Funding agency	Value for money, i.e. efficient use of resources granted within the time frame of the project	Periodic monitoring of achieved results
Incubator & Science Park	Conditions for open innovation processes	Facilitating collaboration efforts via advertising the project
Managers of Österbo dementia care centre	Integration of the project activities in ordinary tasks	Seeking internal legitimacy and acceptance of collaboration among personnel
Municipality	Long-term impact of the results of the project and knowledge spillover about efficiency of working processes and resource utilization	Seeking external legitimacy and working out ways to internally organize for collaborative innovations
Project managers	Fulfilment of the project goals and plan in line with deadlines	Establishing routines for internal and external collaborations fora. Dealing with uncertainties while respecting reporting duties
Testing company(ies)	Knowledge of dementia care to ensure innovative products/services to be, ultimately, commercialized	Accessing infrastructure and gaining of trust to execute testing in a collaborative effective way

the quality of life of individuals with dementia; (2) improve the range of innovative products and services for dementia care; and (3) increase the innovativeness, competitiveness and growth of small and medium-sized companies (SMEs) that focus on technological solutions for dementia care. A series of preparatory activities was coordinated by the strategic developer of the Municipality. Besides the Municipality writing the application, relationships with science incubators and academia were established to create a team of partners that agreed upon the main goals of the project. In addition, the structure of the project organization was defined, while legal aspects that could be relevant for the testing and ethical concerns were addressed as well. The project was funded by EU and the official start-up meeting took place in February 2018. *Tensions* in this stage concerned the need to agree upon the resources that partners would need to invest in the project and respective responsibilities. Additionally, a central tension emerged because of ethical considerations of testing in a dementia care centre. People with dementia are intellectually impaired and cannot agree to and fully participate in such testing, which was supposed to be the crucial element of the project. Therefore, precautionary measures had to be taken.

In the *initiation stage*, the employees of Österbo were informed about the project and its aim. They were invited to participate in workshops in which they interacted with the project managers and innovation adviser. The aim of these workshops was to identify urgent issues and needs that the entrepreneurs should consider when ideating products/services to be tested. Another aim of these workshops was to prepare the employees to participate in open innovation processes where they would meet and collaborate with entrepreneurs. In this stage, some of the employees were appointed as ambassadors of the project and interested companies approached. At the same time, the project managers worked on advertising, a call for applications, on contracts and on a confidentiality policy related to the potential entrepreneurs that would test their products/services in the living lab. In this stage, *tensions* appeared when the call for applications and contracts between the municipality and the testing companies had to be prepared and signed. The initial documents were long and complex due to the formal requirements of the Municipality and the funding agency, regarding diversity, gender equality, ethical considerations and transparency. The request to filling out these documents posed a challenge to the potential testing companies, which asked for simple procedures due to limited time, resources and previous experience with EU-funded projects.

The *collaboration stage* started in October 2018 once the company applications were screened by the steering group, suggesting candidates for testing based on the feedback received by the project managers, who had talked to the applicants. The candidates were presented to the employees in workplace meetings and the ambassadors in a workshop devoted to the project. Afterwards, the ambassadors met the companies in two sessions. In the first session, the companies presented themselves and interacted with the employees to create a common understanding of the challenges of dementia care. In the second session, the companies presented the first prototype of the solution they wanted to test and the employees could assess the idea. The ideas that were considered worth being tested by the employees moved on to the next stage. Only one company made it to the actual testing in the first round of applications. Two additional rounds were initiated and dialogues with additional companies were held. However, these rounds were not completed due to the pandemic. In the collaboration stage, *tension* regarding project outcomes was visible as personnel showed resistance to the living lab. At the same time as the project goals promised better life conditions for people with dementia, the personnel were afraid that the testing companies' new digital solutions would either steal their jobs or cause an increased workload. The personnel's fear of losing their jobs due to digitalization was expressed in internal project meetings and explained their initial resistance to the establishment of a living lab at Österbo. Another source of tension became evident when some companies that had applied for testing saw the project as a marketing opportunity for existing products rather than a collaboration aiming at innovating dementia care.

The *testing stage* started in the Spring 2019, after some delay caused by technical problems. The company installed a button in each room of two departments of Österbo. The personnel had to press the button once they had delivered the medicines to the person living in the room. This information was transferred to a screen summarizing the medicine delivery situation in the department. The testing was effective because the personnel could deliver a better and more secure service to the persons living in the departments that constituted the living lab. Not only the percentage of medicine delivery deviation was reduced, but also the personnel's job satisfaction increased. Moreover, the company developed a product that was later commercialized. Once the pandemic hit, the company decided not to remove the buttons immediately but allowed Österbo's two departments to keep using them. However, further testing possibilities, which were discussed, could not be executed. During the testing stage, *tension* was related to personnel's unhappiness with the testing company altering their daily routines due to the need to test innovative solutions. Complaining comments were, for example, expressed by some employees in a department meeting. In addition, during this stage another source of tension became evident due to the pandemic. Given the ban on entering elderly care centres, the project was first suspended and then stopped. Tension existed between project managers, municipality managers and the science incubators striving for the survival of the project, for continuing successful improvements and learnings, and the EU being obliged to stop the project due to difficulties in meeting deadlines and attaining project targets.

The *evaluation and reporting stage* started towards the end of 2020 and finished in Spring 2021, after negotiations with the funding agency. The project management team, steering group and funding agency met on several occasions, and the decision to stop the project on 31 December 2020 was

Table 6.2 Tensions of the DIDEC project

Tension type	Tensions	Challenges for controls
Competing demands related to resources and desired results	Long-term *versus* short-term project goals and results	Improvement inwork conditions and life for people with dementia versus fulfilment of tight project targets in the 3 years' time frame
Competing demands related to the project process	Flexible *versus* standardized methods	Allowing the trial-and-error method to deal with uncertainties in the testing stage *versus* following the predetermined principles and activities of the living lab
Competing demands related to organizational structure and relationships	External pressure *versus* internal legitimacy	Dealing with the extraordinary activities of the testing versus complying with the ordinary job tasks

made. Reports assessing the results of the project were prepared and sent to the funding agency. A workshop with the ambassadors was held to inform them about the situation and ask them for feedback to be considered regarding a potential new project to be executed once the pandemic was over. In the evaluation and reporting stage, another source of *tension* emerged due to the different interests of the project managers and science incubators on the hand and the funding agency on the other. Since DIDEC was funded by public money, the project managers had to report important results to the funding agency. Some of the indicators which were regularly followed up were: (a) the number of companies that received support from the project; (b) the number of companies that tested their products/ideas in the living lab; and (c) employment growth due to the project. The use of indicators proved to be somewhat problematic because the indicators addressed long-term effects that were difficult to accomplish within the deadline of the project, such as employment growth. This difficulty was raised by the project managers and discussed on several occasions by the steering group. It was also communicated to the funding agency. Moreover, it was argued about whether those indicators were the best choices for evaluating the success and results of the DIDEC project. Learnings, new relationships, changed attitudes towards dementia, innovation and digitalization, and an increased interest in the project from external parties (including potential testing companies), which science incubators and managers stressed as important success factors, were not given similar priority by the EU.

In sum, the project managers had to deal with the three types of tensions mentioned before. These tensions challenged the project control system, as illustrated in Table 6.2.

From balancing different control forms to the crisis

The project managers introduced different control forms to deal with the challenges generated by the tensions of the DIDEC project. Stakeholders' different interests, mindsets and goals were reflected in the tension related to long-term and short-term time perspectives. Being a publicly and externally funded project meant that formal controls, such as periodic reporting, contracts, procurement regulations and ethical/secrecy standards, had to be put in place from the very beginning, as happened in the initiation stage. Many of these formal control mechanisms thus derived from requirements of the municipality and the funding agency and were implemented to guarantee an efficient use of resources and the achievement of desired results.

However, some formal controls were also initiated and designed by the project managers with the aim of communicating and creating a shared understanding of the project and its activities. Examples of regularly used formal controls were scheduled meetings, process plans, and work models of the project organization and innovation process. As the project was developing, informal controls, such as dialogue and enhanced trust, were more and more important to ensure the success of the project. Observations point to the importance of engaged and open-minded project managers able to initiate informal activities and events with the aim of motivating, empowering and creating new knowledge. Considering that the employees within healthcare systems and municipalities are exposed to many projects and new initiatives – sometimes with few results (see Abrahamsson & Agevall, 2010) – it is not strange that a project like DIDEC encountered some initial resistance. However, DIDEC seemed to differ from many other projects and initiatives in one central aspect: the personnel were listened to and were able to perceive that they made an impact. The important role of the personnel was emphasized early in the DIDEC project, by giving them a prominent position in the project and by having the personnel represented by ambassadors.

A combination of formal and informal controls did thus solve tensions related to the project process as well as to the project organization structure and relationship. Balancing the use of both formal and informal controls was beneficial in regard to the tension between the strict requirements of the municipality and the funding agency, regarding, for example, diversity, gender equality and ethical considerations, and the need for simple application procedures as expressed by the companies facing resources scarcity. The long and complex document, which should ensure the fulfilment of these requirements, initially caused problems for the companies that were applying. The project managers decided to complete the document in dialogue with the companies, accomplishing a better result and with the positive effect of getting to know the companies and their entrepreneurs.

The project managers had to interact with many stakeholders to make the project work. Accountability towards a wide range of stakeholders besides the funding agency needed to be ensured. The use of the web page and social media to disseminate information, besides the participation in conferences and fairs, contributed to increasing DIDEC's visibility and transparency of action (Argento & Lövstål, 2021). All in all, there was a constellation of controls in various parts of the project organization, and the project managers performed a balancing act by using the controls that fit the needs of each stage of the project implementation.

Once the ambassadors and other personnel became more positive towards the idea of testing new products and came to understand their potential contribution to the co-creation of new digital solutions in the field of dementia care, the Covid-19 pandemic exploded. This unexpected crisis created an extra challenge for the DIDEC project managers and owner. The uncertainties related to the possibility of testing at Österbo and the availability of the EU funds absorbed energy and affected the enthusiasm that had been built up very patiently (Argento & Lövstål, 2021). In other words, the balancing act worked well until it was threatened by the Covid-19 crisis when the priorities changed, and formal controls prevailed. The balance between informal and formal controls, which were taming the competing demands of the involved stakeholders and related tensions, could not be sustained because physical meetings, testing and concrete collaborations – that is, the assets of the project – were not feasible anymore. The project-related tensions turned into real dilemmas because it became impossible to reach the short-term project targets stated in the funding agreement as the funder could not prolong deadlines. Several companies were ready to test their products but could not do so because of the pandemic, which suggests how, as uncertainty increases, the requirement of predictability remains.

Due to the power of the funding agency and the tightening of formal results control, a lot of added value went lost. The DIDEC project produced many positive results that go beyond the strict text of the funding agreement. For example, the testing company developed a better understanding of the procurement regulations and practices within municipalities, which might be useful to prevent tensions stemming from the competing demands related to relationships. Another positive effect of DIDEC was a better atmosphere and working climate at the dementia care centre whose employees had started to have a more open-minded mindset. A final positive effect was the increased understanding gained by managers and other parties on how to accomplish successful organizational changes within municipalities.

In sum, the various tensions were dealt with through the implementation of different control forms which reflected the managers efforts to enact a balancing act that was hampered by the uncertainties of an innovation project and the sudden Covid-19 crisis. The crisis accelerated the need for achieving results and reducing uncertainties which would have been tolerated otherwise. The inflexible funding practices, which did not leave room for major deviations from plans and deadlines, decided the fate of a collaborative innovation project that was leading to success.

Discussion and conclusions

Considering the common practice of implementing projects in the public sector (Fred, 2020; Nilsen & Feiring, 2022), and in line with what extant management control literature highlights (Pan Fagerlin & Lövstål, 2020; Ylinen & Gullkvist, 2014), the combination of different types of control can impact the performance of collaborative innovation projects. The DIDEC project shows how the control forms to be used to monitor the project's results and processes must be matched with the temporary nature of the project organization (see also Turner & Müller, 2003) and the specific circumstances at stake (Godenhjelm & Johanson, 2018; Kober & Thambar, 2022). The project control system needs to deal with tensions stemming from competing demands related to (1) resource availability and interpretations of desired results; (2) project processual aspects; and (3) project organization structure and relationship issues. Specifically, controls must handle the tensions emerging from close relationships in the core project organization, as well as more distant ones between the project organization and external stakeholders. Similarly, the project control system needs to balance both bureaucratic and contractual accountability mechanisms, to prevent opportunistic behaviour and to limit the range of actions, as well as softer control mechanisms aimed at trust building and shared understanding (Edelenbos & Eshuis, 2012; Grafton and Mundy, 2011; Mundy, 2010; Seal & Vincent-Jones, 1997; Six, 2013; van der Kolk et al., 2020; Vosselman and van der Meer-Kooistra, 2009). The findings show that the tensions of a collaborative innovation project can be solved through informal controls based on dialogue, mutual commitment and trust among involved parties (Edelenbos & Klijn, 2007; Klijn et al., 2010).

The findings also show how the effectiveness of a project control system is affected by a sudden crisis. When the Covid-19 pandemic hit, the activities of the project, the testing of new products, could not no longer be executed. Despite the partial good results achieved so far, the funding agency decided to stop the funding and this resulted in the end of the project because the targets set in the funding agreement could not be achieved, which is in line with other studies on EU-funded projects (Büttner & Leopold, 2016; Godenhjelm et al., 2015). Tight formal control bound to a contract prevailed, while potentially new solutions for people with dementia and business development opportunities have gone lost. This means that the balancing act put in place by project managers, Österbo managers and employees to overcome tensions and achieve the goals of the project was hampered by formal controls with a financial and quantitative focus. The balance, progressively achieved by dynamically combining different control forms (Mundy, 2010) depending on the needs at stake in various parts of the project organization and stages of the project implementation, was only temporary. While the project managers could downsize the dominance of rigid formal controls in favour of informal ones, thereby establishing a dynamic balance, such balance was disrupted by the crisis, which witnessed how EU-funding policies and regulations, reliant on rigid formal controls (Büttner & Leopold, 2016), do not match with the spirit of innovation (see Lövstål & Jontoft, 2017). Yet the unbalanced combination of control forms was a necessary choice externally imposed rather than a voluntary decision of the project managers.

The findings presented in this chapter add new dimensions to current debates on the tensions in project organizations. It specifically sheds light on the positive effects generated by balancing formal control (expected deliverables, timelines, budgets) and informal control (trust, dialogue, support) in public sector collaborative innovation projects. This chapter offers theoretical contributions to the literature on how interactions between controls forms can enhance and/or diminish control effectiveness (van der Kolk et al., 2020) by providing empirical insights from collaborative innovation processes in the public sector. Previous public management and management control literature on inter-organizational relationships has not deeply accounted for the competing demands and tensions taking place within a temporary collaborative innovation project engaging different types of stakeholders across organizational boundaries. This chapter contributes to these streams of literature by moving beyond the debate on the substitutive/complementary role of certain control forms. It unravels the tensions and control solutions both at the project level and at the inter-organizational level, thereby also enriching the body of knowledge about projects in the public sector (Fred, 2020; Godenhjelm & Johanson, 2018; Nielsen & Feiring, 2022). This chapter adds to the literature by considering the power dynamics that become explicit in a crisis whose effects were captured, from a methodological point on view, via interventionist research (Suomala et al., 2014; Lukka & Wouters, 2022) and direct access to a real-life setting that provided a fertile soil for data collection over three and a half years.

The chapter illustrates how tensions, first being approached as dualities in which competing demands are dealt with simultaneously (Lövstål & Jontoft, 2017), turn into real dilemmas which cannot be solved. The EU, while recognizing the value of the project, had to stick to its funding policies and regulations. In such situations, having established a project control system, consisting of a combination of formal and informal controls that managed the tensions arising in the project, could not be of help. In this respect, differently from Kober and Thambar (2022), who claimed that controls can be helpful to navigate a crisis, we argue that relying on strict EU funding can hamper the possibility for controls to solve tensions in a project because safeguarding behaviour increases.

Finally, yet importantly, the chapter provides practical implications. The findings point at important challenges and potential solutions that can benefit municipality managers, dementia care centres (i.e. managers, health professionals), and entrepreneurs that engage in the healthcare sector. Efforts in creating mutual understanding and trust, in addition to a good dose of patience, facilitate the achievement of the goals set in a project plan. Investing in relationships can provide long-term effects that span beyond the deadline of the project, and the accumulated learnings should not get lost with the official finalization of the project. However, this is challenging when crises occur. While the crisis offered interesting opportunities to study how relationships evolve over time and the role of different control forms therein, it also represents a contingency that limited this study. Future research could delve deeper into how informal controls can foster learning and actually support the formal ones in projects that are not affected by a crisis like the global pandemic, and foster better understanding of the effectiveness of project control systems as a means of innovating public service delivery.

References

Abrahamsson, A., & Agevall, L. (2010). Immigrants caught in the crossfire of projectification of the Swedish public sector: Short-term solutions to long-term problems. *Diversity and Equality in Health and Care, 7*(3), 201–209.

Adler, P. S., & Chen, C. X. (2011). Combining creativity and control: Understanding individual motivation in large-scale collaborative creativity. *Accounting, Organizations and Society, 36*(2), 63–85.

Agger, A., & Sørensen, E. (2018). Managing collaborative innovation in public bureaucracies. *Planning Theory, 17*(1), 53–73.

Almqvist, R. (2001). Management by contract: A study of programmatic and technological aspects. *Public Administration, 79*(3), 689–706.

Argento, D., Kaarbøe, K., & Vakkuri, J. (2020). Constructing certainty through public budgeting – budgetary responses to the COVID-19 pandemic in Finland, Norway and Sweden. *Journal of Public Budgeting, Accounting & Financial Management, 32*(5), 875–887.

Argento, D., & Lövstål, E. (2021). *DIDEC – A living lab comes to life*. Faculty of Business Report 1: 2021. Kristianstad University Press.

Argento, D., & Peda, P. (2015). Interactions fostering trust and contract combinations in local public services provision. *International Journal of Public Sector Management, 28*(4/5), 335–351.

Artto, K., Kulvik, I., Poskela, J., & Turkulainen, V. (2011). The integrative role of the project management office in the front end of innovation. *International Journal of Project Management, 29*(4), 408–421.

Blomberg, J. (2013). *Myter om projekt* [Myths about projects]. Studentlitteratur.

Brankaert, R., & den Ouden, E. (2013). Setting up a LivingLab for innovation in the dementia care chain, a case study of the PhysiCal. *ISPIM Conference Innovating in Global Markets: Challenges for Sustainable Growth*. Helsinki.

Bürkland, S., Zachariassen, F., & Oliveira, J. (2019). Meeting up for management control: Bracketing interaction in innovation development. *Qualitative Research in Accounting & Management, 16*(1), 144–178.

Büttner, S. M., & Leopold, L. M. (2016). A "new spirit" of public policy? The project world of EU funding. *European Journal of Cultural and Political Sociology, 3*(1), 41–71.

Chenhall, R. H. (2003). Management control systems design within its organizational context: Findings from contingency-based research and directions for the future. *Accounting, Organizations and Society, 28*(2/3), 127–168.

Collier, P. M. (2005). Entrepreneurial control and the construction of a relevant accounting. *Management Accounting Research, 16*(3), 321–339.

Davila, A., Foster, G., & Oyon, D. (2009). Accounting and control, entrepreneurship and innovation: Venturing into new research opportunities. *European Accounting Review, 18*(2), 281–311.

Dekker, H. (2004). Control of inter-organizational relationships: Evidence on appropriation concerns and coordination requirements. *Accounting, Organizations and Society, 29*(1), 27–49.

Ditillo, A., Liguori, M., Sicilia, M., & Steccolini, I. (2015). Control patterns in contracting-out relationships: It matters what you do, not who you are. *Public Administration, 93*(1), 212–229.

Edelenbos, J., & Eshuis, J. (2012). The interplay between trust and control in governance processes: A conceptual and empirical investigation. *Administration & Society, 44*(6), 647–674.

Edelenbos, J., & Klijn, E. H. (2007). Trust in complex decision-making networks. A theoretical and empirical exploration. *Administration & Society, 39*(1), 25–50.

Fred, M. (2020). Local government projectification in practice – a multiple institutional logic perspective. *Local Government Studies, 46*(3), 351–370.

Gaim, M., & Wåhlin, N. (2016). In search of a creative space: A conceptual framework of synthesizing paradoxical tensions. *Scandinavian Journal of Management, 32*(1), 33–44.

Gaim, M., Wåhlin, N., & Clegg, S. (2018). Analyzing competing demands in organizations: A systematic comparison. *Journal of Organization Design, 7*(1), 1–16.

Gascó, M. (2017). Living labs: Implementing open innovation in the public sector. *Government Information Quarterly, 34*(1), 90–98.

Godenhjelm, S., & Johanson, J. E. (2018). The effect of stakeholder inclusion on public sector project innovation. *International Review of Administrative Sciences, 84*(1), 42–62.

Godenhjelm, S., Lundin, R. A., & Sjöblom, S. (2015). Projectification in the public sector – the case of the European Union. *International Journal of Managing Projects in Business, 8*(2), 324–348.

Grafton, J., & Mundy, J. (2011). Collaboration and control: Managing tensions in competitive interorganisational relationships. *CIMA Research Executive Summary Series, 7*(3), 1–5.

Hakanen, T., & Jaakkola, E. (2012). Co-creating customer-focused solutions within business networks: A service perspective. *Journal of Service Management, 23*(4), 593–611.

Högberg, L., Sköld, B., & Tillmar, M. (2018). Kontroll eller förtroende? En balansgång på offentliga marknader. *Organisation & Samhälle, 2*, 56–61.

Klein Woolthuis, R., Hillebrand, B., & Nooteboom, B. (2005). Trust, contract and relationship development. *Organization Studies, 26*(6), 813–840.

Klijn, E. H., Edelenbos, J., & Steijn, B. (2010). Trust in governance networks: Its impacts on outcomes. *Administration & Society, 42*(2), 193–221.

Kober, R., & Thambar, P. J. (2022). Paradoxical tensions of the COVID-19 pandemic: A paradox theory perspective on the role of management control systems in helping organizations survive crises. *Accounting, Auditing & Accountability Journal, 35*(1), 108–119.

Laya, A., Markendahl, J., & Lundberg, S. (2018). Network-centric business models for health, social care and wellbeing solutions in the internet of things. *Scandinavian Journal of Management, 34*(2), 103–116.

Lee, S. (2022). When tensions become opportunities: Managing accountability demands in collaborative governance. *Journal of Public Administration Research and Theory, 32*(4), 641–655.

Lee, S., Park, G., Yoon, B., & Park, J. (2010). Open innovation in SME's: An intermediated networked model. *Research Policy, 39*(2), 290–300.

Lewis, L., Isbell, M. G., & Koschmann, M. (2010). Collaborative tensions: Practitioners' experiences of interorganizational relationships. *Communication Monographs, 77*(4), 460–479.

Lukka, K., & Wouters, M. (2022). Towards interventionist research with theoretical ambitions. *Management Accounting Research, 55*, 100783.

Lövstål, E., & Jontoft, A. M. (2017). Tensions at the intersection of management control and innovation: A literature review. *Journal of Management Control, 28*(1), 41–79.

Merchant, K. A., & Van der Stede, W. A. (2017). *Management control systems: Performance measurement, evaluation and incentives* (4th ed.). Pearson Education.

Mundy, J. (2010). Creating dynamic tensions through a balanced use of management control systems. *Accounting, Organizations and Society, 35*(5), 499–523.

Nilsen, H. M., & Feiring, E. (2022). Local public health projectification in practice: A qualitative study of facilitators and barriers to a public health plan implementation. *Scandinavian Journal of Public Health*, 1–8.

Näslund, L. (2018). Förtroende och tillit–vad är det? *Organisation & Samhälle, 2*, 18–23.

Nyland, K., Morland, C., & Burns, J. (2017). The interplay of managerial and non-managerial controls, institutional work, and the coordination of laterally dependent hospital activities. *Qualitative Research in Accounting & Management, 14*(4), 467–495.

Organization for Economic Cooperation and Development (OECD) (2015). *Addressing dementia: The OECD response*. OECD Health Policy Studies. OECD. http://dx.doi.org/10.1787/9789264231726-en.

Pan Fagerlin, W., & Lövstål, E. (2020). Top managers' formal and informal control practices in product innovation processes. *Qualitative Research in Accounting & Management, 17*(4), 497–524.

Potočnik, K., Verwaeren, B. & Nijstad, B. (2022). Tensions and paradoxes in creativity and innovation. *Journal of Work and Organizational Psychology, 38*(3), 149–163.

Pradies, C. et al. (2021). The lived experience of paradox: How individuals navigate tensions during the pandemic crisis. *Journal of Management Inquiry, 30*(2), 154–167.

Ramirez, R. (1999). Value co-production: Intellectual origins and implications for practice and research. *Strategic Management Journal, 20*(1), 49–65.

Seabrooke, V., & Alisoun, M. (2014). Early intervention and dementia care: innovation and impact. *Quality in Ageing and Older Adults, 15*(1), 34–45.

Seal, W., & Vincent-Jones, P. (1997). Accounting and trust in the enabling of long-term relations. *Accounting, Auditing & Accountability Journal, 10*(3), 406–431.

Sharma, G., & Bansal, P. (2017). Partners for good: How business and NGOs engage the commercial–social paradox. *Organization Studies, 38*(3–4), 341–364.

Six, F. (2013). Trust in regulatory relations: How new insights from trust research improve regulation theory. *Public Management Review, 15*(2), 163–185.

Smith, W. K, Erez, M., Jarvenpaa, S., Lewis, M. W., & Tracey, P. (2017). Adding complexity to theories of paradox, tensions, and dualities of innovation and change: Introduction to organization studies special issue on paradox, tensions, and dualities of innovation and change. *Organization Studies, 38*(3–4), 303–317.

Smith, W. K., & Lewis, M. W. (2011). Toward a theory of paradox: A dynamic equilibrium model of organizing. *Academy of Management Review, 36*(2), 381–403.

Stevens, V., & Agger, A. (2017). Managing collaborative innovation networks. Practical lessons from a Belgian spatial planning initiative. *Journal of Public Administration and Governance, 7*(3), 154–173.

Suomala, P., Lyly-Yrjänäinen, J., & Lukka, K. (2014). Battlefield around interventions: A reflective analysis of conducting interventionist research in management accounting. *Management Accounting Research, 25*(4), 304–314.

Thomas, A. B. (2004). *Research skills for management studies*. Routledge.

Turner, J. R., & Müller, R. (2003). On the nature of the project as a temporary organization. *International Journal of Project Management, 21*(1), 1–8.

Van der Kolk, B., van Veen-Dirks, P. M. G., & ter Bogt, H. (2020). How combination of control elements create tensions and how these can be managed: An embedded case study. *Management Accounting Research, 48*, 100677.

Van der Meer-Kooistra, J., & Vosselman, E.G.J. (2000). Management control of interfirm transactional relationships: The case of industrial renovation and maintenance. *Accounting, Organizations and Society, 25*(1), 51–77.

Van Dooren, W., Bouckaert, G., & Halligan, J. (2010). *Performance management in the public sector*. Routledge.

Van Marrewijk, A., Clegg, S. R., Pitsis, T. S., & Veenswijk, M. (2008). Managing public–private megaprojects: Paradoxes, complexity, and project design. *International Journal of Project Management, 26*(6), 591–600.

Vosselman, E., & Van der Meer-Kooistra, J. (2009). Accounting for control and trust building in interfirm transactional relationships. *Accounting, Organizations and Society, 34*(2), 267–283.

Ylinen, M., & Gullkvist, B. (2014). The effects of organic and mechanistic control in exploratory and exploitative innovations. *Management Accounting Research, 25*(1), 93–112.

7

ENGAGING COMMUNITIES IN INFRASTRUCTURE BUILDING

How governments can learn from social movements

Suresh Cuganesan and Alison Hart

Introduction

Major public infrastructure projects, where governments and private sector entities come together to invest in and develop transport, energy and social assets for the community, are one of the most prominent socio-economic phenomena of today. An estimated US$3 trillion will be invested to develop infrastructure through projects globally in the next decade (Global Infrastructure Hub, 2020). Done well, infrastructure development enables new ways of working and living, stimulates improvements in living standards and accommodates urbanization and population growth. However, as history shows, these types of projects often cause community backlash, mass protests and poor civic engagement, as well as result in poor socio-economic outcomes. California's US$77 billion bullet train project; Stuttgart 21, a US$9 billion railway and urban development project in Germany; and Melbourne's US$20 billion ultimately abandoned East West Link Road project are just a few examples of infrastructure projects which were problematic due to poor engagement by government authorities with the broader public.[1]

At the heart of the challenge facing government authorities is that major infrastructure projects typically disrupt local lifestyles, amenities and the environment (van den Ende & van Marrewijk, 2015). Accordingly, project proponents confront a public seeking greater involvement in decision-making and understanding of process, particularly in democratic societies. Sophisticated social movements are increasingly prevalent, organizing community action against infrastructure projects and bringing small, resource-poor, disparate individuals and groups together into coalitions powerful enough to stop infrastructure projects (Novy & Peters, 2012; Teo & Loosemore, 2017). Too often, government bodies have relied on their bureaucratic authority to push infrastructure projects through, rather than "bringing the public along". As prior research shows, these approaches often result in the erosion of public trust in stated project benefits, in extensive community conflict and citizen protest, leading in turn to excessive project delays and budget overruns, to projects being cancelled and to infrastructure not fit-for-purpose (Flores Dewey & Davis, 2013; Di Maddaloni & Davis, 2018). If infrastructure development is to occur, then government authorities have to confront a significant collective action problem – how to engender public support even if these types of projects cause disruption to amenities, lifestyle and the environment.

The notion of government authorities engaging more effectively with the public resonates with broader ideas that government should more meaningfully demonstrate values comprising civic

DOI: 10.4324/9781003295945-10

engagement, democracy and social justice (Bryson et al., 2014; Denhardt & Denhardt, 2015). Within the public management literature, proclamations that "government should invest more in developing public support for the development of public infrastructure" (Willems et al., 2017, p. 325) are well made, but there is little in the way of insight and guidance on how government authorities should specifically go about this task and what challenges they are likely to face, especially in light of increasingly prevalent social movements adept at organizing public support against proposed infrastructure developments. Rather than see social movements in a negative light as obstacles to be removed, this study proposes that government authorities can usefully learn from the strategies that social movements employ to build and harness public support in their opposition to infrastructure projects.

To investigate how government authorities address the aforementioned collective action problem, and what they might learn from social movements opposing infrastructure development, the study applies a social capital lens to the case of the East West Link (EWL) infrastructure project in Melbourne, Australia. This infrastructure development proceeded to the stage where legally enforceable construction contracts were entered into with the private sector, but was eventually abandoned due to mass public backlash, with contracts subsequently cancelled at a further cost of approximately US$1 billion. As such, this chapter considers this to be an exemplar case with much potential for learning.

The study identifies strategies that government authorities should employ to build and harness social capital with the public as they propose infrastructure development. Doing so is more likely to result in infrastructure developments that have the appropriate support of the public, being delivered on time and on budget.

Social capital, infrastructure projects and public engagement

Social capital as a concept has been widely employed in public management research. Over time, the concept of social capital as a resource that enables collective action and consequential mutual benefits for an aggregate of actors has come to be well established (Putnam et al., 1994; Woolcock, 2010; Engbers & Rubin, 2018). This use of social capital follows most closely the work of Putnam, where social capital refers to "networks, norms, and social trust, that facilitate coordination and cooperation for mutual benefit" (1995a, p. 66) and enables diverse participants to act collectively (Woolcock, 2010).

In research on the rise of social capital over the previous two decades, Woolcock notes that the "seminal work of [...] especially Putnam [...] on civic participation and democracy has provided the inspiration for most of the current work" on social capital across a wide range of research areas, including work and organizations, and democracy and governance (2010, p. 472). Putnam sees social capital as formed through democratic governance and civic engagement, thereby enabling governments to achieve their public objectives: "the performance of governments and other social institutions is powerfully influenced by citizen engagement in community affairs, or what [...] I term [...] social capital" (Putnam, 1995b, p. 664). This reading of social capital as a means of enabling collective action and allowing governments to perform more effectively makes it appropriate for the study – projects to develop public infrastructure are essentially collective action endeavours where the community has significant influence on whether envisioned socio-economic outcomes are realized. The implication of this is that not only is social capital within a community important – a point that prior public management research emphasizes – but it is also important that government authorities develop social capital with the public if they are to perform more effectively.

Indeed, while government entities can rely on their authority and resources to push through infrastructure development, history shows such approaches are problematic for achieving project outcomes (Flores Dewey & Davis, 2013). These approaches also contradict what should be the essentially democratic nature of infrastructure policy. In a liberal democracy there will always be an active and vocal opposition which does not agree with all the policies of government. This particularly requires governments to observe all due process and ensure the public as taxpayers and users can appreciate the benefits of large and costly infrastructure projects. The implication for government authorities leading projects is that a shift in strategy is required, from one of simply seeking to "manage" and appease stakeholders that may pose a risk to the project, to the adoption of a public engagement approach that builds social capital – specifically connecting to the public and enabling both shared understandings in the value and benefits of the infrastructure investment, as well as trust that decision-making about trade-offs and adverse impacts will be fair and just.

Supporting this further, prior studies of infrastructure development projects demonstrate the benefits of governments building social capital with the public. Research on contexts where infrastructure projects experience extended delays or cancellation highlight: diverse networks of opposition such as experts, local governments, community members and other influential entities juxtaposed against government authorities and a small group of entities supporting the project (Corvellec, 2001); how project authorities rely on their apparent legitimacy via bureaucratic authority, the law or technical expertise, instead of building public support (Flores Dewey & Davis, 2013; Novy & Peters, 2012); and a failure to build ties to the public (van den Ende & van Marrewijk, 2015). Studies also show how public support can be generated by government entities through sharing information; encouraging citizen interaction and commentary about the project; enabling physical participation through site tours; and conducting transition rituals that help legitimize the project and communicate accomplishments (van den Ende & van Marrewijk, 2014; van den Ende & van Marrewijk, 2015; Willems et al., 2017). Social capital is clearly implicated in how public infrastructure projects progress and are shaped through engagement with the public.

When considering how government entities can build social capital with the public, it is important to acknowledge that they increasingly confront social movements that are seeking to do the same but for opposing ends. Social movements rely on public endorsement and support to mobilize opposition to infrastructure projects (McAdam, 2011; Novy & Peters, 2012). As "collectivities acting with some degree of organization and continuity [...] for the purpose of challenging or defending extant authority" (Snow et al., 2004, p. 11), social movements rely on the ability of key actors in the movement to connect to community members and groups and build shared understandings and emotive ties (McAdam, 2011; Novy & Peters, 2012). Consequently, public administrators and bureaucrats need to understand how this occurs and affects their own strategies of public engagement in building support for the proposed infrastructure (Di Maddaloni & Davis, 2018; Novy & Peters, 2012; Teo & Loosemore, 2017).

In applying a social capital lens, the study draws upon the field of management studies to focus on the ways that entities might build social capital and how these strategies influence specific social capital dimensions. Management studies propose that social capital consists of three dimensions comprising structural, relational and cognitive capital (Nahapiet & Ghoshal, 1998). Structural capital is concerned with the overall pattern of connections within the network, such as the presence or absence of ties, and the density and connectivity of those ties. Relational capital focuses on the extent to which emotions and feelings such as trust apply to these connections. Cognitive capital encompasses shared understandings and cognitive schemas of meaning, vision and goals. This three-dimensional categorization has been utilized widely across diverse research areas (Inkpen & Tsang, 2005; Pillai et al., 2017; Tsai & Ghoshal, 1998). Accordingly, it is applied to examine how the government authorities leading the EWL project and the social movement (largely composed of community groups) opposing them, competed for the support of the public.

Research methods

Case setting

The case chosen was retrospective. It comprised the ultimately unsuccessful bid to build Stage One of the EWL, a planned two-stage toll road and tunnel designed to alleviate congestion in Melbourne, Australia's fastest growing city. The EWL enjoyed extensive government support and advanced to the point of entering into legal contracts with private-sector consortia for its building. However, it was eventually cancelled, with the government of the day paying significant penalties. Consistent with "theoretical sampling" (Strauss & Corbin, 1998), the cancellation of the EWL was chosen for analysis on the basis it was a highly relevant example of both the importance of public engagement in the proposing of infrastructure projects and the challenges encountered in so doing. The use of a single case study is appropriate given the exploratory nature of the research and the study's interest in sequences (social capital building and use) of actions and effects over time (Langley, 1999).

Government authorities proposing the EWL were headed by the Linking Melbourne Authority (LMA) acting on behalf of the Victorian government and working with various state government departments and authorities, including the Victorian Department of Transport, Planning and Local Infrastructure and VicRoads. Other allies and participants aligned with the LMA over time came to include the Federal Coalition Government, industry groups such as the Master Builders Association, road lobby groups such as the Royal Automobile Club of Victoria, some unions that hoped to gain jobs from the project, and various private-sector entities interested/involved in its construction, at their peak comprising 22 separate entities (hereafter referred to simply as LMA).

Those opposing the EWL comprised a social movement that was an alliance of over 100 groups and bodies, coalesced around the Yarra City Council (YCC) – the main local government area through which the tunnel was to be built – and quickly included local resident groups and peak public transport advocacy groups as other influential actors. This anti-EWL movement eventually also included citizen advocacy groups representing diverse interests such as the environment, heritage, sports clubs and public parks. Additionally, some unions, six inner city local government bodies ("Councils"), various state and federal political parties (including the Greens, Socialists and ultimately the State Labor Party opposition) joined the movement opposing the EWL.

Data collection

Archival data sources comprising contemporaneous public records, personal accounts and physical artefacts representing both sides of the contest over the EWL were selected for analysis. This allowed development of a chronology of events over the approximately two-and-a-half-year period of interest. In addition, analysis of archival documents provided access to records of the reactions to, and effects of, strategies pursued by significant actors as these unfolded. Use of archival documents for this purpose is consistent with prior studies of controversies about infrastructure projects over time (e.g. Corvellec, 2001; Novy & Peters, 2012). As noted by Bowen (2009), "documents provide a means of tracking change and development […] [particularly] where events can no longer be observed" (pp. 30–31).

Data sources were also triangulated, paying particular attention to collecting as complete and balanced a set of documents as possible, and ensuring multiple sources were available for all examples discussed (Bowen, 2009). Beginning with broad key term searches of media and journal databases, the main daily newspapers – local, regional, interstate and national – provided a rich stream of data (including quotes and interviews from relevant parties), enabling a mapping of the project process. This produced an extensive list of major groups and individuals involved. Recognizing the importance of social media for management and accounting research, this list was then used to search primary sources such as government departmental, corporate and activist group websites, including real-time blogs, forums and other social media, which is increasingly utilized to advantage by social movements (Jeacle, 2020). Initially, documents produced about the EWL consisted mainly of government information announcing the project and consultation processes, and flyers and websites from those entities actively opposed to the project. Over time, this expanded as all major political parties became involved, as well as the local and national media and many citizen and diverse advocacy groups, which contributed blogs, flyers and posters. Coding and "snowballing" from reference lists, further searches were carried out to verify specific elements of the project, eventually utilizing 244 separate physical and electronic documents comprising thousands of pages.

Data coding and analysis

To make sense of the longitudinal data, a temporal bracketing strategy was employed (Langley, 1999) where the time period of interest was decomposed into three phases. The first phase, "establishment" (May 2012–mid-2013), was mainly concerned with the LMA and opposition groups reaching out to others to establish their networks and build social capital. In the second phase, "escalation" (mid-2013–mid-2014), the LMA, as well as the social movement opposing them, increased use of social capital, expanded arguments for/against the EWL and commenced overt confrontation. The final phase, "resolution" (mid-2014–November 2014), covers events leading to the eventual outcome for the project, characterized by the LMA and the social movements' intensive direct attacks on each other.

The unit of analysis was then focused upon, namely, the strategies taken by both pro- and anti-EWL networks to build and use social capital in supporting and opposing the EWL. An inductive approach informed by grounded theory was utilized to identify and analyse these (Strauss, 1987). This focused on the actions in which the LMA, the State Coalition Government and influential actors in the anti-EWL movement engaged. This proceeded as a series of iterations between data and construct development, drawing on literatures of interest and back again (Strauss & Corbin, 1998). Both authors jointly analysed and coded the actions identified, interacting regularly to discuss and resolve ambiguities and inconsistencies. Through this process the protagonists' actions were grouped into three main strategies: creating public connections, enhancing public legitimacy and responding to counterarguments.

In the *creating public connections* strategy, those supporting and opposing the EWL engaged in broad-based informing of the general public and targeted the mobilizing of specific entities as active network participants. The *enhancing public legitimacy* strategy comprised entities coordinating in signals of public support to legitimize their viewpoint, utilizing expert reports and other "facts" and evidence to strengthen arguments to support their case. Finally, important actors on each side engaged in a strategy of *responding to counterarguments* by dismissing or disputing facts and evidence presented by the other side, or questioning opposing experts' credentials. In a final phase of analysis, data according to concepts of structural, relational and cognitive capital was coded to determine the social capital effects of these strategies. The results of the analysis process are presented next.

Results

Results are presented in terms of the three strategies the protagonists used to build and use social capital. Creating public connections manifested in all three phases of the study, while enhancing public legitimacy and responding to counterarguments manifested in the first two (establishment and escalation) and the last two (escalation and resolution) respectively. The following subsections detail how each side used these strategies across the relevant phases and the particular social capital effects (summarized in Tables 9.1, 9.2 and 9.3).

Creating public connections

Looking at the creating public connections strategy, development of relational and/or cognitive capital was observed to enable structural capital and stronger ties to be built more rapidly. Both sides used this strategy during the establishment and escalation phases, albeit to varying extents (see Table 7.1).

In May 2012 during the establishment phase, the anti-EWL social movement with the YCC at its core announced its opposition to the EWL, engaging in broad-based informing, disseminating opinions and knowledge about the merits of public transport over roads, and highlighting the authorities' failure to release a business case for the EWL that would reveal its cost-benefit impact. Through this strategy, cognitive capital and shared understandings were developed with numerous already formed public transport advocacy groups (e.g. Public Transport Users Association; PTUA) about the EWL representing poor value for the money. Along with the EWL's potential disruptive effects, these were common themes in actions such as doorknocks, leaflet distribution, market stalls and displays centred around the Melbourne inner suburbs most impacted by the project.

Targeting local residents bereft at the disruption and prospect of losing their properties, the anti-EWL movement also built relational capital, forming emotive ties to residents who, angry at the disruption to community and the environment, formed new groups (e.g. Residents Against the Tunnel) and mobilized existing groups (including groups concerned with the EWL's impact on the natural environment) to join the anti-EWL movement (Jackson, 2014). This strategy thus generated relational capital, underpinning structural connections in the social movement.

Slower to initiate, the LMA attempted to spread their view that "EWL would […] boost accessibility […] and deliver substantial economic benefits to Melbourne and Victoria" (Linking Management Authority, 2013, Sec 7, 1). However, the LMA's attempts to create public connections suffered from their inability to address local resident concerns about the extent to which the EWL would disrupt their lives, concerns the anti-EWL movement had been active in raising. The LMA also engaged in limited specific discussions with resident groups in Melbourne's eastern suburbs likely to benefit from the EWL's effects on traffic congestion. Overall, however, the inability to provide specific details to demonstrate mitigation of negative impacts and ongoing refusal to release the EWL's business case as evidence of benefits, meant the LMA struggled to create sufficient relational and cognitive capital to grow their network. Indeed, there appeared to be a level of mistrust created towards the project arising from this early inaction.

As events moved into the escalation phase, the anti-EWL movement successfully mobilized to achieve scale shifts and diversify its network, with deliberate expansion from the most directly impacted inner-city communities to include outer suburbs and regional areas (Petit, 2015). Utilizing resources and evidence generated through a "Trains Not Toll Roads" (TNTR) campaign (see following section), they represented the EWL as a missed opportunity to invest in sorely needed public transport. Thus, they enlisted the active participation against the EWL of citizens in outlying areas which were poorly serviced by public transport (Legacy, 2015). This cognitive capital building initiative gained widespread press coverage and helped demonstrate that resistance to the EWL was not reflective of a not-in-my-backyard (NIMBY) mindset (Legacy, 2015).

During this phase, the LMA, forging new connections to pro-roads and industry lobby groups with a shared understanding of the benefits of investing in roads, gained some structural capital underpinned by cognitive capital. Additionally, the federal government announced road infrastructure such as the EWL as its priority, with faster movement of goods and people benefitting the state economy, and thus the public. Seeking to build cognitive capital by winning public transport advocates to their network, government authorities announced an A$108m public transport upgrade package linked to the EWL, claiming the new tunnel would remove up to 30% of daily traffic, paving the way for public transport improvements. However, public transport user groups greeted this announcement

Table 7.1 Creating public connections strategy and social capital effects – main patterns only

Phase		Structural Capital Effects	Relational Capital Effects	Cognitive Capital Effects
Establishment	**Pro-EWL**	(+) Selection of the LMA in March 2013 as responsible authority for the EWL provides it centrality (alongside state government) amongst network of government and private-sector entities involved in planning and early works.	(−) The LMA's broad-based informing has negative effects due to inability to answer resident questions about the EWL's local impacts, especially those identified by anti-EWL network; results in public mistrust in EWL corridor suburbs.	(−) Targeted mobilizing of resident groups in areas to benefit from reduced congestion through the EWL creates some positive reactions. However, lack of detail in the LMA's public information sessions and failure to release business case (amplified by anti-EWL network), limit the LMA's ability to create shared understanding about benefits of project amongst resident and pro-public transport groups.
	Anti-EWL	(+) The YCC's broad-based informing about anti-EWL campaign in 2012 results in early alliances with pro-public transport groups and connections with local resident groups in the EWL corridor.	(+) Anti-EWL movement effective in arguing the EWL's negative impacts on residents. Grassroots campaign creates strong affect-based relational ties with fearful and concerned resident and environmental groups.	(+) Scale of investment in the EWL, failure to invest in public transport alternatives and to release business case create shared understanding with pro-public transport groups the EWL is not value for money vis-à-vis public transport.

Escalation	**Pro-EWL**	(+) Broad-based informing continues to result in new connections forming with industry groups, motoring organizations and federal government.	(+) Connections to industry groups and motoring organizations based on understanding faster movement of people and goods important, while federal government shares view roads are prioritized. (−) State government announcement of A$108m public transport package intended to engage public transport groups has opposite effect; seen as insignificant relative to the EWL's cost and symbol of disregard for public transport.
	Anti-EWL	(+) Achieve scale-shifts through targeted mobilization of outer Melbourne and regional groups.	(+) Ties to more geographically distant resident groups achieved based on shared understanding of insufficient investment in public transport to service outer Melbourne and regional areas.
Resolution	**Pro-EWL**		
	Anti-EWL	(+) Targeted mobilization of political entities culminates in ties to main state opposition party which eventually announces it will cancel the EWL project if elected.	(+) Ties with opposition party politicians underpinned by growing understanding this is a widespread voter concern/electoral issue.

Note: Pro- or Anti-EWL refers to entities engaging in strategy, +/− refers to direction of effect.

101

with scepticism when compared with the A$6–8 billion investment in the EWL, perceiving it as reflective of government disregard for public transport.

By the resolution phase, only the anti-EWL movement was still creating public connections and growing its network. It gained a critical ally during this time with the main state opposition party unequivocally committing to cancel the EWL, even if contracts were signed pre-election. The anti-EWL movement's strong campaigning had led the opposition party to the growing understanding that the EWL was now a significant electoral issue with broad community support for the anti-EWL movement. This ally was to prove vital for the eventual success of the anti-EWL social movement (see subsection titled "The outcome").

Enhancing public legitimacy

The enhancing public legitimacy strategy comprised networks using social capital they had built to organize public displays of support, utilizing facts and evidence to collectively demonstrate the merits of their desired outcome. Limited use of this strategy by both networks manifested in the establishment phase, but increased as the dispute escalated (see Table 7.2).

In the establishment phase, the LMA relied mainly on actions aimed at creating legitimacy and momentum for the EWL. The LMA, together with its related government departments, announced funding to commence development of detailed plans and timelines for signing contracts with private-sector consortia to build the EWL. The use of its authority in this way was designed to indicate the EWL would progress to construction without delay. It also resulted in structural capital for the LMA as various private-sector entities commenced early engagement for the tender process on the shared understanding that contracts would be entered into within the advertised time frame.

Meanwhile, the anti-EWL movement utilized evidence through the YCC-initiated TNTR campaign. Reinforcing shared understandings that the EWL was an investment in the wrong transport mode, experts produced evidence at campaign events and rallies that alternative rail investment would, for far less funding, provide much greater traffic congestion relief.

In the escalation phase, both sides attempted to enhance their public legitimacy. The LMA had already mobilized the federal government as an active supporter, with pledged federal infrastructure funding of A$3 billion for both stages of the EWL helping improve perceptions the EWL was value-for-money for Victoria. The LMA also released traffic forecasts showing significant projected time savings for peak-hour motorists using the EWL. Providing some evidence of its benefits, this initially contributed cognitive capital for the LMA; however, the effect of this was quickly countered by the anti-EWL movement's response strategy (described in the following subsection).

In comparison, the anti-EWL movement engaged in diverse actions. Using local resident groups, they encouraged and facilitated dissemination of personalized news stories from local residents. Even the most conservative of Melbourne newspapers ran stories noting "public sympathy for the 92 households whose properties will be compulsorily acquired" (Panahi, 2013). Such stories stimulated feelings of solidarity, generating relational capital amongst those opposing the EWL. Leveraging this, the anti-EWL movement was able to organize local resident rallies and public meetings regularly attracting 200–500 people throughout 2013–2014. It also continued to utilize experts, such as a PTUA-organized forum with an academic expert in government contracts providing evidence that governments could, and indeed do, legally break contracts (Herington, 2014; Petit, 2015).

Additionally, the anti-EWL movement leveraged the scale shift it had achieved by this time to organize diverse and massive displays of support. The organization of peak-hour vigils at prominent prospective EWL sites continued weekly from mid-2013 until November 2014. Attended by a demographically broad range from grandmothers to school students, these vigils encouraged further support-building across the community (Petit, 2015). Orchestrated by the anti-EWL campaign, large

Table 7.2 Enhancing public legitimacy strategy and social capital effects – main patterns only

Phase		Structural Capital Effects	Relational Capital Effects	Cognitive Capital Effects
Establishment	**Pro-EWL**	(+) State government signalling funding commitments and time frame to sign contracts; latter results in connections with private-sector consortia interested in bidding for project.		(+) Signalling time frame for signing contracts to build EWL creates understanding amongst private-sector consortia that government is fully committed to EWL.
	Anti-EWL			(+) Well-known credible transport experts presenting project-specific facts at anti-EWL movement events broadens the shared understanding that EWL is an investment in wrong transport mode.
Escalation	**Pro-EWL**			(+) Organizing federal government support of A$3b reduces some concerns about cost of the project to Victorian taxpayers and reinforces understanding amongst EWL supporters the project represents value for the state. (+ **until discredited**) Releases traffic forecasts produced by its experts that evidences EWL as solution to peak traffic crisis (has limited effect due to anti-EWL's response).
	Anti-EWL	(+) Continued production of knowledge-based claims and growing public demonstrations of support for anti-EWL movement causes majority of members of government-linked planning committee to resign, announcing their lack of support for the EWL.	(+) Personalized news stories about residents losing homes and/or having their lifestyles disrupted elicit sympathy and reinforce feelings of solidarity amongst those opposing the EWL. In turn, this has important effect on the ability to organize further displays of support, regularly attracting 200–500 attendees to local rallies/meetings.	(+) Protest marches attracting large crowds of 2,000–3,000 and the generation of more than 1,500 submissions opposing the EWL to planning authority reinforce shared view that the broader public sees the EWL as the wrong project for the state. (+) Continued production of claims about the EWL's flaws and how governments can legally cancel contracts contributes further to shared view the EWL is a flawed and cancellable project.

Note: Pro- or Anti-EWL refers to entities engaging in strategy, +/– refers to direction of effect.

public transport rallies attracted crowds of 2,000–3,000 people during late 2013–2014, and when final plans for the EWL were submitted to the planning authority, it received more than 15,00 submissions in opposition, with few in support.

In response to this cumulative enhancing of the public legitimacy of their case against the EWL, important allies of the LMA began to shift allegiance. Specifically, in December 2013, five of the six members of the state government committee on planning resigned, with the former chair publicly revealing concern about spending on the EWL at the expense of public transport (Dow, 2013). In enhancing the legitimacy of their case for the EWL's cancellation, the anti-EWL movement had sim-ultaneously grown cognitive capital, with effects also on relational and structural capital.

Responding to counterarguments

In the escalation and resolution phases, both sides were observed responding to their counterclaims. These comprised challenges to the relational and cognitive capital they had developed (see Table 7.3).

In the escalation phase, the pro-EWL conservative press described protesters as "professional agitators […] [a] ratbag gang of unionists, unwashed hippies […] and progress-hating layabouts" (Panahi, 2013). Similarly, the transport minister criticized attendees at a project consultation meeting as "rent-a crowd" (Gordon & Tapper, 2013). Through this response, they sought to divide their oppos-ition and erode relational capital within the social movement. However, when subsequent media reports showed attendees to be genuine, concerned local residents, the opposite effect occurred, with bonds amongst resident groups strengthening based on their highlighted shared identity (Gordon & Tapper, 2013). Responding to growing protests, the State Government challenged their legitimacy, enacting an "anti-protest" amendment to the "move-on" laws in late 2013. Dubbed "The Silencing Act" by the anti-EWL movement, this action backfired when it led to important unions withdrawing support for the project, thus negatively impacting structural capital for the LMA (Jackson, 2014).

While the anti-EWL movement only utilized this strategy in the resolution phase, their attacks were multifaceted. Specifically, they discredited the cognitive capital the LMA were seeking to build. For example, when the LMA quoted a commissioned report stating the EWL would save an average 27 minutes in morning peak hour (Savage, 2014), the anti-EWL lobby pointed out the government's own departments did not approve the report's authors as authorized traffic forecasters, and used video of a cheap dash-mounted clock to show the morning peak-hour trip only took 22 minutes currently. The video flooded social media and was widely reported in the daily press, challenging claims that the LMA was making about the EWL's congestion savings.

The anti-EWL social movement also questioned the authenticity of the LMA's engagement with the public. Questioning the consultation process conducted by the LMA, the YCC and other local councils embarked on well-publicized legal challenges to the EWL centred on the legitimacy of the approval process in the "absence of a transparent and viable business case" (Cook, 2014). Exacerbating the perception that the process was not truly consultative, the independent government authority making recommendations on planning approval for the EWL was required to assess the merits of the project plans without access to the full business case or the final design plans, while tender consortia were given less than a month to alter prospective designs in light of recommendations from this committee (Herington, 2014).

The anti-EWL movement was also able to access a report by independent transport experts sys-tematically discrediting many of the LMA's published figures. It showed projected traffic benefits had been substantially exaggerated and the real cost to taxpayers of the eastern section of the EWL would be nearly double the initial LMA estimate (Dodson et al., 2014). Widely reported in the weeks before the Victorian State election in daily media and on blogs and websites of anti-EWL groups (Edwards, 2014), this struck at the heart of the argument that the EWL was a beneficial and cost-effective investment and eroded the LMA's cognitive capital. In response the government treasurer,

Table 7.3 Responding to counterarguments strategy and social capital effects – main patterns only

STRATEGY		*Structural Capital Effects*	*Relational Capital Effects*	*Cognitive Capital Effects*
Escalation	**Pro-EWL**	(–) Government decision to target protesters by amending "move-on" laws results in important unions discontinuing support for the project when they realize the wider potential impact of anti-protest laws.	(–) pro-EWL authorities repeatedly sought to divide protesters by questioning the authenticity of those protesting and attending local resident consultations. However, lack of supporting evidence meant rather than dividing protesters, it led to perceptions of the LMA as dismissive of local concerns over the project, enhancing solidarity of local resident opposition.	
	Anti-EWL			
Resolution	**Pro-EWL**			(–) The LMA and its allies claim report by independent transport experts is ideologically biased. However, LMA produced no supporting evidence, adding to a growing perception of government as dismissive of concerns about the EWL. (+) State premier's claim the EWL would save average 27/33 minutes in morning/afternoon peak challenged through video of dashboard clock indicating morning peak trip currently only 22 minutes.
	Anti-EWL			(+) Planning approval characterized as unduly hasty and so discredits "genuineness" of the LMA's public consultations. (+) Independent transport experts produce report indicating the EWL's cost likely to be double the initial LMA estimates and traffic congestion benefits much less. This report widely disseminated by anti-EWL movement and media, supporting the claim the EWL is a costly investment in the wrong transport mode.

Note: Pro- or Anti-EWL refers to entities engaging in strategy; +/– refers to direction of effect.

rather than producing additional facts and evidence, argued that the report was ideologically biased and he saw no "need to engage with a bunch of left-wing academics with a clear anti-roads agenda" (Edwards, 2014). Overall, with a greater evidence base to discredit claims, the actions of the anti-EWL movement had achieved significant impact in undermining the cognitive capital of the government.

The outcome

The LMA completed the tender process, and with authority from the state government proceeded to sign project contracts with a private-sector consortium, despite significant opposition. However, with the main opposition party now an ally of the anti-EWL social movement, the EWL became the significant issue in the upcoming state election. The government was voted out of office in November 2014, with discontent over the EWL considered the major factor. One of the first actions of the incoming government was to officially cancel the EWL. Central to the anti-EWL movement's victory had been its ability to create public connections with a wide and ever-expanding range of allies underpinned by shared understandings of the EWL's flaws as well as emotive-based affiliation, ties that ultimately included entities with the ability to cancel the EWL:

> In the early days the fight was led by those closest to the threat [...] As the opposition grew, new organizations blossomed or formed alliances that included individuals and groups of a variety of political persuasions but with a common objective to defeat the East West Link.
>
> *(Petit, 2015)*

Discussion

It is important for government authorities involved in infrastructure development to consider how they can engage more effectively with the public. In the case study, it was the specific role of the LMA and allied government entities to deliver public infrastructure projects. They possessed advantages in terms of authority, superior financial resources to commission expert investigations and reports, and greater information about the project, time frames and impact vis-à-vis the social movement. Despite these, the anti-EWL movement was able to overcome their apparent disadvantages because they built and harnessed social capital with the public in more effective ways vis-à-vis the LMA. It is proposed that government can learn from social movements that mobilize and direct public support effectively, rather than seeing them, as previous studies of infrastructure development suggest, as obstacles that are either to be ignored or removed. The study thus contributes to the public management literature by identifying strategies that need to be considered by infrastructure project proponents as part of their engagement with the public.

First, government authorities need to be more proactive and rethink their approach to creating public connections around specific infrastructure development projects. In contrast to the LMA, the anti-EWL social movement led by the YCC was more aggressive and faster in growing their network of relationships. This involved developing structural capital comprising ties to different entities characterized by shared understandings and cognitive capital, as well as relational capital (refer Table 9.1). Its prompt commencement of broad-based informing gave access to diverse pro-public transport allies that could be mobilized to help enhance public legitimacy in the establishment phase. Similarly, its targeted mobilization of local residents before the LMA did so, meant it was able to amplify concerns that the LMA could not address when it attempted to create public connections. In marked contrast, the approach by the pro-EWL authorities to create public connections was less intense and purposeful. The LMA was successful in creating ties to some resident groups, motoring and industry associations and the federal government. However, it was less active in creating public connections over the escalation and resolution phases, instead relying on its bureaucratic authority, a finding that resonates with prior studies of infrastructure projects (see Flores Dewey & Davis, 2013; Novy & Peters, 2012).

Second, government authorities should consider how they can create virtuous cycles of building social capital through creating public connections and harnessing this to enhance public legitimacy so that authentic public support can be cultivated and demonstrated for proposed infrastructure developments. Here the strategies of the anti-EWL social movement are instructive. Not only did they develop ties and trust within their network of public connections, but they then utilized these to access allies' time (e.g. demonstrations of support), financial resources (e.g. to directly invest in the EWL or challenge it), expertise (e.g. production of evidence), and experiences (e.g. residents allowing access to personal life-stories) to represent the EWL as neither value for money nor beneficial to the community. While this strategy used social capital in pursuit of the contested outcome, it simultaneously had a number of positive effects for social capital (see Table 9.2).

These purposeful cyclic combinations of creating public connections and enhancing public legitimacy were important for the events that unfolded and the final outcome. Specifically, having enlisted pro-public transport experts and groups as allies, the anti-EWL movement used social capital with these specialists to enhance the legitimacy of their case against the EWL with the public through the TNTR campaign. The development of evidence and resources that the campaign enabled was subsequently used in targeted mobilization of residents in areas distant to where the EWL was being built. The social movement was then able to utilize these ties to organize non-locals in displays of support, legitimizing its case further by demonstrating that opposition to the EWL was a widespread concern, rather than a case of NIMBY-ism. Having utilized its social capital to achieve this, it was finally able to enlist the main opposition party into its network. This was critical for the social movement, because it now had an ally that, if elected, would have formal authority over the EWL's fate. These virtuous cycles of purposefully creating public connections to build social capital, followed by the use of social capital to enhance public legitimacy and further build social capital, were not matched by the LMA.

Finally, in responding to counterarguments, the anti-EWL movement produced and disseminated credible alternative representation of the cost and time-saving benefits of the project. This strategy shifted the social capital differential between the anti-EWL movement and the pro-EWL authorities further in the social movement's favour (see Table 9.3). While it is noted that accounting research establishes the contested and fragile nature of financial and non-financial numbers and their effects, which can often comprise unintended consequences for those that promulgate them (e.g. see Christensen et al., 2019), in contrast to the anti-EWL movement, the government authorities did not respond with evidence-based counterclaims, largely relying on an approach to dismiss compelling counterevidence and question the authenticity of those opposing the project. In a world where multiple "evidence bases" can be mobilized to support both the case for and against infrastructure projects, government authorities' dismissal of counterarguments can threaten not only the economics (completion on time and to budget) of infrastructure development projects, but also democratic outcomes such as public inclusiveness and transparency.

Conclusion

This study examined through a social capital lens, the situation where government authorities propose infrastructure development projects and social movements contest this. It finds that the process of proposing infrastructure developments to the public can be contested when government authorities fail to engage in a portfolio of social capital-building strategies that social movements typically utilize. These comprise: creating public connections, enhancing public legitimacy, and responding to counterarguments.

More specifically, government authorities need to be more proactive and rethink their approach to creating public connections around specific infrastructure development proposals. In addition, they should seek to create virtuous cycles of building social capital through creating public connections and harnessing this to enhance public legitimacy. Finally, government authorities have to meaningfully engage with the counterarguments mobilized by social movements advocating against infrastructure development through evidenced-based approaches, rather than mere dismissal. Through these strategies, both the economics of infrastructure developments and their democratic outcomes can be enhanced.

The EWL case illustrates the importance of evidence and openness in the co-determination of public investments (Denhardt & Denhardt, 2015). Social movements and their constituent community groups increasingly mobilize their own scientists, experts and economic modellers to provide alternative views on the impacts of proposed projects. Consequently, project authorities cannot assume their claims about the impact and value of their projects will be unquestioningly accepted. They need to think about how they can be more credible, especially in the early phases when important project detail is yet to be shaped. For project authorities, utilizing actions such as early community engagement and "co-creation" of plans and strategies, may go some way towards enabling social capital building with resident and influential community groups (see Blomkamp, 2018).

However, it is possible that infrastructure proponents may be constrained in their use of social capital-building strategies vis-à-vis those that contest the development. Structural and/or institutional factors may operate to impede governments' use of social movements' strategies. For example, the EWL's proponents arguably were limited in their ability to develop relational capital and the associated deep emotive ties with particular groups because they had to act in the broader "public interest". Future research should examine this possibility of differential access to social capital arising from constraints on strategies available to government, and the implications for governments' engagement with the public when proposing infrastructure projects. Further to this, how governments may better utilize social media and internet-based campaigns, which are rapidly becoming the dominant tools of social movement groups, is an area which could benefit from future study (Jeacle, 2020).

In closing, the limitations of the research require acknowledgement. The single case study approach and the particular project analysed may place limitations on its transferability to other situations. Another limitation relates to the use of archival data, which may be incomplete or partial, insofar as it reflects the perspectives of those originally capturing events and the actions of those involved. Despite these limitations, the strategies identified and how they might be used appropriately are important for public sector managers to think through, as they seek greater civic engagement and democratic outcomes in the context of infrastructure development. These dimensions are important to manage and account for in the building of infrastructure.

Note

1 Currency conversion uses rates applicable at the time of the project and reported values are approximate only.

References

Blomkamp, E. (2018). The promise of co-design for public policy. *Australian Journal of Public Administration*, *77*(4), 729–743.

Bowen, G. A. (2009). Document analysis as a qualitative research method. *Qualitative Research Journal*, *9*(2), 27–40.

Bryson, J. M., Crosby, B. C., & Bloomberg, L. (2014). Public value governance: Moving beyond traditional public administration and the new public management. *Public Administration Review, 74*(4), 445–456.

Christensen, M., Skærbæk, P., & Tryggestad, K. (2019). Contested organizational change and accounting in trials of incompatibility. *Management Accounting Research, 45*, 100641. https://doi.org/10.1016/j.mar.2019.03.001

Cook, H. (2014, 21 July). Yarra council joins Moreland to fight East West Link. *The Age*. www.theage.com.au/ victoria/yarra-council-joins-moreland-to-fight-east-west-link-20140721-zv688.html

Corvellec, H. (2001). Talks on tracks – debating urban infrastructure projects. *Studies in Cultures, Organizations and Societies, 7*(1), 25–53.

Denhardt, J. V., & Denhardt, R. B. (2015). The new public service revisited. *Public Administration Review, 75*(5), 664–672.

Di Maddaloni, F., & Davis, K. (2018). Project manager's perception of the local communities' stakeholder in megaprojects: An empirical investigation in the UK. *International Journal of Project Management, 36*(3), 542–565.

Dodson, J., Low, N., Hayward, D., Stone, J., Gleeson, B., Currie, G., & Legacy, C. (2014). *Tunnel vision or world class public transport: How cancelling the East West Link can fund better transport alternatives for Melbourne*. Melbourne: RMIT/Melbourne University.

Dow, A. (2013, 13 December). Doubts over planning strategy after key advisers quit. *The Age*. www.theage.com. au/victoria/doubts-over-planning-strategy-after-key-advisers-quit-20131212-2z8lz.html

Edwards, J. (2014, 11 November). Victorian election 2014: East West Link could cost almost $18b, academics say. *ABC News*. www.abc.net.au/news/2014-11-11/east-west-link-could-cost-up-to-24178b-academics-say/ 5881252

Engbers, T. A., & Rubin, B. M. (2018). Theory to practice: Policy recommendations for fostering economic development through social capital. *Public Administration Review, 78*(4), 567–578.

Flores Dewey, O., & Davis, D. E. (2013). Planning, politics, and urban mega-projects in developmental context: Lessons from Mexico City's airport controversy. *Journal of Urban Affairs, 35*(5), 531–551.

Global Infrastructure Hub (2020). Global infrastructure outlook. https://outlook.gihub.org/

Gordon, J., & Tapper, G. (2013, 4 September). Reveal costs of projects: Eddington. *The Age*. http://ezproxy.libr ary.usyd.edu.au/login?url=http://search.proquest.com/docview/1429414055?accountid=14757

Herington, A. (2014, 29 April). East West Link planning process leaves Melbourne's public in the dark. *The Age*. www.theage.com.au/comment/east-west-link-planning-process-leaves-melbournes-public-in-the-dark-20140428-zr0nz.html

Inkpen, A. C., & Tsang, E. W. K. (2005). Social capital, networks, and knowledge transfer. *Academy of Management Review, 30*(1), 146–165.

Jackson, S. (2014). Silencing Act targets tunnel protestors. *PEN Melbourne Quarterly*, 29 August. https://suejack sonnews.blogspot.com/2014/08/silencing-act-targets-tunnel-protestors.html

Jeacle, I. (2020). Navigating netnography: A guide for the accounting researcher. *Financial Accountability & Management, 37*(1), 88–101. https://doi.org/10.1111/faam.12237

Langley, A. (1999). Strategies for theorizing from process data. *Academy of Management Review, 24*(4), 691–710.

Legacy, C. (2015). Transforming transport planning in the postpolitical era. *Urban Studies, 53*(14), 3108–3124.

Linking Management Authority. (2013). *Comprehensive Impact Statement. Eastern Section*. Department of Transport, Planning and Local Infrastructure, State Government of Victoria. November.

McAdam, D. (2011). Social movements and the growth in opposition to global projects. In W. R. Scott, R. E. Levitt, & R. J. Orr (Eds.), *Global projects: Institutional and political challenges* (pp. 86–110). Cambridge University Press.

Nahapiet, J., & Ghoshal, S. (1998). Social capital, intellectual capital, and the organizational advantage. *Academy of Management Review, 23*(2), 242–266.

Novy, J., & Peters, D. (2012). Railway station megaprojects as public controversies. The case of Stuttgart 21. *Built Environment, 38*(1), 128–145.

Panahi, R. (2013, 11 November). Protesters' arrogance undermines their cause over East West Link. *Herald Sun*. www.heraldsun.com.au/news/opinion/protesters-arrogance-undermines-their-cause-over-east-west-link/ story-fni0fhh1-1226756866171?nk=18c879ddf505631afb18c22b3e59f9c7-1457507878

Petit, M. (2015, 21 May). East West Link: From "done deal" to dead end. *The Northsider*. http://thenorthsider. com.au/east-west-link-from-done-deal-to-dead-end/

Pillai, K. G., Hodgkinson, G. P., Kalyanaram, G., & Nair, S. R. (2017). The negative effects of social capital in organizations: A review and extension. *International Journal of Management Reviews, 19*(1), 97–124.

Putnam, R. D. (1995a). Bowling alone: America's declining social capital. *Journal of Democracy, 6*(1), 65–78.

Putnam, R. D. (1995b). Tuning in, tuning out: The strange disappearance of social capital in America. *PS: Political Science and Politics, 28*(4), 664–683.

Putnam, R. D., Leonardi, R., & Nanetti, R. Y. (1994). *Making democracy work: Civic traditions in modern Italy*. Princeton University Press.

Savage, A. (2014, 7 August). East West Link: Government claims traffic study demonstrates faster travel times. *ABC News*. www.abc.net.au/news/2014-08-06/study-says-ewl-to-cut-travel-times/5651502

Snow, D. A., Soule, S. A., & Kriesi, H. (2004). Mapping the terrain. In V. Taylor, N. Van Dyke, D. A. Snow, S. A. Soule, & H. Kriesi (Eds.), *The Blackwell companion to social movements* (pp. 3–16). Blackwell.

Strauss, A. L. (1987). *Qualitative analysis for social scientists*. Cambridge University Press.

Strauss, A. L., & Corbin, J. (1998). *Basics of qualitative research: Techniques and procedures for developing grounded theory*. SAGE.

Teo, M. M., & Loosemore, M. (2017). Understanding community protest from a project management perspective: A relationship-based approach. *International Journal of Project Management, 35*(8), 1444–1458.

Tsai, W., & Ghoshal, S. (1998). Social capital and value creation: The role of intrafirm networks. *Academy of Management Journal, 41*(4), 464–476.

van den Ende, A. L, & van Marrewijk, A. H. (2015). Rebalancing the disturbance: Shock-absorbing platforms in urban mega-projects. G. Grabher & J. Thiel (Eds.), *Self-induced shocks: Mega-projects and urban development* (pp. 177–200). Perspectives in Metropolitan Research 1. Jovis Verlag.

van den Ende, L., & van Marrewijk, A. (2014). The ritualization of transitions in the project life cycle: A study of transition rituals in construction projects. *International Journal of Project Management, 32*(7), 1134–1145.

Willems, T., Verhoest, K., Voets, J., Coppens, T., Van Dooren, W., & Van den Hurk, M. (2017). Ten lessons from ten years PPP experience in Belgium. *Australian Journal of Public Administration, 76*(3), 316–329.

Woolcock, M. (2010). The rise and routinization of social capital, 1988–2008. *Annual Review of Political Science, 13*, 469–487.

8

STRATEGIC MANAGEMENT ACCOUNTING FOR CHANGE AND FLEXIBILITY

Kim Eriksson, Linda Höglund and Maria Mårtensson

Introduction

Management accounting is based on the idea of linking strategic objectives with operational targets. This assumes that strategies are constructed with long-term objectives and are linked with calculative practices to operationalize strategic plans into actions at an operational level. This link, which is somewhat complicated (see Kornberger & Carter, 2010; Skærbæk & Tryggestad, 2010), is sometimes expressed as a central aspect of management accounting, and occasionally labelled "Strategic Management Accounting" (SMA) (Nixon & Burns, 2012). Part of the complexity is that the SMA tools that are used tend to take a short-term perspective, ignoring the important aspect of long-term strategy work, such as making priorities based on long-term objectives. In other words, there is often a tension in SMA between long-term objectives and short-term evaluations (Höglund et al. 2018).

The idea of SMA in public sector organizations received gained academic interest and has become one aspect of understanding strategy work (Höglund et al., 2021b) and management control (Modell, 2012). Some studies have taken an interest in the construction of strategy and strategic work (e.g. Llewellyn & Tappin, 2003; Kornberger & Carter, 2010; Hansen Rosenberg & Ferlie, 2016; Höglund & Svärdsten, 2018; Bryson & George, 2020), while some have studied SMA in a public sector context (Cuganesan et al., 2012; Modell, 2012; Begkos et al., 2019; Höglund et al., 2021a); others have taken an interest in the alignment among the authorizing environment, public value creation and operational capacity as an expression of strategic management accounting (Bruns, 2014; Bracci et al., 2019; Steccolini, 2019; Höglund et al., 2021b).

Despite the interest in strategy work and management accounting in the public sector, few have investigated how public sector organizations use strategic management in practice (Höglund & Mårtensson, 2019). As a result, there have been several calls for studies of how strategic management tools are used in practice (Johnsen, 2015, 2016; Höglund et al., 2018) as well as for studies on the use of SMA tools (Nixon & Burns, 2012; Höglund et al., 2021a). Thus, so far, we have rather limited knowledge about how SMA tools are used in practice in the public sector. Therefore, the purpose of this chapter is to enhance our knowledge about SMA in the public sector context.

We have two theoretical starting points. First, we use the term "SMA tools", and we take a broad view of the term, including frameworks, concepts, models and methods (Jarzabkowski & Kaplan, 2015). Second, we approach the empirical material as an issue of strategizing, meaning that we take an activity-based view in this chapter focusing on the doings of people in terms of how people use SMA tools in their local context (Jarzabkowski & Fenton, 2006; Jarzabkowski & Kaplan, 2015).

DOI: 10.4324/9781003295945-11

Strategizing can be viewed as a complex set of activities and tools that practitioners perform and use (Begkos et al., 2019), which are: those planning, resource allocation, monitoring and control practices, and processes through which [SMA] is enacted (Jarzabkowski & Fenton, 2006, p. 632). These starting points mean that our theoretical focus is on the activities that make up (or do not make up) SMA in practice and the tools used.

To address this purpose, we studied strategy and management accounting in the Swedish Public Employment Service (SPES), a central government agency in Sweden. We interviewed 38 operational managers and controllers at the SPES. One reason for our study was that in 2020, a new strategic direction was introduced to manage changes in the agency's environment along with a balance scorecard (BSC). In previous research, the BSC was described as an SMA tool (e.g. Modell, 2012; Raschid et al. 2020) and we decided to study its use more closely in operative units and sections. Based on this, the following research question that guided this chapter is: *How is the BSC used by a public sector agency as an SMA tool?*

The next section presents the SPES, and the following section presents the literature review. After the literature review, the method section is presented. Following the method section is the analysis where three narratives are described, and in the last section is the concluding discussion presented.

The case of the SPES: a continuously changing agency

The SPES has several responsibilities and tasks, a central one being the facilitation of matching jobseekers and employers in the Swedish labour market. Other responsibilities include providing unemployment insurance and helping individuals with disabilities integrate or reintegrate into the labour market. The SPES is also organized into several units throughout Sweden.

In the Swedish context, it is important to recognize that central government agencies are autonomous. This means that by law, a minister cannot exercise control over or intervene in agencies' work (Government Office of Sweden, 2014). The Swedish government governs agencies through instructions, tasks, laws and financial frameworks. In terms of SMA tools, central government agencies are free to choose, formulate and use their own strategies and management accounting tools. Agencies do imitate each other, and powerful actors socially impose certain tools of accounting and control. For example, a strategy discourse was developed due to reforms in the late 1980s, which led to the introduction of strategies and the BSC in several agencies, which were initiated by private sector consultants among others (Modell, 2012).

The SPES has been subjected to continuous changes. Since 2014, SPES had been subject to internal changes, including a "renewal journey" initiated by the Director General in which, for instance, SMA tools were changed; a major reorganization in the agency took place; increasing emphasis on digitalization; and a faster rate of changes in the agency due to the Covid-19 pandemic, according to some of the interviewees. Moreover, changes were not only initiated internally in the agency. For instance, geopolitical changes such as the "immigration crisis" of 2015 contributed to increasing the number of people registered at the SPES. Additionally, after the 2018 election, the governing coalition decreased the SPES budget, forcing the agency to reduce its staff by 4,500 employees (it had approximately 13,500 employees before) and close several physical offices in Sweden. Hence, the agency has been subjected to changes internally as well as externally. All the changes over time created a view that, paraphrasing some of the interviewees, "you need to love change to work at SPES".

New strategies were formulated at the SPES in 2020 for 2026, and the BSC was introduced. The strategic plan contains five areas that are important to focus on for 2026. The areas are: (i) a unified view of the agency's role and mission; (ii) being a modern and efficient agency; (iii) being accessible to everyone; (iv) being a hub in a system with a multiplicity of actors; and (v) being a trust-based, inclusive, and developing workplace (SPES, 2020b). Together these areas aim to set out a general direction for the SPES and describe what the future agency should look like. Other changes linked with the strategy are (i) moving from local dependence to digital independence; (ii) moving from the client (jobseekers and employers) to the client's case; and (iii) moving from generalist to specialist (SPES, 2020b). One ambition of the internal changes is to contribute to effective and available support for customers (customer perspective), improved productivity and working environment for staff (*employee* perspective), and more efficient matching on the labour market by focusing on value creation and efficient use of the agency's resources (assignment perspective).

The BSC is based on three perspectives, each of which has objectives, measurements and activities. These perspectives are a *customer perspective* focusing on simplifying and shortening the path to jobs and studies; an *employee perspective* focusing on creating conditions for employees to thrive, develop and perform; and an *assignment perspective* focusing on creating efficient operations and well-functioning administration (SPES, 2020c). Moreover, the BSC is used as a way of prioritizing at the operational level in the SPES. That is, the scorecard visualizes and emphasizes performances and activities that units and sections are to focus on.

The scorecard created at the SPES is different from the way Kaplan and Norton (1992) designed the BSC. The BSC contains three perspectives and the strategic plan is indirectly linked to it. This means that the strategic plan functions as a framework for the whole agency, while in the "original" BSC, the strategic plan would have been operationalized to strategic objectives. At the SPES, the process is that the top management creates a national operational plan with objectives that are influenced by the strategic plan, the instructions, the appropriation directions from the government and the financial frameworks for the agency. The national operational plan is then translated into a BSC, including objectives, measurements and activities at the regional level, and that BSC is then translated to the units. Hence, the BSC is indirectly linked to strategies. For this chapter, the SPES becomes a context to study the use of an SMA tool that is characterized by change and at an operative level where SMA is used.

Strategic management accounting and the public sector

To study the use of SMA, we need some understanding of SMA and also of what we know about SMA in a public sector context. While we argue that we know little about the use of SMA tools, we do know something about SMA in a public sector context.

To begin with, there are several definitions and positions on how SMA can be understood (Langfield-Smith, 2008; Nixon & Burns, 2012). A common way of understanding SMA is that it creates relationship(s) between strategic management and calculative practices (Höglund et al., 2021a). Calculative practices, in broad terms, include tools for accounting such as performance measurements, cost calculations and budgets that make units, people and processes visible so they can be acted on (Miller, 2001). Strategic management, in a public sector context, can be viewed as strategy formulation and implementation that includes strategic planning to formulate strategies to achieve long-term objectives (Bryson & George, 2020). Putting this together, SMA becomes a set of management accounting practices that have a strategic orientation and can therefore be used for the implementation of strategy, planning, evaluation and control of activities directed towards long-term strategic intentions and objectives in combination with short-term objectives (Simmonds, 1981; Roslender & Hart, 2003; Langfield-Smith, 2008). However, it should be mentioned that the relationship between strategy and management accounting is not necessarily unidirectional. As an example, Skærbæk and Tryggestad (2010) show how accounting played a role in the reformulation of strategy (see also Kober et al., 2007; Kornberger & Carter, 2010).

There have been calls for more research about SMA and the importance of the public sector context for SMA (Cuganesan et al., 2012; Rashid et al., 2020; Höglund, et al., 2021a). Public sector organizations operate in a context where a multiplicity of demands and needs are often inconsistent but need to be managed (Jacobs & Cuganesan, 2014). Research on SMA in this context appears to highlight a couple of aspects despite being described as scant (Malleret et al., 2015).

First, some studies about SMA in the public sector assume that strategies and management accounting are used to create competitive advantages (Agasisti et al., 2008; Lachmann et al., 2013). This is based on a traditional view of strategy that conceptualizes it as unidirectional and deliberate, and situates strategy in a stable context inspired by Porter's (1985) ideas of strategic positioning and competitive advantage (see Malleret et al., 2015). One example is a study by Lachmann et al. (2013), who explored the determinants and effects of the use of SMA tools by addressing strategic positioning and competitiveness in relation to risk management and investments. The competitive advantage assumption does not consider the context in which public sector organizations are regulated. Additionally, in the context of the public sector, this assumption that is embedded in the idea of SMA (Simmonds, 1981; Nixon &Burns, 2012), does not take into consideration the enactment of SMA by practitioners, specifically the strategizing activities and what practitioners do in practice (Bryson & George, 2020).

Second, one stream of studies that has moved away from the traditional view on strategic management and its external focus on competitive advantages, has taken an interest in strategizing as a way of understanding SMA in the public sector. Strategizing is an approach to focusing the analysis on the complex set of activities and tools that practitioners perform in an organization in relation to strategy (Begkos et al., 2019; Bryson & George, 2020), in our case SMA. Studies on strategizing illustrate that management accounting is used to strategize as a coping mechanism in response to financial problems (Begkos et al., 2019); that management accounting enables and constrains strategic intents at operational levels (Höglund et.al., 2018); and that alignment of strategic intents, for instance, through efficiency and minimizing costs via SMA tools also aim to direct attention to strategic intents (Cuganesan et al., 2012). Together, these studies highlight challenges and struggles that actors in public sector organizations face when working with SMA, and some ways that SMA is enacted in public sector organizations.

Third, SMA tools are shaped by and entangled with political regulation (Modell, 2012; Bobe et al., 2017; Höglund et al., 2018; Höglund et al., 2021a). For example, Modell (2012) shows that strategies are translated into BSC and later reconstructed and translated to target maps because of regulatory pressures via budgetary constraints as well as ambitions to align the public sector organization closer with political directives. Modell (2012, p. 285) suggests that sometimes political regulation creates internal short-term focus as regulatory pressures change SMA from a "broad and open-ended quest for better alignment with political regulation" to a focus on certain newly prioritized and short-term issues through performance measurements. According to this argument, SMA sometimes becomes closely associated with regulations that create short-term sightedness in terms of priorities and agendas that constrain long-term strategic management (Modell, 2012; Höglund et al., 2018; Höglund et al., 2021a).

In summary, so far, we have limited knowledge about SMA in the specific context of the public sector and even less about the use of SMA tools in the public sector. This is partly due to a view of SMA from a strategic management perspective privileging the ideas of strategic positioning and competitive advantages; this is a perspective that has no interest in the strategizing activities within an organization and the use of SMA tools by a public organization and its managers and employees. However, previous research suggests that we need to not only take on a strategizing perspective to better understand SMA but also to understand how political regulation affects the use of SMA tools.

Method

The empirical material for this chapter is part of a longitudinal research project that studied management accounting and control change over eight years (2014–2021) at the SPES. During the research project, over 250 interviews, a media study, observations and a document study were conducted. This chapter is primarily based on interviews with 38 operational managers (first- and second-line managers) and controllers working operatively with the BSC. The interviews were conducted digitally in 2021 and varied between 45 and 90 minutes, were transcribed verbatim, and all of them addressed SMA and change. Our interest in conducting the interviews was to understand the practices of operational managers and controllers concerning strategy and management accounting using the BSC as an SMA tool.

We also analysed documents. Those used in this chapter were sent to us by respondents. We ended the interviews by asking for documents describing strategies, work processes and the BSC in the agency as a whole and the units and sections. Sixty documents were sent to us, including the BSC for the unit. The documents contributed to creating a context as well as an understanding of the scope, translation and definitions of strategy and management accounting at the SPES, to name a few examples. For example, when some respondents talked about the BSC, the document with the BSC helped us understand the different objectives and measurements in the local BSC. Thus, the documents enabled us to put the interviews in context, and the other way around as well.

In analysing the empirical material, a reflexive methodology guided the thematization and analysis in this chapter (Alvesson & Sköldberg, 2018), which means that the analysis was written iteratively, moving between the empirical material, reading up on SMA research, putting words to "what is going on here" and so forth. The thematization of the empirical material and the contribution was created by highlighting dominant and recurring narratives. The analysis process described below is presented as a linear process, but the process was iterative.

After the interviews were conducted, a storyline was written. The text was empirical and written based on the question "*how can we understand strategy, management accounting and changes?*" in the case organization; the document was 69 pages with an initial thematization. From the empirical storyline, we wrote the first draft on how SMA tools are used in the agency and a couple of empirical findings began to emerge. For example, we identified a few recurring narratives, three of which are presented in the analysis. Hence, our approach in this chapter has been to theorize from "locally emerging concepts" (see Alvesson & Deetz, 2000) and not take our starting point from a set of predefined concepts.

As we identified some recurring narratives, we interpreted them in relation to the literature on SMA in public sector organizations. This interpretative work enabled us to outline the analysis, answer the research question and also make theoretical contributions. We gained an insight into the use of an SMA tool in analysing the narratives in which the operational managers and controllers described how they work concerning strategy and the balanced scorecard; we also interpreted a flexibility idea that was linked with the narratives. By analysing the narratives and the way they were constructed, we found that they rested on the idea of creating flexibility. Hence, our interpretations of the material, research on SMA and the writing of the contribution developed in two steps. The analysis is addressed in the next section.

Narratives about the use of an SMA tool

The BSC is used in several ways at the SPES by the operational managers and controllers. In this section, we analyse how they use and interpret the BSC in their local context.

Reactive management and control

Our results show that the BSC is used as reactive management and control. This means that the BSC is employed as a tool for reacting and adapting to external changes. The narrative builds on the idea that the scorecard is a way of adapting to contextual changes, for example, changing priorities from the government. In the upcoming section, we provide examples of statements from the interviewed respondents.

One manager gave an example of how the BSC is used as a way of managing external changes affecting the SPES by reacting to political changes due to the COVID-19 pandemic:

> But then, as you said, new priorities come along, and that alone – it might be that we're not at all done with an activity, and all of a sudden there's a new directive and we have to reprioritize. It's happened. The pandemic last year, we at SPES got a lot of funding [from the government] to offer Support and Matching services to jobseekers pretty much from day one. So we increased our Support and Matching services from June of last year to December by 2,000 people.
>
> *(R26, Unit manager)*

In this case, the BSC was used as a tool to reprioritize and make new priorities visible by changing the scorecard based on changing financial conditions from the government. For the SPES, the Covid-19 pandemic meant that the newly unemployed were being prioritized over the long-term unemployed, and that the basic functions of the agency would be digital. New activities and objectives were added to the scorecard. For example, as one controller told us (R24), the BSC came to focus on securing compensation for the unemployed and ensuring that people were enrolled as the influx of the unemployed was greater than before the pandemic.

Another example is when the scorecard is used to capture changes in the funding of prioritized areas or in the refocusing of the agency's work. For instance, the government uses changes in the SPES budget to highlight areas in need of prioritization, which is made visible and operationalized by changing the scorecard. A manager described recent changes focusing on the long-term unemployed that were added to the scorecard:

> At the moment there's an incredible focus as an assignment from the government, too, that we're to have activities, active measures for our long-term unemployed. Unemployment is decreasing, but long-term unemployment is increasing. So what are we doing there? [...] One activity [in the scorecard] can be that someone attended a vocational training course, maybe there's not an obvious employer, so the person needs help from an [external] actor.
>
> *(R36, Unit manager)*

The scorecard is used, as the remarks from the manager suggest, to react to changes by introducing new activities and objectives. Interestingly, the managers, as well as others, point to the link between the scorecard, especially the assignment side of the scorecard, and political initiatives.

To sum up, our results show that the BSC is used to construct reactive management and control. The narrative concerns the relationship between the SPES and their context, such as the government. However, there is also a narrative related to changes constructed in relation to an internal view of managing changes more generally. This leads us to the next section, which points out that the BSC is used as a tool for active management and control.

Active[1] management and control

Our results also show that when the BSC is used, it is not only used as reactive management and control but also as active management and control, that is, an active narrative. These narratives depend on the perspective taken on the BSC at the SPES, such as external or internal. From an internal perspective, our results show how the scorecard is used as a way of continuously changing priorities, objectives and activities in the units and sections that come from changes in internal processes, issues and priorities. As in the previous section, we provide some examples of statements from the interviewed respondents.

One controller gave an example, in a general sense, of how new issues and questions are added to the BSC.

> [I]f there are other issues to be added to the agenda, I think this should be visible in the planning. And our way of tackling it has been to have some kind of *active scorecard*, where we say, "OK, now we're doing this activity". So that's the activity that goes in there, and maybe the other one is finished or needs to be deleted. So it reflects what's really on the table and feels important.
>
> *(R20 Operations controller, italics added)*

As the controller puts it, active management and control are created as issues, questions and priorities that come to matter and need to be focused on are added to the BSC. One example of a priority for some of the units at the time of the study was to develop cooperation with the local authorities and folk high schools to ensure access to training facilities as a solution to manage unemployment during the Covid-19 pandemic, and this priority was added to the scorecard.

One aspect of the active usage of the BSC is that it is revised every third month. During the revision, the scorecard is adjusted to changes in the agency or changes affecting the agency. One manager explained that the process of updating the BSC is based on quite short cycles.

> Given that we have quite short cycles – we follow up on the scorecards every third month and adjust them. Now they look pretty similar, the first and second quarter this year, for example.
>
> *(R10, Unit manager)*

Similarly, one controller stated that the BSC is an "active" tool because the scorecard is continuously adapted:

> Now we change it a bit now and then, *to work more actively and update the scorecard more often*, so it will more clearly focus on what we're to achieve in the next three months. Sort of like that. It might be a bit shorter or longer term, too, of course.
>
> *(R24, Operations controller, italics added)*

One aim of using the BSC is to make changes operationalizable, which suggests that changes that the SPES is subjected to become manageable by changing the scorecard every third month, thereby creating active management and control through revisions.

The active use of the scorecard was not only a question of making changes to it, but also, as several other interviewees told us, the BSC is present in their everyday work. For example, the scorecard is active because it is present in activities such as meetings. One section manager explained:

> It's not just a document you take out and rewrite a couple of times a year; it's with you all the time. It's what we base our follow-ups on, it's what we base our management meetings on. *So it's very active.*
>
> *(R34, Section manager, italics added)*

The section manager emphasized that the scorecard is present in, and is the basis of, evaluations, dialogues and management meetings. The dialogues in which the BSC is used to discuss performance take place at different organizational levels among regional managers and section managers, section managers and unit managers, and unit managers and employees, which vary on a weekly and/or monthly basis. The BSC is used for planning, monitoring and evaluating performance and activities throughout different organizational levels.

Our results show a recurring narrative about active management and control where the BSC is used as a tool to capture updates, changes, issues and questions that are internally initiated, which means the BSC is given active characteristics. It is an internal view and description of the use of the BSC. While there are some differences between the active and the reactive narratives, they also overlap in the sense that the scorecard is used to manage changes and make issues and priorities visible and manageable. A key difference in the narratives is that active management and control are often expressed as managing internal changes and issues. The reactive narrative is used as the BSC becomes a tool to react to external changes and issues. Thus, the narratives resemble each other.

A question here is, why is there a need for both reactive and active management and control in the agency? The short answer is that the agency is constantly changing. As described in the presentation on the SPES, the agency changes often and changes are initiated both internally and externally. Against this background, the two narratives are connected to recurring changes that the agency's managers and employees have to manage. The two narratives suggest that the scorecard is used to adjust priorities and activities concerning these changes. One central issue is, what consequences are created by the use of the BSC? This led us to the next narrative.

Short-term perspective

Our results show that when the BSC is used, it also constructs a short-term perspective: management and control in the units and sections are directed towards questions, issues and performances that are managed "here and now". This could be because we have mainly interviewed people on the operative level. However, the BSC creates circumstances in the units and sections where short-sightedness is emphasized as something good. As in the previous sections, we will provide some examples of statements from the interviewed respondents.

One unit manager gave an example of the short-term perspective by pointing out the difference in planning horizons between the SPES and another central government agency.

> we have very short-term perspectives at SPES. But when I talk to the Swedish Social Insurance Agency's local office, they say that they do three-year operational plans. That sounds like a dream come true to me. But then they have to be revised all the time. We do two months at a time. That's what it's like at our agency.
>
> *(R27, Unit manager)*

The unit's planning horizon, based on the BSC, is two months, and this suggests that the unit's perspective is more or less in conflict with strategic ideas of creating a long-term perspective. The short-term perspective is not only based on the units' and sections' planning, but also on the fact that the contents of the scorecard change. For example, one controller described the ongoing changes in the BSC as taking place one to three times a year when objectives and/or measurements are changed, for instance, by being removed or replaced (R31).

In addition, another controller argued that changes in the scorecard from management come abruptly and are not explained:

The challenge has perhaps not been that they change it, but that they change it and a new score-card pops into your inbox. "Here's a new scorecard". OK, so what does this mean? You can see what's been changed, that's clearly indicated, but it's not clear what that means, we have to work that out for ourselves. So that's a new assignment for us: OK, how do we interpret this? Something was removed, something that maybe a section manager worked a lot on, and now we have to explain to that section manager that, hey, it's gone now. You don't have to do it anymore. Or do you? Maybe, I don't know. Because it's not clear why a certain thing's been removed, it's only clear that it's not on the scorecard anymore.

(R28, Operations controller)

This statement exemplifies how top management tends not only to identify a need for changes without explaining it further down in the organization on an operative level but also to stimulate a short-term perspective that challenges strategy work as it gets detached from the operative level. The lower levels do not understand the changes and they create a short-term focus on acting and reacting in the here and now. The main idea of SMA is thus challenged as it is intended to provide a long-term per-spective that connects the strategic and operative levels using SMA tools such as the BSC.

Another example of short-term focus and detachment between strategy work at a top management level and the operative day-to-day activities is given by a section manager:

But the future and the present don't go hand in hand. We're not in sync. And I think it's important to us locally to signal that we really want to be there, but we're here with our 7,000 clients standing here […] wanting help. […] To put it briefly, I'd say that I think we have different expectations and impressions of our target group and what we can offer our clients. And it's not in sync. […] But I stand by what I say. I've said it before. I think our top manage-ment don't understand what that means. They want to create a nice model. And it is very nice, but it's not based in reality.

(R19 Section manager)

What we want to highlight with this statement is that several of the interviewees argued that the strategy is not grounded in their reality. This reasoning can be viewed in contrast to that of the Director General, who wrote that the strategic plan aims to contribute to "giving direction and meaning to our work" (Director General of SPES, 2020a, p. 19). Instead, SMA becomes detached from the respondents' operations.

Overall, managers and controllers expressed a perspective of being unable to have a long-term perspective due to a general lack of knowledge. "Not knowing" becomes a contrast to the idea that the combination of strategy and management accounting creates direction, clarity and a long-term perspective. The interviewees, in contrast, suggested pondering, having a two-month focus and being prepared for changes in priorities. Moreover, a degree of scepticism can be read into the comments quoted here and their argument can be paraphrased as "the strategies will change" and "strategy is a nice document, but not for us".

When SMA is practised, it is constructed from a short-term perspective, which most of the interviewees who work with operational matters described. However, this contrasts with some ideas about how SMA is practised, that is, linking a long-term perspective and operative management con-trol with SMA tools such as BSC. Instead, when the operational managers and the controllers relate to strategy and work with management accounting, it is a question of managing changes and it is based on the premise of working in the short term. The scorecard can be changed without explan-ation, reacting to changes, with strategies being detached from reality and ending up feeling that it is impossible to work with a long-term focus.

Concluding discussion

The purpose of this chapter has been to enhance our knowledge of SMA in a public sector context by studying the use of an SMA tool. Strategy discourse has influenced management accounting and control in public sector organizations (Nixon & Burns, 2012), and calls for studies about SMA and the use of SMA tools have been made (cf. Cuganesan et al., 2012; Rashid et al., 2020; Höglund et al., 2021a). We have illustrated the narratives are *reactive management and control*, *active management and control*, and a *short-term perspective* regarding how an SMA tool is used. The narratives contribute to our understanding of SMA in public sector organizations in a couple of ways.

First, studies on SMA in the public sector that focused on strategizing illustrate, for example, that SMA becomes a tool used to cope with issues such as financial constraints (Begkos et al., 2019), or that SMA is used to direct actions towards strategic intents (Cuganesan, et al., 2012); instead, we propose that the enactment of SMA is about attributing characteristics to SMA, such as reactive, active and short-term characteristics. Our argument and contribution are that attributing characteristics to SMA tool(s) becomes a way of enacting SMA in the public sector context, in addition to aligning SMA tools to strategic intents (Cuganesan et al., 2012), or as a coping mechanism (Begkos et al., 2019).

Second, our analysis also demonstrates that SMA is given a capturing role in this case. For example, SMA is used to capture changes in issues, questions, prioritizations, activities and objectives, which are both internally and externally initiated. The capturing role illustrates, like some previous studies, that the SMA tool is used for managing and internalizing changes in public sector organizations' environment (Modell, 2012; Höglund et al., 2021a). Like previous research, this points to the importance of regulation and political initiatives that intervene and affect the use of SMA, and that SMA becomes focused on short-term issues (Höglund et al., 2021b). While, for instance, Modell (2012) shows how strategy was reconstructed over time, we point to recurring changes being managed through attributing SMA tool characteristics and capturing and making changes operationalizable at an operative level in an agency. SMA in this context is used to enable adaptation to change at an operative level by capturing, for instance, new issues, priorities, activities and objectives that are related to changes.

Third, if we look at all three narratives together, we can see that they are not only constructed on change but also on the neoliberal idea of flexibilization. That is, flexibility has become a strategic imperative in contemporary organizations and has become a "sought-after characteristic of new post-bureaucratic organisation" (Alawattage & Wickramasinghe, 2018, p. 168). Today's management discourse holds a strong belief in flexibility, emerging from neoliberal ideas and the need to have more "organic" and "flexible" organizational forms and management practices, which strives to overcome the perceived rigidity and inefficiency of more "bureaucratic" structures and practices (duGay et al., 2005). Hence, in a neoliberal discourse, conditions are produced for the flexible individual in the flexible organization to respond to and enact (market) changes by, for example, promoting entrepreneurial behaviour and being externally oriented (Axelsson et al., 2018; Alawattage & Wickramasinghe, 2018, 2022).

Flexibilization is, Alawattage and Wickramasinghe (2022) write, "simultaneously macro and micro, political and techno-managerial" (p. 536), to enhance the ability to create value by responding to changes, which means that change are both politically and managerially initiated. In our case, SMA links to both macro and micro changes. Macro changes, such as a political initiative to redirect efforts on the labour market, become operationalized via SMA. The macro changes point to the role that SMA has in capturing regulations and political initiatives in public sector organizations (Modell, 2012; Höglund et al., 2021a). Micro changes, such as managerial ideas about creating ideas regarding the future via a strategy (cf., Kornberger, 2013) and addressing internal issues, processes and priorities simultaneously, are aimed to be captured by using flexible SMA. The use of SMA through the active narratives, for instance, suggests that the use of SMA is to capture and react to changes from politics, the environment and management quickly.

One reason to use an SMA tool, in this case, is to enable flexibility, which is driven by both political and managerial interventions and contributes to creating flexible management and control as well as flexible managers and employees. We mean that the use of SMA in the three narratives is about creating and maintaining a flexible agency that can manage, react and adapt to changes. However, in the strategy literature, the desire for flexibility in terms of goals, strategies and processes needs to be viewed in relation to stability and long-term perspectives (Bryson & George, 2020), especially in the context of the public sector (Höglund & Mårtensson, 2019). We, rather, mean that public sector agencies use the BSC as an SMA tool for flexibilization purposes, that is, to create a flexible agency using flexible SMA.

In relation to Alawattage and Wickramasinghe (2022), we propose that the SMA tool is used to create flexibility; that is, SMA becomes an aspect of enabling flexibilization and reproducing a neoliberal discourse. Flexibilization, then, is not only a question of the individuals, the organizations, and the society in general but also, in this case, the SMA tools that are used. It suggests that we perhaps must understand SMA in public sector organizations as a short-term, flexibility-seeking tool(s). In our case, SMA is adjusted, modified and altered to enable a flexible agency. This provides a contrast to the idea of SMA providing long-term direction and a degree of stability (Langfield-Smith, 2008; see also Nixon & Burns, 2012). Or in our case, SMA becomes a malleable, responsive and fluid practice in relation to changes and the desire for flexibility in contemporary public management discourse.

Throughout our case, we illustrate how an SMA tool is used and enacted in a public sector context, which has been given little attention in previous research. We show the strategizing activities (doings and use) of an SMA tool by operational managers and controllers that make up SMA in a context where change is prevalent. In conclusion, our analysis in this chapter shows that the use of SMA in a public sector context is characterized by attributes given to an SMA tool, managing and internalizing changes, and used to capture several issues. We propose that the notion of flexibilization is a way of understanding how SMA is used, as the dream of being flexible also characterizes the studied agency's operational managers and controllers and how they use SMA.

Lastly, if strategy and strategic work (Llewellyn & Tappin, 2003; Kornberger & Carter, 2010), management accounting and an idea of linking these together (Cuganesan et al., 2012; Modell, 2012; Höglund et al., 2021a) matter in public sector organizations, there is time for research to analyse its interplay and consequences without naive ideas of an unproblematic linking and use of SMA. For instance, what are some consequences of SMA for public organizations to carry out their essential mission and contribute to societal values? It cannot, reasonably, be unproblematic.

Note

1 A word about translation. In Swedish, the narrative is expressed as a reoccurring characteristic given to SMA as *levande styrning*. It is a challenge to translate *levande styrning* into English. A few words that it is possible to use are active, vital and vivid. We choose to translate it as "active" because the use of the word *levande* means to create management and control that is engaging, creates engagement, aims to create action, and is possible to change.

References

Agasisti, T., Arnaboldi, M., & Azzone, G. (2008). Strategic management accounting in universities: the Italian experience, *Higher Education, 55*(1), 1–15.

Alawattage, C., & Wickramasinghe, D. (2018). *Strategizing management accounting: Liberal origins and neoliberal trends*. Routledge.

Alawattage, C., & Wickramasinghe, D. (2022). Strategising management accounting: liberal origins and neoliberal trends. *Accounting, Auditing and Accountability Journal, 35*(2), 518–546.

Alvesson, M., & Deetz, S. (2000). *Doing Critical Management Research*. SAGE.

Alvesson, M., & Sköldberg, K. (2018). *Reflexive methodology: New vistas for qualitative research*. SAGE.

Axelsson, K., Höglund, L., & Mårtensson, M. (2018). Is what's good for business good for society? Entrepreneurship in a school setting. In U. Hytti, R. Blackburn, & S. Tegtmeier (Eds.), *The dynamics of entrepreneurial contexts: Frontiers in European Entrepreneurship research*. (pp. 54–75). Edward Elgar.

Begkos, C., Llewellyn, S., & Walshe, K. (2019). Strategizing in English hospitals: Accounting, practical coping and strategic intent. *Accounting, Auditing and Accountability Journal, 32*(5), 1270–1296.

Bobe, B. J., Mihret, D. G., & Obo, D. D. (2017). Public-sector reforms and balanced scorecard adoption: An Ethiopian case study. *Accounting, Auditing and Accountability Journal, 30*(6), 1230–1256.

Bracci, E., Papi, L., Bigoni, M., & Gagliardo Deidda, E. (2019). Public value and public sector accounting research: A structured literature review. *Journal of Public Budgeting, Accounting and Financial Management, 31*(1), 103–136.

Bruns, H. J. (2014). Accounting change and value creation in public services – do relational archetypes make a difference in improving public service performance? *Critical Perspectives on Accounting, 25*(4–5), 339–367.

Bryson, J. M., & George, B. (2020). Strategic management in public administration. In J. M. Bryson & B. George (Eds.), *Oxford research encyclopedia of politics* (pp. 1–26). Oxford University Press.

Cuganesan, S., Dunford, R., & Palmer, I. (2012). Strategic management accounting and strategy practices within a public sector agency. *Management Accounting Research, 23*(4), 245–260.

du Gay, P., Salaman G., & Rees B. (1996/2005). The conduct of management and the management of conduct: Contemporary managerial discourse and the constitution of the "competent" manager. *Journal of Management Studies, 33*(3), 263–282. Edited version, 2005, 40–57.

Government Office of Sweden (2014). How Sweden is governed. www.government.se/how-sweden-is-governed/

Hansen Rosenberg, J., & Ferlie, E. (2016). Applying strategic management theories in public sector organizations: Developing a typology. *Public Management Review, 18*(1), 1–19.

Höglund, L., Holmgren Caicedo, M., Mårtensson, M., & Svärdsten, F. (2018). Strategic management in the public sector: How tools enable and constrain strategy making. *International Public Management Journal, 21*(5), 822–849.

Höglund, L., Holmgren Caicedo, M., Mårtensson, M., & Svärdsten, F. (2021a). Strategic management accounting in the public sector context: The case of the Swedish Transport Administration. *Journal of Public Budgeting, Accounting and Financial Management, 33*(4), 468–486.

Höglund, L., & Mårtensson, M. (2019). Entrepreneurship, a strategic management tool for renewal – the case of the Swedish public employment service. *Administrative Sciences, 9*(76), 1–16.

Höglund, L., Mårtensson, M., & Thomson, K. (2021b). Strategic management, management control practices and public value creation: The strategic triangle in the Swedish public sector. *Accounting, Auditing and Accountability Journal, 34*(7), 1608–1634.

Höglund, L., & Svärdsten, F. (2018). Strategy work in the public sector – a balancing act of competing discourses. *Scandinavian Journal of Management, 34*(3), 225–232.

Jacobs, K., & Cuganesan, S. (2014). Interdisciplinary accounting research in the Public Sector: Dissolving boundaries to tackle wicked problems. *Accounting, Auditing and Accountability Journal, 27*(8), 1250–1256.

Jarzabkowski, P., & Fenton, E. (2006). Strategizing and organizing in pluralistic contexts. *Long Range Planning, 39*(6), 631–648.

Jarzabkowski, P., & Kaplan, S. (2015). Strategy tools-in-use: A framework for understanding "technologies of rationality" in practice. *Strategic Management Journal, 36*(4), 537–558.

Johnsen, Å. (2015). Strategic management thinking and practice in the public sector: A strategic planning for all seasons? *Financial Accountability and Management, 31*(3), 243–268.

Johnsen, Å. (2016). Strategic planning and management in local government in Norway: Status after three decades. *Scandinavian Political Studies, 39*(4), 333–365.

Kaplan, R. S., & Norton, D. P. (1992). The Balanced Scorecard: Measures that drive performance. *Harvard Business Review*, January-February, 71–79.

Kober, R., Ng, J., & Paul, B. J. (2007). The interrelationship between management control mechanisms and strategy. *Management Accounting Research, 18*, 425–452.

Kornberger, M. (2013). Disciplining the future: On studying the politics of strategy, *Scandinavian Journal of Management, 29*(1), 104–107.

Kornberger, M., & Carter, C. (2010). Manufacturing competition: How accounting practices shape strategy making in cities. *Accounting, Auditing and Accountability Journal, 23*(3), 325–349.

Lachmann, M., Knauer, T., & Trapp, R. (2013). Strategic management accounting practices in hospitals: Empirical evidence on their dissemination under competitive market environments. *Journal of Accounting and Organizational Change, 9*(3), 336–369.

Langfield-Smith, K. (2008). Strategic management accounting: How far have we come in 25 years? *Accounting, Auditing and Accountability Journal, 21*(2), 204–228.

Llewellyn, S., & Tappin, E. (2003). Strategy in the public sector: Management in the wilderness, *Journal of Management Studies, 40*(4), 955–982.

Malleret, V., de La Villarmois, O., & Levant, Y. (2015). Revisiting 30 years of SMA literature: What can we say, think and do? HEC Paris, Research Paper. No. ACC-2015–1081.

Miller, P. (2001). Governing by numbers: Why calculative practices matter. *Social Research, 68*(2), 379–396.

Modell, S. (2012). Strategy, political regulation and management control in the public sector: Institutional and critical perspectives. *Management Accounting Research, 23*(4), 278–295.

Nixon, B., & Burns, J. (2012). The paradox of strategic management accounting. *Management Accounting Research, 23*(4), 229–244.

Porter, M. E. (1985). *Competitive advantage: Creating and sustaining superior performance*. Free Press.

Rashid, Ali, M. M., & Hossain, D. M. (2020). Revisiting the relevance of strategic management accounting research. *PSU Research Review, 4*(2), 129–148.

Roslender, R., & Hart, S. J. (2003). In search of strategic management accounting: Theoretical and field study perspectives. *Management Accounting Research, 14*(3), 255–279.

Simmonds, K. (1981). Strategic management accounting. *Management Accounting, 59*, 26–29.

Skærbæk, P., & Tryggestad, K. (2010). The role of accounting devices in performing corporate strategy. *Accounting, Organizations and Society, 35*(1), 108–124.

Steccolini, I. (2019). Accounting and the post-new public management: Re-considering publicness in accounting research. *Accounting, Auditing and Accountability Journal, 32*(1), 255–279.

Swedish Public Employment Service (SPES). (2020a). Arbetsförmedlingen: Arbetsmarknadsmyndigheten i samtid och framtid. Diarienummer: Af-2020/0012 1748.

Swedish Public Employment Service (SPES). (2020b). Strategi för kundarbete.

Swedish Public Employment Service (SPES). (2020c). PowerPoint presentation. Styrkort, sammanhang och sammanfattning.

9

MACHINE LEARNING ALGORITHMS AND PUBLIC DECISION-MAKING

A conceptual overview

Floris van Krimpen, Hans de Bruijn and Michela Arnaboldi

Introduction

This chapter is about the use of machine learning (ML) algorithms in public sector decision-making. Much has been published in recent years on the role ML can play in decision-making processes. Practical examples are decision-making processes to identify tax fraud, to support decision-making regarding early release from prison (Berk, 2017), and to prioritize supervision activities (Lorenz, Erp, & Meijer, 2022). Public decision-making has several special characteristics, which can have a significant impact on the effectiveness or legitimacy of algorithm usage.

Why public decision-making matters. First, decisions by governments are often high-impact decisions for citizens and organizations. A licence may or may not be granted or an organization may or may not be faced with an enforcement agency. Second, citizens and individuals often have no exit option (they cannot divert to other parties) because these decisions are based on authority, which only governments have. Third, because of this dominance of governments, public decision-making is bound by particular procedural principles, including transparency, explainability and accountability. Algorithmic decision-making can be at odds with these principles – for example, it is not always sufficiently transparent about which data led to which decision (Burrell, 2016).

The multiple layers of public decision-making. Public decision-making can involve at least two levels: 1) An individual level. Government decisions can relate to individual citizens or organizations. A government may impose a tax charge, provide a benefit or grant a permit. Decision-making on these matters, especially when large numbers of decisions have to be made, is often data-intensive and algorithms play an important role. 2) A collective level. This involves strategic decisions or policy decisions. An enforcement agency has limited capacity and thus has to make strategic choices about which potential lawbreakers to target. Algorithmic decision-making can play an important role in these choices. The same applies to policy-making processes. The development of policies is data-intensive and so algorithms can be an important vehicle for effective decision-making.

The ambiguities of public decision-making. Some public decisions have an unambiguous structure: if one or more conditions are met, a particular decision follows. Decision-making is self-executing. For instance, anyone breaking the speed limit will be fined a certain amount. But many decisions – both individual and collective – are not self-executing. They are decisions that come with ambiguity: the data and information used can be questioned, and normative questions about fairness and equality, for example, often come into play. When a law enforcement agency decides to

DOI: 10.4324/9781003295945-12

conduct additional scrutiny of certain companies, the question can be asked whether this decision is based on the right data and whether the decision is fair to these companies. When a welfare benefit is denied, the question can also be asked whether the right information was available and whether the denial was proportionate. These ambiguous issues are also known as "wicked problems" (Head, 2019; Hisschemöller & Hoppe, 1995; Rittel & Webber, 1973). Public decisions can thus have the above characteristics – high impact, no exit option, special procedure requirements – and also involve wicked issues. This makes the question of the effectiveness and legitimacy of algorithm use even more urgent.

The importance of public decision-making characteristics. The literature related to ML algorithms in the public sector is growing. Some scholars have started to study algorithms for public decision-making (Hartmann & Wenzelburger, 2021; van der Voort, Klievink, Arnaboldi, & Meijer, 2019) and have made comments about legitimacy issues with the introduction of ML algorithms (König & Wenzelburger, 2021; Veale & Brass, 2019), but the current literature lacks fails to recognize the importance of the characteristics of public decision-making and to discuss how these peculiarities need special attention when ML algorithms are used in decision-making processes. Furthermore, the inherent tension that exists between the wickedness of public decision-making and the use of ML algorithms is underexplored.

This chapter focuses on the question of *what the wicked nature of public decisions means for the use of ML algorithms.* To answer this question we carried out a narrative literature review of the state of the art of ML algorithms in the public sector. We squared this review with literature that discusses the specificities of public sector decision-making discussed in section 2. This literature includes studies such as those by Cohen, March and Olsen (1972). De Bruijn and Ten Heuvelhof (2018), and Teisman, 2000. This chapter aims to synthesize the knowledge related to our main question and bring additional theoretical concepts to the world of public sector decision-making with ML algorithms.

The remainder of this chapter is structured as follows. In the next section, we elaborate our theoretical framework, pointing out characteristics important for public decision-making. The third section illustrates our methodology. Then, the results of our review are presented. The fifth section discusses the meaning of those results in light of current literature. Finally, the sixth section concludes the chapter.

Machine learning and public decision-making: type 1 and type 2 decisions

ML is a technology that has gained a lot of popularity in the past decade and is being discussed as an instrument that will have a profound effect on the economy and workforce (Brynjolfsson & Mitchell, 2017). ML is defined as "a core branch of AI that aims to give computers the ability to learn without being explicitly programmed" (Samuel, 2000). Essentially, ML is the capability of software or a machine to improve the performance of tasks through exposure to data and experience (Luxton, 2016). A typical ML model first learns the knowledge from the data it is exposed to and then applies that knowledge, for example, to make predictions. While the adoption of ML-based technologies is already becoming widespread in the commercial sector, the public sector is lagging behind in comparison (Desouza, Dawson, & Chenok, 2020). However, attention has been growing and investment in technologies that are based on ML has been one of the most important strategies of the public sector in several countries around the world in recent years (Sousa, Melo, Bermejo, Farias, & Gomes, 2019).

Regardless of the type of application, ML implies the definition of a decision-making process concerning a problem. Even in simple applications, such as automated responses, ML applications "decide" how to respond in the face of specific questions posed by the users. The level of criticality of the decision-making process is, however, higher or lower depending on the type of problem faced.

The literature on public decision-making distinguishes between two types of problems, which we call type I and type II problems here. We hereby briefly explain the distinction between the two problems to set the background for the literature review. An overview of these distinctions related to decision-making is provided in Table 9.1. The premise of the research reported in this chapter is that ML-based decision-making might lend itself mainly to type I decisions. However, decision-making often involves type II problems– and the question is what this means for valuing algorithmic decision-making. There are four fundamental differences between the two when making decisions (De Bruijn & Ten Heuvelhof, 2018).

First, type I decision-making involves structured problems. A structured problem can be unambiguously defined and therefore often has one best solution. Type II decision-making involves unstructured or "wicked" problems. The problem is ambiguous and can sometimes be defined in completely different ways – or even be seen as a non-problem (Head, 2019; Hisschemöller & Hoppe, 1995).

Second, type I decision-making involves a single problem owner. One-actor decision-making means that this one actor can decide how to define a problem and what the right solution is. Type II decision-making is multi-actor decision-making. Multiple actors are involved in this decision-making, who have different values and interests. Moreover, when a problem is wicked, there is a lot of room for these actors to come up with their own interpretation and preferred solution (Adam & Kriesi, 2007; Klijn & Koppenjan, 2000).

Third, in type I decision-making, problems are often stable, meaning that there is a problem definition, which does not change. When there are wicked problems in a multi-actor context, problems are often dynamic – type II decision-making. When power relations between actors shift, the problem definition may shift – and hence the desired solution (De Bruijn & Ten Heuvelhof, 2018).

Fourth, type I decision-making often proceeds linearly, and type II decision-making non-linearly. Decision-making is often a power struggle between actors who adhere to different problems and solutions. Such a power struggle involves iterations, accelerations and delays, and redefinition of problems and solutions. Decision-making is a messy process – the literature talks about "garbage can decision-making", "windows of opportunity", and governance by randomness (Cohen et al., 1972; Kingdon, 2011; Teisman, 2000).

The essential difference between type I and type II decision-making (see Table 9.1) is the structured versus the unstructured or wicked nature of problems. When a problem is wicked, a multi-actor context becomes problematic and decision-making will be much more dynamic. We, therefore, elaborate on the concept of wicked problems here to point out the criticality concerning ML applications.

There are several definitions of wickedness in the literature (Alford & Head, 2017; Head, 2019; Rittel & Webber, 1973) that all have their specific perspectives or peculiarities. Most of these definitions have in common that they discuss ambiguity related to facts and norms. Therefore, we use the definition developed by Hisschemöller and Hoppe (1995) because it captures the essence of what wicked problems entail, namely, that they are ambiguous. Table 9.1 has two axes.

1. Consensus or dissensus about norms. The question of whether something is a problem or not is partly determined by normative views. There may be consensus or dissensus about these normative views. Take abortion, for example – there are completely different normative views on abortion,

Table 9.1 Differences between type I and type II decision-making

Type I decision-making	Type II decision-making
Involves structured problems	Involves wicked problems
Involves a single problem-owner	Involves multi-actor decision-making
Deals with stable problems	Deals with dynamic problems
Proceeds linearly	Proceeds non-linearly

roughly speaking: the pro-choice and the pro-life view. An example of normative agreement: the value of "equal opportunities" is generally endorsed by all – there is consensus that this is a key value in democratic societies. Consensus or dissensus may also concern the weighing of a set of different values. Usually, in public sector issues, different values have to be weighed (e.g. fairness, transparency, affordability, accessibility and cost-effectiveness). The parties involved may or may not agree on the right trade-off between these values. This issue becomes a crucial point in ML development, where criteria for decision-making and variables of inclusion or exclusion need to be set.

2. The unambiguity or ambiguity of facts. Do the facts allow only one conclusion? Or are they multi-interpretable – and therefore more ambiguous? If someone drives through a red light and is flashed, there is an unambiguous set of facts: it is clear which car drove through which red light, and when. The constellation of facts might also be more ambiguous. What were the consequences of a tax cut? This might be open to debate because there are many intervening variables. Some will say that it promoted inequality, and others will say that it led to economic growth and more opportunities for everyone. In this case, the impact for ML applications can also appear during the operational running of the application, when a new input is arriving or because a new "ambiguous category" of user emerges.

Table 9.2 summirizes the two axes, pointing out four quadrants that are discussed below.

In quadrant I, we find structured problems, which in most cases have one right answer (De Bruijn & Ten Heuvelhof, 2018). If someone drives through a red light (problem), this person will be fined (solution). In quadrant II, the main disagreement is normative – we know what an abortion factually means, but we disagree about the normative question. In quadrant III, the situation is reversed: normatively speaking, there is consensus, but the disagreement is about factual causes and consequences.

The quadrant on the lower right (quadrant IV) contains wicked problems – the essence of which is that they have no unambiguous problem definition and no unambiguous solution (Hisschemöller & Hoppe, 1995). Every problem definition and solution can be questioned. For example, suppose a TSO (an electricity transmission system operator) wants to roll out high-voltage cables. Different stakeholders may have different views on the facts: on the necessity of the cables, given the number of customers; on the effects on health; on the impact or the market value of houses close to the cables. Furthermore, there are different values at stake – economy, ecology, health – that require a trade-off. Different stakeholders will have different opinions on the right trade-off.

Methodology

To investigate and synthesize the knowledge related to the question of what the wicked nature of public decisions means for the use of algorithms and to bring additional theoretical concepts to the world of public decision-making with ML algorithms, we carried out a narrative literature review (Baumeister & Leary, 1997; Webster & Watson, 2002), which was articulated in these phases: initial

Table 9.2 Summary of wicked problems

	Facts unambiguous	*Facts ambiguous*
Consensus about norms	I	III
	Running a red light	Equal opportunities
Dissensus about norms	II	IV
	Abortion	Roll-out of overhead power lines

search and selection of papers; extension of papers portfolio with a snowball approach (Wohlin, 2014); qualitative paper analysis; discussion among authors and synthesis.

For the selection of papers, we used Scopus, focusing on peer-reviewed journals, book chapters and conference papers; written in English; within the social science area. This latter choice is appropriate for the objective of the paper and to have an interdisciplinary range, as this area allows. A systematic search for eligible studies was not carried out, on purpose, given the blurred boundary of the topic under study. However, we comprehensively covered the topic in question.

Search terms included three areas of terms: (i) "machine learning", "algorithms", "big data"; (ii) "public sector", "public administration"; (iii) "decision-making", "decision". These terms were connected with the Boolean elements "AND" and "OR" iteratively to maximise an ample but focused search. The choice to include the third area (iii) was made to make sure the set of literature was focused enough to obtain relevant results.

After the first iteration abstracts were read by us, the authors, we started another search with the snowball method (Wohlin, 2014). The selection terms were integrated; we also integrated papers appearing in the reference list of the first-round documents (after the screening of the title and abstract); we followed authors that emerged as relevant for the topic in the first round. The inclusion within the final set was also based on the criteria used for the inclusion in the starting set. However, in this step in the process, the abstract, introduction and conclusions of the papers were scanned to decide on inclusion or exclusion. Further, exemptions were made for more technically oriented papers cited by already included papers. These technically oriented papers serve to better describe the concept of ML. Also, exemptions were made for literature that describes core concepts from public administration literature helpful to further clarify challenges. Finally, we also searched Google for any other material related to the topic under investigation (through the final set of keywords); they included policy papers and practitioner reports. This was key to further clarifying concepts with empirical examples. The focused selection led to 28 articles.

Figure 9.1 reports the chronological spread. In particular, it indicates that especially from 2016 onwards, attention has been growing for ML algorithms in the public sector. Based on these statistics, it might be argued that after a peak of interest in 2019, attention has declined. However, this could be because, especially in the early phases, there has been attention to the broader topics of algorithms or AI in the public sector instead of ML specifically.

Data analysis was articulated in two steps. Firstly, we carried out a concept-centric analysis, guided by the elements highlighted in the previous section. The contributions were first classified according to their main objectives. The main concepts that appeared within the individual contributions were

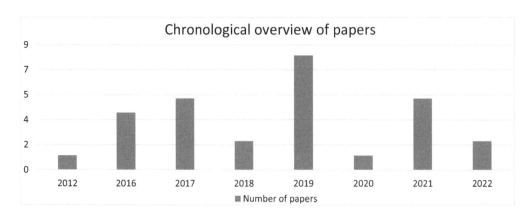

Figure 9.1 Chronological overview of papers.

then identified, within the final boundary of the aim of this research. Next, a cross-sectional analysis of the contributions was done to identify recurring and common concepts.

The second step of the data analysis was carried out with a theory-building aim. We entered more specifically into the topic under investigation guided by the framework provided in section 2 concerning the wicked context of public decision-making. In this step, researchers need several confrontations in pairs and altogether, given that the wicked nature was sometimes present although not underlined with this term.

The final discussion led to an overview that distinguishes between different perspectives related to decision-making and ML algorithms in the wicked context of public decision-making. Firstly, decision-making with algorithms, and secondly, decision-making about algorithms, divided between decision-making about the development of the ML algorithm and the subsequent use of an ML algorithm.

Results

In this section, we discuss the results of the narrative literature review. The issue of decision-making, wicked problems and ML algorithms is a multilayered phenomenon, where a distinction can be made between:

(1) decision-making with algorithms: an algorithm is used to make a decision;
(2) decision-making about algorithms: decision-making about (2a) the development of an algorithm and (2b) the subsequent use of an algorithm.

Decision-making with ML algorithms

Most benefits and challenges are described in more generic literature that discusses at both relatively higher and broader levels, such as Katzenbach and Ulbricht (2019); Wirtz, Weyerer, and Geyer (2019); and Zuiderwijk, Chen, and Salem (2021). However, also more focused technical papers such as Alexopoulos et al. (2019) or Domingos (2012) and papers from legally oriented scholars such as Barocas and Selbst (2016); Coglianese and Lehr (2017, 2018); Kroll et al. (2017); and Liu, Lin, and Chen (2019) are found within this analysis.

ML algorithms result in better decision-making

Here we discuss the potential benefits. Within the reviewed literature, the benefits mostly mentioned are those of efficiency and accuracy; learning processes; objectivity and innovation; and trust.

Efficiency and accuracy. Two of the most mentioned benefits are efficiency and accuracy. Many indicate that AI, in our case ML, can make public decision-making more accurate (Alexopoulos et al., 2019; Eggers, Schatsky, & Viechnicki, 2017) and more efficient (Alexopoulos et al., 2019; Domingos, 2012; Mehr, 2017; Zuiderwijk, Chen, & Salem, 2021). Suppose an enforcement agency, with its limited capacity, has to select the inspectees they pay attention to. This is a continuous and dynamic process. An algorithm can help select the inspectees because it can prioritize cases based on a risk score. In this example, the work becomes more accurate because the ML algorithm helps select those cases that are most interesting. In essence, the algorithm helps strategically choose these cases. Also, the work becomes more efficient because the ML algorithm saves time and resources in the process of determining the cases to inspect. This prioritization based on risk score is also one of the benefits mentioned by Zuiderwijk et al. (2021) as "risk identification and monitoring benefits".

Learning processes. ML systems contribute to organizational learning processes. ML systems can continuously improve and, in addition, enable team-based and mixed-initiative learning. The continuous improvement relates to the fact that ML systems can self-improve by being fed with new historical data (Alexopoulos et al., 2019). Team-based and mixed-initiative learning entails that ML methods now have the capability of working together with humans. Machines and humans can learn together in a mixed way. For example, a machine can extract information from data sets, while humans suggest hypotheses to be tested based on the extracted data sets (Alexopoulos et al., 2019). Thus, learning occurs in a joint effort between the human and the machine. Often, such benefits are a means to an end of becoming more accurate and efficient. However, the notion of public decision-making that can be continuously improved and in which new learning mechanisms can occur between algorithms and humans should be highlighted.

Objectivity and innovation. The use of ML can also have the benefit of the appearance of objectivity (Lorenz et al., 2022). An example here is the use of "robot judges". Human judges can be biased and different judges can, in equal situations, give different rulings. A judge may be tired – and this may affect a ruling (Crootof et al., 2019). The robot judge can contribute to objectifying judicial decisions. Further, this might also give the appearance of innovativeness (Kuziemski & Misuraca, 2020). The logic goes that a government that relies on innovative, technical tools becomes more objective because of the nature of these tools.

Trust. Objectivity and innovativeness, in turn, might increase satisfaction and trust in the government (Dwivedi et al., 2021). Governments are bound by being objective. Citizens expect governments to treat them equally. The premise is that an objective government treats people equally. Thus, the appearance of objectivity and innovativeness contributes to the legitimacy of the government.

Related to benefits, studies points out that ML has the potential to increase the accuracy and efficiency of decision-making. Further, ML algorithms give the possibility to continuously improve public decision-making by facilitating team-based learning between algorithms and humans. Lastly, by the appearance of innovativeness and objectivity, the legitimacy of government and trust in government can be increased.

ML algorithms result in poorer decision-making

There is also much evidence in the literature that the use of algorithms has significant harmful effects. Dwivedi et al. (2021) mention that challenges range from ethical issues, such as the possibility of discrimination, to matters at the level of technology and technology implementation or data challenges. This section discusses the relevant challenges separately. Multiple scholars also mention legally related issues such as Dwivedi et al. (2021), Wirtz et al. (2019),and Zuiderwijk et al. (2021). Our analysis as well includes this legal perspective, also through elaborating on the work of scholars who discuss particular challenges of ML concerning the rule of law, such as Barocas and Selbst (2016); Coglianese and Lehr (2017, 2018); Kroll et al. (2017); and Liu, Lin, and Chen (2019).

Discrimination. Generally, ethical challenges are mentioned by all the studies we reviewed, and discrimination is often the most critical issue. Discrimination refers to making a distinction between people or groups of people based on the group, class or category to which those people belong. Thus, the challenge of discrimination relates to preventing inequality and unfairness (Thierer, Castillo, & Russell, 2017; Wirtz, Weyerer, & Geyer, 2019). Inherent to the nature of ML, if the data the model is trained on is discriminatory, then the model will become discriminatory. The prejudice in the data becomes "baked into the model"(Barocas & Selbst, 2016). A straightforward example is biased data that has racial prejudices. Consequently, the model might be discriminatory.

Lack of transparency. Transparency is also mentioned from multiple perspectives. The argument is that the opacity of ML systems is a threat to the legitimacy of public decision-making processes (Danaher, 2016). The question becomes whether decisions made or supported by a potentially opaque system or algorithm are accepted as rightful by those affected by the decisions. Furthermore, it raises the issue of whether the current rules of accountability are "fit for purpose". That is, can they cope with new requirements due to ML? Responses from the legal literature provide some insight concerning these questions. Coglianese and Lehr (2018) try to answer the question whether governing utilizing algorithmic systems can be squared with legal principles of governmental transparency. They conclude that the relative inscrutability of ML algorithms does not pose a legal barrier to their responsible use by governmental authorities. Also in an earlier study, Coglianese and Lehr (2017) state that if ML algorithms are properly understood, their use by governmental agencies can fit within legal parameters. However, the opposite response comes from Liu et al., 2019. From an examination of the *State vs. Loomis* case in the US, they conclude that the algorithmization of government functions poses a threat to, among other things, transparency. They show that in this particular case, there was a lack of understanding regarding the effects of the implementation of an ML tool and consequently, the necessity to open up the legal black box was not present for the defendants. Naturally, also for practitioners, transparency is mentioned as a challenge. ML algorithms are often adopted as a black box. The algorithms are opaque and it is unclear how the algorithms work, while they are being used for making socially consequential predictions (Burrell, 2016).

Lack of accountability. Accountability is a key legal principle in a democracy. An argument often made is that transparency is a way of making algorithms accountable. Legal scholars like Kroll et al. (2017) mention that they want to challenge the dominant position in the legal literature. They indicate that solving the challenge of accountability by making algorithms transparent is undesirable and not always possible. Rather, we can use technological tools, more specifically computational methods, to adhere to legal standards of accountability. They mention the methods of software verification, cryptographic commitments, zero-knowledge proofs and fair random choices. These methods can guarantee that decisions are made in an accountable way, without the necessity of a fully transparent model. Concerning accountability, Liu et al. (2019) also have their say, noting that to solve this challenge, we need to treat seriously the black box problem of these algorithms. The black box symbolizes the idea of not being able to look inside the ML algorithm (Burrell, 2016).

Breaching privacy. Is the data that is being used actually in line with privacy regulations? Concerning this point, Wirtz et al. (2019) mention that this is particularly about whether data from individuals is collected and processed with consent from these individuals and in line with existing regulations.

Value conflicts. A last challenge, which is particularly relevant but mentioned only scarcely, is that of value conflicts. In the case of ML algorithms, conflicting challenges and benefits have to be weighed against each other. Choices have to be made that are value-laden (Veale & Brass, 2019). Take, for example, the values of accuracy and data privacy (Arnaboldi, de Bruijn, Steccolini, & Van der Voort, 2022). The use of personal data can contribute to the accuracy of public decision-making, but there is also the value of privacy that needs to be safeguarded. This value conflict requires a trade-off, which is partly contextual: different contexts may result in different trade-offs (De Bruijn, 2021). Other values might be part of the trade-off, for example, safety, sustainability and equity.

Some of the challenges, such as discrimination (or bias), are related to the data that is the basis of the ML algorithms. Data is one of the main building blocks of ML algorithms. A lack of quality and quantity of input data (Dwivedi et al., 2021) can affect the quality of public decision-making. The algorithm is only as smart as the data from which it learns (Wirtz et al., 2019). A way to deal with discrimination might be to have more and better data that is used to train better algorithms. However, with the increasing complexity of ML algorithms, accountability and transparency issues increase. This illustrates that challenges are not necessarily solved by better data. Trade-offs are involved in dealing with such challenges. To complicate matters even more, these trade-offs are also dynamic, meaning that they can change over time.

There is overwhelming evidence that ML algorithms for public decision-making raise a host of issues that need to be addressed. As illustrated, the notion should also be taken into account that many of the challenges are closely connected and should be considered interdependent (Wirtz et al., 2019).

Decision-making about ML algorithms

As stated, the issue of algorithms and decision-making is a multilayered phenomenon. Algorithms can be used to make decisions about wicked problems. Before this, decisions were made on the development and use of algorithms.

The development and use of an algorithm is a process in which multiple stakeholders are involved (Lorenz et al., 2022; van der Voort et al., 2019; Zweig, Wenzelburger, & Krafft, 2018). Zweig et al. (2018) can be described as an eight-step process: 1) algorithm development, 2) algorithm implementation, 3) algorithm selection, 4) data collection, 5) data selection, 6) design and training of the system, 7) the embedding of the system in the societal process, and 8) feedback. We might be tempted to pay particular attention to steps 7 and 8 when the ML algorithm is used for decision-making – but these steps are preceded by a whole process of development of the ML algorithm. To understand the use in the final steps (7 and 8), the entire process is relevant. At every step in that process, different stakeholders are involved. For example, a data scientist has to make a decision about the data to include and the algorithm to use. The data has been labelled by someone with domain knowledge. Then, a model will be trained on the labelled data. The type of model has to be chosen by someone. It might be that a different stakeholder has to determine how the ML tool is embedded into the actual daily practice of decision-makers. With a finished model, a person responsible for decision-making processes in the organization has to decide whether and how the model will be integrated into an actual decision-making process that also involves many actors with different perspectives.

The development of ML algorithms is the result of countless interactions like these and other interactions between actors. Because of the many interactions and many ways in which a final ML algorithm can be developed, decision-making processes related to algorithms are very dynamic. The "right way" to use an algorithm is a wicked problem; actors will disagree about the right way; and actors might gain or lose power, which can make the decision-making process a very dynamic endeavour.

On top of this, algorithms are not stand-alone objects but are relational. They belong to a larger algorithmic system "which involves an intricate, dynamic arrangement of people and code, where multiple insiders cooperate and work on the design and implementation of the algorithmic logic" (Janssen & Kuk, 2016, p. 374). The more complex this algorithmic system, the less predictable algorithm development will be. Algorithms are developed in organizational contexts with different intentions and actual effects (Meijer, Lorenz, & Wessels, 2021). In one organization, there might be a higher level of digital discretion than in the other (Young, Bullock, & Lecy, 2019). Digital discretion refers to the distinction between human and machine agents and the relationship between these two. Numerous other organizational variables might have an impact on the use and impact of ML algorithms – for example, the degree of operational autonomy, digital competence or organizational checks and balances. Thus, algorithms and their effects should be understood as an organizational outcome rather than solely based on the technological features of algorithms (Meijer et al., 2021).

A story of amplification

So far so good. Now let's bring in the element of wickedness. Decision-making using algorithms can lead to better and more poor decision-making. The use of ML algorithms for type II decision-making amplifies many of the shortcomings already prevalent within ML algorithms and public decision-making.

Amplification of bias. Algorithms are often biased, and bias might become "baked into the model" (Baro-cas & Selbst, 2016). Now relate this to the concept of wickedness. Decision-making processes related to wicked problems require the weighing of different values. These processes are multi-actor processes and can be power games par excellence, in which the values of the most powerful actors will dominate. Suppose a powerful actor values a rigorous approach towards fraud related to governmental benefits and wants to use an ML system to investigate potential fraud. This rigorous approach can imply that the value of preventing fraud outweighs other values, for example, proportionality. Because of this rigorous approach, there is little room for doubt and someone may be easily marked as potentially fraudulent. This rigorous approach will be reflected in the data that an ML model is trained on. Thus, because a powerful actor values this rigorous approach, it will be embodied in the algorithm.

Amplification of the lack of transparency. Section 2 shows that decision-making processes are often non-linear – decision-making is an opaque, capricious process and it is not transparent concerning what actors have what impact on the ultimate decisions. This is inherent to the wicked character of problems and the many actors involved in the decision-making process. Now, suppose that in this process one or more actors use algorithms – this does not make the process less opaque. On the contrary, since the development of these algorithms was also an opaque process, the decision-making only becomes less transparent. The lack of transparency is amplified.

Amplification of the lack of accountability. Accountability issues might also be amplified. Accountability issues in regular public decision-making relate to the multi-actor nature of decision-making and the problem of "the many hands". As described before, the introduction of ML algorithms adds another layer of hands, namely, that related to the algorithm. In public decision-making, it is not always clear who should be held accountable for particular decisions. When an ML algorithm is present in the decision-making processes, that makes it even harder to talk about accountability. Thus, the introduction of the ML algorithm leads to an amplification of the accountability challenge.

Amplification of disputes on value trade-offs. There is a need for value trade-offs. The literature shows that algorithmic decision-making comes with debatable value trade-offs, in a context where wicked problems must be solved. Wicked problems are already characterized by dissensus about the underlying values and value trade-offs. So there is already a conflict of values when wicked problems are on the agenda. And again, this conflict of values is amplified by the use of algorithms, because these algorithms represent a value trade-off that is often disputable. So, an algorithm with a disputable value trade-off is used to solve a wicked problem, which requires a value trade-off that is inherently disputable.

This amplification of the drawbacks of algorithmic decision-making also finds a cause in the prior process of development. If algorithms are ultimately used for decision-making on wicked issues, then decision-making on the development and use of algorithms is also wicked.

To illustrate this, we can take two benefits of the use of ML algorithms: they can result in more efficient and more accurate decision-making. However, when it comes to wicked problems, there is a fundamental issue: there is no unambiguous definition of a problem – and therefore efficiency and accuracy cannot be defined unambiguously. Suppose an inspection agency wants to detect fraudulent inspectees. This is a wicked problem: one of the questions is, for what measure of accuracy will developers optimize the algorithm? Will they optimize the algorithm to catch as many fraudulent inspectees as possible? Or to make as few as possible wrong accusations? These two approaches may lead to completely different outcomes. Or let's take the question of who should be inspected and who should not be inspected. Research shows that there is a variety of criteria relevant here (Goosensen, 2021). These criteria require a trade-off, and the weighing of the criteria is not unambiguous – or, put differently, is a wicked activity.

To conclude, a story of amplification emerges when we confront the literature about public decision-making with ML algorithms. There is an amplification of many issues that are already prevalent when we are dealing with multi-actor decision-making on wicked issues. This has mainly to do with the fact that ML algorithms themselves can be considered multi-actor and wicked, while they are also coming into the context of multi-actor decision-making on wicked issues.

Discussion

Our findings suggest that applying ML algorithms for public decision-making creates an amplification of many of the shortcomings prevalent in both. Especially public decision-making often concerns decision-making about type II problems. The characteristics of these problems, squared with the drawbacks of ML algorithms create amplification. The amplified shortcomings regard an amplification of bias, an amplification of the lack of transparency, an amplification of the lack of accountability, and finally an amplification of disputes of value trade-offs. The findings suggest that this has partially to do with the fact that before algorithms are used in the wicked multi-actor context of public decision-making, there is decision-making about the development of ML algorithms, which is also a multi-actor and wicked process.

This is a finding that builds on previous literature that started to acknowledge the importance of the development process of ML algorithms (van der Voort et al., 2019; Zweig et al., 2018). Within this literature, it is emphasized that stakeholders such as data scientists, designers and decision-makers all play a critical role in decision-making processes that are based on data or algorithms (van der Voort et al., 2019). This study concludes similarly. What this study specifically adds is the additional claim that shortcomings of either public decision-making or ML algorithms are amplified when ML algorithms are used for public decision-making. Our study brings forward that the involvement of multiple actors in the development process and the wickedness of the decisions involved, is one of the key issues, rather than technical issues with the algorithms. In that sense, our study also relates to previous literature that discusses technical solutions for challenges such as transparency or accountability (Belle & Papantonis, 2021; Kroll et al., 2017). The message we offer is not that these technical approaches have no value. On the contrary, what we do emphasize is that when algorithms are being applied for so-called type II decision-making, much more is going on and only technical solutions are problematic because they do not go to the root of the problem.

There might be multiple potential avenues for dealing with ML algorithms when applied to type II decision-making. What these suggestions all have in common is the importance of the human factor. We emphasize that awareness of the importance of the human factor is something that should be prevalent in all public decision-making dealing with ML algorithms.

Co-produce decision-making. The first suggestion is connected to the question of what role ML can play in decision-making processes. If ML becomes a substitute for human-based type II decision-making, we might expect the outcome of ML to be heavily criticized, often because of the high personal importance of the problems (Wenzelburger, König, Felfeli, & Achtziger, 2022). Thus, we argue for ML that facilitates human-based decision-making. Two variants might be possible. 1) A variant of competition, where ML-based decision-making does not replace human decision-making but competes as an additional tool. When ML-based decision-making leads to other outcomes than human-based decision-making, it can trigger learning processes – actors may reconsider their original decision and subsequently take a better or better-substantiated decision. 2) A variant of cooperation. For example, ML-based decision-making only concerns a limited number of aspects of the decision to be taken, especially those aspects that are less wicked. Decision-making remains human-based, but human decision-makers are partly supported.

Organize for a variety of perspectives. Secondly, wickedness implies the existence of multiple perspectives. Using only one algorithm in such a context is remarkable. A variety of perspectives requires variety in algorithms. We argue that a variety of algorithms is introduced in public decision-making. For example, when dealing with algorithms, we can have ML algorithms based on different data sets, or use different types of algorithms that support the same decision. Also, variety in the integration into decision-making processes is needed. Instead of having an algorithm supporting decision-making, we can aim for variety in decision-making mechanisms. Thus, an ML algorithm supports decision-making, but also decision-making without algorithms or an algorithm that is verified by a human instead of vice versa. In line with "the algorithmic colleague" from the study of Meijer et al. (2021), we argue that the algorithm should be an instrument of knowledge rather an instrument that should be followed.

Build institutions. Thirdly, a focus is needed on developing the institutions within and outside of organizations that can deal with the complexity of developing, implementing and using ML algorithms. Suppose an inspectorate is shifting from a situation in which solely inspectors are selecting inspectees, towards a situation in which inspectors are supported by ML algorithms in selecting their inspectees. To ensure transparency, accountability or fairness, a big organizational challenge awaits this inspectorate. How do we organize in the new situation? How do we make sure that the inspector uses ML algorithms? There might be great importance in building checks and balances in the chain from algorithm development to algorithm use (Arnaboldi et al., 2022). There is already institutional complexity in the old situation, and even more so in the new situation. By institution building, we can start to create some "rules of the game" for ML algorithms in a public sector context.

Naturally, the present study has its limitations. This study brings together different types of literature. It connects literature on algorithms in the public sector to literature focusing on public decision-making. As a consequence, it brings together many concepts that are not often connected. A limitation of this study is especially this connection of many concepts, as it might create confusion.

Finally, we provide several suggestions for future research. As we have tried to conceptually bring together a variety of concepts, our main suggestion is to bring the study of ML algorithms to the empirical context, as also suggested by others (Veale, Van Kleek, & Binns, 2018). Firstly, future research can focus on empirically studying the use and development of ML algorithms for public decision-making. This chapter brought forward the importance of the human factor. But how are public sector professionals dealing with these types of ML algorithms for public decision-making? Secondly, future research can focus on empirically studying the institutions present in the entire process from design to use, or on studying institutions that are effective in ensuring transparency, accountability and fairness.

Conclusion

In the introduction, we asked what the wicked nature of public decisions means for the use of ML algorithms. Our study suggests that the wicked nature of public decision-making has consequences for how we should look at ML algorithms, how we develop ML algorithms, and how we use ML algorithms in the context of public decision-making, especially when ML algorithms are applied for type II decision-making. The main finding of the study is the existence of the amplification of challenges such as a lack of transparency, a lack of accountability and disputes on value trade-offs. This amplification of challenges finds its cause partially in the development process of ML algorithms, which we can consider a wicked and multi-actor process. In turn, the ML algorithm is then applied in a wicked and multi-actor context as well. The contribution of our study to the literature is mainly related to this notion of amplification. Earlier scholars did not specifically take into account the core principles of public decision-making. Since this study brings together a variety of concepts from different disciplines, there is also a potential pitfall, namely that the number of concepts obfuscates the central message of this chapter. Specifically, the human with and within the ML algorithm matters. However, since our study is based on a review of the literature, our suggestion is to start empirically studying the wicked and multi-actor nature of ML algorithms in their actual contexts (Veale et al., 2018). As stated, the growing use of ML algorithms in the public sector amplifies many common challenges in public decision-making. Fortunately, there are multiple ways forward to deal with these challenges. By employing co-production, organizing for variety, and by institution building, some of these amplifications can be condensed.

References

Adam, S., & Kriesi, H. (2007). The network approach. In P. A. Sabatier (Ed.), *Theories of the Policy Process* (2nd ed., pp. 129–154). Routledge.

Alexopoulos, C., Lachana, Z., Androutsopoulou, A., Diamantopoulou, V., Charalabidis, Y., & Loutsaris, M. A. (2019). How machine learning is changing e-government. In *Proceedings of the 12th International Conference on Theory and Practice of Electronic Governance* (Vol. Part F1481, pp. 354–363). ACM. https://doi.org/10.1145/3326365.3326412

Alford, J., & Head, B. W. (2017). Wicked and less wicked problems: A typology and a contingency framework. *Policy and Society, 36*(3), 397–413. https://doi.org/10.1080/14494035.2017.1361634

Arnaboldi, M., de Bruijn, H., Steccolini, I., & Van der Voort, H. (2022). On humans, algorithms and data. *Qualitative Research in Accounting and Management, 19*(3), 241–254. https://doi.org/10.1108/QRAM-01-2022-0005

Barocas, S., & Selbst, A. D. (2016). Big data's disparate impact. *California Law Review, 104*(671), 671–732. https://doi.org/10.2139/ssrn.2477899

Baumeister, R. F., & Leary, M. R. (1997). writing narrative literature reviews – Bausmeister & Leary. *Review of General Psychology, 1*(3), 311–320.

Belle, V., & Papantonis, I. (2021). Principles and practice of explainable machine learning. *Frontiers in Big Data, 4*(July), 1–25. https://doi.org/10.3389/fdata.2021.688969

Berk, R. (2017). An impact assessment of machine learning risk forecasts on parole board decisions and recidivism. *Journal of Experimental Criminology, 13*(2), 193–216. https://doi.org/10.1007/s11292-017-9286-2

Brynjolfsson, E., & Mitchell, T. (2017). What can machine learning do? Workforce implications. *Science, 358*(6370), 1530–1534. https://doi.org/10.1126/science.aap8062

Burrell, J. (2016). How the machine "thinks": Understanding opacity in machine learning algorithms. *Big Data and Society, 3*(1), 1–12. https://doi.org/10.1177/2053951715622512

Coglianese, C., & Lehr, D. (2017). Regulating by robot: Administrative decision making in the Machine-learning era. *Georgetown Law Journal, 105*(5), 1147–1223.

Coglianese, C., & Lehr, D. (2018). Transparency and algorithmic governance. *Administrative Law Review, 71*(1), 18–38.

Cohen, M. D., March, J. G., & Olsen, J. P. (1972). A garbage can model of organizational choice. *Administrative Science Quarterly, 17*(1), 1. https://doi.org/10.2307/2392088

Crootof, R., Bernstein, D., Bloch-Wehba, H., Dayrit, J., Pasquale, F., Re, R., … Surden, H. (2019). Columbia Law Review Forum technological-legal lock-in. *Columbia Law Review, 119*(2016), 233–251.

Danaher, J. (2016). The threat of algocracy: Reality, resistance and accommodation. *Philosophy and Technology, 29*(3), 245–268. https://doi.org/10.1007/s13347-015-0211-1

De Bruijn, H. (2021). *The governance of privacy*. Amsterdam University Press.

De Bruijn, H., & Ten Heuvelhof, E. (2018). *Management in networks* (2nd ed.). Routledge–Taylor & Francis Group. https://doi.org/10.4324/9781315453019

Desouza, K. C., Dawson, G. S., & Chenok, D. (2020). Designing, developing, and deploying artificial intelligence systems: Lessons from and for the public sector. *Business Horizons, 63*(2), 205–213. https://doi.org/10.1016/j.bushor.2019.11.004

Domingos, P. (2012). A few useful things to know about machine learning. *Communications of the ACM, 55*(10), 78–87. https://doi.org/10.1145/2347736.2347755

Dwivedi, Yogesh K. et al. Artificial intelligence (AI): Multidisciplinary perspectives on emerging challenges, opportunities, and agenda for research, practice and policy. *International Journal of Information Management, 57*(2021), 101994.

Eggers, W. D., Schatsky, D., & Viechnicki, P. (2017). AI-augmented government: Using cognitive technologies to redesign public sector work. *Deloitte Center for Government Insights*, 1–24. www2.deloitte.com/content/dam/insights/us/articles/3832_AI-augmented-government/DUP_AI-augmented-government.pdf%0Ahttps://www2.deloitte.com/us/en/insights/focus/cognitive-technologies/artificial-intelligence-government.html

Goosensen, H. R. (2021). *Inzicht in de praktijk van het toezicht: Een empirisch onderzoek naar het verloop van operationele inspectieprocessen in de luchtvaart en zeevaart*. [Doctoral dissertation, TU Delft University]. https://doi.org/10.4233/uuid:62e7441c-72c7-4445-bf72-fb8ef047308e

Hartmann, K., & Wenzelburger, G. (2021). Uncertainty, risk and the use of algorithms in policy decisions: A case study on criminal justice in the USA. *Policy Sciences, 54*(2), 269–287. https://doi.org/10.1007/s11077-020-09414-y

Head, B. W. (2019). Forty years of wicked problems literature: Forging closer links to policy studies. *Policy and Society, 38*(2), 180–197. https://doi.org/10.1080/14494035.2018.1488797

Hisschemöller, M., & Hoppe, R. (1995). Coping with intractable controversies: The case for problem structuring in policy design and analysis. *Knowledge and Policy, 8*(4), 40–60. https://doi.org/10.1007/BF02832229

Janssen, M., & Kuk, G. (2016). The challenges and limits of big data algorithms in technocratic governance. *Government Information Quarterly, 33*(3), 371–377. https://doi.org/10.1016/j.giq.2016.08.011

Katzenbach, C., & Ulbricht, L. (2019). Algorithmic governance. *Internet Policy Review, 8*(4), 1–18. https://doi.org/10.14763/2019.4.1424

Kingdon, J. W. (2011). *Agendas, alternatives, and public policies* (2nd ed.). Longman.

Klijn, E. H., & Koppenjan, J. F. M. (2000). Public management and policy networks. *Public Management: An International Journal of Research and Theory, 2*(2), 135–158. https://doi.org/10.1080/14719030000000007

König, P. D., & Wenzelburger, G. (2021). The legitimacy gap of algorithmic decision-making in the public sector: Why it arises and how to address it. *Technology in Society, 67*(July). https://doi.org/10.1016/j.techsoc.2021.101688

Kroll, J. A., Huey, J., Barocas, S., Felten, E. W., Reidenberg, J. R., Robinson, D. G., & Yu, H. (2017). Accountable algorithms. *University of Pennsylvania Law Review, 165*(3), 633–705.

Kuziemski, M., & Misuraca, G. (2020). AI governance in the public sector: Three tales from the frontiers of automated decision-making in democratic settings. *Telecommunications Policy, 44*(6), 101976. https://doi.org/10.1016/j.telpol.2020.101976

Liu, H. W., Lin, C. F., & Chen, Y. J. (2019). Beyond state v loomis: Artificial intelligence, government algorithmization and accountability. *International Journal of Law and Information Technology, 27*(2), 122–141. https://doi.org/10.1093/ijlit/eaz001

Lorenz, L., Erp, J. Van, & Meijer, A. (2022). Machine-learning algorithms in regulatory practice agencies. *Technology & Regulation*, 1–11. https://doi.org/10.26116/techreg.2022.001

Luxton, D. D. (2016). *An introduction to artificial intelligence in behavioral and mental health care: Artificial intelligence in behavioral and mental health care.* Elsevier. https://doi.org/10.1016/B978-0-12-420248-1.00001-5

Mehr, H. (2017). Artificial intelligence for citizen services and government. *Harvard Ash Center Technology & Democracy* (August), 1–16. https://ash.harvard.edu/files/ash/files/artificial_intelligence_for_citizen_services.pdf

Meijer, A., Lorenz, L., & Wessels, M. (2021). Algorithmization of bureaucratic organizations: Using a practice lens to study how context shapes predictive policing systems. *Public Administration Review, 81*(5), 837–846. https://doi.org/10.1111/puar.13391

Rittel, H. W. J., & Webber, M. M. (1973). Dilemmas in a general theory of planning. *Policy Sciences, 4*(2), 155–169. https://doi.org/10.1007/BF01405730

Samuel, A. L. (2000). Some studies in machine learning using the game of checkers. *IBM Journal of Research and Development, 44*(1/2), 206–226. https://doi.org/10.1147/rd.441.0206

Sousa, W. G. de, Melo, E. R. P. de, Bermejo, P. H. D. S., Farias, R. A. S., & Gomes, A. O. (2019). How and where is artificial intelligence in the public sector going? A literature review and research agenda. *Government Information Quarterly, 36*(4), 101392. https://doi.org/10.1016/j.giq.2019.07.004

Teisman, G. R. (2000). Models for research into decision-making processes: On phases, streams and decision-making rounds. *Public Administration, 78*(4), 937–956. https://doi.org/10.1111/1467-9299.00238

Thierer, A. D., Castillo, A., & Russell, R. (2017). Artificial intelligence and public policy. *SSRN Electronic Journal*. https://doi.org/10.2139/ssrn.3021135

van der Voort, H. G., Klievink, A. J., Arnaboldi, M., & Meijer, A. J. (2019). Rationality and politics of algorithms. Will the promise of big data survive the dynamics of public decision making? *Government Information Quarterly, 36*(1), 27–38. https://doi.org/10.1016/j.giq.2018.10.011

Veale, M., & Brass, I. (2019). Administration by algorithm? Public management meets public sector machine learning. In K. Yeung & M. Lodge (Eds.), *Algorithmic regulation* (pp. 1–30). Oxford University Press. https://doi.org/10.31235/osf.io/mwhnb

Veale, M., Van Kleek, M., & Binns, R. (2018). Fairness and accountability design needs for algorithmic support in high-stakes public sector decision-making. In *Proceedings of the 2018 CHI Conference on Human Factors in Computing Systems* (pp. 1–14). ACM. https://doi.org/10.1145/3173574.3174014

Webster, J., & Watson, R. T. (2002). Analyzing the past to prepare for the future: Writing a literature review. *MIS Quarterly, 26*(2), xiii–xxiii. https://doi.org/10.1.1.104.6570

Wenzelburger, G., König, P. D., Felfeli, J., & Achtziger, A. (2022). Algorithms in the public sector. Why context matters. *Public Administration* (November), 1–21. https://doi.org/10.1111/padm.12901

Wirtz, B. W., Weyerer, J. C., & Geyer, C. (2019). Artificial intelligence and the public sector –applications and challenges. *International Journal of Public Administration, 42*(7), 596–615. https://doi.org/10.1080/01900 692.2018.1498103

Wohlin, C. (2014). Guidelines for snowballing in systematic literature studies and a replication in software engineering. *ACM International Conference Proceeding Series*. https://doi.org/10.1145/2601248.2601268

Young, M. M., Bullock, J. B., & Lecy, J. D. (2019). Artificial discretion as a tool of governance: A framework for understanding the impact of artificial intelligence on public administration. *Perspectives on Public Management and Governance*, 301–313. https://doi.org/10.1093/ppmgov/gvz014

Zuiderwijk, A., Chen, Y., & Salem, F. (2021). Implications of the use of artificial intelligence in public governance: A systematic literature review and a research agenda. *Government Information Quarterly* (May 2020), 101577. https://doi.org/10.1016/j.giq.2021.101577

Zweig, K. A., Wenzelburger, G., & Krafft, T. D. (2018). On chances and risks of security related algorithmic decision making systems. *European Journal for Security Research, 3*(2), 181–203. https://doi.org/10.1007/s41125-018-0031-2

PART IV

Performance management and public value

10

THE PERFORMANCE FRAMEWORK OF THE EU BUDGET

A path to public value creation?

Giuseppe Grossi and Sara Giovanna Mauro

Introduction

Recently, the debate among academics and practitioners on the role(s) and function(s) of the public budget has been growing, even as a consequence of the period we live in. Migrant and refugee crises during the war emergency in Ukraine, as well as economic and social crises determined by the Covid-19 pandemic and the war, are placing increased attention on the need to create public value and pursue good results by using public resources, but how to define and measure them and how to allocate resources to them is challenging (Anessi-Pessina et al., 2020; Grossi et al., 2020; Grossi & Vakulenko, 2022).

The academic debate on this topic is strongly influenced by the continuous development in the paradigms, frameworks and conceptual approaches leading the reform path in the public sector (Mauro, 2021). Since the end of the 1980s, the development of New Public Management (NPM) has inspired the adoption of managerial reforms in the public sector, specifically supporting the use of performance measurement and management systems (Hood, 1995), with consequent impacts on budgeting, in the search for efficiency and effectiveness. In this context, the practice of performance-based budgeting has attracted new attention given its focus on the use of performance information to inform the budgeting process in order to improve the use of resources and overall performance. Then, the development of New Public Governance (NPG) and public value has emphasized democratic and public values over efficiency and effectiveness (Moore, 1995; Osborne, 2010; Almqvist et al., 2013; Grossi & Argento, 2022). The specific debate on public value has grown significantly, focusing on the key goal of governments, namely public value delivery. However, defining what public value or public values are, is a challenging issue (Alford et al., 2017; Bozeman, 2007; Moore, 1995); consequently, the accounting and accountability implications are difficult to detect and manage. Despite the attention paid to public value and the growing recognition of the relevance of public value delivery in public sector accounting (e.g. Bracci et al., 2019; Steccolini, 2019), accounting scholars still pay limited attention to this topic and the empirical investigation of public value budgeting is limited.

The rationale beyond this research aim is that the adoption of performance budgeting can be motivated by the need for managing the budget rationally and improving its performance, increasing the efficiency and effectiveness of the use of public resources and thus improving the delivery of public services. The improvement of performance and public services can be translated into the improvement of the value delivered to the community by the use of public resources and the provision

DOI: 10.4324/9781003295945-14

of effective services. Accordingly, performance-based budgeting can assume more relevance if it is suitable for enhancing the creation of public value. This issue is analysed in the unique setting of a supranational organization, the European Union (EU), where growing attention is paid to the concepts of performance and value.

The present research aims to analyse the extent to which the approach to budgeting can reflect and address the need to measure and manage performance, taking into consideration also public value creation.

The EU has a unique system of institutions (European Commission, European Parliament, European Council, Council of the European Union, Court of Justice, European Central Bank and European Court of Auditors); bodies (the European Economic and Social Committee, the European Committee of the Regions, the European Ombudsman, the European Data Protection Supervisor); and over 30 decentralized agencies. The 2021–2027 multiannual financial framework (MFF) is central to the EU's economic policy framework. Its role is even more relevant today, considering the crucial challenges the EU and its Member States must deal with, such as the effects of the Covid-19 pandemic and the war in Ukraine. Several expectations are placed on the EU budget, such as helping to address the ongoing health emergency; kick-starting the recovery; steering economies, and societies towards a more sustainable, digital, and resilient future; and strengthening the EU's geopolitical role. The European Commission (EC) is thus fully committed to guaranteeing the achievement of its objectives of the EU budget and creating added value to its Member States (Cipriani, 2021). In this context, it is crucial to understand how the EU sets its performance budget and in what way performance is conceptualized and measured to also guide the delivery of public value.

The research was carried out by reviewing available documents concerning the EU budget (e.g. budgeting and performance documents, frameworks and guidelines available on the EU website or made available to the researchers) and by interviewing EC experts dealing with the EU budget process and reforms.

The purpose of the chapter is to shed light on how the EC compiles its performance budget and whether and how this approach is suitable for addressing the need to consider public value, contributing to the underdeveloped streams of literature on both performance budgeting at the EU level and on public value budgeting.

The chapter is structured as follows. The next section briefly reviews the literature on performance-based budgeting, and the third section summarizes the recently growing debate on public value budgeting. The fourth section illustrates the research method, while the fifth explains the budgeting process and framework at the EU level. The sixth section discusses the extent to which the EU budget is built in accordance with the model of performance budgeting and whether the adopted approach to budgeting is suitable for fostering public value creation and disclosure. The last section draws conclusions from the research.

The journey of performance-based budgeting

The label "performance-based budgeting" is used to refer to a budgeting practice built on the use of performance information to influence and guide budgetary decision-making. Despite this practice not being new, it has gained renewed attention in the spirit of NPM. Indeed, this reform movement emphasizes the relevance of measuring performance in order to improve efficiency and effectiveness (Hood, 1995). The use of performance information is expected to improve the decision-making process of public sector organizations as a means of managerial rationality: a management instrument used for rationality and performance improvement (Vakkuri, 2010). Accordingly, the key reasoning beyond performance-based budgeting is that a "performing state" needs a "performing budget" (Schick, 2003). To this purpose, in theory, the key element that characterizes performance-based budgeting is the orientation towards performance. Performance information is expected to be used in the different phases of the budgeting cycle, from its elaboration to its implementation and audit. For instance, in the preparation of the budget, performance information can be used to decide the number of resources to allocate to the different programmes on the basis of the results achieved or to achieve. In the audit phase, a control can be done to assess how the resources allocated have been spent and whether the targets have been achieved or not. In practice, the types of performance information used and the extent to which they are used can vary significantly. Accordingly, the history of performance-based budgeting is characterized by a variety of approaches used to translate the concept of performance-based budgeting into practice. This is in relation to whether the performance information concerns the past (results obtained) or the future (results to achieve, targets); whether it is reported but not explicitly used to inform the budgeting process or used, along with other information, to inform budget decisions, without any automatic or mechanical linkage between targets or performance results and funding; or whether it is used to create a direct link between results and resources (OECD, 2007). More recently, it has been recognized that the focus on the managerial impacts and the changes in organizational behaviour determined by the adoption of performance-based budgeting can be more relevant (Downes et al., 2017) than the direct changes in the allocation process.

The implementation of performance-based budgeting has not in fact always been considered successful. Firstly, the rationality expectations around the use of the tool do not take into account the fact that it does not always simplify the work of managers but can increase ambiguity and the difficulties that need to be coped with because of bounded rationality (Grossi et al., 2018; Vakkuri, 2010). Consequently, several challenges have been widely discussed in the literature (Ho, 2011; Pitsvada & LoStracco, 2002; Schick, 2003), limiting the potential role performance-based budgeting can play in fulfilling its functions. In this regard, it has been claimed that performance-based budgeting can be more successful as a communication tool than as a resource allocation tool. Following this perspective, performance-based budgeting can achieve more promising results if not considered exclusively as an allocation tool and if multiple activities are managed and integrated, such as multiyear budgetary planning and policy planning, emphasizing the management side of the practice (Ho, 2018).

Due to its potential positive results and its multiple challenges, performance-based budgeting has a long history and has undergone several changes over time (Schick, 2014). It was developed in the USA in the early part of the twentieth century, expanding in the 1950s (Ho, 2019). It gained new emphasis in the era of NPM (Anessi-Pessina et al., 2016; Hijal-Moghrabi, 2017), as a consequence of the increasing attention paid to measuring and managing performance. It still attracts attention, not only in Anglo-Saxon countries, where the focus on this practice has been historically more relevant, but also in other developed countries and in countries in transitional and developmental conditions and in relation to other recent and innovative budgeting practices (De Vries et al., 2019; Park, 2019). The focus on performance-based budgeting can come from central or local governments but also from the level of international and supranational institutions. For instance, the Organization for Economic Co-operation and Development (OECD) network of Senior Budget Officials (SBO) has set up a Performance and Results Network to emphasize the relevance of the practice, and several surveys managed by the OECD have been carried out annually to evaluate the extent of the adoption and implementation of performance-based budgeting. As discussed specifically in this chapter, the EU has also shown interest in performance-based budgeting since 2015, and the EU system of budgeting and results is quite advanced, scoring higher than any OECD country in the standard index of performance budgeting frameworks (Downs et al., 2017). However, much less attention is paid in the academic debate to the adoption of these budgeting practices at the EU level.

Public values for budgeting

Despite the growing recognition of the relevance of public value delivery in public sector accounting (e.g. Bracci et al., 2019; Steccolini, 2019), only limited attention has been devoted to public value budgeting (Chohan & Jacobs, 2017, 2018; Douglas & Overmans, 2020).

According to Moore (2014), the most problematic area of public value is measurement. The balanced scorecard approach was used by Moore in his public value scorecard model, in which the original dimensions of Kaplan and Norton's scorecard were replaced by three main elements that managers are expected to focus on in creating public value: creating trust and legitimacy; improving operations and services; and envisioning social results (Moore, 1995, pp. 71–76). Talbot proposed a public value creation framework based on five dimensions in order to manage the process of public value creation: social results focus; trust and legitimacy focus; services focus; resources focus; and processes (Talbot, 2011, p. 32). The dimension of results shows clearly the sort of tensions that have to be traded off or balanced in creating public value. It clearly captures many traditional dilemmas (between co-efficiency, equity and democracy) in public management and provides a useful analytical framework for thinking about the main dimensions of public value creation (Talbot, 2011)

The difficulties in defining the meaning of public values and in identifying suitable ways for measuring public value result also in the scarce empirical research on public value budgeting, which contributes to making the definition and implementation of public value budgeting even more problematic.

According to Douglas and Overmans (2020), an attempt to define the meaning of public value budgeting stresses the call for coordination and integration between funds and other public, private and community resources, for the involvement of societal stakeholders, for continuous updates to the ongoing budget and, generally, for more communication. These authors (2020) formulate several propositions regarding how the principles of a public value approach could affect government budgeting. One of the key ideas is that, to create public value(s), it is essential to engage multiple stakeholders who can contribute to the delivery of public value with their resources and inputs. Accordingly, one significant contribution of the public value literature is the way in which it draws attention to questions about the public purposes that are or should be served by organizations in all sectors, by intra- and cross-sector collaborations. In this regard, Moore (2013) recognizes the contribution made by users, civil society organizations and other private actors to public value production. Public sector organizations are engaged in knowledge sharing, coordination and dialogue with a broad range of actors from state, market and civil society. The attempt to link public value creation to dialogue with multiple actors is built on the idea that the focus on public value is a game changer that transforms the governance of the public sector and opens it up to the market and civil society. These governance developments are concerned with new ways of enabling citizen participation (via, for example, consultation forums and arenas with citizens and users), working together to co-decide how citizens' needs will be met and how public services can improve their quality of life. Citizens can be directly engaged in public decision-making, including strategic, long-term financial planning and budgeting (e.g. Fung, 2006; Torfing et al., 2012; Vangen et al., 2015). From the public value perspective, this must be through some form of representative and participatory democracy, as well as through participation by citizens (Talbot, 2011).

According to the literature on the topic, the principal value delivered by public sector organizations is the achievement of the politically mandated mission of the organization and the fulfilment of citizens' aspirations that were reliably reflected in that mandate. Notably, the value of government bureaucracies is not well measured by financial performance (Moore, 2000). According to Moore (1995), there are five levels in public value creation: namely, quantity and quality increase in public activities; cost reductions; better understanding of citizens' needs and then satisfying those needs; increased fairness in the public sector; and better skills. Papi et al. (2018) presented a multidimensional model, regarding what public value is and how it can be also created, which can be used to measure the public value generated by public sector organizations. In their model, public value is generated when social, economic and intangible values are higher than the associated sacrifices. Social values are related to citizens' satisfaction with public services in qualitative, quantitative, temporal and monetary terms. Economic value, based on the perspective of the public organization, is related to its economic performance, financial stability and efficiency. The intangible values are related to the basic elements of public sector organization, such as its internal organization; its human resources; the relationships with other public, private and non-profit organizations; and its ability to understand changes in the external environment (Papi et al., 2018, p. 505). Despite these examples, the systematic literature review of Bracci et al. (2019) still shows a limited number of accounting studies and the need to achieve a deeper understanding of public value conceptualization, creation and measurement tools.

Guthrie et al.'s (2014) edited book started a dialogue about public value management, measurement and reporting concerning theory and practice; it comprises a collection of chapters with theoretical and empirical investigations that have contributed to the ongoing debates in the literature (Guthrie & Russo, 2014). Cuganesan et al. (2014) emphasize the link between network governance and public value in the case of Australia, pointing to the need for further studies to explore the role of public value and performance measurement practices in a network governance context, which is characterized by inter-organizational collaboration and co-production of service delivery. In the same vein, Spano (2014) argues that public value can be measured at both the organizational and the network level, considering a group of organizations working together. There is a growing number of calls for more practical contributions to the implementation of public value, also using action research (Cuganesan et al., 2014). Chohan and Jacobs (2017) show how "public value in politics" can be achieved by integrating public value in budgeting to enhance the democracy and efficiency of the legislative budget offices. They contrast the higher public value contribution of the advisory role in the case of the US with the costing position in the case of Canada. Chohan and Jacobs (2018) suggest that the use of "public value as rhetoric" in budgeting is a function of contractor values held by citizens, which politicians and public managers must reconcile. We will focus on the case of the performance framework for the EU budget, how the EU sets its performance budget and whether this approach is suitable to guide the delivery of public value.

Research method

The purpose of this chapter is to shed light on how the EU compiles its performance budget and whether and how this approach is suitable for addressing the need to produce public value, contributing to the underdeveloped streams of literature on both performance budgeting at the EU level and public value budgeting.

For this purpose, the research was carried out by reviewing available documents concerning the EU budget (e.g. budgeting and performance documents, frameworks and guidelines available on the EU website or made available to the researchers) and by interviewing European Commission experts dealing with the EU budget process and reforms.

In particular, two informants were interviewed to discuss the history, state of the art and prospect of performance budgeting at the EU level and its suitability for enhancing a focus on public value. The two interviewees work as a senior economist and a policy officer at the EU Directorate General (DG) for Budget and have long experience at the EC. The interview was carried out online, and 75 minutes of conversation were transcribed and analysed.

In addition to the interview text and interviewers' notes, as well as the examination of the official websites and videos, the analysis focused on the budgetary documents of the EU, such as: the EU's

145

2021–2027 long-term budget and NextGenerationEU (NGEU); the Performance Framework for the EU budget (Volumes I, II and III); the EU Budget Focused on Results; and so on. These multiple sources of information were jointly analysed, as discussed in the following sections.

The following findings are then based on the analysis of published documents supplemented with interviews with EC experts.

The EU budget: process, actors and artefacts

Public budgeting is particularly relevant at the EU level, since it is an important tool whereby institutions account for the resources used to a variegated set of numerous stakeholders. Accordingly, the process through which the budget is set, authorized, implemented and audited is very complex and quite different from the budgets of national and local governments.

The EU budget is mainly dedicated to investments and presents a multilevel structure. Its principal revenues are raised by the EU in the form of Member States' contributions, and most EU expenditure is handed back to Member States through a balance of allocative, redistributive and stabilizing measures related to several policy areas and spending programmes. The objectives usually stem from Commission policies, political priorities or international agreements. Currently, the largest share of the budget is dedicated to building a greener and more resilient Europe. Other shares of the budget are directed to ensuring a successful digital transition, strengthening cohesion policies (to help poorer regions in the EU), and nurturing innovation. Finally, other areas of expenditure include combating illegal migration, improving border management and enhancing security. For this reason, the EU adopts long-term spending plans, known as multiannual financial frameworks (MFFs) that run for a period of five to seven years; the current MFF runs from 2021 to 2027. The unanimity of EU Member States – required to set a seven-year MFF – makes finding a compromise between different national interests and stances crucial (Cipriani, 2021). This long-term budget sets out the EU's spending priorities and limits, and the MFF is thus central to the EU's economic policy framework, defining the ceilings for the different headings. Then, the annual budget falls under the MFF.

The budget formulation requires the involvement of the multiple directorate-generals (DGs), which formulate their proposals to be sent to the DG budget. The requests should also be justified through the use of performance information, which can provide support for the requests for specific amounts of resources in terms of results achieved/to achieve. On the basis of this information, the DG budget coordinates the consequent budget hearings, with the aim of drafting and steering the budget. The DG budget has the responsibility for preparing the Commission's budget proposals, which are then negotiated and agreed by the European Parliament and the Council. Among its different functions, the DG budget also has to propose and negotiate, together with the European Parliament and the Council, any new sources of revenue to the EU budget, manage the treasury function, prepare and publish the EU annual accounts, report on implementation of the EU budget and work together with EU countries to guarantee that the EU budget is well spent.

In the context of budget preparation, there is more room to use performance information to evaluate new projects to be financed, considering their potential impacts, and to evaluate previous programmes in terms of what has and what has not worked. The EU budget purposes several objectives in a cross-cutting perspective, for example, cohesion, transport, energy and research spending. The objectives and indicators for each programme over the multiannual period are incorporated into programme statements, which are annexes to the draft budget. After the approval of the MFF, the different DGs can ask, every year, the DG budget for revisions, also using in this case performance information to support their requests, but the flexibility is more limited, given that the general framework has already been set. The following figure (Figure 10.1) depicts the simplified process of the elaboration and approval of the EU budget.

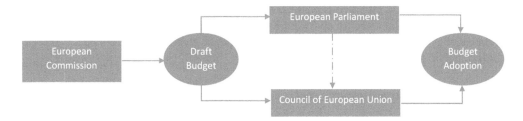

Figure 10.1 EU budget: actors and process.

After the allocation of the budget, every DG has the task of implementing its financed programmes. The annual management performance report will then report the results achieved from a back and forward perspective.

If, during the year, unexpected events occur, it will be necessary to intervene and revise budget allocations, finding additional resources or reallocating the existing ones. Although, in this phase, performance information may also play a role, in practice, it is particularly challenging, and decisions are rarely taken on the basis of performance evaluations. Once the budget has been approved, the Commission is responsible for managing it, while, annually, it is the European Parliament that assesses the implementation of the previous year's budget.

Concerning the reporting phase, a dual accounting system is in place that includes financial statements (balance sheet, statement of financial performance and comprehensive explanatory notes), compiled according to International Public Sector Accounting Standards (IPSAS), and budgetary implementation reports, which give a detailed record of budget implementation (Grossi & Soverchia, 2011). The budgetary accounts are based on the modified cash accounting principle, which means that transactions (expenditure and income) are recorded only when cash is paid out or received. With specific reference to reporting on the performance of the EU budget, each Commission DG produces an annual activity report for the previous financial year, to account for their performance during the past year, including information on results obtained and resources spent, compared with what was stated at the beginning of the year in the DG's annual management plan. This allows analysis of whether DGs were able to achieve targets set in their strategic/management plans. Together with the consolidated annual accounts, these annual reports are part of the Integrated Financial and Accountability Reporting, which also includes the annual management and performance report (AMPR), produced every year by the Commission to discuss the results achieved with the EU budget and how the previous year's budget was managed. At a further level of detail, Annexe 3 of this report includes an overview of the programme's performance (Programme Performance Overview; PPO), detailing the performance information on a programme-by-programme basis.

Finally, the budget is audited internally by the Commission Internal Audit Service (IAS) and externally by the European Court of Audit (ECA), which also takes into account in its analysis the performance dimension. Specifically, the IAS has the goal of providing independent and objective assurance as to the effectiveness and efficiency of the risk management, control and governance processes. The ECA audits the reliability of the EU accounts and the legality and regularity of the transactions, and the ensuing statement of assurance is published in the annual report. Interestingly, for the first time in 2020, a specific and separate annual report on the performance of the EU budget was published, covering the performance of spending programmes. This suggests the growing relevance of the performance dimension of the EU budget. As suggested by some practitioners, the audit opinion should focus more on the operation of the Commission's internal control framework and devote more attention to "value for money", thus enhancing the creation of a performance culture (Cipriani, 2021). Given the extraordinary times we live in, the EC is fully committed to ensuring that the 2021–2027 MFF is as effective as possible in achieving its budget programmes and key objectives, as well as delivering value for all EU citizens. To this purpose, the management, reporting and assessment of performance can contribute to strengthening the control over the efficiency and effectiveness of public spending.

The EU journey towards performance: a path to public value creation?

The EU budget is divided into headings – or spending categories – and programmes, with each programme supporting a different policy area and group of beneficiaries, although there are some cross-cutting priority areas that are financed by multiple programmes. The current budget is made up of seven headings and more than 40 programmes, each of which has an "intervention logic": objectives, targets and performance requirements are set specifically per programme, recognizing formally and explicitly the relevance of performance information. This performance orientation has been strengthened with the introduction of the initiative titled "EU Budget Focused on Results" (BFOR), launched in 2015 in order to improve the effectiveness of the budget and support the achievement of EU goals. The official statements of politicians also reveal that the attention paid to performance and value is visible: "Every action we take must deliver maximum performance and value added" (Jean-Claude Juncker, President of the European Commission in 2015).

A performance budgeting system has indeed been established for the EU budget, with the adoption of the MFF 2014–2020. According to the BFOR initiative, a programme's performance framework is designed to provide budgetary authorities with ex-ante and ex-post performance information relevant to decision-making during the budgetary procedure. The system is reinforced with the publication of an Integrated Financial Reporting Package, which guarantees the reporting of performance information. Following a step-by-step process, EU actors have put increasing efforts into this process of reform, and the "performance framework for budget" was then introduced to reinforce the previous BFOR initiative, in order to make the link between resources and performance even stronger. Given the current size and role of the EU budget, maximizing its performance is of the utmost relevance to the budgetary authorities.

The "performance framework for the EU budget", introduced under the 2021–2027 MFF, includes detailed information on the programmes for each heading, reporting objectives, mission, actions to be taken and challenges to be addressed; the overall resources allocated; and the indicators to be used to monitor the achievement of the objectives. However, there is no direct link between indicators, objectives and resources allocated, since these latter pieces of information are reported with reference to the overall programme. The AMPR discusses the implementation of the EU budget in its second volume, whose annexe provides an overview of the EU budget performance. In the annexes of the last volume of the AMPR, it is possible to find detailed programme-by-programme performance overview (PPO). Indeed, in the PPO, the resources executed and the results achieved are reported for each programme, followed by a qualitative and textual assessment. If we focus on this annexe and take as an example the first heading, "single market, innovation and digital", we can find information on objectives, executed commitments and payments, key performance indicators with targets and results, concrete examples of achievements and a qualitative assessment of performance. With reference to the Horizon 2020 programme, part of the heading "single market, innovation and digital", key performance indicators such as "cross-sector and cross-country circulation of researchers" and "researchers who have access to research infrastructures" have been adopted and associated with targets and results, with the indication of the progress towards the target. An example of an indicator classified as an impact indicator is the following: "Creation, growth & market shares of companies having developed FP innovations". This is done for each heading. In total, more than 750 indicators are defined, with a prevalence of output indicators and limited use of impact indicators.

Based on these considerations, it can be stated that, in general, recalling the classification of performance budgeting experiences made by the OECD, it is possible to recognize a kind of performance-informed budgeting, according to which, performance information is produced, reported in the budget documents and used to some extent to support budget decisions. During the budgeting process at the EU level, performance information can be used to support the DGs' requests for resources and to evaluate the results achieved through the programme's implementation. In some cases, a more advanced and sophisticated approach to performance budgeting is also evident, which recalls direct performance budgeting (OECD, 2007), according to which, performance information is used to directly influence the allocation of resources, as in the case of the Recovery and Resilience Facility (RRF), centrepiece of NextGenerationEU.

The 2021–2027 MFF and NGEU have strengthened the EU budget's focus on economic, social and environmental values. The current MFF dedicates €374 billion to this goal (including €274 billion for regional development and cohesion), plus over €774 billion from the RRF and REACT-EU within NGEU. The RRF offers large-scale financial support for investments and reforms, including green and digital transitions, to make national economies more resilient. It is structured around six pillars: green transition; digital transformation; economic cohesion, productivity and competitiveness; social and territorial cohesion; health, economic, social and institutional resilience; and policies for the next generation. The RRF is really focused on achieving public values, as it helps the EU reach its target of climate neutrality by 2050 and facilitate digital transition. The Member States submit national plans with clear milestones and targets related to their investments, which are then evaluated by the Commission. In preparing their requests, given the six pillars of the RRF, the Member States should guarantee their contribution to each of those areas. For instance, they are required to dedicate at least the 37 per cent of the expenditures to climate objectives (https://ec.europa.eu/economy_fina nce/recovery-and-resilience-scoreboard/index.html). The assessment of the contributions to the objectives is calculated by relying on what indicated in the annexes of the RRF regulation. Milestones and targets are elaborated by each Member State with reference to their investments, and in addition, common indicators are elaborated to show the progress of the implementation of the recovery and resilience plans towards common objectives and the overall performance of the RRF. For instance, the number of young people aged 15–29 years receiving support, or the additional operational capacity installed for renewable energy are indicators used for each Member State to calculate the individual and overall contribution to the pillars financed by the RFF. This contributes to measure the overall value created by the EU funds.

The RRF is "performance-driven by design, as payments are explicitly linked to Member States' fulfilment of milestones and targets linked to investments and reforms in the national recovery and resilience plans financed through the Facility", as stated in the Performance Framework for the EU Budget (Volume I). Payments under the RRF will be linked to performance. The EC will authorize disbursements based on the satisfactory fulfilment of a group of milestones and targets reflecting progress on the reforms and investments of the plan. Since disbursements can take place a maximum of twice a year, there cannot be more than two groups of milestones and targets per year. In this case, resources are allocated to Member States on the basis of the achievement of objectives:

We do not ask for invoices; we ask for results.

(Interviewee)

According to the interviewees, this model should be extended and also applied to the other programmes, and for this purpose they recognize:

The best we can do is to provide more and more performance information.

(Interviewee)

The rationale behind this statement is that, by defining relevant and multiple performance infor-mation, more pressures can be exerted on those who have to implement the projects, reinforcing their accountability; at the same time, such information can support those who have to approve the budget and carry out long-term evaluation and impact assessment:

The performance information should be there. This is our task.

(Interviewee)

According to the interviewees, the performance measurement system can be considered mature at the EU level, given its ability both to set what to achieve and to monitor what has been done with the money allocated, according to a feedback loop perspective. In this regard, it is useful to recall that specific documents are compiled annually to report performance information and allow accountability for results (e.g. AMPR). Significant investments have been made to support per-formance reporting.

However, to be reinforced, performance budgeting still requires investments and time. Its imple-mentation is not without difficulties, as demonstrated by the efforts put into providing suggestions and elaborating proposals for the further development of an integrated budget performance frame-work to be applied to all spending programmes (Becker et al., 2016).

One of the key challenges identified concerns the "distance" between the level at which budget decisions are taken and the level at which the results of the policies financed and implemented are produced. Indeed, it is difficult to monitor and collect information on the "local" effects of the programmes decided and financed at the EU level. The EU budget is implemented mainly by the Commission and the Member States. Only 18 per cent of the EU budget is directly managed by the Commission, including its delegation and executive agencies. Finally, 8 per cent of the EU budget is managed indirectly by international organizations, decentralized agencies, third countries and so on. The main share of the EU funds (74 per cent) is spent together with Member States under what is known as shared management. The authorities in the Member States (for instance, the ministries for regional development), rather than the Commission itself, manage the expenditure, under the super-vision of the Commission.

A second challenge concerns the risk of information overload. As often occurs, the performance information produced does not always correspond to the information needs perceived by the different actors. This is complicated by the coexistence of multiple different actors with diverse perspectives, such as the Member State governments, the budgetary authorities and the EU institutions. From the perspective of the EU, it can also be difficult to collect information from the multiple Member States.

A third "structural" limit is represented by the MFF, which sets indications for a long period of time, limiting the possibilities of intervening and revising the allocations based on performance results. The flexibility is limited.

However, as stated in the interviews,

There is value in predictability.

(Interviewee)

Indeed, it is assessed as positive that the next trends in resource allocation are known in advance, thanks to the MFF. In response to the criticisms and challenges that have emerged during the implementation of performance budgeting, several improvements have been achieved over the years, according to the interviewees, and they can be summarized as follows:

- The midterm evaluations have been made available in a timely way, in order to provide effective support to the decision-making process;
- Indicators for each programme have been streamlined and revised, to address the risk of overload;
- New methodologies have been developed to calculate the EU's contribution to relevant issues and drive cross-cutting policy objectives (e.g. climate change, gender equality etc.), but there is still a need to invest in these issues to allow an aggregate analysis of the impacts of the programmes financed by the EU;
- A renewed methodology, based on EU coefficients, has been used for the horizontal priorities in the EU budget, to improve accountability and transparency;
- Performance reporting has also been strengthened by the creation of ad-hoc web pages.

When discussing the future prospects of performance budgeting, awareness of the potential relevance of this practice clearly emerges, along with the parallel need to make further investments, in order to strengthen the capacity to assess the impact of EU financing and base the allocation decisions on such a foundation. The evaluation of the impact is strongly connected to the creation of public value.

In the European context, it is in fact important to make the measurement of public value possible, as the EU budget is characterized by a subsidiary approach, whereby:

We can intervene only if we produce certain value.

(Interviewee)

Quantifying the value added by the EU budget is a recognized challenge. Currently, the impact assessment has replaced the value measurement, but performance and value are two different concepts, both difficult to measure, interlinked but distinct. In light of the consideration of the value created by the EU budget, the 2021–2027 budget is stated to be different from the previous one, according to the budget document:

When the EU pools its resources and finances in policy areas such as research and border protection at EU level, it achieves better results than the EU Member States could manage acting on their own. EU action in these policy areas brings EU added value.

Based on the official budgetary documents, the policy areas to be financed more significantly are identified in a way that is suitable for increasing the value added by the EU budget, and "This makes the current long-term budget a truly modern budget", according to the interviewees. Thus, every euro allocated should bring added value (European Commission, 2019); the analysis of the empirical material points out that, in the context of the EU budget, "value added" is more frequently discussed than "public value" (Rubio, 2011). However, it is widely agreed among scholars and practitioners that there is no shared meaning and definition of the concept and, consequently, it is difficult to measure it. Value added can be intended as the value added by the EU through the allocation of resources and the financing of projects, in comparison to what Member States could do without the EU budget. However, different perspectives may also be adopted, with reference to benefits arising from good management and implementation, or to positive side effects stemming from EU spending interventions (European Union, 2018; Rubio, 2011). Focusing on added value ex ante or ex post is also a challenge.

Overall, it is recognized that measurement of the value added is difficult because its quantification and its overall value cannot be reduced to a calculation of financial benefits, as it includes other dimensions. At the moment, increasing efforts are put into measuring impacts, but these indicators still call for further development.

An ad-hoc section of the EC website is dedicated to "EU budget added value". This section appears to have been built mainly to strengthen accountability and transparency, arrange events on the public budget, create opportunities and channels to facilitate citizen participation, and to try to clarify budget roles and key features. The EU budget should be compiled through some form of representative – and also sometimes participatory – democracy, as well as through participation by citizens. Currently, there are some existing participatory spending tools in parts of the EU budget – such as Community-Led Local Development (CLLD) within Cohesion Policy Funds regulations (OECD, 2022). However, this area remains in need of investment. In addition, among the key challenges officially recognized in determining where the money should go, there is indeed the making of the EU budget as an EU value-added budget, which should be able to: 1) achieve the objectives set out in the Treaties; 2) provide for EU-wide public goods; and 3) uphold European values (European Union, 2018).

Conclusions

The EU system of budgeting for performance and results, as demonstrated by the BFOR initiative and the "performance framework for the EU budget", is quite advanced and unique, including strengths and weaknesses that are also seen at national levels. Indeed, in 2015, the EC launched the BFOR initiative, aimed at strengthening the systematic focus on performance and results, while making it easier for citizens and stakeholders to understand the objectives and impacts of the EU budget. Then, the new "performance framework for the EU budget" under the 2021–2027 MFF introduced several innovations and several tools, useful for defining objectives and monitoring their progress for all EU programmes, including those financed by NGEU. Overall, the performance measurement system can be considered mature at the EU level, given its ability both to set what to achieve and to monitor what has been done with the money allocated, from a performance-based perspective. Several specific documents are elaborated on annually, to report performance information and allow accountability for results (e.g. AMPR). Significant investments have been made to provide a more systematic ex-post account of performance against headline targets (Downs et al., 2017). The EC implements this framework in collaboration with other EU institutions (the European Parliament and Council and the ECA) and the Member States, with the aim of ensuring that the unprecedented size of the EU budget will deliver its full potential, to increase public value not only at the national level but also at the European level.

Overall, performance information is reported and used to some extent to influence decision-making; in a few cases, such as the RFF, the link between results and resources is more direct. Indeed, more recently, the 2021–2027 MFF and NGEU have strengthened the EU budget's focus on performance and public value. The EC is thus as fully committed to making its budget perform well as to strengthening the ability to reach its objectives and create added value for the EU and Member States (Cipriani, 2021). Nevertheless, there is still a need to invest in performance budgeting, in order to further improve the performance measures and information available and, consequently, strengthen their use in the budgeting process. In particular, the assessment of the impact and the value created by the financed programmes is at the top of the EU's priorities. Indeed, on the one hand, performance budgeting is motivated by managerial rationality, which focuses on and drives the production of performance information for informing decision-making, and, on the other hand, a public value approach to budgeting is relevant to allow dialogue with multiple stakeholders and their engagement (Talbot,

2011). These two approaches can be linked if we consider that the ultimate goal of using performance information in the budgeting process is to improve results in terms of the efficiency and effectiveness of public service delivery and also public value creation and more focus on social, democratic and participatory values (Moore, 1995; Moore, 2000). To facilitate the assessment of impacts and value created, the dialogue with the multiple involved stakeholders can be crucial to facilitate the process of information elaboration, collection and analysis. To this latter purpose, stakeholder engagement is crucial. In the context of the EU budget, it has been recognized that, to reinforce the value added, the focus on impact measurement should be increased.

The research findings show that the performance framework in place is quite developed, although impact indicators are still less developed compared to other indicators. Further investments are required to develop measures and indicators suitable for strengthening the measurement of impacts produced from multiple perspectives and thus enhancing a control over the value created. In the context of the EU budget, it has been recognized that to reinforce the value added, a focus on impact measurement should be reinforced. The capacity to measure the impact generated and the value added is also crucial for legitimacy and accountability purposes, and significant pressures are put on these issues. The RRF provides an example of investment programmes where results are crucial to obtain resources and there is an effort to measure coherently the results achieved by the different Member States, thus allowing a final common assessment of the overall contribution given by the EU funds to the achievement of public goals.

The EC is thus already focusing on the development of suitable financial and non-financial indicators to evaluate the overall impact generated and the current performance framework for budget supports, as well as to enhance the analysis of performance in terms of public value creation (Moore, 1995; Moore, 2000; Talbot, 2011). However, despite the recognized relevance of measuring the "value added", it is worth pointing out the need to focus on "public value", trying to best conceptualize it by recognizing its multiple aspects in the context of the EU and measuring them. Further research can contribute to this stream of research by investigating empirically the potential approaches to be adopted to enhance public value measurement and budgeting, starting from the current budgeting practices and creating a link among them.

References

Alford, J., Douglas, S., Geuijen, K., & 't Hart, P. (2017). Ventures in public value management: Introduction to the symposium. *Public Management Review, 19*(5), 589–604.

Almqvist, R., Grossi, G., van Helden, & Reichard, C. (2013). Public sector governance and accountability. *Critical Perspectives on Accounting, 24*(7–8), 479–487.

Anessi-Pessina, E., Barbera, C., Langella, C., Manes-Rossi, F., Sancino, A., Sicilia, M., & Steccolini, I. (2020). Reconsidering public budgeting after the COVID-19 outbreak: key lessons and future challenges. *Journal of Public Budgeting, Accounting & Financial Management, 32*(5), 957–965.

Anessi-Pessina, E., Barbera, C., Sicilia, M., & Steccolini, I. (2016). Public sector budgeting: a European review of accounting and public management journals. *Accounting, Auditing & Accountability Journal, 29*(3), 491–519.

Becker, W., Dominguez-Torreiro, M., & Saisana, M. (2016). *Monitoring & Reporting EU Budget Performance to 2020 and Beyond: A JRC proposal.* European Commission.

Bozeman, B. (2007). *Public values and public interest – counterbalancing economic individualism.* Georgetown University Press.

Bracci, E., Papi, L., Bigoni, M., Deidda Gagliardo, E., & Bruns, H. (2019). Public value and PSA research: A structured literature review. *Journal of Public Budgeting, Accounting & Financial Management, 31*(1), 103–136.

Chohan, U. W., & Jacobs, K. (2017). Public value in politics: A legislative budget office approach. *International Journal of Public Administration, 40*(12), 1063–1073.

Chohan, U. W., & Jacobs, K. (2018). Public value as rhetoric: A budgeting approach. *International Journal of Public Administration, 41*(15), 1217–1227.

Cipriani, G. (2021). Improving the accountability of the EU budget's multi-level implementation: Strengthening the contribution of the European Court of Auditors. *German Law Journal, 22*, 466–489.

Cuganesan, S., Jacobs, K., & Lacey, D. (2014). Beyond new public management: Does performance management drive public value in networks? In J. Guthrie, G. Marcon, S. Russo, S & F. Farneti (Eds.), *Public value management, measurement and reporting* (pp. 21–42). Emerald Group.

De Vries, M. S., Nemec, J., & Špaček, D. (2019). *Performance-based budgeting in the public sector*. Springer International.

Douglas, S., & Overmans, T. (2020). Public value budgeting: Propositions for the future of budgeting. *Journal of Public Budgeting, Accounting & Financial Management, 32*(4), 623–637.

Downes, R., Moretti, D., & Sherie, N. (2017). Budgeting and performance in the European Union: A review by the OECD in the context of EU budget focus on results. *OECD Journal of Budgeting, 1*, 1–60.

European Commission. (2019). *The EU budget at a glance*. https://commission.europa.eu/publications/eu-bud get-glance-0_en

European Union. (2018). *EU budget focused on results – methodology*. https://commission.europa.eu/strategy-and-policy/eu-budget/performance-and-reporting/programme-performance-statements/introduction-and-met hodology_en

Fung, A. (2006). Varieties of participation in complex governance. *Public Administration Review, 66*(1), 66–75.

Grossi, G., & Argento, D. (2022). The fate of accounting for public governance development. *Accounting, Auditing and Accountability Journal, 35*(9), 272–303.

Grossi, G., Ho, A., & Joyce, P. (2020). Budgetary responses to a global pandemic: International experiences and lessons for a sustainable future. *Journal of Public Budgeting, Accounting & Financial Management, 32*(5), 737–744.

Grossi, G., Mauro, S. G., & Vakkuri, J. (2018). Converging and diverging pressures in PBB development: The experiences of Finland and Sweden. *Public Management Review, 20*(12), 1836–1857.

Grossi, G., & Soverchia, M. (2011). The European Commission adoption of IPSAS to reform financial statement. *Abacus: A Journal of Accounting, Finance and Business Studies, 47*(4), 525–552.

Grossi, G., & Vakulenko, V. (2022). New development: Accounting for human-made disasters – comparative analysis of the support to Ukraine in times of war. *Public Money & Management, 42*(6), 467–471.

Guthrie, J., Marcon, G., Russo, S., & Farneti, F. (2014). *Public value management, measurement and reporting*. Emerald Group.

Guthrie, J., & Russo, S. (2014). Public value management: Challenge of defining, measuring and reporting public services. In J. Guthrie, G. Marcon, S. Russo, & F. Farneti (Eds.), *Public Value management, measurement and reporting* (pp. 3–17). Emerald Group.

Hijal-Moghrabi, I. (2017). The current practice of performance-based budgeting in the largest US cities: An innovation theory perspective. *Public Performance & Management Review, 40*(4), 652–675.

Ho, A. T. K. (2011). PBB in American local governments: It's more than a management tool. *Public Administration Review, 71*(3), 391–401.

Ho, A. T. K. (2018). From performance budgeting to performance budget management: Theory and practice. *Public Administration Review, 78*(5), 748–758.

Ho, A. T. K. (2019). Performance budgeting in the US: A long history of institutional change. In In A. Ho, M. de Jong, & Z. Zhao (Eds.), *Performance budgeting reform: Theories and institutional practices* (pp. 53–70). Routledge.

Hood, C. (1995). The "new public management" in the 1980s: Variations on a theme. *Accounting Organisations and Society, 20*(2/3), 93–109.

Mauro, S. G. (2021). *Budgeting and performance management in the public sector*. Routledge.

Moore, M. H. (1995). *Creating public value: Strategic management in government*. Harvard University Press.

Moore, M. H. (2000). Managing for value: Organizational strategy in for-profit, nonprofit, and governmental organizations. *Nonprofit and Voluntary Sector Quarterly, 29*(1 suppl), 183–204.

Moore, M. H. (2013). *Recognising public value*. Harvard University Press.

Moore, M. H. (2014). Public value accounting: Establishing the philosophical basis. *Public Administration Review, 74*(4), 465–477.

Organization for Economic Cooperation and Development (OECD). (2007). *Performance Budgeting in OECD Countries*. OECD.

Organization for Economic Cooperation and Development (OECD). (2022). *Engaging citizens in Cohesion Policy DG Region and OECD Pilot Project Final Report*. OECD Public Governance Working Paper No. 50. OECD.

Osborne, S. P. (2010). Introduction: The (new) public governance: A suitable case for treatment? In S. P. Osborne (Ed.), *center The New Public Governance?* (pp. 17–32). Routledge.

Papi, L., Bigoni, M., Bracci, E., & Deidda Gagliardo, E. (2018). Measuring public value: A conceptual and applied contribution to the debate. *Public Money & Management, 38*(7), 503–510.

Park, J. H. (2019). Does citizen participation matter to performance-based budgeting? *Public Performance & Management Review, 42*(2), 280–304.

Pitsvada, B., & LoStracco, F. (2002). Performance budgeting-the next budgetary answer. But what is the question? *Journal of Public Budgeting, Accounting & Financial Management, 14*(1), 53–73.

Rubio, E. (2011). *The added value in EU budgetary debates: One concept, four meanings.* Policy paper. Notre Europe-Jacques Delors Institute.

Schick, A. (2003). The performing state: Reflection on an idea whose time has come but whose implementation has not. *OECD Journal on Budgeting, 3*(2), 71–103.

Schick, A. (2014). The metamorphoses of performance budgeting. *OECD Journal on Budgeting, 13*(2), 49–79.

Spano, A. (2014). How do we measure public value? From theory to practice. In J. Guthrie, G. Marcon, S. Russo, & F. Farneti (Eds.), *Public value management, measurement and reporting* (pp. 353–373). Emerald Group.

Steccolini, I. (2019). Accounting and the post-new public management: Re-considering publicness in accounting research. *Accounting, Auditing and Accountability Journal, 32*(1), 255–279.

Talbot, C. (2011). Paradoxes and prospects of "Public Value". *Public Money & Management, 31*(1), 27–34.

Torfing, J., Peters, B. G., Pierre, J., & Sørensen, E. (2012*). Interactive governance: Advancing the paradigm.* Oxford University Press on Demand.

Vakkuri, J. (2010). Struggling with ambiguity – Public managers as users of NPM-oriented management instruments. *Public Administration, 88*(4), 999–1024.

Vangen, S., Hayes, J. P., & Cornforth, C. (2015). Governing cross-sector, inter-organisational collaborations. *Public Management Review, 17*(9), 1237–1260.

11
REFLECTING ON PUBLIC VALUE IN COVID-19

Usman W. Chohan

Introduction

Public value theory (PVT) enjoys much currency in contemporary public administration/public management pedagogy, and it also serves as a discourse for hundreds of academic publications per year (Hartley et al., 2017, p. 670). This would lead one to expect a flurry of PV-related research during the coronavirus pandemic, because so many scholars are familiar with its contours and recognize its academic and practitioner appeal, and also because there are many synergistic elements between PV and the wider literatures of public management, accounting and public administration. Yet in the process of writing my most recent book, *Pandemics and Public Value Management* (Chohan, 2022), I came to observe a dearth of PVT interest in the emergent conditions of Covid-19-stricken societies, as well as in how PV's analyses might inform these conditions.

In dissecting the problem of *why* there has been such scant Covid-19 literature with a PV orientation, I arrived at three conclusions. First, PV suffered from a certain naivete which precluded it from examining crises and other destructive categories of social experience. Second, a long-standing public administration/public management literature which dealt with crises and disasters already existed (hereafter: the crisis-administration literature; "CAL") and therefore offered a natural beacon to scholars wishing to contextualize Covid-19. Third, a frenetic pace of interesting research was being undertaken by scholars in the accounting-accountability literature (hereafter: A-A), which offered important glimpses into the nature of Covid-19's multilayered societal effects that eclipsed the efforts being made among PV scholars (Leoni et al., 2021b).

The first point of naivete speaks to the contention that "PVT is premised on normalized, *peacetime* conditions of genteel democratic engagement among public value agents" (Chohan, 2022, p. 3, emphasis in the original), which is why it is not well suited to covering what are termed *wicked problems,* which is to say, those social issues that are deemed more intractable, far-reaching, amorphous and multifaceted (Roberts, 2000; Head & Alford, 2015). In the recent past, efforts made by leading PV thinkers on wicked problems, such as the global migrant (refugee) crisis (see Geuijen et al., 2017), have been found sorely lacking, to the extent that "PVT's contribution towards framing and understanding (before even getting to resolving) wicked problems has yet to be adequately evidenced," and that current efforts "to grapple with the complexity, interdependence, and magnitude of international problems and transformations simply doesn't do justice to those problems" (Chohan, 2021, p. 2).

DOI: 10.4324/9781003295945-15

The naivete arises from the pedagogical leanings of the theory (Williams & Shearer, 2011) and its "generally optimistic tenor" (Chohan, 2022), which veer it towards putting a positive spin on public management for a practitioner audience (Stoker, 2006; Hartley et al., 2017). It exhorts aspiring public managers to channel a "restless value-seeking imagination" (Benington & Moore, 2011, p. 3), and to engage in value co-creation with other stakeholders (Best et al., 2019), while aiming to "imbue public sector managers with a greater appreciation of the constraints and responsibilities within which they work" (Williams & Shearer, 2011, p. 1367). Such positivity adds to its undoubted allure (Hartley et al., 2017; Prebble, 2012; Alford & O'Flynn, 2009), but it also blinds public managerial pedagogy to the "opposite" of PV, which might alternately be termed: disvalue (Esposito & Ricci, 2015), PV destruction (Spano, 2009), and/or PV failure (Bozeman, 2002). These terms are interchangeable for the purpose of discussion here because they require more rigour and elaboration before they might be differentiated, but the commonality between them lies in their allusion to destructive categories of social experience.

The second point of a large crisis-administration literature (CAL) is also important because the existence of such a vast corpus of research offers immense depth, richness of experience and renewed substance for scholars; and so, there is a natural tendency among scholars to turn towards this long-standing tradition when attempting to contextualize crisis conditions in a society. CAL has a long tenure in public management and public administration (Rosenthal et al., 1989; 't Hart, 1993), and it views public managers as being "tested" by crises (Drennan et al., 2014), where their "success" equates in large part to their resilience in withstanding adversity (Boin & Lodge, 2016). The evolution of this literature has permitted a wide coverage of disaster-related themes, including: public manager decision-making (Rosenthal and Kouzmin, 1997), lesson-drawing/learning (Stern, 1997; Nohrstedt et al., 2021), (de)centralization (T'hart et al., 1993), interdependence (Perrow, 1984; Beck, 1992), public attitudes (Boin et al., 2008), risk typologies (Pescaroli & Alexander, 2016 , critical infra-structure (O'Sullivan et al., 2013), "adhocracy" and ad-hoc approaches (Mintzberg & Alexandra, 1985), performative roles (Boin et al., 2013), and pragmatism (Kaushik & Walsh, 2019), among many others. It is beyond the scope of this chapter to indulge in a fuller review, but one is compelled to venture a glimpse into the many facets that CAL has long examined. However, the more important point remains that scholars of public management would naturally gravitate towards CAL or A-A when examining crisis contexts such as Covid-19, and indeed they did.

The third point of a rich accounting-accountability (A-A) literature is equally important because of its success in a dual effort during Covid-19. On the one hand, A-A scholarship has sought to draw lessons for accounting and accountability from the pandemic, and on the other, its enquiry is evolving dynamically to provide interpretative meaning to the crisis the befell societies during the pandemic. In addition to the role of accounting in disaster contexts (Ahrens & Ferry, 2021; Sargiacomo et al., 2021b; Leoni et al., 2021a-b), which mirrors the area of interest in the CAL literature, there have been important manifestations of accounting in the context of traumas, as in a "mourning" process (Yu, 2021), or one that takes shape through to the end of life (Le Theule et al., 2021), as well as one which mobilizes societies towards accountability during and after "supreme emergency" (Sian & Smyth, 2021). Critical perspectives (notably in the Foucauldian tradition) have been deployed to examine biosecurity (Antonelli et al., 2021), and governmentality (Sargiacomo et al., 2021a) has made mani-fest during the pandemic (Ahrens and Ferry, 2021), along with studies that have sought to examine accounting and accountability at both central and local levels of government (Parisi & Bekier, 2021; Padovani & Iacuzzi, 2021). It has also taken an interest in the social conditions that shape pandemic-related outcomes (Andrew et al., 2021, 2022), and in the remedial measures that might be undertaken to bolster accounting and accountability practices going forward (Rinaldi, 2022; Landi et al., 2021)

Because of the combination of a rich crisis-administration literature, a vibrant literature in accounting-accountability, and general naivete that accompanies PVT's optimistic tenor, one found the stark absence of PV literature in the Covid-19 pandemic's aftermath. This gap behooved me to select attentively from what is otherwise a rich area of public management/public administration research, and curate from that assortment a set of PV-related areas which required the most urgent attention (Chohan, 2022). This included: value conflict (see review in DeGraaf et al., 2016), PV in the post-Truth era (see review in Chohan, 2019), multilateral PV (see review in Chohan, 2020, pp. 61–88), vaccine nationalism (Ruchtsman, 2021), comparative PV (see Casula and Pazos-Vidal, 2021), and PV in developing countries (Samaratunge & Wijewardena, 2009). This rich panoply was really nothing more than an incipient effort to achieve a dual (inductive-deductive) purpose: to use the lens of the Covid-19 pandemic to inform PV's reasoning and precepts, and to deploy PV lenses to better explain and understand the conditions (both in terms of the "public" and in terms of "values") that arose during the pandemic.

To repeat the broad findings of each chapter, where each one could be treated as a separate and stand-alone work, would be maladroit at this juncture, but it is important to iterate that the exploration of that book still left much unmapped and unconsidered, a point which was raised at length in the conclusion of the book, but that has yet to be addressed. This chapter thus offers an opportunity to take the same exploration forward by highlighting and expanding upon select reflections identified in that concluding chapter which warrant further scholarly attention. These reflections pertain to the public management/administration literature, and serve as invitations for scholars in these fields to proactively engage along the lines of enquiry set out in this chapter. As such, the remainder of this chapter comprises a set of reflections (at times phrased as propositions) which present scholars, particularly in the PV tradition, with some points of introspection, research and further investigation.

Reflecting on public value in Covid-19

One might begin by reflecting upon what has occurred since the onset of the Covid-19 pandemic in terms of the pandemic having forced people, both as individuals and as collectives, to revisit *what* they value, and *how much* they value the things that they claim to value (Daniel et al., 2020). This was in fact the very premise of *Pandemics and Public Value Management* (Chohan, 2022): that there was a focusing event which led the *public* to re-examine their *values,* thus invariably resonating with PVT's raison d'être of studying the public and its values. In other words, the private and public reappraisal of what values are worth holding on to, and indeed what is valuable at all, ushers one towards a path of lesson-drawing from the pandemic. This chapter focuses on six points of reflection, where the first three pertain to the role of agents in PV: civil society, private interests and a "global public", while the last three points pertain to the processes and outcomes of the pandemic.

In terms of the agents, the absence of a global effort to combat Covid-19 (as manifested by a sense of "world-public" as singular agent) meant that sufficient concerted energy was not mustered towards so grave a threat. At the same time, civil society's role became more prominent wherever traditional structures of value creation and accountability were left wanting. Furthermore, private interest played an excessively large role, at times to the detriment of PV preservation. Reflecting on these agents allows for finer attenuation of PV study in both a Covid-19 and a post-Covid context. In terms of processes and outcomes, the excess politicization of accounting for loss warrants keener attention for the attainment of accountability for the outcomes of the pandemic. This is equally true for the accounting of success and failures among societies, where there were interesting case studies that prima facie would not have been expected to perform as well (or as poorly) as they did in the pandemic. Additionally, it is important to reflect on how Covid-19 helped us pierce the veil of societies in a manner that would otherwise have been very difficult, by casting a penetrating gaze on long-standing issues that now warrant accounting and accountability in terms of PV outcomes. The points of reflection are enumerated in Table 11.1 as well.

Table 11.1 Points of reflection from the Covid-19 pandemic for public value

Theme	Brief Explanation
Agency	
The Global Public	The transboundary nature of the Covid-19 pandemic required large-scale international coordination as a consolidated global public, but this was often sorely lacking. The lack of global coordination forced countries to seek suboptimal national-level approaches, many of which failed to preserve adequate PV.
Civil Society	Although the public keenly looked to politicians and public managers for leadership and for answers during the turbulence of the Covid-19 pandemic, civil society in fact played a very important role in preserving PV, and especially so in developing countries where public administration was weakly positioned for the Covid-19 pandemic's onslaught.
private interest	Private power and private interests have dominated during the Covid-19 pandemic to an excessive degree, which has worked against global PV efforts at many levels, including: scientific collaboration, vaccine profiteering, travel bans and exacerbated economic inequalities, among others.
Process & Outcomes	
Politics in Accounting	Lives were politicized and then lost. The element of accounting for the sick and for the dead became a political issue both within societies and among them, and most commonly so where lives were being most affected by the pandemic.
Accounting for success	There have been many surprising successes and failures in terms of PV preservation over the course of the pandemic, with many societies that were thought to be more resilient proving fragile, and other ostensibly fragile publics proving more resilient than expected.
Piercing the veil	The Covid-19 pandemic pierced the veil of societies and brought long-standing structural inequalities and social disharmonies front and centre, thus magnifying existing factors of public disvalue for many publics.

Source: author elaboration.

The world public

One might begin with the notion of what the "public" meant during Covid-19, given the global and transboundary nature of the crisis. As a contagious respiratory virus, Covid-19 could and would spread easily across national boundaries, and this quick expansiveness made it necessary to galvanize a global effort of working in close coordination to stem the tide of the virus. Yet the cultivation of a well-united *Weltgemeinschaft* ("world public"; see Künneth & Beyerhaus, 1975), would have necessitated pillars of multilateral cooperation, notably under the stewardship of agencies such as the World Health Organization (WHO), to receive the necessary legitimacy, operational resources and recognition of value (which are ingredients of the PV strategic triangle) so as to mobilize the international community effectively. In the absence of a widespread recognition of the need for cooperation in fighting the common cause of Covid-19 internationally, publics were left with national-level, and in the worst cases, subnational-level, strategies to combat the virus (Parisi & Bekier, 2021; Padovani & Iacuzzi, 2021). Such strategies were evidently suboptimal, drawing upon reduced PV operational resources and failing to extend beyond localized remits, thus leaving publics to the predations of the virus over multiple waves.

One must also recognize that, aside from leading to far less sickness and far fewer deaths, a well-coordinated global response to Covid-19 would have also cost much less in purely monetary (accounting) terms. For example, Varoufakis has estimated that the Group of Seven (G7) developed countries could have spent just $USD 39 billion to "vaccinate humanity" against Covid-19, but instead printed $USD 9,000 billion "on behalf of big Finance" (Varoufakis, 2021). Much of the stimulus printed in the G7 countries was certainly misdirected towards corporate (private) interests, as opposed to direct interventions to assist members of the public, due to which, corporations were much more frequently the beneficiaries of government assistance over families in need (Ding et al., 2021). Therefore, the absence of a consciousness of *Weltgemeinschaft* led to inefficient, suboptimal and ultimately destructive PV outcomes.

Pre-pandemic PV research has also lamented the absence of global responses to wicked problems in PV (see Geuijen et al., 2017), but the Covid-19 pandemic brought the absence of international into efforts into sharp relief and with greater urgency. Since the time of PVT's introduction in the early 1990s, never had a global wicked problem been made to feel as acute in the necessity for global action. Yet the ability to muster a worldwide response to any event has been limited in our lifetimes by a multitude of factors, and an increasing thread in PV research has drawn attention to common causes while recognizing that creating value for a global public is fraught with inherent challenges (Chohan, 2020).

For example, the weaknesses of international bodies such as the WHO diminished their leadership potential during the crisis (Harrington, 2021; Hanrieder, 2020), while vaccine nationalist policies led to a self-defeating logic which kept a large part of the world's population still unvaccinated as of this writing (February 2022). This is how the omicron variant of Covid-19 appeared in a portion of the Global South that was largely left unvaccinated (Pulliam et al., 2021). Politicians and public managers in the Global North were profoundly deluded in thinking that national-level responses could protect them from PV destruction, and so further mutations risk evolving as of this writing, at the same time that a global response to the crisis, and thus value preservation for the global public, remains as remote a PV goal as ever. The need for a sense of global public is, therefore, a point that requires intense reflection.

Civil society

PV is a theory which first and foremost situates the public manager as the agent at the centre, and then focuses on her relationships with the politician and the citizen to argue for the co-creation of value (Chohan, 2020). By framing the public manager as protagonist (Alford & O'Flynn, 2009; Benington & Moore, 2011), however, PVT has a tendency to overlook the importance of civil society in PV creation, and instead treats citizens as collective customers rather than as proactive drivers of value (Samaratunge & Pillay, 2011; Benington, 2009; Chohan, 2019, 2021). In the Covid-19 pandemic, however, civil society played a meaningful role in determining the degree of PV preservation that societies achieved, and this was particularly true in developing countries where governments' wherewithal and operational resources were limited (Cordelia et al., 2020; Chohan, forthcoming). Indeed, civil society filled both a public health role and an economic role, with the former pertaining to citizen compliance with strictures (such as lockdowns) as well as reinforcement of information-sharing networks (see Rural Support Program, 2020), and the latter pertaining to charitable assistance to poor segments which were disproportionately affected by the pandemic. In the accounting literature, it has been found that "supreme emergency" leads to a more prominent presence of civil society as agent of public accountability (Sian & Smyth, 2021).

PVT must pay greater attention to the role of civil society as an active participant in the processes of value creation and preservation (Benington, 2009; Lowndes et al., 2006), and the theory must also must also continue to expand its focus of research into the developing world (Samaratunge & Pillay, 2011; Chohan, 2019; Cordelia et al., 2020). Public health governance research itself has long recognized the importance of civil society in leading pandemic preparedness efforts (see review in White & Banda, 2016), and the lessons of this literature are re-manifesting in the Covid-19 pandemic. Intuitively, the public must be a proactive co-creator and co-preserver of value in the sort of mass mobilization that is required to face crisis conditions. The Covid-19 pandemic offers interesting lenses through which to see where civil society has bridged the gap of operational resource deficit, and also served as an enabling actor for better PV outcomes in conditions of compliance with public health best practices. Therefore, the role of civil society in PV preservation offers a necessary point for further reflection.

Private interest

Pandemics serve as important test cases for the public mobilization of collective efforts to fight an unseen enemy with patience and solidarity. However, the Covid-19 pandemic has served, sadly, to illustrate the predominance of private interest at many levels where PV outcomes have been dismally affected (see also Andrew et al., 2022). One speaks here of *excessive* private interest, whereby the public's values would be overridden by the tenor of private pursuits. This could be observed at many levels during the Covid-19 pandemic. For example, the privatization of profits from vaccines, as opposed to making vaccines into a public good freely accessible to all citizens, translated into severely suboptimal outcomes, both within publics where inequality of access persisted (Andrew et al., 2021), and certainly *between* publics where many nations in fact still have not (as of this writing) been able to vaccinate even half of their populations (see also Varoufakis, 2021).

As another example, the corporate gorging of stimulus funds (Ding et al., 2021) as a competing interest against larger direct transfers to the public meant that stock markets and corporate earnings during the pandemic were stellar in many sectors, but at the same time, excessive deaths occurred and members of the public went through undue hardship. Corporate power also advocated staunchly, in some cases, for maintaining economic activity when lockdown measures might be far more appropriate, in a sort of private-based rationality of the *necroeconomy* (Darian-Smith, 2021; Haskaj, 2018) and *necropolitics* (Mbembe, 2008), where some could be made to die for a "greater good" that was in fact an agenda of narrow benefit. A parallel Foucauldian treatment of *necropolitics* has occurred in the accounting literature, which has studied the nature of accounting for biosecurity (Antonelli et al., 2021), and of new governmentality (Sargiacomo et al., 2021a).

As but one more example, the private-oriented nature of non-compliance with government strictures (such as mask mandates or lockdowns, see Haeder, 2021) led to public risk and PV destruction, even though in some cases the private rationality of such behaviour might be appreciated at the individual level (Gans, 2020), it would nonetheless jeopardize PV preservation. One notes, therefore, that the usurpation of a PV problem by private modes of rationality and interest has precluded the resolution of the pandemic in a manner that would minimize both economic costs and public health damage.

PV itself has not adequately grappled with the neoliberal logic of marketization (Dahl & Soss, 2014), which serves as the background noise for articulating excessive privatized pursuits (Chohan, 2021, 2022). Private interest continues to remain a blind spot in PV, given that its core agents are politicians, public managers and civil society; and as mentioned in the previous point, civil society too remains under-researched. Further, PV research must therefore actively incorporate the presence of private interest in PV (see Chohan, 2020), and the pandemic offers an opportune moment of reflection on the subject, while also bolstering the case for such research interest.

The politics of accounting

Accounting has had a "pervasive role" during the Covid-19 pandemic (Leoni et al., 2021a), and in what has been recognized as the political nature of accounting (Allawattage & Wikremasinghe; 2008; Cooper, 1980), specifically in the accounting of sick and dead bodies (see body counts in Perouse et al., 2016). The miscounting/underaccounting of deaths and cases became a distressing and crucial issue in many countries during the Covid-19 pandemic (Kiang et al., 2020), and one vulnerable to excessive politicization. It is also, needless to say, a philosophical issue for public accountants to consider in the course of their research and praxis. The way in which body counts were hidden, downplayed or deliberately left uncounted meant that the "accounting" of life in a crisis context was deficient, which also played into the public accountability of governments mismanaging their crisis (Leoni et al., 2021a-b). At times, it was ineptitude at work, but at other times, various authors argue that it was also "decision-making proceeding by a wilful ignorance and pseudo-management of a range of 'uncomfortable knowledge'", (Ortega & Orsini, 2020, p. 1262).

There is a pressing need for accounting to serve as both comfortable and uncomfortable knowledge, in order for it to serve the purposes of accountability, and therefore those of PV management. It is difficult to ignore the observation that countries with significant post-Truth predilections were more adversely impacted by the miscounting of cases and deaths, as can be observed in the cases of Brazil (de Lima, 2022; Ortega & Orsini, 2020), India (Chatterjee, 2020), and the United States, all of which left deaths unrecorded with politics in mind. Lives and deaths thus became a political issue during the Covid-19 pandemic, an accounting metric with which to play political games and conceal ineptitude and mismanagement, while trying to allay the public's fears and its rage. This has been examined in the context of "accounting as mourning" (Yu et al., 2021).

Recent research has argued that accounting must grapple not just with natural disaster contexts but with broader social crises (Leoni et al., 2021b), a point that has been brought into sharp focus with the Covid-19 pandemic. The nature of accounting is different in crises (Rouleau et al., 2021), and public accounting research must expand on the (tragic) opportunity that the Covid-19 pandemic provides (Chohan, 2021). PV destruction, insofar as the measurement of value is concerned (Papi et al., 2018), finds ample exploratory scope in the pandemic's context because "large losses of human life are arguably the ultimate category in measuring destruction of value" (Chohan, 2019, p.117). The key reflection here, then, is that the overall public sector accounting literature finds common cause with PV in seeking to have accounting for sickness and death serve as means towards accountability.

Beyond the numbers: success and failure

Although no society was sufficiently prepared for the Covid-19 pandemic, there were measures of ex-ante pandemic preparedness which suggested that developed countries such as the United States were best positioned to withstand and manage the risks associated with large-scale epidemiological contagion (Holmberg & Lundren, 2018). The converse assumption was that other (mostly developing) countries were ill-prepared for pandemics and would quickly falter in a sufficiently large epidemiological crisis (Nguyen & Bresee, 2013; Sambala et al., 2018; Cordelia et al., 2020). However, the "winners and losers" of the Covid-19 pandemic turned out to be quite different from what one might have assumed ex ante. The United States, for example, suffered the highest number of cases and deaths in the world, and many European countries were also early victims of the pandemic to a significant extent.

On the other hand, several developing countries, such as Pakistan, managed the pandemic through a concentrated PV approach that involved all PV actors: politicians, public managers and civil society (Chohan, forthcoming). Such countries, despite having been written off at the outset of the pandemic (Sambala et al., 2018), succeeded despite PV limitations including fewer operational resources and weaker government legitimacy (nodes of the PV strategic triangle, see Alford & O'Flynn, 2009). How could this be possible? New research is examining the "policy mix" (Chohan, forthcoming) and the influence of values (Chohan, 2022) as it impacts the outcomes of societies during crises (Leoni et al., 2021b), finding that a response oriented towards PV preservation and towards a sound policy mix can help even the seemingly underequipped (or altogether unequipped) to withstand turbulent periods (see also Ansell et al., 2021; Ahrens & Ferry, 2021; Sargiacomo et al., 2021).

Further research and reflection are still required, but the fait accompli of successful crisis mitigation, which is a subject of long-standing interest in the CAL (Rosenthal & Kouzmin, 1997; Stern, 1997; T'hart et al., 1993; Perrow, 1984; Beck, 1992), has been evident thus far in the Covid-19 pandemic. To set things in perspective, the *Economist's* Global Normalcy Index, which used various metrics to compare the current conditions of societies relative to pre-pandemic normalcy, rated Pakistan among the top three countries *in the world*, next to New Zealand and Hong Kong, two wealthy island nations with small populations (*The Economist*, 2021). For a country so large to attain such outstanding results was considered a "puzzling" feat (Shah & Xing, 2020), but what might be even more puzzling is why some well-endowed developed nations fared so poorly as well.

This is not to say that the wider cohort of developing countries necessarily outperformed the developed world – far from it, they struggled with their limited PV endowments, particularly when "calculable" comparisons (Parisi & Beckier, 2021) are made in the post-vaccination phase, since many developing countries did not (and still later would not) receive vaccines in sufficient quantities or in a timely manner. Nevertheless, the array of countries in terms of their relative rankings in cases and deaths paints a very mixed picture, far different from what might have been assumed before the pandemic itself hit. The puzzling nature of such outcomes, and the ability to account for such outcomes, remains a fascinating PV-oriented question, and one that speaks to accountability and accounting: where going beyond the numbers is necessary.

Piercing the veil

Many of the disturbing elements of PV destruction that were witnessed during the Covid-19 pandemic were in fact the product of pre-existing social conditions (Chohan, in press), which were only brought to the point of eruption by the pandemic itself. These pre-existing social conditions have been the object of study in many branches of the social sciences, but not particularly so in the PV literature, which is in large part explained by the theory's naivete, as mentioned earlier in this chapter. PV's tendency towards studying "normalized, *peacetime* conditions of genteel democratic engagement" (Chohan, 2022, p. 3, emphasis in original) must be rebalanced with a more sober appraisal of disaster contexts (Sargiacomo et al., 2021a-b), accounting to the end of life (Le Theule et al., 2021), and the role of public management and administration in such conditions (Nohrstedt et al., 2021; Casula & Pazos-Vidal, 2021). The long-standing conditions that were simmering beneath the surface of society when the Covid-19 pandemic hit, included "social inequalities" in the broadest sense (see Andrew et al., 2021; Sancino et al., 2020), but they could also be studied and contextualized through lenses such as race (Wright & Merritt, 2020), class (Gaynor & Wilson, 2020), gender (Viswanath & Mullins, 2021), and caste discrimination and Islamophobia (Kinnvall, 2019; Wojczewsk, 2020),

In a larger sense, then, the Covid-19 pandemic pierced the veil of societies and with great ferocity brought deeply rooted social problems to the foreground. The turbulence of the Covid-19 pandemic (Ansell et al., 2021; Ahrens & Ferry, 2021; Rinaldi et al., 2020) magnified the fissures, widened the gaps and tore into the social fabric. But then, one must ask, what is to be done about these inequalities? Is there any indication that these will be mitigated? The forms of economic and public health responses undertaken during the pandemic do not suggest that inequalities are being actively addressed (Andrew et al., 2021, 2022). There is, perhaps, an efflorescence of sympathetic PV rhetoric among politicians (see Chohan & Jacobs, 2018; Gelmini et al., 2021) regarding the mitigation of inequalities, but there is little to suggest, as the fallout from the Covid-19 pandemic subsides and countries pursue some degree of normalcy (Andrew et al. 2022), that inequalities within and among publics are to be addressed with a "restless, value-seeking imagination" that PV expects (Benington & Moore, 2011, p. 3).

One must therefore reflect on what is fleeting and what is lasting in terms of the Covid-19 pandemic. What people valued before, during and after the pandemic may be impacted by transitory turbulence, or it may leave lasting scars. The scarring of societies is an element that would require deeper PV engagement that is multi-stakeholder in nature and accountable in its structuring. This is no mean feat, but it speaks to CAL's public policy verdict on lesson-drawing from crises (Stern, 1997; Nohrstedt et al., 2021, T'hart et al., 1993, Boin et al., 2008). This literature argues that learning from crises is rarer than one would be led to believe, and both the learning during a crisis (intracrisis) and learning between crises (intercrisis) should be seldom expected. In that case, it is one's duty to reflect on what might be learned from the unique manner in which the Covid-19 pandemic pierced the veil of societies.

Conclusion

The manner in which the foregoing points have been posited for scholarly reflection and invitations to further research is invariably cursory. Nevertheless, it seeks to point to a deficit in PV research regarding destructive categories of social experience, a task that has been relegated to other literatures including CAL and A-A. Yet turbulent and destructive events such as the Covid-19 pandemic must be attended to with greater intellectual alacrity, for they are likely to repeat themselves in the times ahead. Indeed, there should be scant doubt that pandemics will, sadly, reoccur in the future. This can be stated with some degree of confidence because of the way in which publics are evolving/devolving today. Publics are increasingly encroaching upon the natural world, whether in terms of resource extraction, demographic expansion or physical-spatial occupation. Meanwhile, the quality of public service provision is inconsistent, fragile and/or unevenly distributed, not least in terms of healthcare, sanitation and security. At the same time, the structures of accounting and accountability are being tested in a great many ways, and are the subject of continual scholarly interest and study (Ahrens & Ferry, 2021; Sargiacomo et al., 2021a-b; Yu, 2021; Le Theule et al., 2021; Antonelli et al., 2021; Sian & Smyth, 2021; Parisi & Bekier, 2021; Padovani & Iacuzzi, 2021).

The public managers of the future must therefore prepare themselves for resilient responses that can help publics withstand future PV-destructive events (Mintzberg & Alexandra, 1985; Boin et al., 2013; Kaushik & Walsh, 2019). But looking towards future eventualities should not detract from the dangers that lie in the immediate present. It would be unwise, for example, to speak of the Covid-19 pandemic as if it were a thing of the past, since it continues (as of this writing) to erupt in sustained waves around the world, at times more devastating in some countries than previous waves were. Reflection is often seen as an ex-post activity, but public sector accountants, managers, professionals and officials are compelled to reflect on something that is still underway and at risk of worsening at any juncture. In other words, the act of reflection, as posited in this chapter, should not lead to the conclusion that victory should be declared as of yet.

PVT, as discussed in the introductory section of this chapter, has proven largely ill-equipped or at least somewhat disinterested in the Covid-19 crisis. It was argued (see also Chohan, 2022) that this is attributable to the dominance of CAL & A-A, as well as the naive temperament of PV towards destruction and disvalue. These obstacles must be overcome for a wider intellectual engagement to occur that is mediated through the lens of PV. The points of reflection in this chapter, which were merely suggested in another work but have been accorded far greater elaboration here, appear to offer something valuable for future research endeavours. What is "valuable," and what is valued, must be revisited in light of the new experiences that publics have undergone during the Covid-19 pandemic. It must be dually inductive-deductive: PV can help inform the lived experience and the public managerial challenge; while these can inform PV in turn. Ultimately, there is much more value preservation and creation that is required before a day should come that the scars of the Covid-19 pandemic shall truly begin to heal; and reflecting upon PV in the Covid-19 pandemic is but a first step towards the anticipation of that day.

References

Ahrens, T., & Ferry, L. (2021). Accounting and accountability practices in times of crisis: a Foucauldian perspective on the UK government's response to COVID-19 for England. *Accounting, Auditing & Accountability Journal, 34*(6), 1332–1344.

Alawattage, C., & Wickramasinghe, D. (2008). Appearance of accounting in a political hegemony. *Critical Perspectives on Accounting, 19*(3), 293–339.

Alford, J., & O'Flynn, J. (2009). Making sense of public value: Concepts, critiques and emergent meanings. *International Journal of Public Administration, 32*(3/4), 171–191.

Andrew, J., Baker, M., Cooper, C., & Tweedie, J. (2022). Wealth taxes and the post-COVID future of the state. *Critical Perspectives on Accounting*, 102431.

Andrew, J., Baker, M., & Guthrie, J. (2021). Accounting, inequality and COVID-19 in Australia. *Accounting, Auditing & Accountability Journal, 34*(6), 1471–1483.

Ansell, C., Sørensen, E., & Torfing, J. (2021). The COVID-19 pandemic as a game changer for public administration and leadership? The need for robust governance responses to turbulent problems. *Public Management Review, 23*(7), 949–960.

Antonelli, V., Bigoni, M., Funnell, W., & Cafaro, E. M. (2021). Accounting for biosecurity in Italy under COVID-19 lockdown. *Accounting, Auditing & Accountability Journal, 35*(1), 120–130.

Beck, U. (1992). *Risk society: Towards a New Modernity*. Polity.

Benington, J. (2009). Creating the public in order to create public value? *International Journal of Public Administration, 32*(3/4), 232–249

Benington, J., & Moore, M. H. (2011). *Public value: Theory and practice*. Palgrave Macmillan.

Best, B., Moffett, S., & McAdam, R. (2019). Stakeholder salience in public sector value co-creation. *Public Management Review, 21*(11), 1707–1732.

Boin, A., Kuipers, S., & Overdijk, W. (2013). Leadership in times of crisis: A framework for assessment. *International Review of Public Administration, 18*(1), 79–91.

Boin, A., & Lodge, M. (2016). Designing resilient institutions for transboundary crisis management: A time for public administration. *Public Administration, 94*(2), 289–298.

Boin, A., McConnell, A., & 't Hart, P. (Eds.) (2008). *Governing after crisis: The politics of investigation, accountability and learning*. Cambridge University Press

Bozeman, B. (2002). Public-value failure: When efficient markets may not do. *Public Administration Review, 62*(2), 145–161.

Casula, M., & Pazos-Vidal, S. (2021). Assessing the multi-level government response to the Covid-19 crisis: Italy and Spain compared. *International Journal of Public Administration, 44*(11–12), 994–1005.2

Chatterjee, P. (2020). Is India missing COVID-19 deaths? *The Lancet, 396*(10252), 657.

Chohan, U. W., & Jacobs, K. (2018). Public value as rhetoric: A budgeting approach. *International Journal of Public Administration, 41*(15), 1217–1227.

Chohan, U. W. (2019). *Public value and budgeting: International perspectives*. Routledge.

Chohan, U. W. (2020). *Reimagining public managers: Delivering public value*. Routledge..

Chohan, U. W. (2021). *Public value and the digital economy*. Routledge.

Chohan, U. W. (2022). *Pandemics and public value management*. Routledge.

Chohan, U. W. (in press). The return of Keynesianism? Exploring path dependency and ideational change in post-covid fiscal policy. *Policy and Society*, puab013, https://doi.org/10.1093/polsoc/puab013

Chohan, U. W. (forthcoming). Analyzing sound COVID-19 policy responses in developing countries: Case study of Pakistan. *Studia z Polityki Publicznej/Public Policy Studies*.

Cooper, D. (1980). Discussion of towards a political economy of accounting. *Accounting, Organizations and Society, 5*(1), 161–166.

Cordelia, O. N., Ngozi, N. H., & Ebuka, A. A. (2020). Accountability and transparency in nation building: a covid-19 experience in sub-Saharan Africa. *International Journal of Public Policy and Administration Research, 7*(1), 23–33.

Dahl, A., & Soss, J. (2014). Neoliberalism for the common good? Public value governance and the downsizing of democracy. *Public Administration Review, 74*(4), 496–504.

Daniel, E., Bardi, A., Fischer, R., Benish-Weisman, M., & Lee, J. A. (2020). Changes in personal values in pandemic times. *Social Psychological and Personality Science,* 13(2), 572–582. https://doi.org/10.1177/194855 06211024026

Darian-Smith, E. (2021). Dying for the economy: Disposable people and economies of death in the global north. *State Crime Journal, 10*(1), 61–79.

De Graaf, G., Huberts, L., & Smulders, R. (2016). Coping with public value conflicts. *Administration & Society, 48*(9), 1101–1127.

de Lima, J. P., Pereira de Castro Casa Nova, S., Filgueiras Sauerbronn, F., & Castañeda, M. (2022, December). "Is it just a little flu"? Producing a news-based counter account on Covid-19 discursive crises in Brazil. *Accounting Forum.* https://doi.org/10.1080/01559982.2022.2149441

Ding, W., Levine, R., Lin, C., & Xie, W. (2021). Corporate immunity to the COVID-19 pandemic. *Journal of Financial Economics, 141*(2), 802–830.

Drennan, L. T., McConnell, A., & Stark, A. (2014). *Risk and crisis management in the public sector.* Routledge.

The Economist. (2021). Global normalcy index. www.economist.com/graphicdetail/tracking-the-return-to-normalcy-after-covid-19

Esposito, P., & Ricci, P. (2015). How to turn public (dis)value into new public value? Evidence from Italy. *Public Money & Management, 35*(3), 227–231.

Gans, J. (2020). *Economics in the age of Covid-19.* MIT Press.

Gaynor, T. S., & Wilson, M. E. (2020). Social vulnerability and equity: The disproportionate impact of COVID-19. *Public Administration Review, 80*(5), 832–838.

Gelmini, L., Minutiello, V., Tettamanzi, P., & Comoli, M. (2021). Rhetoric, accounting and accountability: COVID-19 and the case of Italy. *Sustainability, 13*(8), 4100.

Geuijen, K., Moore, M., Cederquist, A., Ronning, R., & Van Twist, M. (2017). Creating public value in global wicked problems. *Public Management Review, 19*(5), 621–639.

Haeder, S. F. (2021). Joining the herd? US public opinion and vaccination requirements across educational settings during the Covid-19 pandemic. *Vaccine, 39*(17), 2375–2385.

Hanrieder, T. (2020). Priorities, partners, politics: The WHO's mandate beyond the Crisis. *Global Governance: A Review of Multilateralism and International Organizations, 26*(4), 534–543.

Harrington, J. (2021). Indicators, security and sovereignty during Covid-19 in the Global South. *International Journal of Law in Context, 17*(2), 249–260.

Hartley, J., Alford, J., Knies, E., & Douglas, S. (2017). Towards an empirical research agenda for public value theory. *Public Management Review, 19*(5), 670–685.

Haskaj, F. (2018). From biopower to necroeconomics: Neoliberalism, biopower and death economies. *Philosophy and Social Criticism, 44*(10), 1148–1168.

Head, B., & Alford, J. (2015). Wicked problems: Implications for public policy and management. *Administration & Society, 47*(6), 711–739.

Holmberg, M., & Lundgren, B. (2018). Framing post-pandemic preparedness: Comparing eight European plans. *Global Public Health, 11*, 99–114.

Kaushik, V., & Walsh, C. A. (2019). Pragmatism as a research paradigm and its implications for social work research. *Social Sciences, 8*(9), 255.

Kiang, M. V., Irizarry, R. A., Buckee, C. O., & Balsari, S. (2020). Every body counts: measuring mortality from the COVID-19 pandemic. *Annals of Internal Medicine, 173*(12), 1004–1007.

Kinnvall, C. (2019). Populism, ontological insecurity and Hindutva: Modi and the masculinization of Indian politics. *Cambridge Review of International Affairs, 32*(3), 283–302

Künneth, W., & Beyerhaus, P. (1975). *Reich Gottes oder Weltgemeinschaft: Die Berliner Ökumene-Erklärung zur utopischen Vision des Weltkirchenrates.* Verlag der Liebenzeller Mission.

Landi, S., Costantini, A., Fasan, M., & Bonazzi, M. (2021). Public engagement and dialogic accounting through social media during COVID-19 crisis: A missed opportunity? *Accounting, Auditing & Accountability Journal, 35*(1), 35–47.

Le Theule, M. A., Lambert, C., & Morales, J. (2021). Accounting to the end of life. Scarcity, performance and death. *Critical Perspectives on Accounting,* 102377.

Leoni, G., Lai, A., Stacchezzini, R., Steccolini, I., Brammer, S., Linnenluecke, M., & Demirag, I. (2021a). The pervasive role of accounting and accountability during the COVID-19 emergency. *Accounting, Auditing & Accountability Journal, 35*(1), 1–19.

Leoni, G., Lai, A., Stacchezzini, R., Steccolini, I., Brammer, S., Linnenluecke, M., & Demirag, I. (2021b). Accounting, management and accountability in times of crisis: lessons from the COVID-19 pandemic. *Accounting, Auditing & Accountability Journal, 34*(6), 1305–1319.

Lowndes, V., Pratchett, L., & Stoker, G. (2006). Local political participation: The impact of rules-in-use. *Public Administration, 84*(3), 539–561

Mbembe, A. (2008). *Necropolitics* (Steven Corcoran, Trans.). Duke University Press.

Mintzberg, H., & Alexandra, M. (1985). Strategy formation in an adhocracy. *Administrative Science Quarterly, 30*(2), 160–197. https://doi.org/10.2307/2393104

Nguyen-Van-Tam, J. S., & Bresee, J. (2013). Pandemic preparedness and response. In Robert G. Webster, Arnold S. Monto, Thomas J. Braciale, and Robert Lamb (Eds.), *Textbook of influenza* (pp. 453–469). Wiley Online Library. https://doi.org/10.1002/9781118636817.ch28

Nohrstedt, D., Mazzoleni, M., Parker, C. F., & Di Baldassarre, G. (2021). Exposure to natural hazard events unassociated with policy change for improved disaster risk reduction. *Nature Communications, 12*(193). https://rdcu.be/cgnBx

Ortega, F., & Orsini, M. (2020). Governing Covid-19 without government in Brazil: Ignorance, neoliberal authoritarianism, and the collapse of public health leadership. *Global Public Health, 15*(9), 1257–1277.

O'Sullivan, T. L., Kuziemsky, C. E., Toal-Sullivan, D., & Corneil, W. (2013). Unraveling the complexities of disaster management: A framework for critical social infrastructure to promote population health and resilience. *Social Science & Medicine, 93*, 238–246.

Padovani, E., & Iacuzzi, S. (2021). Real-time crisis management: Testing the role of accounting in local governments. *Journal of Accounting and Public Policy, 40*(3), 106854.

Papi, L., Bigoni, M., Bracci, E., & Deidda Gagliardo, E. (2018). Measuring public value: a conceptual and applied contribution to the debate. *Public Money & Management, 38*(7), 503–510.

Parisi, C., & Bekier, J. (2021). Assessing and managing the impact of COVID-19: A study of six European cities participating in a circular economy project. *Accounting, Auditing & Accountability Journal, 35*(1), 97–107.

Perouse, M. A., Minor, E., & Sinha, S. (2016). *Violence, statistics, and the politics of accounting for the dead.* Springer.

Perrow, C. (1984). *Normal accidents.* Basic Books.

Pescaroli, G., & Alexander, D. (2016). Critical infrastructure, panarchies and the vulnerability paths of cascading disasters. *Natural Hazards, 82*(1), 175–192.

Prebble, M. (2012). Public value and the ideal state: Rescuing public value from ambiguity. *Australian Journal of Political Administration, 71*(4), 392–402.

Pulliam, J. R., van Schalkwyk, C., Govender, N., von Gottberg, A., Cohen, C., Groome, M. J., ... & Moultrie, H. (2021). SARS-CoV-2 reinfection trends in South Africa: analysis of routine surveillance data. *Infection, 1*, 2.

Rinaldi, L. (2022, March). Accounting and the COVID-19 pandemic two years on: insights, gaps, and an agenda for future research. *Accounting Forum*, 1–32. https://doi.org/10.1080/01559982.2022.2045418

Rinaldi, L., Cho, C. H., Lodhia, S. K., Michelon, G., & Tilt, C. A. (2020, July). Accounting in times of the COVID-19 pandemic: a forum for academic research. *Accounting Forum, 44*(3), 180–183.

Roberts, N. (2000). Wicked problems and network approaches to resolution. *International Public Management Review, 1*(1), 1–19.

Rosenthal, U., Charles, M. T., & 't Hart, P. (1989). The world of crises and crisis management. In U. Rosenthal, M. T. Charles, & P. 't Hart (Eds.), *Coping with crises* (pp. 3–35). Charles Thomas.

Rosenthal, U., & Kouzmin, A. (1997). Crises and crisis management: Toward comprehensive government decision making. *Journal of Public Administration Research and Theory, 7*(2), 277–304.

Rouleau, L., Hällgren, M., & de Rond, M. (2021). Covid-19 and our understanding of risk, emergencies, and crises. *Journal of Management Studies, 58*(1), 245. https://doi.org:10.1111/joms.12649

Rural Support Program (RSP). (2020). Pakistan's rural communities fight against Covid-19. www.RSP.org/index.php/pakistans-rural-communities-fight-covid-19/

Rutschman, A. S. (2021). Is there a cure for vaccine nationalism? *Current History, 120*(822), 9–14.

Samaratunge, R., & Pillay, S. (2011). Governance in developing countries: Sri Lanka and South Africa compared. *International Journal of Public Administration, 34*(6), 389–398.

Samaratunge, R., & Wijewardena, N. (2009). The changing nature of public values in developing countries. *International Journal of Public Administration, 32*(3–4), 313–327.

Sambala, E. Z., Kanyenda, T., Iwu, C. J., Iwu, C. D., Jaca, A., & Wiysonge, C. S. (2018). Pandemic influenza preparedness in the WHO African region: are we ready yet? *BMC Infectious Diseases, 18*(1), 1–13.

Sancino, A., Garavaglia, C., Sicilia, M., & Braga, A. (2020). New development: COVID-19 and its publics – implications for strategic management and democracy. *Public Money & Management*, 1–4.

Sargiacomo, M., Corazza, L., D'Andreamatteo, A., Dumay, J., & Guthrie, J. (2021a). COVID-19 and the governmentality of emergency food in the City of Turin. *Accounting, Auditing & Accountability Journal, 34*(6), 1457–1470.

Shah, P. T., & Xing, L. (2020). Puzzling increase and decrease in COVID-19 cases in Pakistan. *New Microbes and New Infections, 38*(10), 91–93

Sian, S., & Smyth, S. (2021). Supreme emergencies and public accountability: The case of procurement in the UK during the Covid-19 pandemic. *Accounting, Auditing & Accountability Journal, 35*(1), 146–157.

Spano, A. (2009). Public value creation and management control systems. *International Journal of Public Administration, 32*(3–4), 328–348.

Stern, E. (1997). Crisis and learning: A balance sheet. *Journal of Contingencies and Crisis Management, 5*(2), 69–86.

Stoker, G. (2006). Public value management: A new narrative for networked governance? *American Review of Public Administration, 36*(1), 41–57.

T'Hart, P. (1993). Symbols, rituals and power: The lost dimensions of crisis management. *Journal of Contingencies and Crisis Management, 1*(1), 36–50.

T'Hart, P., Rosenthal, U., & Kouzmin, A. (1993). Crisis decision making: The centralization thesis revisited. *Administration & Society, 25*(1), 12–45.

Varoufakis, Y. (2021). G7 Central Banks printed $9000 billion on behalf of Big Finance but skimped on $39 billion that would have vaccinated Humanity. Interview, Democracy Now! www.yanisvaroufakis.eu/2021/06/21/g7-central-banks-printed-9000-billion-on-behalf-of-big-finance-but-skimping-on-39-billion-that-would-have-vaccinated-humanity-democracy-now/

Viswanath, S., & Mullins, L. B. (2021). Gender responsive budgeting and the COVID-19 pandemic response: A feminist standpoint. *Administrative Theory & Praxis, 43*(2), 230–244

White, K., & Banda, M. (2016). The role of civil society in pandemic preparedness. *Innovation in global health governance* (pp. 123–146). Routledge.

Williams, I., & Shearer, H. (2011). Appraising public value: Past, present and futures. *Public Administration, 89*(4), 1367–1384.

Wojczewski, T. (2020). Populism, Hindu nationalism, and foreign policy in India: The politics of representing "the people". *International Studies Review, 22*(3), 396–422.

Wright, J. E., & Merritt, C. C. (2020). Social equity and COVID-19: The case of African Americans. *Public Administration Review, 80*(5), 820–826.

Yu, A. (2021). Accountability as mourning: Accounting for death in the time of COVID-19. *Accounting, Organizations and Society, 90*, 101198.

12

THE USE OF PERFORMANCE MEASURES IN THE UK'S CORONAVIRUS CRISIS

Implications for stakeholder engagement and performance management

Suzana Grubnic and Geoffrey Heath

Introduction

Whilst the engagement of citizens and stakeholders in public services has been increasingly investigated, their involvement in performance measurement and management is still an under-researched aspect in the accounting literature. In this chapter, we aim to address this research gap by illustrating the way in which performance information was presented and used by the UK government and other interested parties during the early stages of the Covid-19 pandemic (from winter 2020, to autumn 2021). The performance information was presented in creative, novel and increasingly sophisticated ways by the government and other stakeholders. Furthermore, the ways in which this information was used by stakeholder groups is also of great significance as public health data was translated into information for performance evaluation and accountability.

In order to explore the issues, we frame our discussion by theorization which draws on the concepts of instrumental, communicative and value rationality, deliberative democracy and agonistic pluralism. These concepts have the potential to reveal rich insights, as they relate to dialogue, participation, cooperation and contestation, and this is enhanced by adopting a perspective which, unusually, embraces both agonism and deliberation. The framings have been little used in the accounting academic literature to date, although they are not entirely absent (see, for example, Ferry & Slack, 2022). However, they have significant potential for shaping perceptive insights into performance evaluation, as we aim to demonstrate here. In addition, from the framings and our empirical findings, we propose various themes for future research concerning performance evaluation, all of which relate to the presence or absence of engagement in the triangular stakeholder relationship between government, experts and citizens. These themes have considerable potential for interdisciplinary work, as advocated by, for example, Steccolini (2019). The chapter may be particularly relevant, therefore, to readers interested in interdisciplinary and critical approaches to accounting, accountability, governance and management control.

In the chapter, we set out the background to events and experiences relating to the Covid-19 pandemic in the UK and the way in which it was handled there. The theoretical discussion follows and then the focus is placed on three stakeholders who are particularly significant in this context: the government, scientific experts (especially a group known as Independent SAGE), and the general public. Their responses towards policy and performance evaluation during the period are examined. Another

DOI: 10.4324/9781003295945-16

significant contribution is made by presenting a future research agenda. We conclude by bringing together the theoretical frameworks and our findings, stressing the need to hear many voices in crises.

Background

The Covid-19 pandemic has had devastating consequences in terms of deaths and impaired lives in the UK, as elsewhere. In turn, policies to counter the virus have affected personal liberties, economic activity, mental health, children's education and care for other medical conditions, inter alia.

In January 2020, the risk from Covid-19 to the public in the UK was regarded officially as low and in February 2020, SAGE (the government's scientific advisory body) argued against restricting mass gatherings. However, the official position was revised rapidly and, at the end of March 2020, the first national lockdown was instituted. A series of further lockdowns, "tiering" (quasi-lockdowns of differing intensity in different places) and temporary relaxations followed. The Test and Trace scheme was launched in May 2020, and a mass vaccination programme began in December 2020, with over 80 per cent of the adult population fully vaccinated by September 2021 (House of Commons Health & Social Care and Science & Technology Committees joint report, 2021). During this period, regular television broadcasts concerning the progress of the pandemic were an important part of the government's public health communications strategy, but they also "accidentally" provided information for evaluating the government's performance. In this case, the indicators "led to the government itself becoming politically accountable" (Broadbent, 2020, p. 529).

Numerous academic accounting papers concerning the Covid-19 pandemic have been published (for helpful surveys, see Leoni et al., 2021, and Rinaldi, 2022). Mitchell et al. (2021) evaluated performance in three comparable European countries: Germany, Italy and the UK, using mortality rates as an overall performance indicator. Germany performed notably better and the UK notably worse before the development of vaccines against the virus. When the Covid-19 outbreak began, the UK was unprepared and slow to react. Consequently, the first lockdown was dangerously delayed. Subsequently, there was a rapid move to reducing restrictions as infection rates fell with economic values and personal freedoms being reasserted (Mitchell et al., 2021). This took place in a context of continued attrition of health and social care resources since 2010, which meant that the challenges of dealing with the pandemic were compounded by austerity policies (Heald & Hodges, 2020; Ahrens & Ferry, 2021). Moreover, the previous, well-regarded national performance measurement systems had been weakened, leading to "executive-dominated budgeting used as a sticking-plaster" (Ahrens & Ferry, 2021, p. 1339).

During the lockdown period, restrictions were introduced, for example, on gatherings and travel; hospital capacity increased; and Covid-19 patients were prioritized, although this had a negative effect on other patients (Joint Report, 2021). However, there was a scandal of particularly high death rates in care homes, because older patients were discharged to them from hospitals without testing for Covid-19. Staff in care homes were also worse equipped with personal protective equipment (Broadbent, 2020). In addition, data on the impact of the COVID-19 pandemic on adult social care was limited because integration into the national information system for health was lacking (Ahrens & Ferry, 2021).

Surveillance systems were developed tracking:

1. Hospital capacity through availability of beds, ICU places, ventilators, protective equipment; and
2. Covid-19 spread through infection rates, deaths, excess death and R number.

(Mitchell et al., 2021).

Communication of key measures was essential to the government's effort to obtain the cooperation of citizens early in the pandemic (Broadbent, 2020). UK official measures which were reported daily comprised:

- testing times,
- infection rates,
- hospitalizations and
- deaths

(Mitchell et al., 2021)

Innovative forms of presentation, such as heat maps, were used to communicate information.

However, classic problems associated with perverse incentives emerged, affecting the reliability of data. For example, with personal protective equipment, quantity not quality was measured and prioritized. There were different ways of calculating R rates and death rates, which affected communication. In the case of Covid-19 tests, the number sent out was measured, not tests taken, so targets seemed to be met (Mitchell et al., 2021). Broadbent (2020) argues that manipulation of data in respect of both death rates and testing led to an erosion of trust in government.

The joint report found that the UK response to the Covid-19 crisis was both too slow and too reactive, with too little learning from international experience. The impact of the Covid-19 pandemic was uneven across the population, with older people, ethnic minorities and people with learning difficulties suffering particularly. Moreover, the pandemic put massive strain on the social care sector, which was already under huge pressure. In contrast, the development and delivery of vaccines was "one of the most successful and effective initiatives in the history of UK science and public administration" (Joint Report, 2021, p. 133). This resulted from a collaborative approach, embracing local National Health Service (NHS) organizations, which redeemed the persistent failings of other parts of the national response. Again, at the onset of the emergency, there was a pre-existing significant lack of doctors, beds and ICU capacity in the NHS. For the future, therefore, more resilience in the healthcare system is needed (Joint Report, 2021).

The joint report stressed that public health communications which are clear, consistent and transparent, are key to the public's understanding of the issues and to their compliance with guidelines. The initial messaging was assessed as strong and effective, but communications became increasingly complex, hard to understand and divergent across the UK over time. Another report by the House of Commons Public Administration and Constitutional Affairs Committee (2021) held that accountability requires open and honest presentation of the information underlying decisions, while acknowledging uncertainties in the data. Moreover, there is a moral imperative on government to clearly justify its decisions regarding the virus, given the level of sacrifice by the public they entailed. However, communication was not always open enough, accountabilities were unclear, and some government communications may have been shaped to create a favourable impression. They held that decisions concerning lockdown and "tiering" were insufficiently transparent, leading to confusion and mistrust, and the data underpinning those decisions were not clarified. Similarly, the joint report recommended that SAGE advice to government, minutes and papers should be published promptly to allow rapid response and challenge.

Theory

Performance management

Performance measurement concerns the collection and categorization of information about how successful a network, organization, unit or individual has been in achieving explicit or implicit aims and objectives. *Performance evaluation* refers to judgements made about performance in relation to precise or less defined comparators, such as targets, standards, benchmarks, trends or "rules of thumb". In the case of the pandemic, targets, standards and past performance were unavailable, so performance was compared to other countries or to, say, an intuition that this level of deaths was unacceptable. *Performance management* is the use of performance information by managers to achieve the plans and targets which are derived from the organization's strategic objectives. Other stakeholders may be in a position to evaluate, but not to manage performance.

Performance evaluation is useful for organizations to identify divergence from targets and high-light areas for more detailed investigation, learning and improvement, provided that its limitations are recognized. De Bruijn (2002) suggests the benefits of performance management can include pro-viding transparency; giving incentives for good performance; motivating innovation; improving the quality of policy- and decision-making; and facilitating citizens' engagement. Similarly, van Dooren et al. (2015) suggest that performance information can be used for designing policies, allocating resources and responsibilities, controlling implementation and evaluating results and accountability. However, these benefits do not come automatically (de Bruijn, 2002; van Dooren et al., 2015). De Bruijn (2002) suggests design principles for successful performance management include facilitating interaction between management and professionals in developing performance measures; building variety and redundancy into the packages of performance indicators; and incorporating dynamism into performance management systems.

Many problems arise when performance indicators are used misguidedly. A badly designed set of indicators can generate perverse incentives and unintended effects. The behavioural aspects of performance evaluation are significant, and unintentionally motivating dysfunctional behaviour is an enduring problem. The indicators can come to be seen as ends in themselves rather than as ways to learning and dialogue, with unmeasured or unmeasurable aspects of performance neglected. Indicators may be treated as definitive rather than raising issues for exploration. Schemes may promote gaming (Heath et al., 2018). However, Dugdale (2018), for example, has argued that various unintended consequences caused by excessive use of top-down targets can be avoided through decentralization and empowerment. While these issues affect all organizations, the nature and context of public sector organizations make them more acute there (Heath et al., 2018). Nevertheless, attempts to measure and manage performance are a long-standing feature of the public services, despite the inherent difficul-ties, and effective performance evaluation schemes can be developed (Heath et al., 2018).

A conventional, top-down, instrumentally rationalistic approach to performance management can be criticized for being formalistic and managerialist (Heath et al., 2018). Consequently, well-known approaches like the Balanced Scorecard and Simons' Levers of Control adopt the perspective of management and are only concerned with formal aspects of the organization, although what happens informally is significant. Tessier and Otley (2012), therefore, criticize Simons' framework for treating employees as passive recipients of control packages and disregarding their potential contri-bution to the design of control systems. This suggests the possibility of performance being managed deliberatively in organizations, reflecting communicative rationality (Broadbent & Laughlin, 2009). Indeed, more participative and dialogic ways of evaluating performance could be adopted, involving a range of stakeholders. (See, for example, Barbera et al., 2021.)

Rationality, values and deliberation

For Weber, rational human action can arise from either a concern with achieving given ends, known as *instrumental* or *purpose* rationality, or with conscious principles irrespective of outcomes, known as *value* or *substantive* rationality (Schipper, 1996). In value rationality, ultimate principles govern action irrespective of the prospects of success, and, therefore, rational social action can be based on ethical, aesthetic or religious values. Instrumental rationality is enacted when a formal process of finding the (one and only) best way to achieve an objective is carried out by weighing the various means to achieve an end. In enacting instrumental rationality, aims may be taken for granted, but disputation about values by the stakeholders in a decision is vitally important.

Thus, Rutgers (2019) argues that values relate to ultimate aims, objectives or goals, whereas purposes relate to the (intermediate) ends which are necessary/sufficient preconditions for achieving ultimate aims or are at least supportive of them. Therefore, purpose rationality both always *contains* but also *conceals* an underlying value rationality, while ends (and indeed means) are contestable. Consequently, "instrumental and substantive rationality [...] need to be maintained [...] in a state of mutual interaction" (Gregory, 2007, p. 240).

Like Weber, Habermas regards the exclusive use of instrumental rationality as unhelpful. It separates competitive markets, hierarchical bureaucracies and public policy from the everyday world (Schipper, 1996). A public realm is desired, therefore, where priorities for collective action can be set in open, reflective debate. This is the logic of *communicative rationality* (Healey, 1997). The concept of the Ideal Speech Situation (ISS), in which decisions are reached through dialogue without coercion, has been associated with communicative rationality (Pallerm, 2000). This requires decisions be made on the basis of consensus, defined as not just accepting a decision but also accepting the reasons for that decision: "In deliberative contexts [...] the only force which is supposed to count is 'the force of the better argument'" (Elster, 1998, p. 103). From this, a concept of *deliberative democracy* was developed whereby the common interest emerges through a public process of discourse and debate (Benhabib, 1996).

Dryzek (2000) holds that democratic legitimacy requires that all individuals subject to a collective decision should participate in authentic and effective deliberation about that decision. Thus, for advocates of deliberation, democracy entails more than merely electing representatives periodically, and encompasses participation, authentic debate and informed consent in decision-making. Benhabib (1996) argues that deliberative democracy is proceduralist, recognizes conflicts of interests and values, and favours a plurality of modes of association. Habermas himself eventually came to a theory of deliberative democracy which stressed the pluralistic complexity of modern society rather than the ISS (Dryzek, 2000).

The ISS can be criticized for assuming that there *is* a common interest, which will emerge via dialogue and consensus and for "assuming away" power and hegemony (Pallerm, 2000). Consequently, the issue of how supposedly "coercive" measures, such as voting, can be arranged fairly and effectively would be disregarded. However, Mansbridge (1996), in her conception of deliberation, held that democracies must have both reasoned persuasion and power as different material interests and competing values may be irreconcilable. Hendriks (2009) then distinguishes between "power-over" and "power-with"/"power-to". "Power-with" or "power-to" develops through communal activity and seeks empowerment rather than domination, unlike "power-over". Deliberative forums can promote moves from "power-over" to "power-with" through communication, especially when trust has been established (Hendriks, 2009).

For difference democrats, debating the common good rather than questions of identity and difference, favours the articulate and well educated and, therefore, discriminates against the oppressed, while disregarding the pluralist nature of modern societies (Young, 1996). Some supporters of deliberative democracy demand democratic deliberations only through "reasoned argument", but difference democrats favour other forms of communication such as "greeting, rhetoric and storytelling" (Young, 1996, p. 129). However, Dryzek argues that a variety of ways of communicating can be accepted and contestation encourages reflection. Moreover, workable agreements where, after deliberative scrutiny different participants agree a course of action for different reasons, can be satisfactory (Dryzek, 2000). Bargaining or voting, following rational debate, can be accepted on practical grounds and the ISS, reasoned argument and "strong sense" consensus are increasingly seen as neither possible nor necessary in practice (Curato et al., 2017).

Mouffe (1999) recognizes that deliberative democracy holds morality and justice to be central issues in politics, but she claims that it omits the political dimension, and its advocates are naive about power, conflict and hegemony. Moreover, she argues that, without some constraints on public deliberation, no communication could ever take place because there needs to be an authority to enforce the rules of debate. Power is inevitable in social relations and, therefore, it is desirable to devise forms of authority which are compatible with democratic values. She thus proposes a model of *agonistic pluralism*, which recognizes that antagonism is inherent in all human society, but conflict is contained by the exercise of legitimate power rather than deliberative democracy. Agonistic pluralism recognizes the role of conflict, power and emotion in decision-making. However, as Kapoor (2002) argues, Mouffe's unwillingness to adopt some form of communicative rationality leaves how to adjudicate between competing "pluralisms" unresolved. Indeed, the willingness of some advocates of deliberative democracy to forgo the ISS, "strong sense" consensus and only reasoned argument, limits the critique. Interestingly, Mouffe recently proposed "a combination of different forms of democratic participation" where "direct forms of democracy might be suitable in some cases and a variety of participative ones in others [...] in conjunction with representative institutions" (Mouffe, 2018 p. 69).

Nowadays, deliberative democracy "comes in many shapes and sizes" (Hendriks, 2009, p. 175), and there are versions which seem quite close to Mouffe's view of democratic participation. There has been increased use of different kinds of deliberative processes by governments and others since the 1990s, showing public deliberation takes place in many ways in many venues with different modes of discourse being variously appropriate. Moreover, "deliberative pluralism" (p. 176) recognizes not only that there are different forms of deliberation, but that other forms of decision-making are sometimes more appropriate. Well-known experiments with participatory democracy in Porto Alegre, Kerala and elsewhere, demonstrate empirically that institutions combining representative and deliberative democracy can be devised effectively. This also seems consistent with an agonistic version of deliberation, which holds that participants can debate and agree decisions communicatively, despite having different views, interests and values (Bennington & Hartley, 2019; Wankhade et al., 2022).

Instrumental rationality is related to rational-legal authority and transactional performance management systems, and communicative rationality to reflexive authority and relational performance management systems (Broadbent & Laughlin, 2009). Excessive reliance on instrumental rationality can lead to managerialism and, hence, to imposed and often simplistic performance indicators; whereas, approaches such as deliberative democracy, which are based on communicative rationality, enable participation. However, some versions of deliberative democracy have been criticized for overemphasising consensus, while agonistic pluralism incorporates notions of conflicting interests and values (and, implicitly, therefore, value rationality) but may not emphasize consensus enough. An emerging "agonistic deliberation" may be conducive to balancing communicative, instrumental and value rationality according to circumstances.

Methods

Data for the chapter was derived from several sources linking to the three stakeholder groups focused upon within the chapter.

Government – The authors accessed 91 televised briefings that were provided by the prime minister and/or members of his Cabinet together with members of the government's scientific advisers from the @10downing street YouTube channel. Additionally, the authors downloaded the slides, data sets and transcripts that accompanied each coronavirus press conference, focusing on the performance information (see www.gov.uk/government/collections/slides-and-datasets-to-accompany-coronavi rus-press-conferences). The data was accessed between 9 March 2020, when the briefings began, and 5 November 2020.

Independent Science Experts – The authors accessed and viewed the weekly public briefings of Independent SAGE and downloaded and examined the reports and slides published by the expert scientists and professionals from their dedicated website (see www.independentsage.org). The authors focused on the time period between 26 June 2020 (when the first briefing was streamed live) and December 2020. Data was also accessed from The Great Barrington Declaration website (see https:gbdeclaration.org) for an alternative view on the pandemic.

The Public – In the main, the authors relied upon opinion polls published by YouGov and reports published by the House of Commons on 12 October 2021.

In addition, an emerging recent accounting literature on the pandemic and accounting (and related aspects, such as accountability, governance, management control and performance management) was investigated and a more long-standing interdisciplinary literature on rationality, deliberation and agonistic pluralism was also addressed.

The sources were analysed individually by each of the authors, with a particular emphasis on developments in the presentation and use of performance measures between March and December 2020. Key developments and changes were discussed, leading to a synthesis of views. The suggestions for further research emerged through a similar process towards the end of the writing of the chapter.

Stakeholders

Government

As outlined earlier, the UK government moved from assessing the coronavirus threat as low on 22 January, 2020, to moderate on 30 January and to high on 12 March (Department of Health and Social Care Press Release, 12 March 2020). The decision was based on modelling information produced at Imperial College and the London School of Hygiene and Tropical Medicine. As well as healthcare demand, the information involved infectivity rates, transmissions, disease progression and estimates of deaths in the UK (see, for example, Ferguson et al., 2020).

The government utilized performance measures and charts in an original way in televised briefings to influence citizen behaviour. Between 16 March and 26 June 2020, the government's scientific and medical advisers from SAGE presented the latest statistics relating to the virus. Given fears on trans-mission rates and the potential impact on the NHS, the government introduced the "R" (reproduction) value to the general public and stressed that an R value of 1 or more was indicative of virus growth. As the R value was higher than 1 at the start of the pandemic, the government appealed to the public to wash hands, use face masks, maintain physical distance and to self-isolate. These were to help con-tain the disease and protect the NHS from being overwhelmed while allowing more time for medical research. Communication of the R value was complemented with charts showing numbers of virus cases. The R value performance metric was then communicated during the enforced three-month lockdown from March 2020, with the government emphasizing the need for continued individual and community cooperation.

In an attempt to further engage the general public, the presentation of performance information evolved over the course of the first lockdown period. From presenting relatively simple charts, the government progressed to showing more sophisticated charts with seven-day averages to slides containing both charts and key statistics. From the second week of May 2020, the government presented charts alongside daily statistics such as the number of confirmed cases and the number of deaths where Covid-19 was confirmed or suspected. Although the slides contained more information, the presentation contained both "snapshot" information and trends.

The UK government used the performance metrics *both* to inform government policy and to justify government policy to the public at large. When they extended the lockdown period for at least three weeks in April, it was claimed that the government had followed the scientific and medical advice received "very carefully and deliberately" (Prime Minister's Office, 16 April 2020). Similarly, in May 2020, the prime minister announced a conditional plan for lifting lockdown restrictions, citing sustained falls in the death rate, sustained and considerable falls in the rate of infection, and an R value below 1 (Prime Minister's Office, 10 May 2020).

However, despite government claims of being guided by the science and data, and of matching governmental actions to performance metrics, this was not always the case. For example, SAGE discussed a short period of England-wide rules in September (*The Guardian*, 18 September 2020), referred to as a circuit breaker, noting rapidly increasing infections and an R rate well above 1 (SAGE, 30 October 2020). In response, the prime minister announced that the government would not hesitate to impose further restrictions (Prime Minister's Office, 30 September 2020). However, further restrictions were not put in place in England, despite worsening performance metrics, until 31 October (more than eight weeks after a suggestion of a circuit breaker based on performance metrics), when the prime minister finally announced a second lockdown in England (Prime Minister's Office, 31 October 2020).

While reluctant to impose short-term restrictions after the first national lockdown, the UK government did use performance metrics and charts to instigate local and regional lockdowns. On 4 July 2020, for example, the government put into force the first local lockdown in Leicester and parts of Leicestershire. From September to October 2020, the government then used performance metrics to rationalize local restrictions by introducing a three-tier system, and in December 2020 to reintroduce a tiered system and add a fourth tier (see Ahmad et al., 2021).

Although intended principally as public health guidance, the government used performance information during the early press briefings to discharge political accountability and enable democratic accountability (see Broadbent, 2020; Ferry et al., 2021). For example, following criticism of a failure to test people for the virus and trace contacts of those testing positive, an ambitious target of 100,000 tests a day by the end of April 2020 was announced (Department of Health and Social Care, 2 April 2020). Subsequent press briefings culminated with the health secretary proclaiming that the government target had been met; although this was debatable (Broadbent, 2020).

Independent science experts

Independent SAGE is a group of academics from mathematics, public health, virology and behavioural science who acted as a counterweight to the government and its official advisers during the period of the pandemic (Clarke, 2021; McKee et al., 2022). They worked alongside experts in investigative journalism known as "The Citizens" (McKee et al., 2022). Other groups of scientists and individuals also offered advice on policy concerning the virus. For example, the Great Barrington group of infectious disease epidemiologists and public health scientists advocated protecting only the vulnerable and building up herd immunity (Great Barrington Declaration, 2020). However, Independent SAGE had a high profile and seems to have been particularly influential.

Independent SAGE used performance metrics and performance charts to engage with the government and public, to create and promote better understanding, and to counter the spread of the infection by advising on safeguards and publishing guidance. Members clarified their role as "knowledge brokers" (McKee et al., 2022, p. 4), simultaneously sharing acquired expertise in multiple disciplines while creating space to listen to public concerns. During their weekly online sessions, a mathematician presented the UK's most recent Covid-19 published data and then answered questions from the public and other stakeholders.

In June 2020, Independent SAGE presented charts on the number of UK Covid-19 deaths; new hospital admissions with Covid-19; the number of new people with a positive Covid-19 test result; the number of new infections in the UK per day; and NHS Test, Trace and Isolate results. The charts were compiled based on information from multiple sources including the government's daily figures, the Office of National Statistics, and the NHS Test, Trace and Isolate service. The Independent SAGE members utilized the charts to argue for caution following the restrictions. The views of Independent SAGE as a group, and those of individual members, were clear and unequivocal: wearing face masks is important, and the reduction in physical distancing rules by the government was premature. The presentation of the performance charts was intended to support weight to the argument that 4 July should not be treated as freedom day.

Independent SAGE used evidence regularly in the form of performance charts as a vehicle to influence the policies of the government. This contrasts to the advisory role of SAGE, and the positioning of some leading academics. Professor Spiegelhalter, of Cambridge University, stated: "Policy decisions are political decisions, which require a form of weighing up a range of consequences and values that is beyond a single scientific discipline" (quoted in Clarke, 2021, p. 3). On science and policy, the Independent SAGE group positioned themselves as "issue advocates" (Pielke, 2007), with a focus on reducing the spread of the infection (McKee et al., 2022, p. 3). Professor Pillay, chair of Independent SAGE, argued: "science has had to be political" (quoted in Clarke, 2021, p. 2).

As an example of the use of performance measures and policy, Independent SAGE documented and published plans and guidance following a rise in infections during autumn 2020. On 18 September 2020, the charts presented by Independent SAGE during their public briefing showed the number of new confirmed Covid-19 cases in the UK, a graphic of positive cases by age group shown in the form of a heat chart; a graphic of positive cases by geography in the form of a shaded map of the UK; and numbers of hospital admissions. They referred to a statement from the chief executive of one of Birmingham's large hospitals: "We have seen hospital admissions double in a week and I expect it to double in the next week again – it's an exponential curve. We are in the foothills of that curve" (Independent SAGE, 18 September 2020). As a pre-emptive measure to prevent a second national lockdown, Independent SAGE presented an "emergency ten-point plan", which was also published by the *British Medical Journal* on 20 September 2020. It distinguished between immediate measures and a strategy for building a functional testing system. In mid-October 2020, Independent SAGE escalated their concerns, and published an "Emergency six-week plan for England in response to rising cases, hospitalisations and deaths" (Independent SAGE, 16 October 2020), noting that their September plan was not implemented by the government, and voicing their belief that the then-current tiered system in England was insufficient to reverse the growth of the pandemic. In agreement with SAGE, Independent SAGE called for a short circuit breaker, including the closure of schools, non-essential retail and businesses, leisure and hospitality sectors and places of worship.

In addition to attempting to influence policy decisions, Independent SAGE opposed government decisions, such as the "Eat Out to Help Out" scheme launched in August 2020. They criticized the government for encouraging members of the public to dine out while simultaneously seeking to minimize transmission. Also, they advised the government to adopt a zero-Covid strategy. The scientists pointed to countries with tight control of the virus, such as Taiwan, South Korea, Finland and Norway, and argued that strong suppression would ultimately allow economic recovery with a relatively lower impact on gross domestic product.

From the start of the pandemic, Independent SAGE were vocal in speaking for marginalized groups such as children, the elderly, people with disabilities and black and minority ethnic populations. The Group published a report on the evidence of disparities in the impact of Covid-19 in black and ethnic minority populations and called for the mandatory collection and reporting of ethnicity data in health and social care (Independent SAGE, 3 July 2020). Responding to the lockdown in Leicester in

June 2020, Independent SAGE acknowledged the city as a place of multiple cultures and traditions; highlighted the risks of racist groups blaming ethnic minorities; and called for a response led by local government.

The public

In this section, we draw, with due caution, on data from opinion polls carried out by YouGov, a UK polling organization. The first series of data elicits opinions of *whether the government was handling the virus somewhat or very well* (YouGov, 2022). In March 2020, around the time it had become clear the UK and devolved governments needed to take some action, positive views were at about 50 per cent, and this moved up quickly to 70 per cent (presumably, a "rally round the flag" effect"), followed by a steady decline to just under 40 per cent by late spring. Positive responses stabilized at around 40 per cent through the summer and then declined further to about 30 per cent in the autumn of 2020. There was then a fairly steady improvement to about 60 per cent by late spring and early summer of 2021, but this was followed by a sharp decline to around 25 per cent by July 2021. There was then a "jagged plateau" at around 35 per cent–40 per cent for the rest of 2021, which continued in 2022. Indeed, apart from a large improvement in spring 2021 and an equal decline in summer of that year, approval of the government's performance, according to YouGov, was at 30 per cent–45 per cent throughout the period from July 2020 to spring 2022; reflecting a fair degree of scepticism.

The temporary improvement in the assessment of the government's performance seems related to the development and delivery of vaccines to prevent the virus and improved treatment of serious cases (for example, through better use of ventilators). Another poll by YouGov (2021) compared attitudes about *how well the Government was handling the pandemic across a number of categories* in October 2020 and March 2021. At the latter date, 86 per cent approved of the government's handling of the roll-out of vaccines (a question which was not applicable in October 2020). Similarly, 71 per cent believed that people with the virus were getting the best possible care, compared to 41 per cent in October. There were improvements in other categories, that is, working towards long-term solutions (35 per cent–59 per cent), reducing the number of people who caught Covid-19 (27 per cent–58 per cent), giving financial support to people unable to work (41 per cent–54 per cent), and protecting the British economy (39 per cent–47 per cent). In contrast, the two categories where the government's performance was most highly rated in October 2020 showed declines: ensuring continuing education for children (from 65 per cent to 58 per cent) and protecting people's jobs (from 56 per cent to 52 per cent). Overall assessment of the government's performance would involve these aspects as well as the health aspects, of course, but at this point the success of the vaccine programme seems to have (if only temporarily) restored approval.

It is informative here to examine the actions as well as the opinions of the public. Advice on potential behaviour was given to the government by a subgroup of SAGE and, initially, policy was based on a fear that the British public would not accept a lockdown or a test and trace system, or would only accept them for a short time. This delayed the imposition of necessary measures. However, it turned out that the UK public was very compliant with lockdown and test and trace and other required rules, such as those around social distancing, mask wearing, and self-isolation, despite the restrictions eventually imposed being "unprecedented" and "draconian" (Joint Report, p. 45). This suggests that the government's communications approach, despite its limitations, had some effectiveness both as an instrument for protecting public health and for facilitating performance measurement (albeit unintentionally).

Research agenda

Our preliminary analysis on the creation and use of performance measures during the Covid-19 crisis in the UK suggests potential avenues for future research. The broad themes presented below could be interlinked and are not intended to be exhaustive. They derive from reflection on our analysis, discussion and theoretical framing of the relationship between the three key stakeholders and the desirability of more participatory performance evaluation. As such, they may be particularly relevant to scholars interested in critical and interdisciplinary approaches to accounting. The common features of these pathways is the role of performance in the triangular relationship between three stakeholder groups: government, experts and citizens. The question then arises as to whether the process of performance management is dominated by instrumental rationality. or is characterized by a balance of communicative, instrumental and value rationality. The theoretical perspective we have adopted (which can be summarized as "agonistic deliberation") is well suited to exploring these issues. However, any researchers who take up these proposals might equally adopt other theoretical positions usefully.

Performance measures during a crisis

A scientific basis for informing a crisis has arguably been legitimized during the pandemic and paves the way for future studies on the role of performance measurement and management at times of crisis. While the literature is replete with the unintended consequences of performance management in not-for-profit settings (see, for example, Bevan & Hood, 2006; Franco-Santos & Otley, 2018), an emphasis on the "here and now" suggests the potential for more positive outcomes.

Future research could consider the use of single and collective measures by a chosen nation during the pandemic, or offer a comparative study analysing the presentation of metrics in countries underpinned by different political ideologies (see study by Mitchell et al., 2021, on performance management in three European countries). On a single measure, the UK Covid-19 broadcasts were instrumental in introducing the "R" measure into the lexicon of the general public which was utilized to indicate the growth or otherwise of the virus. There is scope, therefore, to investigate performance measures and "norm dynamics" (see Finnemore & Sikkink, 1998), analysing factors that contributed to the indicators acquiring a taken-for-granted quality. More broadly, a content analysis of the performance measures and charts utilized by the UK government during the televised broadcasts have the potential to reveal insights into government perceptions of the crisis, the assumed role of the government in managing the crisis, and implications for citizenship (see study by Andreouli & Brice, 2021, analysing political rhetoric and the construction of citizenship).

Performance measures and modelling

The Covid-19 pandemic has the potential to revitalize studies on the selection, presentation and use of performance measures in public services. A key novelty during the pandemic was the presentation of performance measures following the insights of data modellers such as the Imperial College Covid-19 Response Team. As an example, the insights took the form of presenting different policy options on total deaths and critical care (ICU) bed requirements in the NHS and showed worst-case scenarios. The insights informed the government/scientist narrative when presenting current performance metrics during televised briefings, and presumably informed the choice of performance measures to display. Rather than benchmark performance information against an aspirational state, an exploration of the potential use of mathematical models to inform performance targets could be beneficial. In turn, real data following public service interventions have a role in scrutinizing assumptions underpinning forecasts and reappraising models.

Performance measures and accountability

The construction and enactment of accountability is a field that also has the potential for renewal following the pandemic. As observed by Broadbent (2020), government reporting of measures, such as deaths and the number of tests undertaken, had a role in achieving the cooperation of citizens and, concurrently, in discharging political accountability. Meanwhile, drawing on the House of Commons Public Administration and Constitutional Affairs Committee findings, Ferry et al. (2021) argue that an increased focus on performance data both served to persuade the general public to act in specific ways and to enable democratic accountability. The presentation of performance information during a crisis impacts on the discharge of accountability as (1) outcomes partly depend upon collective efforts (a point repeatedly reiterated by the UK government); and, (2) performance statistics are subject to misrepresentation (as reported by Broadbent, 2020). As a further point, as argued by Kettell and Kerr (2022), there is scope to depoliticize actions and to remove decision-making from the arena of accountability, as well as to politicize strategies and thereby take credit (p. 12). Thus the UK government claimed to follow the science during some points in the televised briefings, while emphasizing discretionary choices at other points. Therefore, it is timely to further explore "defensiveness" as a pre-emptive move by government and the implications for the discharge of accountability, both in terms of the role of the accountor and accountee.

Communication and performance measures

Referring to the visual charts produced by individual data scientists and (re)produced by collective groups such as Independent SAGE, it is evident that the communication of performance information has evolved in novel and intriguing ways. It would be useful, therefore, to examine the charts over time, and to assess correspondence with the "objects" they purport to represent (see the work of Dambrin & Robson (2011) on inscriptions). Given that individual members of the scientific community have presented charts with commentary on social media, it could be insightful to conduct a study on the key messages taken from the charts with and without commentary by sections of the general public. This could provide learning on the role of narrative statements when presented alongside charts and help inform communication strategies in seeking a healthier society.

Referring to the public briefings provided by the prime minister and senior government officials, one potential opportunity for research could be to consider how the government used performance information to justify limitations on human activity and, conversely, to encourage a return to pre-pandemic life.

Performance measures and stakeholder engagement

Independent SAGE, individual scientists and public health experts provided a structured and systematic challenge to the government on the UK response to the Covid-19 pandemic. While the discussions and work of SAGE were criticized as opaque (see, for example Bowsher et al., 2021), Independent SAGE committed to acting as a transparent source of scientific advice (McKee et al., 2022), and called for government responses commensurate to the available evidence. There are two lines of research that warrant further investigation. Firstly, the possibilities and limitations of performance information in influencing government action during a crisis. A common refrain of Independent SAGE and other public health experts centred on the delay of government action following the release of evidence sets including transmission rates. However, given that the UK government did act on evidence, albeit after a lapse of time, a deeper exploration of factors that contributed to a convergence between science (performance metrics) and policy could be beneficial. Secondly, noting the critiques of the Government Select Committee on health inequalities by marginalized groups, such as people with learning disabilities (see House of Commons report, 21 September 2021), a study on the role of independent experts and performance information and risk assessments is timely. There is scope, for example, to build on the concept of surrogate accountability as presented by Rubenstein (2007) with a particular focus on information.

Discussion and conclusion

Ahrens and Ferry (2021) hold that accounting could potentially increase popular acceptance of measures imposed during the crisis by explaining in detail the options available and reasons behind government decisions, rather than relying mainly on fear. The analysis presented here supports this. During the early period of the pandemic, information concerning the progress of the virus was presented in innovative ways with the purpose of shaping behaviour to meet public health needs in the emergency. The briefings were largely successful in persuading citizens to adhere to public health guidelines. Moreover, they also functioned "accidentally" to provide performance evaluation information (notwithstanding the doubts that have been raised about the reliability of some of the information being presented). This success in communication is in marked contrast to the government's performance dealing with the virus itself, at least, until vaccines were available. The general consensus in the growing literature is that government performance in the UK was below that of other comparable countries in the early stages of the pandemic. However, the development and delivery of the vaccine programme went a considerable way in reducing hospitalizations and deaths. It seems reasonable to infer that the somewhat sceptical attitude towards the government's perform-ance by the public, evident in the polling data we have examined, may have been partly formed by the presentations of data concerning cases, hospitalizations, death rates and so on.

We have identified various stakeholder groups who are interested in how the government performed in discharging responsibilities in relation to the Covid-19 pandemic and focused on three groups of stakeholders of particular significance: the government, independent experts and the public. The interrelationships between such groups and performance management is an important topic, yet under-researched, and has considerable implications for society (see Barbera et al., 2021). To explore this, we have adopted theoretical framings which provide a new insight on performance measure-ment. These framings have been relatively little used in the accounting academic literature to date, yet have great potential for providing perceptive insights. The chapter brings together the concepts of deliberative democracy and agnostic pluralism in ways in which reveal some convergence despite their different origins (Wankhade et al., 2022). The resulting notion, which might be called "agonistic deliberation", helps illuminate the issues and emergent performance measurement in the UK during the Covid-19 crisis. In a crisis, we would argue, it is particularly desirable to allow many voices to be heard; both to recognize a common citizenship and to access vital information which would not otherwise be available. For example, the care home scandal could have been avoided if care home managers, residents and their families had been consulted.

Thus, it might be proposed that there was deliberation between the government and the scientists, both affiliated and non-affiliated (independent to the government), but limited input by the public. However, the government retained the power to make final decisions and disregard advice proffered from formal, let alone informal scientific sources. Deliberation, therefore, was not only agonistic but also limited. Nevertheless, although Independent SAGE was disappointed with some responses from the government, Clarke (2021) suggests that it may have influenced the government in "eventually imposing one of the strictest lockdowns in the world" (p. 3).

Therefore, some degree of communicative rationality was at play between the government and Independent SAGE, but instrumental rationality was more dominant between the government and the general public. The government and professional scientists put forward convincing arguments through the presentation of technical information, a communication "device" which ordinary citizens did not have at their disposal. However, the impression of a "top-down" approach is somewhat moderated by the work of Independent SAGE in communicating with the public and trying to engage them. Therefore, the situation may be seen as somewhat ambiguous, although we would argue that in emergencies, particularly, such as the coronavirus pandemic, a more pluralist and polyvocal approach is desirable. Similarly, Ahrens and Ferry (2021) identified a persistent failure in government accounts to fully utilize calculative processes to address equity as well as efficiency and to facilitate user engagement, which remained the case during the Covid-19 pandemic.

Independent SAGE saw its role as involving both *evidence* and *engagement* and sought to draw attention to groups who had been particularly affected by the crisis but whose views were not prominent (e.g. disabled people, care home residents and their families, and members of the Black, Asian and Minority Ethnic community). This position was criticized by some other scientists who held that the role of science is to *inform* but not *influence* governments, which would then implement policy in an instrumentally rational way. We suggest, however, that it is helpful for independent experts to participate in agonistic deliberation where communicative and value rationality are in play. In this case, weighting the lives of the elderly against the economy or other health concerns and the education of children requires value judgements, and Independent SAGE did not inhibit other scientists, who held different views about the trade-offs, from taking part in the debate.

Another contribution of our chapter is a detailed research agenda, which will facilitate further exploration of the issues across a number of themes: performance measurement in crises; the roles of communications and modelling in performance management; performance and accountability; and performance metrics and stakeholder engagement. It is hoped this categorization will help researchers in the future to investigate this socially significant topic further and in depth. For example, the ways in which presentations were used to communicate public health information, so that it could be readily grasped by the lay public, was a significant achievement. Exploring the details of how this was done would be a worthwhile topic for further research. Again, the briefings were intended to be, and largely functioned as, a tool for top-down implementation of policy rather than for agonistic deliberation involving many voices. The implications of this could be the basis of another productive study.

While both authors of this chapter are accounting academics, we have drawn on our experience of working in interdisciplinary teams and from critical perspectives to present an original take on performance evaluation in the public sector, which should be of wide interest. The topics and conceptual frameworks discussed here are clearly relevant to an audience drawn from a range of disciplines and can facilitate further research from different perspectives. Another contribution, therefore, is to highlight the need for research which investigates the engagement of citizens and/or stakeholders in public sector performance management and to begin to address this research gap. To do so, we have adopted a theoretical stance based on a version of participative democracy which recognizes agonism. The chapter, therefore, should be useful to scholars both within and outside the accounting discipline.

References

Ahmad, S., Connolly, C., & Demirag, I. (2021). Testing times: Governing a pandemic with numbers. *Accounting, Auditing & Accountability Journal, 34*(6), 1362–1375. https://doi.org/10.1108/AAAJ-08-2020-4863

Ahrens, T., & Ferry, L. (2021). Accounting and accountability practices in a time of crisis: A Foucauldian perspective on the UK Government's response to COVID-19 for England. *Accounting, Auditing & Accountability Journal, 34*(6), 1332–1344. https://doi.org/10.1108/AAAJ-07-2020-4659

Andreouli, E., & Brice, E. (2021). Citizenship under COVID-19: An analysis of UK political rhetoric during the first wave of the 2020 pandemic. *Journal of Community and Social Psychology, 32*(3), 555–572. https://doi.org/10.1002/casp.2526

Barbera, C., Sicilia, M., & Steccolini, I. (2021). A conceptual analysis on the role of citizens in public services' performance assessment. Draft Paper, EIASM Public Sector Conference.

Benhabib, S. (1996). Toward a deliberative model of democratic legitimacy. In S. Benhabib (Ed.), *Democracy and Difference* (pp. 67–94). Princeton University Press.

Bennington, J., & Hartley, J. (2019). Action research to develop the theory and practice of public value as a contested democratic practice. In A. Lindgreen, N. Koenig-Lewis, M. Kitchener, J. Brewer, M. Moore, & T. Meynhardt (Eds.), *Public Value: Deepening, enriching, and broadening the theory and practice* (pp. 143–158). Routledge.

Bevan, G., & Hood, C. (2006). What's measured is what matters: Targets and gaming in the English public health care system. *Public Administration, 84*(3), 517–538. https://doi.org/10.1111/j.1467-9299.2006.00600.x

Bowsher, G., Bernard, R., & Sullivan. R. (2021). A health intelligence framework for pandemic response: Lessons from the UK experience of COVID-19. *Health Security, 18*(6), 435–443. http://doi.org/10.1089/hs.2020.0108

Broadbent, J. (2020). The response to Covid-19 in England: Political accountability and loss of trust. *Journal of Accounting & Organizational Change, 16*(4), 527–532. https://doi.org/10.1108/JAOC-07-2020-0093

Broadbent, J., & Laughlin, R. (2009). Performance management systems: A conceptual model. *Management Accounting Research, 20*(4), 283–295. https://doi.org/10.1016/j.mar.2009.07.004

Clarke, L. (2021). Covid-19's rebel scientists: Has iSAGE been a success? *British Medical Journal*, 375. https://doi.org/10.1136/bmj.n2504

Curato, N., Dryzek, J., Ercan, S., Hendriks, C., & Niemeyer, S. (2017). Twelve key findings in deliberative democracy research. *Daedalus, 146*(3), 28–38. https://doi.org/10.1162/DAED_a_00444

Dambrin, C., & Robson, K. (2011). Tracing performance in the pharmaceutical industry: Ambivalence, opacity and the performativity of flawed measures. *Accounting, Organizations and Society, 36*(7), 428–455. https://doi.org/10.1016/j.aos.2011.07.006

De Bruijn, H. (2002). *Managing performance in the public sector*. Routledge.

Department of Health and Social Care. (2020). COVID-19: Government announces moving out of contain phase and into delay. Gov.UK. Press Release, 12 March. www.gov.uk/government/news/covid-19-government-announces-moving-out-of-contain-phase-and-into-delay

Dryzek, J. (2000). *Deliberative democracy and beyond: Liberals, critics, contestations*. Oxford University Press.

Dugdale, D. (2018). Management control systems: Theory and lessons from practice. In E. Harris (Ed.), *The Routledge companion to performance management and control* (pp. 13–38). Routledge.

Elster, J. (1998). Deliberation and constitution making. In J. Elster (Ed.), *Deliberative democracy* (pp. 97–122). Cambridge University Press.

Ferguson, N. M., Laydon, D., Nedjati-Gilani, G., Imai, N., Ainslie, K., Baguelin, M., Bhatia, S., Boonyasiri, A., Cucunubá, Z., Cuomo-Dannenburg, G., Dighe, A., Dorigatti, I., Fu, H., Gaythorpe, K., Green, W., Hamlet, A., Hinsley, W., Okell, L. C., van Elsland, S., Thompson, H., Verity, H., Volz, E., Wang, H., Wang, Y., Walker, P. G. T., Walters, C., Winskill, P., Whittaker, C., Donnelly, C. A., Riley, S., & Ghani, A. C. (2020). Impact of non-pharmaceutical interventions (NPIs) to reduce COVID-19 mortality and healthcare demand. *Imperial College COVID-19 Response Team*, 16 March. www.philipcaputo.com/wp-content/uploads/2020/03/Imperial-College-COVID19-NPI-modelling-16-03-2020.pdf

Ferry, L., Hardy, C., & Midgley, H. (2021). Data, trust, democracy and Covid-19: The first parliamentary assessment of the UK government's approach to data during the pandemic. *Public Money & Management*, 676–678. https://doi.org/10.1080/09540962.2021.1946311

Ferry, L., & Slack, R. (2022). (Counter) accounting for hybrid organising: A case of the Great Exhibition of the North. *Accounting, Auditing & Accountability Journal, 35*(3), 681–705. https://doi.org/10.1108/aaaj-12-2019-4303

Finnemore, M., & Sikkink, K. (1998). International norm dynamics and political changes. *International Organization, 52*(4), 887–917. https://doi.org/10.1162/002081898550789

Franco-Santos, M., & Otley, D. (2018). Reviewing and theorizing the unintended consequences of performance management systems. *International Journal of Management Reviews, 20*, 696–730. https://doi.org/10.1111/ijmr.12183

Great Barrington Declaration. (2020). https://gbdeclaration.org

Gregory, R. (2007). New public management and the ghost of Max Weber. In T. Christensen & P. Lægreid (Eds.), *Transcending new public management: The transformation of public sector reforms* (pp. 221–244). Ashgate.

The Guardian. (2020, 18 September). PM considers imposing Covid "circuit break" across England. www.theguardian.com/world/2020/sep/18/circuit-break-plans-for-england-to-prevent-new-covid-lockdown

Heald, D., & Hodges, R. (2020). The accounting, budgeting and fiscal impact of COVID-19 on the United Kingdom. *Journal of Public Budgeting, Accounting & Financial Management, 32*(5), 785–795. https://doi.org/10.1108/JPBAFM-07-2020-0121

Healey, P. (1997). *Collaborative planning*. Palgrave.

Heath, G., Radcliffe, J., & Wankhade, P. (2018). Performance management in the public sector: The case of the English ambulance service. In E. Harris (Ed.), *The Routledge companion to performance management and control* (pp. 417–438). Routledge

Hendriks, C. (2009). Deliberative governance in the context of power. *Policy and Society, 28*(3), 173–184. https://doi.org/10.1016/j.polsoc.2009.08.004

House of Commons Health & Social Care and Science & Technology Committees. (2021). Coronavirus: lessons learned to date report: government response. Accessed online at https://publications.parliament.uk/pa/cm5 802/cmselect/cmhealth/92/9203.htm

House of Commons Public Administration and Constitutional Affairs Committee. (2021). *Government Transparency and Accountability during Covid-19: The Data Underpinning Decisions*. Eighth Report of Session 2019–21, 15 March. https://committees.parliament.uk/publications/5076/documents/50285/default/

Independent SAGE. (2020). *Disparities in the Impact of COVID-19 in Black and Minority Ethnic Populations: Review of the Evidence and Recommendations for Action*. The Independent SAGE Report 6, 3 July 2020. www.independentsage.org/wp-content/uploads/2020/09/Independent-SAGE-BME-Report_02Jul y_FINAL.pdf

Independent SAGE. (2020). *Emergency Six-Week Plan for England in Response to Rising Cases, Hospitalisations and Deaths – 16 October 2020*. The Independent SAGE Report 18, 16 October 2020. www.independentsage. org/emergency-plan-for-stopping-the-spread-of-covid-19-in-england/

Independent SAGE. (2020). *Latest Numbers on Covid-19 in the UK – 18 September 2020*. www.independents age.org/latest-numbers-on-covid-19-in-the-uk-18-september-2020/

Kapoor, I. (2002). The devil's in the theory: A critical assessment of Robert Chambers' work on participatory development. *Third World Quarterly, 23*(1), 101–117. https://doi.org/10.1080/01436590220108199

Kettell, S., & Kerr, P. (2022). "Guided by the science": (De)politicising the UK government's response to the coronavirus crisis. *British Journal of Politics and International Relations, 24*(1), 11–30. https://doi.org/10.1177/ 13691481211054957

Leoni, G., Lai, A., Staccezzini, R., Steccolini, I., Brammer, S., Linnenluecke, M., & Demirag, I. (2021). Accounting, management and accountability in times of crisis: Lessons from the COVID-19 pandemic. *Accounting, Auditing & Accountability Journal, 34*(6), 1305–1319. https://doi.org/10.1080/0143659022 0108199

Mansbridge, J. (1996). Using power/fighting power/the polity. In S. Benhabib (Ed.), *Democracy and difference* (pp. 46–66). Princeton University Press.

McKee, M., Altmann, D., Costello, A., Friston, K., Haque, Z., Khunti, K., Michie, S., Oni, T., Pagel, C., Pillay, D., Reicher, S., Salisbury, H., Scally, G., Yates, K., Bauld, L., Bear, L., Drury, J., Parker, M., Phoenix, A., Stokoe, E., & West., R. (2022). Open science communication: The first year of the UK's Independent Scientific Advisory Group for Emergencies. *Health Policy, 126*(3), 234–244. https://doi.org/10.1016/j.health pol.2022.01.006

Mitchell, F., Nørreklit, H., Nørreklit, L., Cinquini, L., Koeppe, F., Magnacca, F., Mauro, S. G., Jakobsen, M., Korhonen, T., Laine, T., & Liboriussen, J. M. (2021). Evaluating performance management of COVID-19 reality in three European countries: A pragmatic constructivist study. *Accounting, Auditing & Accountability Journal, 34*(6), 1345–1361. https://doi.org/10.1108/AAAJ-08-2020-4778

Mouffe, C. (1999). Deliberative democracy or agonistic pluralism. *Social Research, 66*(3), 745–758.

Mouffe, C. (2018). *For a left populism*. Verso.

Pallerm, J. R. (2000). An empirical-theoretical analysis framework for public participation in environmental impact assessment. *Journal of Environmental Planning and Management, 43*(5), 581–600.

Pielke, R. A., Jr (2007). *The honest broker: Making sense of science in policy and politics*. Cambridge University Press.

Prime Minister's Office. (2020). Foreign Secretary's statement on coronavirus (COVID-19): 16 April 2020. Gov.UK. www.gov.uk/government/speeches/foreign-secretarys-statement-on-coronavirus-covid-19-16-april-2020

Prime Minister's Office. (2020). Prime Minister announces new national restrictions. Press Release, 31 October 2020. Gov.UK. www.gov.uk/government/news/prime-minister-announces-new-national-restrictions

Prime Minister's Office. (2020). Prime Minister's statement on coronavirus (COVID-19): 10 May 2020. Gov. UK. www.gov.uk/government/speeches/pm-address-to-the-nation-on-coronavirus-10-may-2020

Prime Minister's Office. (2020). Prime Minister's statement on coronavirus (COVID-19): 30 September 2020. Gov.UK. www.gov.uk/government/speeches/prime-ministers-statement-on-coronavirus-covid-19-30-septem ber-2020

Rinaldi, L. (2022). Accounting and the COVID-19 pandemic two years on: Insights, gaps and an agenda for the future. *Accounting Forum*. https://doi.org/10.1080/01559982.2022.2045418

Rubenstein, J. (2007). Accountability in an unequal world. *Journal of Politics, 69*(3), 616–632.

Rutgers, M. (2019). The rationalities of public values: conflicting values and conflicting rationalities. In A. Lindgreen, N. Koenig-Lewis, M. Kitchener, J. Brewer, M. Moore, & T. Meynhardt (Eds.), *Public Value: Deepening, enriching, and broadening the theory and practice* (pp. 40–53). Routledge.

SAGE. (2020). SAGE 59 minutes: Coronavirus (COVID-19) response, 24 September 2020. Published 30 October 2020. www.gov.uk/government/publications/sage-59-minutes-coronavirus-covid-19-response-24-september-2020

Schipper, F. (1996). Rationality and the philosophy of organisation. *Organization, 3*(2), 267–289. https://doi.org/10.1177/135050849632010

Steccolini, I. (2019). Accounting and the post-new public management: Re-considering publicness in accounting research. *Accounting, Auditing & Accountability Journal, 23*(1), 255–279.

Tessier, S., & Otley, D. (2012). A conceptual development of Simons' Levers of Control Framework. *Management Accounting Research, 23*(3), 171–185. https://doi.org/10.1016/j.mar.2012.04.003

Van Dooren, W., Bouckaert, G., & Halligan, J. (2015). *Performance management in the public sector*. Routledge.

Wankhade, P., Heath, G., & Murphy, P. (2022). Re-imagining ambulance services through participation and deliberation. In J. Diamond & J. Liddle (Eds.), *Reimagining public sector management* (Vol. 7, *Critical perspectives on international public sector management*, pp. 139–156). Emerald.

YouGov. (2021, 29 March). Opinion of government handling of the pandemic has improved in most aspects since October. https://yougov.co.uk/topics/politics/articles-reports/2021/03/29/opinion-government-handling-pandemic-has-improved

YouGov. (2022, 17 March). COVID-19 government handling and confidence in health authorities. https://yougov.co.uk/topics/international/articles-reports/2020/03/17/perception-government-handling-covid-19

Young, I. (1996). Communication and the Other: Beyond deliberative democracy. In S. Benhabib (Ed.), *Democracy and difference* (pp. 120–136). Princeton University Press.

PART V

Risk management and disclosure

13

FRAMING RISK MANAGEMENT WITHIN MANAGEMENT CONTROL SYSTEMS

Andre Rodrigues, Adina Dudau, Georgios Kominis
and Alvise Favotto

Introduction

Public sector organizations (PSOs) must be vigilant in their efforts to identify and mitigate risks that can impact their operations, services and stakeholders. In order to effectively navigate a constantly changing environment, these organizations must anticipate, account for and respond to a range of risks. PSOs are exposed to both internal and external risks, which can have significant impacts on their operations, performance and ability to achieve their objectives (Hood & Peters, 2004). Internal risks can arise from within the organization and include issues such as financial mismanagement, fraud or non-compliance with regulations (Power, 2004). At the same time, risks can originate from the broader external environment in which the PSO operates, including changes in the political or economic landscape, natural disasters or cyberthreats (Islam & Tareque, 2022). PSOs may face idiosyncratic risks, such as changes in government policies or funding cuts and austerity measures which can have significant implications for their operations and ability to deliver services to the public (Bracci et al., 2015).

According to Hood and Young (2005), internal risks in PSOs can lead to loss of credibility and public trust, while external risks can result in policy failures, strategic misalignments and ineffective delivery of services. Therefore, PSOs need to implement appropriate risk management to mitigate the impact of both internal and external risks, ensure accountability and enhance performance. As Power (2004, p. 62) succinctly puts it, "the rise of risk management is simply an efficient response to the fact that the world has become more risky and dangerous".

Theorizing around how risk management is to be integrated withing an organization's control framework remains an ongoing endeavour, especially when it comes to PSOs (e.g. Ittner & Keusch, 2017; Rana et al., 2019b). In this chapter we take stock from prior research in this space and leverage insights provided by scholarship on management control systems (MCSs) to propose a theoretical framework that allows us to analyse the complex relationship between risk and control in PSOs. Specifically, our discussion is intended to offer insights into the following questions:

i. How do management control systems and risk management relate to each other conceptually?
ii. How can management control systems be configured in ways that incorporate effective risk management?
iii. How can public sector organizations adapt their management control systems to manage risks effectively?

DOI: 10.4324/9781003295945-18

By addressing these questions, we offer a conceptual contribution towards understanding the interplay between risk and control. In addition, by proposing a theoretical foundation for understanding the interactions between risk management and MCSs, this chapter endeavours to assist practitioners in assessing the effectiveness of existing risk-management practices and in identifying areas for improvement.

The chapter proceeds as follows: we discuss risk, uncertainty and risk management, highlighting the need for them to be integrated into MCSs; we then examine their configurations through the lenses of well-known levers of the control framework. We conclude by discussing ways of embedding risk management in an organization's (notably, a PSO's) control system.

Setting the scene

Risk and uncertainty

In the public sector context, notions of risk have "exploded" (Holzer & Millo, 2005; Power, 2005) well beyond the finances of PSOs. For example, while the intense scrutiny of PSOs by politicians and the civil society is hardly new, this has been increasingly understood in the language of risk as "reputational" or "litigation" risks that PSOs must monitor and control for (Lacey et al., 2012; Rika & Jacobs, 2019; Kominis et al., 2022).

There is no widely accepted definition of "risk" (Aven & Renn, 2009), but for the purposes of our research, we subscribe to the definition given by Sitkin and Pablo (1992), who describe it as "the extent to which there is uncertainty about whether potentially significant and/or disappointing outcomes of decisions will be realized" (p. 9). There are in fact many other definitions, and in order to provide further views on the conceptualization of risk, we also highlight Aven and Renn's (2009) statement that "risk refers to uncertainty about and severity of the events and consequences (or outcomes) of an activity with respect to something that humans value" (p. 6). It is evident from these definitions that the notion of risk is intimately related to the notion of uncertainty, as argued by Boholm (2019), who asserts that "the everyday concept of risk combines uncertainty and adversity" (p. 728).

Conceptually, the notions of risk and uncertainty are connected through the estimated probability of an event occurring and its potential consequences: a risky situation is one where the probability of it occurring and the distribution of its outcomes are known a priori, or can be calculated, while an uncertain situation is one whose probability and outcomes are widely unknown, according to a classic study by Knight (2012; originally published in 1921). Essentially, uncertainties are risks that are hard to measure – they are essentially "unknown unknowns". This distinction is important in a management control context: managing risk has different requirements from managing uncertainty (Mousavi & Gigerenzer, 2014; Teece et al., 2016).

This traditional duality between risk and uncertainty has recently been challenged in an attempt to make uncertainty measurable and controllable (Power, 2007). Researchers and practitioners have suggested alternative typologies of risks based on, for example, their tangibility (Gephart et al., 2009); interconnectedness with ethical conduct and societal expectations; or degree of organizational awareness (Andersen et al., 2014). As risk overtakes uncertainty in scholarly debates, the risk management function in PSOs has gained strategic prominence, at the interface between strategic priorities and organizational controls (Andersen, 2016).

Management control systems: levers of control

Merchant and Van der Stede (2017) provide a generic definition of MCSs as "systems that managers use to ensure the behaviours and decisions of their employees are consistent with the organization's objectives and strategies" (p. 8). This evolved from a focus on budgetary control (Anthony, 1965) and opened out to broader perspectives (Chenhall, 2003; Bisbe & Otley, 2004), including behavioural aspects (Alvesson & Kärreman, 2004), "targeting minds, through norms, emotions, beliefs and values, [and intending] to affect behaviour indirectly" (p. 425). This behavioural approach is per se a reflection of a less formal view of MCSs and empowers the employees, and it is an adequate approach to risk management, to counteract known limitations of the more established risk-management tools (Braumann et al., 2020).

Beyond targeting behaviour, MCSs are organizational information-seeking and gathering, accountability and feedback mechanisms designed to help the organization adapt in a timely fashion to changes in its substantive environment (Lowe, 1971). Those changes are meant to reconcile differences between organizational strategic objectives and actual results (Lowe, 1971). This view of MCSs is consistent with that proposed by Ewusi-Mensah (1981, p. 314), who suggested organizations were "adaptively rational" systems which survive successful interaction with their environment. From this evolutionary perspective, MCSs are the channels through which information and incentives are provided to decision makers within organizations so that they can remain viable as change takes place (Emery & Trist, 1965; Terreberry, 1968).

Within the MCS literature, Simons' (1995) levers of control framework holds a prominent place. It suggests that overall organizational control comes from four complementary control systems (or levers): boundary controls delineating the acceptable domain of conduct; belief systems inscribing organizational culture in terms of accepted values, rules and routines; diagnostic controls measuring how organizational objectives are met when compared to preset objectives; and interactive controls gathering information from all organizational levels and enabling organizational learning (Tessier & Otley, 2012). Each lever of control assumes an understanding of risk. Indeed, these levers "are the mechanisms managers can adjust to control risk as a company pursues its strategy" (Simons, 1999, p. 92). On the one hand, boundary and diagnostic systems play a role in shaping an organization's understanding of risk associated with its operations and current strategy: boundary controls help identify acceptable domains of operation in the face of "defined business risks" (Simons, 1995, p. 39), while diagnostic control systems help identify and monitor key risk factors with a critical effect on organizational success. On the other hand, through interactive controls, organizations monitor and gather information on future strategic uncertainties that may impinge on an organization's prospects (Simons, 1991), and belief controls frame such endeavours.

Not only are there diagnostic and interactive control systems in organizations' overall control strategies, but there are also interactive and diagnostic ways in which decision makers use MCSs (Tessier & Otley, 2012) to respond to change or uncertainty in their operating environment. In this sense, all four MCSs can be used diagnostically to monitor the extent to which an organization is on track to meet its objectives, or to interactively stimulate information gathering about strategic uncertainties and organizational dialogue around them (Simons, 1991, p. 50).

Interactive control systems – or any control system used interactively – have an attention-focusing function and are meant to facilitate the generation and analysis of information about future strategic uncertainties and their potential outcomes. They are also ideally placed to turn immeasurable uncertainty into measurable risk (Kominis et al., 2022), as they enable dialogue between organizational members at different hierarchical levels (Simons, 1995). As such, they entail the intensive, personal involvement of managerial staff and prolonged communication (Tessier & Otley, 2012). Organizations can use any MCS interactively by shifting the emphasis away from the monitoring of known determinants of organizational success to discussing and rather exploring the unknown: unknown factors which may affect the development and success of future strategies (Widener, 2007; Kominis & Dudau, 2012; Tessier & Otley, 2012).

Despite its prominence in the MCS literature, Simons' (1995) levers of control framework does not stand without criticism. In their attempt to develop and improve this framework, Tessier and Otley

(2012) argue that in the labelling assigned by Simons (1995) to the positive and negative dimensions of controls (characterizing them as respectively "good" or "bad"), he is using non-neutral terms, despite affirming that "neither control is bad" (Tessier & Otley, 2012, p. 173). Having perceived this as a limitative ambiguity, the authors prefer the use of the words "enabling" and "constraining" to refer to the dual role of controls, and consequently distinguish this dualization of role from the actual objectives of a control, which may be focused on either compliance or performance. In doing so, Tessier and Otley (2012) contest the vague definitions used by Simons (1995) in his levers of control framework, arguing that rather than looking at the descriptive identification of how controls can be used (referring to Simons' (1995) definitions of diagnostic and interactive controls), one should look at the "objectives of control (performance and compliance) and organizational level (operational and strategic)" (Tessier & Otley, 2012, p. 177).

Focusing specifically on the objectives of control, a concept that has emerged from the work of Adler and Borys (1996) concerning different forms of bureaucracy, a distinction must be made regarding enabling and coercive controls. These terms refer to, respectively, perceptions of good control (fostering performance), or bad control (encouraging compliance), according to the potential outcome that such a control would represent. While the former will encourage a performance-oriented risk-management culture (in which risks are considered opportunities for progression), the latter is likely to lead to a compliance-oriented risk-management culture (in which risks are perceived as threats) (Gong & Subramaniam, 2020).

This participation from employees in the organization control system is also further emphasized by Tessier and Otley (2012) as one of their divergences from Simons' (1995) levers of control framework, noting that Simons (1995) only recognizes formal interactions from senior management with the lower hierarchical levels of the organization, and does not consider employees as actors of major relevance in the organization control system, as has been broadly argued and evidenced in the MCS and risk-management literature.

When it comes to the implementation of MCSs in PSOs, it is important to note that these "are often administered through coercive control" (Bracci et al., 2021a, p. 4), despite the implication that these two forms of control in PSOs have "shared values around managing risks and use of MCS" (Gong & Subramaniam, 2020, p. 2432) and are yet to be empirically addressed (Gong & Subramaniam, 2020).

Risk management

Risk management is generally accepted to be a value-adding activity for organizations (Godfrey et al., 2009). The usefulness of risk management applies not only to severe unexpected events, such as for example the Covid-19 crisis (Ansell, Sørensen, & Torfing, 2021), in which risk management emerged as a key function for organizations to support their organizational resilience (Metwally & Diab, 2022), but also in more stable environments, with the aim of navigating change (Sax & Torp, 2015). Internally, "risk management is an integral component of a successful organization's strategy and operation" (Burnard & Bhamra, 2011, p. 5584). It supports organizations in pursuit of objectives defined as strategic (Arjaliès & Mundy, 2013), as well as enhancing their capacity to "anticipate and respond to adversity" (Williams et al., 2017, p. 733).

The Covid-19 crisis has highlighted, among others, the risks related to "the importance of financial management, well-being budgeting, the security and stability of supply chain management, indigenous and gender equity, national safety and cyber security, climate change management, and rebuilding public trust in government" (Rana et al., 2022. p. 363), notably for PSOs.

The risk-management paradigm in organizations has been evolving from a silo-based approach to a more holistic one (Gordon et al., 2009), in an attempt to consider systematically all the risks that an organization might face (Sax & Torp, 2015), within the context of an integrated management approach (Power, 2009) and a strategic risk-management perspective (Drew et al., 2006). This new holistic approach has come to be known as enterprise risk management (ERM) (Braumann, 2018). In the literature, ERM assumes the role of "a key resource in the design of risk management systems" (Sax & Torp, 2015, p. 1452). ERM can be characterized as "the main form taken by firms' increasing efforts to organise uncertainty" (Arena et al., 2010, p. 659).

ERM proposes a holistic approach to risk management, following mechanisms for managing known risks, as well as being proactive towards uncertain conditions. The latter are defined as "emergent risks" (Andersen et al., 2014) due to their possible but as yet undefined effects on organizational objectives. ERM leverages the complementarity between Simons' (1995) diagnostic and interactive MCSs. It brings together processes intended to diagnostically manage the effect of known risks. At the same time, in an interactive fashion, ERM encourages managers to gather information about and discuss the impact of unpredictable eventualities that can represent threats or opportunities for the organization (Andersen et al., 2014).

Risk management is of strategic importance for organizations, and for that very reason the whole paradigm of ERM shifts "from a compliance-focused to a strategy-focused model" (Rana et al., 2019b, p. 148). In order for an ERM framework to be successful, it is necessary to ensure that the process of managing risks is strategic in nature (Mikes, 2009), and that it is a practice based on the organizational context, meaning it should consider "the business environment, the stage of [a] firm's growth, and their position in the industry life cycle" (Drew et al., 2006). Despite its strategic nature, ERM puts employees at the centre by empowering them to be part of the risk-management system and therefore creating a culture that supports the development of an appropriate environment for managing risks. Failure to properly consider employees' roles and responsibilities towards managing risk might constrain the success of ERM (Drew et al., 2006). Organizational leaders play a role in the success of ERM, and it has been empirically proven that participative leadership styles enhance the risk-management performance of an organization (Sax & Torp, 2015), by "setting the tone" in risk management (Braumann et al., 2020).

Furthermore. empirical research evidences that "proactive ERM culture and practices can only be triggered when senior leaders move beyond a compliance mindset" (Gong et al., 2022, p. 372). Adding to this argument, it is important to note that recent research concerning ERM has focused increasingly on the responsibilities of organizational leaders with regards to risk management (Barrett, 2022, p. 409).

ERM has its fair share of critics, notably in relation to "the manner in which we trade off the risk of harm associated with an activity, against the benefits that might accrue from that same activity" (Smith & Toft, 1998, p. 7). Power (2009) alerts us to the possibility that the implementation of a risk-management framework without considering its limitations (for example the fact that its embeddedness in the organization is limited) can lead to the establishment of a flawed risk-management system, and an organization that attempts "the risk management of nothing" (2009), the "risk management of everything" (Power, 2004), or the "discipline of everything and nothing" (Braumann, 2018, p. 242). The notion of establishing risk management as part of an organization's strategic management requires thoughtful consideration of the place of risk management in an organization, and this is especially difficult because aligning strategic management and risk management requires the identification of converging points in practices that work with different drives and aim at different objectives.

Although "risk management has been increasingly influential in local public service practices in recent decades" (Ferry & Eckersley, 2022, p. 365), risk management has been given limited attention in public sector settings. Notable exceptions include Smith and Toft (1998), Palermo (2014), Carlsson-Wall et al. (2019), Bracci et al. (2021a, 2021b), Alsharari (2022), and Mahama et al. (2022). Despite some renewed interest in this topic, much work remains to be done. Nevertheless, we now have some evidence of the extent to which senior management in PSO settings have made an attempt to manage pre-identified risks, typically in a "diagnostic" fashion. For example, Rana et al. (2019a) show evidence of partial integration of risk-management and control systems through legislative reform in the Australian public sector which introduced the idea of a "risk culture" that civil servants had to operationalize into risk processes and performance targets (Rana et al., 2019a, p. 40). Similar examples emerged in Birmingham (Woods, 2009) and UK higher education (Power et al., 2009; Soin et al., 2014). Not only have PSOs started realizing the importance of understanding and managing strategic uncertainties (Power, 2007; Power et al., 2009), but they have also started designing inter-active systems to uncover such emergent risks (Scheytt et al., 2006).

Following Hood's "new public management" (1995, p. 93), which characterizes a transfer of public accountability from political to managerial actors with the aim of modernizing the public sector, public organizations are expected (and even required) to be able to control risks, leading to what Hood and Miller called the "new world of generic risk management" (Hood & Miller, 2009, p. 3), and what Palermo (2014) described as "new risk management". This refers to "organisational arrangements that are generic, integrated and holistic, reflecting private sector literature on Enterprise Risk Management (ERM)" applied to PSO settings (Palermo, 2014, p. 339).

This shift of responsibility is very significant for the management of risks in PSOs, particularly given that "research shows that managers tend to underestimate the magnitude and probability of risks" (Rana et al., 2019b, p. 149). Therefore it should be noted that the effective deployment of ERM can mitigate this liability, since the existence of a formalized ERM framework induces participation by senior management in risk management (Sax & Torp, 2015), which is a broadly consensual *sine qua non* condition for the effectiveness of any organization in risk management.

This conceptualization underlines the validity of ERM as a risk-management framework and reinforces the need for it to encompass a "generic, integrated and holistic" (Palermo, 2014, p. 349) management of risks.

It is worth pointing out that although ERM may be applied to both private and public sector organizations, the kinds of risk that each type of organization aims to manage vary greatly. While private organizations may be focused "towards mitigating the risk in sustaining profitability" (Bracci et al., 2021a, p. 1), PSOs should focus on "ensuring an uninterrupted service delivery against internal and external risks and to uphold public accountability" (Bracci et al., 2021a, p. 1).

All in all, the risk-management function appears to have gained strategic prominence in PSOs that have to interface expanding understandings of risk with their strategic priorities (Andersen, 2016). Although there is general agreement and ample empirical evidence that MCSs play a central role in private firms in identifying and managing an inclusive array of idiosyncratic risks and their poten-tial effects on organizational objectives (Bhimani, 2009; Mikes, 2009; Soin & Collier, 2013), with a few notable exceptions (see Power et al., 2009; Woods, 2009), this terrain has remained substantially uncharted with respect to PSOs. Perhaps more importantly, the extant literature does not explicitly theorize the extent to which MCSs design can capture notions of risk. We argue that Simons' (1995) classification of control systems based on their managerial use represents a suitable point of departure for eliciting such understanding.

Risk management through management control systems

Control systems configuration

There are two main perspectives on how to approach management control combinations (Grabner & Moers, 2013), either "as a package" (Malmi & Brown, 2008; O'Connor et al., 2011; Bedford & Malmi, 2015), which builds upon a configuration perspective, or "as a system" (Widener, 2007; Grabner, 2014), which is based on a complementarity perspective. It is, however, clear that individual management control elements can be both independent from each other and interdependent (Bedford, 2020), as well as that there is no perfect MCS configuration and no consensus on how to reach and research MCS optimality (Merchant & Otley, 2020).

Grabner and Moers (2013) further developed this distinction by arguing that a "package" of controls consists of a "complete set of control practices in place, regardless of whether the management control practices are interdependent and/or the design choices take interdependencies into account" (2013, p. 410). A "system", on the other hand, comprises controls that are interdependent by design. This view sets interdependency between practices as the key factor in distinguishing between a "system" or a "package" approach to management control configurations (Choi, 2020; Martin, 2020). Therefore, any management control practice influences, and is influenced by other such practices. Failure to recognize this interdependency may have "the potential for serious model underspecification" (Chenhall, 2003, p. 131). For all intents and purposes, though, the discussion of the configuration of an MCS "as a package" or "as a system" should not limit our understanding of it, because an MCS cannot simply be defined as a package or a system, and the way it is configured depends on its degree of internal consistency (Merchant & Otley, 2020). This means that an internally consistent MCS can be considered a system, while inconsistent practices that do not consider the integration between control practices are likely to be classified as a package.

Going beyond this distinction, Otley (2016) argued that informal processes are an important component of the MCS package, playing a key role in the functionality of the system. This argument has been further advanced by Demartini and Otley (2020), who have leveraged on the loose coupling theory to demonstrate how informal controls can be combined with more formal elements of control in order to increase or decrease the internal consistency of the system to make it better fit a specific context. A higher degree of internal consistency fosters stability, resulting in, for example, increased control and efficiency, while a lower degree of internal consistency fosters flexibility, more specifically, for example, greater adaptability and innovation (Orton & Weick, 1990; Demartini & Otley, 2020).

With regards to the configuration of control systems for effective management of risk, ERM posits that risks shall be managed in a holistic and integrated fashion, so ERM is a systematic control practice that requires the MCS of the organization to be highly (and adequately) integrated, meaning that organizationally speaking, risk management is a "concept of integration rather than a separate function" (Bracci et al., 2021a, p. 6).

Given that the management of risks is in fact a component of MCSs (Chenhall & Euske, 2007; Gordon et al., 2009; Otley, 2016; Braumann et al., 2020; Bracci et al., 2021a), and that MCS design influences the capacity of an organization to effectively manage risks (Ittner & Keusch, 2017; Braumann, 2018; Rana et al., 2019a; Rana et al., 2019b; Braumann et al., 2020; Posch, 2020; Vasileios & Favotto, 2022), we argue that research into risk management in the context of an MCS cannot ignore the systemic and holistic nature of that management. An MCS should therefore be considered as nothing but a system that, as discussed, may have a higher or lower degree of internal consistency.

How do we implement risk management through MCSs?

For Simons (2000), the antecedents of MCSs are strategic uncertainty and risk. In his levers of control framework, Simons (2000) theorized about the tensions that need to be considered in management, noting that "balancing these tensions is at the heart of implementing strategy" (p. 13), underlining that the ultimate purpose of any organization is to create value, and an MCS should serve that purpose. This creation of value is subjective, and it is important to emphasize that diverse stakeholders have different perspectives of what is of value for an organization. Ultimately, Simons' conceptual framework rests on the idea that control of an organization's strategy is effectively achieved by balancing the opposing forces generated by different levers. While each lever has idiosyncratic features, "at the heart of implementing strategy" (Simons, 2000, p. 3) lie the ways in which these levers work together, complement each other, and are ultimately designed to reach equilibrium (see e.g. Kruis et al., 2016). Drawing on Simons (1995), we propose three theoretical standpoints for observing the extent to which equilibrium between opposing control forces is pursued and maintained.

First, belief and boundary systems of control function together to frame the "strategic domain" (Simons 1995, p. 157) of an organization, while diagnostic and interactive control systems work in combination to shape "the implementation and formulation of strategy" (Simons 1995, p. 157). Drawing on this distinction, Widener (2007) argues that belief and boundary systems are considered to address a variety of "strategic" risks and uncertainties, including operational, technological and competitive factors. Meanwhile, diagnostic and interactive controls are primarily used to manage operational risks in daily activities. In a study on private sector organizations, she finds that firms facing higher degrees of operating risks are more likely to use performance measurement systems both diagnostically and interactively. She also finds that organizations are more likely to rely on belief systems, such as mission statements and organizational values, when facing higher levels of strategic risk and uncertainty. Surprisingly, Widener (2007) does not find evidence of the use of boundary systems to mitigate strategic risks, which possibly suggests that mission and value statements are likely to embed and communicate key aspects of an organization's risk culture. At the same time, acceptable boundaries are more likely to be communicated operationally, for instance, by embedding risk metrics into diagnostic controls. This evidence is echoed in public sector research by Ferry et al. (2017, p. 236), who report public managers' expectations of belief systems to be conducive to "an environment in which innovation, risk-taking and creativity can flourish".

Our second theoretical standpoint is that of positive versus negative control systems. Simons (1995) recognizes that two levers of control – belief and interactive systems – create "positive forces", which are deemed to "motivate organisational participants to search creatively and expand opportunity space" (p. 158). Such positive forces are counterbalanced by two "negative systems", that is, boundary and diagnostic controls. Organizations leverage these negative forces to "constrain search behaviour and allocate scarce attention" (p. 158). Empirical research suggests that belief systems are used to foster a culture informed by flexibility and creativity that allows organizations to seize opportunities while being capable of reacting to environmental shocks effectively (Heinicke et al., 2016; Speklé et al., 2017). At the same time, interactive controls direct the organization's attention towards key strategic uncertainties (Posch, 2020). These levers are deemed to produce a positive tension towards awareness and adaptability to strategic risks. In turn, diagnostic and boundary systems are intended to balance such tension. Boundary systems enable managers to communicate to employees identified risks that need to be avoided and they thus "provide structure" (Speklé et al., 2017, p. 73). That is, they compose a framework within which flexibility and creativity can be fostered whilst guaranteeing appropriate behaviour (Heinicke et al., 2016). Diagnostic controls, such as risk-adjusted performance measures, can embed risk considerations in result-oriented MCSs and feedback mechanisms (Posch, 2020). Posch (2020) shows that risk-focused results (i.e. diagnostic control) and risk-related information sharing (i.e. interactive controls) are used in a complementary way and "address each-other weaknesses" (p. 13) to pursue risk effective management in private sector organizations.

Our third theoretical argument is that the discussion concerning the implementation of MCSs in the public sector requires us to acknowledge the need for a balance between the incorporation of a compliance-oriented risk-management culture, which is the natural pathway for PSOs in their current settings, and the change in PSOs to a more performance-oriented type of organization, in order to respond to public and contextual expectations and needs. This change should not in any way represent a decrease in an organization's capacity to manage risks, as argued by Mahama et al. (2022), who propose that "ERM maturity is positively associated with public sector organisations' service delivery performance" (p. 3). We aim precisely with this chapter to provide a solid contribution to the important contemporary discussion concerning "whether PSOs must maintain their coercive style of hierarchy within a strict regulatory environment or whether they should promote an enabling style" (Bracci et al., 2021a, p. 6).

Finally, the empirical work mobilizing the Levers of Control framework is appropriate for both private (Braumann et al., 2020; Posch, 2020) and public organizations (Ferry et al., 2017), as it sheds light on the dynamic interaction between core beliefs regarding risk and risk appetite and the design of diagnostic and interactive controls. Specifically, these studies find a top-down relation between guidelines regarding risk management, organizations established via formal and informal belief systems, and the design and functioning of diagnostic and interactive controls. In addition, this litera-ture highlights the role interactive controls play in pointing out strategic risks via practices including information gathering and face-to-face discussion of unstructured information. The latter suggests a "bottom-up" relationship between these levers of control.

Overall, Simons' conceptual framework and the associated empirical literature (e.g. Mundy, 2010) enable managers to reflect on risk-control relationships from three perspectives: (1) belief and boundaries levers can be seen to influence an organization's risk culture and risk appetite, while diagnostic and interactive controls are likely to be employed to manage operational risks that may hinder strategic implementation. (2) Belief systems and interactive systems can reinforce a culture that embraces to risk. These "positive forces" are compensated by communicating risks to be avoided through boundary systems and risk-adjusted performance measures. (3) Formal and informal belief systems inform the design of diagnostic and interactive control as well as their interaction. Alongside contributing to manage operating risks, interactive control systems are found to play a key role in generating awareness around strategic risks and uncertainties, with implications for the framing of the strategic domain belief and the configuration of boundary systems.

Conclusion

In this chapter, we have argued the case for using Simons' (Simons, 1995) levers of control frame-work as a lens through which to conceptualize the complex interaction between risk and control in public sector settings. Starting from the recognition that PSOs are under increasing pressure to design systems and processes which enable them to identify and manage a wide range of risks and uncer-tainties, we offer a framework within which this interplay can be better understood and thereby allow researchers and practitioners alike to consider a number of key areas. These include the dynamic tension that inevitably exists between creativity and control and the competing risks these entail; the applicability of risk-management tools (for example, ERM) and the way in which these can poten-tially be integrated and retooled within pre-existing management control packages; and the possible limitations that such reliance on management control systems entails for the understanding and man-agement of risk in public sector organizations – a key consideration for the long-term viability and success of a PSO.

Fundamentally, the proposed framework makes a case for the design of an MCS that can manage risk in a holistic way. The levers of control framework is structured on the assumption that the essence of control lies in the successful management of the tensions between innovation and predictability, enablement and coercion, current and future strategy (Simons, 1995). All these are associated with risks and uncertainties of a different nature, and the key MCS design consideration for PSOs is how to strike an acceptable balance between the risks associated with opportunity-seeking behaviours and those associated with "check box" compliance, although acknowledging that risk management integration into PSOs requires "a radical cultural shift and strategy development" (Rana et al., 2022, p. 362).

Perhaps more importantly, the model makes it possible to reconcile operational controls for risk with the guidance offered by systems of belief and core values that underpin PSOs. The framework can thus help distil a comprehensive understanding of the "risk appetite" an organization has. Scholars in this domain have warned against "impoverished" understandings of such a vital construct for managers and regulators (Andreeva et al., 2014). Understanding risk appetite is frequently reliant on making operations controllable or auditable via ad-hoc risk measurement systems. The conceptual map provided by Simons' framework allows for the fact that PSOs are value-laden with respect to risk and it opens up the possibility of conceiving of risk appetite as a "dynamic organizational process involving values as much as metrics" (Power, 2009, p. 849).

Future research should focus on how and to what extent PSOs and private sector organizations manage risks differently, as well as how recent events, such as the pandemic, geopolitical tensions and conflicts; the climate crisis; and the economic recession have increased our understanding of the level of uncertainty to which organizations are exposed and have produced practical changes in organizations' risk-management frameworks.

References

Adler, P. S., & Borys, B. (1996). Two types of bureaucracy: Enabling and coercive. *Administrative Science Quarterly, 41*(1), 61–89.

Alsharari, N. M. (2022). Risk management practices and trade facilitation as influenced by public sector reforms: institutional isomorphism. *Journal of Accounting & Organizational Change, 18*(2), 192–216.

Alvesson, M., & Kärreman, D. (2004). Interfaces of control: Technocratic and socio-ideological control in a global management consultancy firm. *Accounting, Organizations and Society, 29*(3–4), 423–444.

Andersen, T. J. (2016). Introduction: Strategic risk management. In T. J. Andersen (Ed.), *The Routledge companion to strategic risk management* (pp. 21–30). Routledge.

Andersen, T. J., Garvey, M., & Roggi, O. (2014). *Managing risk and opportunity: The governance of strategic risk-taking*. Oxford University Press.

Andreeva, G., Ansell, J., & Harrison, T. (2014). Governance and accountability of public risk. *Financial Accountability & Management, 30*(3), 342–361.

Ansell, C., Sørensen, E., & Torfing, J. (2021). The COVID-19 pandemic as a game changer for public administration and leadership? The need for robust governance responses to turbulent problems. *Public Management Review, 23*(7), 949–960.

Anthony, R. N. (1965). *Planning and control systems: A framework for analysis*. Harvard Business School.

Arena, M., Arnaboldi, M., & Azzone, G. (2010). The organizational dynamics of Enterprise Risk Management. *Accounting, Organizations and Society, 35*(7), 659–675.

Arjaliès, D.-L., & Mundy, J. (2013). The use of management control systems to manage CSR strategy: A levers of control perspective. *Management Accounting Research, 24*(4), 284–300.

Aven, T., & Renn, O. (2009). On risk defined as an event where the outcome is uncertain. *Journal of Risk Research, 12*(1), 1–11.

Barrett, P. (2022). Managing risk for better performance – not taking a risk can actually be a risk. *Public Money & Management, 42*(6), 408–413.

Bedford, D. (2020). Conceptual and empirical issues in understanding management control combinations. *Accounting, Organizations and Society, 86*, 101187.

Bedford, D., & Malmi, T. (2015). Configurations of control: An exploratory analysis. *Management Accounting Research, 27*, 2–26.

Bhimani, A. (2009). Risk management, corporate governance and management accounting: Emerging interdependencies. *Management Accounting Research, 20*(1), 2–5.

Bisbe, J., & Otley, D. (2004). The effects of the interactive use of management control systems on product innovation. *Accounting, Organizations and Society, 29*(8), 709–737.

Boholm, M. (2019). How do Swedish Government agencies define risk? *Journal of Risk Research, 22*(6), 717–734.

Bracci, E., Humphrey, C., Moll, J., & Steccolini, I., 2015. Public sector accounting, accountability and austerity: More than balancing the books? *Accounting, Auditing & Accountability Journal, 28*(6), 878–908.

Bracci, E., Mouhcine, T., Rana, T., & Wickramasinghe, D. (2021a). Risk management and management accounting control systems in public sector organizations: a systematic literature review. *Public Money & Management, 42*(6), 395–402.

Bracci, E., Tallaki, M., Gobbo, G., & Papi, L. (2021b). Risk management in the public sector: A structured literature review. *International Journal of Public Sector Management, 34*(2), 205–223.

Braumann, E. (2018). Analyzing the role of risk awareness in enterprise risk management. *Journal of Management Accounting Research, 30*(2), 241–268.

Braumann, E., Grabner, I., & Posch, A. (2020). Tone from the top in risk management: A complementarity perspective on how control systems influence risk awareness. *Accounting, Organizations and Society, 84*, 101128.

Burnard, K., & Bhamra, R. (2011). Organisational resilience: Development of a conceptual framework for organisational responses. *International Journal of Production Research, 49*(18), 5581–5599.

Carlsson-Wall, M., Kraus, K., Meidell, A., & Tran, P. (2019). Managing risk in the public sector – the interaction between vernacular and formal risk management systems. *Financial Accountability & Management, 35*(1), 3–19.

Chenhall, R. (2003). Management control systems design within its organizational context: findings from contingency-based research and directions for the future. *Accounting, Organizations and Society, 28*(2–3), 127–168.

Chenhall, R., & Euske, K. (2007). The role of management control systems in planned organizational change: An analysis of two organizations. *Accounting Organizations and Society, 32*(7–8), 601–637.

Choi, J. (2020). Studying "and": A perspective on studying the interdependence between management control practices. *Accounting, Organizations and Society, 86*, 101188.

Demartini, M. C., & Otley, D. (2020). Beyond the system vs. package dualism in performance management systems design: A loose coupling approach. *Accounting, Organizations and Society, 86*, 101072.

Drew, S. A., Kelley, P. C., & Kendrick, T. (2006). CLASS: Five elements of corporate governance to manage strategic risk. *Business Horizons, 49*(2), 127–138.

Emery, F. E., & Trist, E. L. (1965). The causal texture of organizational environments. *Human Relations, 18*(1), 21–32.

Ewusi-Mensah, K. (1981). The external organizational environment and its impact on management information systems. *Accounting, Organizations and Society, 6*(4), 301–316.

Ferry, L., Coombs, H., & Eckersley, P. (2017). Budgetary stewardship, innovation and working culture: Identifying the missing ingredient in English and Welsh local authorities' recipes for austerity management. *Financial Accountability & Management, 33*(2), 220–243.

Ferry, L., & Eckersley, P. (2022). Budgeting and governing for deficit reduction in the UK public sector: Act four – risk management arrangements. *Public Money & Management, 42*(6), 365–367.

Gephart, R. P., Van Maanen, J., & Oberlechner, T. (2009). Organizations and risk in late modernity. *Organization Studies, 30*(2–3), 141–155.

Godfrey, P., Merrill, C., & Hansen, J. (2009). The relationship between corporate social responsibility and shareholder value: An empirical test of the risk management hypothesis. *Strategic Management Journal, 30*(4), 425–445.

Gong, M. Z., & Subramaniam, N. (2020). Principal leadership style and school performance: Mediating roles of risk management culture and management control systems use in Australian schools. *Accounting & Finance, 60*(3), 2427–2466.

Gong, Z., Vesty, G., & Subramaniam, N. (2022). Risk as opportunity in schools: An economies of worth perspective. *Public Money & Management, 42*(6), 371–378.

Gordon, L., Loeb, M., & Tseng, C. (2009). Enterprise risk management and firm performance: A contingency perspective. *Journal of Accounting and Public Policy, 28*(4), 301–327.

Grabner, I. (2014). Incentive system design in creativity-dependent firms. *Accounting Review, 89*(5), 1729–1750.

Grabner, I., & Moers, F. (2013). Management control as a system or a package? Conceptual and empirical issues. *Accounting, Organizations and Society, 38*, 407–419.

Heinicke, A., Guenther, T. W., & Widener, S. K. (2016). An examination of the relationship between the extent of a flexible culture and the levers of control system: The key role of beliefs control. *Management Accounting Research, 33*, 25–41.

Holzer, B., & Millo, Y. (2005). From risks to second-order dangers in financial markets: Unintended consequences of risk management systems. *New Political Economy, 10*(2), 223–245.

Hood, C. (1995). The "new public management" in the 1980s: Variations on a theme. *Accounting, Organizations and Society, 20*(2), 93–109.

Hood, C., & Miller, P. (2009). Public service risks: What's distinctive and new? *Risk and Public Services, 1*(1), 2–3.

Hood, C., & Rothstein, H. (2001). Risk regulation under pressure: Problem solving or blame shifting? *Administration & Society, 33*(1), 21–53.

Hood, J., & Young, P. (2005), Risk financing in UK local authorities: Is there a case for risk pooling?, *International Journal of Public Sector Management, 18*(6), 563–578.

Islam, M., & Tareque, M. (2022). Public sector innovation outcome-driven sustainable development in Bangladesh: Applying the dynamic autoregressive distributed lag simulations and Kernel-based regularised least square machine learning algorithm approaches. *Journal of Public Policy, 1–32*

Ittner, C., & Keusch, T. (2017). Incorporating risk considerations into planning and control systems. In M. Woods & P. Linsley (Eds.), *The Routledge companion to accounting and risk* (pp. 150–171). Routledge.

Kominis, G., Dudau, A., Favotto, A., & Gunn, D., 2022. Risk governance through public sector interactive control systems: The intricacies of turning immeasurable uncertainties into manageable risks. *Public Money & Management, 42*(6), 379–387.

Kominis, G., & Dudau, A. I. (2012). Time for interactive control systems in the public sector? The case of the Every Child Matters policy change in England. *Management Accounting Research, 23*(2), 142–155.

Kruis, A.-M., Speklé, R. F., & Widener, S. K. (2016). The levers of control framework: An exploratory analysis of balance. *Management Accounting Research, 32*, 27–44.

Lacey, D., Cuganesan, S., Goode, S., & Jacobs, K. (2012). Celebrating adversity: Inter-organizational dependence and public sector performance reporting in the Australian Federal Police. *Public Administration, 90*(2), 393–411.

Lowe, E. A. (1971). On the idea of a management control system: Integrating accounting and management control. *Journal of Management Studies, 8*(1), 1–12.

Mahama, H., Elbashir, M., Sutton, S., & Arnold, V. (2022). Enabling enterprise risk management maturity in public sector organizations. *Public Money & Management, 42*(6), 403–407.

Malmi, T., & Brown, D. A. (2008). Management control systems as a package – opportunities, challenges and research directions. *Management Accounting Research, 19*(4), 287–300.

Martin, M. A. (2020). An evolutionary approach to management control systems research: A prescription for future research. *Accounting, Organizations and Society, 86*, 101186.

Merchant, K. A., & Otley, D. (2020). Beyond the systems versus package debate. *Accounting, Organizations and Society, 86*, 101185.

Merchant, K. A., & Van der Stede, W. A. (2017). *Management control systems: Performance measurement, evaluation and incentives* (4th ed.). Pearson.

Metwally, A. B. M., & Diab, A. (2022). An institutional analysis of the risk management process during the COVID-19 pandemic: Evidence from an emerging market. *Journal of Accounting & Organizational Change.* ahead-of-print.

Mikes, A. (2009). Risk management and calculative cultures. *Management Accounting Research, 20*(1), 18–40.

Mousavi, S., & Gigerenzer, G. (2014). Risk, uncertainty, and heuristics. *Journal of Business Research, 67*(8), 1671–1678.

Mundy, J. (2010). Creating dynamic tensions through a balanced use of management control systems. *Accounting, Organizations and Society, 35*(5), 499–523.

O'Connor, N. G., Vera-Muñoz, S. C., & Chan, F. (2011). Competitive forces and the importance of management control systems in emerging-economy firms: The moderating effect of international market orientation. *Accounting, Organizations and Society,* 36(4–5), 246–266.

Orton, J., & Weick, K. (1990). Loosely coupled systems: A reconceptualization. *Academy of Management Review, 15*(2), 203–223.

Otley, D. (2016). The contingency theory of management accounting and control: 1980–2014. *Management Accounting Research, 31*, 45–62.

Palermo, T. (2014). Accountability and expertise in public sector risk management: A case study. *Financial Accountability & Management, 30*(3), 322–341.

Posch, A. (2020). Integrating risk into control system design: The complementarity between risk-focused results controls and risk-focused information sharing. *Accounting, Organizations and Society, 86*, 101126.

Power, M. (2004). The risk management of everything. *Journal of Risk Finance, 5*(3), 58–65.

Power, M. (2005). The invention of operational risk. *Review of International Political Economy, 12*(4), 577–599.

Power, M. (2007). *Organized uncertainty: Designing a world of risk management.* Oxford University Press.

Power, M. (2009). The risk management of nothing. *Accounting, Organizations and Society, 34*(6), 849–855.

Power, M., Scheytt, T., Soin, K., & Sahlin, K. (2009). Reputational risk as a logic of organizing in late modernity. *Organization Studies, 30*(2–3), 301–324.

Rana, T., Hoque, Z., & Jacobs, K. (2019a). Public sector reform implications for performance measurement and risk management practice: Insights from Australia. *Public Money & Management, 39*(1), 37–45.

Rana, T., Wickramasinghe, D., & Bracci, E. (2019b). New development: Integrating risk management in management control systems – lessons for public sector managers. *Public Money & Management, 39*(2), 148–151.

Rana, T., Wickramasinghe, D., & Bracci, E. (2022). Editorial: Management accounting and risk management – research and reflections. *Public Money & Management, 42*(6), 361–364.

Rika, N., & Jacobs, K. (2019). Reputational risk and environmental performance auditing: A study in the Australian commonwealth public sector. *Financial Accountability & Management, 35*(2), 182–198.

Sax, J., & Torp, S. S. (2015). Speak up! Enhancing risk performance with enterprise risk management, leadership style and employee voice. *Management Decision, 53*(7), 1452–1468.

Scheytt, T., Soin, K., Sahlin-Andersson, K., & Power, M. (2006). Introduction: Organizations, risk and regulation. *Journal of Management Studies, 43*(6), 1331–1337.

Simons, R. (1991). Strategic orientation and top management attention to control systems. *Strategic Management Journal, 12*(1), 49–62.

Simons, R. (1995). *Levers of control: How managers use innovative control systems to drive strategic renewal.* Harvard Business School Press.

Simons, R. (1999). How risky is your company? *Harvard Business Review, 77*, 85–95.

Simons, R. (2000). *Performance measurement and control systems for implementing strategy.* Prentice Hall.

Sitkin, S. B., & Pablo, A. L. (1992). Reconceptualizing the determinants of risk behavior. *Academy of Management Review, 17*(1), 9–38.

Smith, D., & Toft, B. (1998). Risk and crisis management in the public sector: Editorial: Issues in public sector risk management. *Public Money & Management, 18*(4), 7–10.

Soin, K., & Collier, P. (2013). Risk and risk management in management accounting and control. *Management Accounting Research, 24*(2), 82–87.

Soin, K., Huber, C., & Wheatley, S. (2014). Management control and uncertainty: Risk management in universities. In D. Otley & K. Soin (Eds.), *Management controls and uncertainty* (pp. 178–192). Palgrave Macmillan

Speklé, R. F., Van Elten, H. J., & Widener, S. K. (2017). Creativity and control: A paradox – evidence from the levers of control framework. *Behavioral Research in Accounting, 29*(2), 73–96.

Teece, D., Peteraf, M., & Leih, S. (2016). Dynamic capabilities and organizational agility: Risk, uncertainty, and strategy in the innovation economy. *California Management Review, 58*(4), 13–35.

Terreberry, S. (1968). The evolution of organizational environments. *Administrative Science Quarterly, 12*(4), 590.

Tessier, S., & Otley, D. (2012). A conceptual development of Simons' Levers of Control framework. *Management Accounting Research, 23*(3), 171–185.

Vasileios, G., & Favotto, A. (2022). New development: Management control for emergent risks in the public sector – a levers of control perspective. *Public Money & Management, 42*(6), 417–419.

Widener, S. K. (2007). An empirical analysis of the levers of control framework. *Accounting, Organizations and Society, 32*(7–8), 757–788.

Williams, T., Gruber, D., Sutcliffe, K., Shepherd, D., & Zhao, E. (2017). Organizational response to adversity: Fusing crisis management and resilience research streams. *Academy of Management Annals, 11*(2), 733–769.

Woods, M. (2009). A contingency theory perspective on the risk management control system within Birmingham City Council. *Management Accounting Research, 20*(1), 69–81.

14

FINANCIAL VULNERABILITY AND RISK DISCLOSURES IN AUSTRALIAN UNIVERSITIES

Jodie Moll

Introduction

This chapter examines the situation facing universities since the Covid-19 pandemic began. In 2019, reports were received about the coronavirus disease (Covid-19) in Wuhan, China. In January 2020, the World Health Association declared Covid-19 a global public health emergency, and they characterized it as a pandemic in March that year. The Australian government's response was swift. It shut its borders to travellers from mainland China on 1 February 2020 and to all international travellers on 20 March 2020 (Anonymous,2020; Deloitte, 2019). Some states also imposed lockdowns and introduced social distancing measures to curb the spread of the virus. In the months that followed, headlines like this appeared in the media:

"Top Unis Face $1.2bn coronavirus hit".

Dodd et al., 2020

"From boom to gloom: it'll be a long, difficult road back to prosperity".

Foo, 2020

In response to government measures introduced because of the pandemic, Universities Australia forecast a revenue reduction of $A 16 billion between 2020 and 2023. This reduction is mainly because of foreign student income, which was expected to fall primarily due to international border closures. In Australian universities, foreign student income has become a critical component of income, especially since there is a lack of regulation of international student tuition fees (Babones, 2019). Today, foreign student income is about $A 37 billion a year (Department of Education, Skills and Employment 2021c; Smyth et al., 2020, p. 13; Wei & Gekara, 2022). This dependence on international income is perhaps most noticeable when we compare the enrolment of students in the 1990s with today. In 1990, 24,998 international students were enrolled in higher education institutions, compared to 460,068 domestic students (Department of Education, Training and Youth Affairs, 2001). Today, there are 469,248 international students, compared to 1,042,345 domestic students enrolled in Australian institutions (Department of Education, Skills and Employment, 2022; Department of Education, Skills and Employment 2021a). About one-third (131,442 students) of international students enrolled in Australian higher education institutions come from China. However, in some states, such as NSW,

DOI: 10.4324/9781003295945-19

the number of students from China is much higher. Many, including the NSW Audit Office, have long argued that institutions that have taken this approach and have not diversified their revenue sources put themselves at financial risk (Babones, 2019; Bolton, 2019; Primrose, 2019), especially given emerging geopolitical challenges (Guthrie et al., 2022).

Before the pandemic, questions were raised about the sector's financial health, especially considering the neoliberal agenda of successive governments that focused on competition and corporate-style management (Christopher & Sarens, 2015; Croucher & Lacy, 2020; Guthrie et al., 2022; Martin-Sardesai et al., 2021; Parker, 2011; Parker, 2020). Many universities have become large commercial enterprises looking to provide mass global education to boost their profits. Evaluation and accountability have become the lifeblood of these organizations (Jarvis, 2022).

Since the Covid-19 pandemic began, universities in Australia have been forced to rethink their operations. Although the response of individual institutions to the pandemic and immediate financial challenges has been diverse, a common strategy has been to cut jobs, with about 17,300 jobs made redundant in the sector in 2020 (Universities Australia, 2021). Many universities have also imposed a freeze on recruitment. Other strategies have been to move courses online, and sometimes, for the first time, they have been made available to international students studying abroad, increasing student enrolment choice (c.f. Audit Office of New South Wales, 2022).

New risks are associated with such changes. Academics working in institutions that have used such measures have an added challenge of maintaining the quality of delivery and student experience, especially when staff–student ratios have changed. Many academics may also be inexperienced in facilitating learning and developing assessments online, requiring them to learn new skills. One question to consider is how the time needed to develop skills for online teaching has affected research and, in turn, institutions' ranking. Existing workload models may not consider these new tasks, leading to employee burnout (Ross, 2022c). Online delivery of courses also raises questions about the fees set, particularly since teaching costs can be reduced in an online environment. Students may not want to pay the same fees as when the delivery mode was in person and permitted interaction between students and teachers. Some universities have cut courses. Some universities now offer shorter courses. In some institutions, managers took voluntary pay cuts. They also delayed salary increases for others. There have also been reports that uUniversity leaders have delayed capital works. They cut travel budgets. Some universities have tried to improve their financial resilience by selling, leasing or repurposing surplus land and buildings.

This chapter has two objectives: first, to foster an understanding of the financial impact of the health crisis to determine whether it has been as catastrophic as university leaders predicted. Previous studies, such as Irvine and Ryan (2019), which examined the sector's financial health before Covid-19, expressed concerns that the university sector was at risk of becoming vulnerable if it did not diversify its income. Guthrie et al. (2022) repeated the study by Irvine and Ryan et al. (2022), using the data in university financial statements from 2008 to 2020 to assess the sector's financial health. They also added Merton's default probability measures to evaluate financial health. Although they discovered significant revenue increases over this period, they also found that spending such as non-academic salaries, building and infrastructure, and general expenditures have risen. They propose three future scenarios (i.e. optimistic, probable and pessimistic) and consider how universities could react to make them more resilient. The optimistic scenario proposed that student numbers might return to 78 per cent of the pre-Covid-19 numbers by 2030. The probable scenario was that student numbers might be 52 per cent of 2019 by 2030. The pessimistic scenario was that they might be 38 per cent of student numbers by 2030. They argue that

all three require vice-chancellors to grapple with overreliance on international onshore student fees and face the triple threat of increasing tensions with China, rising competition with the quality and number of Chinese universities, and unsustainable undergraduate operating and funding model from the Commonwealth Government. (p. 2227)

They also suggest short-term measures such as developing micro-credential programmes in fintech, data visualization and sustainable investment expertise.

Second, the chapter contributes to the literature that focuses on risk framing and the communication of risk information (Power, 2007). Risk communication is required to ensure stakeholders understand risk management decisions (Hardy et al., 2020). Annual reports act as accountability instruments since management must publicly disclose their material risk exposures in these documents. Risk communication can also serve other purposes, such as persuading stakeholders to change their behaviour, including developing a state of preparedness (Hardy et al., 2020). For instance, risk disclosure can help other institutions identify risk objects, calculate the probability of risks occurring, and stress-test various responses. Disclosing information about their risk practices is one-way institutions can prepare for what comes next and benefit the entire sector.

A small set of papers focusing on the importance of Annual Reports in risk reporting already exists (Abraham & Cox, 2007; Guthrie et al., 2020; Linsley & Shrives, 2006). Prior research has found risk reporting in Annual Reports to be inadequate. For example, studies investigating risk reporting practices in countries such as Italy and the UK have found that risk reporting is of poor quality. Abraham and Cox (2007, p. 244) argue, for example, that the information published in Annual Reports is too short and relies on language that is "boilerplate", meaning that risk disclosures are not sufficiently detailed for decision-making by stakeholders.

Two recent studies on risk reporting in the higher education sector make similar observations. Carnegie et al. (2021a) examined the extent to which the university's Annual Reports disclosed the organization's financial risks. This study analysed the 2019 Annual Reports of eight public universities in Victoria, Australia. Although the publication of these reports was often delayed, and the Australian government had instantiated measures to curb the spread of Covid-19, Carnegie et al. (2021a) found that universities disclosed little information in the reports about the impact of Covid-19 on students, staff and operations. In a subsequent article, Carnegie et al. (2021b) extended their review to include the 2019 Annual Reports of the 37 public universities. The lack of risk disclosures in these reports from institutions dependent on international student income led Carnegie et al. (2021b, unpaged) to the conclusion that reports in this sector provide "fake accountability" and "distorted transparency". This lack of disclosure is surprising, given that there is a Voluntary Code of Best Practice for the Governance of Australian Public Universities in Australia that many universities have endorsed. The Code of Best Practice states that the university's Annual Report should "include a report on risk management within the organisation" (see section 11).

In this chapter, we expand on the studies of Carnegie et al. (2021a; 2021b), examining the risk disclosures of 37 public universities in the 2019 and 2020 Annual Reports to deepen our understanding of the risk work undertaken by universities in the current situation.

We divide the rest of the chapter into five sections. In the next section, we discuss the research method. A look at the revenues of public universities follows this. In particular, we pay close attention to any change in international student revenues between 2019 and 2020. In section 4, we consider the financial performance of these public universities since Covid-19 began. Section 5 focuses on the risks disclosed by universities in the 2019 and 2020 Annual Reports. We consider the results in the last section and suggest future research areas.

Research method

The primary data for this chapter are the 2019 and 2020 Annual Reports of 37 public universities in Australia. We downloaded each institution's Annual Reports from its particular website. Some universities publish two volumes of Annual Reports every year. We include both volumes in the data set analysed. Most Annual Reports are over 100 pages, with some over 200 pages. We performed the analysis in two phases. First, we retrieved 2019 and 2020 revenue and financial performance information from the 2020 Annual Reports. Next, we conducted a content analysis focused on risk disclosures in the Annual Reports.

We used Provalis Wordstat 9, content analysis and text mining software to analyse the reports. The use of the software helped ensure that data was consistently analysed (Krippendorff, 2019). Keyword and phrase retrieval was based on both sentences and paragraphs, and focused on risk, the Covid-19 pandemic, international students, budget and cybersecurity. We identified these search terms based on Carnegie's studies (2021a, 2021b) and from reading the risk-related sentences in the Annual Reports. We also added variations on terms. For instance, "risk" included "risks". There was also a search for the co-occurrence of the Covid-19 pandemic and for each of these terms. Besides a count, the software identifies the sentence or paragraph containing the keywords or phrases. We provide some excerpts to show the types of disclosures. We also evaluated the differences in reporting between the years. One limitation of the text mining approach is that we have not identified when headings and words used in the table of contents contain the keywords or phrases, and these are included in the count.

Findings

We structure the findings section into three parts. First, we analyse the revenue and income of universities to understand the financial impact of the Covid-19 pandemic on specific higher education institutions. Next, we consider each university's financial performance. Finally, we review disclosures in the Annual Reports related to risk work.

Revenue

In Australia, the Higher Education Support Act (2003) regulates the provision of funding to public universities. Part of the funding universities receive for domestic students is allocated to student places through the Commonwealth Grant Scheme. When government provides funding, it considers delivery costs in various areas. Domestic students are also required to pay tuition fees, and the amount they pay depends on their field of study. In 2021, law, accounting and commerce students could expect to pay up to $14,500 to study, compared to those in dentistry and medicine, who can expect to pay up to $11,300 (Department of Education, Skills, and Employment, 2021d). Many students benefit from government help through the Higher Education Loan Programme.

Other grants are also available to universities for various initiatives, including equal opportunities and research. In terms of international fees paid by students, universities determine the fees they want to charge. Table 14.1 shows the proportion of international students enrolled at public universities between 2017 and 2020. The difference between the number of international students and the total number students in 2020 was insignificant; it was more than in 2018 and 2017.

Table 14.1 Students undertaking higher education at Australian higher education providers*

Year	2017	2018	2019	2020
Total Number of Students	1,513,383	1,562,520	1,609,798	1,622,867
International Students	431,438	479,987	521,948	489,234

* Includes all higher education providers, not just public-funded ones.

Source: Adapted from 2020 Student Time Series. Available from www.dese.gov.au/higher-education-statistics/resources/2020-student-summary-time-series

Table 14.2 shows the revenue and income of universities for 2019 and 2020. Of the 37 universities in Australia, 30 (81 per cent) reported a decline in revenue, with the largest, Australian National University (ANU), at 15.3 per cent. The average total reduction in revenue in the higher education sector was about 3.41 per cent in 2020 (see Table 14.1). By comparison, Charles Darwin University reported the highest percentage growth in revenue, at 13.83 per cent, of the institutions reporting

Table 14.2 Revenue and income by university*

Institution	2019	2020	Change $'000	Change %
The University of Sydney	2,740,320	2,644,430	-95,890	-3.50%
Australian Catholic University	549,703	548,139	-1,564	-0.28%
Australian National University	1,531,979	1,297,514	-234,465	-15.30%
Central Queensland University	487,171	449,963	-37,208	-7.64%
Charles Darwin University	270,849	308,305	37,456	13.83%
Charles Sturt University	616,811	569,210	-47,601	-7.72%
Curtin University	969,944	902,715	-67,229	-6.93%
Deakin University	1,320,511	1,224,003	-96,508	-7.31%
Edith Cowan University	481,528	477,218	-4,310	-0.90%
Federation University	376,550	343,309	-33,241	-8.83%
Flinders University	527,561	532,198	4,637	0.88%
Griffith University	1,031,828	967,763	-64,065	-6.21%
James Cook University	504,079	476,465	-27,614	-5.48%
La Trobe University	867,426	786,186	-81,240	-9.37%
Macquarie University	1,027,337	974,088	-53,249	-5.18%
Monash University	2,798,746	2,705,723	-93,023	-3.32%
Murdoch University	395,659	378,671	-16,988	-4.29%
Queensland University of Technology	1,160,763	1,054,164	-106,599	-9.18%
RMIT	1,379,547	1,308,399	-71,148	-5.16%
Southern Cross University	291,286	314,245	22,959	7.88%
Swinburne University	772,654	745,154	-27,500	-3.56%
University of Adelaide	971,780	976,906	5,126	0.53%
University of Canberra	314,235	312,402	-1,833	-0.58%
University of Melbourne	2,853,644	2,664,107	-189,537	-6.64%
University of New England	341,209	347,924	6,715	1.97%
University of New South Wales	2,235,490	2,162,167	-73,323	-3.28%
University of Newcastle	833,942	794,924	-39,018	-4.68%
University of Queensland	2,194,156	2,119,635	-74,521	-3.40%
University of South Australia	684,676	696,051	11,375	1.66%
University of Southern Queensland	327,359	344,972	17,613	5.38%
University of Sunshine Coast	310,157	321,578	11,421	3.68%
University of Tasmania	769,330	712,927	-56,403	-7.33%
University of Technology, Sydney	1,097,766	1,058,767	-38,999	-3.55%
University of Western Australia	1,057,625	968,870	-88,755	-8.39%
University of Wollongong	686,995	620,343	-66,652	-9.70%
Victoria University	484,406	474,294	-10,112	-2.09%
Western Sydney University	906,376	887,897	-18,479	-2.04%

* Note this is not based on the consolidated income figures, as changes in student fee income affect the parent company's operations.

Source: Based on the revenue disclosed in the Comprehensive Income Statement, Institutional Annual Reports 2020.

improvements. Although not all universities reported financial losses, the decision by universities to cut costs was widespread. For example, Charles Darwin (2021, p. 51) noted the need to conserve the budget. Measures they used included deferring staff

recruitment and making other structural changes to improve their sustainability.

Of total income, Australian government grants were the largest source of revenue in 2020, at about A$12.1 billion, an increase of 1.2 per cent compared to 2019 (Department of Education, Skills and Employment 2021b).

International student income represents about A$9.2 billion of the A$34.6 billion income in the sector. Table 14.2 shows the proportion of income from international student fees. In 11 universities, international student income accounts for over 30 per cent of their income. Table 14.3 compares the change in the income earned by international fees in 2020 and 2019. Eleven universities have seen a decline in international student income of over 10 per cent.

University financial performance

An analysis of the university's net operating results shows that 14 universities reported a deficit for their operations in 2020. Macquarie University, University of Wollongong and Central Queensland University reported the biggest changes in net operating results. Although not all Annual Reports for 2021 were available when this chapter was written, there is evidence of significant improvements in the financial situation at many universities since that year. For example, in their review of NSW Annual Reports, the Audit Office of New South Wales (2022, p. 10) reported that at least in this state, all ten universities had reported positive net results in 2021 compared to the four in 2020. In Queensland and Victoria, all but one university in each state made a profit in 2021 (Auditor General's Office of Victoria, 2022; Queensland Audit Office, 2022).

Risk work

This section considers universities' risk work that is disclosed in the 2019 and 2020 Annual Reports. In the reports, universities identified multiple factors or "risk objects" impacting their financial health, including uncertainty about government support and funding, market competition and government measures introduced in response to the Covid-19 pandemic. Statements like the following that UTS included in their 2020 Annual Report were common:

> This updated risk assessment indicated UTS continued to face the significant challenge of having a resilient business model with a diversity of markets, revenue streams and delivery methods to cope with high impact, low likelihood risk events (e.g. pandemic), changes in government policy, aggressive market competition and opportunities to tap into new or emerging markets.
>
> *UTS, 2021, p. 29*

Universities including ANU, Charles Sturt University, Deakin University, Flinders University, Griffith University, Macquarie University, QUT, RMIT, the University of Sydney, UNE University of Newcastle, University of Woolongong, UQ, Victoria, Western Sydney University and UTS also identified cybersecurity as a potential risk affecting their operations.

Regarding changes in their risk work, some universities now claim that they review their risk management strategies more frequently. For instance, Victoria University (2021) reported,

> In 2020, in light of the Covid-19 pandemic and changes in the operating environment, strategic and enterprise risks were more frequently reviewed and revised, based on extensive

Table 14.3 International student fees income as a proportion of revenue*

Institution	2020 Total Revenue $'000	2020 International Student Fees $'000	Fees/ Total Revenue %
James Cook University	476,465	73,884	16%
The University of Sydney	2,644,430	1,105,200	42%
Australian Catholic University	548,139	78,678	14%
Australian National University	1,297,514	248,071	19%
Central Queensland University	449,963	122,254	27%
Charles Darwin University	308,305	50,619	16%
Charles Sturt University	569,210	113,503	20%
Curtin University	902,715	160,909	18%
Deakin University	1,224,003	395,830	32%
Edith Cowan University	477,218	119,767	25%
Federation University	343,309	125,225	36%
Flinders University	532,198	102,395	19%
Griffith University	967,763	189,571	20%
La Trobe University	786,186	159,238	20%
Macquarie University	974,088	301,880	31%
Monash University	2,705,723	982,634	36%
Murdoch University	378,671	80,621	21%
Queensland University of Technology	1,054,164	221,204	21%
RMIT	1,308,399	454,396	35%
Southern Cross University	314,245	98,320	31%
Swinburne University	745,154	150,054	20%
University of Adelaide	976,906	254,148	26%
University of Canberra	312,402	69,529	22%
University of Melbourne	2,664,107	845,596	32%
University of New England	347,924	28,187	8%
University of New South Wales	2,162,167	671,350	31%
University of Newcastle	794,924	113,709	14%
University of Queensland	2,119,635	648,903	31%
University of South Australia	696,051	150,019	22%
University of Southern Queensland	344,972	48,706	14%
University of Sunshine Coast	321,578	46,306	14%
University of Tasmania	712,927	130,101	18%
University of Technology, Sydney	1,058,767	405,079	38%
University of Western Australia	968,870	139,737	14%
University of Wollongong	620,343	144,558	23%
Victoria University	474,294	98,973	21%
Western Sydney University	887,897	148,785	17%

Source: Based on the revenues disclosed in the annual income statement, institutional Annual Reports 2020, and course fees and fees as per the notes of the financial statements.

consultation within the university, and reported to the Compliance, Audit and Risk Committee and Council itself. Where appropriate, new risks were identified and included. (p. 56)

The University of the Sunshine Coast (2021, p. 43) also reported that "a more dynamic approach to responding to risks was also needed given the identification and management of risks associated with COVID-19".

Others explained that their approach was to consult more extensively to ensure that risks were identified and strategies developed in response. For instance, the University of Melbourne Annual Report comments: "The 2020 annual review of the University Risk Register involved iterative consultations with responsible owners and stakeholders to ensure that all key risks due to COVID-19 were appropriately identified, assessed and mitigated" (University of Melbourne, 2021, p. 109).

Some universities, such as Central Queensland University (CQU), have detailed their practices. For instance, CQU (2021, p. 21) explained that they had identified 36 key risks that "had the potential to cause significant disruption to CQU's operations during the height of the pandemic event and the immediate financial challenges". They also discussed their risk register and risk appetite in the narrative sections of the report.

Like Carnegie et al. (2021a), we analysed the locations of Covid-19 disclosures. Table 14.6 is an adaptation of Carnegie et al. (2021a). We examine the 2019 and 2020 Annual Reports and show in Table 14.6 the parts of the Annual Reports where universities made Covid-19 risk disclosures. As indicated in Table 14.6, 18 of the Chancellor Statements in the Annual Reports commented on Covid-19 risks compared with 21 Vice Chancellor Statements. The chancellor and vice chancellor issued a joint statement about Covid-19 in 13 of the 2020 and 2019 Annual Reports.

Next, we considered the frequency (See Table 14.7) of risk and risk-related terms like Covid-19, international students, budget and cyber-security. Aside from COVID-19, which increased in usage from 287 to 4107, there was no notable change in the use of other words. We looked for the co-occurrence of risks and Covid-19 in university disclosures. In 2020, there was a significant increase in disclosures related to the Covid-19 pandemic. But there is little change in other risk discussions. For example, the co-occurrence of the terms "risk" and "international students" remained unchanged in the 2019 and 2020 reports. There was also little change between the 2019 and 2020 reports in disclosures focused on risk and international students.

We have included risk and cybersecurity in our search for co-occurrences, as these terms were identified in the risk disclosures in many reports. Universities have become more dependent on information technology because of state border lockdowns. Many now offer more online courses, increasing the possibility of cyberthreats.

Table 14.8 analysed the text in the Annual Reports focusing on the co-occurrence of risk and identified types of risks. As stated in the table, the number of sentences and paragraphs, including both risk and Covid-19, increased in the 2020 Annual Report compared with 2019. We found little difference in the frequency of reporting of most other identified risks in the 2019 and 2020 Annual Reports.

Finally, we investigated the disclosure of specific risk frameworks that provide the architecture for risk work at universities, including ISO31000, Enterprise Risk Management Frameworks and the Code of Best Practice for the Governance of Australian Public Universities (see Table 14.9).

ISO31000 Risk Management provides guidelines for organizations to adapt to their circumstances to identify and manage risk objects. However, it is not intended to provide certification for organizations. Enterprise Risk Management Frameworks are designed to help organizations plan and manage how they will achieve their risk management goals. Using these types of frameworks can give stakeholders confidence that they are ready to respond to environmental changes. Deakin University (2020), for example, explained the importance of such frameworks in the following terms, adoption of ISO31000 "enables the executive to understand, manage and satisfactorily control risk exposures" (p. 55).

The Code of Best Practice for the Governance of Australian Public Universities states in section 11 that "the annual report of a university should include a report on risk management within the organisation".

Table 14.4 Total international student fees*

Institution	2019 $'000	2020 $'000	Change $'000	Change %
James Cook University	82,350	73,884	-8,466	-10.28%
The University of Sydney	1,061,900	1,105,200	43,300	4.08%
Australian Catholic University	75,505	78,678	3,173	4.20%
Australian National University	328,942	248,071	-80,871	-24.59%
Central Queensland University	175,961	122,254	-53,707	-30.52%
Charles Darwin University	37,896	50,619	12,723	33.57%
Charles Sturt University	154,394	113,503	-40,891	-26.48%
Curtin University	166,046	160,909	-5,137	-3.09%
Deakin University	412,658	395,830	-16,828	-4.08%
Edith Cowan University	116,744	119,767	3,023	2.59%
Federation University	151,609	125,225	-26,384	-17.40%
Flinders University	98,577	102,395	3,818	3.87%
Griffith University	193,891	189,571	-4,320	-2.23%
La Trobe University	203,927	159,238	-44,689	-21.91%
Macquarie University	323,688	301,880	-21,808	-6.74%
Monash University	1,003,980	982,634	-21,346	-2.13%
Murdoch University	84,002	80,621	-3,381	-4.02%
Queensland University of Technology	245,423	221,204	-24,219	-9.87%
RMIT	522,502	454,396	-68,106	-13.03%
Southern Cross University	73,996	98,320	24,324	32.87%
Swinburne University	180,009	150,054	-29,955	-16.64%
University of Adelaide	254,730	254,148	-582	-0.23%
University of Canberra	67,216	69,529	2,313	3.44%
University of Melbourne	904,733	845,596	-59,137	-6.54%
University of New England	27,923	28,187	264	0.95%
University of New South Wales	767,565	671,350	-96,215	-12.54%
University of Newcastle	121,921	113,709	-8,212	-6.74%
University of Queensland	678,865	648,903	-29,962	-4.41%
University of South Australia	147,047	150,019	2,972	2.02%
University of Southern Queensland	46,724	48,706	1,982	4.24%
University of Sunshine Coast	63,857	46,306	-17,551	-27.48%
University of Tasmania	139,636	130,101	-9,535	-6.83%
University of Technology, Sydney	366,814	405,079	38,265	10.43%
University of Western Australia	151,018	139,737	-11,281	-7.47%
University of Wollongong	179,971	144,558	-35,413	-19.68%
Victoria University	107,865	98,973	-8,892	-8.24%
Western Sydney University	163,456	148,785	-14,671	-8.98%

* Note this is not based on consolidated income figures, as the parent company's operations are affected by changes in student fee income.

Source: Based on the revenue disclosed in the comprehensive income statement, institutional Annual Reports 2020.

Concluding comments

This chapter has considered universities' financial position and risk management disclosures. The Annual Reports show the Covid-19 pandemic to have significantly influenced many universities' financial positions. Although the Annual Reports suggest that many experienced financial challenges during the Covid-19 pandemic, recent reports suggest this to be short term, and most are now reporting positive financial positions (Forsyth, 2022; Ross, 2022b). Many institutions' improvement

Table 14.5 Net operating result*

Institution	2019	2020	Change $'000	Change %
The University of Sydney	177856	106563	-71293	-40.08%
Australian Catholic University	45034	31374	-13660	-30.33%
Australian National University	316502	-17699	-334201	-105.59%
Central Queensland University	3413	-33172	-36585	-1071.93%
Charles Darwin University	-8762	42806	51568	-588.54%
Charles Sturt University	5904	18986	13082	221.58%
Curtin University	82,054	-1,098	-83152	-101.34%
Deakin University	107345	32112	-75233	-70.09%
Edith Cowan University	36491	23662	-12829	-35.16%
Federation University	36724	3871	-32853	-89.46%
Flinders University	25080	37795	12715	50.70%
Griffith University	53213	-5057	-58270	-109.50%
James Cook University	10383	13953	3570	34.38%
La Trobe University	19338	-51450	-70788	-366.06%
Macquarie University	2041	-52723	-54764	-2683.19%
Monash University	229999	267277	37278	16.21%
Murdoch University	19996	-10961	-30957	-154.82%
Queensland University of Technology	88391	25218	-63173	-71.47%
RMIT	43088	-78773	-121861	-282.82%
Southern Cross University	15787	-2780	-18567	-117.61%
Swinburne University	33748	-35666	-69414	-205.68%
University of Adelaide	42947	40816	-2131	-4.96%
University of Canberra	19207	29363	10156	52.88%
University of Melbourne	320485	178222	-142263	-44.39%
University of New England	-4845	-18995	-14150	292.05%
University of New South Wales	30584	-24167	-54751	-179.02%
University of Newcastle	64974	5861	-59113	-90.98%
University of Queensland	131810	82928	-48882	-37.09%
University of South Australia	20939	21085	146	0.70%
University of Southern Queensland	5580	12580	7000	125.45%
University of Sunshine Coast	19909	24085	4176	20.98%
University of Tasmania	72371	18019	-54352	-75.10%
University of Technology	27599	-43075	-70674	-256.07%
University of Western Australia	115422	58089	-57333	-49.67%
University of Wollongong	3400	-52780	-56180	-1652.35%
Victoria University	30336	5724	-24612	-81.13%
Western Sydney University	19084	21979	2895	15.17%

* Note this is not based on the consolidated income figures, as the parent company's operations are affected by changes in student fee income.

Source: University Annual Reports 2020.

in financial position can partly be traced back to international students returning to Australia faster than expected (Ross, 2022a). So what is the future for this sector and the organizations that have made significant cuts during the crisis?

Although we do not know what will happen in the future, it is plausible that the higher education sector will face sustained periods of fiscal austerity because the government must redirect public funding to meet the ongoing and rising costs in the health sector (OECD, 2021). If this happens,

Table 14.6 Locations of 2019 and 2020 annual report Covid-19 disclosures

Institution	Year	Parts of Annual Report where COVID-19 disclosures were made				
		CS	VCS	MCVC	OS	NND/TNN
James Cook University	2019	NA	NA	No	No	0/29
	2020	NA	NA	Yes	Yes	2/29
The University of Sydney	2019	NA	NA	No	Yes	32/34
	2020	NA	NA	Yes	Yes	2, 22, 34/35
Australian Catholic University	2019	NA	No	NA	Yes	1/24
	2020	Yes	Yes	NA	Yes	1/24
Australian National University	2019	NA	No	NA	No	summary of significant accounting policies, 0/6
	2020	NA	Yes	NA	Yes	1.2F/6
Central Queensland University	2019	No	No	NA	No	0/32
	2020	Yes	Yes	NA	Yes	1, 3.2, 5, 6, 7, 8, 9, 17/31
Charles Sturt University	2019	No	No	NA	Yes	15/15
	2020	Yes	Yes	NA	Yes	1, 19/38
Charles Darwin University	2019	NA	NA	No	Yes	41/45
	2020	NA	NA	Yes	Yes	1/40
Curtin University	2019	No	Yes	NA	No	29/31
	2020	Yes	Yes	NA	Yes	1/31
Deakin University	2019	No	No	NA	No	20/27
	2020	No	Yes	NA	Yes	1, 7, 21, 22, 26/28
Edith Cowan University	2019	No	No	NA	No	31/39
	2020	Yes	Yes	NA		1/37
Federation University	2019	No	No	NA	No	29/29
	2020	Yes	Yes	NA	Yes	30/30
Flinders University	2019	Yes	No	NA	Yes	38/45
	2020	Yes	Yes	NA	Yes	34, 45/45
Griffith University	2019	NA	NA	Yes	Yes	22/27
	2020	NA	NA	Yes	Yes	1, 4, 7, 14, 16, 22/27
La Trobe University	2019	No	No	NA	No	29/35
	2020	No	Yes	NA	Yes	Notes "About this report", 10, 14, 17, 27, 29, 32/34
Macquarie University	2019	NA	No	NA	No	30/35
	2020	NA	Yes	NA	Yes	1, 2, 3, 4, 21, 31/36
Monash University	2019	NA	Yes	NA	No	35/43
	2020	NA	Yes	NA	Yes	1, 7, 8, 10, 11, 12, 14, 16, 17, 19, 20,21, 25, 35, 44/46
Murdoch University	2019	No	No	NA	No	25/32
	2020	Yes	Yes	NA	Yes	1/32
Queensland University of Technology	2019	NA	NA	No	Yes	1/29
	2020	NA	NA	Yes	Yes	1, 2, 4, 8,15, 17,18, 20/29
RMIT	2019	No	No	NA	No	38/44
	2020	Yes	Yes	NA	Yes	1,28, 39/45
Southern Cross University	2019	NA	NA	NA	Yes	27/32
	2020	NA	NA	NA	No	1,19, 27/32

(*Continued*)

Table 14.6 (Continued)

Institution	Year	Parts of Annual Report where COVID-19 disclosures were made				
		CS	VCS	MCVC	OS	NND/TNN
Swinburne University	2019	No	No	NA	No	20/28
	2020	Yes	Yes	NA	Yes	10,12,22,30/30
University of Adelaide	2019	No	No	NA	Yes	23/37
	2020	Yes	Yes	NA	Yes	25/39
University of Canberra	2019	No	No	NA	No	28/32
	2020	No	Yes	NA	Yes	1/32
University of Melbourne	2019	No	No	NA	No	27/34
	2020	Yes	Yes	NA	Yes	1, 33/34
University of New England	2019	No	No	NA	Yes	14, 30/35
	2020	No	Yes	NA	Yes	34/39
University of New South Wales	2019	NA	NA	Yes	Yes	40/41
	2020	NA	NA	Yes	Yes	2, 41/42
University of Newcastle	2019	NA	NA	No	No	28/32
	2020	NA	NA	Yes	Yes	1, 9, 11, 14, 15, 29, 31/32
University of Queensland	2019	NA	No	NA	No	33/34
	2020	NA	Yes	NA	Yes	1, 3, 20/34
University of South Australia	2019	No	No	NA	Yes	34/38
	2020	Yes	No	NA	Yes	10, 35/39
University of Southern Queensland	2019	No	No	NA	No	0/26
	2020	Yes	Yes	NA	Yes	2, 7, 15, 27/28
University of Sunshine Coast	2019	NA	No	NA	No	0/21
	2020	NA	Yes	NA	Yes	1, 2, 3, 4, 6, 12/22
University of Tasmania	2019	NA	NA	No	No	24/28
	2020	NA	NA	Yes	Yes	1/28
University of Technology Sydney	2019 (2 reports)	NA	NA	Yes	Yes	27/28
	2020 (2 reports)	NA	NA	Yes	Yes	1, 31, 34/34
University of Western Australia	2019	Yes	No	NA	Yes	7/7
	2020	Yes	Yes	NA	Yes	1, 3, 7/7
Victoria University	2019	No	No	NA	No	34/40
	2020	Yes	Yes	NA	Yes	1,4,18,22,26,27,29/43
Western Sydney University	2019	NA	NA	No	No	39/39
	2020	NA	NA	Yes	Yes	0/38
University of Wollongong	2019	NA	No	NA	Yes	43/47
	2020	NA	Yes	NA	Yes	1,44 /49

Note: CS = Chancellor's Statement
VCS = Vice-Chancellor's Statement
MCVC = Message of Chancellor and Vice Chancellor
OS= Other sections of the Annual Report
EO = Events occurring after the reporting period impacting 2020 or 2021 and beyond
NND/TNN = Number of Note of COVID-19 disclosure / Total Number of notes
Not applicable (NA)

Source: Adapted from Carnegie et al. (2021a) and updated with 2021 data.

Table 14.7 Word frequency

Word	Year		
	2019	2020	2019 & 2020
Risk*	4331	4299	8630
Covid-19**	287	4107	4394
International Students	543	486	1029
Budget	280	294	574
Cybersecurity	162	164	326

*Also includes risk-related expressions
** Also includes coronavirus pandemic

Table 14.8 Co-occurrence of "risk" with identified risks*

Co-occurrence	Year	
	2019	2020
Sentences: Risk and Covid-19	12	123
Paragraphs: Risk and Covid-19	30	155
Sentences: Risk and International Students	5	6
Paragraphs: Risk and International Students	5	6
Sentences: Risk and Cybersecurity	21	22
Paragraphs: Risk and Cybersecurity	24	25
Sentences: Risk and Budget	22	21
Paragraph: Risk and Budget	27	27

institutions will have to reconsider their priorities for the future. Some tough decisions may need to be made about what they can do to make institutions less vulnerable. This underscores the need for universities to use high-quality information for decision-making. However, it has been reported that this information is lacking in many institutions. For example, in 2019, Deloitte (2019, p. vii) found that about 60 per cent of universities use activity-based costing and that "most importantly, there was scope to improve the accuracy of their cost allocation process over time." If this is correct, this raises the question: What tools do these institutions use when they consider themselves financially vulnerable and need to decide where to save costs? What data informs these decisions? And do the tools they use undermine or help them improve their ability to respond to disruptions while achieving their key mission to educate and advance knowledge? We need more research to answer these questions.

In addition, the Covid-19 pandemic is a timely reminder of the need for diversification in those institutions that enrol large numbers of international students. The government has recognized that universities face increasing risks to "business resilience" when the optimal student mix is not considered. In February 2022, the government published a discussion paper in which it proposes a series of voluntary guidelines to support institutions looking to optimize their student mix. In their discussion paper, the government also proposes several strategies universities could use to diversify their student mix, such as increasing the visibility of their diversification efforts and increasing enrolment in undersubscribed programmes through marketing in target markets (Australian Government, 2022, p. 13). Already, some institutions have taken seriously the pandemic's lessons, particularly the importance of diversity in income streams. New offers for international students, such as 20 per cent fee remissions and scholarships at institutions like the University of Melbourne and the University of

Table 14.9 Governance of risk: The risk frameworks disclosed in the Annual Reports*

Institution	ISO31000	Enterprise Risk Management Framework	Code of Best Practice for the Governance of Australian Public Universities
James Cook University		Y	Y
The University of Sydney			Y
Australian Catholic University			
Australian National University	Y	Y	Y
Central Queensland University	Y	Y	Y
Charles Darwin University		Y	Y
Charles Sturt University	Y	Y	Y
Curtin University		Y	Y
Deakin University	Y		Y
Edith Cowan University	Y		Y
Federation University			Y
Flinders University	Y		Y
Griffith University	Y	Y	Y
La Trobe University	Y		
Macquarie University			Y
Monash University	Y	Y	
Murdoch University	Y		Y
Queensland University of Technology		Y	Y
RMIT		Y	Y
Southern Cross University	Y		Y
Swinburne University	Y		Y
University of Adelaide			Y
University of Canberra	Y		Y
University of Melbourne	Y		Y
University of New England	Y	Y	Y
University of New South Wales			Y
University of Newcastle	Y	Y	Y
University of Queensland		Y	Y
University of South Australia			
University of Southern Queensland	Y		
University of Sunshine Coast	Y	Y	Y
University of Tasmania			Y
University of Technology Sydney	Y		Y
University of Western Australia	Y		
University of Wollongong	Y		Y
Victoria University	Y		
Western Sydney University	Y	Y	

* Note that there were cases of auditor reports indicating compliance with ISO31000.
** Y indicates the use of this Framework.

Sydney, aimed at students from under-represented countries such as Armenia and Georgia, suggest newly developed understandings of risk may be emerging. The risk appetite in some institutions may be changing. Such changes represent important opportunities for future research to deepen our understanding of risk work, including how such institutions represent, manage and intervene in risk.

Besides understanding the financial impact of the pandemic, the chapter also considers the extent of risk disclosure in this sector. In this respect, it extends previous studies by Carnegie et al. (2021a;

2021b). Like Carnegie's studies of the 2019 Annual Reports of Australian universities, we found that risk disclosures by higher education institutions lack detail or are not included in the Annual Reports even in times of financial vulnerability. Many institutions claim to use ISO 131000 and Enterprise Risk Management Frameworks. Many have voluntarily agreed to comply with the Code of Best Practice for the Governance of Australian Public Universities, but how these frameworks influence day-to-day risk work remains unclear. Differences in risk disclosures also suggest that the maturity of risk management varies, with some institutions' disclosures emphasizing the regular manner in which they update risk registers and use other risk tools.

In conclusion, Australian universities have not shown a commitment to transparent reporting on issues that make them vulnerable and expose their financial sustainability to risk or the interventions they have made or are making, even during the pandemic. However, stakeholders know that uncertainty is inevitable. Organizations that do not provide accurate risk information, including how risk-intelligent decisions have been made, may face additional risks; they may create stakeholder mistrust among those who see certain institutions as ill-prepared to respond to future disruptions. Future research could usefully examine how these disclosures shape stakeholder perceptions about how well the institution is organized to respond to future disasters.

References

Abdelrehim, N., Linsley, P., & Verma, S. (2017). Understanding risk disclosures as a function of social organisation: A neo-Durkheimian institutional theory-based study of Burmah Oil Company 1971–1976. *British Accounting Review, 49*(1), 103–116.

Abraham, S., & Cox, P. (2007). Analysing the determinants of narrative risk information in UK FTSE 100 annual reports. *British Accounting Review, 39*(3), 227–248.

Audit Office of New South Wales. (2022). *Universities 2021*. www.audit.nsw.gov.au/our-work/reports/universities-2021.

Auditor General's Office of Victoria. (2022). *Results of 2021 Audits: Universities*. www.audit.vic.gov.au/report/results-2021-audits-universities.

Australian Government. (2022). *International Student Diversity at Australian Universities*. Discussion Paper. www.dese.gov.au/download/13264/international-student-diversity-australian-universities-discussion-paper/25546/international-student-diversity-australian-universities-discussion-paper/pdf/en.

Babones, S. (2019). *The China student boom and the risks it poses to Australian universities*. Analysis Paper 5. Centre for Independent Studies. www.cis.org.au/wp-content/uploads/2019/08/ap5.pdf

Bolton, R. (2019, 20 August). Unis risk a catastrophic hit due to reliance on China. *Australian Financial Review*. www.afr.com/policy/health-and-education/unis-risk-catastrophic-hit-due-to-reliance-on-china-20190820-p52ivu

Carnegie, G. D., Guthrie, J., & Martin-Sardesai, A. (2021a). Public universities and impacts of COVID-19 in Australia: Risk disclosures and organisational change. *Accounting, Auditing, and Accountability, 35*(1), 61–73.

Carnegie, G. D., Martin-Sardesai, A., Marini, L., & Guthrie Am, J. (2021b). "Taming the black elephant": Assessing and managing the impacts of COVID-19 on public universities in Australia. *Meditari Accountancy Research, 30*(6), 1783–1808.

Central Queensland University. (2021). *CQ University, 2020 Annual Report*. www.cqu.edu.au/__data/assets/pdf_file/0037/189685/cquniversity-annual-report-2020.pdf.

Charles Darwin University. (2021). *Charles Darwin University Annual Report: 2020 Year in Review*. www.cdu.edu.au/files/2021-07/cdu-annual-report-2020.pdf

Christopher, J., & Sarens, G. (2015). Risk management: Its adoption in Australian public universities within an environment of change management – A management perspective. *Australian Accounting Review, 25*(1), 2–12.

Coronavirus travel restrictions block arrivals from China, as Government warns visas could be cancelled. (2020). ABC News. www.abc.net.au/news/2020-02-02/coronavirus-china-slams-us-ban-as-who-warns-local-outbreaks/11921416

Croucher, G., & Lacy, W. B. (2020). The emergence of academic capitalism and university neo-liberalism: Perspectives of Australian higher education leadership. *Higher Education, 83*(2), 279–295.

Deakin University. (2020). *Deakin University 2019 Annual Report*. www.deakin.edu.au/__data/assets/pdf_file/0006/2147415/Deakin-Annual-Report-2019.pdf

Deloitte. (2019). *2019 Transparency in Higher Education Expenditure for Publication.* Department of Education, Skills and Employment, Australian Government. www.dese.gov.au/higher-education-publications/resources/2019-transparency-higher-education-expenditure-publication

Department of Education, Skills and Employment. (2022). *International Student Numbers by Country, by State and Territory.* Department of Education, Skills and Employment, Australian Government. www.education.gov.au/international-education-data-and-research/international-student-numbers-country-state-and-territory

Department of Education, Skills and Employment, Australian Government. (2021a). *2020 Student Summary Tables.* www.dese.gov.au/higher-education-statistics/resources/2020-student-summary-tables

Department of Education, Skills and Employment, Australian Government. (2021b). *2020 University Finance Summary Information.* www.dese.gov.au/higher-education-publications/resources/2020-university-finance-summary-information

Department of Education, Skills and Employment, Australian Government. (2021c). *2020 University Finance Summary Information.* Department of Education, Skills and Employment. www.dese.gov.au/higher-education-publications/resources/2020-university-finance-summary-information

Department of Education, Skills and Employment, Australian Government. (2021d). *2021 Commonwealth Supported Places and HECS-HELP Information.* (1449–9282). www.studyassist.gov.au/sites/default/files/2021_csp_and_hecs-help_booklet.pdf

Department of Education, Training and Youth Affairs, Australian Government. (2001). *Time Series Data 1949–2000.* www.dese.gov.au/higher-education-statistics/resources/time-series-data-1949-2000

Dodd, T., Creighton, A., & Rowbotham, J. (2020, 19 February). Top unis face $1.2bn coronavirus hit. *The Australian.*

Foo, M. (2020, 19 May). From boom to gloom: It'll be a long, difficult road back to prosperity. *The Australian.*

Forsyth, H. (2022, 27 July). Australian vice-chancellors have forfeited public trust. *Times Higher Education.* www.timeshighereducation.com/blog/australian-vice-chancellors-have-forfeited-public-trust

Guthrie, J., Linnenluecke, M. K., Martin-Sardesai, A., Shen, Y., & Smith, T. (2022). On the resilience of Australian public universities: Why our institutions may fail unless vice-chancellors rethink broken commercial business models. *Accounting and Finance, 62*(2), 2203–2235.

Guthrie, J., Manes Rossi, F., Orelli, R. L., & Nicolò, G. (2020). Investigating risk disclosures in Italian integrated reports. *Meditari Accountancy Research, 28*(6), 1149–1178.

Hardy, C., Maguire, S., Power, M., & Tsoukas, H. (2020). Organising risk: Organization and management theory for the risk society. *Academy of Management Annals, 14*(2), 1032–1066.

Irvine, H., & Ryan, C. (2019). The financial health of Australian universities: Policy implications in a changing environment. *Accounting, Auditing, and Accountability Journal, 32*(5), 1500–1531.

Jarvis, D. S. L. (2022). Work, risk and academic labour. In C. L. Peterson (Ed.), *Identifying and managing risk at work: Emerging issues in the context of globalisation* (pp. 157–172). Routledge.

Krippendorff, K. (2019). *Content analysis: an introduction to its methodology* (4th ed.). SAGE.

Linsley, P. M., & Shrives, P. J. (2006). Risk reporting: A study of risk disclosures in the annual reports of UK companies. *British Accounting Review, 38*(4), 387–404.

Martin-Sardesai, A., Guthrie, J., & Parker, L. (2021). The neoliberal reality of higher education in Australia: How accountingisation is corporatising knowledge. *Meditari Accountancy Research, 29*(6), 1261–1282.

Organization for Economic Cooperation and Development (OECD). (2021). *The State of Higher Education: One Year into the COVID-19 Pandemic.* www.oecd-ilibrary.org/docserver/83c41957-en.pdf?expires=1661430839&id=id&accname=guest&checksum=75AEC7629967699FE42BD280FA699412

Parker, L. (2011). University corporatisation: Driving redefinition. *Critical Perspectives on Accounting, 22*(4), 434–450.

Parker, L. D. (2020). Australian universities in a pandemic world: Transforming a broken business model? *Journal of Accounting & Organisational Change, 16*(4), 541–548.

Power, M. (2007). *Organised uncertainty: Designing a world of risk management.* Oxford University Press.

Primrose, R. (2019, 11 November). Australian business schools immune to reliance on Chinese students. *Financial Times.* www.ft.com/content/6c9ff7f2-df9d-11e9-b8e0-026e07cbe5b4

Queensland Audit Office. (2022). *Education 2021.* www.qao.qld.gov.au/reports-resources/reports-parliament/education-2021

Ross, J. (2022a, 19 July). Australia "back in the fold" for foreign students. *Times Higher Education.* www.timeshighereducation.com/news/australia-back-fold-foreign-students

Ross, J. (2022b, 3 May). Australian universities report record earnings despite pandemic. *Times Higher Education.* www.timeshighereducation.com/news/australian-universities-report-record-earnings-despite-pandemic

Ross, J. (2022c, 18 August). Overworked academics "give away one-third of their time". *Times Higher Education.* www.timeshighereducation.com/news/overworked-academics-give-away-one-third-their-time

Smyth, J., Pong, J., & Jack, A. (2020, 19 February). Coronavirus exposes Western universities' reliance on China. *Financial Times*. www.ft.com/content/b3429de6-4dec-11ea-95a0-43d18ec715f5

Universities Australia. (2021, 3 February). *17,000 Uni jobs lost to COVID-19*. www.universitiesaustralia.edu.au/media-item/17000-uni-jobs-lost-to-covid-19/

University of Melbourne. (2021). *Annual Report 2020*. https://about.unimelb.edu.au/__data/assets/pdf_file/0023/349142/University-of-Melbourne-2020-Annual-Report.pdf

University of Technology Sydney. (2021). *2020 UTS Annual Report: Review of Operations*. (Vol. 1). www.uts.edu.au/sites/default/files/2021-06/gsu-aboututs-utsannualreport-2020-vol1.pdf

University of the Sunshine Coast. (2021). *USC Annual Report 2020*. www.usc.edu.au/about/reports/annual-report.

Victoria University. (2021). *Victoria University 2020 Annual Report*. www.vu.edu.au/sites/default/files/annual-report-2020.pdf

Wei, R., & Gekara, V. (2022). Australia's higher education sector in the eye of the COVID-19 storm. In F. Netswera, A. A. Woldegiyorgis, & T. Karabchuk (Eds.), *Higher education and the COVID-19 pandemic: Cross-national perspectives on the challenges and management of higher education in crisis times* (pp. 81–99). Brill.

15

PUBLIC VALUE ACCOUNTING AS AN INTEGRATING MECHANISM BETWEEN PERFORMANCE AND RISK

Enrico Bracci, Enrico Deidda Gagliardo,
Giorgia Gobbo and Mouhcine Tallaki

Introduction

Performance management (PM) and risk management (RM) represent two interconnected systems towards public Value (PV) creation. While PM is instrumental to support politicians and managers of the organization towards the improvement of societal, economic and environmental well-being, the key objective of RM in public services is to protect/create PV (Fletcher & Abbas, 2018). PV is here defined as the ability to improve the well-being of the community (Moore, 1995; Deidda Gagliardo, 2002, 2015). In this context, governments have defined the legislative context for the development of an internal control system integrated with RM frameworks (Bovaird & Quirk, 2013; Thomas & Davies, 2005; Vann, 2004). The integration of RM within other managerial systems and PM is considered beneficial for the organization (FRC, 2005). The literature shows that public administrations design and implement risk-based control systems arbitrarily, so there is an issue of appropriate integration between RM in management accounting and control systems, and a radical cultural shift is still required (Bracci et al., 2021).

This chapter examines the recent reform brought about in Italy with the decree law 80/2021. Said reform changed the PM system of the Italian public administration. The main innovation is represented by the "integrated plan of activities and organization" (PIAO), which incorporates both performance objectives and RM analysis and treatment, in the PV creation perspective. Italian public administration, from 2022 onwards, in planning their performance must consider both PV objectives, organizational PM, and RM objectives.

Through multiple-case study from Italian regions, the chapter will present some of the first experimentation of the PIAO to understand its functioning, and inductively understand the conceptual integration between PV, PM and RM. More specifically, the following research question is set: What tools, processes and actors contribute to making PV an integrating mechanism between PM and RM?

The rest of this chapter is structured in the following manner: the second section will discuss the literature on PM, RM and PV. The third section will address the recent reform that introduced the PIAO in Italy. The fourth section will detail the methodology, before describing the main results. The last section will discuss and conclude with the implications emerging from the case study.

DOI: 10.4324/9781003295945-20

Performance management, risks and public value: a literature review

Since the 1980s, a process of reforms has involved public sector organizations worldwide. Inspired by the neoliberal state and new public management (NPM), reforms have focused on competition and market issues to enhance performance and maximize the level of efficiency, effectiveness and productivity of public service organizations. The process of reform has revealed the need to assess performance (Pollitt & Bouckaert, 2004). In fact, various managerial tools like management control systems (MCSs), PM and RM have been introduced in the context of public organizations. These managerial tools and other related issues have conditioned public debates since the 1980s (Hood, 1995). Recently, the financial crisis, the subsequent budget pressure and the Covid-19 crisis have refocused and intensified the interest on RM and other risk-related issues like PM (Bastida et al., 2022; Soin & Collier, 2013). While PM is instrumental to support politicians, and managers of the organization towards the improvement of societal, economic and environmental well-being, the key objective of RM in public services is to protect/create PV (Fletcher & Abbas, 2018, Gobbo, 2021).

PM is functional to support organizations and politicians in decision-making processes, but also to establish a dialogue between the administrative and political components (Kloot et al., 2000). It also plays an important role in accountability processes (Kloot et al., 2000). However, in the context of the public sector, financial performance prevailed over other non-financial measures (Ricci & Civitillo, 2018). The dominance of financial performance has been criticized by various authors (Jones & Pendlebury, 2010) as it could give rise to negative consequences (Ricci & Civitillo, 2018). In addition, financial performance has also been criticized for overlooking social equity outcomes (Kroll, 2017).

Performance is not only financial, but can also be related to other qualitative and social dimensions, that is, the quality of actions and the quality of achievement. In this sense, the performance is configured as the performance of sustainable results and refers both to outputs and outcomes (Van Dooren et al., 2010). Also, Boyne (2002, p. 19) highlighted that performance is related to various qualitative dimensions. The author reported that performance dimensions include outputs (quantity and quality); efficiency (cost per unit of output); outcomes (formal effectiveness, impact, equity cost per unit of service outcome); responsiveness (consumer satisfaction, citizen satisfaction, staff satisfaction, cost per unit of responsiveness); and democratic outcomes (probity, participation, accountability, cost per unit of democratic outcome). Considering the nature – quantitative and qualitative – of performance dimensions, "public value literature may help in making more sense of performance" (Van Dooren et al., 2010, p. 31). Bracci et al., (2014) emphasized the need to consider performance and its measurement within the PV framework and strategy, as the PV paradigm considers *citizens' expectations in respect to government and public services* (Moore, 1995). In this regard, participation of citizens and other stakeholders is an important issue for the PV creation (Yang, 2016). This is because participation contributes to identifying and increasing understanding about public values (Nabatchi, 2012); reduces disagreement in interpretations; helps translate subjective and abstract value in actions (Yang, 2016); and consequently improves the decision-making process.

Performance, as it has been conceptualized under the label of NPM, undermines the core values of public service organizations, because the logic of the market and competition, on which the NPM is based, have led to a focus on aspects concerning efficiency gains and cost savings (O'Flynn, 2007). PV has shifted the attention towards social value that cannot be addressed by the market, competition logic and economic efficiency. PV is a broader concept that considers performance not only in financial terms. It goes beyond the concept of performance as a simple achievement of goals and considers the effect on society in term of value created (Blaug et al., 2006). Therefore, the PV approach acts as an organizational flywheel for the generation of fair and sustainable outcomes (Papi et al., 2020), and contributes to creating conditions for public sector change (Marcon, 2014). In this sense, performance represents the engine of the NPM, and every engine needs a flywheel. The PV approach is the flywheel that guides and regulates the process towards sustainable goals. The concept of PV, since its introduction in 1995 (Moore, 1995; Deidda Gagliardo, 2002, 2015), has continued to attract growing interest among public scholars. It has become pervasive but with the difficulty if theorization, operationalization and measurement (Bracci et al., 2019; Salemans & Budding, 2022). The conception of PV represented a turning point for public management. The latter has shifted from a logic inspired by the neoliberal state and new public management, where competition and the principles of the free market guide the decision-making process of policymakers, to a logic based on the PV created for the citizen and for future generations (Benington, 2009). Accordingly, the PV conception considers the citizen and the user as central to the decision-making process by emphasizing policy and the process of implementation in terms of value created (Moore, 1995). In doing so, the PV approach can improve performance by reducing conflicting values between stakeholders (Andersen et al., 2021) and by considering multilevel networks and the interaction between actors of the network (Cuganesan et al., 2014). PM and PV are related as the PV can frame and guide policy and goals towards performance. In fact, performance can be conceptualized as the "realization of public values such as efficiency, effectiveness, equity, robustness, openness, and transparency" (Van Dooren et al., 2010, p. 50). The inability of public administrations to emphasize the creation of PV both in the processes initiated and in the desired results, represents a limit to the improvement of performance (Issa & Masanja, 2022).

Improving performance requires attention to minimize the risks of damaging public values (Yuzhakov et al., 2020). In fact, RM can promote performance (Hinna et al., 2018; Rana et al., 2019; Gobbo, 2020), improve goal setting (Capaldo et al., 2018), and enhance learning in PM (Hinna et al., 2018). Barrett (2019, p.1) reported that "a better focus on risk management in producing required outcomes would contribute significantly to better performance and to greater public support and involvement." RM is part of the managerial system since it is not independent of other management processes (Hutter & Power, 2005). Therefore, its integration into the business processes is fundamental for its functioning (FRC, 2005). Accordingly, RM processes should be related to the organizational and suborganizational objectives, accounting and auditing norms, and performance systems (Power, 2009). Integration of RM within the internal processes, the relationships between management control, accounting, and RM have been addressed only to a minimal extent in the academic literature. Therefore, little has been investigated, also, on the perception and implementation of RM at various organizational levels (Bhimani, 2009). More so, regulations and reforms in the public sector are often superficial or give only general indications to implement RM (Kolisovas & Andrius, 2011), leaving large margins of subjectivity to public managers. Thus, except for the regulatory initiatives and often superficial efforts to implement a RM framework, little has been done to practically establish an overall internal public sector control system on an RM basis (Kolisovas & Andrius, 2011).

The goal of this chapter is to investigate the adoption of a PV perspective, through a participative approach, as an integrating device between RM and PM. This determines the adoption of a participative approach, which is a hybrid mode of decision-making and service provision where a public organization engages stakeholders in a formal, consensual and collective decision-making process to identify and create value (Thompson & Rizova, 2015; Yang, 2016). In this sense, we claim that RM integrated into internal process enhances performance, and that RM is PV creating. In fact, Thompson and Rizova (2015, pp. 571–572) highlighted that risk management is potentially value creating and its potential tends to increase over time. Although PV research is widespread, empirical studies are lacking and there is little support regarding the shift towards the PV paradigm in the public sector

(Guarini, 2014). The chapter contributes to the literature by analysing a case study from Italy. The case study analysed highlights how the PV paradigm is like a flywheel in governing the integration of RM into the performance system.

The context: the PIAO

The Italian public administration is experiencing a new reform season, supported by the European funds related to the National Recovery and Resilience Plan (NRRP). The latter can lead to economic and social growth if, in addition to the investment plan, a reform plan and a monitoring system are provided. This monitoring system must not only be aimed at certifying the expenses made but must also be centred on the value generated by the investments themselves.

One of the important reforms (decree law 80/2021) is the PIAO, which is conceived to replace several specific planning documents. This new Plan aims to incorporate both performance objectives and RM analysis and treatment into the perspective of PV creation (Moore, 1995; Deidda Gagliardo, 2015), through a monitoring system with a focus on the effective results of the various programmes. The reform, therefore, provides for the redevelopment of strategic planning and monitoring tools, aimed not only at reducing the number of documents provided but also at defining their use, within an integrated planning framework.

Figure 15.1 (Deidda Gagliardo, Saporito, 2021) shows the contents and structure of the PIAO, provided in a "standard scheme" defined by the legislation. The PIAO is a multi-year programmatic

	SECTION 1) **Administration details**		
PROGRAMMING	**SECTION 2)** **Public Value, Performance, Risk**		
	Sub-section PUBLIC VALUE Improvement of the users and stakeholders' well-being in the different perspectives [economic, social, environmental, health etc.] generated by planning strategies, measurable in terms of impacts		
	Subsection PERFORMANCE MANAGEMENT Performance objectives and indicators functional to PV creation		Subsection RISK MANAGEMENT (focus anti-corruption risk) Risk management measures functional to the PV protection
	SECTION 3) **ORGANIZATION and HUMAN CAPITAL HEALTH** Organizational development actions (i.e. smart working, hiring and training) functional to performance objectives and risk management measures and, therefore, to PV creation and protection		
	Organizational Health		Professional health
	Subsection Organizational structure	Subsection Smart working organization	Subsection Human capital hiring plan Human capital training plan
	SECTION 4) **MONITORING**		

Figure 15.1 Contents and structure of the PIAO.

document (three years with annual update) comprising four sections: 1) administration details; 2–3) integrated programming; 4) integrated monitoring.

The second section deals with the planning of public value and performance objectives in an integrated way with corruption risk management. This planning is further integrated with the administration's human resource planning. For this reason, the second section consists of three subsections:

- PUBLIC VALUE subsection: in which one or more objectives of PV are aimed at responding to the needs of context are defined. The section also presents the expected results in terms of PV objectives (outcome/impacts), planned in coherence with the financial planning documents, the actions aimed at improving the physical and digital accessibility of citizens to the services offered by the administration. The administration selects some PV objectives, also with reference to the measures of equitable and sustainable well-being (i.e. Sustainable Development Goals of the UN Agenda 2030);
- PERFORMANCE MANAGEMENT subsection: in which operational objectives of PV creation are defined. The objectives and performance indicators are defined in term of efficiency and effectiveness.
- In the CORRUPTION RISK MANAGEMENT subsection, RM measures are defined which allos for the creation of the planned PV. In this perspective, the RM system protects the creation of PV because it prevents risky events.

The third section, "ORGANIZATION AND HUMAN CAPITAL", is articulated in three subsections:

- ORGANIZATIONAL STRUCTURE: in this the administration presents the organizational model adopted (i.e. organization chart; levels of organizational responsibility and the average number of employees);
- SMART WORKING ORGANIZATION: subsection that indicates the strategy and objectives related to the development of innovative work organization models. In particular, the subsection contains: the enabling factors (i.e. technological platforms, professional skills), the objectives within the administration, and the contributions to improving performance, in terms of efficiency and effectiveness (i.e. perceived quality of smart working, reduction of absences);
- HUMAN CAPITAL HIRING AND TRAINING PLAN: in this subsection the administration presents the strategic planning of human resources, aimed at improving the quality of services. Human capital training is also planned by identifying strategic priorities in terms of requalification of skills.

As shown in Figure 15.1, the "programmatic logic" of the PIAO can therefore be summarized with the following formula: more organizational and human health, less corruption risk, more performance, more PV.

The contents and structure of the PIAO are organized according to a programmatic logic based on the following principles:

- Vertical integration (cascading logic), from PV to strategic objectives, to operational objectives, to annual actions;
- Horizontal integration: between PM objectives and RM measures;
- Finalization: towards the generation (through PM) and protection (through corruption RM) of PV.

Cases of integrated programming in the Italian Regions: objectives and methodology

This section describes the FORMEZ PA PROJECT[1] entitled *"The Territorial Public Value of the Regions. Towards the PIAO"*,[2] finalized to train and support some Italian Regions in the introduction of the PIAO. One of the authors of this chapter took an active part in the Formez PA project.

From the above-mentioned research objective – aimed at inductively understanding the conceptual integration between PV, performance and risk – the following research question has arisen: What tools, processes and actors contribute to the quality integrated and participatory programming?

Adopting an explorative approach, a longitudinal multiple case study was conducted on five Italian Regions (Regione Basilicata, Regione Emilia-Romagna, Regione Friuli Venezia-Giulia, Regione Liguria, Regione Toscana) that voluntarily joined the workshop.

The experiment was conducted from June 2021 to July 2022 using the focus group tool; 20 focus groups were held (four for performance, anticorruption and organizations sections, and eight for the Public Value section). The focus groups had an average duration of two hours. For each Region, a team of facilitators was identified consisting of three members: one coordinator and two collaborators. All focus groups were conducted in virtual meeting mode, and were recorded and subsequently transcribed.

From a methodological point of view, the chapter adopts a descriptive-exploratory methodology (Creswell, 2013) divided into three phases (deductive, exploratory and feedback). In the deductive phase (June 2021–September 2021), following the analysis of the literature and legislation in the process of being issued, the integrated programming tool and process were developed and the composition of the team of actors involved in the integrated programming process was also defined (heads of the four sections of the PIAO).

In the exploratory phase (October 2021–May 2022), training sessions were carried out on the contents of the PIAO sections and subsequently focus groups were conducted, called "Innovation Labs", guided by the team of facilitators. The Innovation Labs were conducted by adopting an action research methodology (Argyris, 1985), with one of the researchers having the role of facilitator.

At the end of the exploratory phase, a grid of measurement of the programmatic quality of the tool, of the process and of the actors was applied (Yu et al. 2011; Deidda Gagliardo et al., 2020) in order to realize a cross-comparison (Gustafsson, 2017) of multiple cases (Yin, 1994; Baxter & Jack, 2008) and obtain empirical evidence on the successes and criticalities of integrated programming. The grid makes it possible to measure the level of quality with reference to the five criteria chosen by the Dipartimento della Funzione Pubblica: 1) simplification, 2) selectivity, 3) adequacy of objects and anti-corruption measured, 4) integration, 5) finalization towards PV creation.

In the feedback phase, an event was held with all the project participants (Dipartimento della Funzione Pubblica, Regions and team of facilitators) in order to determine the usefulness of the tool in integrated programming from a PV-creation perspective. The event was conducted using the semi-structured interview method.

Integration between performance and risk management through public value paradigm in the Italian Regions

The results of the project are presented below with reference to the three phases of the methodology used.

Deductive phase

The first result of the research brings out a model consistent with the legislation tool that introduced the PIAO (Figure 15.2). The PIAO model must be designed as an Integrated Plan between the different

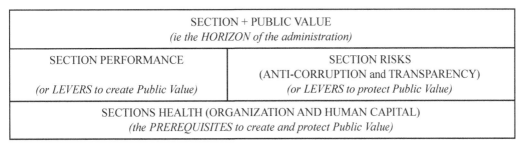

SECTION + PUBLIC VALUE
(ie the HORIZON of the administration)

SECTION PERFORMANCE	SECTION RISKS
	(ANTI-CORRUPTION and TRANSPARENCY)
(or LEVERS to create Public Value)	*(or LEVERS to protect Public Value)*

SECTIONS HEALTH (ORGANIZATION AND HUMAN CAPITAL)
(the PREREQUISITES to create and protect Public Value)

Figure 15.2 The PIAO model.

Source: Deidda Gagliardo (2022).

programmatic perspectives towards the horizon of the generation of PV, and must be prepared through the rationalization and functionalization of the contents: the PIAO must be synthetic. Therefore, we need to identify a few priority contents. The PIAO will have to be useful to improve the well-being of citizens; therefore, we need to include content functional to the PV that we want to achieve.

The model proposed gave more importance to the integration between PM and RM through the PV paradigm. The model schema considers the various sections of the PIAO with more focus on integration and the role of PV. The conceptualization of the model considers the relationship between PM, RM and PV highlighted in the literature. The object of the experimentation was the integrated planning of PM and RM to create PV in terms of employment impact. In particular, this employment policy was focused on NEETs, that is, young people aged between 15 and 29 who do not study and do not work. Considering the role of participation in the identification and creation of PV, the implementation and testing of the model in the Regions that have chosen to join the project, has been done from a participatory perspective. In fact, for each Region, a team of facilitators was identified consisting of three members: one coordinator and two collaborators. Training sessions were carried out on the contents of the PIAO sections and subsequently focus groups were conducted, called "Innovation Labs", guided by the team of facilitators.

Exploratory phase

The results of the second phase of the Formez PA Project were measured in terms of the quality level of the instrument, the preparation process and the actors involved. As shown in Table 15.1, the criteria considered to measure quality are: 1) simplification, 2) selectivity, 3) adequacy of objects and anti-corruption measured, 4) integration, 5) finalization towards PV creation. Each of the five criteria contains a specific number of quality items, and the combination of items allows for the calculation of the quality level of each criterion, which has values in a range [0, 100]. Assuming that each of the criteria has the same weight for the quality of the PIAO, the synthetic overall quality indicator is obtained as the arithmetic mean of the five criteria, which therefore have a single associated weight equal to 1/5. The evaluation of the criteria used a dichotomous method for four criteria (integration, functionality, actors and process), and a proportional method for the adequacy criterion. The evaluation of the quality level of the first group of criteria is carried out using dummy variables: within each criterion, the presence of an item is equivalent to number 1, while 0 is selected by the evaluator in case of the absence of the requirement. Therefore, a value of the specific quality indicator (e.g. integration) equal to 0 corresponds to the absence (according to the evaluator) of all the items within the PIAO, while a value of the specific quality indicator equal to 100 is the result of all ten items as present.

The evaluation of the quality level of the adequacy criterion through a proportional method is based on the presence of specific characteristics of the indicators (e.g. size, baseline, target, source)

Table 15.1 The evaluation grid

Criteria	Item				
	1	2	3	4	5
ADEQUACY	Objectives (PM) and measures (RM) concise, clear, time-based	Multidimensional objectives and measures	Baseline for each objective and measure	Multi-year target for each objective and measure	Data source for each objective and measure
INTEGRATION	Objectives of PV vertically integrated with the critical issues/opportunities of the context	Strategic objectives vertically integrated with the objectives of PV	Operational objectives vertically integrated with strategic objectives	Organizational actions vertically integrated with the operational and strategic objectives of creating PV	Corruption RM measures planned in an integrated manner with the operational objectives
PUBLIC VALUE FUNCTIONALITY	The specific operational objectives are functional to the creation of the expected PV	Corruption RM measures are functional to the protection of the expected PV	The organizational actions are functional to the creation and protection of the expected PV	The organizational actions are functional to the creation and protection of the expected PV	The recruitment and professional training actions are functional to the creation and protection of the expected PV
ACTOR	Policymaker indication in the PV Section	Stakeholder indication in the PV Section	Indication Head of the Performance Section	Indication Head of the Corruption Risks Section	Indication Head of the Organization and Human Capital Section
PROCESS	Linking PV with context analysis	Stakeholders involved in the validation of the PV objectives	The TEAM responsible for the Corruption Risks subsection also participated in the drafting of the Performance subsection	The TEAM responsible for the Performance subsection also participated in the drafting of the Corruption Risks subsection	The TEAM responsible for the subsections Performance and Corruption Risks also participated in the drafting of the Organization and Human Capital Sections

Table 15.2 The average quality of the PIAO

ADEQUACY	83%
INTEGRATION	96%
FUNCTIONALITY TO PUBLIC VALUE	92%
ACTORS	96%
PROCESS	88%
AVERAGE QUALITY OF PIAO	91%

associated with the objectives of the various programmatic sections or subsections (Public Value, Performance, Anti-corruption, Organization). Therefore, for each item, the evaluator inserts a value from 0 to 100, based on how many objectives of the specific programmatic section or subsection satisfy each quality item with respect to the total objectives programmed in that section or subsection (e.g. in the case of the absence of impact indicators linked to the PV objectives, the evaluator will insert a value of 0, while if half of the PV objectives include impact indicators, the evaluator will insert a value of 50).

The criteria considered made it possible to evaluate the basic elements of the model, namely: integration between PM and RM, the role of the PV paradigm, and participatory implementation. In Table 15.2 are shown the average results of the application of the grid to the five Regions involved.

An average vertical (between VP and PM) and horizontal (between PM and RM) integration of 96% is observed. The Regions have demonstrated a good competence to develop objectives of PV consistent with the analysis of the context; the coherence between PV objectives, strategic objectives and related operational objectives is also developed satisfactorily. The Regions have developed an excellent horizontal programmatic integration between expected performance and corruptive RM measures: risk measures have been identified for each operational objective to protect the PV.

Satisfactory results in terms of integration were also achieved thanks to the good level of adequacy (83%) of the sections of the PIAO: excellent identification of the PV and of the strategies for its creation; excellent identification of indicators (and anti-corruption measures), targets and related data sources.

The analysis of the average finalization of the PV confirms an excellent capacity (92%) of the Regions to plan in an integrated way through the PIAO using the PM and the RM as levers of value creation and protection respectively.

Finally, with reference to the actors involved in the PIAO, almost all the Regions (96%) clearly identified the responsibility of the Integration Team with reference to each section. The average quality of the process is also good (88%), and is attributable to the active involvement of stakeholders in the planning phase of the PV, and to the presence of the Integration Team.

Feedback phase

In the feedback phase, the computer-assisted theoretical thematic analysis of the semi-structured interviews carried out in the final event of the FORMEZ PA Project was conducted. The analysis brought out some main issues relating to integration between PM and RM through the perspective of creating PV. The main results are discussed below, which presents some passages from the interviews with the Project participants.

The interviews revealed how the PV paradigm applied in the PIAO implementation process represented a guiding element. On the one hand, the PV approach has made it possible to identify clear and shared objectives, and on the other hand, it has improved the performance and the integration between PM and the RM process. As affirmed by some participants:

Public Value is a real cultural paradigm shift in which well-being becomes the driving and motivating element for public personnel. (Representative of Liguria Region)

Stakeholders play a very important role both in the planning phase and in the evaluation of the public value. (Manager, Public Function Department)

The Innovation Labs have led to a cultural awareness of the programming methods useful for generating value starting from the knowledge of the context and with the involvement of the stakeholders. (Representative of Friuli Venezia Giulia Region)

The Innovation LAB has improved the PM system by reducing the performance objectives by 25% and increasing their quality in a way that is functional to the generation of value. (Representative of Basilicata Region)

The PV measures the effect of an administration's policies on the reference context. PV is a broader concept that considers performance not only in financial terms. It goes beyond the concept of performance as a simple achievement of goals and considers the effect on society in terms of value created (Blaug et al., 2006). Therefore, the PV approach acts as an organizational flywheel for the generation of fair and sustainable outcomes (Papi et al., 2020), and contributes to creating conditions for public sector change (Marcon, 2014). Accordingly, the PV conception considers the citizen and the user as central to the decision-making process by emphasizing policy and the process of implementation in terms of value created (Moore, 1995).

Improving performance requires attention to minimize the risks of damaging public values (Yuzhakov et al., 2020). In fact, RM can promote performance (Hinna et al., 2018; Rana et al., 2019; Gobbo, 2020), improve goal setting (Capaldo et al., 2018), and enhance learning in PM (Hinna et al., 2018). Barrett (2019, p. 1) reported that "a better focus on risk management in producing required outcomes would contribute significantly to better performance and to greater public support and involvement." Thompson and Rizova,(2015, pp. 571–572) highlighted that "risk management is potentially value creating and its potential tends to increase over time". RM is part of the managerial system since it is not independent of other management processes (Hutter & Power, 2005). Therefore, its integration into the business processes is fundamental for its functioning (FRC, 2005). Accordingly, RM processes should be related to the organizational and suborganizational objectives, accounting and auditing norms, and performance systems (Power, 2009). The literature shows that public administrations design and implement risk-based control systems arbitrarily, so there is an issue of appropriate integration between RM in management accounting and control systems, and a radical cultural shift is still required (Bracci et al., 2021).

With the PIAO, the control programming system was renewed above all thanks to the integration between the actors, which was the engine for improving the planning by addressing the performance and risk management measures in an integrated way towards the Public Value. (Representative of Basilicata Region)

Need for integration between tools starting from the integration between people's skills. (Representative of Emilia-Romagna Region)

As reported by some interviewers, the PV paradigm is a new concept for public organizations, and various public managers did not know the concept before the start of the experimentation. This confirmed the inability of public administrations to emphasize the creation of PV both in the processes initiated and in the desired results, which represents a limit to the improvement of performance (Issa & Masanja, 2022). Performance and PV are related as the PV can frame and guide policy and goals towards performance. In fact, performance can be conceptualized as the realization of public values such as efficiency, effectiveness, equity, robustness, openness, and transparency (Van Dooren et al., 2010, p.50).

Closing remarks

The present chapter aimed at analysing the theme related to the integration between PM, RM and PV management. The current literature is scant, particularly from an accounting perspective (Bracci et al., 2019, 2022). We focused on a recent reform in the Italian public administration that introduced the so-called PIAO, an integrated plan where PM and RM, among the others, are to be planned in coherence with the PV to be created. This paradigmatic change was observed through a multiple case study during the first experimentation with the PIAO implementation in five Italian Regions.

The results support the argument in the literature that putting the perspective of PV at the centre of the planning process reduces the cultural and ideological barriers that led to the failure of most of the previous PM system reforms (Mauro et al., 2019). Indeed, the PV literature argued that public managers' and employees' intrinsic motivation remains anchored to some public values (Bozeman & Moulton, 2011). The PV dimension within the PIAO represents the flywheel towards which organizational PM objectives and RM objectives can be oriented in a coherent manner. After decades of NPM reforms where short-term performance, and which were mainly linked to financial performance and efficiency, represented the overall objectives, the PIAO reforms steer public sector organizations towards a PV governance perspective. This calls for further studies to analyse the effects of this reform and whether it can keep its promises.

Moreover, the research has shown the importance of central government methodological and practical support of public organizations in the reform implementation process. Sharing the principles, the tools and the knowledge is key to reducing a priori barriers, to increase the comparability of the implementation and the quality of the management tools implemented. Although public values and publicness may sound more attuned to a public sector ethos (Mériade & Qiang, 2015), any reform may encounter resistance and strategic behaviour, leading to loose coupling (Lukka, 2007).

This chapter contributes to the ongoing debate related to the integration of managerial systems, and between PM systems and RM systems by integrating the perspective of PV management as a flywheel to move beyond NPM and neoliberal logic more in general. In so doing, we concur with the need to bring back PV(s) into the political as well as the managerial agenda and the related reforms (Bracci et al., 2021; Steccolini, 2019). The turbulent times characterizing many national and international contexts increase the urgency to (re)centre public service organizations towards the creation of PV, and in line with global challenges, like the SDGs (Bastida et al., 2022). The Covid-19 pandemic, the Russian invasion of Ukraine and the frequent climate emergencies (e.g. heatwaves, droughts) make this challenge timely and compelling.

Notes

1 Formez PA–Service, Assistance, Studies and Training Centre for the Modernization of PA is a private association of public administration headquartered in the Presidency of the Council of Ministers (Dipartimento della Funzione Pubblica) (www.formez.it/).
2 FORMEZ PA PROJECT is part of the wider project titled Participation of Citizens and Users in the Process of Measuring Organizational Performance, born from the institutional agreement between the Dipartimento della Funzione Pubblica and Formez PA, signed on 27 December 2019.

References

Andersen, L. B., Brewer, G. A., & Leisink, P. (2021). Stakeholders, public value(s), and public service performance. In P. Leisink, L. B. Andersen, G. A. Brewer, C. B. Jacobsen, E. Knies, & W. Vandenabeele (Eds.), *Managing for Public Service Performance: How People and Values Make a Difference* (pp. 25–44). Oxford University Press.

Argyris, C., Putnam, R., & McLain Smith, D. (1985). *Action science – concepts, methods and skills for research and intervention.* Jossey-Bass.

Barrett, P. (2019). New development: Managing risk for better performance – not taking a risk can actually be a risk. *Public Money & Management, 42*(6), 408–413.

Bastida, F., Bracci, E., & Hoque, Z. (2022). Accounting for unstable environments in the public sector: managing post-COVID-19 times. *Journal of Public Budgeting, Accounting & Financial Management, 34*(1), 1–26.

Baxter, P., & Jack, S. (2008). Qualitative case study methodology: Study design and implementation for novice researchers. *The Qualitative Report, 13*(4), 544–559.

Benington, J. (2009). Creating the public in order to create public value? *International Journal of Public Administration, 32*(3–4), 232–249.

Bhimani, A. (2009). Risk management, corporate governance and management accounting: Emerging inter-dependencies. *Management Accounting Research, 20*(1), 2–5.

Blaug, R., Horner, L., & Lekhi, R. (2006). *Public Value, Politics and Public Management: A Literature Review.* Work Foundation. https://westminsterresearch.westminster.ac.uk/item/9234y/public-value-politics-and-public-management-a-literature-review

Bovaird, T., & Quirk, B. (2013). *Risk and resilience.* University of Birmingham, Institute of Local Government Studies. www.birmingham.ac.uk/Documents/college-social-sciences/government-society/inlogov/publications/2013/chapter-5-bovaird-quirke.pdf

Boyne, G. A. (2002). Public and private management: What's the eifference? *Journal of Management Studies, 39*(1), 97–122.

Bozeman, B., & Moulton, S. (2011). Integrative publicness: A framework for public management strategy and performance. *Journal of Public Administration Research and Theory, 21*(Supplement 3), 363–380.

Bracci, E., Deidda Gagliardo, E., & Bigoni, M. (2014). Performance management systems and public value strategy: A case study. In J. Guthrie, G. Marcon, S. Russo, F. Farneti (Eds.), *Public value management, measurement and reporting* (vol. 5, pp. 129–157). Emerald.

Bracci, E., Gobbo, G. , & Papi, L. (2020). The integration of risk and performance management: the role of boundary objects. *Journal of Public Budgeting, Accounting & Financial Management, 34*(1), 139–161.

Bracci, E., Papi, L., Bigoni, M., Deidda Gagliardo, E., & Bruns, H.-J. (2019). Public value and public sector accounting research: a structured literature review. *Journal of Public Budgeting, Accounting & Financial Management, 31*(1), 103–136.

Bracci, E., Saliterer, I., Sicilia, M., & Steccolini, I. (2021). Accounting for (public) value(s): Reconsidering publicness in accounting research and practice. *Accounting, Auditing and Accountability Journal, 34*(7), 1513–1526.

Capaldo, G., Costantino, N., Pellegrino, R., & Rippa, P. (2018). The role of risk in improving goal setting in performance management practices within public sector: An explorative research in courts offices in Italy. *International Journal of Public Administration, 41*(12), 986–997.

Creswell, J. W. (2013). *Qualitative inquiry & research design.* SAGE.

Cuganesan, S., Jacobs, K., & Lacey, D. (2014). Beyond new public management: Does performance measurement drive public value in networks? In J. Guthrie, G. Marcon, S. Russo, F. Farneti (Eds.), *Public value management, measurement and reporting* (vol. 5, pp. 21–42). Emerald.

Deidda Gagliardo, E. (2002). *La creazione del valore nell'ente locale.* Giuffrè.

Deidda Gagliardo, E. (2015). *Il valore pubblico: la nuova frontiera della performance.* Rirea.

Deidda Gagliardo, E., Papi, L., Gobbo, G., & Ievoli R. (2020). La qualità programmatica dei Ministeri. Evidenze empiriche dall'analisi dei Piani della Performance. *RIREA, 3,* 318–335.

Deidda Gagliardo, E., & Saporito R. (2021). Il PIAO come strumento di programmazione integrata per la creazione di Valore Pubblico. *Rivista Italiana di Public Management, 4*(2), 196–236.

Financial Reporting Council. (2005). *Internal Control-Revised Guidance for Directors on the Combined Code.* www.frc.org.uk/getattachment/fe1ba51a-578d-4467-a00c-f287825aced9/Revised-Turnbull-Guidance-October-2005.pdf

Fletcher, K. C., & Abbas, A. E. (2018). A value measure for public-sector enterprise risk management: A TSA case study. *Risk Analysis, 38*(5), 991–1008.

Gobbo, G. (2021). *Un modello di integrazione tra risk management e performance management per la creazione di Valore Pubblico.* Giuffrè.

Guarini, E. (2014). Measuring public value in bureaucratic settings: Opportunities and constraints. *Studies in Public and Non-Profit Governance, 3,* 301–319.

Gustafsson, J. (2017). *Single case studies vs. multiple case studies: A comparative study.* Academy of Business, Engineering and Science, Halmstad University, Sweden. www.diva-portal.org/ smash/get/diva2:1064378/FULLTEXT01.pdf

Hinna, A., Scarozza, D., & Rotundi, F. (2018). Implementing risk management in the Italian public sector: Hybridization between old and new practices. *International Journal of Public Administration, 41*(2), 110–128.

Hood, C. (1995). The "new" public management in the 1980s: Variations on a theme. *Accounting, Organisations and Society, 20*(2–3), 93–109.

Hutter, B., & Power, M. (Eds.). (2005). *Organizational encounters with risk.* Cambridge University Press. https://doi.org/10.1017/CBO9780511488580.

Issa, F. H., & Masanja, E. P. (2022). Change for performance improvement in the Tanzania Ports Authority, a public sector organization in Tanzania. *International Journal of Public Leadership, 18*(4), 337–354. https://doi.org/10.1108/IJPL-12-2021-0061/FULL/HTML

Jones, R., & Pendlebury, M. (2010). *Public sector accounting* (6th ed.). Pearson Education.

Kloot, L., Martin, J., Kloot, L., & Martin, J. (2000). Strategic performance management: A balanced approach to performance management issues in local government. *Management Accounting Research, 11*, 231–251.

Kolisovas, D., & Andrius, Š. (2011). Risk management in Lithuania's public sector: Starting point, current situation and future perspectives. *Intellectual Economics, 5*(4), 547–559.

Kroll, A. (2017). Can performance management foster social equity? Stakeholder power, protective institutions, and minority representation. *Public Administration, 95*(1), 22–38.

Lukka, K. (2007). Management accounting change and stability: Loosely coupled rules and routines in action. *Management Accounting Research, 18*(1),–101.

Marcon, G. (2014). Public value theory in the context of public sector modernization. In J. Guthrie, G. Marcon, S. Russo, & F. Farneti (Eds.), *Public value management, measurement and reporting* (vol. 5, 323–351). Emerald.

Mauro, S. G., Cinquini, L., & Pianezzi, D. (2019). New public management between reality and illusion: Analysing the validity of performance-based budgeting. *British Accounting Review, 53*(6), 1–16. https://doi.org/10.1016/j.bar.2019.02.007

Mériade, L., & Qiang, L. Y. (2015). Public values on the public/private boundary: the case of civil servant recruitment examinations in China. *International Review of Administrative Sciences, 81*(2), 282–302.

Moore, D. M. H. (1995). *Creating public value: Strategic management in government.* Harvard University Press.

Nabatchi, T. (2012). Putting the "public" back in public values research: Designing participation to identify and respond to values. *Public Administration Review, 72*(5), 699–708.

O'Flynn, J. (2007). From new public management to public value: Paradigmatic change and managerial implications. *Australian Journal of Public Administration, 66*(3), 353–366.

Papi, L., Ievoli, R., Gobbo, G., Deidda Gagliardo, E., & Bacchini, F. (2020). Il Valore Pubblico come volano per finalizzare le performance di filiera dei Ministeri verso il Benessere Equo e sostenibile, *Azienda Pubblica, 4*(2020), 339–362.

Pollitt, C., & Bouckaert, G. (2004). The nature of public management reform. In *Public management reform: A comparative analysis* (pp. 6–23). Oxford University Press.

Power, M. (2009). The risk management of nothing. *Accounting, Organizations and Society, 34*(6–7), 849–855.

Rana, T., Wickramasinghe, D., & Bracci, E. (2019). New development: Integrating risk management in management control systems – lessons for public sector managers. *Public Money and Management, 39*(2), 148–151.

Ricci, P., & Civitillo, R. (2018). Italian public administration reform: What are the limits of financial performance measures? In E. Borgonovi, E. Anessi Pessina, & C. Bianchi (Eds.), *Outcome-based performance management in the public sector* (pp. 121–140). Springer International.

Salemans, L., & Budding, T. (2022). Operationalizing public value in higher education: The use of narratives as an alternative for performance indicators. *Journal of Management and Governance, 26*(2), 337–363.

Soin, K., & Collier, P. (2013). Risk and risk management in management accounting and control. *Management Accounting Research, 24*(2), 82–87.

Steccolini, I. (2019). Accounting and the post-new public management: Re-considering publicness in accounting research. *Accounting, Auditing & Accountability Journal, 32*(1), 255–279.

Thomas, R., & Davies, A. (2005). Theorizing the micro-politics of resistance: New public management and managerial identities in the UK public services. *Organization Studies, 26*(5), 683–706.

Thompson, F., & Rizova, P. (2015). Understanding and creating public value: Business is the engine, government the flywheel (and also the regulator). *Public Management Review, 17*(4), 565–586.

Van Dooren, W., Bouckaert, G., & Halligan, J. (2010). *Performance management in the public sector.* Routledge.

Vann, J. L. (2004). Resistance to change and the language of public organizations: A look at "clashing grammars" in large-scale information technology projects. *Public Organization Review, 4*(1), 47–73.

Yang, K. (2016). Creating public value and institutional innovations across boundaries: An integrative process of participation, legitimation, and implementation. *Public Administration Review, 76*(6), 873–885.

Yin, R. K. (1994). Discovering the future of the case study. Method in evaluation research. *Evaluation Practice*, *15*(3), 283–290.

Yu, C. H., Jannasch-Pennell A., & Digiangi, S. (2011). Compatibility between text mining and qualitative research in the perspectives of grounded theory, content analysis, and reliability. *Qualitative Report, 16*(3), 730–744.

Yuzhakov, V. N., Dobrolyubova, E. I., Pokida, A. N., & Zybunovskaya, N. V. (2020). Evaluating performance of regulatory enforcement activities by businesses: Key trends. *Public Administration Issues, 2*, 32–53.

16

NEW REALITIES OF RISK MANAGEMENT IN THE PUBLIC SECTOR

Anil K. Narayan and John Kommunuri

Introduction

The Covid-19 pandemic has highlighted the growing importance of risk and crisis management in the contemporary public sector. The global pandemic has forced many governments to respond quickly to safeguard the health and livelihoods of their populations by relaxing budgeting and spending rules, fast-tracking decision-making, and removing bureaucratic obstacles that prevented public service managers' capacity to act quickly. The Covid-19 pandemic has also fundamentally changed the risk landscape in the public sector as governments have taken direct roles in the management of the economic and societal issues, including the need to address complex factors such as inequality, growth, health and well-being, sustainability and climate change (World Economic Forum, 2022). Finding new ways to manage the uncertainties associated with the pandemic has exposed the public sector to a new set of risks related to balancing health and economic imperatives, finding alternative service delivery methods, and placing greater reliance on digital technologies (World Economic Forum, 2022). Pre-Covid-19, the public sector was largely risk averse (Bozeman & Kingsley, 1998), with accountability systems built around avoiding risks and uncertainties (Bastida et al., 2022). The Covid-19 pandemic and the post-pandemic reality have intensified the public sector's interest in and the centrality of risk management work (Bracci et al., 2021).

This chapter explores the new realities of risk management in the public sector with respect to the current and post-Covid-19 era challenges. The purpose is to present the implementation needs and the advantages of an enterprise risk management (ERM) system for public entities. The methodology adopted is a narrative literature review aimed at providing an assessment of relevant literature on the topic. The chapter offers a theoretical contribution to the needs and benefits of adopting ERM systems in the public sector, as well as their relationship with governance, management control systems (MCSs), and digital technologies. It brings to the fore the importance of a holistic, comprehensive and consolidated approach to help address many emerging challenges of risk management in the public sector.

The chapter is structured as follows: First, it provides a review of literature on risk management in the public sector. This is followed by a discussion of the new realities of risk management in the current Covid-19 era and the post-Covid-19 risk management challenges. We then discuss how an ERM approach with an enhanced risk governance, MCSs and the use of digital technologies will help manage the new realities of risk in the public sector. Finally, we provide a summary and conclusion.

DOI: 10.4324/9781003295945-21

Risk management in the public sector

Risk management in the public sector is complex and challenging mainly because the institutional settings of public sector organisations (PSOs) are generally large and complex, with high levels of bureaucracy and regulation, and also subject to wide-ranging societal interests and political influences (Ahmeti & Vladi, 2017; Braig et al., 2011; Ene & Dobrea, 2006; Leung & Isaacs, 2008; Nilsen & Olsen, 2007). Furthermore, studies reveal that conflicts exist between the norms, values and beliefs of multiple social systems, making PSOs complex (e.g. Greenwood et al., 2011). Such complexities push PSOs into contestation and conflict (Battilana & Dorado, 2010) and, as a result, impact their performance (Tracey et al., 2011). Moreover, the service delivery of PSOs is often hampered by diverse social, political, operational, institutional and global issues (e.g. Covid-19), which are expected to be managed in conjunction with emerging states of risk and uncertainty (Fleming et al., 2016). Dealing with the degree and complexity of risks and balancing conflicting demands and their resultant threats is an endless struggle for PSOs (Ahmeti & Vladi, 2017; Laguecir et al., 2020). Hence, there is a need for PSO transformation in organizational structures and processes to enable managers to respond to the changing needs and demands and manage risks effectively (Carlsson-Wall et al., 2016).

The risk management literature reveals that risk has been conceived and managed in different ways in the public sector. Traditionally, PSOs were risk averse (Bozeman & Kingsley, 1998), and their accountability system was built around avoiding risks and uncertainties (Bastida et al., 2022). Thus, little attention was paid to developing formal risk identification and management systems in PSOs. It was not until the late 1980s that risk management became an emerging element in New Public Management (NPM) implementation in the public sector (Lapsley, 2009). NPM promoted an entrepreneurship culture, encouraging public sector managers to be innovative and optimize opportunities through risk management. In addition, introducing an enterprise culture gave managers much-needed freedom from public sector bureaucracy and made them more receptive to risk-taking behaviour and engaging in appropriate risk management practices (Mahama et al., 2020).

Black (2005) states that risk management has mobilized the interest of regulators and policymakers. Relevant regulatory changes have made risk management a tool for effective service delivery and accountability (Barrett, 2014; Palermo, 2014). These regulatory initiatives are used to implement risk management frameworks and fulfil the PSO's mission (Kolisovas & Andrius, 2011). However, Kolisovas and Andrius (2011) express that the efforts to implement the risk management framework have so far been superficial, and little has been done to establish an overarching internal public sector control system for risk management. Some studies warn that this may cause risk management practices to be distorted from their rationale (Huber, 2009), while seeking to convey legitimacy and manage reputation (Bhimani, 2009; Power, 2009).

The Organization for Economic Cooperation and Development, the World Bank and other public sector organizations advocated their special interest in risk management (Black, 2005; Boin & Lodge, 2016; Osgood et al., 2007). Risk management practices are now prominent in countries like New Zealand, Australia, the UK and Canada (Barrett, 2014; Bui et al., 2019; Rana et al., 2019b; Woods, 2009). Additionally, several reforms over the past four decades have directed PSOs to focus on accountability, effective service delivery, performance and risk management (Palermo, 2014; Schillemans, 2016). But Huber (2009) observes that most PSOs deal with their risks on an ad-hoc basis and use a standardized model primarily to convey legitimacy. Within the categories of risks, the political, strategic, financial, operational and data-related risks are often managed by higher-level management, leaving document compliance and the maintaining of audit trails to the lower-level employees (Carlsson-Wall et al., 2019). Reminiscent of the traditional public sector compliance culture with extensive rules and regulations (Mahama, 2020), some PSOs limit their risk management to the accountability function by focusing on "processes, auditable trails, and documentation" (Lapsley, 2009, p. 16).

Bracci et al. (2021), in a structured literature review from 1990 to 2018, found a growing research interest in various aspects of the impact and diffusion of risk management practices and systems (Palermo, 2014; Rocher, 2011; Vinnari & Skærbæk, 2014; Woods, 2009; Carlsson-Wall et al., 2019) and integration of risk management within organizational processes (Rana et al., 2019a). However, despite increasing attention to risk management in the public sector, Bracci et al. (2021) suggested that more research is needed to open the black box and avoid the symbolic use of risk management. Surprisingly, the Covid-19 pandemic has immensely changed the risk landscape in the public sector and added another layer of complexity and further intensified the public sector's interest in and focus on risk management.

Though PSOs have sought better ways of managing risk using formal risk management tools and frameworks (Hinna et al., 2018), there have been calls for risk management frameworks to progress beyond compliance with a comprehensive strategy and process approach (Rana et al., 2019a), and integrate risk management with other organizational processes and systems (Christopher & Sarens, 2018; Hinna et al., 2018). The purpose is to have an integrated approach covering various aspects of MCSs (Rana et al., 2019a), performance measurement and accountability (Barrett, 2014; Hood & Smith, 2013; Palermo, 2014). However, to build up an efficient and properly integrated risk management, PSOs should locate organizational or structural factors, which some studies have indicated as risk management building blocks (Bracci et al., 2021; Capaldo et al., 2018; Hinna et al., 2018). The building blocks include the development of risk culture, the roles and responsibilities of risk managers and the role of technologies (Bracci et al., 2021).

The following section discusses the new realities of risk management in the current Covid-19 era and the post-Covid-19 risk management challenges.

The Covid-19 pandemic and the new realities of risk management

The Covid-19 pandemic has exposed the public sector to the new realities of risk management. It has led several countries to realize the vulnerability of their health, education, economic and social systems. Developed countries like the US and the UK have come to see the vulnerability of their production and public health systems, and found it difficult to increase production and manage supply chains for food and essential medical supplies, particularly medicine, protective equipment, ventilators and test kits (Mazzucato & Kattel, 2020). Moreover, international border closures due to the Covid-19 pandemic have exposed the public higher education system to strategic, operational and financial risk resulting from over-reliance on international student markets, particularly China (Carnegie et al., 2022; Martin-Sardesai et al., 2021). The financial and social impact is deeply felt in the higher education sector worldwide, especially in leading international student destination countries like the US, the UK and Australia (Carnegie et al., 2022).

The responsibility for societies' long-term resilience and stability lies with the public sector (Mazzucato & Kattel, 2020). In the pre-Covid-19 time, the public sector was largely risk averse (Bozeman & Kingsley, 1998), with the sector's accountability system built around avoiding risks and uncertainties (Bastida et al., 2022). However, the pandemic has highlighted that the pre-Covid-19 view of risk has been at the expense of long-term vision setting and has left many PSOs with reduced capacities in the face of the crisis, especially healthcare capacity to handle emergencies. This is essentially because the public sector was a frequent target of NPM reforms before the pandemic. Managerial reforms such as outsourcing, cost-cutting and financializaton of the economy have resulted in the erosion of public sector capacity and the capability to provide essential services (Mazzucato & Kattel, 2020).

The Covid-19 crisis has fundamentally changed the external risk landscape, with governments worldwide forced to take direct roles in safeguarding the health and livelihoods of their population and managing the economy. As a result, the risks that the public sector faces today and post-Covid-19 have significantly shifted in areas of public policy expectations, operational and strategic functions, and service delivery. While the government response has been out of necessity, the pandemic has emphasized that governments can no longer be risk averse and put society at risk when it comes to providing essential public services.

PSOs will need to navigate complex policy factors arising from the crisis, such as inequality, growth, sustainability and climate change. Besides having a clear understanding of multiple, complex, interrelated risk factors, public sector managers' appetite for risk needs to align with societal values, strategies, capabilities and the rapidly changing external risk landscape. Moreover, risk management needs to be an ongoing and integral part of essential public service delivery rather than a periodic response function (Collins et al., 2020). Hence, PSO managers will need a clear understanding of the potential risks and how they affect their operations, service delivery and people.

Concerns expressed by Mazzucato and Kattel (2020) also highlight that an overemphasis on financial cost efficiency at the expense of long-term vision setting has hampered public sector capacity to: adapt and learn, align public services and citizen needs, govern resilient production systems, and govern data and digital platforms. As a result, the public sector's vulnerability has been highlighted, and the need for government to rebuild public sector capacity and capabilities in critical areas of public service has been emphasized. This rebuilding of the capacity and capabilities will become possible through effective risk management policies and strategies. Thus, the pandemic has forced public sector managers to take a relook at their risk management approaches and make efforts to switch from the traditional way of avoiding risks to becoming more innovative and receptive to risk-taking behaviour.

In the literature, risk management has been viewed as a governance tool (Mikes, 2011; Power, 2007) and as a tool to support policy choices and decision-making (Hutter, 2005; Hutter & Power, 2005). However, in PSOs, risk management has been critiqued as a "reputation management strategy" (Power et al., 2009), as having only a symbolic use (Bracci et al., 2021), as seeking to convey legitimacy (Bhimani, 2009), and as often used as defensive management to avoid blame (Palmero, 2014). Avoiding risk inhibits entrepreneurial spirit, and the wholesale adoption of risk management techniques could hold up and even imprison organizational thinking (Power, 2007).

Effective risk identification and suitable management systems are essential to optimize opportunities and support capacity and capability building. There is a need for a well-connected public sector with functional collaborations between different PSOs (e.g. healthcare, finance, economic planning, social welfare, education, technology and infrastructure entities). Hence, managing risks with interconnected government services will increase the complexity of risk management in the public sector as PSOs must manage their risks and the risks that come with interconnected government services. The new reality is that PSOs can no longer think about risk in purely static, financial terms that counter societal expectations (Jain et al., 2022). For example, healthcare capacity constraints have influenced the way many countries managed the Covid-19 pandemic, suggesting more investment in their dynamic capabilities and capacity to provide essential public services.

Furthermore, the more complex risks arising from new forms of collaboration between different PSOs will need to be managed on an ongoing and continuous basis rather than just maintaining a short-term or fixed-term focus (Fleming et al., 2016; Rana et al., 2019a). Risk management cannot be a stand-alone activity and merely a matter of compliance, but should be integrated with PSOs' organizational processes by linking strategic planning, budgeting, decision-making, performance monitoring and reporting. This underlies the importance of having an ERM system that takes a more holistic approach to identifying and assessing risks from all areas of PSOs to manage less in "silos" and more in an integrated and continuous manner. Linking risk factors with calculative mechanisms such as budgets should help make better decisions on delivering quality public services and better outcomes (Barret, 2014; Rana et al., 2019a; Rana & Hoque, 2020).

Moreover, the Covid-19 pandemic has highlighted the central role of MCSs in managing risks in the public sector (Bracci et al., 2021). Several researchers have drawn attention to accounting control mechanisms such as budgeting and performance management to help decision-makers address post-Covid-19 challenges. Bastida et al. (2022) reported that the Covid-19 pandemic increased budget constraints, and PSOs are expected to develop risk-aware accountability and control systems. With increased budget constraints, performance budgeting is expected to emerge (Bastida et al., 2022; Douglas & Overmans, 2020). Anessi-Pessina et al. (2020) suggest that budgets should be more resilient to an external crisis by having anticipatory and coping roles. To navigate a crisis, Kober and Thambar (2022) suggest that MCSs must simultaneously pursue short-term/operational and long-term/strategic objectives. This will avoid narrowly adopting a constraining approach and widen the choice of strategic opportunities the crisis may bring about (van der Kolk et al., 2015). Carnegie et al. (2022) have called for an urgent transformation in public universities' financial reporting to adequately disclose and manage significant risks. This is after they found the low quality of risk disclosures associated with COVID-19 in the financial reporting of Australian public universities.

Budget deficits and government debt have increased dramatically in most countries, prompted by COVID-19 stimulus packages to sustain employment and companies (Bastida et al., 2022). Public sector efficiency is expected to be a key driver in the new reality as governments are forced to do more with fewer resources in future years. With the government exercising spending controls and making budget cuts to address the debt burden, PSOs could be exposed to much greater risks in terms of not meeting programme outcomes, downsizing, or even slowing down of business operations. A comprehensive understanding of how risks may develop over time and careful risk management will be required to ensure this does not happen. The COVID-19 pandemic has demonstrated that government service delivery can be effective and efficient by working in a connected and collaborative manner. An integrated risk management system linking strategic planning, budgeting and decision-making will help ensure intended outcomes are achieved (COSO, 2017).

The pandemic has also transformed the future of work and the workforce. Remote and flexible working, working with diverse teams and heavy reliance on digital technology have become the pandemic and post-pandemic new reality. This presents complex issues and a new set of risk management challenges in the public sector. Hence, PSOs will need to properly assess and manage numerous risks associated with new working conditions and new approaches to service delivery and to working with technology. Particular attention needs to be given to risk management of employees' emotional and physical well-being, to the risk resulting from loss in productivity and efficiency, to employee performance-related risks, to the risk of not having the required capacity and capability to provide required services, and to the risk of shortage of new skills. Moreover, the Covid-19 pandemic has accelerated the digital technology transformation across the public sector to enable staff to work remotely and share information between and across departments and PSOs in a more connected way. This has intensified technology disruption, data protection and privacy, and cybercrime risks. These risks will require ongoing and proactive management to avoid potential breaches.

The pandemic has brought to the fore an entirely new set of challenges related to an uncertain and volatile future. The new reality is that good risk management must provide a consistent approach to systematically identifying, assessing and seizing opportunities. Information technology provides the mechanism for the collection and collation of all risk-related information in an integrated manner (Woods, 2009). The information system must support the phases of risk identification, assessment and reporting processes, including providing useful information to help reduce the uncertainty of the risk estimates (Dittmeier, 2015). Managing risk in an increasingly volatile and complex public sector environment calls for proactive and integrated solutions.

The next section discusses how an ERM approach with an enhanced risk governance framework, an integrated MCS and the use of digital technologies will help manage the new realities of risk in the public sector.

Enterprise risk management

ERM has been increasingly recognized as offering an integrated risk management framework that promises to meet the new challenges in public sector risk management (Bracci et al., 2021; Rana et al., 2019a). ERM is

> a process, effected by an entity's board of directors, management and other personnel, applied in strategy setting and across the enterprise, designed to identify potential events that may affect the entity and manage risks to be within its risk appetite, to provide reasonable assurance regarding the achievement of entity objectives.
>
> *COSO, 2004*

This definition indicates that ERM captures not simply financial risks but all risks from potential events that influence the achievement of an organization's objectives.

As Rana et al. (2019a) noted, ERM involves shifting from a top-down, silo-based approach to an integrated approach that cuts across different internal departments and involves external constituents where everyone has risk management responsibility. This approach allows PSOs to look at specific areas of risk and the larger picture by effectively assessing, controlling, exploiting opportunities, nd monitoring risks from all sources to achieve their goals (Leung and aacs, 2008). Under ERM, everyone will clearly understand the potential risks and how they affect their operations, service delivery and people. Also, ERM helps identify risks and opportunities that can negatively or positively influence an organisaiion's ability to achieve its desired objectives (COSO, 2009; Huber, 2009). This will make public sector managers more receptive to risk-taking and help extract risk opportunities instead of simply avoiding them. In addition, ERM enables the alignment of risk appetite with societal values, strategies, capabilities and the changing external risk landscape.

The new realities of the pandemic require the public sector to be well connected with functional collaborations between different PSOs (e.g. healthcare, finance, economic planning, social welfare, education, technology and infrastructure entities) to implement whole-of-government programmes. This increases the complexity of risk management as PSOs need to manage their risks and the risks that come with interconnected government services. ERM provides a clear understanding of multiple, complex and interrelated risk factors by taking a more holistic approach, identifying and assessing risks from all areas of PSOs to manage less in "silos" and more in an integrated manner. In addition, it enables risks arising from new forms of collaboration between different PSOs to be managed on an ongoing and continuous basis rather than just maintaining a short-term or fixed-term focus (Fleming et al., 2016; Rana et al., 2019a). However, the key challenge for ERM adoption is integrating all processes and systems, improving capability and coordination, and providing stakeholders with a unified risk picture.

The recent health, social, economic and financial crises due to the Covid-19 pandemic have challenged the service delivery capacity of PSOs. ERM recognizes that risk management cannot be a stand-alone activity and is not merely a matter of compliance. Therefore, integration is critical, and ERM provides integration with other organizational processes (e.g. strategic planning, budgeting, decision-making) to make risk management an ongoing and integral part of essential public service delivery rather than a periodic response function. Integration with organizational processes will ensure that risk related to service delivery capacity and capability is proactively managed. With strategy driving decision-making, budgeting and the achievement of organizational goals, aligning ERM with strategic objectives will help PSOs identify and manage their most critical risks effectively. Effective risk management should assist in the efficient allocation of resources and build public sector capacity and capability.

ERM integration with organizational processes and strategy provides opportunities for PSOs to move from compliance to a comprehensive approach to risk management. By aligning with the company's strategy, ERM involves employees at all levels of the organization in its implementation process. This enables risk to be managed at the operational and strategic levels. It also helps create greater awareness of risk issues essential in establishing a sustainable and integrated corporate risk culture. Capaldo et al. (2018) noted that without an effective risk culture in an organization, individual perceptions of risk are insufficient for developing a real propensity to take risks.

Though ERM employs a top-down process for determining, evaluating, assessing, controlling and monitoring all risks that a business faces (Tuddenham & Baird, 2007), it is an enterprise-wide commitment rather than just a management initiative, and the use of ERM as a strategic management tool will help boost PSOs' performance. ERM is a multidirectional iterative process in which almost any component in the process can and does influence another. To rein in the risks a business confronts, ERM extends the financial risk management stream to non-financial risks and helps management design proper and effective risk management practices and strategies. Various frameworks provide guiding principles to assist risk managers in ERM design and implementation. However, even within the public sector, frameworks differ from organization to organization (Hoyt & Liebenberg, 2011; Kommunuri et al., 2016), and implementation issues require careful attention as frameworks may not provide all the necessary tools to facilitate its application (De Souza et al., 2012; Caron et al., 2013).

Managers should not assume that ERM refers unequivocally to a coherent set of practices (Power, 2007). Moreover, if regulators pressure managers to integrate various risk categories into corporate governance, it may result in the risk management of nothing instead of everything (Power et al., 2009). Therefore, a moderate and a more optimistic view of risk management is needed as it may be highly unlikely to calculate and manage every individual risk and integrate it into the whole risk management strategy. However, it is important to consider how risks are organized, which involves more than calculating each risk and reflecting on how to improve the way they are organized in the future (Hardy et al., 2020). To face the challenges of the new realities of the Covid-19 pandemic, PSOs must ensure a good risk governance system, proper integration of risks with MCS, and efficient use of the latest digital technologies.

Enterprise risk management and governance

Risk management is considered the backbone of good governance (Hood & Nawaz, 2004; Miller et al., 2008). For successful implementation and effective operation of ERM, an integrated approach encompassing every level of corporate governance is required (Wood & Randall, 2005). Sound corporate governance mechanisms with functional ERM and internal control systems effectively police internal operations to prevent miscues that would potentially threaten organizational legitimacy. ERM proposes an integrated structure of all risks an organization faces and aligns risk management with the organization's corporate governance and strategy. Such alignment helps enhance the risk governance framework and provide a strategic perspective of risks. The Covid-19 crisis has magnified the need for a robust risk governance framework to provide rapid responses and mobilize resources. In the new reality, an enhanced risk governance framework will provide a strategic perspective of risks, help prioritize limited resources, act proactively and make timely decisions.

The prime responsibility of governance is to ensure the integrity of the company's systems of risk identification, assessment and management. Effective risk governance through ERM facilitates early risk identification, good risk assessment and timely communication of risk information (Tuddenham & Baird, 2007). Risk identification is the most critical stage in the entire risk management process, as any mistakes made at this stage are likely to lead to incorrect risk analysis, assessment,and response.

Establishing a sustainable and integrated corporate risk culture that creates greater awareness of risk issues is also essential to effective risk identification and management. Capaldo et al. (2018) warn that without an effective risk culture in an organization, individual perceptions of risk are insufficient for developing a real propensity to take risks.

Risk assessment of the Covid-19 pandemic based on scientific data and epidemiological models resulted in a high degree of agreement among policymakers on the strategies and measures needed to suppress virus transmission (Hale & Webster 2020). Policy consensus was strengthened as increasing data became available from the large body of evidence and analysis relating to previous coronaviruses (Paules et al., 2020) and data from the earliest affected countries, notably China and Italy (Phull, 2020).

To implement ERM, senior leadership support is critical to the programme's success. Having a chief risk officer (CRO) role helps management set a strong tone at the top to assign responsibilities, oversee the risk management process and maintain constant responsibility. Assigning the right risks to the right people and driving meaningful conversations with department heads are crucial for effective ERM implementation. The senior management may stay focused on strategy and performance management but often neglect to challenge the capabilities from a risk perspective. Therefore, developing a strong risk culture with risk management capabilities and establishing a robust risk management operating model is warranted. A risk committee will help monitor risks, oversee the coordination, and advise management on risk strategy. Effective risk communication is essential for public sector organizations to develop and maintain public confidence (Smith & McCloskey, 1998). Risk reporting based on the risks identified and assessment of controls enables management to prioritize controls in order of their effectiveness.

The Covid-19 pandemic has highlighted the importance of timely communication of risk-related information. The pandemic was foreshadowed by the SARS outbreak of 2003–2004. Despite some early warning signs of the spread of the coronavirus, communication failure was costly, especially in China and the US, where policymakers actively suppressed or disregarded early risk-related information until it was too late to contain the outbreak (Collins et al., 2020). However, the communication of risk-related information within and between different groups, such as scientists, policymakers and the public, both nationally and internationally, helped reduce uncertainty and facilitate robust risk assessment (Collins et al., 2020). There were numerous other challenges related to risk communication, such as communicating the severity of the risk, instilling urgency without creating panic or despair, and communicating consistent messages to very different audiences. Assessing risk perceptions by considering individual and societal opinions in shaping protective behaviours, balancing health and economic impacts, or determining the level of isolation and lockdowns that is appropriate for the government to enforce was not easy. PSOs should learn from the pandemic experience that speed of action is a critical success factor in risk management.

Enterprise risk management and management control system

Risk management is a cornerstone of management control in modern society (Bhimani, 2009), and the pandemic has highlighted the crucial role of MCSs in managing risks in the public sector (Bracci et al., 2021). Effective MCSs help PSOs identify, assess and mitigate significant threats and enhance opportunities (Rana et al., 2019a). With an integrated framework, ERM acts as an important control mechanism that enhances organizational performance (Adam et al., 2023; Hyot & Liebenberg, 2011; Malik et al., 2020; Wang et al., 2018). MCSs comprise strategic planning, budgeting, decision-making, performance monitoring, and reporting tools. These tools give direction to the management regarding their behaviour and decisions related to achieving organizational goals and setting strategies (Merchant & Otley, 2006).

Effective MCSs are very much needed in complex settings of PSOs (Jarvinen, 2016; Schaffer et al., 2015) and are valuable in managing complex and competing institutional demands (Carlsson-Wall et al., 2016). Some suggest specific management controls such as budgets, balanced scorecards and performance measurement (Amans et al., 2015; Sundin et al., 2010) for successful risk management. The integrated ERM framework ties risk management to management controls, links to organizational goals and strategy, management style and culture, monitoring and coordination. ERM and MCSs play a fundamental role in identifying and implementing PSOs management choices and taking corrective actions to reduce and overcome uncertainties. Integrating ERM with MCSs provides an effective management framework to face unexpected challenges and enhance organizational performance. It helps proactively engage leaders from across PSOs to determine mitigation and response efforts.

However, due to a continuous focus on compliance and regulatory requirements, PSOs are under pressure which could slow down the formal implementation process, thereby hindering the benefits of risk management. This may also result in the minimal integration of risk management with MCSs. Vinnari and Skaerbaek (2014) suggest that the formal risk management structure can destabilize existing informal practices. Crawford and Stein (2005) suggest that integrating risk management with other organizational processes requires developing a culture of second-order change to encourage the culture of ongoing learning.

In the public sector, some risks are managed outside formal risk management systems, leading to tensions between formal and informal approaches to risk management (Carlsson-Wall et al., 2019). However, that tension is not static and may eventually turn into a hybridized mode of interaction (Carlsson-Wall et al., 2019; 2021). A slightly different view from Oulasvirta and Anttiroiko (2017) is that if organizations do not see immediate benefits from implementing risk management, they could start with a silos approach and slowly integrate individual risks into a formal risk management framework, which may yield greater benefits from this hybridized approach. Similarly, Fleming et al. (2016) emphasizes the importance of adopting soft rather than hard (a regulation-drive) risk management as it enhances organizational learning and innovation. Risk managers can be a source of innovation when PSOs adopt a soft relational approach rather than a hard or technocratic and regulation-driven approach.

Moreover, Barrett (2016) hints that, though risk management is expected to involve everyone in the organization, it is mostly isolated within the internal audit function. In PSOs, risk management is traditionally limited to an accountability function and is often used to avoid blame. Though the reliance on legislative requirements as frameworks is needed, the PWC (2015) report documents the growing adoption of private sector approaches to ERM in PSOs. While integrating risk and control systems in organizations is important, it has been neglected for a long time (Arena et al., 2011). For effective ERM implementation, the top management needs to build a risk-awareness culture with a strong tone at the top (Simkins, 2008). Lack of awareness or interest in risk may result in negligence of responsibility. As the focus of risk management shifts from compliance to a greater managerial approach, MCSs could play a key role in implementing an organization's ERM by directing management behaviour towards efficiencies (Rana et al., 2019a).

Risk reporting is an important component of MCSs. However, if it is unconnected from business strategy and performance, it can be merely a matter of compliance, defeating risk management's purpose. Carnegie et al. (2022) have called for an urgent transformation in public universities' financial reporting to adequately disclose and manage significant risks. With ERM, PSOs will manage less in 'silos' and more in an integrated and continuous manner. Therefore, risk reporting and management will improve by strengthening the vertical and horizontal communication of risks, reporting near misses, and communicating risk digitally (Agarwal & Kallapur, 2021).

The Covid-19 pandemic has forced PSOs to depend closely on their MCSs, such as in terms of budgeting and strategic planning (Bastida et al., 2022). With rising government debt and budget constraints, public sector efficiency will be a key driver in the new reality as governments are compelled to do more with less resources in future years. Anessi-Pessina et al. (2020) suggest budgets should be more resilient to external crises by playing anticipatory and coping roles. A comprehensive understanding of how risks may develop over time and of careful risk management will be required to ensure spending controls and budget cuts do not expose PSOs to much greater risks in terms of not meeting programme outcomes or having the dynamic capabilities and capacity to provide essential public services.

The Committee of Sponsoring Organisations (COSO 2017) framework proposes management think strategically about the existing and emerging risks that could affect their operations and determine whether a strategy works in tandem with risk appetite and how it will help drive them to set objectives to allocate resources efficiently. Also, as more complex risks arise from new forms of collaboration between different PSOs, these will need to be managed on an ongoing and continuous basis rather than just maintaining a short-term or fixed-term focus (Fleming et al., 2016; Rana et al., 2019a). Kober and Thambar (2022) suggest that management control systems must simultaneously pursue short-term/operational and long-term/strategic objectives. This will avoid narrowly adopting a constraining approach and widen the choice of strategic opportunities a crisis may bring about (van der Kolk et al., 2015).

Enterprise risk management and digital technologies

Risk management is not a stand-alone activity but must be integrated with other corporate processes and systems (Hinna et al., 2018). Information technology plays a central role in supporting the integrated ERM by providing a mechanism for the collection and collation of both performance and risk-related information (Woods, 2009). A good information technology system will support all phases of the integrated ERM, enabling early identification and assessment of risk from all sources and providing useful information to manage risks (Dittmeier, 2015). The Covid-19 pandemic has accelerated the digital technology transformation across the public sector to enable staff to work remotely and share information between and across departments and PSOs in a more connected way. At the same time, it has intensified technology disruption risks, data protection and privacy risks, and cybercrime risks. The new reality is that these risks will require ongoing and proactive management to avoid potential breaches.

Regarding data and digital technologies, governments have also performed differently in the Covid-19 crisis, showing once again that throwing money at a problem is not viable if core capacities and capabilities are not there or have been outsourced. For example, Singapore had invested heavily in its government digital service unit and was able to utilize the tracking applications to trace the viral spread (Mazzucato & Quaggiotto, 2020). South Korea adopted a very aggressive high-tech tracking approach (a result of completely redrawing its pandemic response legislation after the SARS debacle), but the government also opened up real-time data on mask stocks and pharmacy locations, so that start-ups and citizens were able to build a number of add-on services that helped ensure a more effective and safe distribution (Mazzucato & Quaggiotto, 2020). However, many Western governments were slow to react as their legal and technical infrastructure around data is insufficiently developed. For instance, the UK only tested a tracing app in June 2020.

Digital technologies are of strategic importance and fundamental for organizations' operations (Anderson et al., 2020; Klein & Todesco, 2021), enabling the transformation of business activities, processes and competencies to leverage changes and opportunities. In emergencies such as the Covid-19 pandemic, digital technologies are hailed as enablers to ensure business continuity and assist in resolving challenges that arise in the wake of such emergencies (Golinelli et al., 2020). The Covid-19 pandemic has intensified existing trends of digitalization that are challenging organizations. While delivering Microsoft's earnings report, CEO Satya Nadella stated, "we have seen two years' worth of digital transformation in two months" (Spataro, 2020). Since the Covid-19 pandemic has swiftly moved organizations and consumers to digital channels, organizations across sectors have realized the importance of scaling artificial intelligence (AI) and analytics to update demand patterns and reconsider supply chains. Also, the efficient use of high-level digital technologies is crucial to keep businesses running during a crisis (Chamola et al., 2020) as they improve resilience and support management decision-making.

Digital technologies (e.g. mobile and collaborative technologies, the internet of things, big data analytics, blockchain technology and AI crosslink organizations' operational and value creation processes. For example, AI is being deployed in healthcare to understand disease transmission, improve infection detection rates, create an epidemic intelligence dashboard through data analytics, develop trivial vaccines and treatments, and assess the pandemic's impact on socio-economic aspects (Bullock et al., 2020). However, Kane et al. (2015) suggest that organizations should have the appropriate capabilities and talent to experiment and conceptualize how digital technologies will affect business processes and models.

Developing and adopting dynamic capabilities are fundamental to organizational success (Teece, 2017). Dynamic capabilities group organizational skills, processes and routines that differentiate organizations in dealing with risks and bridge the gap between an organization's existing capabilities and the changing external environment. Managers are critical in aligning the organization's resources and capabilities with the changing and unprecedented external environment. For example, the global health crisis caused by the Covid-19 pandemic has changed the external environment. To respond to the challenges of this pandemic and the changing external pressures, a high level of digital maturity is needed (Priyono et al., 2020). Past evidence shows that digital technologies mitigated the SARS pandemic's health crisis in 2003 (Katz et al., 2020). Additionally, more advanced digital technologies developed recently can help PSOs better sense opportunities, exploit those opportunities and transform their processes and systems to effectively face the challenges of the Covid-19 pandemic. During the pandemic, a high level of digital activity enabling online interactions with the clients, online sales and applications to conduct and collect payments was reported (Klein & Todesco, 2021).

Though digital technologies as a form of dynamic capabilities are associated with reduced business risks, limited research has been done on digital technologies and AI to reduce the consequences of the Covid-19 pandemic in PSOs (Piccialli et al., 2021). AI enables PSOs to navigate complex risk scenarios and optimise costs through predictive maintenance. In addition, the dynamic capabilities assist them in adjusting their resources and processes to gain and sustain competitive advantages in the changing Covid-19 context. As a set of dynamic capabilities, AI and its subsets provide a framework to approach the impact of AI on the way PSOs deal with the pandemic's challenges. It paves the way for them to find new venues (sensing capabilities), exploit available opportunities (seizing capabilities), and bring changes to their operational processes (transforming capabilities) (Teece et al., 2016; Warner & Wager, 2019). Hence, PSO managers must leverage technology to meet new demands in order to pivot their operations, boost efficiency and reduce their exposure to risk.

Summary and conclusion

The Covid-19 pandemic has changed the external risk landscape and exposed the public sector's vulnerability to risk management. In the new reality, the public sector managers can no longer be risk averse and think about risk in purely static, financial terms and as merely a matter of compliance. The risk appetite must align with societal values, strategies and the changing external risk landscape to ensure society is not at risk when providing essential public services. The crisis has highlighted the need for the public sector to develop the capacity and capability to manage risks in critical areas of public service delivery. With the increasing complexity of risk arising from new forms of collaboration and interconnected government services, it has become essential that risk management become an integral and ongoing part of essential public service delivery rather than a periodic, short-term or fixed-term response function.

ERM offers an integrated risk management framework designed to eliminate silos and provide a holistic perspective of risks so they can be managed proactively and continuously. Its integration with organizational processes of strategic planning, budgeting, decision-making, performance monitoring and reporting helps prioritize resources, make timely decisions and accomplish strategic objectives. Also, ERM will provide a strategic perspective on all risks to improve governance and establish a sustainable and integrated corporate risk culture that creates greater awareness of risk issues. The importance of timely communication and the reporting of risk-related information cannot be overemphasized. A robust risk governance framework aligned with ERM will help provide rapid responses and mobilize resources to manage risks effectively.

Integrating ERM with MCSs is vital in managing risks in the public sector. Effective risk management control processes will ensure that the risk tolerance levels for the set risk appetite are maintained at all levels of the organization. The pandemic and the post-pandemic realities are that budget deficits and government debt have increased dramatically, forcing governments to exercise spending controls and make budget cuts. The Covid-19 pandemic has also transformed the future of work and the workforce with new forms of risks associated with new working conditions, new approaches to service delivery, risk of loss in productivity and efficiency, risk of shortage of new skills and the need to work with technology. Integrating ERM with MCSs promises improved strategic planning, budgeting and decision-making beyond mere financial compliance. An integrated ERM will unquestionably direct risk management behaviour towards improved efficiency, accountability and performance. It will help develop a strong risk culture.

A key element of the ERM process is the use of digital technologies to provide a centralized source of risk information and facilitate risk management in an integrated manner. The Covid-19 pandemic has accelerated the use of digital technologies, and PSOs must embrace the digital revolution to improve risk management. The use of digital technologies will ensure proactive management of all risks, especially through proper monitoring, review and the taking of corrective actions before a risk event takes place. Risk managers will need a deep understanding of data, analytics and technology to ensure they are utilized effectively to manage all risks.

The aim of this chapter was to present the new realities of risk management in the public sector with respect to the current and post-Covid-19 pandemic challenges. The chapter contributes to new ways of managing the uncertainties associated with the pandemic, which has exposed the public sector to a new set of risks related to balancing health and economic imperatives, finding alternative service delivery methods and experiencing greater reliance on digital technologies. Risks and uncertainties are here to stay, and the Covid-19 pandemic has accelerated the need for the public sector to refresh and strengthen its approach to risk management. The chapter makes a theoretical contribution to advance knowledge on the need and benefits of adopting ERM systems, as well as their relationships with governance, MCSs and digital technologies. To meet the increasingly volatile and dynamic risk environment of the future, PSOs require more agile risk management and an enterprise-wide view of all risks so that they can be managed effectively. An integrated ERM offers many advantages and, if implemented properly, promises to elevate risk management from compliance to a more proactive and comprehensive strategy.

The views presented in this chapter represents an important area for further debate and future research. Future research could look at the benefits of the inclusion of digital technologies in ERM and functional collaborations between different PSOs to implement whole-of-government risk management programmes and strategies.

References

Adam, M., Soliman, A. M., & Mahtab, N. (2023). Measuring enterprise risk management implementation: A multifaceted approach for the banking sector. *Quarterly Review of Economics and Finance*, 87, 244–256. https://doi.org/10.1016/j.qref.2021.01.002

Agarwal, R., & Kallapur, S. (2021). Four ways to improve risk reporting. *California Management Review, 63*(4), 52–65.

Ahmeti, R., & Vladi, B. (2017). Analysis of international risk management standards (advantages and disadvantages). *European Journal of Research and Reflection in Management Sciences*, 5, 323–329.

Amans, P., Mazars-Chapelon, A., & Villesèque-Dubus, F. (2015). Budgeting in institutional complexity: The case of performing arts organisations. *Management Accounting Research, 27*, 47–66.

Anderson, R. M., Heesterbeek, H., Klinkenberg, D., & Hollingsworth, T. D. (2020). How will country-based mitigation measures influence the course of the COVID-19 epidemic? *The Lancet, 395*(10228), 931–934. https://doi.org/10.1016/S0140-6736(20)30567-5

Anessi-Pessina, E., Barbera, C., Langella, C., Manes-Rossi, F., Sancino, A., Sicilia, M., & Steccolini, I. (2020). Reconsidering public budgeting after the COVID-19 outbreak: Key lessons and future challenges. *Journal of Public Budgeting, Accounting & Financial Management, 32*(5), 957–965. https://doi.org/10.1108/JPB AFM-07-2020-0115

Arena, M., Arnaboldi, M., & Azzone, G. (2011). Is enterprise risk management real? *Journal of Risk Research, 14*(7), 779–797. https://doi.org/10.1080/13669877.2011.571775

Barrett, P. (2014). Risk management – how to regain trust and confidence in the government. *Public Money & Management, 34*(6), 459–464. https://doi.org/10.1080/09540962.2014.962376

Barrett, S. (2016). *Effects of information technology risk management and institution size on financial performance* [Unpublished doctoral dissertation]. Walden University.

Bastida, F., Bracci, E., & Hoque, Z. (2022). Accounting for unstable environments in the public sector: managing post-COVID-19 times. *Journal of Public Budgeting, Accounting & Financial Management, 34*(1), 1–26. https://doi.org/10.1108/JPBAFM-09-2021-0136

Battilana, J., & Dorado, S. (2010). Building sustainable hybrid organisations: The case of commercial microfinance organisations. *Academy of Management Journal, 53*(6), 1419–1440.

Bhimani, A. (2009). Risk management, corporate governance, and management accounting: Emerging interdependencies, *Management Accounting Research, 20*(1), 2–5.

Black, J. (2005). The emergence of risk-based regulation and the new public risk management in the United Kingdom. Public Law, 3, 512–548. Public law - Dialnet (unirioja.es)

Boin, A., & Lodge, M. (2016). Designing resilient institutions for transboundary crisis management: A time for public administration. *Public Administration, 94*(2), 289–298.

Bozeman, B., & Kingsley, G. (1998). Risk culture in public and private organisations. *Public Administration Review, 58*, 109–118.

Bracci, E., Tallaki, M., Gobbo, G., & Papi, L. (2021). Risk management in the public sector: A structured literature review. *International Journal of Public Sector Management, 34*(2), 205–223. https://doi-org.ezproxy.aut. ac.nz/10.1108/IJPSM-02-2020-0049

Braig, S., Gebre, B., & Sellgren, A. (2011). *Strengthening risk management in the US public sector*. McKinsey Working Papers on Risk, No. 28. www.mckinsey.com/capabilities/risk-and-resilience/our-insights/strengthen ing-risk-management-in-the-us-public-sector#/

Bui, B., Cowdery, C., & Wang, Z. (2019). Risk management in local authorities: An application of Schatzki's social site ontology. *British Accounting Review, 51*, 299–315. https://doi.org/10. 1016/j.bar.2019.01.001

Bullock, J., Luciano, A., Pham, K. H., Lam, C. S. N., & Luengo-Oroz, M. (2020). Mapping the landscape of artificial intelligence applications against COVID-19. *Journal of Artificial Intelligence Research, 69*, 807–845.

Capaldo, G., Costantino, N., Pellegrino, R., & Rippa, P. (2018). The role of risk in improving goal setting in performance management practices within the public sector: Explorative research in courts offices in Italy. *International Journal of Public Administration, 41*(12), 986–997.

Carlsson-Wall, M., Iredahl, A., Kraus, K., & Wiklund, M. (2021). The role of management controls in managing heterogeneous interests during extreme situations: The Swedish migrant crisis in 2015. *Qualitative Research in Accounting and Management, 18*(1), 1–25.

Carlsson-Wall, M., Kraus, K., Meidell, A., & Tran, P. (2019). Managing risk in the public sector – the interaction between vernacular and formal risk management systems. *Financial Accountability & Management, 35*, 3–19.

Carlsson-Wall, M., Kraus, K., & Messner, M. (2016). Performance measurement systems and the enactment of different institutional logics: Insights from a football organisation. *Management Accounting Research, 32*, 45–61.

Carnegie, G. D., Guthrie, J., & Martin-Sardesai, A. (2022). Public universities and impacts of COVID-19 in Australia: Risk disclosures and organisational change. *Accounting, Auditing & Accountability Journal, 35*(1), 61–73.

Caron, F., Vanthienen, J., & Baesens, B. (2013). A comprehensive investigation of the applicability of process mining techniques for enterprise risk management. *Computers in Industry, 64*(4), 464–475.

Chamola, V., Hassija, V., Gupta, V., & Guizani, M. (2020). A comprehensive review of the COVID-19 pandemic and the role of IoT, drones, AI, blockchain, and 5G in managing its impact. *IEEE Access, 8*, 90225–90265.

Christopher, J., & Sarens, G. (2018). Diffusion of corporate risk-management characteristics: Perspectives of chief audit executives through a survey approach. *Australian Journal of Public Administration, 77*(3), 427–441.

Collins, A., Florin, M. V., & Renn, O. (2020). COVID-19 risk governance: Drivers, responses, and lessons to be learned. *Journal of Risk Research, 23*(7–8), 1073–1082.

Committee of Sponsoring Organisations of the Treadway Commission (COSO). (2004). Enterprise Risk Management-Integrated Framework. www.coso.org.

Committee of Sponsoring Organisations of the Treadway Commission (COSO). (2009). COSO internal control integrated framework: Guidance on monitoring internal control systems. Volume 3: Examples. www.coso.org/Shared%20Documents/CROWE-COSO-Internal-Control-Integrated-Framework.pdf

Committee of Sponsoring Organisations of the Treadway Commission (COSO). (2017). Enterprise risk management – integrating with strategy and performance. www.coso.org/enterprise-risk-management

Crawford, M., & Stein, W. (2005). "Second-order" change in UK local government: The case of risk management. *International Journal of Public Sector Management, 18*(5), 414–423. https://doi.org/10.1108/095135 50510608877

De Souza, R. S., Gomes, S. M. S., Bruni, A. L., De Oliveira, G. G., Sampaio, M. S., & De Faria, J. A. (2012). Enterprise risk management and performance improvement: A study with Brazilian non-financial firms. *Performance Measurement and Management Control: Global Issues*, 275–298.

Dittmeier, C. (2015). *La governance dei rischi. Un riferimento per gli organi e le funzioni di governo e controllo.* EGEA SpA.

Douglas, S., & Overmans, T. (2020). Public value budgeting: Propositions for the future of budgeting. *Journal of Public Budgeting, Accounting & Financial Management, 32*(4), 623–637. https://doi-org.ezproxy.aut.ac.nz/10.1108/JPBAFM-05-2020-0066

Ene, N. C., & Dobrea, C. R. (2006). Adapting risk management principles to the public sector reforms. *Administratie si Management Public, 6*(1), 126–130.

Fleming, S., Osborne, S., & Kinder, T. (2016). Risky business – reconceptualising risk and innovation in public services. *Public Money & Management, 36*(6), 425–432.

Golinelli, D., Boetto, E., Carullo, G., Nuzzolese, A. G., Landini, M., & Fantini, M. P. (2020). Adoption of digital technologies in health care during the COVID-19 pandemic: Systematic review of early scientific literature. *Journal of Medical Internet Research, 22*(11), e22280. https://doi.org:10.2196/22280

Greenwood, R., Raynaud, M., Kadesh, F., Micelotta, E. R., & Lounsbury, M. (2011). Institutional complexity and organisational responses. *Academy of Management Annals, 5*(1), 317–371.

Hale, T., & Webster, G. (2020). Oxford COVID-19 Government Response Tracker. www.bsg.ox.ac.uk/resea &rch/research-projects/oxford-covid-19-government-response-tracker

Hardy, C., Maguire, S., Power, M., & Tsoukas, H. (2020). Organising risk: Organization and management theory for the risk society. *Academy of Management Annals, 14*(2), 1032–1066.

Hinna, A., Scarozza, D., & Rotundi, F. (2018). Implementing risk management in the Italian public sector: Hybridisation between old and new practices. *International Journal of Public Administration, 41*(2), 110–128.

Hood, J., & Nawaz, M. S. (2004). Political risk exposure and management in multi-national companies: Is there a role for the corporate risk manager? *Risk Management, 6*(1), 7–18.

Hood, J., & Smith, T. (2013). Perceptions of quantifiable benefits of local authority risk management. *International Journal of Public Sector Management, 26*(4), 309–319. https://doi.org/10.1108/IJPSM-01-2012-0016

Hoyt, R. E., & Liebenberg, A. P. (2011). The value of enterprise risk management. *Journal of Risk and Insurance, 78*, 795–822.

Huber, C. (2009). Risks and risk-based regulation in higher education institutions. *Tertiary Education and Management, 15*(2), 83–95. https://doi.org/10.1080/13583880902869554

Hutter, B., & Power, M. (Eds.). (2005). *Organisational encounters with risk.* Cambridge University Press.

Hutter, B. M. (2005). *The attractions of risk-based regulation: Accounting for the emergence of risk ideas in regulation*, Vol. 33. CARR.

Jain, R., Nauck, F., Poppensieker, T., & White, O (2022). Meeting the future: Dynamic risk management for uncertain times. *McKinsey Quarterly*, Issue 1. www.mckinsey.com/business-functions/risk-and-resilience/our-insights/meeting-the-future-dynamic-risk-management-for-uncertain-times

Järvinen, J. T. (2016). Role of management accounting in applying new institutional logics. *Accounting, Auditing and Accountability Journal, 29*(5), 861–886.

Kane, G. C., Palmer, D., Phillips, A. N., Kiron, D., & Buckley, N. (2015). Strategy, not technology, drives digital transformation. *MIT Sloan Management Review and Deloitte University Press, 14*(1–25).

Katz, R., Jung, J., & Callorda, F. (2020). Can digitisation mitigate the economic damage of a pandemic? Evidence from SARS. *Telecommunications Policy, 44*(10), 102044.

Klein, V. B., & Todesco, J. L. (2021). COVID19 crisis and SMEs responses: The role of digital transformation. *Knowledge and Process Management, 28*(2), 117–133.

Kober, R., & Thambar, P. J. (2022). Paradoxical tensions of the COVID-19 pandemic: A paradox theory perspective on the role of management control systems in helping organisations survive crises. *Accounting, Auditing and Accountability Journal, 35*(1), 108–119. https://doi.org/10. 1108/AAAJ-08-2020-4851

Kolisovas, D., & Andrius, Š. (2011). Risk management in Lithuania's public sector: Starting point, current situation, and future perspectives. *Intellectual Economics, 5*(4), 547–559.

Kommunuri, J., Narayan, A., Wheaton, M., Jandug, L., & Gonuguntla, S. (2016). Firm performance and value effects of enterprise risk management. *New Zealand Journal of Applied Business Research, 14*(2), 17–28.

KPMG. (2022). The new reality for government: Post-pandemic global insights for the public sector: Dynamic risk assessment in the public sector. KPMG Global (home.KPMG)

Laguecir, A., Kern, A., & Kharoubi, C. (2020). Management accounting systems in institutional complexity: Hysteresis and boundaries of practices in social housing. *Management Accounting Research, 49*, 1–14.

Lapsley, I. (2009). New public management: The cruellest invention of the human spirit? *Abacus, 45*(1), 1–21. https://doi.org/10.1111/j.1467-6281.2009.00275.x

Leung, F., & Isaacs, F. (2008). Risk management in public sector research: Approach and lessons learned at a national research organisation. *R&D Management, 38*(5), 510–519.

Mahama, H., Elbashir, M., Sutton, S., & Arnold, V. (2020). New development: Enabling enterprise risk management maturity in sector organisations. *Public Money & Management, 42*(6), 403–407. https://doi.org/10.1080/09540962.2020.1769314

Malik, M. F., Zaman, M., & Buckby, S. (2020). Enterprise risk management and firm performance: Role of the risk committee. *Journal of Contemporary Accounting and Economics, 16*(1). https://doi.org/10.1016/j.jcae.2019.100178

Martin-Sardesai, A., Guthrie AM, J., & Parker, L. (2021). The neoliberal reality of higher education in Australia: How accountingisation is corporatising knowledge. *Meditari Accountancy Research, 29*(6), 1261–1282. https://doi-org.ezproxy.aut.ac.nz/10.1108/MEDAR-10-2019-0598

Mazzucato, M., & Kattel, R. (2020). COVID-19 and public-sector capacity. *Oxford Review of Economic Policy, 36*(Supplement_1), S256–S269.

Merchant, K. A., & Otley, D. T. (2006). A review of the literature on control and accountability. *Handbooks of management accounting research*, 2, 785–802. Elsevier.

Mikes, A. (2011). From counting risk to making risk count: Boundary-work in risk management. *Accounting, Organisations, and Society, 36*(4–5), 226–245.

Miller, P., Kurunmäki, L., & O'Leary, T. (2008). Accounting, hybrids, and the management of risk. *Accounting, Organisations, and Society, 33*(7–8), 942–967.

Nilsen, A. S., & Olsen, O. E. (2007). Resistance or acceptance? Mitigation strategies in risk management. *Risk Management, 9*(4), 255–270.

Osgood, D. E., McLaurin, M., Carriquiry, M., Mishra, A., Fiondella, F., Hansen, J., Peterson, N., Ward, N., & Malawi, I. (2007). *Designing Weather Insurance Contracts for Farmers in Malawi, Tanzania, and Kenya: Final Report to the Commodity Risk Management Group*. ARD, World Bank. International Research Institute for Climate and Society (IRI). Columbia University.

Oulasvirta, L., & Anttiroiko, A.-V. (2017). Adoption of comprehensive risk management in local government. *Local Government Studies, 43*(3), 451–474. https://doi.org/10.1080/03003930.2017.1294071

Palermo, T. (2014). Accountability and expertise in public sector risk management: A case study. *Financial Accountability & Management, 30*(3), 322–341.

Paules, C. I., Marston, H. D., & Fauci, A. S. (2020). Coronavirus infections – more than just the common cold. *JAMA, 323*(8), 707–708.

Phull, A. (2020, 20 March). What we must learn from Wuhan. *Op-Med*. https://opmed.doximity.com/articles/what-we-must-learn-from-wuhan?_csrf_attempted=yes.

Piccialli, F., di Cola, V. S., Giampaolo, F., & Cuomo, S. (2021). The role of artificial intelligence in fighting the COVID-19 pandemic. *Information Systems Frontiers, 23*(6), 1467–1497.

Power, M. (2007). *Organised uncertainty designing a world of risk management*. Oxford University Press.

Power, M. (2009). The risk management of nothing. *Accounting, Organizations & Society, 34*, 849–855.

Priyono, A., Moin, A., & Putri, V. N. A. O. (2020). Identifying digital transformation paths in the business model of SMEs during the Covid-19 pandemic. *Journal of Open Innovation: Technology, Market, and Complexity, 6*(4), 1–22. https://doi.org/10.3390/joitmc6040104

PwC. (2015). *Enterprise Risk Management in the Public Sector: Survey Results*. Association for Federal Enterprise Risk Management and PwC. www.aferm.org/wp-content/uploads/2015/10/AFERM-ERM-Public-Sector-Survey-2015.pdf

Rana, T., & Hoque, Z. (2020). Institutionalising multiple accountability logics in public services: Insights from Australia. *British Accounting Review, 52*(4), 100919.

Rana, T., Hoque, Z., & Jacobs, K. (2019a). Public sector reform implications for performance measurement and risk management practice: Insights from Australia. *Public Money & Management, 39*(1), 37–45.

Rana, T., Wickramasinghe, D., & Bracci, E. (2019b). New development: Integrating risk management in management control systems – lessons for public sector managers. *Public Money and Management, 39*(2), 148–151. https://doi.org/10.1080/09540962.2019.1580921

Rocher, S. (2011). "Reopening the black box": The story of implementing a risk analysis method in a French local government. *Financial Accountability & Management, 27*(1), 63–82.

Schäffer, U., Strauss, E., & Zecher, C. (2015). The role of management control systems in situations of institutional complexity. *Qualitative Research in Accounting & Management, 12*(4), 395–424.

Schillemans, T. (2016). Calibrating public sector accountability: Translating experimental findings to public sector accountability. *Public Management Review, 18*, 1400–1420.

Simkins, B. (2008). Enterprise risk management: Current initiatives and issues journal of applied finance roundtable. *Journal of Applied Finance, 18*(1), 115–132.

Smith, D., & McCloskey, J. (1998). Risk and crisis management in the public sector: Risk communication and the social amplification of public sector risk. *Public Money and Management, 18*(4), 41–50.

Spataro, J. (2020, 30 April). *2 years of digital transformation in 2 months*. www.microsoft.com/en-us/microsoft-365/blog/2020/04/30/2-years-digital-transformation-2-months/

Sundin, H., Granlund, M., & Brown, D. A. (2010). Balancing multiple competing objectives with a balanced scorecard. *European Accounting Review, 19*(2), 203–246.

Teece, D., Peteraf, M., & Leih, S. (2016). Dynamic capabilities and organisational agility: Risk, uncertainty, and strategy in the innovation economy. *California Management Review, 58*(4), 13–35.

Teece, D. J. (2017). Dynamic capabilities and (digital) platform lifecycles. In *Entrepreneurship, innovation, and platforms*. (Advances in Strategic Management, vol. 37, pp. 211–225). Emerald. https://doi.org/10.1108/S0742-332220170000037008.

Tracey, P., Phillips, N., & Jarvis, O. (2011). Bridging institutional entrepreneurship and the creation of new organisational forms: A multilevel model. *Organization Science, 22*(1), 60–80.

Tuddenham, L., & Baird, J. (2007). The risk management authority in Scotland and the forensic psychiatrist as a risk assessor. *Psychiatric Bulletin, 31*(5), 164–166. https://10.1192/Pb.bp.106.014357

van der Kolk, B., ter Bogt, H. J., & van Veen-Dirks, P. M. G. (2015). Constraining and facilitating management control in times of austerity: Case studies in four municipal departments. *Accounting Auditing & Accountability Journal, 28*(6), 934–965. https://doi.org/10.1108/AAAJ-03-2014-1660

Vinnari, E., & Skærbæk, P. (2014). The uncertainties of risk management A field study on risk management internal audit practices in a Finnish municipality. *Accounting, Auditing & Accountability Journal, 27*(3), 489–526. https://doi.org/10.1108/AAAJ-09-2012-1106

Wang, H., Xiong, W., Wu, G., & Zhu, D. (2018). Public-private partnership in public administration discipline: A literature review. *Public Management Review, 20*(2), 293–316.

Warner, K. S., & Wäger, M. (2019). Building dynamic capabilities for digital transformation: An ongoing process of strategic renewal. *Long-Range Planning, 52*(3), 326–349.

Wood, D., & Randall, S. (2005). Implementing ERM-2: The link with risk management. *Oil & Gas Journal, 103*(12), 20–22.

Woods, M. (2009). A contingency theory perspective on the risk management control system within Birmingham City Council. *Management Accounting Research, 20*(1), 69–81.

World Economic Forum. (2022, January 11). *Global Risks Report 2022*. www3.weforum.org: www.weforum.org/reports/global-risks-report-2022/

PART VI

Sustainability accounting, management and accountability

17

POLYCENTRIC GOVERNANCE AND SDG COMMITMENTS

Public sector responses in challenging times

Carolyn Cordery and Melina Manochin

Introduction

Late in the last century, heightened global awareness of climate change, environmental degradation and unequal wealth and health outcomes led nations to commit to the Millennium Development Goals (MDGs). Following mixed success in developing nations' achievement of the MDGs, all 193 members of the United Nations (UN) committed, in 2015, to achieving 17 Sustainable Development Goals (SDGs) by 2030. Such commitments and demands for innovative policymaking and action to tackle this complex problem, point to the need to operate governance and regulatory regimes that focus on interdependence; allow global, national and local actors to concentrate on areas of specialization; and encourage learning. Vincent and Elinor Ostrom and colleagues (E. Ostrom, 2010a, 2010b; V. Ostrom, 1991; V. Ostrom et al., 1961) outline the need for polycentric approaches to governance of complex problems. In this chapter, we argue that polycentric governance approaches are manifestations of New Public Governance (NPG) (Osborne, 2006). Thus, we use the UN's governance of the SDGs as an opportunity to observe management of polycentric governance within an interdependent system. In particular, we consider how the UN (as a transnational actor) calls member nations to account for their commitments, and enables learning. In so doing, we draw on independent assessments which juxtapose nations' slow progress on the SDGs against UN members' positive statements. This case study is ideal to highlight the challenges faced in a complex fragmented sustainability project, managed under NPG-style polycentric governance. Chaturvedi et al. (2021) are amongst those who state that the SDGs will not be achieved unless there is cross-border cooperation and polycentric governance. The issues arising from polycentrism, as outlined in this case, will continue to drive public sector responses to complex problems, especially in these challenging times. We also acknowledge the impact of the Covid-19 pandemic on SDG progress and make suggestions for practice within an NPG environment.

The chapter continues by introducing polycentric governance, which is then linked to the SDGs for a transnational approach to polycentrism. We examine the manner in which the UN holds nations to account for progress on sustainability, followed by a discussion on the challenges and opportunities for polycentric governance for future policymaking and action during challenging times.

DOI: 10.4324/9781003295945-23

Polycentric governance

While traditional and bureaucratic public administration (PA) focuses on a monocentric "rule of law" and the administering of these rules and guidelines, following the New Public Management (NPM) reforms, markets were increasingly called upon to regulate and manage resource allocations (Osborne, 2006). Under both the PA and the NPM approach, clear identification of principals and agents inform the holding to account (Black, 2008; Lodge & Stirton, 2010). In "rule of law" and market-based approaches, the conformity of participants is underpinned by penalties for non-compliance (McConville & Cordery, 2018). Yet, where there are multiple principals and agents (and none), Osborne (2006) introduces NPG, a concept arising from network theory and recognition of a plural and pluralistic state. NPG seeks to engage more participants than traditional PA and NPM governance and regulation (Trubek & Trubek, 2007), is relational and inter-organizational (and therefore based on legitimacy and trust) (Osborne, 2006), and combines self-regulation and co-regulation (McConville & Cordery, 2018). Polycentric NPG is marked by diversity, is "decentred" across nations and society, and often must accommodate global as well as local actors (Black, 2008; Lodge & Stirton, 2010). NPG approaches which utilize polycentric governance, seek ways for communities to make collective choices on key policy issues, to cooperate in working towards better outcomes, and to learn (Lubell, 2013).

Vincent Ostrom (1991, p. 225) describes a polycentric political system as comprising: "(1) many autonomous units formally independent of one another, (2) choosing to act in ways that take account of others, (3) through [often decentred] processes of cooperation, competition, conflict, and conflict resolution". Thus, idealized polycentrism is self-organizing, self-governing (V. Ostrom, 1991), and, it could be suggested, requires a fundamental appreciation of systemic principles such as inclusiveness and empowerment. Polycentrism is suited to dealing with complex problems such as sustainable development. In particular, Elinor Ostrom (2010a) used the example of climate change as a complex multilevel problem that demands more than a single response, necessitating "experimental efforts at multiple levels, leading to the development of methods for assessing the benefits and costs of particular strategies adopted in one type of ecosystem and compared to results obtained in other ecosystems" (p. 1). Polycentric regulation thus requires a monitoring system to assess results within a context which is conducive to change and experimentation and to learning from those actions.

However, polycentrism is not a panacea (E. Ostrom, 2010a). Black (2008) notes polycentric regulation is "marked by fragmentation, complexity and interdependence between actors" (p. 137). As the state is not the central (or only) regulator, polycentric regulation favours third-party "watchdogs" and new regulatory bodies outside government, including transnational regulators (these latter having gained increased legitimacy) (Black, 2008; Lodge & Stirton, 2010). The boundaries between these multiple regulators are often marked by the problems they work on, creating ambiguity in dealing with the larger issues, exacerbating the challenges of polycentricity. Further, the decentred context allows for overlaps, redundancy and duplication, as some actors will progress more rapidly on certain issues, and use different tools from binding (i.e. more mono-centric) regimes to those that are not (i.e. some tools may be quite "loose") (Jordan et al., 2018). The "efficiency" sought by NPM is unlikely to be evident in the polycentric NPG context.

With numerous formal and informal regulators, the accountability and legitimacy of the regulated and the regulator respectively form prime concerns, especially when the basis of supranational or transnational activities differs from national law and/or structures (Black, 2008). Thus, Black (2008) warns that these various local and global "regulators may attempt to create and manipulate others' perceptions of their legitimacy" (p. 139). She further recognizes that transnational (and supranational) regulators have "liquid authority", requiring them to create and maintain their own legitimacy in order to enforce/change social or community practices to meet their goals (Black, 2017). Supranational regulators operating in a liquid and shifting context without constitutional authority must therefore display their effectiveness, as their regulatory power (and subsequent legitimacy) derives from others within the "system" who hold participants to account (Bryce, 2012). To build trust and to show change towards goals, the regulator should encourage monitoring, innovation and learning (E. Ostrom, 2010b).

With respect to accountability, the lack of simple principal–agent relationships in polycentric regulatory systems (Black, 2008) impacts how accountability is enacted. Despite complexity, Koliba et al. (2011) argue that traditional accountability questions should continue to be asked, stating the necessity of understanding who is responsible for what, to whom accounts of action should be rendered, and how, noting that, if hybrid structures are to deliver effective accountability, a balance must be struck between bureaucracy and collaboration. Yet, accountability and transparency of disclosures depend on the ecosystem within which they operate. With polycentric regimes delivering multiple sources of information for accountability purposes, this potentially leads to fragmentation, specific types of information being illuminated more than others, or merely a lack of overall transparency (Black, 2008; Lodge & Stirton, 2010). Further, with a broad range of stakeholders involved in polycentric governance, stakeholder demands are likely to compete against each other, with the ensuing opposition creating tensions in accountability discharge (Black, 2008; Bovens, 2007).

Lodge and Stirton (2010, p. 408) argue for a "citizen empowerment" view of accountability in polycentrism, one that emphasizes accountability as a forum in which decision-making takes place "in the eye of the public" and enables a wide range of stakeholders to participate.[1] In addition to information availability, such demands for transparency must also be met at an appropriate level. We suggest that multiple layers of action and reporting in a polycentric regulatory system could therefore make it eas(ier) to "pass the buck" to another layer.

As polycentric governance possesses many moving parts, it is unsurprising that policymakers are challenged to continuously adjust proposed actions to deal with complex problems (Jordan et al., 2018). In the following section, we briefly examine challenges to the success of the MDGs which resulted in their replacement by the SDGs. This shows the importance of monitoring as one "adjustment" to deal with a complex problem. Despite a (theoretically) non-hierarchical governance system, in this chapter we ask, how are governments and non-governmental actors held to account against measurable goals, targets and indicators for sustainability? Accordingly, we seek to examine what learnings can be gleaned from how the UN encourages holding to account within its SDG programme. Thus, the next section considers the SDGs within a transnational system.

The SDGs – a transnational perspective of polycentrism

The SDGs follow the prior MDGs which were sponsored by the UN and targeted at developing nations. There were eight MDGs:

1. Eradicate extreme poverty and hunger
2. Achieve universal primary education
3. Promote gender equality and empower women
4. Reduce child mortality
5. Improve maternal health
6. Combat HIV/AIDS, malaria and other diseases
7. Ensure environmental sustainability
8. Develop a Global Partnership for Development.

Additionally, the UN set 18 targets as quantitative benchmarks and a framework of 53 indicators for member states to use in measuring and reporting progress (Ministry of Statistics and Programme

Implementation, 2011 (MoSPI)). Yet, the MDGs achieved mixed success. For example, despite many other South Asian countries meeting most MDG targets, India and Pakistan were unable to achieve many of their goals (Asadullah et al., 2020). Reasons cited included: lack of resources to fund programmes, lack of base data or data that was sufficiently disaggregated, poor measurement practices (including adjustments to goals to suit the available data), differing outcomes in urban versus remote rural areas, and generally a lack of innovation in policymaking and programmes which resulted in stepwise approaches and single programmes rather than integrated policies to deal with human development issues (Asadullah et al., 2020; Development Alternatives, 2016; MoSPI 2017). These data, measurement and policymaking issues are systemic and challenge all new programmes seeking to set and achieve targets. Further, the MDGs lacked UN monitoring and a platform of shared knowledge of good practice that would ensure engagement and inclusivity through the nations tasked with achieving the MDGs.

Given the patchy progress on the MDGs, in a more "ambitious post-2015 development agenda",[2] the UN announced 17 SDGs "to promote prosperity while protecting the planet", and, taking it beyond those countries believed to be "in need of development", all 193 UN member states pledged to achieving the SDGs by 2030 (UN General Assembly, 2015). Compared to the MDGs, the SDGs are more comprehensive, universal and attempt to make explicit linkages between different goals and targets, in order to communicate the integrated nature of successful sustainable development (Monkelbaan, 2019). While this global effort should be an improvement on the MDGs, and could lead to success, the breadth of the SDGs provides policymakers with achievement challenges, especially given the short 2030 deadline. Not least amongst the challenges is that priorities for goal achievement differ between stakeholders and regions, although these stakeholders frequently agree that climate action is most important (Monkelbaan, 2019). Further, financing to underpin programmes, especially in developing countries, is scarce (Southern Voice, 2020).[3] Additionally, the political nature of UN member states' engagement with the SDG process, with power struggles and unresolved contestations, leaves Chaturvedi et al. (2021) doubting the SDGs will be achieved.

Fuelling this gloomy outlook, is the recognition that achieving the SDGs is both a complex and an urgent task. Hierarchical styles of governance will be insufficient for the UN to drive forward SDG achievement at national and local levels. As it has little direct power to successfully demand hierarchical compliance and the problem is complex, if it is to manage networks and funding, the UN (as a supranational regulator) must use polycentric approaches to governing sustainability, building its own legitimacy (Monkelbaan, 2019). Monkelbaan (2019) argues that a joined-up "pluralistic approach, partnerships and 'bottom-up' action" (p. 28) is needed to link the UN's global agreements with target setting and local implementation. Hence, we ground our discussion on the SDG challenges within polycentric NPG, positing that the UN and governments will prioritize their SDG agreements and act as partners, negotiating consent, working with citizens and multiple stakeholders to implement the SDGs successfully. This echoes Ostrom et al.'s (1961) explanation of polycentrism including many parties that are independent of each other but jointly form complex modular systems to govern.

The fragmentation and complexity highlighted by Black (2008) is evident throughout the SDG ecosystem. The UN itself is not merely a single organization, but comprises different organizations working on issues,[4] many of which are related to sustainable development. Through these operational arms, it must manage its liquid form of legitimacy and authority (Black, 2017) if it is to progress through the political minefield of sustainable development (Chaturvedi et al., 2021).

Member states that have agreed to implement the SDGs are autonomous. Therefore, they translate SDGs locally to inform their policymaking in context. Many nations have established new bodies to coordinate and/or develop policy as a way to break down silos and manage SDGs nationally. These member states' public servants derive actions from these new policies, using different tools to motivate the diverse range of stakeholders to action. For example, in member states with federal systems such as Australia, India and the US, semi-autonomous states decide whether and how to achieve certain goals; federal states may need incentives to align to national goals. Our attention in this chapter is on India and a domain (per Ostrom, 2010a) which has developed an initiative aiming to transform districts seen as needing greater levels of development (described as "aspirational districts") as a way to help that member state achieve its SDGs overall.[5] Seeking "low-hanging fruits for immediate improvement", a nationally based nodal think tank – NITI Aayog – selected districts for inclusion that it considered deprived against key health and education metrics, as well as lacking in sufficient basic infrastructure.[6] This programme's strategy is to aim for: Convergence of Central & State Schemes, Collaboration at all levels down to districts, and Competition among districts (the three C's) (UNDP, 2020). Key to tracking progress against the programme's metrics is a baseline ranking of each district and almost real-time progress based on 49 indicators (81 data points) from five identified thematic areas. Presentation of progress includes how close (or distant) each aspirational district is from states that are achieving at a high level (NITI Aayog, 2018). To encourage competition, these metrics are posted online in summary form, with users being able to drill down to the district level.[7] The United Nations Development Programme's (UNDP's) (2020) appraisal recognizes this programme is one way that India incentivises subnational and local governments to localize global goals, and improve people's lives. Although this domain-specific programme is at an early stage, the UNDP (2020) lauds the quantitative metrics gathered, notes progress on the targets in all districts, and its qualitative analysis also shows progress. In particular, the UNDP (2020) notes that districts where the aspirational districts programme had improved healthcare infrastructure, coped better with the effects of the Covid-19 pandemic. This mixed-methods approach to appraisal reflects Ostrom's (2010b) encouragement to reflect multiple frameworks and theories to understand complexity. The operation of "double polycentrism" (Jordan et al., 2018) can be observed in the locally led programme that provides an example of how other nation states can decentre and motivate sustainability governance.

In addition to managing federal states and districts, member states' national governments committing to the SDGs must also manage autonomous private sector corporates. Legislation is a common tool to encourage certain behaviours. For example, national governments might incentivize corporate behaviour through Emissions Trading Schemes (ETS), require Corporate Socially Responsible (CSR) actions and reporting thereof, or demand reports and actions on climate risks under the Taskforce for Climate Financial Disclosure (TCFD) initiative. Nevertheless, Monkelbaan (2019) notes that the greatest number of corporates is small to medium-sized enterprises (SMEs), and may therefore show little interest in transnational goals, given SMEs often lack the ability to engage in development at a basic level. Yet, recognition of interdependence is required (Black, 2008; V. Ostrom, 1991; V. Ostrom et al., 1961); this is evident, for example, in TCFD disclosures of scope three Greenhouse Gas Emissions which require measurements down the supply chain from large corporates to the smallest supplier.

The SDG motto (to "leave no-one behind") reminds member states that non-governmental organizations (NGOs) and citizens are also important actors in the SDG polycentric space, both to be nudged to change citizens' behaviours, as well as being stakeholders that should be encouraged to demand accountability (Southern Voice, 2020). Essential to accountability is improved access to data and analysis to assist citizens in assessing progress on local and global goals (Abhayawansa et al., 2021). Abhayawansa et al. (2021) provide an Australian example where, in order to implement the SDGs, a local government reported the alignment of NGO strategies with their own. Possibilities for citizens and NGOs to be involved in NPG-type projects to help design development programmes was not mentioned, however.

Further, national and transnational actors work in specialist areas towards SDG achievement. For example, Mahon and Fanning (2019) consider regional ocean governance at an ecosystem level. In addition to the intergovernment bodies under the FAO Regional Fisheries Bodies programme and the UNEP's Regional Seas programmes, Mahon and Fanning (2019) found numerous treaties, conventions and consortia undertaking initiatives which would assist in achieving SDG6 and 14, although they also note gaps in coverage. Unless all actors work collaboratively (Chan et al., 2015), the SDGs may experience the same fate as the MDGs.

In addition to coordination challenges, goal achievement is also impacted by an uncertain and unpredictable environment (as can be seen with the Covid-19 pandemic, and the environment, such as floods, earthquakes). Therefore, reporting and monitoring are important in ensuring SDG progress.

Voluntary national reviews

To monitor member states' progress towards the SDGs, from September 2013, the UN established a High-Level Political Forum (HLPF) on Sustainable Development, replacing its Commission on Sustainable Development, which had met annually since 1993.[8] Monkelbaan (2019, p. 38) states that, globally, the HLPF is "the key forum for follow-up and review" and that peer review will assist in bringing about mutual accountability on SDG implementation. Concerns that this type of accountability is voluntary (Chaturvedi et al., 2021) highlight one of the challenges of polycentric sustainability governance. Jordan et al. (2018) also note that the multiple actors within polycentric governance bring further challenges for coordination, consistent and comparable evaluation and sharing. Nevertheless, the HLPFs convene a broad group of stakeholders, as the annual meetings are preceded by multi-stakeholder forums on science, technology and innovation (UN General Assembly, 2015).[9] At a global level, the mandate of the HLPF is to:

> facilitate sharing of experiences, including successes, challenges and lessons learned, and provide political leadership, guidance and recommendations for follow-up. It will promote system-wide coherence and coordination of sustainable development policies. It should ensure that the [SDG] Agenda remains relevant and ambitious and should focus on the assessment of progress, achievements and challenges faced by developed and developing countries as well as new and emerging issues.
>
> *(UN General Assembly, 2015, para. 82)*

Despite these brave words, Abhayawansa et al. (2021, p. 2) confirm the challenges in developing SDG strategies, recommending that: "government accountability processes are critical to member states' implementation of SDGs" if they are not to mimic the partial success of MDGs. At the HLPFs, member states are encouraged to submit and publicly present Voluntary National Reports (VNRs) that are country-led, track progress and to take a longer-term orientation, as well as being "open, inclusive, participatory and transparent [...] [with a] particular focus on the poorest, most vulnerable and those furthest behind" (UN General Assembly, 2015, para. 74). Further, in signing up to the SDG accord, member states agreed to be held accountable for "effective implementation of our commitments [...] [by providing] for systematic follow-up and review at the various levels" (UN, 2015, paras. 45, 47). The HLPF has the central role of overseeing global-level accountability. VNRs are therefore both a report and a vital practice in the polycentric governance framework.

Nevertheless, Chaturvedit et al. (2021) are concerned these reviews are voluntary, and yet the UN deems VNRs to be the "cornerstone" to bring about accountability. This raises the possibility that some member states will not report, or that they will make choices about reporting that provide aspirational statements, but little detail on achievement. For example, while there has been a "groundswell" of interest in reducing climate change (Chan et al., 2015), Chan et al.'s (2018) analysis of progress towards 52 climate actions announced in the UN's Climate Summit in Paris in 2014 (COP 21), finds a disjuncture between the actions nations planned and those that they are actually implementing. Additionally, 40 per cent of the nations that had implemented climate actions were high-income countries belonging to the Organization for Economic Cooperation and Development (a further 23 per cent were upper-middle-income countries), with a disproportionately low percentage of lower-middle-income and low-income countries implementing their climate action plans (Chan et al., 2018). Unsurprisingly, Chan et al. (2018) argue that, as well as holding nations accountable for their promises, the UN must find more effective ways to support developing nations, to incentivize private sector entities and to ensure even progress across all actions. Our discussion of the Indian case above illustrates attempts to bring about progress through creating vertical independence between multiple actors, including corporates, NGOs and citizens.

Building on these concerns about promises and voluntary monitoring, we undertook a high-level analysis of the VNRs to consider their role within the SDG project. We accessed documents and websites focused on VNRs to analyse the formats used by nations, as well as accessed independent feedback on these reports. We sought to understand how the HLPF's VNRs operated as an account-ability mechanism and (similar to Chan et al.'s (2018) findings) whether developing nations are less likely to engage in the VNR process, particularly since the UN General Assembly (2015, para. 74) notes that developing countries will need "enhanced capacity-building support [...] including strengthening of national data systems and evaluation programmes" to achieve SDG success.

Since 2016, as can be seen from Table 17.1, a great majority of UN members have presented at least one VNR; an average of 41 VNRs have been presented at each HLPF with a number already promised at the 2022 HLPF. Further, each HLPF focuses on a specific set of goals, recognizing the cross-cutting nature of the issues. It is encouraging to note that the member states that have submitted VNRs are spread across the range of developed to least-developed nations (and some have submitted more than once).

Since the earliest presentations, the Division for Sustainable Development in the UN's Department of Economic and Social Affairs (UNDESA–DSG) (2018a, 2018b, 2019) has summarized the key messages of VNRs presented in each year. Their report on the 2017 VNRs (UNDESA–DSG, 2018b, para. II) is introduced by statements lauding these reports as "an inspiring repertoire of country profiles in action", while recognizing the challenges of implementation. As an example of an economy in transition, 2017 was the first year that India presented a VNR reporting "in depth" on progress towards SDG goals 1, 2, 3, 5, 9, 14 and 17, as did nine other countries (UNDESA–DSG, 2018b). For each SDG, India detailed newly developed programmes along with plans for further investment. No details were provided of new funding sources, despite India's narrow tax base and the significant international investment required to assist India in achieving the SDGs (Cordery et al., 2022). Of par-ticular mention in the 2017 VNR are the Indian government's initiatives "to transform the innovation and entrepreneurship landscape in the country", including the India Innovation Index Framework (NITI Aayog, 2017, p. 24).

The UN also made positive comments following the 2018 HLPF where "the benchmark for the VNRs is being raised every year" (UNDESA–DSG, 2018a, para. 4), also observing that member states

Table 17.1 Total VNRs from 2016 to 2022 by categorization of economy

Type of economy[10]	# Participating	%	Reports	%
Developed	40	20.6%	52	20.4%
Developing	92	47.4%	123	48.2%
Economies in Transition	17	8.8%	23	9.0%
Least developed	45	23.2%	57	22.4%
	194	100.0%	255	100.0%

appeared to recognize the need to engage more meaningfully with stakeholders and align the SDGs with national plans and targets. Similarly positive, the 2018 and 2019 summary reports mentioned the work of the International Organization of Supreme Audit Institutions (IOSAI) to gather assurance on the readiness to report against the SDGs, although their reports provided no results of these "readiness audits" (UNDESA–DSG, 2018a, 2019).[11] The tenor of the VNR 2019 summary again lauded the "showcasing" of national achievements and improvements in the VNRs, but also highlighted the data challenges, congratulating member states that had developed national indicators (UN Department of Economic and Social Affairs Division for Sustainable Development Goals, 2019) (as evident with the India Innovation Framework).

Against this positive rhetoric, and from within the same UN Department, the Committee for Development Policy (UNDESA–CDP) is less sanguine about the VNRs and their contribution to the SDG effort. This is at first obvious from the titles of their annual reports, which include "what do VNRs (still not) tell us/reveal" (UNDESA–CDP 2018, 2019, 2020, 2021). These reports analyse cross-cutting issues – particularly the overarching aim of the SDGs to "leave no-one behind", and efforts towards global partnership – whether the theme was included in the relevant VNR and whether the VNR presented a strategy to address that theme. Many 2018 VNRs focused on gender, disability and the elderly alone, rather than the wide-ranging social and environmental challenges they faced. Thus, the UNDESA–DP (2018, p. 15) notes that "countries often remain vague in discussions on strategies towards implementing it". Further, they observe little integration of policy, nor information on outward-reaching global partnership (NITI Aayog, 2017; UNDESA–CDP, 2018). In the report on 2018 VNRs, the UNDESA–CDP (2019) scores the proportion of each SDG covered, showing the prevalence of global partnership by counting the number of times the term was mentioned. The UNDESA–CDP (2019, p.4) suggests global partnership (and sustainable development finance) is "central to the 2030 Agenda". These two different committees' reports provide evidence of the variety of viewpoints on the VNRs, even from within the UN. This could be seen as a further challenge of polycentrism.

As noted, Supreme Audit Institutions (SAIs) have also undertaken a monitoring role by independently and proactively auditing "the preparedness for implementation of SDGs in their national context" and through these performance audits, nudging "national governments into action by providing constructive recommendations at an early stage" (INTOSAI & IDI, 2019, p. 8). While Monroe-Ellis (2018) (Auditor General of Jamaica and a Carribbean leader) states that, globally, these performance audits have improved processes, programmes and structures – both in government and SAIs – upon examining the individual SAIs' performance reports, we note that, without exception, they opine that member states have made little progress and more action is needed. This chimes with the UNDESA (2021) report which found that "regrettably the SDGs were already off-track" when the Covid-19 pandemic occurred. That report further notes the pandemic has diverted member states away from dealing with anything but immediate circumstances.

The UNDESA–CDP (2020, 2021) presents two further reports, acknowledging the impact of the Covid-19 pandemic on SDG achievement. The 2020 report mentions only that member states' VNRs discussed how the pandemic may impact the achievement of SDG3 (Good health and well-being). In 2021, the critique of VNRs sought to ascertain the wide-ranging effects of the pandemic on member states' achievement, yet the UNDESA–CDP (2021) reports disappointment that when member states' VNRs mentioned the pandemic, they failed to highlight how it had impacted issues such as gender diversity (e.g. more women lost jobs, family violence increased) or income inequality. As they report:

> the crisis has touched all segments of the population, all sectors of the economy, and all areas of the world [...] [but] the effects are not felt equally and in the same ways [...] it is now widely

acknowledged that COVID-19 is widening inequalities within and between countries due to the structural vulnerabilities [...] Prospects for SDG implementation are uncertain in a post-pandemic economy.

(UNDESA–CDP, 2021, p. 44)

In addition to the pandemic, however, "violent conflicts, increasing migration and numbers of refugees, as well as climate change as a global challenge" have redirected the foci of many member states, potential financiers and supporters (Chaturvedi et al., 2021, p. 3). Hence, UNDESA–CDP (2020, 2021) regret that the "leaving no-one behind" agenda has been reduced, so that rather than lowering inequity overall, most member states focus on specialized programmes for specific groups. The cost of implementing the SDGs, monitoring systems and of policy coherence are also less likely to have been covered in VNRs published in 2019 and 2020. Thus, the UNDESA–CDP (2020, 2021) argue for more evidence-based VNRs, that VNRs should outline member states' capacity needs, and for the UN to draw on NGOs' "shadow accounts" that identify gaps in VNRs and would lead to solution-based discussions taking place, especially in respect of SDG 17 (strengthening partnerships).

Hence, while the HLPF and their associated VNRs should combine voluntary accountability with "learning opportunities", it is likely that member states also grapple with liquid forms of legitimacy in the multi-stakeholder, complex NPG ecosystem. Thus, the public nature and ceremony involved in HLPFs where VNRs are presented, mean they become a space for positive spin and a lack of accountability. Stakeholders must turn to different ways of assessing member states' accountability.

In addition to the HLPF, the UN has established a global registry of voluntary commitments, multi-stakeholder partnerships and different action networks focused on SDG implementation.[12] This Partnership Platform recognizes the disaggregated nature of multiple non-state coalitions and regulators and includes a wide diversity of "partners" across the different SDGs. While this may suggest a solidification of the UN's liquid authority, it does not diminish the UN's need to maintain legitimacy across a very broad range of actors. In addition, examination of the details shows that many of these actors are from the developed world (the global north), and the authority of these network actors in less-developed nations is not clear. We now turn to discuss what this SDG case study can tell us about NPG-style polycentric governance.

Discussion and conclusion

This chapter seeks to analyse public sector responses to member states' SDG commitments in challenging times through the lenses of polycentric governance and the overarching NPG paradigm. In doing so, we analyse how the UN, as a transnational body, holds member states accountable to their SDG commitments. We recognize there is wide variety of actors and institutions operating at global and domain levels, and therefore this chapter is limited by focusing only on the UN. Without the ability to force penalties for non-compliance (McConville & Cordery, 2018), the UN is in a liquid space (Black, 2008), necessitating ongoing negotiations to ensure its own legitimacy. The UN doesn't demand mono-centric accountability from member states which committed to the SDGs, but seeks member states' voluntary accountability through VNRs and annual HLPFs. Allowing voluntary accountability not only develops a monitoring regime and enhances trust (Ostrom, 2010b), but it also enhances learning through a myriad of activities prior to the HLPFs, and through the Partnership Platform by which groups bring like-minded stakeholders together. Ideally, this allows member states to experiment and learn from each other (Jordan et al., 2018), but the political nature of global governance challenges nations' legitimacy and reduces the likelihood this will be reported, even when it occurs. Further, the voluntary and decentred nature of reporting is likely to reflect a proliferation of different reporting frameworks, leading to a lack of comparability and consistency from which others can learn (Jordan et al., 2018).

Thus, the UN SDGs, with their byline of "leave no-one behind", signal the need to address climate change not only through domain- and global-level policymaking and action, but also through creating vertical independence between multiple actors, corporates, NGOs and citizens. It is a highly hybrid way of approaching an incredibly complex system to bring sustainable development, worldwide. Such polycentrism is becoming a more common way of governing in the NPG era (Osborne, 2006; E. Ostrom, 2010b, 2010a; V. Ostrom et al., 1961).

Polycentric governance is evident from the UN's encouragement of member states to engage more participants in their reporting and to build relationships as recommended by NPG principles (Osborne, 2006; Trubek & Trubek, 2007). Of particular interest is the underpinning slogan to "leave no one behind" and citizen empowerment (Lodge & Stirton, 2010). NPG concepts should preference the wide availability of information. Despite slogans and systemic principles of inclusiveness and empowerment, UN members are fully autonomous nation states, leading to a fragmented regulatory space. The SDGs represent a complex sustainability problem where interdependence (whether actioned or not) means many stakeholders and actors are impacted by action and inaction (Black, 2008; E. Ostrom, 2010a; V. Ostrom, 1991). Thus, the SDG ecosystem meets the three principles outlined by Ostrom (1991) (independence, interdependence and decentred practice). While idealized polycentrism is self-organizing and self-governing (V. Ostrom, 1991), for member states to achieve SDGs within this complex interdependent sustainability ecosystem, it is imperative that stakeholders call actors to account. Further, given the need to overcome the "stepwise" policymaking that contributed to the failure of the MDGs, innovation and new ways of policymaking and practice are required. As such, we see "double polycentrism" (Jordan et al., 2018) in India's Aspirational Districts programme, where a domain-level programme decentres sustainability governance through motivating districts to achieve goals in certain areas. Nevertheless, there is scant research on how NGOs and other civil society actors participate in polycentric regimes and, specifically, hold governments to account for their commitments to the SDGs (Jordan et al., 2018).

The UN instigated monitoring and learning through its HLPF and VNRs to attempt to require accounts of action that will enable these hybrid structures to deliver effective accountability (Koliba et al., 2011). Yet, the HLPF and attendant VNRs are not the only opportunity for calling to account globally. As can be seen from this brief review, multiple sources of information exist, and transparency through reports and websites leads to particular items being highlighted, with other (perhaps not so positive) information being more hidden (Black, 2008; as we might expect from Bovens, 2007). While these VNRs and other monitoring have shortcomings, the UN SDGs are relatively unique in embedding monitoring into the promises made (Jordan et al., 2018). The challenge within a polycentric regime is to design regulation that has monitoring at its heart and can identify and hold to account those actors which fulfil their commitments, and those that fall short.

The challenges of sustainability are myriad within the SDG ecosystem. Managing such a large project requires measurement and action at many levels, not only global and domain (regional-local). Polycentrism by its very definition within NPG approaches (Osborne, 2006; E. Ostrom, 2010a, 2010b) necessarily engages many parties, and therefore holds promise for future styles of public governance. Nevertheless, the challenge is that polycentrism can lead to a lack of accountability "on the ground" and to high-level goals not being met, unless public policymakers embed monitoring as an essential feature of polycentric regimes.

Notes

1 Lodge and Stirton (2010) also examine "fiduciary trusteeship", "consumer sovereignty" and "surprise and mistrust" as views on accountability, but "citizen empowerment" more closely matches the goals of the SDGs to leave no one behind, as well as those of NPG.
2 See: www.un.org/millenniumgoals/.

3 As also attested to at COP27, see, for example, https://unfccc.int/news/cop27-reaches-breakthrough-agreem ent-on-new-loss-and-damage-fund-for-vulnerable-countries

4 For example, the Food and Agriculture Organization of the United Nations (FAO), United Nations Children's Fund (UNICEF), United Nations Department of Economic and Social Affairs (UNDESA), United Nations Development Programme (UNDP), United Nations Environment Programme (UNEP), United Nations Economic and Social Commission for Asia and the Pacific (UNESCAP), United Nations Framework Convention on Climate Change (UNFCCC), United Nations Industrial Development Organization (UNIDO), and the United Nations Office for disaster risk reduction (UNISDR).

5 See: www.niti.gov.in/sites/default/files/2022-04/Stories_of_Change_2022_1.pdf

6 These are: health and nutrition, 30 per cent; education, 30 per cent; agriculture and water resources, 20 per cent; basic infrastructure, 10 per cent; and financial inclusions and skill development, 10 per cent.

7 See http://championsofchange.gov.in/site/coc-home/

8 https://sustainabledevelopment.un.org/hlpf.

9 Unlike the prior MDGs, monitoring is an integral part of the SDGs. In addition to the HLPF and VNRs noted in this chapter, different goals encourage reporting – for example, the SDG target 12.6 encourages "companies, especially large and transnational companies, to adopt sustainable practices and to integrate sustainability information into their reporting cycle".

10 As classified by the United Nations. www.un.org/development/desa/dpad/wp-content/uploads/sites/45/WES P2020_Annex.pdf

11 In respect of India, the report highlighted many shortcomings (Comptroller and Auditor General of India, 2019).

12 https://sdgs.un.org/partnerships.

References

Abhayawansa, S., Adams, C. A., & Neesham, C. (2021). Accountability and governance in pursuit of Sustainable Development Goals: Conceptualising how governments create value. *Accounting, Auditing & Accountability Journal, 34*(4), 923–945. https://doi.org/10.1108/AAAJ-07-2020-4667

Asadullah, M. N., Savoia, A., & Sen, K. (2020). Will South Asia achieve the Sustainable Development Goals by 2030? Learning from the MDGs Experience. *Social Indicators Research, 152*, 165–189.

Black, J. (2008). Constructing and contesting legitimacy and accountability in polycentric regulatory regimes. *Regulation & Governance, 2*(2), 137–164. https://doi.org/10.1111/j.1748-5991.2008.00034.x

Black, J. (2017). "Says who?" Liquid authority and interpretive control in transnational regulatory regimes. *International Theory, 9*(2), 286–310. https://doi.org/10.1017/S1752971916000294

Bovens, M. (2007). Analysing and assessing accountability: A conceptual framework. *European Law Journal, 13*(4), 447–468. https://doi.org/10.1111/j.1468-0386.2007.00378.x

Bryce, H. J. (2012). Review Essay: Polycentric governance, capital markets, and NGOs as regulatory bodies: Expanding the scope of Ostrom's Understanding Institutional Diversity. *Politics & Policy, 40*(3), 519–535.

Chan, S., Falkner, R., Goldberg, M., & van Asselt, H. (2018). Effective and geographically balanced? An output-based assessment of non-state climate actions. *Climate Policy, 18*(1), 24–35. https://doi.org/10.1080/14693 062.2016.1248343

Chan, S., van Asselt, H., Hale, T., Abbott, K. W., Beisheim, M., Hoffmann, M., Guy, B., Höhne, N., Hsu, A., Pattberg, P., Pauw, P., Ramstein, C., & Widerberg, O. (2015). Reinvigorating international climate policy: A comprehensive framework for effective nonstate action. *Global Policy, 6*(4), 466–473. https://doi.org/10.1111/ 1758-5899.12294

Chaturvedi, S., Janus, H., Klingebiel, S., Xiaoyun, L., de Mello e Souza, A., Sidiropoulos, E., & Wehrmann, D. (2021). *The Palgrave handbook of development cooperation for achieving the 2030 Agenda.* Palgrave Macmillan. https://doi.org/10.1007/978-3-030-57938-8

Cordery, C., Arora, B., & Manochin, M. (2022). Public sector audit and the state's responsibility to "leave no-one behind": The role of integrated democratic accountability. *Financial Accountability & Management, 39*(2), 304–326. https://doi.org/10.1111/faam.12354

Development Alternatives. (2016, February). *Tracking the Global Goals in India Project: Assessing the SDGs in Indian Context.* www.devalt.org

International Organization of Supreme Audit Institutions, & INTOSAI IDI Development Initiative. (2019, July). *Are Nations Prepared for Implementation of the 2030 Agenda? Supreme Audit Institutions' Insights and Recommendations.* www.idi.no/work-streams/relevant-sais/auditing-sdgs/sdgs-prcparcdness-audit/idi-ksc-2030-agenda

Jordan, A., Huitema, D., Schoenefeld, J., van Asselt, H., & Forster, J. (2018). Governing climate change: The promise and limits of polycentric governance. In *Governing climate change: Polycentricity in action?* (pp. 357–383). Cambridge University Press. https://doi.org/10.1017/9781108284646

Koliba, C. J., Zia, A., & Mills, R. M. (2011). Accountability in governance networks: An assessment of public, private, and nonprofit emergency management practices following Hurricane Katrina. *Public Administration Review, 71*(2), 210. http://search.proquest.com/docview/940861621?accountid=8330%5Cnhttp://jn8sf5h k5v.search.serialssolutions.com/directLink?&atitle=Accountability+in+Governance+Networks%3A+An+ Assessment+of+Public%2C+Private%2C+and+Nonprofit+Emergency+Management+Practices+Fol

Lodge, M., & Stirton, L. (2010). Accountability in the regulatory state. In R. Baldwin, M. Cave, & M. Lodge (Eds.), *The Oxford handbook of regulation* (pp. 397–419). Oxford University Press. https://doi.org/10.4324/ 9781315183770

Lubell, M. (2013). Governing institutional complexity: The ecology of games framework. *Policy Studies Journal, 41*(3), 537–559. https://doi.org/10.1111/psj.12028

Mahon, R., & Fanning, L. (2019). Regional ocean governance: Integrating and coordinating mechanisms for polycentric systems. *Marine Policy, 107*(April), 1–8. https://doi.org/10.1016/j.marpol.2019.103589

McConville, D., & Cordery, C. J. (2018). Charity performance reporting, regulatory policy and standard-setting. *Journal of Accounting and Public Policy, 37*(4), 300–314. https://doi.org/10.1016/j.jaccpubpol.2018.07.004

Ministry of Statistics and Programme Implementation. (2011). *Millenium Development Goals India Country Report 2011*. www.undp.org/india/publications/millennium-development-goals-india-country-report-2011-0

Ministry of Statistics and Programme Implementation. (2017). *Achieving Millennium Development Goals Target Year Factsheet – India*. www.mospi.gov.in/sites/default/files/publication_reports/MDG_Final_Country_repo rt_of_India_27nov17.pdf

Monkelbaan, J. (2019). *Governance for the Sustainable Development Goals: Exploring an Integrative Framework of Theories, Tools, and Competencies*. Springer Nature Singapore.

Monroe-Ellis, P. (2018). We have to be a beacon: Jamaica's AG reflects on SAI's SDG journey. *International Journal of Government Auditing, 45*(4), 4–5.

NITI Aayog. (2017). *Voluntary National Review Report on the Implemetation of Sustainable Development Goals*. www.niti.gov.in/sites/default/files/2019-01/Final_VNR_report.pdf

NITI Aayog. (2018). *Deep Dive: Insights from Champions of Change: The Aspirational Districts Dashboard*. www.niti.gov.in/sites/default/files/2018-12/FirstDeltaRanking-May2018-AspirationalRanking.pdf

Osborne, S. P. (2006). The new public governance? *Public Management Review, 8*(3), 377–387. https://doi.org/ 10.1080/14719030600853022

Ostrom, E. (2010a). *Background Paper to the 2010 World Development Report: A Polycentric Approach for Coping with Climate Change*. No. 5095, Policy Research Working Paper. October 2009.

Ostrom, E. (2010b). Beyond markets and states: Polycentric governance of complex economic systems. *American Economic Review, 100*(3), 641–672.

Ostrom, V. (1991). *Meaning of American federalism: Constituting a self-governing society*. Institute for Contemporary Studies.

Ostrom, V., Tiebout, C. M., & Warren, R. (1961). The organization of government in metropolitan areas: A theoretical inquiry. *American Political Science Review, 55*(4), 831–842.

Southern Voice. (2020). *Global State of the SDGs: Three Layers of Critical Action*. Report 2019.

Trubek, D. M., & Trubek, L. G. (2007). New governance & legal regulation: Complementarity, rivalry, and transformation. *Columbia Journal of European Law, 13*, 1–26.

United Nations Department of Economic and Social Affairs. (2021). *The Sustainable Development Goals Report 2021*. https://unstats.un.org/sdgs/report/2021/The-Sustainable-Development-Goals-Report-2021.pdf

United Nations Department of Economic and Social Affairs Committee for Development Policy. (2018). *Voluntary National Review Reports – What Do They Report?* Issue CDP Background Paper No. 46. https:// sustainabledevelopment.un.org/content/documents/20549CDPbp201846.pdf

United Nations Department of Economic and Social Affairs Committee for Development Policy. (2019). *Voluntary National Reviews Reports – What do they (not) tell us?* Issue CDP Background Paper No. 49. www. un.org/development/desa/dpad/wp-content/uploads/sites/45/publication/CDP-bp-2019-49.pdf

United Nations Department of Economic and Social Affairs Committee for Development Policy. (2020). *Voluntary National Reviews Reports: What do they (not) reveal?* Issue CDP Background Paper No. 50. www. un.org/development/desa/dpad/wp-content/uploads/sites/45/publication/CDP-bp-2020-50.pdf

United Nations Department of Economic and Social Affairs Committee for Development Policy. (2021). *What Did the 2020 Voluntary National Review (VNR) Reports Still Not Tell Us?* Issue CDP Background Paper No. 52. www.un.org/development/desa/dpad/wp-content/uploads/sites/45/publication/CDP-bp-2021-52.pdf

United Nations Department of Economic and Social Affairs Division for Sustainable Development Goals. (2018a). *2018 Voluntary National Reviews Synthesis Report*. https://sustainabledevelopment.un.org/content/documents/210732018_VNRs_Synthesis_compilation_11118_FS_BB_Format_FINAL_cover.pdf

United Nations Department of Economic and Social Affairs Division for Sustainable Development Goals. (2018b). *Synthesis of Voluntary National Reviews 2017*. https://sustainabledevelopment.un.org/content/documents/17109Synthesis_Report_VNRs_2017.pdf

United Nations Department of Economic and Social Affairs Division for Sustainable Development Goals. (2019). *2019 Voluntary National Reviews Synthesis Report*. https://sustainabledevelopment.un.org/content/documents/252302019_VNR_Synthesis_Report_DESA.pdf

United Nations Development Programme. (2020). *Aspirational Districts Programme: An Appraisal*. www.niti.gov.in/sites/default/files/2022-09/UNDP-Assessment-of-ADP.pdf

United Nations General Assembly. (2015). Transforming Our World: The 2030 Agenda for Sustainable Development. *A/RES/70/1*. https://doi.org/10.1891/9780826190123.ap02

18

ACCOUNTABILITY AND SUSTAINABILITY IN THE PUBLIC SECTOR

An impression management perspective for research

Delfina Gomes, Adelaide Martins and Manuel Castelo Branco

Introduction

The nature of each crisis influences official policies concerning public services. The health crisis with the outbreak of Covid-19 and the *new normal* that was created by it has demonstrated that "decades of a misplaced focus on privatization, outsourcing, and static efficiency have left many governments with reduced options and capacities in the face of the crisis" (Mazzucato & Kattel, 2020, p. 265; see also Ansell et al., 2021). The pandemic revealed that unequal conditions created by neoliberalism are limiting the ability of governments to guarantee future collective welfare (Andrew et al., 2020). Governments operated under conditions of deep uncertainty, and a trade-off between public health and economic damage characterized many national public policies (Heald et al., 2020). Climate change, migration crises, modern slavery and a war in Europe have also added to this reality, which created new demands for governments concerning sustainability issues and policies.

Governments and public-sector entities play a critical role since the public sector is considered a steward for sustainability issues (Kaur & Lodhia, 2019). Accountability mechanisms are among the most significant instruments with which governments ensure and enhance the performance of public-sector organizations (Schillemans, 2016). Consequently, public-sector accounting and accountability systems play a key role and are implicated in the debates and actions surrounding social and environmental issues (Bracci et al., 2015; O'Regan et al., 2022).

The pressures on the public sector to be accountable for its actions are greater than ever. The public sector carries "responsibility for the long-term resilience and stability of societies, and for shaping public outcomes through policy-making and public institutions" (Mazzucato & Kattel, 2020, p. 257). Public accountability is established as a pillar of democracy; however, the concept may have become rhetorical (Manes-Rossi, 2019). The literature has shown that reassuring statements in sustainability reporting are often not genuine and have little to do with existing practices and performance (Boiral, 2013; Boiral et al., 2021). Impression management is often considered the tool that disseminates a myth of accountability (Solomon et al., 2013), but it may also play a critical role in constructing organizational and national sustainability identities and the corresponding images. Though in essence being a "theory" of the individual, it has been applied to explain discretionary disclosure practices in organizational contexts (Merkl-Davies & Brennan, 2011). This chapter addresses the following question: How can sustainability-related disclosures' impression management help evaluate what public-sector entities should be accountable for and how such accountability may be discharged?

DOI: 10.4324/9781003295945-24

Accountability is context specific (Almqvist et al., 2013), being subject to modifications, depending on cultural, political and social factors (Manes-Rossi, 2019; Steccolini, 2004). The literature on sustainability has mainly focused on disclosures by private-sector companies and has neglected sustainability in public organizations (e.g. Boiral, 2013; Chiba et al., 2018; Guthrie et al., 2010). However, as highlighted by Kaur and Lodhia (2019, p. 498), "[t]he public sector is a significant employer and provider of services and consumer of resources; therefore, it has a significant impact on national and international progress towards sustainable development". The role of governments and other public entities in sustainable development has been reinforced with the development of the 2030 Agenda for Sustainable Development. Besides the impact on all sections of society, government bodies must develop national targets and plans to meet the sustainable development goals (SDGs) established by the Agenda and at the same time play an active role in their implementation (Kaur & Lodhia, 2019; Pizzi et al., 2020). Hence, as discussed below, a different and more constructive use of impression management strategies with a view to creating an identity and image of the public sector in general and of public-sector organizations in particular that are consistent with the role they play in the prosecution of SDGs, is crucial.

Adopting Ricoeur's (1992) vision of the ethical intention, and grounded on the capabilities approach (Sen, 1999), we consider that the responsibilities of those who provide public goods and services should be defined and assessed in terms of their contribution to the safeguarding of humanity and impacts on individual and collective capabilities. We view the ethics of public service as an ethics of care, having as its central tenet "meeting the needs of others for whom one is given responsibility" (Rauh, 2018, p. 247), implying "an openness to dialogue" (p. 248), which we consider a crucial notion when addressing accountability in the public sector. This chapter offers a reflection on how accounting and accountability systems can contribute to stimulating a deeper social concern for the public sector, particularly in its responsibility and accountability regarding sustainability in challenging times, and the crucial role that impression management can have in such contribution. By bringing together the literature on accountability and sustainability in the public sector and developing a framework to evaluate what public-sector entities should be accountable for and how such accountability is discharged, we contribute to stimulating research concerning sustainable practices for public services (Farneti et al., 2019; Guthrie et al., 2010; Niemann & Hoppe, 2018). This will allow future research to question the role governments, governmental agencies/departments, state-owned enterprises and other public-sector entities play in adopting sustainability policies and to make them accountable for their actions.

The chapter proceeds as follows: the next section provides an analysis of the literature on accountability in the public sector, focusing on the concept itself and how it is challenged when complex and uncertain events occur. Section three analyses sustainability disclosure practices, from an impression management perspective. Section four provides a proposal of a formal theoretical framework. The final section provides the concluding comments, including the contributions and suggestions for future research.

Accountability in the public sector

The Covid-19 pandemic has highlighted, with a strong focus on the protection of public health, the relevance of public-sector institutions' capacity to manage emergencies and solve societal challenges (Mazzucato & Kattel, 2020). Particular relevance is attributed to how institutional complexity is managed by organizations over time (Fossestol et al., 2015; McPherson & Sauder 2013; Pache & Santos 2010, 2013). The pandemic has shown the importance of governments' capacity to align public services with the needs of citizens (Mazzucato & Kattel 2020), thus aiming to gain citizens' trust and governance legitimacy (Christensen & Lægreid, 2020). This legitimacy is often connected with accountability (Schillemans. 2008), where political leaders or the heads of public services try to justify the policies and measures taken (Christensen & Lægreid, 2020).

Accountability has been described as a "heterogeneous, complex, chameleon-like and multifaced concept encompassing several dimensions" and meanings (Almqvist et al., 2013, p. 480). One meaning is that of giving and demanding good conduct but with a need for control, allowing the concept to be distinguished from answerability and transparency (Almqvist et al., 2013; Letiche et al., 2022). Bovens (2009, p. 184) concisely defines accountability as a "social relationship in which an actor feels an obligation to explain and to justify his or her conduct to some significant other". However, accountability is not restricted to principal–agent relationships, and numerous types of accountabilities, pertaining to different types of relationships and with a wider range of stakeholders involved, have been identified (Almqvist et al., 2013).

In democratic societies, governments and public-sector entities are scrutinized by multiple accountability forums. This means that the public sector becomes accountable to an increased number of stakeholders, such as government departments, inspections, auditors, critical clients and the media, each with different legitimate interests and conflicting expectations (Demirag et al., 2020; O'Regan et al., 2022; Schillemans, 2016). In this context, accountability can be seen as concerning the management of the relations with these different stakeholders, often with different expectations and objectives, which may often be conflicting (Demirag et al., 2004; Demirag et al., 2020). Recently, more attention has been given to the participation of citizens, clients and societal actors in holding public-sector organizations to account (Brummel, 2021).

The use of multiple accountability mechanisms and the relevance they assumed in public-sector governance and performance has been a reason for the implementation of NPM ideas over the last decades (Rana & Hoque, 2020). These demands for accountability in the public sector have been broadly classified in the literature into two models of institutional logics: individualizing, also known as instrumental or calculative; and socializing, also known as relational or community (Rana & Hoque, 2020). This distinction is the consequence of a more individualizing sense of accountability experienced by people in the public sector, while others experience a more socializing form of accountability (Rana & Hoque 2020).

Vosselman (2016, p. 605) argues for a duality in the framing of accountability, a duality between relational response-ability and instrumentality. The author highlights the potential for frames of relational response-ability, which enable intrinsically ethical behaviour in unexpected circumstances and events. He goes further and argues that such a development is related to a conceptualization of the public organization as moral community rather than market-like organizations in which the Homo Economicus and principal–agency relationships are dominant. This conceptualization of the public organization recognizes that individuals associate with an organization without putting their own interests and calculative behaviour first (Vosselman, 2016). This means that individuals aspire to pursue common goals or shared values and ambitions, although they may unconsciously have their own interests. Instrumental accountability assumes the relation of agency theory, where in a public organization managers must give an account of their conduct, using accounting tools (Rana & Hoque, 2020; Vosselman, 2016). Agent and principal may adopt tricking and deceiving behaviours while pursuing their self-interest. Behaving opportunistically, an individual may "take advantage of the differences in accessibility to relevant information by the parties involved", "hide or distort relevant information", or even "hide certain actions or non-actions" (Vosselman, 2016, pp. 608–609).

To avoid these behaviours, organizational codes of conduct and codes of governance may be adopted, the latter at the country level with the status of law (Vosselman, 2016). However, moral conduct is grounded on formal rules, which means that sources for such type of conduct "include organizational and institutional rules and constraints" and are not restricted to "individual preferences as they are reflected in contractual agreements" (Vosselman, 2016, p. 612). It is noteworthy that in a moral community, virtues are the sources of ethical behaviour. This does not implicate altruism, as Vosselman (2016) argues, but it does imply the recognition that individuals are fallible in their conduct and that economic and opportunistic interests are not the best guide to their actions given the interdependence between them.

A frame of relational response-ability unveils trust, which is the basis for accountability. Trust encourages commitment to the organization, while mistrust involves hard controls against opportunism and self-interest, and generates distance between individuals (Vosselman, 2016). In a moral community, accountability would assume the form of dialogue and not of instrumental practices. Thus, it is important to combine instrumental accountability with a more social and relational form of accountability (Vosselman, 2016; Rana & Hoque 2020). As argued by Vosselman (2016, p. 621):

> In many public organizations, more attention should be given to conditions that promote virtuous behavior. Instead of taming and disciplining individuals, managers and regulators should aim at conditioning networks and relations in these networks. At least, intrinsic motivation and commitment should not be frustrated, but, even better, individual commitments and shared ambitions should be enhanced.

Nonetheless, while there is a recognition that public accountability mechanisms are of crucial importance in democracies and there is a need for more direct and explicit accountability relations between public-sector entities and their clients, as well as with citizens (Bovens, 2007; Schillemans, 2016), the reality is that many dysfunctional effects are reported (Flinders 2011; Schillemans, 2016). Schillemans (2016) argues that there are many accountability failures. These failures may be the result of the heterogeneity and complexity of the interests at stake in the public sector. As argued by Almqvist et al. (2013), "public organizations may tend to opt for ambiguous strategies and goals which are less likely to be rejected by the electorate than clear-cut policies, and will allow the politicians to maintain or increase their political consensus" (p. 480). Accountability to citizens, clients or the public at large – social accountability – has been advanced as the path to a better connection between policy implementation and the interests and needs of citizens and societal stakeholders, but also as a response to a lack of trust in government and governmental institutions (Bovens, 2007; Brummel, 2021). Brummel (2021) argues that social accountability has become an appealing facet of many public management reforms as it emphasizes the direct influence of citizens, clients and societal actors on the providers of public services.

Sustainability disclosure practices – an impression management tool

As mentioned above, while the literature on sustainability has mainly focused on private-sector companies' disclosure practices (Chiba et al., 2018), the reality has changed, and sustainability has gained considerable relevance in the public sector (Niemann & Hoppe, 2018). Public-sector entities are increasingly assuming more responsibility for the resilience and stability of societies, and at the same time being accountable for public outcomes resulting from policymaking (Mazzucato & Kattel, 2020). Public-sector organizations operate within a complex business environment, with pressures to disclose financial and non-financial information, and these circumstances influence their practices of disclosing sustainability information (Argento et al., 2019; Kaur & Lodhia, 2019).

A clear demand to all large private-sector and public-sector entities to increase the disclosure of sustainable information emerges from the United Nations' Sustainable Development Goals and the European Union directive 2014/95/EU (Niemann & Hoppe, 2018), and, more recently, from the proposal for a sustainability reporting directive in the EU and the entry of the International Financial Reporting Standards Foundation into the sustainability reporting field (Giner & Luque-Vílchez,

2022). Governments, and a wide range of public-sector entities, are called to assume an active role in ensuring the pursuance of the SDGs (Kaur & Lodhia, 2019; Pizzi et al., 2020). As acknowledged in SDG 16, partnerships between cross-sectorial entities are paramount in order to accomplish the SDGs and guarantee sustainable development.

The literature has recognized that institutional pressures and a search for social legitimacy are the main drivers of governments and public-sector organizations in the development of sustainability disclosure practices (Chiba et al., 2018; Boiral, 2013). For both private-sector companies and public-sector entities, the disclosure of sustainability information may represent business as usual (Milne & Gray, 2013) and not enhance accountability and contribute to the praxis of sustainability (Dumay et al., 2010). In these situations, sustainability reporting has no benefits for stakeholders and society (Niemann & Hoppe, 2018; Pizzi et al., 2020). Niemann and Hoppe (2018) investigated the evolution of sustainability reporting by six pioneering European local governments. The findings suggest that for those local governments producing stand-alone reports, the pursuit of public legitimacy was an evident objective. The authors claim there is evidence that organizational learning, improved management and positive valued communication with different audiences are an outcome of public-sector sustainability reporting. However, local governments also experienced "reporting fatigue", leading to the discontinuation or radical altering of sustainability reporting practices (Niemann & Hoppe, 2018, p. 202).

Previous research suggests that sustainability disclosure practices are often interpreted as tools for impression management (Chiba et al., 2018; Diouf & Boiral, 2017). The concept of impression management originates in social psychology and was first used by Goffman (1959), who explains it using a dramaturgical metaphor of individuals as actors on a stage playing several roles for an audience. Since then, the construct has been used in organizational research and corporate reporting research from different theoretical perspectives, ranging from agency theory to a critical perspective, as well as sociological and psychological approaches (Merkl-Davies & Brennan, 2011; Perkiss et al., 2021). The perspective on impression management informed by agency theory focuses solely on the relationship between managers and investors. It ignores the role of organizational reporting in mediating the relationship between management and stakeholders and the reporting bias of sustainability performance. The critical perspective regards organizational narrative and disclosure as a means to provide "a hegemonic account of organisational outcomes, often by means of using dominant discourses" (Merkl-Davies & Brennan, 2011, p. 428). Impression management theorists who take a sociological approach have increasingly claimed that the major motive is to manage stakeholders' perceptions of organizations to avoid being viewed unfavourably (e.g. Cooper & Slack, 2015; Leung et al., 2015; Moussa et al., 2022).

From a social psychology perspective, impression management involves "any behavior that has the purpose of controlling or manipulating the attributions and impressions formed of that person by others" (Tedeschi & Riess, 1981, p. 3). In an organizational setting, the aim is to control the information that is presented about the organization (Arndt & Bigelow, 2000; Martins et al., 2020, 2021). The government, and other public-sector entities, by managing the impressions of citizens can influence the "nature of the interactions" (Arndt & Bigelow, 2000, p. 496). Thus, impression management may help to understand, in moments when unpredictable and complex events occur, how public entities react and act to manipulate or gain the trust of stakeholders.

The literature has highlighted that organizations use impression management strategies to manage their legitimacy, image or reputation by communicating their activities and goals (Deephouse & Carter, 2005; Deephouse et al., 2017; Perkiss et al., 2021). Legitimacy and reputation have similar antecedents, social construction processes and consequences, but reputation implies a social comparison among organizations (Deephouse & Carter, 2005). Deephouse et al. (2017, p. 32) defined legitimacy as "the perceived appropriateness of an organization to a social system in terms of rules, values, norms, and definitions". Legitimacy is a perception (Suchman, 1995). The appearance of societal conformity may be achieved through successful manipulation of public expectations and perceptions about the organization (Deephouse et al., 2017; Meyer & Rowan, 1991; Martins et al., 2020, 2021).

The motivation underlying impression management behaviour may be the search for social legitimacy or the improvement of the image among relevant stakeholders, but it can also be to conceal poor performance (Boiral, 2013; Diouf & Boiral, 2017). Based on reports that reached the highest application level of the Global Reporting Initiative (GRI), Boiral (2013) showed that 90 per cent of the significant negative events were not reported and concluded that sustainability reports appear as a form of spectacle and simulacra, given their lack of any impact. Diouf and Boiral (2017) provide insight into the quality and reliability of sustainability reports by analysing the perceptions of socially responsible investment practitioners. The authors explore to what extent the possible discrepancies between GRI framework principles and the quality of sustainability reporting reflect impression management strategies. The findings support the argument that sustainability reports are perceived as an impression management tool used by organizations to highlight the positive outcomes aspects of their sustainability performance and to disguise negative events. The disclosure of positive events while concealing negative ones (a form of "greenwashing") to create a misleadingly positive impression of overall sustainability performance (Marquis et al., 2016), constitutes one of the main criticisms of sustainability reports (Diouf & Boiral, 2017).

Previous studies have demonstrated deficiencies in the sustainability disclosure practices of public sector entities (Chiba et al., 2018; Guthrie & Farneti, 2008; Pizzi et al., 2020; Williams, 2015). Chiba et al. (2018) analysed the credibility of information on the sustainable development outcomes of ministries and agencies of the Quebec provincial government and investigated the factors undermining its quality. They concluded that the disclosed information is inconsistent and incomplete, and pointed out deficiencies in the quality of the monitoring mechanisms used to measure the outcomes. Guthrie and Farneti (2008) and Williams (2015) reached similar conclusions. Similarly, Pizzi et al. (2020) conducted an analysis of 202 entities that operate within the Italian National Healthcare System to evaluate the overall degree of transparency in terms of contribution to the SDGs. The findings suggest that the Italian National Health Service is characterized by a low degree of accountability. The authors conclude that the deficiencies in the reporting of sustainability practices are potentiated by the fact that "public managers are less oriented than private managers to adopt non-financial reporting tools" (Pizzi et al., 2020, p. 445). According to Jamali et al. (2010), in the case of the healthcare system, the managerial structure, ownership and the role of the board of directors influence the degree of accountability, transparency and responsibility.

In sum, public sector organizations are increasingly required to report on their sustainability performance to ensure they are accountable to stakeholders, promote citizens' participation and secure employee commitment to achieving sustainability goals (Chiba et al., 2018; Niemann & Hoppe, 2018). However, the lack of sustainability culture in the public sector increases the lack of trust by stakeholders regarding non-financial information (Pizzi et al., 2020). The impression management behaviour on the part of public sector and private sector entities may result in the exploitation of information asymmetry between organizations and stakeholders (Diouf & Boiral, 2017; Merkl-Davies & Brennan, 2007; Pizzi et al., 2020). Adding to all these issues, impression management behaviours may be stimulated by the usually voluntary nature of sustainability disclosure practices and the lack of regulation (Diouf & Boiral, 2017; Merkl-Davies & Brennan, 2007). Accordingly, the criticism levelled at the private sector also applies to the public sector: sustainability disclosure practices may not have an effective impact on sustainability and enhance accountability but may provide an outlet for "greenwashing" (Dumay et al., 2010) or constitute a "ritualistic myth-building exercise" (Solomon et al., 2013, p. 205).

Notwithstanding the relevance of this "negative" entrenched view of impression management, one has to acknowledge that there is another more "positive" type of impression management. Leary and Kowalsky (1990) recognize the importance of both impression motivation and impression construction. Regarding the first, these researchers refer to "three interrelated yet distinct ways" through which impression management is used: obtaining the desired social and material outcomes and avoiding the undesired ones; maintaining and ameliorating self-esteem; creating or developing identities. Leary and Kowalsky (1990, p. 38) note that although the three types of motives can be regarded as distinct, "specific factors that elicit them overlap substantially". Although the motivation pertaining to identity creation has been underexplored in the management literature, we submit that it is of utmost importance for research on the public sector. We put forward that in the case of the public sector, impression management strategies may be crucial in the constructing of an identity of contribution to sustainable development, as well as of the respective image.

We put forward, in the case of the public sector, Tata and Prasad's (2015) view of impression management in CSR communication as often involving "an attempt to ensure that the image perceived by audiences is accurate" (p. 767) is of great utility. Tata and Prasad (2015) focused on situations in which the CSR image an organization wants to convey is in tune with the respective CSR identity, which they define as "the attributes that collectively represent the characteristics of the organization with respect to CSR" and "what an organization perceives is central and distinctive about itself" (p. 768). Therefore, these researchers explore impression management as a technique that can be used when an organization's image perceived by the audience (current image) does not accurately portray the respective identity (desired image).

An ethical and social model for sustainability-related impression management and accountability

Complex moments, such as the world is currently experiencing, put pressure on governments and public sector entities to act responsibly, but above all, in a sustainable manner and to be accountable for their actions. These pressures are increasing due to the actions of citizens and international organizations (such as the UN), but also of international accounting bodies, such as the International Public Sector Accounting Standards Board (IPSASB), which has very recently launched a consultation paper on "advancing public sector sustainability reporting" (IPSASB, 2022).

To address the challenge of a sustainable future, as Deneulin (2008), we call for a move away from ethical individualism and for a conception of the good for citizens as co-dependent with the common good. The latter is conceived as the good for the community formed by the relationships of which an individual is a part, and both goods imply one another (Deneulin, 2013). As Deneulin (2008) states, referring to Aristotle, if the focus of development is "enhancing the quality of life of human beings, then it cannot ignore that such a human life is a life whose sustenance and meaning can come only through others" (p. 122). Based on Ricoeur's thinking, namely his vision of the ethical intention (the aim of a good life, with and for others, in just institutions) and his vision of the institution as a structure of living-together of a historical community, irreducible to interpersonal relationships (Ricoeur, 1992), Deneulin (2006), emphasizes these characteristics of history and irreducibility to interpersonal relationships.

The perspective above is, we argue, the most adequate to address issues of social responsibility, sustainability and accountability in the public sector. Because of the role played by public sector organizations in the prosecution of sustainable development, it is crucial for them to create an identity centred on their contribution to sustainable development and an image that accurately portrays such identity, as well as develop policies and practices which are in accordance with them and providing accurate accounts of all this. Accordingly, there is the need for a coherent framework on which engagement with sustainability and accountability discharge may be grounded. We submit that such a framework should be based on the capabilities approach – which we view as a normative language for political and social action – in particular the Aristotelian version of it proposed by Deneulin (2008).

Important concepts in the capabilities approach are those of functionings and capability. Human well-being is defined in terms of human functionings, with the concept of capability being defined in terms of functionings. As for the concept of functionings, regarding which Sen (1999, p. 75) recognizes the "distinctly Aristotelian roots", it "reflects the various things a person may value doing or being". The valued functioning can range from "elementary ones, such as being adequately nourished and being free from avoidable disease, to very complex activities or personal states, such as being able to take part in the life of the community and having self-respect" (Sen, 1999, p. 75). Regarding a person's capability, Sen (1999, p. 75) refers to it as consisting of the "alternative combinations of functionings that are feasible for her to achieve". It is, therefore, "kind of freedom: the substantive freedom to achieve alternative functioning combinations" (Sen, 1999, p. 75). Capability is "the opportunity to achieve valuable combinations of human functionings – what a person is capable to do or be" (Sen, 2005, p. 153).

When we consider that the public sector is responsible in most countries for the provision of such fundamental goods and services as those pertaining to health, education, science and public utilities (such as water, gas and energy), it is not difficult to argue for the interest of grounding in such an approach the public sector's engagement with sustainability and the associated image construction and accountability discharge. We agree with Hewitt (2019, p. 406) when he considers the "provision of healthcare", which he argues is uniquely positioned to "directly affect human flourishing", as the main social institution charged with the promotion, restoration and maintenance of health. Furthermore, because those who need such services more are among the most vulnerable in society, this institution is a fundamental concern of justice. Education can be similarly depicted. As Barnett (2021, p. 389) put it, it "may be considered as expanding the individual capabilities of people, providing them with access to the required resources, and ensuring their ability to make decisions that matter to them". We also agree with Mormina (2019), who asserts that

> considering knowledge creation processes as a social good on one hand reaffirms the systemic (social) nature of scientific knowledge (a good *of* society), and on the other makes explicit the relationship between scientific knowledge and its ultimate goal: social transformation (a good *for* society). (p. 685, italics in original)

Based on the belief that the capabilities approach provides the ethical underpinnings for a new public services model, Vizard (2013) puts forward the idea, with which we agree, that the focus of such a model is the expansion of capabilities. The advantages of such a focus pertain to "concentrating directly on intrinsically valuable 'ends' (in the form of central and valuable capabilities) rather than instrumental 'means' (such as income and wealth)" and "capturing the multidimensional nature of equality and inequality (spanning areas such as longevity, physical security, health and education)" (p. 54). This is compatible with an approach to public management that came to be known as the New Public Service approach, developed over 20 years ago by Janet and Robert Denhardt (Denhardt & Denhardt, 2000, 2001, 2003, 2015). Bryson et al. (2014) refer more broadly to an emerging approach to public administration, whose outlines were becoming apparent in frameworks such as the one offered by the Denhardts, which "appears to be the leading contender based on citations" (p. 452). The New Public Service approach, which emerged as a response to NPM (Rauh, 2018) can be thus characterized. It is grounded on the idea that the main responsibility of the government is "to uphold democratic and social criteria", and views public interest as paramount and as the result of a dialogue about the "mutual or overlapping interests" of citizens and other groups (Denhardt & Denhardt, 2001, p. 393). Importantly for our argument, "the conception of accountability embedded in this approach suggests that public servants must attend to more than just the law; they should include community values, political norms, professional standards, and citizen interests" (Denhardt & Denhardt, 2001, p. 393). Moreover, the ethics of public service is an ethics of care, which "holds that care for others and benevolence is a central tenet of moral action" (Rauh, 2018, p. 236).

While instrumental accountability cannot be disregarded, more focus needs to be put on a form of social and relational accountability (Rana & Hoque, 2020; Vosselman, 2016). As argued by Vosselman (2016, p. 605), it is paramount to the

> development of a relational frame of accountability, a frame that enables intrinsically ethical behavior and openness to the future, to the unexpected. [...] such a development is related to a re-conceptualization of the public organization from a market bureaucracy toward a moral community.

In this new conception, trust is the basis for accountability, and virtues are the source of ethical behaviour in a moral community. Governments and public sector entities need to take into consideration the participation of citizens, clients and societal actors, as they increasingly hold public sector organizations to account (Brummel, 2021), and work to gain their trust regarding their discourses and policies (Christensen & Lægreid, 2020). Thus, we argue for critical researchers to adopt a critical lens in the analysis of sustainability discourse and disclosure adopted by the public sector as impression management strategies and to evaluate the ethical and moral principles involved in those practices and disclosures.

We agree with Abhayawansa et al.'s (2021) view of value creation in a public sector context as including the consideration of the prosecution of wealth creation in a gross domestic product growth perspective, but also as going beyond this and including a whole set of other forms of value creation for the society as a whole, from the perspective of various stakeholders. The role of many public sector organizations in the prosecution of SDGs pertains to the definition of strategies and policies on how to best achieve such goals on three different levels, organizationally, nationally and internationally. As argued by Abhayawansa et al. (2021, p. 926), "given the interdependent nature of sustainable development projects, national governance for the SDGs can only be effective when in accord with global governance for sustainability". We believe that a similar statement could be made concerning public sector entities and national government institutions. Beyond these crucial roles, we consider of paramount importance when discussing sustainability and accountability in a public sector context, the acknowledgement of the direct role played by many public sector organizations in achieving such goals (such as the roles of health services organizations in pursuing good health and well-being, or the role of educational institutions in pursuing quality education). However, we consider equally important the role they play in educating for the SDGs. We do not view education as restricted to classrooms. When we think of health literacy or sustainability literacy, we acknowledge the role of other organizations in promoting them. For example, health literacy is now a major preoccupation in clinical practice and for policymakers (Nutbeam et al., 2018). Outside the public sector scope, Hochmuth and Sørensen (2021) refer to it as an important aspect of a company's corporate social reporting strategy.

We put forward idea of shifting attention from the public sector to "publicness" as the central concept, as suggested by Steccolini (2019) and Bracci et al. (2021). As these researchers argue, this concept refers to "the attainment of public goals and interests", rather or less "than to the organizations and concrete spaces where the related activities take place" (Bracci et al., 2021, p. 1514; Steccolini, 2019, p. 262). This is in line with the idea that "care and public services can also be provided in the private context" (Rauh, 2018, p. 250). With this in mind, and focusing on public sector organizations, we view as crucial the engagement in impression management strategies for the creation of organizational/national sustainability identities. One of the most important roles of public sector organizations is that of constructing an identity for themselves and for the nation, which, when referring to sustainable development and SDGs, must include an idea of how such organizations and the nation fit within how the world is pursuing them (or, better put, within the international organization's strategies and policies to pursue them).

We believe that when dealing with the public sector, one should also explore this less negative perspective on impression management, and should consider, as Tata and Prasad (2015, p. 777) do more broadly, that "organizations need to ensure that CSR communication provides a cohesive and complete picture of their CSR identity and image". What is more, agreeing with these researchers but keeping in mind the public sector, we believe that "communicating about CSR can play an important role in organization-stakeholder relations" (p. 777). As Tata and Prasad (2015, p. 777) put it, "an understanding of the organization's CSR philosophies, policies, and activities can allow stakeholder audiences to become more engaged in the issues affecting them and more willing to collaborate with organizations in reaching socially responsible solutions to problems".

From the above, it is not difficult to understand our view that public sector organizations, especially government and public sector entities, use or can use impression management strategies in defining their sustainability engagement strategies, as depicted in Figure 18.1. They must create an organizational identity consistent with the national one (that they also must create) and must strive to live according to such an identity. It is also crucial to create a sustainability image that is consistent with the identity created, and impression management can also be used here to ensure that the sustainability image perceived by the audience is an accurate portrayal of the respective identity.

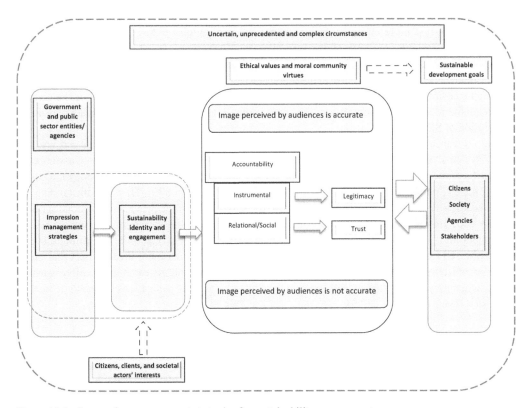

Figure 18.1   Impression management strategies for sustainability engagement.

When communicating their subsequent engagement with sustainability, their policies and practices, and how effective these have been in terms of contributing to the SDGs, one has to keep in mind that such communication is crucial in engaging citizens and keeping them engaged in sustainability issues and enhancing their willingness to collaborate with the public sector in promoting sustainability. Accountability processes and instruments must be consistent with the identities and images mentioned above. In particular, we consider that social and relational accountability must be pursued in a manner consistent with the identities and images impression management has assisted in creating. Hence, it is our view that accountability and impression management in the public sector are (and must be) profoundly imbricated.

Conclusion

This chapter brings together the literature on accountability and sustainability in the public sector and proposes a framework to evaluate what public sector entities should be accountable for and how such accountability may be discharged. The aim is to contribute to stimulating research concerning sustainable practices for public services, specifically to stimulating future research to question the role governments, governmental agencies/departments, state-owned enterprises, and other public sector entities play in adopting sustainable policies and in making them accountable for their actions. We call for critical researchers to adopt a critical lens in the analysis of sustainability discourse and disclosure adopted by the public sector as impression management strategies, and the need to evaluate the ethical and moral principles involved in those practices.

The proposed ethical and social model for sustainability-related impression management and accountability claims to move away from ethical individualism and adopt a conception of the good for the community. Governments and public sector entities must attend to more than just the law. It is paramount that these entities infuse their actions and policies with community values, political norms, professional standards and citizen interests. Accordingly, more focus needs to be put on a form of social and relational accountability, in such a way that potentiates "intrinsically ethical behaviour and openness to the future, to the unexpected" (Vosselman, 2016, p. 605). We view impression management in the public sector through a positive lens and deem it important for the creation of a requisite identity and a corresponding image consistent with the role they (must) play in the prosecution of SDGs.

The relevance of this research stems from the fact that public sector accounting and accountability systems "serve to challenge, reinforce and/or sustain particular representations, assumptions and myths of the value of particular practices, forms of accountability, and ruling conceptions of the public interest, public services and the state" (Bracci et al., 2015, p. 879). This notwithstanding, the public sector is responsible, in most countries, for the largest part of the provision of crucial services, such as education and healthcare. Importantly, public organizations operate in a "complex web of accountabilities" (Brummel, 2021, p. 1047; see also Schillemans, 2016, p. 1402), meaning that they are scrutinized by multiple accountability forums. In addition, given the critical impact that public sector organizations have on the environment and society, accounting research that explores sustainability accounting, accountability and reporting practices by these organizations has become increasingly vital (Kaur & Lodhia, 2019).

References

Abhayawansa, S., Adams, C. A., & Neesham, C. (2021). Accountability and governance in pursuit of Sustainable Development Goals: Conceptualising how governments create value. *Accounting, Auditing & Accountability Journal, 34*(4), 923–945.

Almqvist, R., Grossi, G., Van Helden, G. J., & Reichard, C. (2013). Public sector governance and accountability. *Critical Perspectives on Accounting, 24*(7–8), 479–487.

Andrew, J., Baker, M., Guthrie, J., & Martin-Sardesai, A. (2020). Australia's COVID-19 public budgeting response: The straitjacket of neoliberalism. *Journal of Public Budgeting, Accounting & Financial Management, 32*(5), 759–770.

Ansell, C., Sørensen, E., & Torfing, J. (2021). The COVID-19 pandemic as a game changer for public administration and leadership? The need for robust governance responses to turbulent problems. *Public Management Review, 23*(7), 949–960.

Argento, D., Grossi, G., Persson, K., & Vingren, T. (2019). Sustainability disclosures of hybrid organizations: Swedish state-owned enterprises. *Meditari Accountancy Research, 27*(4), 505–533.

Arndt, M., & Bigelow, B. (2000). Presenting structural innovation in an institutional environment: Hospitals' use of impression management. *Administrative Science Quarterly, 45*(3), 494–522.

Barnett, E. (2021). Towards an alternative approach to the implementation of education policy: A capabilities framework. *Issues in Educational Research, 31*(2), 387–403.

Boiral, O. (2013). Sustainability reports as simulacra? A counter-account of A and A+ GRI reports. *Accounting, Auditing & Accountability Journal, 26*(7), 1036–1071.

Boiral, O., Talbot, D., Brotherton, M.-C., & Heras-Saizarbitoria, I. (2021). Sustainability rating and moral fictionalism: Opening the black box of nonfinancial agencies. *Accounting, Auditing & Accountability Journal, 34*(8), 1740–1768.

Bovens, M. (2007). Analysing and assessing accountability: A conceptual framework. *European Law Journal, 13*(4), 447–468.

Bovens, M. (2009). Public accountability. In F. Ewan, L. Lawrence Jr, & C. Pollitt (Eds.), *The Oxford handbook of public management* (pp. 182–208). Oxford Handbooks.

Bracci, E., Humphrey, C., Moll, J., & Steccolini, I. (2015). Public sector accounting, accountability and austerity: More than balancing the books? *Accounting, Auditing & Accountability Journal, 28*(6), 878–908.

Bracci, E., Saliterer, I., Sicilia, M., & Steccolini, I. (2021). Accounting for (public) value(s): Reconsidering publicness in accounting research and practice. *Accounting, Auditing & Accountability Journal, 34*(7), 1513–1526.

Brummel, L. (2021). Social accountability between consensus and confrontation: Developing a theoretical framework for societal accountability relationships of public sector organizations. *Administration & Society, 53*(7), 1046–1077.

Bryson, J. M., Crosby, B. C., & Bloomberg, L. (2014). Public value governance: Moving beyond traditional public administration and the new public management. *Public Administration Review, 74*(4), 445–456.

Chiba, S., Talbot, D., & Boiral, O. (2018). Sustainability adrift: An evaluation of the credibility of sustainability information disclosed by public organizations. *Accounting Forum, 42*(4), 328–340.

Christensen, T., & Lægreid, P. (2020) The coronavirus crisis–crisis communication, meaning-making, and reputation management. *International Public Management Journal, 23*(5), 713–729.

Cooper, S., & Slack, R. (2015). Reporting practice, impression management and company performance: A longitudinal and comparative analysis of water leakage disclosure. *Accounting and Business Research, 45*(6–7), 801–840.

Deephouse, D. L., Bundy, J., Tost, L. P., & Suchman, M. C. (2017). Organizational legitimacy: Six key questions. In R. Greenwood, C. Oliver, T. B. Lawrence, & R. E. Meyer (Eds.), *The Sage handbook of organizational institutionalism* (pp. 27–54). SAGE.

Deephouse, D. L., & Carter, S. M. (2005). An examination of differences between organizational legitimacy and organizational reputation. *Journal of Management Studies, 42*(2), 329–360.

Demirag, I., Dubnick, M. J., & Khadaroo, I. (2004). A framework for examining accountability and value for money (VFM) in the UK's private finance initiative (PFI). *Journal of Corporate Citizenship, 15*, 63–76.

Demirag, I., Fırtın, C. E., & Bilbil, E. T. (2020). Managing expectations with emotional accountability: Making city hospitals accountable during the COVID-19 pandemic in Turkey. *Journal of Public Budgeting, Accounting & Financial Management, 32*(5), 889–901.

Deneulin, S. (2006). "Necessary Thickening": Ricoeur's ethic of justice as a complement to Sen's capability approach. In S. Deneulin, M. Nebel, & N. Sagovsky (Eds.), *Transforming unjust structures: The capability approach.* (pp. 27–45). Springer.

Deneulin, S. (2008). Beyond individual freedom and agency: Structures of living together in Sen's capability approach to development. In F. Comim, M. Qizilbash, & S. Alkire (Eds.), *The capability approach: Concepts, measures and applications* (pp. 105–124). Cambridge University Press.

Deneulin, S. (2013). Recovering Nussbaum's Aristotelian roots. *International Journal of Social Economics, 40*(7), 624–632.

Denhardt, J. V., & Denhardt, R. B. (2015). The new public service revisited. *Public Administration Review, 75*(5), 664–672.

Denhardt, R. B., & Denhardt, J. V. (2000). The new public service: Serving rather than steering. *Public Administration Review, 60*(6), 549–559.

Denhardt, R. B., & Denhardt, J. V. (2001). The new public service: Putting democracy first. *National Civic Review, 90*(4), 391–401.

Denhardt, R. B., & Denhardt, J. V. (2003). The new public service: An approach to reform. *International Review of Public Administration, 8*(1), 3–10.

Diouf, D., & Boiral, O. (2017). The quality of sustainability reports and impression management: A stakeholder perspective. *Accounting, Auditing & Accountability Journal, 30*(3), 643–667.

Dumay, J., Guthrie, J., & Farneti, F. (2010). GRI sustainability reporting guidelines for public and third sector organizations: A critical review. *Public Management Review, 12*(4), 531–548.

Farneti, F., Guthrie, J., & Canetto, M. (2019). Social reports of an Italian provincial government: A longitudinal analysis. *Meditari Accountancy Research, 27*(4), 580–612.

Flinders, M. (2011). Daring to be a Daniel: The pathology of politicized accountability in a monitory democracy. *Administration & Society, 43*, 595–619.

Fossestøl, K., Breit, E., Andreassen, T. A., & Klemsdal, L. (2015). Managing institutional complexity in public sector reform: Hybridization in front-line service organizations. *Public Administration, 93*(2), 290–306.

Giner, B., & Luque-Vílchez, M. (2022). A commentary on the "new" institutional actors in sustainability reporting standard-setting: A European perspective. *Sustainability Accounting, Management and Policy Journal* (ahead-of-print).

Goffman, E. (1959). *The presentation of self in everyday life*. Doubleday Anchor Books.

Guthrie, J., Ball, A., & Farneti, F. (2010). Advancing sustainable management of public and not for profit organizations. *Public Management Review, 12*(4), 449–459.

Guthrie, J., & Farneti, F. (2008). GRI sustainability reporting by Australian public sector organizations. *Public Money and Management, 28*(6), 361–366.

Heald, D., & Hodges, R. (2020). The accounting, budgeting and fiscal impact of COVID-19 on the United Kingdom. *Journal of Public Budgeting, Accounting & Financial Management, 32*(5), 785–795.

Hewitt, J. (2019). Just healthcare and human flourishing: Why resource allocation is not just enough. *Nursing Ethics, 26*(2), 405–417.

Hochmuth, N., & Sørensen, K. (2021). Corporate application of health literacy. *HLRP: Health Literacy Research and Practice, 5*(3), e218–e225.

International Public Sector Accounting Standards Board (IPSASB). (2022). Consultation Paper. Advancing Public Sector Sustainability Reporting. International Federation of Accountants (IFAC). www.ipsasb.org/publications/consultation-paper-advancing-public-sector-sustainability-reporting

Jamali, D., Hallal, M., & Abdallah, H. (2010). Corporate governance and corporate social responsibility: Evidence from the healthcare sector. *Corporate Governance, 10*(5), 590–602.

Kaur, A., & Lodhia, S. K. (2019). Sustainability accounting, accountability and reporting in the public sector: An overview and suggestions for future research. *Meditari Accountancy Research, 7*(4), 498–504.

Leary, M. R., & Kowalski, R. M. (1990). Impression management: A literature review and two component model. *Psychology Bulletin, 107*(1), 34–47.

Letiche, H., De Loo, I., Lowe, A., & Yates, D. (2022). Meeting the research (er) and the researched halfway. *Critical Perspectives on Accounting*, 102452.

Leung, S., Parker, L., & Courtis, J. (2015). Impression management through minimal narratives disclosure in annual reports. *British Accounting Review, 47*(3), 275–289.

Manes-Rossi, F. (2019). New development: Alternative reporting formats: A panacea for accountability dilemmas?. *Public Money & Management, 39*(7), 528–531.

Marquis, C., Toffel, M. W., & Zhou, Y. (2016). Scrutiny, norms, and selective disclosure: A global study of greenwashing. *Organization Science, 27*(2), 483–504.

Martins, A., Gomes, D., & Branco, M. C. (2021). Managing corporate social and environmental disclosure: An accountability vs impression management framework. *Sustainability, 13*(1), 296.

Martins, A., Gomes, D., Oliveira, L., Caria, A., & Parker, L. (2020). Resistance strategies through the CEO communications in the media. *Critical Perspectives on Accounting, 71*, 102092.

Mazzucato, M., & Kattel, R. (2020). COVID-19 and public-sector capacity. *Oxford Review of Economic Policy, 36*(Supplement_1), S256–S269.

McPherson, C.M., & Sauder, M. (2013). Logics in action: Managing institutional complexity in a drug court. *Administrative Science Quarterly, 58*(2), 165–196.

Merkl-Davies, D. M., & Brennan, N. M. (2007). Discretionary disclosure strategies in corporate narratives: Incremental information or impression management? *Journal of Accounting Literature, 26*, 116–194.

Merkl-Davies, D. M., & Brennan, N. M. (2011). A conceptual framework of impression management: New insights from psychology, sociology and critical perspectives. *Accounting & Business Research, 41*(5), 415–437.

Meyer, J. W., & Rowan, B. (1991). Institutionalized organizations: Formal structure as myth and ceremony. In W. S. Powell, & P. J. DiMaggio (Eds.), *The new institutionalism in organizational analysis* (pp. 41–62). University of Chicago Press.

Milne, M. J., & Gray, R. (2013). W(h)ither ecology? The triple bottom line, the global reporting initiative, and corporate sustainability reporting. *Journal of Business Ethics, 118*(1), 13–29.

Mormina, M. (2019). Science, technology and innovation as social goods for development: Rethinking research capacity building from Sen's capabilities approach. *Science and Engineering Ethics, 25*(3), 671–692.

Moussa, T., Kotb, A., & Helfaya, A. (2021). An empirical investigation of UK environmental targets disclosure: The role of environmental governance and performance. *European Accounting Review, 31*(4), 937–971.

Niemann, L., & Hoppe, T. (2018). Sustainability reporting by local governments: A magic tool? Lessons on use and usefulness from European pioneers. *Public Management Review, 20*(1), 201–223.

Nutbeam, D., Levin-Zamir, D., & Rowlands, G. (2018). Health literacy and health promotion in context. *Global Health Promotion, 25*(4), 3–5.

O'Regan, B., King, R., & Smith, D. (2022). Combining accountability forms: Transparency and "intelligent" accountability in a public service organization. *Accounting, Auditing & Accountability Journal, 35*(5), 1287–1315.

Pache, A.-C., & Santos, F. (2010). When worlds collide: The internal dynamics of organizational responses to conflicting institutional demands. *Academy of Management Review, 35*(3), 455–476.

Pache, A.-C., & Santos, F. (2013). Inside the hybrid organization: Selective coupling as a response to competing institutional logics. *Academy of Management Journal, 56*(4), 972–1001.

Perkiss, S., Bernardi, C., Dumay, J., & Haslam, J. (2021). A sticky chocolate problem: Impression management and counter accounts in the shaping of corporate image. *Critical Perspectives on Accounting, 81*, 102229.

Pizzi, S., Caputo, F., & Venturelli, A. (2020). Accounting to ensure healthy lives: Critical perspective from the Italian National Healthcare System. *Corporate Governance, 20*(3), 445–460.

Rana, T., & Hoque, Z. (2020). Institutionalising multiple accountability logics in public services: Insights from Australia. *British Accounting Review, 52*(4), 100919.

Rauh, J. (2018). Ethics problems in the new public service: Back to a service ethic? *Public Integrity, 20*(3), 234–256.

Ricoeur, P. (1992). *Oneself as another*. University of Chicago Press.

Schillemans, T. (2008). Accountability in the shadow of hierarchy: The horizontal accountability of agencies. *Public Organization Review, 8*(2), 175–194

Schillemans, T. (2016). Calibrating public sector accountability: Translating experimental findings to public sector accountability. *Public Management Review, 18*(9), 1400–1420.

Sen, A. (1999). *Development as freedom*. Alfred A. Knopf.

Sen, A. (2005). Human rights and capabilities. *Journal of Human Development, 6*(2), 151–166.

Solomon, J. F., Solomon, A., Joseph, N. L., & Norton, S. D. (2013). Impression management, myth creation and fabrication in private social and environmental reporting: Insights from Erving Goffman. *Accounting, Organizations and Society, 38*(3), 195–213.

Steccolini, I. (2004). Is the annual report an accountability medium? An empirical investigation into Italian local governments. *Financial Accountability and Management, 20*(3), 327–350.

Steccolini, I. (2019). Accounting and the post-new public management: Re-considering publicness in accounting research. *Accounting, Auditing & Accountability Journal, 32*(1), 255–279.

Suchman, M. C. (1995). Managing legitimacy: Strategic and institutional approaches. *Academy of Management Review, 20*(3), 571–610.

Tata, J., & Prasad, S. (2015). CSR communication: An impression management perspective. *Journal of Business Ethics, 132*(4), 765–778.

Tedeschi, J. T., & Riess, M. (1981). Identities, the phenomenal self, and laboratory research. In J. T. Tedeschi (Ed.), *Impression management theory and social psychological research* (pp. 3–22). Academic Press.

Vizard, P. (2013). Towards a new model of public services: The capability approach and rights-based approaches. In H. Kippin, G. Stoker, & S. Griffiths (Eds.), *Public services: A new reform agenda* (pp. 53–70). Bloomsbury.

Vosselman, E. (2016). Accounting, accountability, and ethics in public sector organizations: Toward a duality between instrumental accountability and relational response-ability. *Administration & Society, 48*(5), 602–627.

Williams, B. (2015). The local government accountants' perspective on sustainability. *Sustainability Accounting, Management and Policy Journal, 6*(2), 267–287.

19

MANAGEMENT CONTROL SYSTEMS AND RISK MANAGEMENT

Mapping public sector accounting and management research directions

Tarek Rana and Lee Parker

Introduction

Risk management in the public sector involves identifying, assessing and mitigating risks associated with public policy, programmes and services (Hinna et al., 2018). Public sector organizations (PSOs) face various risks, including financial, operational, reputational, legal and strategic risks (Bracci et al., 2022; Rana et al., 2019, 2022). Effective risk management is essential to ensure that these organizations can achieve their goals and deliver services to their stakeholders while minimizing potential negative outcomes. This involves identifying potential risks that might arise from policy, programme or service delivery. Such risks include regulation compliance, stakeholder satisfaction or operational efficiency (Hopkin, 2018). Once the risks are identified, they need to be assessed in terms of their potential impact and likelihood of occurring (Chapman, 2001). This assists organizations to prioritize their risk management efforts and allocate resources effectively, and involves implementing strategies to reduce the likelihood of risks occurring or minimize their impact if they do occur (Kaplan & Mikes, 2012). For example, organizations might implement compliance monitoring processes, develop contingency plans or implement internal controls. After implementing risk mitigation strategies, it is important to use management control systems (MCSs) to monitor the effectiveness of these strategies and to detect any new risks that might arise (Vasileios & Favotto, 2022) This enables organizations to adjust their risk management strategies as needed.

Ostrom and Ostrom (1999) emphasize the need for a scientific foundation for public sector risk management, arguing that a rigorous and evidence-based approach is essential for effective risk management. They suggest that PSOs should adopt a systematic approach to risk management involving the development of risk management policies and procedures, establishment of risk management teams and the use of risk management tools and techniques. The importance of risk management in the public sector is also highlighted by the work of Hood and Scott (2000), who argue that risk management is an essential element of the accountable state. The authors suggest that risk management enables PSOs to identify, assess and manage risks effectively while enhancing accountability and transparency in decision-making processes. This is particularly relevant in today's heightened public scrutiny and demand for transparency and accountability. Power (2004) further emphasizes the importance of risk management, arguing that risk is an inherent part of PSOs' operations and that effective risk management is critical to ensuring the successful achievement of organizational

DOI: 10.4324/9781003295945-25

goals. Power (2004) suggests that risk management should be an integral part of the governance process, involving a systematic and structured approach to identifying and managing risks. Hallowell (2002) supports this argument, stating that risk management in the public sector is a critical tool for managing uncertainty and enhancing decision-making processes. He suggests that effective risk management requires a holistic approach involving identifying potential risks, assessing their likelihood and potential impact, and developing and implementing strategies to mitigate or manage them. Vignali (2006) provides empirical evidence of the importance of risk management in the public sector, highlighting the benefits of a proactive and strategic approach to risk management. Her study suggests that effective risk management can improve organizational performance, enhance stakeholder trust and reduce reputational risk.

Recent global events, notably the Covid-19 pandemic, have intensified the interest in understanding risks and risk management practices. Today's supply chains are more dynamic, complex and international, and inevitably more susceptible to the risk of failure in times of global disruption (Leoni et al., 2021, 2022). Contemporary public services operate in an environment where global events such as trade disputes, political relations and natural disasters are more frequent. For example, during the Covid-19 pandemic, countries like Australia experienced a severe disruption of supply chains in many essential public service areas, including food, agriculture, education, health and medical products. The trade relations between Australia–China and US–China also have implications for global supply chains, and PSOs are not immune from the unintended consequences of such disruptions to essential supply chains. Geopolitical uncertainties like these highlight the importance of further research into technology, management control and supply chain risks.

Thus, risk management in the public sector is essential to ensure that public organizations can achieve their goals and effectively deliver services to their stakeholders while minimizing the potential for dysfunctional outcomes. This involves identifying, assessing and mitigating risks through risk management strategies and contingency planning, and communicating effectively with stakeholders about the risks involved. This leads to examining how effectively PSO organizations understand, assess, manage and govern risks in their supply chains and how emerging technologies, such as data analytics, can enhance MCSs. This applies particularly concerning the operation of cultural and technical controls (Mahama et al., 2022), enabling risk management of overall supply chain operations.

This chapter, therefore, discusses the benefits and challenges of using MCSs for supply chain risk management in the public sector. We aim to develop a framework that integrates MCSs and resilience for supply chain risk management in PSOs. This involves analysing chapters of this book to understand how PSOs can use MCSs and resilience as a framework for supply chain risk management. In addition, it proposes how they can embed integrated MCSs and risk management into their governance and accountability practices, and how emerging technologies can play a role in this. In addition, it explores how technology-enabled MCSs can be used to manage such risks. Ultimately, this chapter identifies emerging themes and offers future research directions.

Key public sector risk management themes

Supply chain risk management

This theme focuses on the role of MCSs in managing supply chain risks in the public sector context. Supply chain risk management refers to identifying, assessing and mitigating risks in a supply chain network. This includes risks associated with sourcing raw materials, manufacturing products, transporting goods and delivering products or services to customers (Colicchia & Strozzi, 2012). Effective supply chain risk management ensures that PSOs can maintain operations and deliver products or services to their customers even when disruptions occur (Hohenstein, 2022; Free & Hecimovic, 2021). The public sector increasingly relies on supply chains to deliver goods and services to the community. However, supply chains are inherently complex and dynamic, making them vulnerable to a range of risks that can impact the ability of PSOs to deliver services effectively. The Covid-19 pandemic has highlighted the critical need for effective risk management in the supply chain of healthcare supplies (Moosavi et al., 2022). The pandemic has led to shortages of essential healthcare supplies such as personal protective equipment, ventilators and medical-grade oxygen. These shortages have had significant impacts on the ability of healthcare organizations to provide essential care to patients and have highlighted the need for effective risk management in the supply chain of healthcare supplies (Pournader et al., 2020; Valayutham et al., 2021). Therefore, supply chain risk management is an essential aspect of public sector management, as it enables organizations to identify, assess and manage risks in their supply chains.

MCSs play an important role in identifying and managing risk in the public sector (Rana et al., 2019, 2022). They are designed to assist managers in making informed decisions based on information about the risks involved in their operations and to ensure that these risks are appropriately monitored and managed. In the context of supply chain management, MCSs can help organizations identify and manage risks that arise from their relationships with suppliers, customers and other stakeholders (Nartey et al., 2022). Prior studies identify crucial MCSs essential to ensuring supply chains' operational performance during public health emergencies like Covid-19, including risk management, collaboration, communication and performance measurement. Effective MCSs are critical to ensuring the resilience of supply chains during public health emergencies, and PSOs must invest in these mechanisms to ensure their ability to respond effectively to future crises. This includes risks related to quality, delivery, pricing, and geopolitical, economic and social factors (Nartey et al., 2020). It has been argued that supply chain integration has a significant impact on the design of MCSs in hospitals and that this impact varies depending on the level of supply chain integration and the contingency factors present in the hospital (Nartey et al., 2020). The case of Ghana shows that MCSs are critical to ensuring the operational performance of hospitals, and supply chain integration plays a vital role in shaping the MCS.

One way that MCSs can help manage supply chain risks is by providing real-time information about the status of the supply chain. For example, a system that tracks inventory levels and delivery times can alert managers to potential disruptions before they occur. Similarly, a system that monitors supplier performance can help identify potential quality issues before they become problematic. Another aspect of MCSs is the role that information technology (IT) plays in supply chain management. IT systems can provide real-time visibility into the supply chain, enabling managers to identify and respond to potential risks quickly. For example, an online dashboard that tracks inventory levels, order volumes and delivery times can help managers quickly identify potential supply chain disruptions.

While there is a burgeoning literature in the private sector on risk management and its interrelatedness with MCS practices (Soin & Collier, 2013; Chapman & Kihn, 2009), our understanding of MCS practices for public sector supply chain risk management is underdeveloped. Of course, there are exceptions, such as Louth and Boden (2014), who undertook a study of defence procurement to understand how risk management has become embedded in decision-making processes (Mahama et al., 2022). Prior research highlights how particular moral ideals have provided a rationale for risk-related reforms while also critically engaging with the policy initiatives articulated to transform risk management in the public sector context (Mahama et al., 2022; Rana et al., 2019). Whilst some researchers have undertaken comparative analyses of the adoption of risk management structures across different contexts, others focus on prescribing practices that can potentially ensure effective risk management (Rana et al., 2019).

It has been found that supply chain risk management in the public sector is necessary, and effective supply chain risk management is essential for the success of PSOs (Free & Hecimovic, 2021). Prior studies suggest that risk management should be integrated into the overall supply chain management process, involving a structured and systematic approach to identifying and managing risks (Nartey et al., 2022, 2020; Free & Hecimovic, 2021). Other authors also emphasize the importance of supply chain risk management, suggesting that the public sector is particularly vulnerable to supply chain risks due to the large and complex nature of many public sector supply chains (Singh & Wahid, 2014). They argue that effective risk management requires a collaborative approach involving the engagement of stakeholders across the public sector supply chain. Pournader et al. (2020) support this argument, stating that effective supply chain risk management requires a proactive and strategic approach involving identifying potential risks, assessing their likelihood and potential impact, and developing and implementing strategies to mitigate or manage these risks. They suggest that effective supply chain risk management requires various tools and techniques, including risk mapping, scenario planning and supplier risk assessments. Sodhi and Tang (2012) provide empirical evidence of the importance of supply chain risk management in the public sector, highlighting the benefits of a proactive and strategic approach to risk management. Their study suggests that effective supply chain risk management can improve supply chain performance, enhance stakeholder trust and reduce reputational risk.

While these prior studies have improved our understanding of risk and its management in the public sector, the literature on the implications of MCS in supply chain risk management is scant. The Covid-19 pandemic has highlighted the importance of crisis scenario planning in the public sector (Free & Hecimovic, 2021). The pandemic has caused unprecedented disruption to public sector operations, forcing organizations to adapt to new working conditions and changing demands rapidly. In response, many public sector organizations will likely engage in crisis scenario planning designed to stress test their ability to manage disruption and evaluate the impact of current threats identified in risk assessments (Rickards et al., 2014). The Covid-19 pandemic provides a clear example of the public sector's need for crisis scenario planning. The pandemic has caused widespread disruption to public sector operations, forcing organizations to adapt to new working conditions and changing demands rapidly. As a global crisis, it has also highlighted the importance of risk assessments, with many organizations identifying the risks associated with a global pandemic in their risk assessments prior to the outbreak. However, there is an inadequate understanding of PSOs' processes to identify, assess and manage supply chain risk and how MCSs may be implicated in these processes. This highlights the need for further research to explore the role of data analytics in enhancing MCSs for supply chain risk management in the public sector. By addressing this gap in the literature, our research agenda can contribute to our understanding of the implications of MCSs for supply chain risk management in the public sector. This can help PSOs identify and manage supply chain risks more effectively, enhance their supply chain resilience and improve their overall performance and accountability.

Climate change risk management

Climate change presents significant challenges for risk management, as its effects can be both pervasive and unpredictable, impacting ecosystems, biodiversity and human well-being (Pecl et al., 2017). Climate change risk management has become increasingly important in recent years as the impacts of global warming become more severe and the need for effective action becomes more urgent (Heyd, 2021). However, the Covid-19 pandemic has created additional challenges for climate change risk management as PSOs have struggled to balance the need for climate action with the immediate demands of the pandemic. Thus, the Covid-19 pandemic and climate change are two global challenges that have recently captured the world's attention. The Covid-19 pandemic and climate change are global crises that significantly impact human health and well-being. Covid-19 has caused widespread illness, death and significant economic and social disruption, while climate change is causing more extreme weather events, rising sea levels and the loss of biodiversity, among other impacts. We argue that, while the Covid-19 pandemic presents a danger, we must use MCSs effectively to manage the risk of both the pandemic and climate change to achieve long-term sustainability.

While the two issues are fundamentally different, some meaningful connections between them are more visible through the MCS and risk management lens. One key role of MCSs in managing climate change risks is to enable PSOs to identify and assess climate change risks. According to a study by KPMG (2020), effective risk identification and assessment require a comprehensive approach that includes the identification of climate change risks, the assessment of the potential impacts of these risks, and the development of strategies to mitigate these risks. MCS can help PSOs identify and assess climate change risks by providing a framework for risk identification and assessment and tools for data analysis and modelling. Effective monitoring and reporting is another critical role of MCSs in managing climate change risks. It requires the development of appropriate performance metrics, as well as the implementation of controls to ensure the accuracy and reliability of financial and non-financial data. In this way, MCSs can help PSOs monitor and report climate change risks by providing a framework for performance measurement and reporting, and facilitating data analysis for risk management. Thus, PSOs must ensure that their MCS is designed to manage climate change risks and to ensure their ability to deliver public services in the face of climate change challenges. Let us consider several general challenges of climate change risk management.

Climate change presents a range of risks to PSOs, including physical risks, such as damage to infrastructure from extreme weather events, and transition risks, such as changes in policies and regulations that affect the performance of PSOs. Regarding the issue of uncertainty, climate change is a complex and dynamic phenomenon that is difficult to predict. It involves multiple interconnected factors such as temperature changes, rising sea levels, extreme weather events and precipitation patterns (de Silva et al., 2020). These factors interact in complex ways, and their timing and effects are difficult to predict with certainty. As a result, a high degree of uncertainty is associated with climate change risk management, making it difficult to plan and prepare for potential risks (Simpson et al., 2021). Climate change risk management requires a long-term perspective, as its effects may not be felt for decades (Simpson et al., 2021). This can make it difficult for organizations to prioritize climate change risks over more immediate concerns (Porter et al., 2015).

Furthermore, global climate change risks can have cascading effects across multiple sectors and geographical regions (Dessai et al., 2004). This makes it difficult to isolate and systematically manage individual risks. These challenges are compounded by access to reliable data and information, which may be limited or incomplete in some regions or sectors. This can make it difficult to assess and manage climate change risks effectively.

Climate change risk management is also influenced by political and social factors such as competing priorities, multiple and sometimes conflicting stakeholder interests, and institutional barriers (Lorenzoni et al., 2005). These factors can complicate PSO efforts to address climate change risks in a coordinated and effective manner. To this end, addressing these challenges will require a coordinated and collaborative effort across sectors and stakeholders, and a commitment to ongoing monitoring and adaptation in the face of changing climate conditions. Organizations that can manage climate change risks effectively will be better positioned to achieve long-term sustainability and resilience in the face of an uncertain and rapidly changing climate.

Especially, let us consider the management of climate change risk in the particular context of the public sector. Being a complex and dynamic phenomenon, climate change uncertainty poses significant challenges for risk management within the public sector context (Drennan et al., 2014). PSOs may struggle to identify and prioritize climate change risks, assess their potential impacts and develop effective risk management strategies in the face of uncertainty (Rickards et al., 2014). To assist them, they may need to work collaboratively with other stakeholders, such as researchers, community organizations and private sector actors, sharing information and expertise, identifying emerging risks and developing more effective risk management strategies (Howes et al., 2015).

It is also often the case that PSOs' limited resources can pose significant challenges to climate change risk management. Competing budget demands may threaten the prioritization and allocation of resources to climate change risk management activities, so PSOs may need to adopt a strategic approach to climate change risk management that considers their available resources and competing priorities (Forino et al., 2017). This may involve conducting a thorough risk assessment to identify the most significant climate change risks facing the organization and then prioritizing risk management activities based on their impact and feasibility (Forino et al., 2017). In addition, PSOs may need to seek out alternative sources of funding and support for climate change risk management activities. For example, they may be able to leverage partnerships with private sector actors or seek out grants and other forms of external funding to support their efforts.

Climate change risk management can often be politically charged, with differing opinions and priorities among stakeholders (Few et al., 2007). This can create challenges for PSOs in developing and implementing effective risk management strategies. For example, climate change risk management may be seen as a low priority or even as controversial by some stakeholders, particularly if they do not believe climate change is a pressing issue or have competing interests that they believe should take precedence. Conversely, other stakeholders may view climate change as an urgent and high-priority issue and push for more aggressive risk management strategies that may be difficult to implement or costly to sustain.

Institutional barriers such as bureaucratic structures, siloed decision-making and limited collaboration between agencies can impede the development and implementation of coordinated climate change risk management strategies (Tosun & Howlett, 2021). Action may also require navigating complex regulatory and legal frameworks. For example, regulations may limit the types of actions that PSOs can take to address climate change risks or may require extensive consultation and approval processes that can slow down or impede risk management efforts (Adger et al., 2005). To address these challenges, PSOs may need to communicate openly and transparently with stakeholders to build support for climate change risk management activities (Riege & Lindsay, 2006). This may involve educating stakeholders about climate change's potential risks and impacts and working to identify common ground and shared goals that can guide risk management efforts.

It is also arguable that climate change risk management requires specialized knowledge and expertise, which may be lacking within some PSOs, making it difficult to assess and manage climate change risks effectively (Brown & Osborne, 2013). This problem arises because climate change risk management is a complex and technical field that requires specialized knowledge and expertise, including knowledge of climate science, risk assessment methodologies and risk management strategies. In smaller or less well-funded PSOs, this may be aggravated by inadequate funding, training and staffing capacity. These challenges are further complicated by the rapid and ongoing emergence of new research and practices emerging in this field, so keeping up with these developments and incorporating them into risk management strategies can be beyond the resources of many PSOs. Staff training, expertise capacity building and collaboration with external partners such as academic institutions, industry associations and non-governmental organizations may become immediate potential PSO responses. The long-term perspective required for managing climate change risks poses particular political and strategic prioritization challenges for PSOs that conventionally operate within shorter time horizons and that may be pressured to prioritize more immediate concerns. For example, a PSO may need to allocate resources to address a current public health crisis or respond to a natural disaster, leaving little funding for longer-term climate change risk management activities.

Innovation risk management

While the definition of innovation can vary depending on the context and perspective, scholars have a consensus that innovation involves generating and realizing novel ideas (Chen et al., 2020). Innovation means developing new or improved products, services or processes that create value and drive change (Torugsa & Arundel, 2015). It involves applying creativity and integrating new knowledge, technology and approaches to address existing challenges or create new opportunities (De Vries et al., 2016). In his 2000 paper, Davila draws on Galbraith's concept of uncertainty to examine the relationship between project uncertainty, product strategy and MCSs. The paper argues that project uncertainty is a crucial determinant of product strategy and the design of management control systems. In uncertain environments, organizations must adopt flexible strategies and control systems to adapt to changing conditions and respond to unexpected challenges. The study finds that project uncertainty is positively associated with adopting flexible product strategies and control systems that allow for experimentation and learning.

Furthermore, the study finds that the impact of MCSs on product development performance is contingent on the level of uncertainty in the project environment. In uncertain environments, flexible MCSs that allow for experimentation and learning are associated with higher levels of product development performance. However, in specific environments, more rigid MCSs that emphasize compliance and standardization may be more effective. This is one of the undertheorized and under-researched areas in the public sector service delivery context (Chen et al., 2020; Hartlry et al., 2013; Moore, 2000).

Unlike private sector organizations primarily focused on products and services for generating profits (Bisbe & Otley, 2004), PSOs have the remit to contribute to national and community economies and welfare (De Vries et al., 2016). Accordingly, PSOs are responsible for delivering critical services that affect citizens' lives, such as healthcare, education and infrastructure. Innovation can help PSOs improve processes to deliver these services more efficiently and effectively, thereby enhancing community outcomes and citizens' well-being. Being subject to government oversight and community accountability, PSOs are subject to greater scrutiny and accountability than private sector organizations. However, most public sector innovations have been adopted from the private sector (Chen et al., 2020). They are often held to higher standards of transparency and accountability, and their performance is closely monitored by citizens, elected officials and other stakeholders (Stewart-Weeks & Kastelle, 2015). Innovation can assist PSOs in demonstrating their commitment to improving services, delivering better outcomes for citizens and providing a better way to engage with risk (Osbourne & Brown, 2011). In another study, Brown & Osbourne (2013) proposed a risk-innovation framework for managing risk in PSOs.

For several reasons, innovation is vital in public sector management (Osbourne et al., 2013). First, societal needs and expectations constantly change, and the public sector must adapt to meet these evolving demands. Innovation can help PSOs identify new solutions and approaches to address emerging issues in order to provide better public services. Second, PSOs are currently facing budget constraints, and innovation can help improve efficiency in reducing costs, improving processes and delivering intended outcomes. For example, new technologies and management control processes can streamline operations, improve resource allocation and reduce waste as service quality (or performance) is interlinked with processes. Third, PSOs must engage with citizens to understand their service needs and build trust and support for better government services. Innovation can help improve service performance and citizen engagement using new technologies and platforms, such as social media and online citizen forums. Finally, innovation can help PSOs gather and analyse data more effectively, enabling better decision-making and long-term impactful policy development. This can lead to better processes and outcomes for citizens and more effective use of public resources.

Innovation is a critical element of success in government and the public-purpose sector. Sandford Borins, a prominent scholar in public sector innovation, has identified three prominent types of public sector innovation. These are politically led responses to crises, organizational turnarounds engineered by newly appointed agency heads, and bottom-up innovations initiated by frontline public servants and middle managers (Borins, 2000; 2001). However, the innovation process is complex and multi-faceted and involves three distinct phases: infection, inspiration and implementation (Stewart-Weeks & Kastelle, 2015). Each phase uniquely influences the innovation process and requires specific skills and approaches. The first phase of innovation is infection. In this phase, ideas and concepts are shared and spread throughout the organization. This phase is critical for generating new ideas and identifying areas for innovation. In government and the public-purpose sector, the infection can occur through a range of mechanisms, including formal brainstorming sessions, informal discussions and stakeholder feedback. The second phase of innovation is an inspiration. In this phase, the organization develops and refines ideas into tangible solutions. Inspiration requires creativity, collaboration and a willing-ness to experiment and take risks. In government and the public-purpose sector, inspiration can be fostered by creating innovation labs, pilot projects and cross-sector partnerships. The third phase of innovation is implementation. In this phase, the organization puts the ideas and solutions into action. Implementation requires planning, execution and adapting to changing circumstances. In govern-ment and the public-purpose sector, implementation can be facilitated through agile methodologies, continuous improvement frameworks, and performance measurement and evaluation. To this end, it is essential to note that the three phases of innovation are not necessarily linear and may co-occur or take place in a different order depending on the specific context and circumstances. Additionally, innovation in the public sector requires a unique set of skills and approaches, including the ability to collaborate with diverse stakeholders, manage complex and uncertain environments, and balance competing priorities and demands.

Service delivery is intertwined with processes and innovation (Chen et al., 2020; Torugsa & Arundel, 2016). Processes are interrelated activities that work together to achieve a specific outcome or goal (Moore & Hartley, 2008). In service delivery, processes are the series of steps that a PSO takes to provide a quality service to its (customers) citizens. When the processes are well designed, documented and implemented effectively, they can help ensure that services are delivered consist-ently and efficiently. This can result in better performance and experience for the citizens, who can rely on the service provider to deliver a high-quality service that meets their needs or expectations. Effective processes can also help minimize errors, reduce delays and improve the overall efficiency of service delivery. For example, a well-designed process for handling customer complaints can help ensure that complaints are addressed promptly, consistently and to the customer's satisfaction. On the other hand, poorly designed processes can lead to errors, delays and inconsistencies in service delivery, resulting in a negative customer experience. This can damage the public organization's reputation and lead to lost reputation and trust.

Addressing risks in the public sector and mitigating the associated challenges will require a coordinated effort among PSOs, policymakers and stakeholders to build capacity, foster collabor-ation and prioritize innovation risk management activities (Ansell & Torfing, 2014; Hartley et al., 2013). This may involve investing in MCSs and developing risk management frameworks and tools (Bloch & Bugge, 2013; Koch & Hauknes, 2005). By investing in and promoting innovation in MCSs, PSOs can better prepare for the impacts of risks and build more resilient and sustainable communi-ties in search of public value (Chen et al., 2020; Lusch & Nambisan, 2015; Ansell & Torfing, 2014). There is a strong need for MCS innovation in PSOs to address the changing needs of risk manage-ment and improve government services' efficiency and effectiveness. While evidence suggests that innovation can lead to improved performance, the relationship between innovation and performance is complex and can be influenced by a range of factors (Bisbe & Otley, 2004). However, there is increased interest in examining the relationships between product innovation and the use of MCSs (Bisbe & Otley, 2004; Davila, 2000). Prior research suggests that effective innovation management requires a strategic and coordinated approach that includes the development of a supportive organizational culture, implementing appropriate MCSs, and engaging employees in the innovation process (Bisbe & Otley, 2004). Studies suggest that a participative style of MCS use is particularly effective in facilitating employee engagement and involvement in innovation, leading to improved performance (Bisbe & Otley, 2004; Davila, 2000). These studies suggest that effective MCS design requires a focus on developing performance metrics aligned with organizational goals and objectives, and implementing controls that facilitate innovation and experimentation (Bisbe & Otley, 2004; Davila, 2000). However, understanding how PSOs use formal and informal MCSs to support service innovation has the potential to emerge as a research question. One factor that requires research attention, particularly in the context of PSOs, is the role of MCSs in moderating the relationship between innovation and performance.

To this end, innovation is essential for the public sector to deliver effective and efficient services that meet the evolving needs of citizens. It can help improve processes, reduce costs, increase citizen engagement, enable better decision-making and improve performance. The three phases of innovation – infection, inspiration and implementation – can play a critical role in driving innovation in government and the public-purpose sector. Each of these phases requires specific skills and approaches and can be facilitated through various mechanisms and tools. A participative style of MCS use can significantly enhance the relationship between innovation and performance in PSOs by facilitating employee engagement and involvement in innovation. PSO innovation management requires a strategic and coordinated approach that includes the development of a supportive organizational culture, the implementation of appropriate MCSs, a focus on improving the service delivery process, and engagement of stakeholders in the innovation process. PSOs must ensure that the MCS is designed to facilitate innovation through experimentation and is aligned with organizational goals and strategic objectives. To succeed in innovation, PSOs must be willing to experiment, take risks and embrace change while also focusing on their broader mission and purpose of risk management in the public sector.

Technology and cybersecurity risk management

Technology has become an increasingly important part of public sector operations, enabling PSOs to deliver services more efficiently and effectively (Criado & Gil-Garcia, 2019). Covid-19 has accelerated the adoption and transformation of technologies and digitalization in the public sector (Agostino et al., 2021; Gabryelczyk, 2020). However, with technology comes new risks and challenges that must be managed effectively. Technology risk management is a critical element of success in the public sector and involves identifying, assessing and managing the risks associated with using technology.

Technology risk management is important in the public sector because it helps organizations identify and mitigate risks associated with using technology (Desouza et al., 2020). According to Boehm et al. (2019), technology risks can include cyberattacks, system failures and data breaches, among other things. Technology risks can significantly impact public sector operations, leading to service delivery disruptions, data loss and reputation damage. Effective technology risk management involves various activities, including risk assessment, mitigation and monitoring. Risk assessment involves identifying and evaluating the risks associated with using technology and developing strategies to manage these risks effectively. Risk mitigation involves implementing measures to reduce the likelihood or impact of a risk, such as implementing cybersecurity protocols or disaster recovery plans. Risk monitoring involves regularly reviewing and updating risk management strategies to ensure they remain effective. The use of technology in the public sector is also subject to a range of legal and regulatory requirements, including data protection and privacy laws. Effective technology risk management must consider these requirements and ensure PSOs comply with relevant laws and regulations.

Stakeholders are becoming increasingly concerned as cybersecurity incidents continue to rise (Eaton et al., 2019). Cybersecurity risk management is essential for PSOs, as they increasingly rely on technology to deliver services and manage operations. Cybersecurity risks can lead to significant financial, operational and reputational damage, making effective risk management critical. According to Boehm et al. (2019), cybersecurity risk management involves identifying, assessing and mitigating risks associated with using technology. Effective cybersecurity risk management requires a proactive and strategic approach, which includes identifying and evaluating risks, developing risk management strategies, and monitoring and evaluating risk management efforts.

PSOs face various cybersecurity risks, including data breaches, hacking and malware attacks. These risks can significantly impact service delivery, reputation and trust. Effective cybersecurity risk management requires a range of measures to prevent, detect and respond to these risks, including implementing cybersecurity protocols, conducting regular security assessments, and developing incident response plans. The public sector is also subject to various legal and regulatory requirements related to cybersecurity. According to the European Union Agency for Cybersecurity (2023), public sector organizations must comply with various legal and regulatory requirements related to cybersecurity, including data protection and privacy laws. Effective cybersecurity risk management requires organizations to develop and implement measures to ensure compliance with these requirements, such as data encryption, access controls and regular data backups.

Cybersecurity is often viewed as involving technical controls and security measures to help organizations manage cybersecurity risk (Argaw et al., 2020). Whilst some controls and measures are technical, involving security software and firewalls, there need to be social controls and measures that directly involve organizational members. The organization's experiences with cybersecurity breaches show that myopic technical controls and measures are insufficient to build a cyber-resilient organization. The culture of the organization and the behaviour of employees is critical for an organization's cyber-resilience, as many data breaches in recent times appear to have involved a human element. Cyberthreats are part and parcel of the contemporary digital age, and cyberattacks on PSOs will only continue to become more frequent and sophisticated. PSOs can better protect themselves by fostering cyber-resilience within organizations through developing a risk-aware cybersecurity culture. A resilience perspective will help PSOs develop awareness and establish clear strategies to ensure that employees can contribute to the organization's cybersecurity risk management. This way, alongside technical controls, PSO employees can become part of a more effective cybersecurity control system.

MCSs play a critical role in cybersecurity risk management, enabling organizations to effectively identify, assess and mitigate risks associated with using technology (Haapamäki & Sihvonen, 2019). MCS is a set of policies, procedures and practices that enable organizations to manage risks effectively, including risk assessments, control monitoring and incident response planning. Effective MCSs are critical to cybersecurity risk management in the public sector, as they provide a framework for identifying and managing risks associated with using technology. MCSs for cybersecurity risk management should be designed to provide a comprehensive view of risks and controls across the organization and enable risk management efforts to be aligned with organizational goals and objectives. In addition, MCSs should also include mechanisms for monitoring and reporting on risk management efforts and should be regularly reviewed and updated to ensure they remain effective. PSOs' use of MCS for managing cybersecurity risks is under-researched in accounting, and how PSOs leverage MCS for the strategic management of cybersecurity risks deserves research attention.

We, therefore, contend that a key to creating an influential cybersecurity culture is recognizing that people can represent a formidable first line of defence in safeguarding against cyber risks. However, for PSO cybersecurity resilience, the culture and controls cannot be solely top-down driven but instead need to foster a balance between top-down and bottom-up controls to be effective and impactful. Future research can explore the dynamics between technical versus social cybersecurity measures and control, and top-down to bottom-up approaches to cybersecurity risks. Potential research questions can examine how calculative accounting and technology's pervasive role impact cybersecurity resilience.

Mapping future research directions

Supply chain risk management

Future research can focus on how, in practice, MCSs might contribute to resilience through supply chain risk management. Teasing out these interrelations will enable future research to address some of the following issues:

- To explore the role and implications of regulatory reforms and government policies in the supply chain risk management of PSOs.
- To examine what supply chain risks mean for PSOs and how they account/control/report for risks to their supply chains.
- To discover how supply chain risk management can be integrated into MCSs in PSOs.
- To provide insight into how data analytics and other emerging technologies can enhance MCSs, and how enhanced MCS capability enhances supply chain risk management.
- To identify innovations required for integrated supply chain risk management transformations within PSOs.

Each of these has the potential to bring out significant contributions to the contemporary study of supply chain risk management, particularly in the public sector context. In the course of achieving these goals, future studies can aim to:

- Develop new mechanisms through which risk management ideals/rationalities can be articulated and practised in the supply chain management of PSOs.
- Develop a new framework to classify supply chain risk categories and subcategories for efficient and effective MCSs.
- Develop new data analytics approaches that PSOs can use to enhance their MCSs' ability to support the allocation and prioritization of organizational resources for managing risks in their supply chains.
- Develop an integrated risk management framework by combining data analytics, MCSs and supply chains to identify, measure and manage risks per PSO strategic objectives.
- Develop and participate in international collaboration and build comparative studies on supply chain risk management in various national PSO contexts.

Climate change risk management

There are multiple avenues for climate change risk management research in the public sector, with aspects particularly relevant to public sector accounting and management researchers:

- Assessing current climate change risk management practices: Research is needed to assess the current state of climate change risk management practices within PSOs. This can include ana-lysing existing risk management frameworks and identifying areas for improvement.

- Developing new risk management strategies: Research is required to develop new risk management strategies tailored to the unique needs and challenges of PSOs. This can involve exploring innovative approaches to risk management, such as using artificial intelligence and machine learning to automate risk assessment and management processes.
- Evaluating the effectiveness of risk management strategies: Research is needed to evaluate the effectiveness of existing climate change risk management strategies within PSOs. This can involve assessing risk management initiatives' outcomes and identifying improvement areas.
- Assessing the impact of climate change on PSOs: Research can be conducted to assess the potential impact of climate change on PSOs, including the risks and vulnerabilities associated with different types of climate hazards.
- Identifying best practices and case studies: Research aimed at identifying best practices and case studies of effective climate change risk management within the public sector offers potential insights into implementation processes and their impacts. This can involve analysing successful risk management initiatives and identifying key factors contributing to their success.

In general, climate change risk management research can help PSOs better understand and manage the risks associated with climate change and ultimately enhance their resilience and ability to adapt to a changing climate.

Innovation risk management

Future research is also required to understand the following factors that will increase our understanding of innovation in the public sector and the impacts of innovation on PSOs and the citizens they serve.

- Innovation is crucial for PSOs to meet the changing needs of society, increase efficiency and improve the quality of public services.
- The public sector faces unique challenges to innovation, including bureaucratic structures, regulatory constraints and the need to balance competing priorities.
- Innovation in the public sector can take many forms, including developing new processes, policies, programmes, technologies and partnerships.
- Factors that promote innovation in the public sector include strong leadership, supportive organizational culture, effective collaboration and a willingness to take risks.
- Innovations in the public sector can significantly impact the public they serve, such as improving access to public services, increasing citizen participation and fostering economic and social development.
- Some barriers to innovation in the public sector include a lack of resources, resistance to change and a risk-averse culture.

Innovation risk management in the public sector involves identifying and managing risks associated with implementing new technologies, processes or policies. The following are some potential avenues for research on innovation risk management in the public sector:

- Identifying types of innovation risks: Research can focus on identifying the types of risks that arise from innovation in the public sector. These risks might include technological risks, such as cybersecurity threats, as well as organizational risks, such as resistance to change

- Developing risk management frameworks: Researchers have the opportunity to develop frameworks for managing innovation risks in the public sector. These frameworks might include guidelines for assessing and prioritizing risks and strategies for mitigating or avoiding risks altogether.
- Examining case studies: Case studies of successful and unsuccessful innovation projects in the public sector can provide valuable insights into the risks and challenges of innovation. Researchers can analyse these cases to identify patterns and best practices for managing innovation risks.
- Analysing stakeholder perspectives: Innovation in the public sector often involves multiple stakeholders with diverse interests and priorities. Research opportunities include examining the perspectives of different stakeholders, such as policymakers, public administrators and citizens, to understand better how innovation risks are perceived and managed.
- Evaluating the impact of innovation: Research is needed to evaluate the impact of innovation in the public sector, both in terms of its potential benefits and the risks it poses. This could include assessing the effectiveness of risk management strategies and identifying areas for improvement in future innovation projects.

Overall, research on innovation in the public sector will provide valuable insights into the challenges and opportunities for public sector innovation and can inform efforts to promote innovation and improve the quality of public services.

Technology and cybersecurity risk management

Technology and cybersecurity risks are becoming increasingly prevalent in the public sector, particularly with the increasing use of digital systems and data. Effective technology and cybersecurity risk management are crucial to ensure that PSOs can operate securely and protect sensitive information. The following are some potential avenues for research on technology and cybersecurity risk management in the public sector:

- Assessing the current state of technology and cybersecurity risk management: Research could examine the current state of technology and cybersecurity risk management in the public sector, including identifying common vulnerabilities and weaknesses.
- Developing risk management frameworks: Researchers could build frameworks for managing technology and cybersecurity risks in the public sector. These frameworks might include guidelines for assessing risks, developing mitigation strategies and implementing controls to prevent and detect cybersecurity threats.
- Analysing the effectiveness of cybersecurity controls: Research is needed to evaluate the effectiveness of existing cybersecurity controls in the public sector. This would involve testing controls and assessing their ability to prevent, detect and respond to cybersecurity threats.
- Identifying emerging cybersecurity threats: Researchers must be undertaken to identify emerging cybersecurity threats and potential attack vectors in the public sector. This includes analysing trends in cyberattacks and the evolving tactics used by attackers.
- Examining the role of culture and training in cybersecurity: Research examining the role of organizational culture and training in promoting cybersecurity awareness and reducing the risk of human error is a significant need. This includes identifying best practices for training employees and promoting a culture of cybersecurity awareness.

To this end, research on technology and cybersecurity risk management in the public sector is critical to help PSOs to identify and manage risks effectively and ensure the security of public data and systems.

Conclusion

This chapter focused on MCSs and risk management for public sector management. Drawing on the themes that emerged in this book, in this chapter, our proposal for future research in public sector accounting and management emphasizes the importance of recognizing MCSs and risk management as a social practice that reflects and reinforces societal values and norms. This means that accounting systems can potentially enable and constrain efforts to address emerging challenges the public sector faces. For example, the Covid-19 crisis has highlighted the need for more flexible and responsive accounting systems that adapt to rapidly changing circumstances. Similarly, climate change and supply chain management require accounting systems that account for long-term risks and impacts on social and environmental outcomes.

Furthermore, accounting and accountability systems that prioritize financial performance over social outcomes may not adequately address these emerging challenges and may even incentivize short-term decision-making that could have dysfunctional consequences in the long term. Therefore, policymakers and stakeholders need to engage in critical reflection and dialogue on the role of public sector accounting and accountability systems in addressing emerging challenges. This involves incorporating diverse stakeholder input and considering a range of perspectives when designing and implementing these systems. By doing so, accounting and accountability systems can be better aligned with society's needs and can help promote sustainable development in the public sector. Future research in public sector accounting and management should focus on addressing these emerging challenges and developing accounting and accountability systems that can effectively support PSOs in meeting their goals and responsibilities.

References

Adger, W. N., Arnell, N. W., & Tompkins, E. L. (2005). Successful adaptation to climate change across scales. *Global Environmental Change, 15*(2), 77–86.

Agostino, D., Arnaboldi, M., & Lema, M. D. (2021). New development: COVID-19 as an accelerator of digital transformation in public service delivery. *Public Money & Management, 41*(1), 69–72.

Ansell, C., & Torfing, J. (2014). *Public innovation through collaboration and design*. Routledge.

Argaw, S. T., Troncoso-Pastoriza, J. R., Lacey, D., Florin, M. V., Calcavecchia, F., Anderson, D., … & Flahault, A. (2020). Cybersecurity of hospitals: Discussing the challenges and working towards mitigating the risks. *BMC Medical Informatics and Decision Making, 20*, 1–10.

Bisbe, J., & Otley, D. (2004). The effects of the interactive use of management control systems on product innovation. *Accounting, Organisations and Society, 29*(8), 709–737.

Bloch, C., & Bugge, M. M. (2013). Public sector innovation – from theory to measurement. *Structural Change and Economic Dynamics, 27*, 133–145.

Boehm, J., Evans, H., Jillavenkatesa, A., Nadal, M., Przybocki, M., Witherell, P., & Zangmeister, R. (2019). *2018 National Institute of Standards and Technology Environmental Scan*. NIST Interagency/Internal Report (NISTIR). National Institute of Standards and Technology, Gaithersburg, MD. https://doi.org/10.6028/NIST. IR.8244

Borins, S. (2000). Loose cannons and rule breakers, or enterprising leaders? Some evidence about innovative public managers. *Public Administration Review, 60*(6), 498–507.

Borins, S. (2001). Encouraging innovation in the public sector. *Journal of Intellectual Capital, 2*(3), 310–319.

Bracci, E., Mouhcine, T., Rana, T., & Wickramasinghe, D. (2022). Risk management and management accounting control systems in public sector organisations: a systematic literature review. *Public Money & Management, 42*(6), 395–402.

Brown, L., & Osborne, S. P. (2013). Risk and innovation: Towards a framework for risk governance in public services. *Public Management Review, 15*(2), 186–208.

Chapman, C. S., & Kihn, L. A. (2009). Information system integration, enabling control and performance. *Accounting, Organisations and Society, 34*(2), 151–169.

Chapman, R. J. (2001). The controlling influences on effective risk identification and assessment for construction design management. *International Journal of Project Management, 19*(3), 147–160.

Chen, J., Walker, R. M., & Sawhney, M. (2020). Public service innovation: a typology. *Public Management Review, 22*(11), 1674–1695.

Colicchia, C., & Strozzi, F. (2012). Supply chain risk management: A new methodology for a systematic literature review. *Supply Chain Management: An International Journal, 17*(4), 403–418.

Criado, J. I., & Gil-Garcia, J. R. (2019). Creating public value through smart technologies and strategies: From digital services to artificial intelligence and beyond. *International Journal of Public Sector Management, 32*(5), 438–450.

Da Silva, L. B. L., Alencar, M. H., & de Almeida, A. T. (2020). Multidimensional flood risk management under climate changes: Bibliometric analysis, trends and strategic guidelines for decision-making in urban dynamics. *International Journal of Disaster Risk Reduction, 50*, 101865.

Davila, T. (2000). An empirical study on the drivers of management control systems' design in new product development. *Accounting, Organisations and Society, 25*(4–5), 383–409.

De Vries, H., Bekkers, V., & Tummers, L. (2016). Innovation in the public sector: A systematic review and research agenda. *Public Administration, 94*, 146–166.

Desouza, K. C., Dawson, G. S., & Chenok, D. (2020). Designing, developing, and deploying artificial intelligence systems: Lessons from and for the public sector. *Business Horizons, 63*(2), 205–213.

Dessai, S., Adger, W. N., Hulme, M., Turnpenny, J., Köhler, J., & Warren, R. (2004). Defining and experiencing dangerous climate change. *Climatic Change, 64*, 11–25.

Drennan, L. T., McConnell, A., & Stark, A. (2014). *Risk and crisis management in the public sector*. Routledge.

Eaton, T. V., Grenier, J. H., & Layman, D. (2019). Accounting and cybersecurity risk management. *Current Issues in Auditing, 13*(2), C1–C9.

European Union Agency for Cybersecurity. (2023). A Governance Framework for National Cybersecurity Strategies. www.enisa.europa.eu/publications/a-governance-framework-for-national-cybersecurity-strategies

Few, R., Brown, K., & Tompkins, E. L. (2007). Public participation and climate change adaptation: avoiding the illusion of inclusion. *Climate Policy, 7*(1), 46–59.

Forino, G., von Meding, J., Brewer, G., & Van Niekerk, D. (2017). Climate change adaptation and disaster risk reduction integration: strategies, policies, and plans in three Australian local governments. *International Journal of Disaster Risk Reduction, 24*, 100–108.

Free, C., & Hecimovic, A. (2021). Global supply chains after COVID-19: The end of the road for neoliberal globalisation? *Accounting, Auditing & Accountability Journal, 34*(1), 58–84.

Gabryelczyk, R. (2020). Has COVID-19 accelerated digital transformation? Initial lessons learned for public administrations. *Information Systems Management, 37*(4), 303–309.

Haapamäki, E., & Sihvonen, J. (2019). Cybersecurity in accounting research. *Managerial Auditing Journal, 34*(7), 808–834.

Hallowell, M. R. (2002). Risk management in the public sector. *Risk Analysis, 22*(4), 741–748.

Hartley, J., E. Sørensen, & Torfing, J. (2013). Collaborative innovation: A viable alternative to market competition and organizational entrepreneurship. *Public Administration Review, 73*, 821–830.

Heyd, T. (2021). Covid-19 and climate change in the times of the Anthropocene. *Anthropocene Review, 8*(1), 21–36.

Hinna, A., Scarozza, D., & Rotundi, F. (2018). Implementing risk management in the Italian public sector: Hybridisation between old and new practices. *International Journal of Public Administration, 41*(2), 110–128.

Hohenstein, N. O. (2022). Supply chain risk management in the COVID-19 pandemic: Strategies and empirical lessons for improving global logistics service providers' performance. *International Journal of Logistics Management, 33*(4), 1336–1365.

Hood, C., & Scott, C. (2000). Risk management and the accountable state in the UK. *Journal of Law and Society, 27*(1), 38–60.

Hopkin, P. (2018). *Fundamentals of risk management: Understanding, evaluating and implementing effective risk management*. Kogan Page.

Howes, M., Tangney, P., Reis, K., Grant-Smith, D., Heazle, M., Bosomworth, K., & Burton, P. (2015). Towards networked governance: improving interagency communication and collaboration for disaster risk management and climate change adaptation in Australia. *Journal of Environmental Planning and Management, 58*(5), 757–776.

Kaplan, R. S., & Mikes, A. (2012). Managing risks: A new framework. *Harvard Business Review, 90*(6), 48–60.

Koch, P., & Hauknes, J. (2005). *Innovation in the public sector*. NIFU STEP.

KPMG. (2020). *Climate disclosures within the annual report. An Australian focus.* https://assets.kpmg.com/content/dam/kpmg/au/pdf/2020/climate-disclosures-within-annual-report-australian-focus.pdf

Leoni, G., Lai, A., Stacchezzini, R., Steccolini, I., Brammer, S., Linnenluecke, M., & Demirag, I. (2021). Accounting, management and accountability in times of crisis: Lessons from the COVID-19 pandemic. *Accounting, Auditing & Accountability Journal, 34*(6), 1305–1319.

Leoni, G., Lai, A., Stacchezzini, R., Steccolini, I., Brammer, S., Linneluecke, M., & Demirag, I. (2022). The pervasive role of accounting and accountability during the COVID-19 emergency. *Accounting Auditing and Accountability Journal, 35*(1), 1–19.

Lorenzoni, I., Pidgeon, N. F., & O'Connor, R. E. (2005). Dangerous climate change: The role for risk research. *Risk Analysis: An International Journal, 25*(6), 1387–1398.

Louth, J., & Boden, R. (2014). Winging it? Defence procurement as risk management. *Financial Accountability & Management, 30*(3), 303–321.

Lusch, R. F., & Nambisan, S. (2015). Service innovation: A service-dominant logic perspective. *MIS Quarterly, 39*, 155–175.

Mahama, H., Rana, T., Marjoribanks, T., & Elbashir, M. Z. (2022). Principles-based risk regulatory reforms and management control practices: A field study. *Accounting, Auditing & Accountability Journal, 36*(3), 773–800. https://doi.org/10.1108/AAAJ-10-2020-4983

Moore, M. H. (2000). Managing for value: Organisational strategy in for-profit, nonprofit, and governmental organizations. *Nonprofit and Voluntary Sector Quarterly, 29*, 183–208.

Moore, M. H., & Hartley, J. (2008). Innovations in governance. *Public Management Review, 10*, 3–20.

Moosavi, J., Fathollahi-Fard, A. M., & Dulebenets, M. A. (2022). Supply chain disruption during the COVID-19 pandemic: Recognising potential disruption management strategies. *International Journal of Disaster Risk Reduction, 75*, 102983.

Nartey, E., Aboagye-Otchere, F. K., & Yaw Simpson, S. N. (2020). The contingency effects of supply chain integration on management control system design and operational performance of hospitals in Ghana. *Journal of Accounting in Emerging Economies, 10*(2), 207–241.

Nartey, E., Aboagye-Otchere, F. K., & Simpson, S. N. Y. (2022). Management control and supply chain operational performance of public health emergency to pandemic control. *Management Research Review, 45*(3), 398–435.

Osborne, S. P., & Brown, L. (2011). Innovation in public services: Engaging with risk. *Public Money & Management, 31*(1), 4–6.

Osborne, S. P., Radnor, Z., & Nasi, G. (2013). A new theory for public service management? Toward a (public) service-dominant approach. *American Review of Public Administration, 43*, 135–158.

Ostrom, V., & Ostrom, E. (1999). Public sector risk management: A scientific foundation for developing an empirical research agenda. *Public Administration Review, 59*(5), 369–377.

Pecl, G. T., Araújo, M. B., Bell, J. D., Blanchard, J., Bonebrake, T. C., Chen, I. C., … & Williams, S. E. (2017). Biodiversity redistribution under climate change: Impacts on ecosystems and human well-being. *Science, 355*(6332), eaai9214.

Porter, J. J., Demeritt, D., & Dessai, S. (2015). The right stuff? Informing adaptation to climate change in British local government. *Global Environmental Change, 35*, 411–422.

Pournader, M., Kach, A., & Talluri, S. (2020). A review of the existing and emerging topics in the supply chain risk management literature. *Decision Sciences, 51*(4), 867–919.

Power, M. (2004). *The risk management of everything: Rethinking the politics of uncertainty*. Demos.

Rana, T., Wickramasinghe, D., & Bracci, E. (2019). New development: Integrating risk management in management control systems—lessons for public sector managers. *Public Money & Management, 39*(2), 148–151.

Rana, T., Wickramasinghe, D., & Bracci, E. (2022). Management accounting and risk management – research and reflections. *Public Money & Management, 42*(6), 361–364

Rickards, L., Wiseman, J., Edwards, T., & Biggs, C. (2014). The problem of fit: Scenario planning and climate change adaptation in the public sector. *Environment and Planning C: Government and Policy, 32*(4), 641–662.

Riege, A., & Lindsay, N. (2006). Knowledge management in the public sector: stakeholder partnerships in the public policy development. *Journal of Knowledge Management, 10*(3), 24–39.

Simpson, N. P., Mach, K. J., Constable, A., Hess, J., Hogarth, R., Howden, M., … & Trisos, C. H. (2021). A framework for complex climate change risk assessment. *One Earth, 4*(4), 489–501.

Singh, G., & Wahid, N. A. (2014). Supply chain risk management: A review. *International Journal of Supply Chain Management, 3*(3), 59–67.

Sodhi, M. S., & Tang, C. S. (2012). Supply chain risk management. In *Managing supply chain risk*. International Series in Operations Research & Management Science, vol. 172, 3–11. Springer. https://doi.org/10.1007/978-1-4614-3238-8_1

Soin, K., & Collier, P. (2013). Risk and risk management in management accounting and control. *Management Accounting Research, 24*(2), 82–87.

Stewart-Weeks, M., & Kastelle, T. (2015). Innovation in the public sector. *Australian Journal of Public Administration, 74*(1), 63–72.

Torugsa, N., & Arundel, A. (2015). The nature and incidence of workgroup innovation in the Australian public sector: Evidence from the Australian 2001 State of the Service Survey. *Australian Journal of Public Administration, 75*, 202–221.

Torugsa, N., & Arundel, A. (2016). Complexity of innovation in the public sector: A workgroup-level analysis of related factors and outcomes. *Public Management Review, 18*, 392–416.

Tosun, J., & Howlett, M. (2021). Managing slow onset events related to climate change: The role of public bureaucracy. *Current Opinion in Environmental Sustainability, 50*, 43–53.

Vasileios, G., & Favotto, A. (2022). New development: Management control for emergent risks in the public sector – a levers of control perspective. *Public Money & Management, 42*(6), 417–419.

Velayutham, A., Rahman, A. R., Narayan, A., & Wang, M. (2021). Pandemic turned into pandemonium: The effect on supply chains and the role of accounting information. *Accounting, Auditing & Accountability Journal, 34*(6), 1404–1415.

Vignali, C. (2006). Risk management in the public sector: An exploratory study. *International Journal of Public Sector Management, 19*(3), 260–276.

INDEX

Note: Endnotes are indicated by the page number followed by "n" and the note number e.g., 121n1 refers to note 1 on page 121.

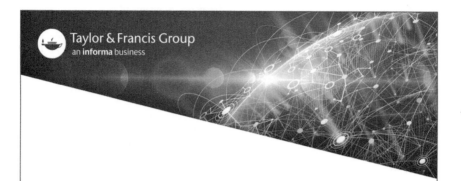